AF326663

ACROSS LATITUDES

The Complete Trilogy

Against the Dusk
Beneath the Purple Dawn
Eastern Light

BRETT ANDREW STRANGE

Atlas Elite Publishing Partners

ISBN: 978-1-972014-10-3

CONTENTS

AUTHOR'S INTRODUCTION

The novel trilogy *Across Latitudes* emerged from the rolling chaos of our contemporary world. I am pleased to now present these three books as a definitive unified series—a *roman fleuve* that follows our time's turbulent currents in a period between 2017 and 2024.

The journey begins in New York City with *Against the Dusk*. Here, we meet our principal protagonists: individuals tethered to violent pasts who are then drawn into a deepening spiral of life-altering decisions, and unfolding conflicts. The narrative then gains momentum in *Beneath the Purple Dawn*, careening through the streets of Istanbul to the different landscapes of California, Paris, Malta, and Sicily. The cycle concludes with *Eastern Light*, which begins in 2022 at the onset of the Russian invasion of Ukraine. As personal and global conflicts deepen, the story shifts to grim battlefields and related clandestine operations.

At its heart, this series follow individuals navigating the stark divide between the West's confused, imperfect democracies and the autocratic, repressive East. Our protagonists fight for freedoms that most in the West consider settled facts rather than distant aspirations. They do so on a deeply personal level, defying surface-level identities in the fearful darkness of long, doubtful nights. Some benefit from ample resources; others must join the front lines barehanded, with nothing but tight fists and raw resolve.

As the author, I found myself more an observer than a master of these fates. Each free agent navigated their own trial by fire. Whether Paul Drake triumphed or succumbed often felt beyond my feeble control. Max Drake's combat fate seemed decided by the dice roll, while Jo Richards brooded and planned of her own accord, existing far beyond the few moments I was permitted to glimpse.

My aim for these books was multifaceted: to craft a story of revenge, weave in elements of romance, deliver an action-packed spy thriller, and document modern warfare. Ultimately, however, my hope is to shine light on human resolve and the nature of authentic freedom. If any of these themes succeed in reaching the reader, I will consider my fictional purpose satisfied.

Prior to Russia's attack, the free world had assumed that a large-scale European war would not happen again. We assumed international law, interconnected markets, and common societal values would shield forty-five million civilians against a predatory neighbor. But today's gleaming progress is not so far removed from prior struggles. Evil old men still clutch to fantastical imperial dreams with grimy fingers. Shielded by nuclear arsenals, these despots and their vile enablers feel safe enough to send young men to the butcher's block without so much as a shrug.

The story also tracks Katya's spiritual reliance on Art. This cerebral metaphysical theme may seem indulgent for a globe-trotting espionage tale but not if we consider how Art and deception share common ground. Senses alone often misperceive reality's noisy inputs unless we shine imaginary magic via dramatic plot, heightened colors, and bold brushstrokes. Art helps to better see, hear, and taste fragments of a broader experiential truth. Character decisions are framed within humanity's long history of spiritual conjectures. Hence art galleries, ancient cathedral, and humble village churches appear as integral settings within a much larger, and longer, imaginary journey.

Any shortcomings of stylistic choices are mine alone. I ask for the reader's indulgence regarding the necessary English translations of dialogue spoken in Russian, Ukrainian, French, and Italian. Furthermore, this definitive complete trilogy edition has been enhanced with referential footnotes to foster a deeper, more immersive engagement with various factual details woven into the narrative's fabric.

In *The Master and Margarita,* Mikhail Bulgakov's devil famously proclaimed that "manuscripts don't burn." Though Bulgakov was born in Kyiv and passed away in 1940—decades before his story finally saw publication in 1973—his words remain prophetic. Such hard-won victory for the written word is best summarized by the Latin maxim: *Vita brevis, ars longa.* May you embrace life's short journey, and this longer journey portrayed here.

—Brett Andrew Strange

Volume 1

AGAINST THE DUSK

Though wise men at their end know dark is right,
Because their words had forked no lightning they
Do not go gentle into that good night.
Good men, the last wave by, crying how bright
Their frail deeds might have danced in a green bay,
Rage, rage against the dying of the light.

—Dylan Thomas, 1951

DISCOVERY

Prologue

"ALL YOURS," the bank officer says unsmiling as he left safety deposit box 4756 on the shiny white tabletop.

Paul Drake pulled the black curtain over the alcove entrance before he sat. The vault's dry air pumped in through the ceiling ducts, smelling vaguely of lemon-scented cleaning fluid; a stark fluorescent light gave everything a hard, artificial sheen.

Paul lifted the deposit box's steel top. Nothing much there: birth certificate, army dog tags, Dad's last letter before he died, Julie's two-carat diamond engagement ring she returned to him at a Boston courthouse. These were distant and immaterial fragments, flotsam of a now dead life.

Paul pulled his own fresh letter from his pocket. Every sentence scribbled last night had been a struggle. But his own words might help since Max had a right to know, especially if it all turned horribly wrong in the not-too-distant future. Truth twists and curls when you are no longer present to tell your own story. The living have their unknown motives; the dead are mute.

```
     Max,


     You hold this letter only because I had
no chance to say goodbye. How I died, I'll
not know. Others may say I committed crimes,
betrayed my country, sold out. Not true. Don't
believe their lies. Everything I did was of my
own free will, for the right purpose. I can't
yet know if we will succeed, but what I've
helped put into motion might save millions,
maybe make right what others ruined before. I
took this path against a cruel enemy, even if
it cost everything.
     Remember the woman in this photo but don't
look for her. She will find you when she knows
it is safe. You can trust her, but only her if
you want to understand to my truth.
```

        Life is a gift. I wish we could have had
more time together, just the two of us. In a
different world, I could have told you what
happened and, more importantly, why. I'm sorry
for the pain that I have caused you and Mom. I
kept secrets only to keep you safe.
        Your brother,
        Paul

Good enough. He'll get it. What more can I say?

Paul reached into his shoulder bag and neatly placed fifty packs of $10,000 bundles into the back of the deposit box. He locked the letter, a computer hard drive, and her photo in the box with a turn of the small key.

The bank officer gave a slight nod as he buzzed open the vault door leading out of the basement. Within minutes, Paul was outside again, downtown on Maiden Lane and Pearl. Manhattan teemed with droves of people crawling in and out of buildings like bees in a hive. A cool breeze mixed the ocean's smell with exhaust fumes and stale, underground subway air.

He walked uptown to slow his mind.

Today was so different from that first cold winter evening nearly two years ago when it all began at The Zephyr Gallery, Twenty-Sixth Street, in Chelsea.

There are certain paintings that communicate across a vast gulf. Art is a lie that enables us to realize the truth. She first showed him that.

That was how it all began on a cold Friday, January 13, 2017.

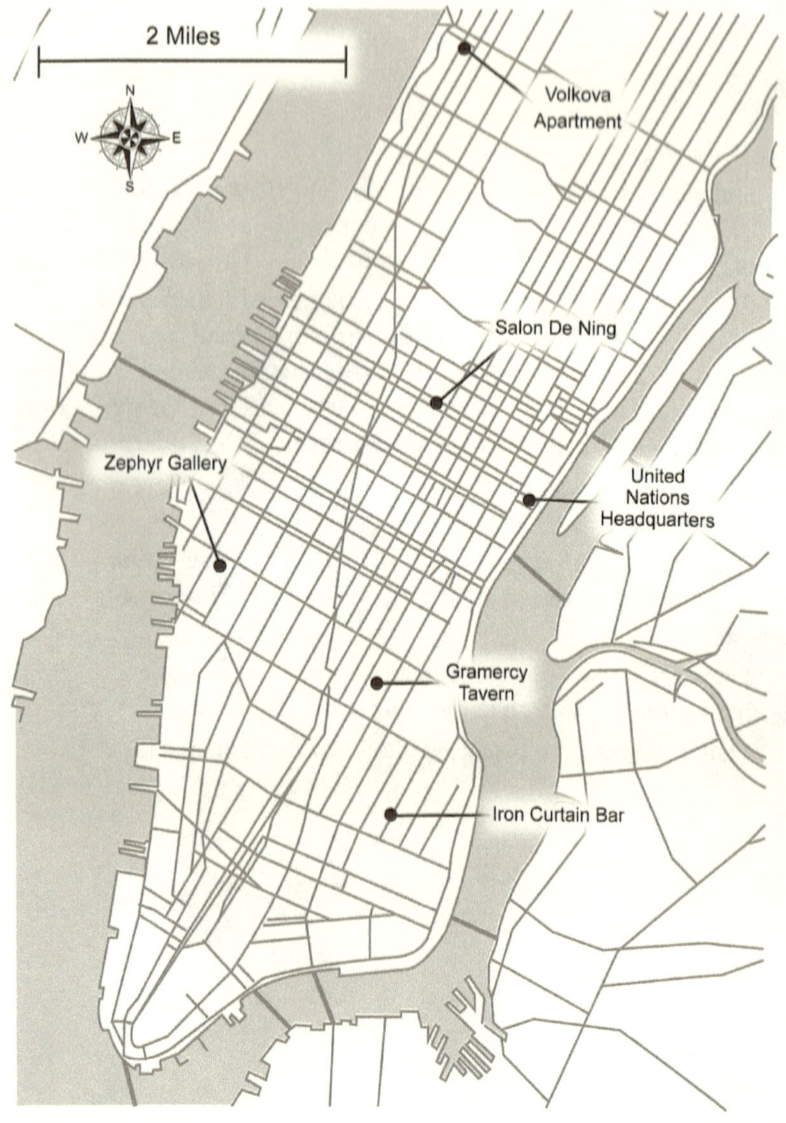

2 Miles
N
W E
S
Volkova Apartment
Salon De Ning
Zephyr Gallery
United Nations Headquarters
Gramercy Tavern
Iron Curtain Bar

1

PAUL DRAKE stopped in front of the large canvas. He stared at the two blue silhouettes embracing in the foreground of a blood-orange sunset. The fierce, imaginative vision inside the white beechwood frame gripped him. The bold lines and masterful details expressed a freedom and creative energy he longed to bring to his own smudged, charcoal-gray life. There was something disturbingly intimate connecting the two outlined forms. Faces were indiscernible, but the imagined forms seemed more authentic than what constantly flickered by in his own daily experience.

Paul had passed the oversized pane glass windows of the Zephyr Gallery in New York City's Chelsea district many times before. Tonight, he entered mostly because of the bracing January cold. There was at least an hour to kill between the end of densely bundled work meetings and the start of yet another cycle of Friday-night drinks. He had mentally turned off the minutiae of interest rates and collateralized debt pools.

"Do you know this artist's work?" a female voice asked from behind in a slight foreign accent, deep and rich.

"I'm afraid not," he replied.

"The painter is Swiss. This is his last major work before he died just a year later."

"I can't say I've seen anything like this," Paul mused. "The figures embracing in the forefront tell a story, but I'm not sure I understand it."

"Maybe there is no stable meaning," the voice conjectured.

Against the Dusk, Oil on Canvas, 72 x 60—Paul read on the small metal tile next to the picture just above the artist's long name.

"Whatever it is called, it is new and different," Paul said. "It's a win for any painter to create something truly memorable today, not just some blob of paint or a silly shock piece."

The woman released a small sigh.

"Yes, art history is long, with few truly great masters. This artist obsessed about how to link his ideas to Plato's theory of forms and the golden ratio. He was searching how to build a new vision out of what he believed are universal principles."

Paul went blank on the relevance of Plato as he turned around to meet the voice's owner. She was exquisite in an elegant white linen suit, with her long, honey-colored hair loosely tied up. A slender neck led up to a delicate, pale face with two striking light blue-green eyes. Odd how he had not even registered her obvious living beauty when he first walked in. The canvases had displaced her; his recent divorce must have also dulled his faculties of observation.

"Care for an espresso?" the woman asked.

"I would like that," he replied automatically.

Paul crossed the floor and sat across from her at a frosted glass table while the espresso machine hummed. She poured the thick black coffee into two tiny white cups.

"Is it always this quiet? Twenty-Sixth Street should be a good location, near enough to the High Line," Paul said, after his bitter first coffee sip.

"I show mostly by appointment," she replied. "Normally, walk-ins do not purchase our kind of art. But occasionally, yes, someone looks at a picture and just falls in love. The art must engage you, or it is nothing. Are you a painter?"

"No. Do I seem like one?" Paul said, deeply flattered at the question. He thought it a curious observation.

"The way you looked at all the pictures and then talked about the last painting seemed very... passionate."

"Passionate? Maybe yes. But I don't have any art skill myself," Paul replied. "I am just envious. Those of us without talents can't communicate so deeply."

"Picasso said it took him four years to paint like Raphael and a lifetime to paint like a child. Average painters let themselves slip into conformity. That is just another type of fear."

Refocused by the espresso's caffeine, Paul observed her more closely as she continued speaking about dead painters—Kandinsky, Beckmann, Braque, El Greco—with a kind of spiritual reverence. Her face was well proportioned, accented by sharp eyebrows and smooth, full lips. Tastefully applied mascara surrounded blue-green eyes that anchored a symmetrical calm. Her accent, her features, and her slightly distant demeanor suggested she had escaped from somewhere cold, corrupt, and tragic. Somewhere in the East. Someplace with vastly different rules governing life.

Paul said he admired David Hockney's colors, knowing just enough to describe the painter's vivid style without betraying his paper-thin knowledge. She replied that her gallery had recently purchased some of Hockney's early work. He knew that her job was to weave a spell on a potential buyer. You didn't spend this kind of money without also buying into the whole universe of trends, countertrends, leading theories, and big, bold creative personas.

The door to the gallery opened, and a couple entered along with a rush of cold air to break their seance.

"I've taken enough of your time. Thank you for the coffee," Paul said as he rose to leave.

She lifted a business card from a platinum case on the table and scribbled rapidly on it with a Montblanc pen.

"If you want to learn about our monthly shows or just talk about the artists we represent, call me. My name is Katya."

"I'm Paul. Thank you for the insights and the lovely espresso." he replied, the oppressively canned and polite words tumbling out of his mouth despite himself.

Then he spilled back out into the vulgar Manhattan evening again, back into the blaring of honking cars, the smell of dirty steam from the subway, and the tangle of his own constantly shifting thoughts. The rest of his evening proceeded in a dull, meaningless fashion: drinks with two friends at an overpriced, pretentious bar, followed by greasy street food in the early morning at Washington Square, crowded with college students stumbling through nocturnal pleasures.

I should have been cleverer, he lamented, regretting he was no art connoisseur by any stretch. He knew nothing about Plato's theory of the forms, nor much about any of those names she rattled off. He reacted to art like a child reacts to new experiences, without any doctrine, philosophy, or heavy expectation. A painting was simply an encounter. His eyes saw what they saw. Maybe they didn't see enough.

———— ✳ ————

The older couple lingered until the gallery's closing time. When they left, Katerina Sergeevna Volkova gathered her belongings into her black Prada purse, turned off the gallery lights, and punched the six-digit security code on the gallery's electronic alarm.

Tonight was busy enough for a cold Friday; she had managed through the lulls by catching up on correspondences with some of her more important buyers. Katya had enjoyed the brief conversation with Paul. His face was handsome enough and curiously sensitive. She didn't have a set type of preferences in men, but she found his look interesting—dark brown hair, clean cut, medium height, athletic. Perhaps he would call her. Perhaps not. *No wedding ring but likely unavailable.*

The winter night had turned very cold as she left the gallery through the back door behind Twenty-Sixth Street. She hailed a cab, gave the taxi driver her uptown address on the Upper West Side, and then sank into the taxi's cracked vinyl back seat. The driver took a left on Forty-Second, then a right on the West Side Highway, running north along the Hudson River.

With the city lights whisking by her, she reflected about her current life in this foreign city—a smoky New World cauldron of commuting office workers, global tourists, ethnic restaurants, college students, fast-walking executives in suits, and, everywhere in the shadows, the homeless, heads bowed, hidden in alleyways and on the fringes of the urban parks. Strange that Manhattan still felt so hard for her, even though it had been four years since Paris and ten years since she had left that more austere St. Petersburg.

Katya was constantly on the move, organizing and thinking, yet she had made few true friends among the many millions packed in around her now. There was only Chloe, a French artist whom she had hired late last year to help with the gallery. She never spoke of her past with Chloe; friends shouldn't be expected to carry old burdens. It was dangerous to reveal too much to anyone. Katya's survival method was always to conserve energy. Every single action needed to have a purpose. If at each step she conserved energy—she believed—then slowly, she would steadily progress, reach a higher, enlightened goal. The gallery helped her focus. The industry fascinated her, how dealers connected artworks with their clients and how tastes and spiritual insights evolved over decades and centuries.[1]

Despite her business goals, Katya had dreamed up a few children's names already, a sign perhaps that one day it might happen. But she wasn't ready to seriously think about children yet. She had only recently become healthy again after those dark years of struggle, and now the gallery consumed most of her time and energy. She pressed her hand to the cold window. *Is it not said that the future is for those who know how to wait?*

The taxi dropped her off at corner of West End and Ninety-Fifth Street. The lights shined from the top floor of her brick building home on Riverside Drive. The old Otis elevator brought her up the five floors to her spacious duplex.

Viktor's face greeted her from the open kitchen on the loft's mezzanine floor.

---

1   In 2017, New York City alone accounted for 40% of the global art market's $64 billion sales, by far the world's largest single-city market. Estimates of the value of public and private collections in Manhattan alone exceed $500 billion.

"Your refrigerator has no real food. Only caviar, dry toast, and some of this disgusting Greek yogurt," her older brother complained in Russian.

"There are fruits in a bowl on the table if you are hungry," Katya replied, also in her native tongue. She kicked off her uncomfortable Jimmy Choo high heels before collapsing limp on to the black leather couch.

"No bread, no meat. Only bird food, books, and lunatic paintings. Why do you live like this?" Viktor asked.

"I don't eat much."

"That's why you look like a ghost," Viktor said.

"So….why are you here?" Katya asked, annoyed that her brother used his spare key to show up unannounced whenever he pleased. She never could anticipate when he would appear, only that when he did, it meant something was breaking in his life. The facial features that came together softly on Katya's face were formed more sharply on Viktor's visage. His face looked unfinished: a Roman nose, severe eyebrows, and piercing, slightly menacing light blue eyes.

"No reason. Is this wrong?"

"You need to call me first."

"*Prostite menya.* Forgive me for intruding," Viktor said with a histrionic bow.

Katya and Viktor had bought the apartment together two years ago from a famous heart surgeon who had moved to a Florida beachfront mansion. Katya's interior designer spent models remodeling the surgeon's dusty prewar room into a chic, spacious penthouse loft—old iron balustrades, tall bookshelves built into the exposed brick walls, and a central exposed spiral staircase that corkscrewed up to the loft's top-level two rooms, with a private rooftop access via an old fire escape stair. From the rooftop, the building commanded partial views of Midtown to the south and the Hudson River to the West.

Sometimes Katya went up there to read and listen to the city's murmurings at night. Her street was old money and old urban people, mostly second and third-generation immigrants keeping to themselves. This was her domain now—an atelier in a quiet uptown neighborhood attached to the enormous city and yet sufficiently apart from its most frenetic core.

"Will you come out with me tonight?" Viktor asked, pouring himself a vodka.

"*Nyet,*" Katya said. "I have a book to read."

"Always reading. Very boring," Viktor said. "I will introduce to one of my handsome Finnish investors tonight. Finnish men are very polite. This one speaks passable Russian."

"Your friends are crooks and pigs," she answered. She had not come to New York and worked so hard to be any man's ornament or incubator. Better to spend the night alone at her *sanctum sanctorum,*[2] conserve her energy. She probably only knew a fraction of her brother's vices. Like many other scions of the elite, many of her old friends, her brother had been spoiled by too much easy money.

"*Dorogaya moya,*" Viktor said, earnestly. "Can you speak to Uncle Yuri? He likes you. You can ask him for favors. Tell him you need cash to buy more paintings from a Christie auction."[3]

"Why should I lie for you?"

"Because Yuri loves you more and he has more power in his little finger than I will ever have."

"Your Cyprus hotel scheme isn't working?" Katya asked.

"Those Muslim contractors screwed me; the bank has tied up my capital."

"How much?"

"More than I have now on hand. If you don't want to lie, then just promise Uncle that I'm good for it and will repay by the summer," Viktor said.

"What about using Alexi's bank?" Katya asked.

Viktor snorted. "Alexi is always pressuring me about more collateral and guarantees. He wants me to fail. No. I need Yuri. This is nothing to him. Everyone obeys him. Yuri trusts you. You are his favorite."

"I'll think about," Katya murmured. She disliked asking Yuri Volkov for more favors. Involving her London-based uncle invited complications. The Volkov business empire quietly supported both of their lifestyles, now that their own father was gone. Without Yuri's influence in finance and government, Viktor would have no investors, no capital, and no legitimate identity. Likewise, it was Yuri's investor consortium that owned the three Zephyr Galleries in Moscow, New York, and Paris. But there were limits to the old man's generosity. He could take it all away if Viktor's petty dramas brought unwanted attention. Asking for more, suddenly and for the wrong reasons, might end badly.

---

2   Latin for 'holy of holies,' referring to sacred, private, or restricted place.
3   British auction house founded in 1776 by James Christie, and currently owned by François Pinault's Groupe Artémis.

"*Harisho*. Good. Think about it. You should come with me on a trip to London to see him," Viktor continued.

"I don't like British food," Katya said.

"Or Paris?" Viktor suggested.

"I have not been back there in years," she said.

"Maybe it is time," Viktor said.

"I will go if and when I need to," Katya shot back. She still blocked out Paris in her mind. She missed the city's cool gray temperament, even though incredible pain also waited there. Rue Perronet in Neilly-Sur-Seine[4] flashed in her mind. She could never go back to that particular tree-lined, quiet street. Only pain waited there.

Viktor finished his drink. He came over to the couch and kissed Katya on her cheek, just as he had always done since they were children.

"I am sorry I mentioned Paris. It hurts me too to think of that too," Viktor said. "I'm not as bad nor as stupid as you think I am. Trust me."

"I don't," she sneered, as he smiled back.

Poor Viktor. Never just be satisfied with a quiet, normal life. He was older than her by five years yet still was that rotten, spoiled boy who pushed other children when he wanted more toys. Always more, more, more. *If father had lived, he would have been different.*

But that was not this reality. Father was gone. Imaginary worlds only existed within the frame of a canvas or in books. In this world, the real and only world she knew, it was too late for Viktor to change.

---

4   An affluent residential commune in the Hauts-de-Seine department, located immediately west of Paris.

2

PAUL RANG Katya's mobile number four days later. Feigning casual, he was surprised when she accepted his afterwork drink offer for a Friday evening. Until that moment, he had feared that Katya's prior friendliness at the Zephyr Galler was an automatic professional routine, or an act of momentary boredom. Hard to believe she accepted.

They met that same evening at Gramercy Tavern[5] in the Flatiron district on Twentieth Street on another cold night. Paul arrived early and held a space for her at the crowded bar. She took off her black leather gloves, gray fur-lined coat, and a white cashmere scarf before ordering a vodka tonic. A faint fragrance of her perfume, perhaps Chanel, lingered. She looked even more attractive tonight, dressed in a dark wool sweater and long pants, more relaxed yet still elegant and poised.

"What kind of vodka?" the bartender asked.

"Russian Standard," Katya said without hesitation in her strange, deep accent. *A good-quality choice*, Paul thought. *Not one of those outrageously expensive vodka brands.*

Paul knew the drinks were going well when she dropped her guard further and began to laugh more freely.

"Are you really that bad of a singer?" she asked after he told her about an awful karaoke dare in front of a hundred strangers during an office party.

"Singing is not my talent," Paul admitted. "Definitely deserved the worst-performer award."

"At least you tried, Paul," she said. "You had courage to expose your flaws."

"I have many."

"We all do. Flaws are human. We should be able to laugh at these."

"How do you laugh?" Paul asked.

"Me? This advice does not apply to me. I am an ice princess without blemish. Isn't that how you see me now?" Katya said, her lips curved slightly.

"Shall we stay for dinner?" Paul asked, feigning cool ambivalence while watching her every gesture.

---

5   Michelin-starred New American restaurant opened in 1994.

"Only if you have time," she said.

Paul seamlessly converted the drinks to dinner by slyly slipping the hostess a hundred-dollar bill. The hostess adjusted her bookings and brought them to a suitable corner table. Paul noticed how an older man and another woman dining at different tables each furtively stole glances at Katya as she walked by. Even here in jaded Manhattan—an island chock-full of fashion models and media celebrities—there was an ineffable quality to how this woman carried herself, as if she had dropped down from a higher astral plane and was only visiting the distracted, cluttered human world for a while.

"Care for some wine, or shall we stick with cocktails?" Paul asked.

"Wine, although Russians are not supposed to step down in our alcohol once we have started the evening. I'll make an exception tonight."

A tall, impeccably dressed sommelier drifted over and began to speak to them of the restaurant's extensive choices.

"California or French?" Paul asked Katya.

"Perhaps a nice Croze-Hermitage tonight," she suggested. By the end of the talk with the sommelier, Katya had switched to French and was asking about the 2005 vintage in the northern Rhône Valley. Paul understood them speaking of a country church in a town called Rasteau.

"*Bonne option, madame,*" the sommelier said as he carried away the wine list and left to search for the bottle in the restaurant's basement cave.

"Your French is fluent," Paul noted.

"Just average. I studied in Paris," she demurred. "And I am not actually a wine snob. I settled on a fair-value-for-money bottle. You will enjoy."

The meal of various chef creations that came out on porcelain plates. Paul searched for subtleties in the wine with his tongue while he listened to her speak of her youth in St. Petersburg and her student days in Paris when she lived in the 5th arrondissement overlooking the ruins of second-century Roman baths. She described how she spent long afternoons debating Sartre's essays and Tolstoy's novels at smokey cafes with classmate friends full of strong opinions on such critical matters.

Paul nodded, vaguely remembering Sartre from his own college days—something about accepting your own radical freedom. Paul had never read much Tolstoy, although he acted as if he had. He recalled Napoleon's invasion of Russia and another book about unhappy nineteenth-century families,[6] loosely recalled from a sophomore world literature course.

---

6   The titles escaping Paul's memory are Tolstoy's *War and Peace,* published in 1868, and *Anna Karenina,* published in 1878.

"You had an interesting life before New York," Paul said.

"My family still owns several apartments near the Jardin de Luxembourg. I haven't been back in years though."

"Why not?"

"I've moved on, that's all," she replied, before the waiter came to take their order for an espresso and grappa.

Finally, at the end of the evening, Paul helped Katya put on her coat and offered to accompany her in a taxi home. She declined and instead gave him a formal double kiss on each cheek.

"Lovely dinner, Paul. I'm glad it worked out tonight. Please call me again," she said, then held her hand out to signal the yellow cab coming down Twentieth Street.

Even the wave of her hand has a subtle artistry, he thought.

After her taxi sped away, Paul walked the rest of his way to his apartment, savoring how the winter cold bit against his skin. Along Madison Avenue, he ruminated on several possible explanations for the mystery of why this jewel of a woman was still single, if indeed she was. He approached the question as an algebra problem with factors that eliminated potential rival suitors:

1. Too classy for casual flings.
2. Not interested in Russian men.
3. Refined aesthetic that veered into the philosophic—hard for most busy professional men to match.
4. Unimpressed by bank accounts; obviously from her rarified, aristocratic demeanor, she had never lacked money.

Still doesn't add up. There must be some factor I'm missing, something wrong with her, some unwise decision or fatal personality flaw, he thought.

Or was this apparent anomaly, Katerina Sergeevna Volkova, simply a reflection of how society itself was infinitely full of different manifestations of the human condition? On some occasions, under confused and chaotic pressures, humanity spits out a rare outlier who does not fit any familiar pattern. Somehow this unique formation of an individual just exists. Because these external conditions are so amorphous and unpredictable, these individuals occasionally exist inexplicably alone.

———— ✳ ————

Dinners and coffees continued. Week by week, with each new interaction, Paul felt an elusive vigor return to his life, as if he was imbibing a new kind of drug to clear out festering maladies.

"What happened to your marriage?" Katya asked him on their fifth outing while she held his hand.

"Nothing happened. It was simply wrong. I am bad at making key life decisions," Paul admitted.

"We often don't know our own real blindness. How did it end?" Katya prodded.

"Julie's dream job in Los Angeles materialized. We both knew it was over, so we decided to separate before we became very ugly. Easier to quit without kids."

"Sounds civilized," Katya said.

"Civilized and loveless," Paul replied, thinking that his past fixations now seemed so trivial. "It is better now. I can focus on my career."

"You enjoy banking work?"

"It serves its purpose. Pays the bills."

"Without hard work, no one would get a catfish out of the pond, and you would never eat," Katya said.

"Precisely," Paul replied. "In American English—stay in the game."

"Do you like children?" Katya probed.

"I do but only if I can be in a better place myself. It wasn't easy after leaving the service. My brother had a harder time of it, after his last tour in Iraq."

"That senseless war must have been a traumatic experience."

"More for my brother than for me," Paul said, then explained more about how Max had struggled for many years after. Her eyes held steady as she listened to his worries about Max's challenges.

"Here's to a new chapter," Katya eventually said to change the mood. She raised her wine glass, then declared: "The future is unwritten."

"To the future," Paul replied as they clanked glasses.

A sharp, new excitement began to animate Paul's bones and skin over the next several weeks. He woke up in the morning with a sense of passionate anticipation. Otherwise, purposeless weekends became purposeful. Friday nights released him from a work week prison tied to calculations and deadlines so he could enter Katya's more authentic world. Past complexities slipped further away each time she a spoke of some new artist or referred to a great European writer. He found himself up late at

Katya took the drink and swallowed it in one gulp. Then she pulled him closer to her and kissed him on the lips. A rush of energy coursed through him as he returned her kiss, surprised himself by how much he longed for her after these many weeks.

Katya embraced him. Her smooth, alabaster body melted his fears. A much more powerful desire to press his skin against hers, to engulf her fully, now possessed him. He caressed her skin and kissed her fragrant, slender neck. She shuddered slightly, then froze.

"Forgive me," she whispered.

"For what?" Paul asked.

"It's not you. It's just hard for me to trust." She slowly pushed him away.

"Turn off the lights now, please," she said.

He switched off the lights while she removed her black silk blouse and wiggled out of her white linen pants.

Katya motioned to below her waist, and he could still see her lean body in the room's pale darkness, illuminated by the city's fluorescent lights shining through the large window. Across Katya's right hip and right leg, and along her lower back, were several large, jagged scars and other cuts that seemed to have been made with a surgeon's knife. The wound must have been from a severe injury, a crash of some sorts.

"I hope you don't find me too ugly now," she whispered.

"No, of course not. It is nothing," Paul said.

"I'm glad you say that. I know it is ugly."

"Nonsense. It is just the two of us now," Paul whispered as he pulled her closer to him.

He felt her very slowly relax her muscles and embrace him. They gave themselves to each other's touch and existed together in the silence, wholly apart from the sharp, complex universe outside. Periodically, almost like clockwork, a police or ambulance siren blared outside, indicating the continued existence of an objective external world beyond the sensations of their two bodies.

After Katya drifted into sleep, Paul lay next to her and watched her sleeping form. Low clouds passed over the black sky to give an eerie electric-blue halo to the urban night outside. *The world is always there*, Paul thought. The sun shines now elsewhere on the planet as it ceaselessly spins, turn after turn, indifferent to human desire and purpose.

During the Iraq War,[9] Paul had seen similar scar wounds on those who had been hit by shrapnel. Here was a record of that same kind of violence on Katya's otherwise smooth ivory skin. Someone had done a skilled job sewing her up. Her hips and back had undergone multiple skin grafts from an expert surgeon, but you couldn't completely repair the damage, no matter how advanced the medical science.

Women can be so self-conscious over such meaningless imperfections, he thought. And with Russians, who can tell? You can never really tell what goes on inside a Russian head. They are a different human type, much harder in their sensibilities with their long winters, bitter history, and very murky souls. A representative specimen was here now, naked and unconscious on his bed.

He touched her honey-colored hair, now spread disheveled over the white linen pillow. Paul didn't know Katya's true mind yet. They had dinners together and shared some conversations. Now they shared their bodies, and she revealed to him her physical flaws. But he had not solved the problem of this observed human anomaly, Katerina Volkova.

The authentic identity of the human being sleeping next to him remained an enigma.

---

9   The Iraq War (2003–2011) began with a U.S.-led invasion to dismantle the government of Saddam Hussein. Following the rapid collapse of the Ba'athist regime, the conflict transitioned into a protracted military occupation.

3

KATYA SLIPPED out very quietly, just before the purple dawn lifted Manhattan into another new day, still untarnished. Paul did not stir as she quietly closed the door behind her. The building's doorman looked up sleepily when she passed through the lobby and exited out to Twenty-Ninth Street. It was hard for Katya to sleep in an unfamiliar bed, especially downtown within the city's ever-humming immensity.

Conserve energy, always conserve, she reminded herself as she hailed a cab to take her back uptown.

Now it was done. She crossed the line last night with Paul. Something was different with him. She felt the possibility of completion, a sense that maybe she could be one part of a greater whole with this partner. Now, after many years alone, this man had connected with her body and inner self. His fingers had passed unflinchingly over her damaged skin, touching the jagged lines along her legs and hips that she otherwise always kept hidden under fabric. His hands touched the imprint of that day in Neilly-sur-Seine.

That secret, horrible day…

Easter Sunday, four years ago…

A very bright and pleasant morning….

Katya saw herself again, opening the red lacquered apartment door on the tree-lined Rue Perronet.

She had asked her father to come to Paris not only because she missed him but also for a more serious reason. They had argued the night before. For months, Katya had urged Sergei to do something more than just paper over the ugly truths of Russian foreign policy. Her father claimed to his supporters that he was a reformer. She was proud of this. She wanted him to live up to his promises, follow words with actions. Otherwise, what was the point of his political position? Just to be a new kind of *apparatchik*[10] under a different flag?

She met her inspiration for more activism months before in the form of an older man, a journalist, Rene Voclain. Rene sat in on her Sorbonne

---

10   A loyal "agent of the apparatus" who manages administrative details, often with negative connotations of being blind and obedient.

graduate political philosophy class. He first approached her as she left the lecture hall on a clear autumn day—a wide smile, open-collared shirt, shoulders held back, clean Italian leather shoes. She agreed to coffee. Soon they were regulars at a café near Place Michel. Rene's father had been a *Pied-Noir*[11] in Algeria; he also felt like an outsider, just like her.

Rene showed her the chapters of the new book he was writing. He was full of passion, purpose, and self-confidence. He wanted more than just to sleep with her like the other men, although he wanted that too. What Rene really wanted was to change the world. He probed, prodded, argued, and cajoled her about her father's politics. So many questions on Russia's role in the Middle East for the book he was writing. If any decent person knew about today's military programs, didn't that leader have a duty to tell the world? Why else had Sergei Volkov set up a special committee for the Duma to independently investigate weapons proliferation? Rene said he could help publish material, but he needed more facts. She gave him as much as she could—Sergei's unpublished speeches, group discussion notes, the names of other political contacts, and even some more sensitive material gathered on chemical laboratories and factories in former Soviet republics. Rene asked her to keep this secret until he was ready to interview her father and his peers and then discuss the best way to publish while still protecting his sources. His book would be groundbreaking. A true new start, a new revolution.

Katya, Elena, and Sergei left the apartment dressed in their Sunday best. They walked to the white Mercedes parked beneath the spreading branches of a gnarled, ancient elm at the start of its seasonal bloom. Katya carried a pastry in her right hand and sipped hot coffee from a plastic cup in her left.

Sergei in the blue suit moved into the driver's seat, while Katya's mother settled into the passenger side next to him. Katya, dressed in a stylish white chiffon dress, paused to place her coffee on top of the car while she finished the slightly sweet *kouign-amann*.

"Hurry up, or we will be late for the services," Sergei said.

"I don't want to spill on white," Katya replied, slightly annoyed.

Katya took her coffee from the car top and swallowed it in one long gulp. Sergei turned the car key just as Katya began to slide her lithe body into the back seat.

---

11   French for "Black-Foot" refers to people of French and other European descent born and raised in Algeria during French colonial rule from 1830 to 1962. Though French citizens, most had a tenuous connection to mainland France.

Suddenly, Katya felt herself hurtling through the air in a blaze of fierce heat.

Then it all went black.

The explosion triggered by the transmission mechanism reverberated for miles. Metal shards from the car's engine blasted more than fifty meters away, shattering several residential windows and catapulting hot debris that burned holes in the square, manicured lawns along Rue Perronet. The detonation emanating from beneath the front engine instantly incinerated the two front-seat passengers. The blast catapulted her body backward, but she was shielded by the heavy car door.

The following morning, the Paris newspapers reported two fatalities and one critical injury from what French police called an all-too-common act of terror. The Russian consulate in Paris issued a warning to its overseas citizens to exercise increased caution, blaming a rise in Middle East tensions. The consulate's short statement condemned violence against her citizens traveling abroad; French authorities offered their full cooperation.

First responders rushed Katya to Bichat-Claude Bernard Hospital, where she remained in critical condition for nearly a week. Then they moved her to other hospitals over the next several months. This was the beginning of her long route of recovery. Ultimately, it took four more surgeries, followed by nine months at a specialized facility in Lausanne before her twelve broken bones and the fractured pelvis all healed and she could finally walk again, at least with a cane.

Rene Voclain, or whoever he was, vanished after this event. Katya should have known something was off when he told her not to take his picture, and how he angrily snatched her phone one time to delete an image she innocently snapped. She had wrongly assumed his anxious outbursts were because of a wife or another mistress, lurking in his past.

In the next several months, Russian security forces arrested many of Sergei Volkov's associates, all on trumped-up charges, and in some cases, no charges at all. Even Yuri was powerless to respond against an unknown culprit. No terrorist group ever came forward to claim direct responsibility or to offer a coherent motivation for the murder of a relatively new member of the Russian Duma. A Moscow-based political supporter had his office raided and his staff harassed after insinuating that not enough was being done to investigate the bombing. After intimidation, no one in Russia asked questions so the bombing was largely forgotten.

The only clear fact that Katya understood was that her own weakness, stupidity, and utter naïveté cost everything. Why had she even cared about politics or tried to interfere with matters she knew nothing about? Such stupidity!

Katya kept one picture of Rene that she managed to hide, but for years now, her uncle Yuri had no luck tracking down additional information on him. It was as if the handsome, struggling, passionate book writer Rene Voclain had never existed.

———— ✳ ————

"Bienvenue monsieur," the hostess said with a smile as a handsome man entered Café Procope[12] in Paris' 6th arrondissement. He wore a wide smile, open-collared shirt, shoulders held back, and clean Italian leather shoes. The hostess found his name in her reception book—Andre Gauthier— before she led him into the crowded interior.

The man, now calling himself Andre, was very fond of this centuries-old café on Rue de l'Ancienne Comédie. Procope was among just a handful of places he could not resist visiting every time he returned to Paris. The cafe's refurbished Pompeian red walls and crystal chandeliers exuded a distinct eighteenth-century charm, reminding him of the world's old excesses and bloody revolutions. Andre nevertheless understood the dangers of overripe routines in any big city, especially one where he had already spent considerable time. Thus, he carefully scanned the other patrons: Japanese tourists, a few scattered businessmen, rich Parisian housewives, and the well-dressed waiters floating between tables. Andre wasn't overly concerned about being recognized. He had the look of a different man now, all carefully crafted. His reddish beard and suntan came from the past three years he had spent mostly in the warmer climates of Istanbul, Amman, and Beirut. Business in those ancient lands had never been better.

Nazir Hassan waited at the reserved round table in the far corner; he had come early as instructed.

"How are you?" Andre asked when he sat down at the small, round table.

"Stairs are climbed step by step," Nazir said.

This thin, ambitious Turk had been ruthlessly efficient these last eighteen months, scurrying around on behalf of several very needful clients. Assad's Syrian generals and Erdogan's Turkish security apparatus kept Nazir active during Syria's long brutal civil war. The Americans were finally out of Iraq, their bravado sucked out by the cruelty and pointlessness of a never-ending occupation. Americans didn't have the stomach for this

---

12   The original café was opened in 1686 by the Sicilian chef Procopio Cutò; a hub of the Parisian artistic and literary activity in the 18th and 19th centuries.

type of conflict. Russia was sending in more special forces to prop up her client states. A new group of Islamic fundamentalists had also emerged with savage tactics against all these political regimes and so-called great power stratagems. Plenty of blood spilled these last ten, twenty, fifty years. Plenty more to come, Andre knew.

He watched the slightly shiny sweat collect on Nazir's temple as the drinks were served. Arranging this meeting implied that Nazir didn't fully trust his previous Istanbul contacts. Turkish military intelligence recently purged two high-ranking generals for perceived transgressions. A new, even more nationalistic military faction was now in charge of dealing with the Syrian border, the Islamic fundamentalists, and the restive Kurds. Nazir would be eager to steer away from stale old loyalties and prove himself anew.

Nazir opened Andre's envelop, then studied the contents.

"Your client can inspect the cargo at this location outside Iskenderun," Andre explained. "Send just one person to inspect, and then you and I will close payment tomorrow night."

"I will arrange. Let it be so."

"Come alone, ten o'clock. Wait outside this church in Clichy, and I will text you." Andre pointed to the church meeting point on a small map; the church was on a quiet street, carefully chosen, in a lower-class Parisian suburb.

Nazir's eyelids fluttered.

"Will this be a problem?" Andre asked.

"No," he said. "No problem."

"Come alone, or no deal."

"Understood. This is a beginning. I have more business for Perses when we have success."

"Very good then, *Inshalla*," Andre assured. He could never really tell with the Turk counterparties. Nazir might fear Perses because of what he's heard, but it is still always wise to be prepared.

He handed Nazir a card with the telephone number of his most talented local woman written on the back.

"A shame to let the city's pleasures slip because of our business. Call this number tonight. Naomi will take care of you," Andre continued. "She's incredible, *mon ami*. Dom Perignon in the finest club, and after this, heaven."

Nazir took the card and Andre changed the subject to avoid appearing too assertive. *Another advantage of Paris*, he thought. Naomi will watch him, maybe even take him to the prepped room at Hotel Regina. If she can pick his phone for a data transfer, a bonus. Mostly these men always did.

———————— ✳ ————————

After the Turk left, Andre finished his coffee alone, ordered another, and spent the next hour reading *Le Figaro* and *Le Monde* before his mind began to retrace the past.

Why reserve this table among ten thousand other choices? He had specifically asked to be seated here.

This was the same corner table he had taken the young Russian girl to, years ago now. The eager politician's attractive daughter had a certain otherworldly presence, that one. He enjoyed the game with her—always more complicated and subtle with a Russian, even if she was only a lovely, inexperienced flower.

Katerina Volkova was also unfinished business.

She was not supposed to be there that morning of the car bombing, but so it went with collateral damage. A miracle she survived. Odd also that Perses still took such a sustained interest in her following that action. Why exactly, Andre still didn't fully understand. There was much that Perses never shared. In fact, after nearly seven years as his agent and courier, Andre had never met the man who paid his fees, arranged political cover, and fulfilled orders involving the most sensitive weapons. They spoke only a few times each year and otherwise communicated only in writing through intermediaries. Andre accepted this fact. Those who needed to know more were told enough. Those who didn't know enough or deviated from rules met the consequences and became examples. Why change this status quo if his own Zurich bank account was now eightfold what it had been just three years ago? Andre fulfilled his part of the machine. The machine rolled on, unobserved and highly successful. The machine served its higher political purpose in this flawed, brutal, unjust world, and it made him rich.

When Andre left Procope, low clouds were beginning to threaten rain. He crossed the River Seine on foot via Pont Royal, then made his way through the Tuileries Garden.

Andre lingered under the shade of a large oak tree to place his mobile call as the air suddenly chilled.

The phone rang half a dozen times before a familiar low female picked up.

"*C'est moi.* It's me." Andre said. "Can you speak?"

"Some," Simone replied in French. "What is it?"

"Only that I think of you," Andre said.

"You never do."

"I do."

"Never."

"You are good?"

"Some days."

"Tired of bagels and pizza?"

"*J'ai besoin de changer*. I need change, Andre," Simone asserted. "Nothing ever happens with your precious Scheherazade. Only drivel about her canvases. She's in love with pictures, that's all. It's very quiet here and I'm bored."

"The brother?" Andre asked.

"Just a hustler. He knows nothing important," Simone said.

"The uncle?"

"I've never seen him."

"Their buyers?"

"I have a list."

"Good."

"No one special," she said.

"What makes you think you know that?" Andre replied tersely, annoyed. "Remember the training I gave to you. Drop the list you have now to Lena."

"I will, but I need more money, like you promised."

"Yes, yes, yes … she will bring you some," Andre said.

"How much longer?" she asked.

"Stop, Simone," Andre said. "When Scheherazade has no more stories, then you can go back to spreading your legs for diplomats. You'll get paid either way, I promise."

"Why are you so cruel?" Simone snapped.

"Why are you so ungrateful?" he replied. "Don't you remember how I found you?"

"I remember."

"Do you want to go back to that?"

"No."

"Have I not given what I promised?"

"*Oui.*"

"Then listen. Don't think. Obey."

"I am grateful. It's just … I don't know. I'm sorry…"

"Make yourself useful. Make them all trust you more. Do your job a little longer, and I promise you, Simone, you will get what you really want, and more."

4

"HOW WAS your trip?" Katya asked after she came up to Paul for a kiss.

"Not easy this time," Paul said. "The client turned us over to the lawyers." Paul's body ached from the long flight and taxi line at JFK. By the time Paul had crossed through the Midtown tunnel, he was glad to refocus on the evening of freedom that awaited him. Katya wait at her favorite spot, the Salon de Ning,[13] an outdoor bar on the top of the Peninsula Hotel. A warmer breeze now pervaded the May evening.

"Are you hungry?" she asked.

"Not yet," Paul said. His whirlwind business trip to Los Angeles had not gone well. Paul had spent the plane ride reviewing the documents and adjusting the forecasts in his planning model.

They found a corner of the rooftop bar overlooking busy Fifth Avenue. Katya ordered two vodka sodas on ice, then talked about a new novel she had begun reading.

Then Paul saw Katya's eyes flash. He turned his head slightly to see a man approach them from the bar area. The man was dressed in a slightly too tight black Italian suit with a purple pocket square conspicuously jutting out of his jacket.

The man gave Katya a kiss on the left cheek then said something in Russian in a somewhat clipped tone. He turned to Paul, smiled, and held out his hand to shake.

"I'm Viktor. Katerina's brother. Who are you?"

"Pleasure. I'm Paul," Paul replied.

"How did you know we'd be here, Viktor?" Katya asked.

"You enjoy the rooftops. You took me here last year for my birthday," Viktor replied obscurely. Katya frowned.

"What has my sister told you about me?" Viktor asked.

"Not much yet, unfortunately," Paul said, turning his gaze to Katya who had never mentioned a brother in New York. Katya squeezed Paul's

---

13 1930-themed lounge designed around the fictional "Madame Ning," featuring opulent, quirky decor like Venetian mirrors, Chinese screens, velvet sofas, and curated travel artifacts before it closed in 2024.

hand and then whispered to him, "Let him speak. Just don't believe a word."

Viktor sat, then chatted breezily about a recent Metropolitan Opera concert he attended and about which Japanese chef in the city served the best omakase. While Viktor's accent was less pronounced, he occasionally put the wrong syllable on some words. *Difficult to mask one's origins from different worlds,* Paul thought.

"You have been dating Katerina for a long time?" Viktor asked.

"Not long," Paul replied.

"Bored with her books yet?"

"Never."

Viktor glanced at his gold-plated Rolex.

"You both will come with me to my party, Katerina?"

"Not tonight, Viktor," Katya replied.

"But Paul has never experienced one of my evenings," he said.

"Paul is tired from his business trip to California," Katya interjected.

"Is he? No…. you *must* come," Viktor insisted, turning now directly to Paul. "I have taken a whole floor tonight. Katya needs to meet her art buyers. And you do not look tired, Paul. Is it past your bedtime?"

"Shall we go for one drink?" Paul asked Katya, curious now why after several months of dating she had never mentioned a brother.

"Briefly then," Katya said.

"There, you see! Settled. Come along then. We pay now and take my driver," Viktor said, throwing down a wad of bills on the table to clear the tab.

At the hotel's entrance on Fifth Avenue, Viktor's burly driver, Anton, waited in a large black SUV. Viktor sat in front.

"Do you like Italian opera, Paul?"

"Some, yes," Paul said.

"Verdi is the best. Am I right, Katya?" Viktor said. "Our mother Elena loved the opera. Elena followed all the Italian singers. She knew more about the Italian opera than Katya does about her crazy paintings."

"No need to speak of Elena tonight. Let's just listen," Katya said cooly.

Viktor turned up the volume of an opera score and hummed softly as Anton snaked his way downtown to Alphabet City[14] near the East Village.

---

14 Named for Avenues A, B, C, and D, which run from Houston Street to 14th Street. Once a high-crime area, it has now transformed into a trendy, bohemian residential district.

The burly driver parked the suburban in an outdoor parking lot on Avenue A, and they walked a block up to an old brick building that looked like a former warehouse. Viktor led them to a nondescript side door without lights or signage. An oversized Latino bouncer then waved the foursome through a narrow hallway toward the music and voices. A steel door and a series of red velvet curtains opened to the club's spacious interior.

Viktor quickly established himself at a table with a bucket of ice and two open champagne bottles. He pasted a wide smile on his face and drifted over to greet two men in suits settled at a corner table beneath a large, modernist chandelier made of shiny red glass. More women in tight bodysuits and high stiletto heels circled.

"Know anyone?" Paul asked Katya.

"Some. Viktor's business team," Katya said. "Most of the women, I do not know. Do you like them?"

"A bit slutty, don't you think?" Paul shouted over the loud music. Other slim women in tight Versace dresses milled around the bar area and the small dance floor, flashing white teeth inside glistening ruby lipped smiles.

"Of course they are sluts. This is my brother's party."

Paul watched how Viktor was invigorated. The women came to him with suggestive pouts and flirtatious glances, and where needed, he introduced them to his guests. Viktor relished his role. He was the maestro of fabulous moments, generous with wads of cash to create a regal experience for all those lucky enough to enter. He directed the evening's theater with the confidence of a rehearsed artist in his own milieu.

"One of my important buyers for the gallery is here, Paul. I should say hello. Do you mind?" Katya asked.

"No, of course not," Paul replied. "Do your thing."

Katya drifted over to an older gray-haired man in a dark blue suit.

A waiter poured more champagne in Paul's glass. The taste was sweet. Then there was a vodka with cranberry juice. Loud music and dancing on the small, cramped dance floor under flashing strobe lights. More lanky women smiled at him and sometimes spoke short phrases as they clanked glasses. The club's lighting gave them all a sexy sheen. His head began to feel light, body warm.

Another champagne came to his hand in a long flute glass.

"Having fun, Paul?" Viktor asked when he drifted by. "I'll take Katya home if you want to taste another dish."

Paul pretended not to hear. He was drenched in sweat now.

Katya was still speaking with her art buyer when Paul slipped out to the back of the club, up a narrow flight of stairs to a small space in an open courtyard in the back of the building. Someone had propped open the back door to let out the smoke and heat. The evening air refreshed him. Finally, no more crashing drumbeats pulsing in his ears.

"Cooler out here," a man said when he saw Paul. He wore horn-rimmed glasses and a tan blazer and was casually smoking in the fresh spring night. The man's face was strangely incongruous, like that of a boy's yet hidden beneath unshaven stubble. His eyes were glassy, slightly bloodshot.

"Yeah, fresh air is good," Paul replied, still trying to clear his head, the alcohol coursing through him.

"Amazing beauties, the women," the man said.

"Some are," Paul said.

"You want one of these sticks," he said, holding out his pack of Marlboros. Paul took one, and the man lit it from a Zippo.

"I'm Arlen," he said, and Paul introduced himself.

"And where are you from?" Paul asked.

"Nowhere exotic. Greenwich, Connecticut," Arlen said.

"Locals are outnumbered tonight," Paul said.

"Hah, who knows anymore? We're just one big planet now, all doing business on the same iPhones and iPads. I spend half my time in Dubai myself."

"You enjoy it there?" Paul asked.

"It has its moments. Tall buildings. Plenty of expats in and out of boomtown. Global capitalism in the desert. Have you been?" Arlen asked.

"Only briefly. I passed through with my unit when I served in the region."

"You served? Good for you. Glad we could help the Sheiks stay safe. Seems like a long time ago, that little Dick Cheney war against Saddam," Arlen said.

"More than ten years now," Paul said.

"We started with UN speeches on destroying weapons of mass destruction and ended with a few hundred thousand dead civilians and a scared guy hiding out in a spider hole.[15] What a shit show. Am I right?"

"A twenty-first-century war. No cheering crowds or French babies to kiss," Paul said, never knowing how to respond to such statements.

---

15 Saddam Hussein was captured on December 13, 2003, discovered in a small, concealed underground bunker—commonly referred to as a "spider hole"—near his hometown of Tikrit. He was tried and executed in 2006.

Paul rarely thought about those desert days. That part of his past was now just a distant dream that belonged to another person altogether. There was no point in surfacing difficult memories. Nothing to gain in replaying a sordid, violent past. It was bad enough how Iraq had scarred his little brother. Max had a rougher time than most. It was tough for him to turn the page as Paul had done for a long time now.

"What's your business with Viktor?" Arlen probed.

"Nothing. Just dating his sister, Katya."

"Sister? Didn't know he had one here."

"And you?" Paul asked.

"I invest with Viktor," Arlen replied, exhaling smoke before he crushed his dying cigarette beneath his loafer and lit another. "I prefer protected transactions."

"Protected transactions?"

"These Russian aristocrats are loaded. They pay up for access. Hard to tell who really controls the companies, but Viktor's family is politically connected. They don't let their own fail."

"That simple?" Paul said.

"Not simple. It isn't all white shoe like JP Morgan or Goldman Sachs. But those guys are bigger crooks. With Russians, you just need to understand their mentality. What they care about. Get inside their heads. Am I right?"

"It's hard to get into anyone else's head, particularly a Russian," Paul countered.

Arlen shrugged, then turned the subject back to more familiar territory of baseball and the current strengths and weaknesses of the New York Yankees' pitching lineup. They slowly finished the cigarettes and tossed the butts on the ground.

"I would very much like to meet your girlfriend, Katya, when you have a chance," Arlen said.

"Let's find her," Paul said.

"Good. Back into the fray."

5

VIKTOR VOLKOV drank a strong cup of coffee as he looked down at the traffic on Houston Street from his top floor apartment window. After a shower and some food, he felt strong again even as the alcohol from last night in Alphabet City still numbed his fingertips.

He glanced at his Rolex: fifteen minutes past noon. He folded his favorite blue Brioni suit into a brown leather Tumi bag, zipped it up, and checked his business class British Airways ticket: JFK to Heathrow, leaving in three hours.

Viktor deemed last night a success. His two superstar showgirls, Sonia and Kim, had done well. The little snot-nosed private family office heir from Los Angeles left with Sonia. Kim had gone to a hotel with one of the corporate lawyers.

These two women were his most reliable soldiers, very discreet with a surprisingly addictive charm. The women pulled you into an alluring illusion of your own virility. They knew the subtle steps of their theater better than any professional playactor. When Sonia brought her drugs, it was just a small amount of ecstasy meant to sweeten the experience but not overwhelm it. They only indulged a little themselves in such forbidden pleasures to keep the mood lively. True professionals, Sonia and Kim. Employees of the year, worth every cent to keep them housed and fed.

London would be easier than New York, he thought. Viktor needed to continue at a faster pace if he was going to pull himself out of his current jeopardy. His last few deals had gone very poorly. His investors would lose millions in Cyprus. This stupid hotel deal had exposed his carelessness. He regretted not understanding the key players in that far-flung country better.

Now Viktor needed to dig himself out. New investment partners would help cover up past mistakes. He especially needed the German banks to trust him. Arlen Cross could help. Arlen knew Hans Vogel. And Vogel had the banks in his pockets, at least according to Arlen.

Viktor lifted his luggage and headed for the lift to the lobby. He straightened his tie while gazing at his somewhat distorted reflection in the elevator's shiny, buffed steel side panels.

Dmitry Medkov waited for Viktor in the lobby, his hands clasped behind his back in a manner that seemed pensive. Dmitry was always ten minutes early for his appointments. Dmitry's black fedora made him seem particularly old-fashioned and slightly comical. *No one wears hats anymore,* Viktor thought, *except these older-generation Soviet types.*

"Good morning," Viktor said in Russian. Viktor always used the polite form of Russian with Dmitry, adding an extra "te" at the end of all his verbs. "Thank you for riding with me to the airport. I know your time is very valuable. I appreciate it."

"The drive is the right direction for me," Dmitry said from behind his small, sliver-rimmed spectacles. The two men walked outside to the waiting car on the street. Dmitry's driver put Viktor's suit bag in the trunk, and the two men settled in the back of the black sedan.

"Shall we listen to your opera while we drive?" Dmitry suggested.

"Yes. Thank you. Verdi, please. La Traviata if you have it,"

Viktor said. Dmitry's driver turned on operatic voices as they drove toward the tunnel that passed below the East River to Queens.

"Do you like Verdi?" Viktor asked.

"I do," Dmitry said, smiling. "But my favorite is Aida."[16]

"Aida, yes, a classic. I should have known you would appreciate an Egyptian tale," Viktor said. "For me, Aida lacks some of the drama of Verdi's earlier work, but perhaps I have not seen the right production. I have only seen it once, in Petersburg. I was disappointed."

As the group operational chief for nearly twenty years, Dmitry Medkov headed security for Yuri Volkov. Dmitry was a scrupulously private man, like Yuri himself. As part of his cultivated anonymity, Dmitry had virtually no online presence. A Google search returned no results in any language except for a record of a very prestigious mathematics prize Dmitry won while still a student in Moscow more than thirty years ago.

Viktor knew that Dmitry lived in several cities, traveling often to inspect and review different businesses. He was perhaps Yuri's most effective and talented operator. Dmitry had also once let slip that he had served in Russia's special forces, the *spetsnaz*.[17] That must have been thirty plus years ago, but even so, Viktor thought it best not to underestimate these old-school types, even if they didn't look like much now in their silly old hats.

The two men spoke as they drove out of the city, across the Manhattan Bridge onto the traffic-ladened, tangled highway toward JFK

---

16   Aida (1871) is a four-act opera by Giuseppe Verdi, celebrated as a masterpiece of the 19th-century repertoire; set in Ancient Egypt during a fictional war with Ethiopia.

17   A syllabic abbreviation for *Spetsialnogo Naznacheniya*, or "Special Purpose", used as an umbrella term for elite special operations.

airport. Dmitry focused his most pointed questions on the newest business partners. Dmitry always took precautions. His surveillance algorithms did the work of a thousand private investigators to pick up any hot button signals. People said and texted stupid things all the time on their mobile phone and computers: adultery, drugs, gambling debts, ill-advised little side businesses. How exactly Dmitry's team first obtained the access and then transformed the unstructured data into intelligence insights remained a deeply embedded secret beyond Viktor's purview. It was just Dmitry's magic, and it worked.

"What do you know of the Mercury Fund?" Dmitry asked.

"Nothing. What is it?"

"You are working with them, no? The director there is Arlen Cross."

"Ah, of course. I don't know what silly word he uses for his funds, but I do know little baby-faced Arlen, yes, yes. He is a *rabotyaga,* a very willing horse."

"Perhaps too willing?" Dmitry said.

"I don't know. Hedge fund boys are greedy and arrogant. He came to me via a recommendation from an Arab, and he has promised to help me. The Arab told me he can be trusted."

"Which Arab recommended him?"

"The boy from the Al Maktoum family. Amir, Ahkmed, Abdul … something like that. I don't remember. The one who only likes redheads."

"Yes, I know Amir. Tread lightly with these people, especially the Al Maktoum group. Amir's family owns most of Dubai. They are not simple," Dmitry cautioned. Viktor felt this was the same cautious speech always, for what felt like countless times.

Verdi's La Traviata ended in a flourish of operatic voices just as the car sped up to the departure gate at JFK's Terminal 2.

"Thank you for your time, Dmitry. I am always happy to see you. Do you think Uncle Yuri would be willing to see me in London?" Viktor asked, saving his most important question for last. Never be too eager.

"Unfortunately, he will be traveling. Perhaps next time."

"Yes. Next time then."

Dmitry Medkov's cold eyes fixated on Viktor. Viktor looked back, straight into his elder's eyes. Viktor suddenly felt himself diminished again, as he always had been with these men in power. Little Dmitry with the hat and glasses always knew more than he let on. These older men would pounce on his mistakes whenever he tried to help himself. It was just their old, unhelpful Soviet habits. Always watching, waiting for weakness, stifling true entrepreneurship.

"Stay very quiet in London, Viktor. Clear?"

"Yes, of course," Viktor replied, then walked into the terminal.

He would solve his own problems without old man Yuri or little, condescending Dmitry interfering. He would find other like-minded cohorts, and soon, in a few weeks, business would be back on track, liquidity issue solved, and everyone happy again.

Arlen Cross looked at his haggard face in the bathroom mirror of his downtown apartment. Red eyes stared back from inside deep circles. He had not slept well after his late evening in Alphabet City on Friday. Too many drinks, too much smoking. He needed most of Saturday to recover. Sunday passed by as a series of errands. Now it was Monday morning again, alarm buzzing at 6:00 a.m. sharp. A new day pounced. He was already exhausted.

Arlen guided the razor across the stubble of his checks and dully acknowledged another day of a life in crisis. How had he crashed this far and this fast? How could everything that he had accomplished be so close now to toppling down?

Arlen ran his razor under hot water and looked at the gold class ring on his left hand. The ring's face had a delicate University of Pennsylvania emblem with the school's founding year of 1740 engraved. He wore the class ring with pride.

He thought of Nick Forrest, his father's roommate from Dartmouth and a Wharton alumnus. Nick first hired him fresh out of school. When Arlen joined Mercury, it was a twenty-person outfit, well respected and successful enough to rent a high floor at the World Financial Center. Arlen was good with clients. He could weave a story that combined a seemingly scientific approach with a salesman's confidence about future outcomes. But even with his skill, the real source of his meteoric success came from his cultivated friendship with Amir Al Maktoum.

Arlen met the reserved Amir during an investing seminar his second year at Wharton.[18] Amir kept a low profile in Philadelphia. Amir had been to various prep schools in the UK, loved Quentin Tarantino films, and hungered for more Western experiences. Amir never spoke about belonging to Dubai's most influential royal family or the massive donations his family made to Wharton's endowment—but Arlen knew, and Amir

---

18   Business school of the University of Pennsylvania. Established in 1881 by industrialist Joseph Wharton, it is the world's first collegiate school of business.

enjoyed Arlen's acumen and hunger for success. They were friends, and friendship mattered.

After their MBA, Amir returned to Dubai. They kept in touch. Amir visited twice each year to see Broadway shows, eat the thick steak at Smith & Wollensky, and finish their evenings with long conversations on how to make even more money. Dubai was booming, all made possible because the US military machine stood ready to protect the "good" Arab countries capable of embracing modern capitalism and, at the very least, staying quiet on Israel and the Palestinians. You couldn't get a proper gin and tonic there, but Dubai was civilized enough for Starbucks and Red Lobster, both in spacious modern malls better than in the States. You needed pleasant mall interiors for those 105-degree afternoons.

When Mercury raised capital for its newest fund, Amir was eager to champion Arlen's cause. A year later, an even larger investment came from a related UEA government agency. Mercury went from a boutique fund manager in the tightly knit world of specialty finance to a darling of the Street. Nick Forrest elevated Arlen to a senior MD status. By thirty-eight, Arlen Cross was rich enough to buy a four-bedroom summer house on Long Island and a bright red convertible Porsche 911 Carrera. Arlen had even begun to date a well-known Milan fashion model he met at a charity gala sponsored by his firm. Good eye candy, although a bit too high maintenance.

But how quickly that had all changed! Today, Arlen's hand trembled slightly as he shaved the stubble beneath his square chin. He couldn't remember enjoying a full night's sleep for at least six months. His light brown hair had turned white in patches along the sides.

It all began to collapse after those people, the so-called authorities, approached him. First came the IRS agent with his beady little eyes and dandruff-covered hair. Somehow, this little tax dwarf had discovered his offshore income from a side project in Dubai that Amir had pulled him into when they first started. It was a harmless little personal friendship project, but Amir's accounting was sloppy. When the IRS accountant looked closer, a few million had been siphoned off to cover lifestyle expenses. Matters turned worse several months ago when his lawyer told him in a hushed and serious tone that prison time was possible. It was in his best interest to cooperate fully with whatever else Uncle Sam demanded.

Disappointingly, none of this unfortunate ordeal was like in the movies. The Treasury agent harassing him now wasn't a sharp-suited beauty but instead looked like a harried schoolteacher. Jo Richards had a hard and mean face and an angular, almost robotic body.

Jo was most intrigued by Mercury's foreign investors—the Al Maktoum family, the German banks, and now most of all these Russians. Jo kept direction for the Russians frustratingly vague: provide access to books and records and learn more about immediate family members, especially the man in London, Yuri Volkov. There was always a weak link somewhere, some disgruntled family member or unsatisfied lieutenant.

Arlen rubbed off the remaining soap from behind his ears with a clean towel. His face was smooth again. His business mask had returned in its clean form, although the whites of his eyes were still a dull bloodshot red.

He switched on his mobile phone.

Three voice mails. Three hundred and twenty-five unread emails. A typical Monday start.

6

JO RICHARDS peered through the glass-enclosed conference room at Mercury's crowded trading floor. The brokers, traders, and analysts were all busily typing on their computers, speaking loudly into phones, and studying graphs and charts on multiple display monitors stacked together. The best of the Ivy League, she lamented, here pursuing their noble tasks to better humanity one trade at a time.

Jo knew that her unannounced office visit at ten o'clock on this busy Monday would certainly unnerve Arlen Cross. Showing up like this at his place of work would remind him how thin the ice was beneath his feet, and if she wanted, she could tap her foot and crack it. Jo needed to scare him because so far Arlen Cross had produced very little of real value. She was running out of patience with his lack of enthusiasm for what she thought was a fair exchange of value in the confidential deal they had struck.

Arlen entered the conference room, shut the door, and sat across from her. He was dressed in a dark blue Italian suit with a pocket square, a pink tailored shirt, and a silk tie tightly wound in a wide Windsor knot.

"Lovely morning," Jo began.

"I'm surprised to see you here," Arlen said gruffly. "How can I help you today, Jo."

"I just wanted to chat," Jo said.

"We're in the middle of trading hours. I have a meeting in twenty minutes. Can't this be handled through my lawyers?"

"Just a few minutes then. For me."

Arlen folded his hands and kept his face placid.

"Any more success on our project?" Jo asked.

"You tell me," Arlen said. "Don't you read all my emails on the mirror site? I've complied with everything that we agreed upon; I think a bit more."

"Yes, that's helpful. You've been good on the computer access and IP addresses, but that's not enough. What else about Hans Vogel?"

"The German banks are financing the transaction. They approved the new loans in just a week. Record time," Arlen explained. "Vogel made it happen. Unusual."

"Anything in writing linking him to this?"

"Of course not."

"Transaction cutouts? Shell companies?"

"I'm looking."

"Look harder. Get something I can work on," Jo said curtly. "Insist you need it for your diligence."

"These Russians are no fools," Arlen protested. "You know better than anyone that most of them grew up playing chess since age four. They don't make amateur mistakes. They are suspicious of everything. They know their business and set up countermeasures."

Here he is, making excuses now and getting nothing done, Jo thought. *Another low-level informant covering old ground, not breaking through, not connecting the dots.*

"What about Yuri Volkov?"

"Nothing yet."

"Viktor's sister?"

"I'm looking."

"Look faster," Jo said. "If your intel had no value, then we can always go back to issuing a subpoena on your tax case. You'll probably be able to pay a stiff monetary settlement if you can convince a judge to settle. The subpoena will be a matter of public record, of course. You would need disclosure to your investors and board."

Arlen winced.

I do have rights. This is America," he said.

"I know you have rights. Yes, of course you do. We all have rights," Jo replied, casually.

She pushed off from the table and rose from the designer chair.

"You're a smart guy, Arlen. Make something happen. Give me something I can use so this goes away. Besides, don't you want to do something to help your country? You've done quite well for yourself by the look of things here at Mercury. Good gig here. Maybe time to give a little back to your fellow citizens. Do it for God and country."

"And if they start suspecting me?"

"I haven't asked you to wear a listening device," she said. "If they accuse you, it's simple: deny, deny, deny, and then deny again. Never tell them what you are doing for me. Never. You'll be fine, Arlen. Trust me."

Jo opened the door herself and walked out of the room.

After Jo left, Arlen returned to his corner office. He sank back on his leather chair.

God and country, my ass. What horseshit.

From his office window, he could see the distant Statue of Liberty, still holding her torch gallantly above New York harbor. Lady Liberty was always standing there, alone in the water, very severe and serious with that pale green copper patina, and the Roman nose. *What was the poem? Send these, the homeless, tempest-tossed to me, I lift my lamp beside the golden door.*[19]

Arlen breathed deeply, then exhaled. He would figure something out to knock this annoying little sharp-toothed monkey off his back.

Arlen glanced down at his Phillip Patek watch. It was already 9:00 p.m. The traffic along the West Side highway was a stop-and-go nightmare. Viktor's invitation to meet uptown after dinner came as a fortunate surprise a week after Jo's visit to his office. A drink only, Viktor offered, to celebrate success and talk about the future.

The taxi left Arlen on a quiet street near Ninety-Fifth Street and Riverside. He walked the remaining few blocks to the five-story apartment building. Viktor buzzed him in through the locked street entrance, and Arlen took the old Otis elevator up, annoyed there was no doorman to help. Arlen fumbled with the iron grate before the elevator gear kicked in. The Otis creaked and moaned slowly up each floor.

Viktor greeted him on the top floor with a strong handshake.

"Come in. Welcome," Viktor said, wearing a burgundy-colored Louis Vuitton silk shirt beneath his black jacket, his long arms sticking out from the sleeves.

"Nice loft," Arlen said.

"This place belongs to my sister. She is the artist, not me."

Katya's private paintings hung in various places on the loft's bare brick wall. Arlen admired one of the larger canvases: an orange cube balanced on one corner in a sea of purple. In truth, none of the art spoke to him. It seemed more like random colors and patterns than visionary artifacts. However, it was easy just to tell others what he thought they wanted to hear. No downside to compliments. Flattery usually worked.

"Shall we take a drink on our rooftop? Katya does not approve when I smoke inside," Viktor said.

Viktor handed Arlen a vodka on ice, and they climbed the old fire escape to the private rooftop. Viktor brought him to the small sitting area with two wicker chairs that overlooked the trees of Riverside Park

---

19   Final lines of "The New Colossus", an 1883 sonnet by American poet Emma Lazarus, written to raise money for the construction of the Statue of Liberty's pedestal.

and Midtown lights to the south. The September night was a balmy sixty degrees.

Viktor pulled out a pack of Sobranie Black,[20] and the two men lit their cigarettes to ease in the night's conversation. Arlen let Viktor speak—bragging about his business successes and natural brilliance. Viktor found positive spin for most of his questionable investments, which under normal circumstances Arlen would never touch. Arlen was too good at spinning stories himself to be impressed by this charlatan.

After Viktor finished his first cigarette, he wrinkled his brows, frowned, and then changed his tone.

"You are pleased with your investment?" Viktor probed.

"Yes, so far. The terms work. I'm glad we did this first one within this calendar year. Our team looks forward to a productive relationship to help you achieve your goals," Arlen said, relying on well-oiled phrases used to bolster confidence.

"Tell me, Arlen, if you want to help me, then why do you hurt me?" Viktor asked.

"What do you mean?" Arlen said.

"You hurt me. I say hurt because this is how I feel."

"Why do I hurt you?" Arlen asked, a nervous tinge passing through him. He did not like how Viktor now squinted.

"You hurt me because you are not what you seem," Viktor said.

Now Arlen's heart skipped a beat. Perhaps it was just bad English. Foreigners always struggled with the nuance. Arlen kept his face expressionless even as a small internal alert mechanism now sprang to attention, flashing caution.

"I don't know what you mean."

"You know."

"Know what?"

"Everything. Your government squeezes you. Then you squeeze me." Viktor clenched his right hand into a tight fist to demonstrate the feeling. "I know you don't really want to hurt me, but when you play games, this embarrasses me. You hurt me."

"I don't understand, Viktor," Arlen continued, sticking to his cover story.

"When you choose to lie, it is worse," Viktor replied calmly. His words hung on the air. Arlen puffed slowly at his cigarette and mentally raced through his current options. Arlen had been in many situations with

---

20   Cigarette brand known for its distinctive aesthetic, featuring black paper and a gold foil filter. Founded in London in 1879.

clients when he was forced to lie. He was good about dissembling facts and promoting alternative fictions when pressured.

"These are strong," Arlen said as he put out the remaining cigarette butt.

Viktor let the silence linger. He offered him another Sobranie from the pack, as if he had suddenly landed Arlen in a confessional booth. Arlen lit the new cigarette and took in a long drag of smoke that he released through his nostrils.

"What do you want me to say, Viktor?" Arlen said.

"Who is Jo?"

Arlen's internal alarm now flashed a brighter orange.

"I don't know any Jo. Who is he?"

"Not he, she. A spook who should mind her own business," Viktor said.

"Never heard of her," Arlen said.

Uncomfortable silence ensued. Arlen tipped the last of the vodka down his throat. *I'm done with this minor league clandestine bullshit*, Arlen concluded.

"Listen," Arlen said. "Let's call it a night, shall we?"

"So soon?"

"Yes, I should get going. Uptight girlfriend needs some attention."

Viktor leaned back in his chair.

Arlen put the empty tumbler on the floor, rose from the wicker chair, and headed for the fire escape in a casual manner.

Arlen felt a firm grab on his right shoulder from behind just as he began to descend the small ladder that led off the rooftop. Another hand came roughly to his left arm.

"What are you doing? Get your hands off me," Arlen hissed, shocked at being physically touched. Even the most contentious business meetings never involved touching. Touching was never allowed!

Viktor's hands were strong; his fingers gripped Arlen's arms until it hurt. Arlen saw rage in Viktor's blue eyes. His face was a distorted mask, like a cornered animal caught in a trap. Then without exchanging words, Arlen grasped the real danger.

Viktor shoved him down fire escape stairs to the next lower level. Arlen felt a sharp pain in his ankle as he fell to the grated metal a floor below. He regained his balance shakily, then pushed against Viktor, who had quickly descended the fire escape after him. Arlen's limbs did not obey his commands. He was shocked to wrestle this way with another grown man.

"Stop it," Arlen said weakly, still not entirely sure how to physically respond. Arlen had always been a poor athlete; his limbs did not obey him. The adrenaline confused his mind. *This isn't really happening. Is it? Is he really doing this to me?*

Viktor pressed Arlen against the iron grating of the fire escape. Arlen pushed back, struggling. Viktor paused as if to catch his own breath.

With one tremendous heave, Viktor came at him again. Viktor grabbed at Arlen's legs, then lifted Arlen's hips with one sweeping motion and pushed him hard over the iron balustrade. Arlen felt his body tilt in space. Then for a just a few seconds, he was tipping over, falling in the air with a horrifying weightlessness, plummeting down in the darkness until, suddenly, a crash, crack, and shudder engulfed his body.

Strangely, after this catastrophic shock, there was no pain. Only a cool and pervasive silence.

Arlen was back in his childhood room, a small place with waxy wallpaper and high windows looking onto a lovely rose garden. Arlen felt very small now. He heard his mother calling him from above someplace. It was her voice, so faint, always very feminine and sweet. She was the only person who had loved him unconditionally. Arlen loved her back when she cradled him in her soft, so soft, arms.

The little, infantile Arlen had been such a helpless child, cooing up at her, looking at her gentle, loving, big brown eyes. Then the image of his mother faded into a swirling cloud, his mind became confused, and like the onset of a drug-induced sleep, his universe went blank. The life Arlen Cross had occupied over thirty-nine years—the entire vast complexity of his lived experiences, his myriad loves, anxieties, triumphs, hopes, sorrows, and fears—ceased permanently to function.

7

VIKTOR VOLKOV stared down at the still body lying in a pool of dirty water next to a garbage dumpster in an alley. Gravity did the dirty work using all those five stories. The living man who had just previously wrestled with him was now just a smashed piece of flesh with a crushed spine.

He deserved it. Pretty boy. Faker. Piece of shit.

Viktor straightened himself up and regained his poise. It didn't go exactly as planned but close enough. He had wanted Arlen to talk more. But it was hard to choreograph perfect outcomes or predict how others would react in stressful situations. At least this was a quick way to solve the main problem. Thankfully, Arlen was mostly quiet about it. He had raised his voice only a little at the end, as one might protest a traffic ticket or complain about a minor domestic problem. These finance types were always lost in their dreaming until too late.

Now Viktor needed to move quickly. When Viktor reentered the penthouse, he stopped. A jangle of keys, then voices came from the main entrance into the living room. He heard Katya's laugh. It was too soon for her return.

"What are you doing up there, Viktor? Who's there with you?" Katya called up.

Paul and Katya peered at him just as Viktor entered the loft's main living room from the fire escape. Now here he was before them, like a child with his hand trapped in a cookie jar. Viktor could manage Katya, but she was with the American boyfriend again. He was a much bigger problem that might require immediate fixing.

"No one. I'm fine."

"You don't look fine," Katya said. "Your nose is bleeding."

"Is it?" Viktor said. Little Arlen must have struck his face.

He wiped the blood away with his sleeve. "There was an ... accident," Viktor replied.

"What kind of an accident?" Paul asked.

"My guest. He slipped just now. He fell," Viktor said. There was no way to hide this from the American now. Paul went to the fire escape and looked down to the dark alley below.

"He fell," Viktor repeated. "Come on. Help me now."

"Help you how?"

"I need to clean this," Viktor said to Paul, as if he were simply asking for help with an oil change.

"We need to call an ambulance," Paul asserted earnestly.

"Nonsense. Too late for that."

"Then we need to call the police." Viktor coldly stared at Paul.

"I told you he slipped and fell," Viktor said sharply.

"I heard you." Paul glanced over to Katya, but she averted his eyes and instead looked down at her shoes.

"No, Paul. Think," Katya said. "We can't."

Viktor checked the apartment windows from different angles to determine any other problems. The other buildings along the alley were quiet with darkened windows. People in this neighborhood kept to themselves, each unit a separate island. Neighbors here insulated their homes from sirens, street noise, and all manner of unknown domestic disputes.

Paul Drake needed time to think. He had asked Katya to leave the theater at intermission. The play was tediously boring. Paul expected a simple detour back to Katya's place to pick up her clothes, then spend the night downtown at his place. Now this. The part of Paul's mind obedient to an idea of an imagined authority called out for him to stop. But his body and the rest of his consciousness stood there as if nothing serious had happened.

Viktor called Anton to bring a car. Then he and Paul took the elevator down to the street. Down at the end of the narrow alley, a limp body lay in darkness behind a steel dumpster.

Paul walked up closely to look at the dead man. He had seen worse in the desert, men lying in the dust, their bodies ripped up by a concealed land mine or a large-caliber weapon. Sometimes it was so bad he couldn't connect the piece of inanimate flesh to have once been human. In contrast, this man's face looked almost peaceful, his features placidly calm after the blunt force trauma of his fall. Then Paul recognized the face: The cocky hedge fund manager. The Dubai guy.

"I know him," Paul said.

"Yes, he was my friend. Now help me."

Paul observed Viktor's logic. Step one: secure all physical evidence. Viktor checked for street cameras. The neighborhood was quiet at night, with only a few passing taxis. Anton drove Viktor's black SUV in reverse down the narrow alley. They wrapped Arlen's body in a tarpaulin canvas, and the two Russians heaved Arlen's body into the SUV's back with a single motion. Viktor took out Arlen's wallet and his phone.

Step two: identify electronic evidence. Viktor gave Arlen's phone to Anton. Then Paul thought, yes, a GPS record, an electronic fingerprint. They will move the phone while the batteries remained charged.

Step three: create an alternate reality. For Arlen's credit cards, the last transaction should not end with a taxi ride to Ninety-Fifth Street. They should use the card in another location. Perhaps swipe the card at some neighborhood store a few blocks from his apartment. Smart way to plant a digital footprint along a different trail.

Finally, there was the fourth and final step: deal with any unintended witnesses.

"You want to help me?" Viktor asked.

"Yes, I do," Paul said. Anton's hulking form loomed nearby.

He gazed at Paul with expressionless eyes. "Get into the car," Viktor said.

"No, I should stay with Katya," Paul said. Viktor paused.

"Get into the car," Viktor said again.

Paul took one step back. It was already getting light now, the morning sky turning a soft blue. Paul was on the street. It would be hard to corner him in this rising daylight without drawing attention.

"I said no," Paul repeated. Aton shifted his weight to the front of his feet and began to reach inside his leather coat.

A dog barked nearby. A man in a sweatsuit was crossing toward Riverside Park, led by a husky golden retriever on its lease. The day was beginning again. More moving parts. Not enough time left to set up the pieces exactly right on the board.

The dog barked again.

"Fine," Viktor acquiesced. "You stay with Katya. Listen to what she tells you and don't be stupid."

Then Viktor went to the driver's seat of the SUV next to Anton. Viktor stared at Paul through the window's dark glass before the SUV moved very slowly down the alley, paused, and turned right.

Paul took the old Otis elevator back up to the apartment, and at each floor, his mind rattled off stray questions and anxieties.

When Paul returned, Katya sat alone in the couch staring blankly ahead, face marble white.

"Viktor wanted me to go," Paul said.

"Smart not to listen," Katya said.

"What now?"

"Trust me. Give me time," Katya said. "I will find us a way out."

"How?" Paul asked.

Paul saw Katya shaking very slightly. She had fallen from her astral plane and was now a thin bundle of nerves. He moved closer to her on the couch.

"I'm sorry, Katya. We can't erase this. You know what just happened," Paul said.

Then he thought, *Yes, I need more time to think. Inaction now means we're both accomplices. The arrow of time moves only in one direction. Too late to go back. Or is it?*

"Yuri can help us," she said.

"Your uncle?"

"Yes. He can help us. I know it."

"Then let's ask."

"Yes. I must now, for you."

CHOICE AND OPPORTUNITY

8

Paris, France.
September 9, 2017. 3 p.m.

PAUL DRAKE peered deeply in the dark, blood-red wine before he savored a first sip. His tongue registered a dry, complex, and earthy taste, which also caused him momentarily to marvel at how easily it had been to cross the Atlantic Ocean overnight. Through the miracle of twenty-first-century commercial aviation, Paul now found himself in a small café on the banks of the Seine.

Paris, unfortunately, was no vacation. Only a week had passed since that night with Viktor, and nothing yet was settled. No bevy of uniformed police had arrived to inspect a suspected crime scene; no cluster of reporters had prowled near Katya's Upper West Side loft. Absolutely nothing had happened.

The days also had done little to determine in Paul's mind what exactly he was going to do next. The only certainty was that he had missed his window of opportunity to leave. Inaction itself was his choice. There was only the journey ahead and waiting choices.

Paul and Katya had both slept during the Air France red-eye flight, with Katya's head resting on his arm most of the way. They avoided the worst of the morning traffic from Charles de Gaulle by arriving in the late morning. The overcast September morning blended its somber tones with rooftops and monuments, giving the capital the appearance of washed-out age, like a faded print made from a restricted color palette.

"Isn't it lovely," Katya said as she saw the Eiffel Tower peak above the rows of well-ordered Haussmann-era rooftops.

"A postcard day," Paul said.

Katya took him to a walk-up apartment still owned by her family in the 6th arrondissement across from the Luxembourg Gardens—a decent one-bedroom, mostly unused. They both took hot showers, brushed teeth, and changed clothes. Thus refreshed, they head to the quiet Café Jacques was tucked away down a smaller, tree-lined street just off the Boulevard de St. Germain. The waiter took them inside to a round table in the back corner. There, they ordered a simple meal of bread, onion soup, cheese, and wine. The Bourgogne pinot noir came first.

"How do you feel now?" she asked.

"Splendid," Paul said after his first sip.

"Good. Perhaps we can stop at L'Eglise de St. Germain later. I love the blue ceiling," Katya said.

They finished the food and were halfway through the bottle of wine when he finally arrived. Katya saw him first through the pane glass window. They rose from their chairs when he entered.

Katya kissed both of Yuri Volkov's cheeks and spoke Russian in a soft tone. Then Yuri held his hand out to Paul, who shook it with a robust, firm grip before he sat down.

"Hello, sir," Paul said, forgetting the more elaborate introduction he had prepared in advance. Yuri Volkov was an imposing man with chiseled features, deep wrinkles, and a trim white beard that enhanced a sage-like visage. His eyes seemed to belong to a being who was contained in this one singular body but had retained access to a much wider set of experiences from myriad past lives.

"You look well, Katerina," Yuri said.

"How was your trip?" Katya asked.

"From London, simple under the water through the tunnel. Just three hours."

Katerina poured Yuri some wine and refilled the other glasses on the table, switching languages for Paul's benefit. Yuri spoke English with the deep, careful voice of a man who had learned the language later in life as a formal exercise.

"It's good you came to me now," Yuri said as he leaned back. "Tell me about yourself, Paul."

As Paul spoke, he formulated in his mind a vision of how he wanted others to see his life. He told Yuri how he had first contemplated an engineering career while at Columbia. Then his plans changed. The Army Reserve called him up, brought him to the Gulf for a so-called War on Terror. He hadn't expected to serve in an active theater, but that was exactly what happened. Two long tours.

After Iraq, the army slung him back home. He chose a banking life in New York City, more fast paced and lucrative than other options.

"Katerina says you work hard," Yuri said.

"I don't come from money," Paul said. "I have done modestly well, but the game is always changing. Many executive layers in big companies. Every few years, another reorg."

"It sounds dehumanizing," Yuri offered.

"In a way," Paul said, thinking of the myriad traps that could derail his career. No one had his back when it came to New York jobs. If Paul had a spare moment, it was best to push ahead on the job, hustle his way forward, maximize his bonus potential, even if there was no higher mission behind making revenue targets each quarter.

They stayed at the small, round table after the waiter cleared their plates, then ordered Alsatian sausages and more onion soup. Yuri continued to ask probing questions intermingled with other casual observations.

The daylight began to fade while the dinner crowd began to arrive. The café became crowded with laughing voices and the clanking of plates and glasses. After the plates were cleared and the bill was paid, Yuri sent a message to his driver from his small mobile phone.

"My train departs at noon tomorrow. I would like to see you again, in the morning before I go," Yuri said. "We can take some exercise at the Jardine de Luxembourg. Shall we say seven sharp?"

"Yes, Uncle, we will see you there."

Yuri's driver had already pulled his car onto the boulevard and moved to the sidewalk to open the door. Yuri kissed Katya on the cheek again, nodded to Paul, and disappeared inside the vehicle.

"Well?" Paul asked.

"I don't know, Paul. My uncle doesn't share his deepest thoughts, but I know he wants to help us. I told him in Russian that I trust you."

"Just that?"

"Trust is everything."

Paul and Katya walked arm in arm down the boulevard de St. Germain toward Place de St. Michel. The ornate Parisian streetlamps shone brightly, traffic was heavy, and the many boutiques teemed with patrons.

Paul thought more about his own smudged, charcoal-gray life before Katya. What he described to Yuri—college, Saddam's desert war, different jobs—all this seemed now to be a series of random events without any deeper purpose. He had been floating in a vast and random sea without any authenticity. The war was violent and intense, but Paul had put on that uniform because external force ordered him, not because he himself believed in its purpose. There was a patriotic mission, but real decisions were out of his control, in the hands of politicians and generals. He realized now that he had never really believed in any of it. The war passed before his eyes as a surreal pantomime of violence, a dream disassociated from his own life. It was the same inauthenticity in his failed married. He was never his real self.

"Don't worry," Katya said. "Yuri will have a good plan."

"I hope so," Paul said.

A plan and a new purpose, Paul thought.

Something about the clean Paris night kept Paul philosophic.

"What did your Sartre say about freedom?" Paul asked Katya.

Katya didn't answer at once but instead thought carefully as they crossed the Pont St. Michel over to the Île de la Cité. The two great towers of Notre Dame Cathedral peaked just above a row of buildings. Tonight, the lights made the city look peaceful, orderly, and very old. He felt as if he could almost see back across these twenty centuries and unravel each layer of stone and brick, back to the Romans when this place was just a tiny outpost. Western civilization, such great progress, and beauty over all these different epochs. *How far we have come*, it struck him. *How far must we go?*

"Sartre said, 'Freedom is what we do with what is done to us.'[21] Make sense to you, Paul?" Katya asked, holding his arm tighter.

"It does."

"Are you free, Paul?" she asked.

"We always have a choice," he said. "I'm not going to be an automaton putting on yet another uniform."

Tonight, here and now, at this moment along history's long continuum, his new freedom felt exhilarating.

---

21   " From Sartre's 1952 work, Saint Genet, Comédien et Martyr. *"L'important n'est pas ce qu'on fait de nous, mais ce que nous faisons nous-mêmes de ce qu'on a fait de nous."*

9

A COLDER MORNING greeted Yuri Vladimirovich Volkov while he awaited alone on a green wooden bench at the northern side of the Jardin de Luxembourg. The grand horse chestnut trees and the paulownias along the garden paths were starting to lose their leaves. The twisted branches reached up into the gray sky, holding their dying, dry leaves in a network of delicate, thin stems.

For his entire adult life, Yuri woke early, usually before sunrise. He long ago recognized that one of his most useful physical attributes was his need for very little sleep to support normal bodily and mental functions. On average, he found just five hours each night sufficient. This very valuable physical gift served Yuri well for many years. He used the gift of more time to read, study, and plan.

Yuri watched the bigger seagulls push off the smaller pigeons near the garden's flat central pool. The last time he had seen the Luxembourg fountain was summer, when it was full of children playing with their model sailboats in the park's central fountain. Today, there were only a few Parisians jogging and walking dogs along the dirt paths that coursed through the manicured lawns in the timeless geometric ovals as originally laid out in the seventeenth century.

Katerina had changed since last time Yuri saw her. Despite the circumstances she now faced, she looked happy. Yuri was glad she had found a separate existence within the New York art scene and her busy work at the Zephyr Gallery; a wise investment to start that business and to have her run it.

Now healthy again, she resembled so much her father, Sergei, in his youth. He could see his brother especially in Katerina's eyes, those mutating blue-green pupils always anchoring her different expressions with absolute constancy. It was as if through her eyes you could see clearly to her soul, while for most others, there was only a shifting, uncertain fog.

The pigeons pecked around him at fallen breadcrumbs. Yuri drifted back into thoughts of his own youth. The world was different thirty-five years ago. His early years in Moscow were the best; he was poorer then, but there was also a sense of hope for an unknown future. Those days were full of big, capital-letter ideologies. He felt a certain pride in the ideal that all men are brothers and that society could grow stronger, progress toward a better union. But that promise had long faded for them all, lost in harsh reality of bloated bureaucracies, failed solutions, and mountains of propaganda lies. Chernobyl[22] had been his personal breaking point. After that, he believed no one.

Sergei had always been there with him. They were a formidable team. Sergei was his more noble half, better than Yuri in all the important ways—friend, thinker, and well-rounded, sensitive human being. Sergei always trusted Yuri. It was Yuri who had introduced Sergei to the younger sister of his school friend, Elena Andropov. Sergei married her just six months later. She was a pretty girl then, like Katerina today. They held their wedding in a simple wooden country church outside St. Petersburg. Elena wore a hand-made lace dress, and Yuri carried the crown over his brother's head. Not a drop of wine was spilled at the wedding, a good omen.

Yuri was in the prime of his life at the dying end of the Soviet era. The chaos began when the state failed, the promise of Communism finally exhausted. Then came a long, hard, thrilling experience without any real authority above them. There was only confusion, power grabs, and new opportunity.

Yuri always had his special skills for finding the useful within any complex problem. This unique gift was a kind of genius that elevated him far above his formal training as an engineer. The Soviet chemical industry was inefficient, but its scientists were highly skilled, and the industry formed a key backbone of a large-scale industrialized economy. Yuri quickly took leadership positions to modernize and transform these hulks. The bankers loved him for this. He gained followers because he delivered a real success they understood. Over time, his stature grew with those who mattered.

Sergei took a different path by studying law and politics. When opportunity arose, Sergei helped align them both with a new breed of influential Moscow government officials. Sergei opened the door, and Yuri walked through it to find the most useful tools and deliver results. No matter how confused the situation, Yuri always devised a path to make money for himself and his allies. Many others failed, gave up, were jailed, or worse. Yuri and Sergei somehow thrived. They stayed free while others were imprisoned. There was plenty of luck with timing too. If he had been five years younger or five years older, then his classmates would not have been in their positions, nor would he have found the opportunities.

---

22   The 1986 Chernobyl nuclear reactor disaster exposed the deep systemic flaws within the Soviet government, fatally shattering public trust and accelerating Mikhail Gorbachev's policy of Glasnost. Cleanup costs crippled an already failing economy, while the botched handling of the crisis ignited powerful independence movements in Ukraine and Belarus.

Equally talented and ambitious men ended up in gulags just a short time earlier, or Putin's cells a short time later.

Today, Russia exchanged the worker's yellow hammer and sickle for the tricolor red, white, and blue. The old ideology was gone, but the Russian empire still spanned more land than any other country on earth. Yuri's own ventures included air and shipping firms in Malta, an extensive agrochemical business in Belarus, and most recently, a high-tech start-up. The dozen IPOs he had pushed over two decades were a boon for himself and his business circle. The English bankers sought him. He collected dividends and read monthly diversified financial reports. His ventures brought improvements to a vast swath of humanity, even if there was no more overt ideological talk of brotherhood and social progress. He was now a man of the West, settled quietly in a stone townhouse near Russell Square, still alive, healthy enough, always occupied, alert, careful.

Yuri saw Katya waving from a distance as she walked toward him with Paul at her side. She greeted him warmly, carrying two paper cups of coffee in her hands while Paul held a third.

"Morning, Uncle. We brought you a hot drink. Did you sleep well?" Katya said in Russian.

"Very well," he said. They engaged in small talk for a few minutes about the fall weather and the garden.

"Would you mind if I speak with Paul alone?" Yuri asked.

"Of course, Uncle. There are many statues to see here. I shall enjoy finding them again," Katya said.

Yuri saw her glance quickly at Paul before she set off walking along one of the many gravel footpaths.

"Please," Yuri said, motioning with his hand for Paul to sit down with him on the green park bench.

"Good coffee," Yuri declared.

"From the boulangerie near our hotel," Paul replied, his neck wrapped in a black wool scarf.

"Paul, if we had more time, I would want to hear more and tell you more. But time is not our friend. You traveled far to have this conversation. I need to make decisions. Let us start with the most important matter," Yuri said. "What do you truly feel about Katerina?"

"I don't know why, but we are kindred spirits. We still don't know each other well, but I've never met anyone with her qualities, her sensitivities. Something in the universe has brought us together," Paul haltingly explained.

"She is fond of you," Yuri said.

"That's what matters," Paul replied. "I am a better person because of her."

"Has Katya told you much about me?"

"Only a little."

"I do business in many countries. I have had success, but it has not been easy. For me, there is only forward, always swimming faster. Now I have wealth and perhaps some power. All can disappear if I don't stay useful. It can end more quickly if I am careless."

"Russia is not an easy place today," Paul opined.

"Not only Russia. There are the Europeans, the Arabs, and now the Chinese. In my world, I see many who feed off the world's mistakes—wars, disease, corruption. The world is full of men looking to profit from chaos, violence, and fear. It is easier to see this now that there are no more ideologies left to hide behind. The world is always changing. We need to change with it," Yuri said. "Now my point. I want to give you a job. Come work at my investment company in New York. Would this suit you?"

"As what?" Paul asked, his face showing surprise.

"Whatever we want to call you. Title is unimportant."

"I know little about your business. How can I help?" Paul asked.

"Work hard, learn, think, adapt. I will match your salary at your bank. If you perform, you will be rewarded in ways you cannot find now. I have my selfish reasons too. I worry about Katya. She has taken so long to get healthy again. Now we have another new problem with her brother. I don't feel that she is safe anymore. I don't trust Viktor's judgment; I never have."

"Why is she not safe?"

Yuri knew his next point would be the most delicate. Americans always seemed to anchor their moral compass on simplistic absolutes. Now Yuri would discover whether this young man was a thinker.

"Do you know about guilt, Paul?" Yuri asked. "I mean the guilt you have when you know you have failed those you love."

"I felt that, yes. From Iraq, I have this guilt. I try to forget now, but sometimes it haunts me," Paul said.

"Those people you saw die were not your loved ones. They were not even your compatriots."

"Some were, but most were strangers. There were women and children. Many children. I do feel guilt at the injustice and pointlessness of it all," Paul confessed. "We may have achieved something, but it was dirty business, like a lie buried. The worst was just coming home and realizing that no one really cared. They shook your hand and told you platitudes about your service, but they didn't really care. They couldn't care because they couldn't understand," Paul said, and looked away.

"What about your family?" Yuri asked.

"I have a younger brother. He served also," Paul said

"Then you will understand me better. I have thought these last few years much about guilt, much about my failures," Yuri continued. "But my guilt has a face I know well. My guilt has Katerina's face. My younger brother, Sergei, was a better person than I will ever be. He was a dreamer. He used his voice to stir up new thoughts in an old country. Dreams were his greatest strength and his curse. It's my fault because success came first for me. I used my success to give my brother his platform. I found a way for him to join our Duma so he could take more real action. I thought the shadow of my success, my importance, would protect him. I was wrong."

Yuri leaned forward and peered directly into Paul eyes. "For four years now, I have been searching for my brother's murderers. Katya should have died that day too from the car bomb. Somehow, just by luck, she lived. Nearly two years of therapy, months in many hospitals. I sent her to the United State to make a new life."

Paul now sat very still, unblinking.

"I looked very hard for these killers that first year. Then the second year came. I continued looking. Here and there, I picked up some breadcrumbs, but this kind of information is not easy to find. My questions were met mostly with real or pretend ignorance. Many were afraid. So, I trade with those whom I think can help me. I give what I can. I take what is useful. Trust no one. Without trust, I mostly overpay and expect to be disappointed.

"Sergei was a pacifist, a reformer," Yuri continued. "My brother put his mind on development, not war. He was against empire building, unnecessary interventions. He spoke out against Russia's occupation of Chechnya and against Assad in Syria. These are not popular views held behind closed doors. Sergei felt that there was more scandal to expose. He was working with a few others, trying to publish more, getting closer to the truth."

"That was enough reason to kill him?" Paul said.

"More than enough. Producing and distributing sarin gas and other nerve agents violates international treaties. Nerve gas is the poor man's atomic bomb. Even the Nazis, who first developed sarin, never used it in combat. Can you imagine? Hitler was a victim himself of mustard gas. The Nazis only used their gas on the helpless, in their camps."[23]

"Who do you suspect?" Paul asked.

"I was told the trigger was Iranian. This is hard to identify. What I do know is that to pull off a daylight murder and then to cover it so well requires resources and precise planning. Possibly Russian. Maybe Syrian or Turkish. I say beware the quiet dog. There are many quiet dogs today. No doubt I am seen as a quiet dog. But I need more than my own suspicion. I need proof.

"The Americans must know something," the old man continued, leaning forward now. "They put their noses in many places, and they have tremendous resources. And if they don't know anything yet, they can help me find out more once I show them my value. I know my true enemy is out there. He sees me, but I can't see him. Do you understand this?"

Yuri looked closely at the younger man seated next to him on the bench. Paul's origin was so different from his own, so much safer. But perhaps Paul's two tours in the desert had shaken away enough of those lazy American illusions. Or perhaps Katya was wrong. Perhaps Paul understood nothing from his active service. Was it wise to trust a foreigner from such a different culture? Americans were always too Manichean with their notions of good and evil, right and wrong. They were fed this like a bad diet of prepackaged food.

"I want to help if I can," Paul said.

"You will need to deceive," Yuri said.

"I understand," Paul said. "I am already involved. I can't go back." Yuri let the silence linger as both men followed the dance of cooing pigeons pecking at breadcrumbs scattered around the bench.

"Good then," Yuri said. "My man Dmitry will contact you after you fly home. He will cover all the details and help you prepare. The US authorities will come to you very soon with questions about their missing informant. I want you to cooperate with them when they do."

"Help the FBI?"

"Give them what we want them to see. Make them see your value. You must have them trust you for any of this to work. You are clean. Cooperation is plausible. Both Katerina and I are trusting you, are we not?"

"And tell them about Viktor?"

---

23   Nazi Germany discovered and produced sarin in 1938. Despite having stockpiles, the Nazis did not use sarin on the battlefield. Rather, the regime used chemical agents—specifically Zyklon B—to murder over one million people in extermination camps.

"Dmitry will help prepare you. He is very good. Tell them enough to believe you more."

"Seems like uneven odds against us," Paul said.

"Why? Because they are bureaucrats, and I am just an old Russian?"

"Because they have resources and legal authority. They can outspend you by many multiples," Paul said.

"I have resources of a different kind. I put little faith in their legal authority over me. I can use one dollar better than any bureaucrat can use ten. Americans are not much different than the Russians when it comes to this. Governments spend because there is a need to spend, not because it solves problems," Yuri said.

"What about Viktor?" Paul asked.

"Since you now work for me," Yuri said, "Viktor will not touch you."

Yuri rose from the bench. "I am glad we have found each other. If you forgive me, now I want time alone with Katya. I do not see her often."

Paul also rose and held out his hand, which the older man shook firmly.

"In Russian, before the hunt, we say a curious thing to wish you good luck: neither fluff nor feathers," Yuri said.

"And how should I reply?" Paul asked.

"You say, 'Go to hell.' In Russian, this is *K'chort u.*"[24]

"*K'chort u,*" Paul repeated.

Yuri smiled, thinking how odd to hear the expression spoken with such bad pronunciation.

———— ✶ ————

Yuri buttoned his long wool coat and walked toward the slender figure of his niece he saw strolling in front of the Palais de Luxembourg.

"It's too bad we don't have more time," Katya said in Russian when Yuri was close enough to hear.

"Never enough time for those we love," Yuri said. He removed his leather gloves to clasp Katya's thin hand in his own. They walked, hands linked, along the gravel path while the working Parisians passed on their way to offices and appointments; small groups of uniformed children hurried their way to school.

---

24   The phrase originated from a hunting superstition: hunters would use reverse psychology to trick eavesdropping evil spirits into believing the hunt would fail. Responding signaled a rejection of the bad luck wish, thereby ensuring success. Russian equivalent of 'Break a leg!'

Katya led Yuri first to a bronze statue of a woman holding a torch straight in the air. The garden's statue was a smaller version of the familiar Lady Liberty holding the flame of freedom and enlightenment in the New York harbor.

"I have always loved this statue," Katya said. "She wasn't always meant to be wearing a Roman tunic. Bartholdi's original design was a statue of an Egyptian woman for the Suez Canal. He called it Egypt Bringing the Light to Asia before he changed to a Roman goddess for the Americans."

"Designs have a way of changing. When we see only the end, we forget the origin," Yuri said.

"Have you also seen the Medici fountain,[25] Uncle?" Katya asked.

"Take me there. Tell me what you know of it," Yuri said.

As they walked through the gardens, Yuri thought, *I should not be here with you today. Sergei and Elena should be in my place. They should be the ones listening to stories about statues and fountains, wars and revolution. You would have been their inspiration, pride, and joy. Instead, only I am here with you. I am a survivor, an old man, while better humans are but dust memories. I have robbed you of your life through my own carelessness.*

"What did you think of Paul?" Katya asked when they reached the Medici fountain. The fountain's placid water reflected gnarled branches placed around the outer rim. A few colored leaves lay scattered around the bronze and marble baroque figures in the center.

"An attentive young man," Yuri said. "Your Paul is a blank slate."

"Is that good?"

"It can be if I write well."

"Then you will help us?"

"I will try. We must help each other," Yuri said. He squeezed Katya's thin hand in his, not yet knowing what to make of the gambit he was about to set in motion.

"Not a day goes by when I do not think of them," Katya said.

"I know it is so, but you live for the future not the past," he replied.

"*Te prav.* You are right."

"*Te yugal lubish?* Do you love him?" Yuri prodded.

"I don't know," Katya replied. "I want to believe again. I don't want to be alone. But it is so hard to know others."

---

25   17th-century monumental grotto commissioned around 1630 by Marie de' Medici, the widow of King Henry IV.

10

"TAKE A seat in here," the young woman told Paul before she shut the door behind herself on the way out.

Paul folded his trench coat over another empty chair. His dark gray suit felt damp from the afternoon rain. Paul realized with some annoyance that his feet were cold; he had stepped into a muddy puddle while exiting the yellow cab in Jersey City. No matter about the rain. At last, the plan was in motion.

The US authorities had approached Paul after just six weeks. That was the time needed to reach a tactical conclusion that either Arlen Cross met an untimely demise, or he had orchestrated an extremely clever exit. The latter was possible but very unlikely. Paul could thank Dmitry Medkov for using this precious interval to prepare him for this moment in Jersey City. Just two days after Paul's return from Paris, his rapid transformation began. He embraced it. Leaving his position at the bank was simple. Paul sent in his resignation via email, put his personal items from his desk in a box, made abrupt farewells to his colleagues, and signed his exit documents promising not to steal the bank's clients or reveal proprietary data. He used unpaid leave to cover the two-week notice period.

"What's next?' his friend Andy asked him with a puzzled expression.

"Private opportunity," Paul said, and left it at that. There was nothing to the job; all the hard work Paul had conscientiously built over four years dissolved quickly. None of that mattered now.

Dmitry first sent Paul to the office of Eastern Finance on the twentieth floor of the Greylock Building on Forty-Second Street, near Grand Central. An office staffer greeted Paul at 7:00 a.m. She equipped him with an access card, laptop, and Bloomberg terminal. Paul kept his interaction with other staff to brief courtesies and routine words. He was just a new consultant brought in to do some necessary chore—a technical expert hired to fix something broken. The managing director of the office, a gray-haired Bulgarian woman, smiled when she saw Paul from across the office floor, huddled in his new twelve-by-eighteen square-foot domain. Like the others, she just left him alone.

Dmitry never came to Eastern Finance's office. Paul met Dmitry a few times at a hotel suite on Sixty-Fourth Street, also at a private room at the University Club on Fifty-Eighth Street, and once at the member lounge at the New York Athletic Club on Central Park South.

"I have only a few weeks to discuss with you what it took me many years to learn. You will need to learn quickly," Dmitry warned Paul at their first meeting. "Let's make our time together pleasant, shall we?"

"I can try," Paul said.

"Have you ever had an acting class?"

"I'm afraid not."

"Think of this as acting. Think of yourself on a stage with a new costume, a new voice. Use your imagination and your memory to become a new person. Only you are not trying to entertain. You are there to help the other actors around you with their scenes."

Dmitry began each session in the late afternoon, usually accompanied by strong black tea. Dmitry's firm attention was that of a coach with a new athlete hired to a key team position, or a producer with a new but untested lead. He started with some cursory questions about Paul's daytime consulting work. What opportunities did Paul see for financing the various logistics businesses? How could he help integrate new technologies?

These discussions didn't last long before Dmitry turned to his games. The US Army had trained Paul in some aspects of counterintelligence, but that was for combat conditions in the desert. Dmitry's training was a far more subtle and psychological art.

First, there was Dmitry's game inspired by Chekov, the early days of the Moscow theater, and the method approach of the great Konstantin Stanislavski.[26] Paul prepared details of an invented character. Then through a short conversation, Paul played out his fictitious role.

Roles changed for each new session: London businessman, UN diplomat, a trade lawyer. Paul let his imagination rove, but invariably, Dmitry distinguished when Paul strayed from the proposed character facts. Paul's first tell was a slight downward gaze when he lacked confidence in the invented persona. Once identified and corrected, the tell moved to Paul's voice via a very slight tempo change. Dmitry then worked to correct.

"Think of yourself as formless. You can be anyone at any time in your mind," Dmitry explained. "It is a matter of intentionality. Change by using your imagination to overpower reality. Become your new person. Inhabit the new place. Lose doubt."

---

26   Konstantin Stanislavski (1863–1938) revolutionized 20th-century acting by shifting performances from melodramatic gestures to, truthful, psychologically realistic human behavior. The precursor to Method acting.

During other sessions, Dmitry rehearsed different types of anticipated interrogation—the typical good/bad cop routine, positive denials, theme development, passive confrontation. Paul replayed responses, feigning answers. Each time, Dmitry gave subtle steerage to keep the interaction cool and subdued.

"In the future, you may become both the interrogated and the interrogator," he cautioned.

Then there were memory and awareness games: Dmitry showed hundreds of photos on a handheld device. Some were simple headshots and others taken in private settings. Paul memorized the identities via a mnemonic method to associate names with very specific facial features. Paul discovered that his human brain had evolved to recognize and retain identities with great specificity. In a week, he could recall more than a hundred associated names; easy once he mastered the technique and paid absolute attention.

"Most people don't really understand their surroundings," Dmitry cautioned. "They walk around 90 percent themselves and, at most, 10 percent others. You need to reverse this. Exist in the minds of those around you."

Finally, there was the hardest lesson: the polygraph machine. This contraption measured his heart rate, blood pressure, and small changes in breathing. The polygraph tested the most critical relationship: that which he held with himself.

Dmitry took Paul to a private apartment located in an old brick building in Murray Hill, with a partial view of the United Nations' austere lone rectangle rising from the East River. A tall, thin man with a ponytail, colorful plaid shirt, and old, brown leather loafers greeted them on the ground floor, first name only: Scotty.

Scotty administered a first polygraph test to calibrate Paul's responses. Then they began practicing how to beat the machine under stressed conditions to mimic a real test. Paul sat uncomfortably on a plastic chair with bright overhead lighting shining on his face. Scotty asked his questions methodically. Dmitry patiently observed.

Paul used a repetitive mantra to visualize a wide-open sea with gently rolling waves splashing on the shore. When Paul invoked this mantra, the ocean waves lapped in. He matched his breathing to the imaginary shore as he answered. Each session, the waves grew louder and more vivid.

"These polygraph machines are just body sensors. The trained mind is the instrument of a detached superego. You must seek the place of this detachment. In this place, you must stay a long time to understand nothingness," Dmitry said.

Even Dmitry seemed pleased with how quickly Paul figured out how to beat the machine.

———— ✳ ————

Thus prepared, Paul Drake waited in the FBI's windowless room in Jersey City. He glanced at his watch: ten minutes already. He stared at a poster of the Grand Canyon on the wall. Why choose such an expansive vista for such a confined room? Paul had never been to the Grand Canyon. Rather than climb up a mountain to its peak, with a canyon, one descends from the top. A curious reversal, just as he had to reverse his thinking: perjury was truth, and truth was whatever he created in the mind.

A quick double knock on the door preceded two figures entering. One was African American, and the other, a dark-haired Caucasian with a chiseled chin and wide lips. They flashed their badges and false smiles, then gave their names before they took the two empty chairs across from Paul: federal agents Marcus Woods and Francis J. Gallo.

"Sorry to keep you waiting," Gallo said. "Thank you for coming on such short notice."

"Not a problem. How can I help?"

"We asked you to come for a missing person investigation on Arlen Cross. This should not take long," Gallo continued.

Marcus Woods looked down at a document in his portfolio. He flipped to the next page and began his questioning.

"Did you have much personal contact with Mr. Cross since you met him?"

"Not much. He came to an art show Katerina held at her gallery downtown. We had drinks afterwards. That was July, I think."

"You were mutually introduced by your girlfriend's brother, Viktor Volkov?"

"Yes, Viktor introduced us," Paul said.

"How would you describe the relationship between Mr. Volkov and Mr. Cross?" Woods asked.

"Friendly. Primarily interested in furthering mutual business."

"Any unusual incidents?"

"None that comes to mind," Paul said.

"Where were you the night of September 2?"

Paul scrolled through his mobile phone calendar, feigning an attempt to recall the details of that night when in truth it was mentally etched in stone.

"Yes, here we are. Now I recall. I went to the theater with Katya to see a play," Paul said. "The Iceman Cometh. Nice production with good acting. I recommend it if you are a fan of O'Neill.[27] I can find the receipt if that is helpful."

"It may be helpful. Did you see Mr. Cross at Ms. Volkova's Ninety-Fifth Street apartment that same evening?" Marcus asked.

"No. We came home later. Why?"

"Mr. Cross did not return to his home after this," Woods explained. Paul reviewed his night's timeline in greater detail, repeating many details for the benefit of accuracy. Then Frank Gallo followed up with a different line of attack.

"Any recent changes in employment?" Gallo asked.

"A new job six weeks ago. A smaller firm providing financial services to foreign industrial companies."

"That's a step down for you, no?" Gallo asked.

"Not really. Most jobs these days don't last long. Viktor introduced me to the opportunity. It provides me more freedom to do what I want. Better pay. I've been promised to work on transactions at senior levels. Project financing, currency hedging, some acquisition work."

"Involving Mercury?"

"They are a priority partner."

"Any difficulties on these transactions? Anything unusual?"

Paul knew that the moment to plant the seed had come. He paused for effect as Dmitry's script demanded and took on his role.

"One real estate transaction in Cypress needed a loan from a consortium of lenders. The Germans were the only parties willing to accept the hard collateral and corporate guarantees," Paul said. "Arlen helped Viktor find a private investing group out of London. They helped, but the structure was unusual."

"Who helped?"

"Viktor bragged to me that Hans Vogel helped facilitate. Apparently, he's a big shot politician."

---

27   Eugene O'Neill's four-act tragedy centering on the lives of social outcasts in a squalid bar premiered in 1946. It takes place in the back room and bar of Harry Hope's saloon and rooming house in New York City during the summer of 1912.

Paul caught a quick exchange of glances between the two agents. Then he described a complicated set of referral arrangements as Dmitry had prepared at just the right level of detail to pique interest. Viktor's dinner with Hans in London was only hearsay, but Paul described enough to capture their prosecutorial imaginations.

"It seems they have given you a great deal of responsibility. Why so much confidence in you?"

"Maybe I impressed them," Paul said.

"They show you details about Hans Vogel?"

"Some."

Woods put his pen down and eased back in the chair.

"Let's pause here. If you don't mind, Paul, please excuse us," Gallo said. Then the two agents left Paul alone in the room again. They had been going at it for nearly two hours.

Paul looked at the poster of the Grand Canyon again. Had he already descended enough? Another thirty minutes passed before Woods opened the door. He came in alone, carrying a set of documents in his hands.

"Thank you for waiting so patiently. Please look through these documents. This is standard procedure in an investigation of this nature. These documents provide you an outline of your legal protections. This also gives a description of criminal and civil penalties related to communicating details of our discussions, should you obtain additional information that is ultimately submitted in court."

"Do I need a lawyer?"

"You are not the subject of any investigation. We need your help. These documents provide you structure and assurances regarding additional conversations we may want to have," Woods said.

"I appreciate that," Paul said.

"Any upcoming travel plans?" Woods asked.

"Not in the immediate future."

"Good. That's all for now, Paul," Woods said as he handed him a business card. "Call me with any questions, any time of the day, any issue. Number on the card."

"Thank you, Marcus," Paul said.

"Thank you for coming to see us today. It means a lot to me that people like yourself are willing to do the right thing, especially a fellow service veteran."

The two men shook hands.

"Someone will be in touch from our side," Marcus said. "I look forward to helping."

11

THE WOMAN who called Paul on his mobile identified herself first as a real estate broker, a simple cover story: "How are you today? Would you be available to come downtown to tour a rental opportunity for about an hour?"

Paul arrived at the older office building wedged within a tight maze of taller downtown towers and a few blocks from city hall. The concrete building was an antiseptic 1970s monstrosity that housed dentist offices, divorce attorneys, and independent financial advisers. Paul found his way to the fourth floor, to a white metal door with a room number but no other signage.

A middle-aged blond woman in large, round glasses greeted him at the door. She was alone in the room, empty except for some cheap office furniture and a bookshelf with a handful of books on foreign affairs, chemistry, and US presidential biographies.

"Ah, come in. Great to meet you. I'm Jo. Water or coffee?"

"Water please."

Jo handed him bottled Evian, and they sat down.

"I've signed your legal documents," Paul said, handing her his envelope. She took it and placed it on the table without unsealing the contents.

"I hope you understand," Jo said. "Everything in this country is so bureaucratic these days. I'm with Shakespeare that we should kill all the lawyers. Amazing I can still buy aspirin without signing some fucking form."

Jo took a quick swig of coffee as they both made casual observations about how the warm weather was global climate change on display. *These types always try to humanize themselves before they get into their true objectives,* Paul thought.

Then Jo started into her pitch. *Is she going to appeal to my patriotism, vanity, or greed? Or a combination?*

Jo began with patriotism.

"Before banking, you served in the military?" she asked.

"Yes, Iraq. Just out of college."

"Army reservist?"

"That's right. An ROTC officer. They put me into intelligence," Paul said. "Not much intelligence happening with that war. Wrong about most of it, bullshit from start to finish."

Jo's lips smiled slightly, but her eyes remained very quiet and still.

"Army must have taught you something."

"In the beginning, yes," Paul replied. "There are no shining knights."

"Maybe only a few," Jo countered. "Serving your country these days takes grit, mental discipline, some madness too. You don't think we accomplished any good in Iraq by taking out Saddam. Nine eleven doesn't mean anything?"

"It does, but those were not Iraqis jets smashing into the Twin Towers,"[28] Paul said.

"Guilt by association."

"And plenty of manufactured lies. Time has passed. Is anyone better off?"

"I understand your bitterness, Paul. I really do. War is an ugly bitch," she countered. "I was the Treasury liaison in Kabul then," Jo said. "Tough assignment. Hated every minute. Three years dealing with trigger-happy Blackwater mercenaries[29] and towel heads who wanted to behead us in the name of Allah. Such is the Taliban."

He shrugged.

"I know you also have a brother who was injured during an incident outside Fallujah?"

"That's right. Max lost sight in an eye and half his spirit."

Patriotism could take Jo's pitch only so far. "Mission accomplished" was always going to be a hard sell. Jo moved on to vanity.

"I need someone like you, Paul. I need help. I believe that you may be well placed to significantly make a difference. Help us get the bad guys. You have somehow begun to touch issues we care about. You can finally use your talents and the training we gave you."

"What issues?"

"His name is Hans Vogel. A politician good at making speeches criticizing NATO but even better at making obscene money for himself when the cameras turn off. He puts his fat, sticky fingers in bad places.

---

28   On September 11, 2001 al-Qaeda terrorists crashed two planes into the World Trade Center and a third into the Pentagon. None of the attackers were Iraqi citizens and any direct links to Iraq were never established.

29   A private military firm founded by Erik Prince that became a primary, yet highly controversial, security contractor for the U.S. government during the Iraq War.

Putin and his cronies love how he keeps Germany open for business. They enable him. We're not fans."

"You want me to help like Arlen Cross did?" Paul said. Jo shook her head sideways.

"Not the same. Arlen already made some poor choices. You are different. You are smarter. National security and the right thing to do for someone with your skills and potential. All these parasites feed off misery. That's not the world we want," Jo said.

"I've done my bit on that already. More than most."

Finally, Jo moved to greed, the most reliable of motivations. Most college students in the Army's Reserve Officers' Training Corps didn't come from money. Maybe the queen's coin would work.

"If your cooperation leads to materially relevant information, then the United States will provide you with a substantial monetary reward. Would that make a difference?"

"It could," Paul said.

"Good. We can be very innovative in this regard to scale up payment," Jo said. "What have they told you of their uncle?"

"Not much."

"And you are not curious about their lifestyles? How they pay for all their prime-location apartments and fancy art galleries?"

"I know something about it," Paul said.

"Do you? Yuri Volkov is a legend. He's one of the most talented industrialists to come out of a bad Soviet system. I'm not interested in the petty scams of the nephew's offshore transactions. Leave that to the taxman. I'm interested in exploring the possibility of a mutually beneficial relationship with Yuri himself. I need to focus on our country's overall strategic goals. The big picture. The fate of humanity. War and peace. This is what gets the attention I need to make a difference with the people who matter. I care about saving lives and stopping tyranny. The lofty shit."

"You are asking me to spy for you?" Jo laughed.

"I don't think any of these Russians trust you enough, including your girlfriend. You may have found out about one of Viktor's poorly conceived business transactions, but he's the family's weakest link. I just want to know more. Dirt is useful. I don't need to trust Yuri, but his Russian friends do, at least to a reasonable degree."

"You think I can help?"

"You can try. Yuri Volkov has brought you in. That's a very rare opportunity. See it? But a clandestine relationship like this must be kept very, very quiet. Game over if any of this leaks. Maybe Yuri gets picked up next time he lands in the wrong airport."

"And how am I supposed to convince this uncle in London to take these risks?"

"I don't know. You're a smart guy. Be resourceful. Find out more about what that old man truly needs. Ask more probing questions. Try to meet him somehow. Take your girlfriend to London. Find out what money can't buy."

Jo looked like an overworked schoolteacher, but she had studied chess like the rest of them. She had her own theater training, someplace down in Northern Virginia.

"Interested?"

"Possibly," he confessed.

"Good," Jo said. "Then we start by nailing our Kraut friend to a cross. Oh, one more item. We need you to take a polygraph test. Would you be available, say, tomorrow morning? I've booked this as a priority with my security team. Standard procedure."

"You don't trust me?"

"I appreciate your military service, and I believe somehow you've stumbled into a unique situation. If we have success, you will be rewarded. But no, I don't trust you. A polygraph will help us start dating. No polygraph, no deal. Is this going to be a problem?"

"No problem. Nothing to hide."

"We're off to the races then," Jo said.

"It seems so. What time is available tomorrow?" Paul said. "And will you be compensating me for my time?"

"Don't worry, Paul. Help me, and I promise you that you'll get what you really want. I'll make it worth your while."

12

HE WAS on the third mile of an early-morning jog along the East River running path when his lungs began to burn. Paul's body had grown weaker these past few years, a side effect of desk jobs tied to computer screens and office conference rooms. Now Paul was determined to change. Armed with a New Year's resolution, he had started with boxing classes, a structured weightlifting program, and morning runs at the crack of dawn. Strong mind, strong body, his father had always told him. It was a simple adage but one that was universally true and had served him well in the past.

Paul sprinted the final hundred meters, then slowed his pace and caught his breath. As his heartbeat slowed, he looked to scan the alerts sent continuously to the mobile phone he always carried. At the end of a long list of messages. There it was—and sooner than expected.

```
    Former German MP Arrested in €50M Tax Fraud and
Money Laundering Raid

    German authorities yesterday arrested prominent
businessman Hans Vogel on suspicions of tax fraud and
money laundering. Federal police detained Mr. Vogel in
an early-morning raid at his private home in Westend.
Prior to founding a private business in 2007, Mr. Vogel
served eight years in the German Parliament, where he
was known for controversial positions on foreign policy
issues. A lawyer for Mr. Vogel did not return comment.
```

Josephine Richards didn't waste time. It was just a month since Paul had handed over Dmitry's technical information. Now, the German police were already knocking down doors and making arrests. Jo must have already marshaled convincing evidence for such a quick win. She found her ways.

Paul put the phone down and reached toward his toes to stretch his hamstrings.

Later in the week, Paul and Jo met for early breakfast at Pershing Square, a diner under the Park Avenue overpass in front of Grand Central. Jo greeted him with a broad smile when he sat down with her at the corner table near the window. The waitress first poured the coffee in two mugs, then took their orders and left them alone.

"Ah coffee, elixir of the gods," Jo said as she took the first sip.

"How did it happen?" Paul said.

"The list and IP address you gave nailed it." Her eyes glowed.

"Not good for Viktor."

"No, but that is just a pawn sacrifice," Jo said. "Now I keep my promises," Jo said.

"You write me a check?"

"Something better. Hans was a good win, something real to showcase. With proof of concept, we take it up a notch. There is a man I know with a special interest in supporting our project. And more importantly, resources to help."

"Didn't you say our secrets need to be ironclad?" Paul said.

"They are, they are. This man has the influence in Washington," Jo explained.

"Another politician?"

"George is many things— patriot, businessman, patron of the arts. I will plant the suggestion that he might rely on your girlfriend's excellent eye for his art needs."

"Art collecting doesn't seem to fit your line of work," Paul said.

"There you are wrong," Jo said. "Art is very much my business. This is how I get what I want, and you get paid. Art's value is what you put into it. Everyone sees something different on the canvas. True subjective value. Eye of the beholder. Am I right?"

Jo put down the empty coffee cup just as the server arrived with a plate of pancakes.

"What is this all about, Jo?" Paul asked. "Why do you need Yuri Volkov?"

"Unfinished business in my favorite part of the world," she continued. "You remember Colin Powell?[30] Not only did we fuck up that region for a generation; today we have a humanitarian disaster in Syria. It's turned into the biggest refugee problem since World War Two. Ten million displaced. Worse than when we started."

"What can we possibly do about that?" Paul said.

"Now that is the right question!" Jo slapped the table. "What can you and I, just two people sitting here, possibly do about that!"

"I'm all ears."

---

30   As U.S. Secretary of State, Powell presented faulty intelligence about Iraq's alleged weapons of mass destruction (WMD) to the UN Security Council in February 2003, using his credibility to build international support for the war.

"The Russians will not accept American private firms to deliver aid to all these suffering masses in Syria. But they might agree to a compromise choice, one of their own."

"Yuri."

"That's right."

"Is there money in it?"

"Always buckets of money. Fortunes made when blood oozes on the streets. These are multimillion-dollar contracts. Enough for Yuri to spread around."

"What's the catch?"

"The catch? A UN presence will help keep millions housed and fed, stop some from flooding Europe as refugees. There is no catch. My art collector is coming this weekend. He wants to meet Katya. Indulge him his moment with her. After they meet, then we can all decide what's next. I'm confident you will help Yuri understand the scale of what I'm putting on the table. This could be the start of a very productive, very lucrative arrangement."

Jo poured more syrup on her pancakes and took a final bite. She left Pershing Square satisfied that Paul had understood. She was making something of this little domestic desk job by going after a new relationship with Yuri Volkov. Those army clowns wanted to sideline her into some meaningless little corner chasing two-bit money launderers. Now she saw a way back into the real action. If George Rutherford agreed to help, then she could do an end run around those Pentagon blockheads. Her creative approach might actually succeed.

It had been more than three years since she stood on that barren hill in Northern Iraq. Local militia took the marines to the bodies a day after the attack. The dead were all wrapped up in white shrouds laid out in parallel rows on the dirty sand. The children were under the smaller shrouds. The shells had destroyed the building, but most had died of asphyxiation, whether smoke or sarin gas. Of course, the Russian government denied involvement. They never would admit blame or complicity in any of these atrocities.

Fucking Russians. They always backed the hardcore killers when it served their interests. Jo was not going to blow a real chance to shove a hot poker up Putin's ass for propping up Al Assad. Then there were the Turks, who wanted nothing less than to destroy any chance for an independent Kurdistan. The Israelis hated Iran and played their own game. And now these new fanatics were trying to set up some dark age caliphate by swinging scimitars in the name of Allah. What a fucking disaster.

Just because Operation Timber Sycamore[31] had been such a failure didn't mean the Seventh Floor wasn't eager to fill this unstable vacuum. Why did lover boy General Petraeus[32] ever greenlight that idiotic arms-smuggling scheme with the Jordanians? These so-called covert programs were a joke when they leaked like a sieve. Might as well call the New York Times with the ops plan. For Timber, some brilliant army mind posted a solicitation for small arms on the internet. Now you could read all about it on Wikipedia. Amateur hour.

She shrugged her shoulders. Now perhaps she could clear away this mess and find a better way.

---

31   CIA-led covert operation aimed at providing weapons and training to Syrian opposition groups. Phased out in 2017 due to limited success, the rise of extremist factions, and reports of weapons being diverted to the black market.

32   David Petraeus resigned as CIA Director on November 9, 2012 after revealing an extramarital affair with his biographer, Paula Broadwell.

13

NAZIR HASSAN looked down from the limestone ridge through a pair of high-powered binoculars. Across a two-kilometer stretch of dry flatland, he saw the small Kurdish village of Sheran, a cluster of stone and mud houses.

Sheran stood on the outskirts of Khobani, just south of the Syrian border with Turkey, about forty kilometers east of the Euphrates River. Khobani began first as an outpost along the Baghdad railway during the waning days of the Ottoman Empire. It was a decent location near to the Euphrates River where seminomadic Kurds could settle and conduct trade. After Syrian independence in 1946, Khobani and its surrounding villages slowly stabilized into a commercial center developing industries related to rock mining, cement production, textiles, and olives. The area's population had reached eighty thousand. Generations lived together. It was rare for families to move either in or out of this community.

Two members of the Turkish intelligence stood next to Nazir, dressed in desert camouflage. The older officer, Colonel Atakan, had insisted that Nazir join this operation as an observer. Atakan was keen to test Nazir's various Russian-made weapons given the high prices recently paid for these illicit tools. A young officer, no more than twenty, set up a tripod with another high-powered scope to observe the distant town.

For the past six months, Khobani had been infested with Islamic State fighters, destroying most of the eastern part of the town in a brutal ground assault. The presence of these terrorists, however, gave Colonel Atakan the pretext to attack another enemy, militia fighters belonging to the Kurdish Worker's Party.[33] Syrian government forces, positioned some fifty kilometers to the south, gave him tacit approval for today's incursion.

The enemy of my enemy is my friend, Atakan understood.

The small village of Sheran had been determined to be a military target based on recent intelligence. This village was now home to more than a hundred young Kurdish fighters. They stored small arms in hidden weapons caches and built a sophisticated tunnel system to navigate underground

---

33 The Kurdish Workers' Party (Partiya Karkerên Kurdistanê, or PKK) is a militant political organization and guerrilla group that has been a central actor in Kurdish nationalism for over four decades.

between their various cells. Five days ago, a group of masked Kurdish fighters had attacked a nearby Turkish border post that was preventing many Kurdish Syrians from entering Turkey. Three Turkish soldiers were killed in that early-morning assault, a cowardly and despicable act that sent Atakan into a fury. The colonel was charged with stamping down such lawless activity. Failure to retaliate forcefully made him look like a weak fool in a time of active conflict.

Yesterday, Atakan and Nazir dressed in plain clothes and began early in the morning. They drove through Sheran's dusty streets in an old white Toyota truck. The village was already in bad shape from street fighting earlier in the year. However, in the past month, a sizable group of Kurds had come together here with the hope of rebuilding. The village was beginning to stir again in small but important ways.

Nazir brought his new device, a Belarus-made handheld GPS target marker no larger than a mobile phone. As they drove through the streets, Nazir registered GPS coordinates of each desired target. Now, the town was prepped.

The three men waited on the dry, hot ridge, while two large desert vultures circled the clear azure sky. Atakan listened to radio communication on a handheld radio unit. Voices involved in the operation announced different steps over the radio. Atakan determined that the assault needed to be a surprise to ensure intended results—air support came at a costly fee. Ten fifteen in the morning was chosen as the optimal time.

A faint rumble in the sky steadily grew in intensity until it became a deafening roar as the Turkish F-16 passed overhead. The plane soared over Sheran and tipped its wing slightly as it made a half circle over the village. After a few seconds, a series of bright explosions tore through a section of low-rise stone and mud houses. Seconds later, after they saw these bright explosions, sound waves reached the observation ridge—a clapping roar confirming the bombs' lethal reality.

Through binoculars, Nazir watched the chaotic scene outside the village's central mosque, where dozens had been milling around rows of outdoor food stands. Now those people were frantically scurrying, like insects on an ant hill kicked over by a malicious child. Some Kurds ran toward many of the collapsed buildings to help family members and friends trapped in the rubble. Fires from a damaged gas station sent up billowing black smoke.

Ten minutes later, a second plane came from the north at a slightly higher elevation, bringing another series of explosions. This time, the bombs scattered over a wider target area, knocking down a municipal building and hitting other residential structures throughout the village. A four-story apartment complex crumbled like an old, dry white cake, pushing out gray dust clouds.

Nazir was much too far way to hear the shouts and cries, if there were any.

Twenty minutes later, the third and final run, this time from an older turboprop military plane. Now there were no fiery explosions. Instead, a cluster of metal canisters dropped like stray confetti. The canisters broke apart on impact around the target area. It was hard to see from this distance, but Nazir knew that gas now filled this area with a noxious haze. *Nerve gas will finish off those now trapped under stones*, Nazir knew. *This little town was the perfect place for an example. No one cares, nor will they send any inspectors this deep into the war zone.*

He put down the binoculars.

"What do you think?" Nazir asked Colonel Atakan in Turkish.

"Effective," Atakan replied. "We have taken the fight to those terrorists."

"What about the children, *Bayim*?" the junior staff officer asked after he took his eyes from his mounted telescope.

"What about them?" Atakan asked.

"One bomb has also hit the school at the south part of the village. I can see it from this distance. Should we send in any medical support?"

The older military man pulled out a pack of cigarettes from his breast pocket. He lifted out a cigarette from the pack, put it between his gray lips, lit it, then puffed out a cloud. Atakan hated the dirty Kurds. The Kurdish Worker's Party was to him the true threat to Turkey's future. The Americans only supported the Kurds because of a common enemy. The previous common enemy had been Saddam's Iraqi regime. Today, it was these black-clad fanatics, waving flags of a new Islamic caliphate. Tomorrow it could be another group.

"Did these cowards show any mercy when they ambushed our boys?" Atakan shot back to his subordinate. "No, they cut them down like animals. Besides, this is Syria. Let the Syrians help their own."

"Yes, *Bayim*," the young officer replied, chastened.

Atakan needed to be brutal. Fear was a great psychological weapon, he understood. Ten years ago, he quashed a similar Kurdish rebellion because of an equally strong stance. Those Kurds feared the gas most of all. Sarin would burn their lungs first, then choke them out in a few minutes. The horrors of gas made even the most diehard rebel think twice about attacking even a single Turkish boy.

Having seen enough of this operation's success, Atakan walked along the ridge to the nearby military truck parked higher up on the ridge. Nazir followed, also with a queer sense of power to have played a role in reigning down such a destructive force on this ancient small town. It was as if they possessed the might of Genghis Khan crushing his enemies without remorse. "When can you arrange delivery of the next shipment?

There is more for us to do thirty kilometers east of here as well," Atakan said.

"As soon as you are ready, *Kardesim.*[34] I'm sure our Russian providers will accommodate."

"Good. It's time to bring back order to our sacred Anatolia." *Business is good*, Nazir thought. Blood begets blood. This single border is five hundred kilometers long, and there are many others like this.

This is just the beginning.

---

34   Turkish word for younger brother, similar to 'my friend' in English.

14

TWILIGHT enveloped Manhattan in a dull yellow light when the tall George Rutherford III crossed Ninth Avenue and approached the Zephyr Gallery on Twenty-Sixth Street. George saw the gallery's modern script signage from across the quiet street. Before drawing closer, he peered through the gallery's front window.

A woman sat alone at a small table facing the entrance; she was writing in a leather journal, intensely focused on the page.

George was pleased. Even from this distance, he thought Katerina Volkova prettier than the coarse photos he saw last night. There was something very serene in how this young woman looked now through the window, waiting for his arrival with her long, honey-colored hair falling over her thin shoulders. George couldn't have asked for a better casting choice for this whole proposal. She was perfect for the role.

At seventy-eight years old, George still felt like a young man in spirit even though his body had begun to fail him in all kinds of inconvenient ways. His wife had died of cancer twenty years before, and now George was settled at his ranch outside of Palm Springs, where the sun kept him warm, and he could manage his affairs in the broad comfort of the open skies and clean continental air. He kept a good diet and exercised every day, thus expecting to live at least another decade or more.

Officially retired from executive roles, George still considered himself a man of action. The reward of immense wealth meant that he didn't need to mix with others or worry about commercial airline headaches. This morning, the chartered Gulfstream left directly from the Palm Strings airport and landed five hours later in Westchester County. As a veteran visitor to Manhattan, he loved to sip the madly frenetic island in small doses: two nights at the Carlyle, dinner at Keens,[35] and at least one martini at Bemelmans.[36]

George Rutherford III held a few core beliefs that had served him well. In his mind, his spectacular success was a direct result of his

---

35   Established in 1885 by Albert Keen, famous for its massive mutton chops, and a ceiling adorned with over 90,000 clay tobacco pipes.
36   Established in 1947, an iconic, historic lounge famous for its original murals painted by Ludwig Bemelmans, author of the Madeline children's books.

personal brilliance and superhuman work ethic. He had earned his success by assiduously devoting every single day for more than half a century to transforming the regional chemical business he had inherited from George Rutherford II into a global industrial giant.

Now in his old age, George thought more about his legacy. His current $3 billion net worth would amply provide for his two sons, their children, and their children's children. But neither son had developed any more impactful vision for humanity. His five grandkids were even worse, all pursuing fanciful lives because they had never struggled themselves. This was the danger with offspring. Even George IV, his eldest, had no vision, no true understanding. They all had grown soft in the belly and assumed freedom and democracy were absolutes. All his spoiled kids wanted were their big houses and long vacations.

George looked elsewhere for his legacy. A decade ago, George breathed new life into the otherwise quiet foundation his father had set up in the 1950s at the height of the Cold War. The Jefferson Foundation promoted American capitalism and democracy abroad. Each year, George happily steered his foundation to donate tens of millions in campaign support to defend the true vision of the founding fathers in the world's difficult places. George made tremendous progress winning over the Permanent Select Committee on Intelligence. He cultivated legislators on Appropriations, Armed Services, Judiciary, and Foreign Affairs Committees. These people, in turn, came to his events, sought his guidance, and gave his foundation the kind of access to government programs and special people otherwise beyond any ordinary citizen.

When Jo Richards reached out on her special project, George took the call. He liked Jo because they agreed on core principles, and she had been out there in the field, a real scrappy fighter. Now she came to him with something new; something daring and brilliant; something to put his mark upon the fate of humanity. Together they would put words into real actions of consequence.

George was frustrated with the mess that those lesser men had made in the Middle East with their catastrophic stupidity. If a young Russian woman somehow fit into this puzzle, then it was imperative that George see her with his own eyes. He needed to decide himself if Jo's fanciful scheme for Syria was real.

Thus, with the great anticipation of a much younger man, George Rutherford III crossed Twenty-Sixth Street and pushed open the glass door to enter the Zephyr Gallery.

"Welcome," Katya said with a smile as she rose to greet her appointed visitor.

"I'm sorry I'm a few minutes late," George said.

"Not at all. You are actually a few minutes early," she said.

"Oh, that's good then. I must have made a mistake with the time. I thought I was late. Very good. Very good."

"I've been told by your staff that you are mostly interested in oil paintings."

Katya gathered a small clipboard with notes, and then they toured the gallery, spending time to visually take in each canvas throughout the different rooms. Katya spoke fluently about painting, describing the context of each artist and the themes each had spent their careers exploring. Some of the paintings evoked traditional motifs, while others were more controlled, mechanical abstractions with a greater sense of form and materiality. Katya described the artists as visionaries who lived in a way that others could not, always fishing for epiphanies out of the dark oceans of the human unconscious. Katya's accent added an intriguing flavor to the expression of her ideas.

One large painting caught George's eye. He stopped in front of two blue figures bathed in the blood orange of a setting sun. The figures embraced in a shimmering, strange light that seemed a combination of the figurative and the purely imaginary.

"This one I like very much," George said.

"Yes. This is called *Against the Dusk*. A masterpiece of color. One of my favorites," Katya said. "Each time I look at it, I draw out a different meaning. What do you see?"

George leaned closer. It was rare now to be challenged to explain how he viewed anything, let alone a strange painting in a high-end Chelsea gallery. George put his face near the canvas to see the painting details and the rhythm of the artist's brush strokes. This picture called on him to examine all the multi-layered nuance that before he missed upon a more superficial viewing.

Now he saw what Katya meant when she spoke of art reaching beyond the mere visual to connect with some deep living core. Strange vision, this one. Pale translucent lines in the background formed a shimmering city against the blood-orange horizon. The artist had brushed in this almost invisible outline so that the picture seemed to shimmer in an out of focus. George stepped back, readjusted his eyes to the full composition, and formulated his thoughts.

"It reminds of time passing, how we are all limited with the very little time we are given. The two figures embrace because they understand the brevity of their spirits and the immensity of the universe beyond this."

"Bravo. You see temporality in the composition," Katya said. "The artist finished this just a year before he died. This is his last major work. Perhaps he was thinking about the end of life."

"Strange color of the sky and in the fury of his brush strokes. It is almost a kind of ... rage," George mused.

"If you wish to get hold of the invisible, you must penetrate as deeply as possible into the visible,"[37] Katya said.

The silence lingered as they both looked.

"Anything else you want to see now?" she finally asked.

"No, thank you. A wonderful, impressive collection," George said.

As George lingered with the canvases, he considered his options. He was still nothing to Katya except another potential buyer interested in modern painting. But her voice had seductively drawn him in. The paintings had somehow induced a deep calm, tinged with childish excitement. He liked very much how he was entirely alone with this shimmering female from a different planet. Now he wanted to reveal himself. There was little time left to lose.

"Did they tell you about me when they made the appointment?" George asked.

"Afraid not. Your foundation only asked for this time slot."

"Well, then I owe you an apology. You should have been told more. And perhaps I should have been more forthcoming myself. Let me correct this now. I did business in Russia many years ago, and during that time, I had the pleasure to meet your father."

George eyed Katya closely to gauge how quickly the blood rushed out of her face. She paused for a slight moment as she took in this new information. Had George revealed himself too soon, too abruptly?

"We met briefly at a conference in Moscow, more than twenty years ago," George said. "I was an early foreign investor at that time, introducing better chemical processes used in heavy industry. Your father and I both shared a vision for a better world. I was a great admirer of his forward thinking on social issues. He was different from the other Russia government people I met. He had vision and the courage to act."

---

37 German Expressionist painter Max Beckmann famously said this in a 1938 London lecture to suggest that to truly understand spiritual or hidden truths, one must first intensely study and deeply engage with the physical, observable world.

"Yes, he had his bright new, liberal ideas, like an American. He paid the price for that," Katya said.

"He believed in the possibility of freedom," George asserted.

"Who is truly free?" Katya asked. "What is freedom?"

"Self-determination. Your gallery here is a kind of pure freedom, no? Look what you have assembled here."

"This gallery? Money buys self-determination. Poor clients don't buy art."

"Exactly, and I want more people to have resources and security to make their own choices," George said.

He continued to explain his politics, giving Katya his vision for a new world of open borders, free elections, superpower cooperation. He spoke of an End to History when elections produced substantive leaders rather than despots, how war zones could be rebuilt and civil institutions strengthened. Radical religious faith would fade away under the progressive forces of open societies. These themes were covered by the half a dozen position papers produced annually by the Jefferson Foundation.

"Well, then. I don't need to lecture you on such matters. I bore you with political fantasies of an old man," George said as he noticed Katya's eyes begin to drift.

"Shall we return to the matter at hand then? The paintings?" George said.

"Which are you most interested in?" Katya asked.

"Great art is a scarce asset. You have already put together a very cohesive collection with a trained eye. I wouldn't want to be outbid by anonymous buyers when these go to auction. Shall I buy it all now?"

Katya paused to refocused on what this crazy old man had just said.

"You mean *all* the paintings in the gallery now?"

"Yes, plus what you keep in inventory. I can also acquire the lithographs you mentioned. I'm no great collector like the Getty family, but I buy art for its scarcity value. The good stuff appreciates at a very attractive rate of return. Your taste is exceptionally good."

"I've never priced out the entire gallery," Katya said. "The cost is significant, and I would need new appraisals for many."

"No, no, no," George said, shaking his head. "I don't need to give you direction on pricing! No doubt you have had the canvases appraised by the right third parties. That's your business. What is profoundly important to me is to restart a friendship. I never had the chance to do anything meaningful with your father or your uncle. Now the world has changed again, and here we are. If there is a need, then I will play my part. I have been told your uncle maybe is involved in a new UN effort in the Middle East. For me, fascinating work."

George watched Katya's lips finally curl into a very slight smile. Now she understood! Marvelous how this young Russian girl's gem-like eyes mutated between green and blue depending on the light, he observed. Katya reached into a small white cabinet behind the table. She pulled out a bottle of Stolichnaya[38] with her right hand and two small shot glasses with her left.

"I suggest we drink to your support and to our future," she said.

Katya poured the vodka. They both swallowed. The vodka went down George's throat smoothly, with only a slight burning at the end. He felt younger already. Katya poured another round.

"Tell me more about your trips to Russia and what you think we can do today to change their politics," Katya said.

This was much better than drinking alone at Bemelmans, George thought. Now he felt like a much younger man, alive again. George had even told his first lie already. He had never met Sergei Volkov in Moscow. This was Jo's invention to humanize his outreach and form a connection with this alluring target. They had profiled her based on an algorithmic assessment on how to win her trust.

He was a man of action now. Wasn't art the lie that made us see the truth? Wasn't his patriotic moment with Katya now so brilliant to be much like his own personal work of art?

---

38   Stolichnaya (often called Stoli) is a well-known brand of vodka that originated in the Soviet Union in 1938. The name is the feminine adjectival form of the Russian word *stolitsa,* which translates to "of the capital city."

15

PAUL ENTERED the Metropolitan Club[39] through the entrance on Sixtieth Street between Fifth Avenue and Madison. It was a very cold December evening, and the traffic snarled throughout the canyons of Midtown's streets.

"Are you here for tonight's event?" the girl at the front desk asked him.

Paul nodded, then signed his name in the registry for tonight's discussion of the Syrian crisis. The UN's emergency relief coordinator, Emil Marek, was the event's main speaker. Emil was to be interviewed by a BBC journalist on the status of ongoing relief programs, followed by cocktails and light hors d'oeuvres.

Three large crystal chandeliers graced the Metropolitan Club's ornate event room. Italian marble bas-reliefs depicting the twelve labors of Hercules covered the walls. This was old New York, reminding Paul of stiff white collars and gilded-age tycoons. He took his seat near the front of the room while men and women in dark suits milled about. He observed many donor groups, a bevy of UN diplomats, foundation representatives, and leaders from Médecins Sans Frontiers, Care, and other notable relief agencies.

After a brief introduction, Emil Marek took his seat for an interview-style discussion with the BBC journalist. Emil began:

"Syria today is a tragedy we have not experienced in our lifetimes. More than two hundred and fifty thousand Syrians have lost their lives in four and a half years of armed conflict. Eleven million others have been forced from their homes into neighboring countries. What is the UN and the donor community doing to alleviate this suffering? Since 2013, we have delivered three million tons of essential food and water to those impacted by this senseless conflict."

Emil Marek's voice boomed deeply. Paul saw him now as one of the few leaders who really cared. He was a dashing figure who commanded all the necessary details and laid out the challenges of large and small humanitarian organizations struggling to keep refugee families alive. He cited the priorities—clean water, food, basic shelter—and brought

---

39   An exclusive, private social club founded in 1891 by financier J.P. Morgan.

attention to how in one country there was peace, affluence, and progress, while at the same time, others suffered war, extreme poverty, and utter despair.

"Ensuring the quality and proper storage of medicine is a priority," Emil finished. "Addressing this will go a long way."

The BBC journalist then opened the discussion to audience questions.

"Can you comment on what the UN is doing to protect the UNESCO heritage site at Palmyra?"[40] one person in the audience asked.

"The destruction of Palmyra is part of this tragedy. Unfortunately, there isn't much we can do now. Jihadist militants from the Islamic State are still fighting to establish a new caliphate in that part of Syria. They have dynamited most of the monumental ruins of that once great city. When peace is restored, my hope is that certain structures, such as the Temple of Bel, can be rebuilt, and we can restore this important culture site."

"How long will the UN's aid commitment last?" came another question.

"Given the entrenched nature of the conflict, we are planning a multiyear assistance program. I'm not optimistic this will be solved anytime soon. We need your help."

It was 9:00 p.m. before Paul and Emil took a short walk from the Metropolitan Club to Vaucluse on Fifty-First Street, where Paul had reserved a table for two. The host took their coats, and then the head waiter led them to a softly lit corner of the restaurant near the window.

"Was tonight's event helpful?" Emil asked.

"Very much," Paul said. "Your explanations were very clear."

"Jo is a good friend of the UN," Emil said discreetly to acknowledge the nature of the dinner introduction. "When she mentioned your employer, I expected someone different."

"Someone older?" Paul offered.

"And a Russian speaker," Emil admitted.

"Perhaps it's time to think of new options. We want to do more and smarter. Tell us how we can help."

"The most acute unsolved problem is the widespread distribution of antibiotics and basic medical needs for very preventable illnesses. The Syrian government has destroyed anything that came close to being called a medical facility. There is still no effective way to deliver medicine and food. We need to get more medical kits from warehouses out to the camps.

---

40 During its two occupations of Palmyra (2015–2017), the Islamic State demolished monuments they deemed idolatrous, beheaded the city's longtime antiquities chief, looted the museum, and financed their operations through the illicit sale of smaller "blood antiquities."

"Two years ago, the UN Security Council established four crossing points in Jordan, Turkey, and Iraq," Emil continued. "Russia has long backed Syria's contention that the cross-border delivery of assistance is aiding the rebels. They've severely restricted what can come through. To the Russians, helping their puppet Assad takes priority."

"Why, after everything he's done?"

"Russia needs access to the Mediterranean, plain and simple," Emil explained. "They need Syria to remain a staunch ally, especially given the conflict with Ukraine and Turkey's role in NATO. Putin's ambassador channels all major decisions on Syria into the UN Security Council, where they have a veto. We can't scale up these aid programs if Moscow says no."

"And the solution?" Paul probed.

"If the border crossings are allowed, I would consider a no-bid contract with a single provider to quickly scale operations. I can recommend this to the Inter-Agency Standing Committee. Washington has balked at many of Moscow's recommendations, and then Moscow does the same. Every vendor needs to thread this needle."

"We can work hard at aligning this," Paul said.

"This is bigger than what any single firm has done in the past," Emil said. "The need is urgent. Aid deliveries are now possible through crossing points at Yaroubia, along the Iraqi border, and Bab al-Salam in Turkey. This alone could reach more than a million civilians."

Emil spoke passionately throughout the remainder of the dinner, until the waiter came with the last coffee and the check. "I appreciate your time," Paul said as he signed the dinner bill. Emil was a consummate professional. He would not reveal himself too much on a first meeting with a stranger, even with Jo's warm introduction.

"When do you think we can receive your detailed contract proposal?" Emil asked as they exited back to Park Avenue.

"End of the week," Paul promised.

Then Emil paused and lowered his voice just a fraction. "You understand that it's not my job to determine why any member country approves or disapproves contracts. My only goal is to support this relief effort no matter what the politics. Lives are at stake here. Tens of thousands of human beings without good options. If food and medicine get to the right places, that's what saves lives. We need to move quickly. Days, not months."

Emil's driver brought up his car and opened the back door.

"Can I take you anywhere?" Emil asked.

"No thank you. I'll walk," Paul said, then turned toward Third Avenue after a final polite handshake.

Paul buttoned his jacket and began to walk downtown. A week was noticeably short. He would need tremendous help to design this quickly. Paul began to mentally check off a list of tomorrow's needs.

When Paul waited for a light change at the Forty-Sixth Street intersection, his eyes caught a backward glimpse of a tall, olive-skinned man walking behind him. This man had been drinking at the restaurant bar during his dinner and had also lingered on the sidewalk when he parted with Emil. Now the man donned a blue baseball hat with an American flag. Odd. He had been trailing behind now for six blocks already.

Paul summoned Dmitry's technique to recall recent faces. Did he see him at tonight's Syrian event? *Focus now. Shift the mind's camera lens back four hours.* A similar figure sat quietly on the back-row chair in front of the marble bas-relief depicting Hercules wrestling with the three-headed Cerberus. Paul turned left toward the East River. The tall man still lingered behind, hands in his pockets, that blue baseball cap pulled down low over his temple to hide his face.

Paul stood on the corner of another intersection as if waiting for a cab. The man also paused, staying a block away across the street. The stalker looked in the opposite direction to avoid eye contact. *Now this is enough*, Paul thought. No crime for having poor taste in hats, but he needed to confront this follower.

When the crosswalk light turned green, Paul pivoted back at a fast gait. The man had already seen Paul's attention, so he quickly adjusted into a light jog, crossed the perpendicular street, then ducked into an alley between two residential brick buildings.

A taxi honked loudly as Paul tried to cross the intersection.

Goddamn New York City drivers.

Paul approached the alley cautiously. He lost sight of the blue cap as the back alley diverged to the left behind more buildings, leading into a small parking lot. Paul followed slowly, until he could see around this corner. A chain-link fence separated the back lots from another egress to the south. The man had swiftly climbed a dumpster, then jumped the fence to reach the alternative exit.

The distant shape scurried an instant more, then was gone.

16

D MITRY MEDKOV took back his passport from the dull eyed customs official at the Odessa International Airport. His plane from London's Heathrow via Istanbul had just touched down four hours before. His bones ached from the long journey.

Dmitry rubbed his hand over his neck and his bald head. He would have only a brief time in Odessa, less than a week.

The young American had surprised them all when he presented them with the no-bid UN contact of this substantial scale and importance. The size of the contract was large, and there was more than just money to be made. This effort served a purpose. If they executed well, lives would be saved. If he failed, more people would perish.

Piotr Verzilov came by car to the airport. At first, Dmitry didn't recognize Piotr when he stepped out. Piotr had grown a thick black beard and no longer looked like the young man Dmitry had known from ten years ago when they last met.

Piotr was not the highest-ranking official within the Ukrainian navy, only a captain first rank, but Dmitry trusted him. Piotr was well placed to arrange the right set of meetings. The naval command in Odessa was a small, tightly knit community. A half dozen people needed to be brought along. And all these men were already in a war mentality because of the annexation of Crimea two years before. They were hungry for action. *A wolf eats standing up*, Dmitry thought. He would find his warriors among such hungry wolves.

"I have arranged for you to meet each of them separately, as you asked," Piotr explained in his Ukrainian-accented Russian as he drove the car.

"Good work. Thank you," Dmitry said.

From the airport, the car entered the old city and slowed down over the uneven cobblestones of the smaller streets. Odessa had once been a thriving port town, a jewel in the Black Sea. But now, everything reeked of age: the limestone baroque buildings, the Potemkin steps that Eisenstein filmed almost one hundred years before[41], those chipped European statues erected for some civic purpose now long lost in the annals of time after successive wars and revolutions.

Dmitry hated all the inefficiencies he saw: the poorly paved roads, the crumbling old city walls, and the soot smeared on the commercial signs. Odessa promise had been clouded by the turmoil of centuries, world wars, and decades lost in the wilderness of a repressive Soviet ideology. The rest of the world simply moved on, while Odessa stood still, like an aged parent left forgotten in a nursing home.

Piotr drove Dmitry to his hotel in the old city. Dmitry showered and ate some stale black bread, and then they started with the first of a series of meetings. There was already a small UN contract in place with Yuri's shipping subsidiary, MSA, to ship tents, potable water, and basic food stuff into southern Turkey. But what Emil now needed was a major escalation of these activities, with new destinations for the massive camps that had sprung up around Aleppo, and some also in Jordan and Turkey. Emil needed both air and sea transport; the operation required military clearance from multiple countries, especially Turkey. Feeding and sheltering millions of people in the desert was a massive task. MSA was just one of many parts in this vast undertaking.

For the next three days, Dmitry's meetings started early in the morning and lasted into the late evenings— "Tell me what you need to deliver on these goals. How much will it cost? What permissions do we need? When can you start?" It was like the old days when the system collapsed, and you just had to figure things out without expecting anyone else to supply the answers. Piotr scheduled the final dinner on the last night with the key players from the local government. He chose a quiet restaurant in old Odessa. At the entrance of Restoran Glechik, a bevy of tall, attractive female waiters all dressed in very seductive tight dresses greeted Dmitry. They handed him vodka and bacon served on silver plates, showing him their smooth cleavage in tight shirts with plunging necklines.

The navy men came to the dinner dressed casually in their dark suits, not their white formal uniforms. If they doubted Dmitry, they didn't articulate this to his face. The old balding man was now stepping into their lives with heroic resources and the promise of a UN contract. Dmitry dangled millions of dollars, paid out in cash. Nearly all the key players

---

41   The Odessa Steps sequence from Sergei Eisenstein's 1925 film Battleship Potemkin depicts a brutal massacre of unarmed civilians by Tsarist soldiers during the 1905 Russian Revolution

already had their private companies set up, ready to receive personal commissions. And they were ready for risks.

"We are committed to helping with this crisis," Valentine Kuzoff formally announced when he stood up for a small toast in the middle of the dinner. Valentine was not the most senior among the group, but he was the most charismatic. Others listened to him. Dmitry studied all their faces, their reactions, and their questions, Valentine most of all.

"How many workers here in Odessa will you need?" Valentine asked later in the meal.

"I estimate about two thousand. We will need around-the-clock shifts for the dock workers in the beginning," Dmitry said, thinking that they would need to take over a large swath of the old Odessa shipyard. Regular air shipments would leave from the nearby government airstrip.

If Dmitry made payments of sufficient amounts to the right six people, then these six would facilitate the whole endeavor, he concluded. These six were more important than the two thousand workers, the planes, refrigerated units, and the shipping equipment. The six would in turn incentivize their foreign contacts, and if he made the payments quickly in cash, they would act quickly.

"You think the Turks will be a problem?" Dmitry asked.

"No, only those in Sebastopol," Valentine warned.

All these men here tonight knew why two years ago, Russian special forces and airborne troops landed in the Crimea to seize the navy base as well as the regional political infrastructure. Crimea became Russian Federation territory virtually overnight. Moscow needed secure access to the Mediterranean via the Bosporus Straits. This geopolitical goal had stood in place now for centuries. Lev Tolstoy himself had fought in Crimea one hundred and fifty years ago for Czar Alexander II to secure a similar goal, Dmitry knew.

"The Russians will want observers. A very good job. We have beautiful women," Valentine said.

"I'll pay so they enjoy themselves and work less," Dmitry added.

After a few hours, the dinner moved away from the discussion of business details. The men began to call up patriotic songs as the long-legged women wrapped their slender arms around them. The songs had meaning. They all had grandfathers or great uncles who served in the Red Army those seven decades ago. Stories of sacrifice and the great defense of the nation grew more distant each year, but they still lingered strongly in movies, legends, and song.

The waiters brought in more vodka bottles. The women poured.

The men's voices boomed together, singing the song of Russia's victory over fascism, *Den Pobedy:*[42]

> This Victory Day
> Air saturated with gunpowder, It's a celebration
> With temples already gray, It's joy
> With tears upon our eyes Victory Day!
> Days and nights at blast furnaces, Our Motherland didn't sleep a wink.
> Days and nights a hard battle we fought—We hastened this day as best we could.

It is always these types of men who do the real fighting in every era, Dmitry thought. Dmitry appreciated their spirit, their sense of pride, but he also felt sorry for them today—always outgunned, trampled, underfunded, while the Russians relied on their satellite-guided weapons, laser scopes, and other advanced capabilities. Now was time to fight back, to stand up yet again for democracy, independence, and a better tomorrow.

Dmitry pulled Valentine over to the corner to speak privately. Valentine had drunk nearly a liter of vodka throughout the evening, but his eyes were still alert.

"What else can I do?" he asked.

"Piotr has told me you have served in *spetsnaz.*"

"That's true, my friend. Very proudly for the government of the Ukraine. *Geroiam slava*. Glory to the heroes."

"I need your help selecting the best men for more dangerous work in Syria and Turkey."

"Many of the best are now in Donetsk, I fear."[43]

"This will pay much better. Cash in US dollars. A signing bonus."

Valentine's eyes lit up. "What do you need?"

"Military and logistics skills if you can find them. They will be fully equipped, paid upfront and regularly thereafter."

He nodded his head in confirmation. "How many Russians now in Syria?"

---

42   Victory Day was composed in 1975 for the 30th anniversary of the end of World War II by David Tukhmanov (music) and Vladimir Kharitonov (lyrics); a staple of May Day parades.
43   Following the 2014 Russian-backed insurrection, Donetsk became the center of the self-proclaimed "Donetsk People's Republic" (DPR), a Russian proxy statelet. The region experienced intense fighting, leading to heavy industrial destruction, a ruined economy, and a trench war with Ukraine along a 420-km battleline.

"Many hundreds at least. They are like bees to honey," Dmitry said. "If we're lucky, we'll have our chance to meet them."

The dinner kept on until midnight.

Two of the women offered Dmitry their sexual services after the party, but Dmitry declined and left the restaurant alone. He departed after a series of handshakes. It was never wise to indulge in favors that might expose a personal vulnerability or create a wrong impression of weakness. He needed at least a few hours of sleep to function. He was, after all, getting too old for all this.

———— ✳ ————

Dmitry Medkov put down the cup of strong black tea and looked out across the bay of Odessa to the Black Sea's dark, choppy waters. He checked his watch: 11:00 a.m. The silver-plated samovar on the table was nearly empty, as he had worked nonstop throughout the long flight back. He was still busy signing the remaining documents—everything in this part of the world required an actual ink signature: bank accounts, warehouse leases, permit applications, employment agreements. He steadily attacked a whole stack of them, photocopied in duplicate.

For the past week, Dmitry had drunk tea constantly, never slept more than four hours, and never adjusted his biological clock to the new time zone. This would be the largest operational challenge that Yuri's organization had faced. It was certainly the most politically complex, with tremendous downside risks.

Dmitry heard knocking on his door.

"Ready, sir?" Piotr asked him.

"Yes, yes, let's go," Dmitry answered.

That was it then. In just five days, he had put the whole operation in motion. Complex, yes, but when there was enough money to make everyone happy, the momentum followed. In three weeks, they could make the first maritime shipment to Iskenderun in Turkey. Twice daily flights should begin shortly thereafter.

The antibiotics and other key essentials would be delivered to solve immediate problems for the refugees. He would put Valentine's squad on the ground there, too, for security reasons. Dmitry had also pulled the woman's file: Josephine Richards, West Point graduate, master's degree in chemistry, known expert on chemical weapon conventions, a former Kabul station chief passed over for promotion and sent back to a domestic job. The Americans kept this woman lurking in the shadows.

She had been involved in the region at least since the US toppled Saddam in 2003. What did she really want? What was the price for such lucrative business? Why work so hard to help set this all up?

17

WITH THE windows propped open to let the air circulate in her Manhattan loft, Katya sliced two apples in her kitchen and looked over at Paul, still groggy from a late sleep on Sunday morning.

Paul had begun to work long hours. Since January, they had only seen each other on weekends. Yuri had piled on a whole new urgent set of work. Paul didn't share all these details with Katya, and she didn't ask.

Instead, Katya tried hard to continue with her routines and interests. Last week, she marched with thousands of others to celebrate Earth Day on April 22.[44] The weather was getting strange, much more volatile than in years past. Now winter brought them extremely frigid days; Valentine's Day was the coldest in New York history, while December had been one of the warmest on record. Nature herself seemed to be in rebellion against the intrusion of human will and industry. She was now rejecting humanity's encroachment on her delicate balance, displaying her temper in new and unusual ways. The questions were posed: Who could doubt the science? Were fossil fuels now humanity's greatest threat?

Katya listened. She considered. She mingled with the thousands of people waving flags as they all walked down Fifth Avenue together. The UN secretary told the people, "Take your passion and compassion and build a better, sustainable world." Hollywood celebrities joined the cause; a famous actor addressed the UN assembly with a passionate plea for the world's attention on the melting polar ice caps. Maybe it was true that the entire planet was on an unsustainable path, and the oil pulled so cheaply from the ground was slowly poisoning the planet's ozone layer. The world dies not with a bang but with an exceedingly long and tiresome … whimper.

"You must spend a lot of time reading," Paul said from the living room. Katya snapped her attention back to him. Paul's voice pulled her out of her internal mental chatter. He was browsing through her books—French, Russian, some English—all lined up neatly on the tall bookshelf.

"There have been times when I have read much, yes," Katya said. "I read more as a student. Many nights in bed, alone." She had become the

---

44   Widely recognized as the largest secular observance in the world. While it began as a U.S.-focused protest in 1970, Earth Day has grown into a massive global movement. It now mobilizes an estimated one billion people annually across more than 190 countries.

guardian of these tomes because no one else in her immediate circle now cared or understood. To others, they were just dead trees with ink.

"What is this large one?" Paul said, pulling down a large, leather-bound volume in Cyrillic script.

"*Voyna I Mir.* War and Peace."

"Intimidating size," Paul said, paging through the Cyrillic Russian's indecipherable code.

"You've read this all?" Paul asked.

"Many times."

"For pleasure?"

She smiled.

"You think that strange?" Katya said. "I discover something new whenever I reread. All these people don't fully understand the events happening around them. Napoleon believed he won a victory by taking Moscow, but General Kutuzov saw this differently. Kutuzov retreated, burning the city instead. None of Napoleon's generals fully grasped the winter threat until too late. Nature did the killing with frost and famine. Other characters are just caught in these decisions. No singular history, only versions of histories seen by different eyes. Nothing fated. Small factors tip results. This I find—what is the phrase—a better mental model of our reality."

"I wish I had more time to read," Paul said.

"Shall we see Tolstoy in the theater instead?" Katya asked. "On Broadway they have used *Voyna I Mir* for a new musical. I have seen a billboard for this in Times Square. The show is called *Natasha, Pierre, and the Great Comet of 1812.*" [45]

"Ambitious to make a Broadway musical about Napoleonic Wars," Paul said.

"Let's see what theater writers have invented," Katya said.

Paul gently slid the large volume back on the bookshelf. He walked over and took a slice of the apple she had placed in a bowl on the kitchen table.

"What's bothering you?" he asked.

"Nothing," she replied.

"Is it Viktor?"

"Of course not."

"What then?" Paul asked.

---

45   The Broadway show by Dave Malloy starred singer Josh Groban in the lead of Pierre. There were 368 showings at the Imperial Theatre on 45th Street, Manhattan.

"I don't know."

Paul kissed her neck but did not pursue his line of questions further. He told her instead he was going to shower and change clothes for the day ahead.

Katya drifted over to the window. She looked out to the Hudson River just beyond the trees, a sense of guilt and loss welling up inside whenever she thought too strongly of the lost past. The past was now a drama she could no longer change, full of voices that could no longer speak any new words. Those voices now were forever silent.

———— ✳ ————

On Friday night, Broadway and Forty-Fifth Street hummed with thousands of patrons emptying the many theaters. The sky was clear, and a light breeze helped circulate the warm spring air down Manhattan's cavernous avenues.

"What did you think about it?" Chloe asked Paul as they walked out of the Imperial Theater. Paul surprised both Katya and Chloe by purchasing three perfectly situated orchestra tickets.

Paul and Chloe stood together while Katya refreshed herself in the restroom after the show. Paul was relieved that he didn't need to consume three thousand pages but instead imbibed the musical in just over two hours. He had been working nonstop and needed the mental break.

"That probably wasn't what Tolstoy would have done, but it was ingenious," Paul said. "I still don't understand the part about the comet though."

"Ask Katya about the comet," Chloe said. "That's her thing. Very existential."

Chloe still carried a French accent, and pouting mannerisms. Paul saw her often now at the gallery and sometimes outside after work. Her bohemian charm had crept up on him over the last few months. There was something intriguing and different about Chloe beneath that heavy black mascara and the dyed dark hair.

"It was sweet you invited me," Chloe said.

"Glad you came."

"The casting of a black actress to play Natasha was bold," Chloe said.

"Artistic license," Paul said. "You should appreciate that. She had a very good voice."

"Ha-ha, yes, artists are chameleons," Chloe replied.

"Katya says that you paint?" Paul said.

"I'm not very good."

"I'd like to see your work."

"It's nothing."

"Must be something," Paul said.

"I'm glad you and Katya are getting along," Chloe said. "I hope it lasts."

"There is only being alive and the patterns that block our aliveness," Paul said.

"Aren't you the self-help guru, Paul," Chloe chimed, smiling now.

"That bad?" Paul said.

"Just jealous Katya found you first."

Katya emerged from the theater exit, and the trio continued walking down Tenth Avenue to their next destination.

"Where to next?" Katya asked.

"You will love it," Chloe said. "Just a few blocks away. It's hot and crowded. The jazz is good. *J'adore.*"

They crossed five blocks south and two blocks west. Chloe brought them to a side entrance of the street that led down a tight flight of stairs to a basement door. Chloe pressed a buzzer, and after paying a cash fee, they entered the jazz club's small, atmospheric interior, a converted basement of an old townhouse. Rows of crowded tables encircled a jazz trio already deeply engaged on their second act.

Behind a wooden counter, the bartender shook cocktails into tall glasses. Bottles sat alongside weathered photos of vintage music acts, a trumpet, and woven cabaret-style lamps. Paul waved the bartender over and ordered. They watched as he poured out a gin, a vodka, and a scotch into three tall tumblers. Each took a drink. Chloe spotted an open high-top table in the far corner, and the threesome squeezed their way through a labyrinth of tables and limbs.

Chloe closed her eyes, listened to the jazz, and sipped her drink. The bassist was drenched in sweat, his fingers plucking his instrument in an offbeat rhythm along with the piano player, who glided his long fingers over the keyboard. The set continued energetically for twenty minutes, before a hypnotic trumpet solo changed to a slower pace.

"Let me order us another round," Katya said.

"Not for me," Paul said. "Still nursing this one."

"Chloe?"

"Gin would be lovely."

Katya went back to the bar for another order.

"Do you like it here?" Chloe asked, round eyes now open, looking squarely again at Paul.

"I do," Paul said.

"Better than her boring Tolstoy play?"

"Different," he replied. "No plot needed with jazz."

"Yes, no plot. Just feeling. Just life."

Chloe drew closer to Paul. She leaned her body against his, then casually put her hand on this thigh, hidden under the high-top table.

Paul smelled her pungent perfume mixed with sweat. Paul took a last swig of his scotch and crunched an ice cube in his back teeth.

Chloe moved her hand slowly up Paul's thigh.

"Do you like that?" Chloe whispered, her face now close to her ear.

"I don't know. Should I?" Paul said.

Paul allowed Chloe to move her hand up his crotch and against his better judgment felt himself aroused by her touch.

She rubbed him more with her hand.

"It feels like you like it. Very much. Don't worry. Ice princess doesn't need to know this is what you really want. I won't tell. I can give you more."

Chloe moved her hand away when she saw Katya on the other side of the room, returning with two drinks. Paul shifted his body to the side to hide an unwanted bulge.

"*Merci*," Chloe said nonchalantly as Katya handed her the gin. Then Chloe said something in French to Katya that Paul could not understand. They both laughed together, and Chloe turned back to the music.

The jazz continued for the next hour, and Paul made sure he went back to the bar himself for the next round. When the lights came on at 2:00 a.m., they drifted back up the stairway and back on the street.

"I'll take a taxi back. Don't worry about me," Chloe said.

"We will drive you," Paul said.

"No. Opposite direction. I'm fine," Chloe replied and kept on walking toward Ninth Avenue.

On the cab ride uptown, Katya leaned her head against Paul's shoulder.

"Your friend is quite a character," Paul said. "No boyfriend?"

"Not one she wants to reveal."

"What do you know about her?"

"A good friend. Different. Thank you for inviting her."

"Is her art any good?"

"I've never seen it. She lives in Staten Island. Too far."

Then she lifted her head. "Why are asking about her?"

"I don't know. Probably just the booze."
"What happened?"
"Nothing."
"Are you sure?"
"Friendly drinks," Paul said. Katya furrowed her brow.
"Thin French blood. Can't hold liquor," Katya said.
 "You drank as much," Paul replied.
"Yes, Paul, but I'm Russian. Did you forget?"

18

VIKTOR VOLKOV closed his eyes while a wave of lush symphony music filled his ears. He sat in the mezzanine section of the New York Metropolitan Opera House in rapt attention as the libretto voices cascaded throughout the large hall. The song was carried harmoniously by the violins, cellos, flutes, oboes, and English horns.

Tonight, Viktor decided to push his ever-present anxieties aside. Tonight, he was here to enjoy a lavish production of Verdi's Otello,[46] one of the great composer's last works and a personal favorite. Thus far, the production had not disappointed.

The lead tenor's voice was superb. The baritone playing Iago was also an excellent fit. But the night's greatest voice belonged to the opera's soprano, Sonya Yancheva,[47] who achieved perfection as the doomed Desdemona.

Kim Quoc sat beside him and leaned her cheek against his arm. Viktor was pleased that he had arranged to have this exotic beauty by his side. Kim completed the perfection of this Friday night. Her half-Vietnamese, half-Russian heritage gave Kim such lovely olive skin and delicate, fine bones. Her dark almond eyes fascinated Viktor. Her dark, impenetrable pupils reminded him of alternate realities, other countries in remote Asia that he had never visited but existed elsewhere in a kind of fantasy of potential discovery.

Kim's Russian was not very good, but this didn't matter once you touched her smooth, warm body. The gold dress hugged her slender young curves; the dress's slit ran up the length of her smooth, nubile thigh.

Viktor had dined with Kim at La Bernadine[48] before the show. Viktor relished the restaurant's atmosphere. He quietly enjoyed the choreography of waiters serving the world's best seafood to the well-heeled and satisfied patrons. Viktor sat among these urban elite at a white linen table, wearing

---

46   The opera's original 1887 debut at Milan's La Scala was a historic event; Verdi received 20 curtain calls from an ecstatic crowd.

47   Bulgarian operatic soprano celebrated for her dramatic intensity and versatility in leading roles at the Metropolitan Opera and Teatro alla Scala.

48   Three Michelin star French seafood restaurant founded in 1986 by siblings Maguy and Gilbert Le Coze

his black Armani suit. The dinner's pageantry and the two bottles of white wine served chilled washed down the latest string of business failures.

The opera's last act brought the audience to Desdemona's bedchamber as the libretto reached its tragic conclusion. The voices carried the action as Otello murdered his wife only then to realize just moments later that he had punished her in error. Otello first drew his scimitar but then relinquished it and pulled out a dagger from his robe instead.

"*Ho un'arma ancor!*" I still have another weapon!

In a crescendo of song, Otello stabbed himself. The tenor dragged himself next to his wife. He kissed her gently on the lips.

"*Un bacio ancora! Un altro bacio.*" Another kiss, yet another kiss.

Then the sonorous voices trailed off. Otello collapsed motionless next to the dead Desdemona. The curtain fell into a hushed silence. The violins, oboes, and English horns all ceased.

The packed 3,800-person audience stood together in a wave of adoration. The cast had given a rigorous and expressive three-hour performance. Viktor brought his hands together and vigorously clapped, shouting, "Bravo!" repeatedly to the singers, especially to the soprano, Sonya Yancheva. The troupe gathered, a cluster of elaborate sixteenth-century silk costumes. Sonya gave a slight bow to the audience and then waved them all kisses.

Viktor thought, *yes, my mother was right to love the opera. Civilization at its finest, a great tradition played again across cultures and centuries.* Elena took him often as a boy to the State Chamber music theater in St. Peterburg. She filled his head with composers: Verdi, Mozart, Bizet, Wagner, Puccini. Somehow Elena's passion had stuck. Tonight, he connected with her spirit, lost himself in sound and pageantry. Viktor and Kim lingered inside a while before they walked out after all the others into the open area of Lincoln Square Plaza.

"Let's walk to the hotel tonight," Kim said, holding Viktor's arm. "It is not far. The night feels warm to me." The spring weather tonight was moist. A slight haze diffused the tall building lights, giving the night an eerie but strangely intimate glow. Viktor acquiesced. Why not? It would take almost as much time to hail a taxi with this geriatric crowd lingering around Lincoln Center. They had been sitting and eating for nearly five hours. It would be just a short, pleasant walk while his ears still rung with Desdemona's last tragic farewell to life.

Viktor had arranged a room for Kim at the Hotel Plaza Athénée, his favorite place for special weekend trysts. It was just across the park, a small luxury hotel tucked away in the Upper East Side. No one ever asked questions there. They could sleep late, and he would treat her like his queen there.

Viktor and Kim entered Central Park through the gate on Sixty-Third Street and followed the pathway east. A few other couples strolled along the path in the night's soft darkness, but otherwise the park was empty. To the right, giant towers still under construction along Central Park South reached up to the sky and seemed to lord over him. *All that dirty Arab oil money built those new towers along Billionaire's Row,*[49] Viktor thought. Harder for any government to steal foreign assets assuming valid land titles. All that money created from pulling liquified black carbon from beneath the sand, here recycled into residential slices of these mighty architectural wonders.

Viktor was growing tired of New York. His life in this city had become so uncomfortably complicated. Now because of dead Arlen Cross, old man Yuri trusted him much less. Without even Yuri's tacit support, his own projects moved at a snail's pace.

Maybe it is time to relocate to LA. The weather is much better there. Californians don't linger in the past, he thought. *I'll start again with a new group of partners. A lot of money sloshing around all those entertainment big shots. Change is good. Start fresh again.* He could leave behind that amorphous pool of Russian émigrés spread out throughout the five boroughs. They were always trying to lure his men away, always sniffing around his business. He hated those cheap Brighton Beach *svoloch*. Scum.

Kim stopped at a bench.

"Can I sit? Fucking high heels like sandpaper on my toes," Kim said in her passable Russian. She sat down, untied the leather laces, and took off her black Gucci heels.

"Going barefoot from here?" Viktor asked, annoyed.

"Unless you carry me," she said.

Viktor stood nearby, waiting for his companion to rub her feet. Kim had been the one who had suggested walking across the park, and now she was complaining.

"Did you like the opera?" Viktor asked.

"I don't understand Italian," Kim replied.

"Words are not important. What about the music?" Kim shook her head sidewise, showing ambivalence.

"Tell the truth," he pressed.

"Old style music. I don't like."

---

49   A cluster of ultra-luxury, residential supertall skyscrapers—including Central Park Tower and 111 West 57th Street—located primarily along West 57th Street.

"Was there anything good?"

"Nice costumes and hairstyles," Kim said. "Here, *Lyubimaya moya*, my love, come sit with me." She pulled at his wrist, dragging Viktor down to a park bench.

Viktor obeyed her command.

Kim moved closer to Viktor and began to caress his neck. In the back of his mind, Viktor knew that she was a professional whom he used to lure investors, but tonight, that truth didn't matter. Maybe Kim could join him in LA, the next phase in his journey. She would look good in a bathing suit.

Kim's skin was as smooth as a baby. Viktor ran his hands over her hips, up her waist. He felt her small breasts, and he lightly bit her small ears. Kim's heart was now thumping wildly. She was excited now and kissed him back with a kind of strange ferocity. Viktor wanted to rip her clothes off here alone in the park's darkness.

Then suddenly, Viktor felt Kim lift her body. She pulled herself away and sprung to her feet with catlike agility.

A bulky shadow moved in front of him.

Strong hands pressed against him. Viktor instinctively put up his arms just as quick stabs pierced his chest in sharp, sudden motions. Excruciating pain shot straight into his chest. Thrust after thrust cut through his white shirt into his chest.

Viktor put up his hands to block it, but the sharp steel blade kept jabbing quickly into his stomach, lungs, below his throat.

Jab. Jab. Jab.

The figure pulled away.

Kim gone too.

Pain.

Viktor felt his body slump. He fell, sprawled on the pavement, and gasped. Blood leaked from all the many holes now poked on his chest, thighs, arms, throat, and back. The essence of his body was now coursing away, trickling out with each heartbeat from the darkening mosaic of the small puncture wounds.

Inch by inch, Viktor crawled along the park's asphalt path. His limbs did not obey his command no matter how hard he willed them to do so. Viktor tried to cry for help but heard instead only the faint gurgle of his voice.

Viktor's hands grasped at clumps of grass. Then after several minutes of crawling, he could no longer move his limbs. He decided to lie still. With one final effort, Viktor rolled on his back. Paralyzed, he stared up at the trees and saw the tall towers still lording above him with their final mastery.

Those towers above, still standing. Viktor's breathing grew lighter.

A soprano's soft voice came from someplace in the woods. The voice was singing an aria, beautiful and calming and perfect now. He listened to the song, so beautiful, that was slowing him down with a lovely, fading harmony, beat …

by beat …

by beat …

by beat …

Viktor's menacing blue eyes stayed open, but he saw nothing more out of them. His heart pumped one final time, then his mind failed, and all that he had ever been as a living human being dissolved irreversibly into nothingness.

———————— ✳ ————————

On Saturday morning, visitors to the southwest corner of New York City's Central Park might have thought that a movie or a television series was scheduled to film. An extensive uniformed police presence gathered throughout a small section of the park near Hallett Nature Sanctuary. Officers had spread out ribbons of plastic yellow crime tape to mark a perimeter.

"Do you know what show is filming here?" one middle-aged female jogger asked another runner nearby who had also been turned away from his favorite footpath.

"I don't think it is a show," the other runner replied. "I don't see the camera crew."

"They should be here," the jogger replied, still looking for one of the television or movies crews. Film crews were a common sight. Likewise, she thought that the park was no longer a particularly dangerous part of the city. New York's homicide statistics had been trending down for years—just 615 homicides last year, a remarkably tiny sum for a city of this immense size and density.

The two joggers lingered for a while before they went on their way. The joggers took no notice of a small, thin, inconspicuous, dark-skinned man standing just outside the police tape. The man watched the scene for a while, his hands pensively clasped behind his back. Then he walked leisurely along the asphalt path lined with tall London plane trees.

The man exited the South Gate near the statue of Simon Bolivar on horseback. He crossed over Central Park South and the Avenue of the Americas, then headed west two more blocks. "Welcome back, Mr. Maktoum," the doorman at the Essex House said.

Amir Al Maktoum nodded in return. Amir had been staying at the Essex House for more than a month now. He was treated well by the hotel's staff, although not with the same total deference as in the best hotels of Dubai, despite the generous tips.

Amir had been enjoying his current sojourn to New York. Each day, he would wake up to glorious views looking over the park's green, rectangular landscape. *Without the park, New York would be just another big city,* Amir thought. The city planners had kept the center as a green haven, and this made all the difference. He enjoyed his daily strolls along the gravel paths and liked to mingle with the thousands of strangers.

Central Park's shaded paths served another purpose too last night.

Amir took tea in his room on the thirtieth floor. He ordered a strong jasmine flavor, with a hint of lavender. He read the newspaper and perused a copy of GQ. Then Amir made his phone calls to release the final payment. He had seen with his own eyes that the job was done. Those people in Brighton Beach would do anything for money, and it was a clever, untraceable plan. He didn't want to know more.

Amir touched his Wharton class ring. The ring's face had a delicate University of Pennsylvania emblem with the school's founding year of 1740 engraved. He wore the class ring with pride and thought about his younger days living here in America. Those were the best days of his fortunate life. Of all the most valuable things in the world, perhaps a friendship was worth the most. Friends were irreplaceable in one's short life. This was the least he could do to seek justice for such a devoted friend as Arlen.

———————— ✳ ————————

Jo's phone vibrated and buzzed lightly.

She glanced down at the NYPD alert text. The text reported a homicide last night in Central Park; victim identified as Viktor Volkov.

Done.

Those Arabs finally found the right moment. The less she knew about how they did it, the better. Always a fair price for this kind of dirty work. Sheiks had money to burn.

Funny what really motivates people, Jo considered. The Al Maktoum family would owe her in the future for the tip. Amir's cousins and uncles all had deep connections with the banks and financial institutions throughout the region. With the UEA banks, you could follow the money trail, find your villains scattered around in all the little shitholes in Yemen or Iran. This was a valuable strategic tool for the larger chess game. If she could hand up more gifts like this to the seventh floor, then they would start taking her more seriously again, give her more resources. Jo needed more resources to move mountains.

Viktor was worth the trade. He deserved it.

And better for Paul.

19

"WHAT DO you know about it?" Paul asked as he slid on the wooden New York ferry seat next to Jo.

She waited for him near the bow, pretending to read a newspaper. The ferry boat was mostly empty now that the evening rush hour from Manhattan had run its course. The lights of Brooklyn Heights condominiums shone just beyond Brooklyn Bridge's six-thousand-foot expanse.

Jo had asked Paul to make the 6:54 p.m East River ferry because everyone minded their own business, and the transit allowed for multiple departures. Cold air and the smell of sea made the whole experience refreshing. Even better how the boat's engine generated a steady stream of white noise.

"I don't know much," Jo replied. "NYPD didn't find any useful physical evidence. The girl wasn't in our system. They were seen together at dinner and at the opera. No witnesses after that."

"Could she have done this alone?"

"Unlikely at a hundred pounds. No drugs in Viktor's system. Alcohol below the legal limit."

"That's all you have?" Paul said.

"They found an ice pick nearby, same as from any hardware store."

"What's next?" Paul probed.

"Do you want to stop?" Jo said.

"We can't stop now," Paul said. "UN shipments are moving, and we're making quick progress now in Turkey."

"Good. Let Yuri know I have sourced a loan for him to buy out the partners of MSA, the Maltese firm. No minority partners where we're headed. Have the owners agreed to a price?"

"Fifty million, plus debt."

"Less than expected," Jo said. "Funding this will be easy for our friend in Palm Springs."

The captain blew a loud whistle as the ferry approached the dock. Jo rose.

"It sounds like your Odessa boys are making quick progress. You should see what's happening over there in the region for yourself, Paul.

Always better to take a bit of desert sand into your lungs and see with your own eyes. I'll help you do it, give you some expensive toys," Jo said.

"When?" he asked.

"As soon as you can pack your toothbrush."

She left Paul to disembark with the other passengers. Paul stayed on board for the round trip back to Manhattan. He watched Jo walk down the Brooklyn Point harbor path and exit the ferry station through a turnstile.

———————— ✳ ————————

Katerina Volkova was not surprised when she heard about Viktor. On some unconscious level, she always knew this was coming since her family was cursed.

Now she stood here at Saint Nicolaus,[50] on Ninety-Seventh Street, with Viktor's ashes in the porcelain urn cradled in her hands. *Strange*, she thought, *the entirety of her older brother's existence now only this little pile of galactic dust. Mother, father, brother, all reduced to this nothingness.* Only she remained, a living, breathing, thinking thing.

Viktor's Pominki[51] began sharply at 9:00 a.m. Flowers surrounded Viktor's black-and-white photo taken when he was still a student in St. Petersburg. The bearded priest—dressed in a long black tunic—lit the twisted wax candles. The priest spoke in generalities about the temporal nature of life and the nature of God's relationship to man. The priest had been given very little information for today. He was already uncomfortable with the family's decision to cremate instead of a more traditional orthodox burial. The priest also knew that Viktor had suffered what was considered a bad death not due to natural causes. In such cases, God was not ready to invite those souls into his kingdom. Instead, the soul was trapped here on earth. Precautions were prudent. He advised the family to cover all mirrors and stop their clocks.

Viktor's business team stood respectfully in black suits. Dmitry Medkov, the bald man with the silver-rimmed glasses, seemed to watch them all with careful eyes. Paul came too and stood silently in the corner. Those who showed up on this cold, rainy day did not come out of any affection for Viktor. They came out of a sense of obligation for the nephew of Yuri Volkov. Anything less would look suspicious and ungrateful. Even Alexi arrived with a stoic, somber demeanor. Alexi marshaled some kind

---

50   A designated landmark located at 15 East 97th Street. Completed in 1902 in the Moscow Baroque style, and partially funded by Tsar Nicholas II, serving as the administrative center for the Russian Orthodox Church in North America.

51   Traditional Russian wake or memorial meal held to commemorate the deceased.

words describing Viktor's virtues, although Katya knew that these words were exaggerations. Everyone knew that Alexi always hated Viktor; this turn of events meant more opportunity for him.

Yesterday, the undertaker placed Viktor's body in a cremation chamber, then turned a knob until the fire and heat reduced Viktor's body to ash. Tomorrow, Katya would place these remains in a small mausoleum, a simple space with only his name etched in stone. At least artists left something of themselves in their works, she thought, while Viktor left nothing. Even now, Katya struggled to remember his voice. The present shoved down these memories, forced her to forget, just as she had pushed down the memory of her parents. No ghost could speak. They all were silenced, gagged in the purgatory.

Afterwards, Paul and Katerina walked into the nearby park by themselves. The rain still drizzled down from a heavy canopy of dark gray clouds. Everyone at the church today—including herself—would go the same way as Viktor. They would all end this way. It was only a matter of time. Some sooner than expected.

Paul balanced the umbrella over their heads as they walked tightly together.

"I hate to do this now. But I need to travel. It's important," Paul began.

"Where?"

"Out of the country. Near Istanbul," Paul said.

Katya turned her head to look into Paul's eyes. She feared Paul was beginning to lose his center as he moved further into Yuri's orbit. Paul was working constantly now, slowly spinning away from her with each orbit into a darker, colder world. *If he spins too far out, he'll be lost,* she worried. *Why have I done this to him?*

"I need to go this time. I must help Dmitry and his team. It's just for a few weeks, a month at most. There may be answers for us there."

She held him closer under the umbrella.

"You can only find answers if you know the right questions," Katya said. "Do you know those questions, Paul?"

"I know the most important ones," he replied.

"Does it matter what I think about this?"

"You know it does, but I need your understanding."

"I do understand," Katya said ruefully. "I understand that if you stay too long, you will never come back, ever."

"I will. I'll be careful. It's just a few weeks, a month at most."

She released his arm, then stepped away from him to walk alone under the rain until her honey-colored hair turned a dull and dirty bronze.

20

THE TURKISH Airline Boeing 777 passed without incident over the Atlantic, landing on time at 10:35 a.m. in Istanbul. Paul slept most of the flight, his head propped awkwardly against the plane's window, an eye mask blocking the light. The next domestic Pegasus Air flight to Gaziantep in the southeast was full of local Turks, except for a handful of other European aid workers and some Chinese businessmen making their way deeper into Turkey.

As Paul set down in Gaziantep, he wore the same military boots as he had nine years ago while serving in Iraq. The sun hit his face and arms with that familiar extra kick. He felt the same dust on his skin, the same dry air in his lungs.

Paul found Gaziantep to be strangely lovely the morning of his arrival. The ancient city's stone houses, paved streets, and covered bazaars were interspersed with gardens, vineyards, and olive groves. The limestone hills cut majestically against the morning sky. Life here continued as it always had, just a few dozen kilometers from a Syrian border. Paul could feel the city's long age. It began as Antiochia in the ancient world, and then a millennium later, the Byzantines built Gaziantep Fortress and Ravenna citadel. The Ottomans came for four centuries after the crusades. Then the French and the British took over after the First World War and left after the Second. Now Erdogan controlled Turkey. He was another nationalist leader keen on stamping out any perceived threat from his own people, the Anatolian Turks. The latest sultan in a very long line of them.

A van came for Paul in the afternoon. The driver took him farther east as the cooler evening approached. Around halfway through the drive, more signs of turmoil began to emerge. Paul saw abandoned buildings, damaged army trucks, and lines of people moving on foot from one town to the next, carrying all their worldly possessions in old suitcases and bags.

Most of the refugees did their best to avoid the crowded UN camps. Those seeking work and shelter had forced Turkish authorities to issue tens of thousands of limited work permits. The Syrians took whatever work might be available in the larger cities like Istanbul and Ankara. Those brave enough to risk more could make the next leg of the journey to Greece, perhaps Germany or Italy if they could stomach the risks. But hardline nationalist parties in many neighboring countries pushed against such policies, and more internment-style camps sprang up.

Then there were the Kurds spread out across northern Iraq and in southern Turkey. In the last year, the violence spread to dozens of Kurdish-majority cities: Diyarbakir, Sirnak, Mardin, Cizre, Nusaybin, Yuksekova. These towns had been reduced to rubble. The Islamic State sent in their fighters, and Turkish forces bombed them from the air. Occasionally, a US or a Russian jet broke through the sky with a thunderous clap, launching a satellite-guided missile on some real or perceived high-value target.

At the entrance gate to the camp near Suruç, Paul flashed the badge of a UNHCR medical supply technician, Jo's arranged cover. The camp spread out in the shallow valley—rows of drab, tarpaulin tents and makeshift wooden shelters as far as the eye could see. At least thirty thousand refugees were gathered in this area alone. Other camps elsewhere were much bigger, some hosting as many as a hundred thousand. Médecins San Frontiers doctors established a safe zone for medical treatment and potable water near the camp's entrance. Other relief groups had begun to build more permanent structures. They were all setting up for what they expected would be a very long haul.

Dmitry's MSA team had set up the secure air transport depot to regularly receive shipments via a small airstrip newly created on a flat stretch of dirt. An organized logistics team met the day's first transport plane from Odessa each morning; the crew unloaded crates and sorted the supplies. A second old Soviet propeller plane noisily barreled in sometime in the late afternoon. Barbed wire fences and security cameras surrounded MSA's storage areas to prevent theft. MSA's armed trucks then drove supplies to other camps within the approved radius. Thirteen target sites extended to Turkey, Syria, and northern Iraq. The team tagged its shipments with electronic trackers to curb black marketeering, but once the supplies left the logistics chain, there was little they could practically do to control it.

In the evenings, when the air cooled down, Paul wandered through the camp. He saw mostly women and children dispersed in the hundreds of tents; many husbands and fathers had died in active fighting. The children gathered to play soccer on a central field, using sticks as goal posts. The girls watched in small groups on the sidelines, their black hair covered by hajibs.

If you had enough money somehow to bribe your way to a new place, you paid that price and took that chance for renewal. The thousands here in the camp had no such alternative options. They had lost everything, with nowhere else to go to escape the bloodshed. Today's goal under the hot sun was simply to survive.

—————— ✳ ——————

On Tuesday morning of the next week, Dmitry Medkov stepped off the afternoon transport flight.

"*Priviet*, Paul," he said, his short, stocky body in army fatigues and his quick eyes hidden behind reflective sunglasses.

Paul took Dmitry to the only functioning outdoor restaurant just outside the camp and set upon a small hill. They drank black tea at a cedarwood table positioned beneath a large fig tree. MSA's operational ramp up was now three months old but still evolving rapidly as the fighting shifted from one small town to the next. Food, medicine, and water needed to follow these shifting contours. In just two months, MSA shipped more than $150 million of antibiotics, medical kits, nutritional supplements, grain, packaged poultry, blankets, and condensed milk. Emergency health kits each contained more valuable items, such as surgical tools, sterilizers, and trauma care supplies.

"How long do you think this will go on?" Paul asked. Dmitry gave a wry, slightly forlorn smile.

"Al-Assad is still in power, and his army is well supplied. The Americans are almost all gone, and Kurds still have no country," Dmitry observed. "I don't see an end."

"And Russia?" Paul prodded.

"Putin wins another chess match. You see, Paul, in this old place, every action leads to a reaction, a different blood feud, a new Jihad. Now Syria, Iran, Turkey, and Russia line up on one side, and Israel, Saudi Arabia, and the US on the other. Always another villain: Khomeini, Hussein, Kaddafi, Assad. I can barely pronounce them all."

"And them?" Paul said, nodding his head toward the thousands of people crowding the refugee camp at the foot of the hill.

"As our great Soviet leader Joseph Stalin said, 'The death of one man is a tragedy. The death of a million is a statistic.' Look at those tents down there, Paul. Do you see human tragedies, or do you see statistics?"

Dmitry and Paul finished the tea in silence as they both watched the flow of people mingle throughout the sprawling encampment.

"Now the two of us need to take a drive, Paul. I need your help to bring our new tools to another site," Dmitry said.

They walked over to a black van already loaded with military-grade computer and communication equipment brought over from Odessa. Dmitry had secured most of this from a seller in Tel Aviv using Yuri's influence and Rutherford's money. With Paul's help, Jo's input with the Israelis enabled coveted legal approvals, and the seller's manifest falsely marked the equipment for Eastern Ukraine rather than Turkey. Dmitry took his place in the driver's seat and rolled the jeep out through the camp's secure gate.

Dmitry drove another thirty kilometers along a single dusty road that snaked its way along a tree-lined ridge. Twilight was just beginning to embrace the wide horizon. The sky seemed immense and translucent when they reached another, smaller village nestled in the nearby limestone foothills. The village's two dozen scattered stone houses were dark except for the light shining through just a handful of windows.

An armed guard with a rifle and binoculars stood in a small, three-meter-high wooden guard post that commanded views of the village and the roads below. He was an Odessa man who recognized Dmitry and tipped open the gate to let the van pass. A few other trucks were parked in front of a single-story stone structure next to a smaller domed mosque.

Dmitry knocked on the locked door. The buzzer unlocked, and they entered the first room of the compound. The tall Piotr Vezilov shook Paul's hand and introduced himself.

"What is this place?" Paul asked.

"An old Kurdish militia safehouse. There are many in this area. Most are empty now. Turkish troops have been destroying as many as they can find," Dmitry explained.

"How is our new guest?" Dmitry asked Piotr in English so that Paul could understand.

"Quiet today. It has been three days."

"Let's see if he is ready for us," Dmitry said.

Piotr understood this request and took them farther inside into the compound's labyrinth of tunnels and small rooms. In one storage area, Paul saw a row of weapons against the wall—Israeli-made rifles, Kalashnikovs,[52] boxes of grenades. They also passed a communication room, mess hall, kitchen, and spartan sleeping quarters. At the end of the corridor, Piotr took them down a flight of stairs into another underground space with gray cinder block walls and hallways lit by a string of white neon lights along the ceiling.

---

52   Also known as an AK-47, it is a gas-operated, assault rifle designed by Mikhail Kalashnikov in 1947 and adopted by the Soviet Union in 1949.

Piotr came to the rusted iron door of what looked to be an old holding cell.

Dmitry lifted the panel that covered a small, dirty window so Paul could see inside. The man sitting on the wooden chair had been beaten. His left eye was bruised badly, swollen nearly shut. Dried blood was smeared down his dirty white shirt.

"Who is he?" Paul asked.

"This is Nazir Hassan, a hated man. Our Kurdish friends wanted to shoot him on sight. I paid a very large cash reward to bring him here," Dmitry said. "This one knows more than the others."

"What has he done?" Paul asked.

"He gave up a Kurdish militia location in Syria. The Turks used gas on them. Maybe two hundred were killed, mostly women and children," Dmitry said.

Dmitry reached into his pocket and handed Paul a pack of Marlboros and a lighter.

"Are you ready for our theater game, Paul?" he asked. "Follow my lead. Show our friend your UN badge and your American optimism."

Piotr unlocked the door, and the two men entered. "Hello, Nazir," Dmitry said with some energy.

Nazir peered blankly back. "Who are you?" he asked.

"I'm someone who can help you now," Dmitry began. "Would you like that, my friend?"

Nazir shifted in his chair. Paul slid the pack of Marlboros and lighter across the table. Nazir took it and lit up a cigarette with a blank expression. Dmitry did the same. The two men took long drags in silence, and Dmitry puffed out the smoke through his nostrils.

"Paul is an American with the UN," Dmitry began. "He wants to hear your story. If you provide him a testimony with details and facts, Paul can find you asylum. Get you out of this mess."

"Is this true?" Nazir asked, turning to Paul.

"It is true, yes. I can protect you. I can put it all in writing, all legal, and you can sign it," Paul said, playing along the invented story. "And I'll take you to the US embassy if I think what you tell us can help."

"This is your lucky chance, friend," Dmitry stressed. "Give us something that we can use to bring you to safety. Maybe even tonight. Right. Paul?"

"That's right, later tonight."

Paul placed his phone on the table to record the confession. The theater game continued. They progressed like this for more than two hours. Piotr brought in a bottle of vodka. They drank from three short glasses, Nazir taking the largest swigs and asking for more. Nazir also finished another cigarette pack while he rambled, mentioned names, talked about transactions on behalf of the Syrian army and Turkish intelligence.

Some of the details were muddled because Nazir was kept ignorant of many deals. But slowly a picture began to emerge of an organized network that these struggling governments tapped into to procure a range of deadly weapons—gas-enabled missiles, land minds, rocket launchers, other various conventional small arms, and neurotoxins.

Nazir described an extensive shadow operation with different cells in many cities, involving layers of control and a sophisticated, apparently well-funded set of resources. This group only dealt with Russian allies and carefully avoided attention. Most of the items were made in one of the ex-Soviet republics, according to Nazir. But he didn't know this for certain since he wasn't an expert and just followed orders.

"The man you say you met in Paris. Was it this man?" Dmitry asked.

He slid a photo of Rene Voclain on the table. The image Katya snapped five years ago showed a roguishly handsome man with reddish-brown hair, brown eyes, and a square jaw.

Nazir looked at the photo and nodded.

"Look closely. Are you sure?" Dmitry prodded.

"He had a beard, but it is the same man—Andre," Nazir confirmed. "But I never met Perses."

Dmitry's ears perked.

"Who?" Dmitry prodded.

"Perses. They all work for him," Nazir said.

Dmitry pressed for more details as they lingered on the subject. Nazir admitted that he had heard of the name Perses only in secondhand discussions. These were in apocryphal stories from Jordanian and Iranian secret police describing Perses's ruthless tactics. In one story, a buyer who allegedly violated terms of a transaction was killed by cyanide slipped into his tea at an airport lounge. Another story involved an entire family's death by apparent gas suffocation while at a luxury hotel in San Tropez.

"Yes, Perses. He keeps them all together. Perses can procure everything needed. They all fear him. The Russians support him, but he is a man without borders."

"If you've never seen him, maybe he's a myth?" Paul prodded.

"As God is my witness, I tell you the truth of what I hear about the devil," Nazir insisted.

Dmitry squinted his eyes while Paul poured the last of the vodka into Nazir's empty glass. Nazir was slowly running out of new facts, and various details began to seem vague and partially invented. Nazir had been sitting in this underground cell for three days now, suffering beatings, intentional sleep deprivation, and the likelihood of what he must have understood were his final days. Now Dmitry's theater game gave Nazir a slight glimmer of hope. He began to ask Paul more questions about the next steps to bring him to the US embassy. Paul remained firmly in character, a beacon of hope.

"Will you testify to everything you've told us?" Paul asked. "It's important you don't leave anything out. If you don't tell me here, I can't make the case at the US Embassy and then we can't protect you."

Nazir insisted it was all so. Then he covered his hands over his face, and his trembling lips began to mumble prayers in Turkish.

Dmitry glanced at his watch and motioned for Paul to turn off the audio recorder on his phone.

"You have done well, my friend. It is good that you tell us these things. Get some rest," Dmitry said. The two interrogators rose. Piotr unbolted the door to let them out.

Outside the cell, Paul felt drained.

"You did well, Paul," Dmitry said. "He believed in you like angel Gabriel come down from heaven to wash away his sin."

Paul then saw a bearded Kurdish man dressed in black fatigues sitting in the corner of a small alcove across from Nazir's holding cell. The Kurdish man tapped his foot impatiently.

"We're finished now," Dmitry called to the man.

The bearded man nodded and rose to his feet. When he stood up, Paul could see that he was a towering figure with a thick neck and hulking arms. He gripped a rusty metal pipe in his hand.

Piotr opened Nizar's cell door for the man to enter, then sealed it shut again.

"Who was that?" Paul asked.

"The Kurd who brought us Nazir. His 11-year-old son and wife died in the air attack that Nazir helped the Turks set up," Dmitry explained. "My payment covered only limited interrogation time. The rest, I do not control."

From behind the door, Paul first heard two voices loudly talking in Turkish. Then came muffled shouts, followed by horrifying screams of slow anguish. Dmitry and Piotr headed back up the stairs, while Paul lingered there until Nazir's screaming stopped and a long, deep, unsatisfied silence ensued.

21

JO RICHARDS was in her downtown office when the unscheduled call came in over the secure line from the UNHCR camp in Suruç, Turkey. She hung up the other line and took the inbound.

"We have a problem on the ground. I need your help," Paul said, his voice breaking up over the poor connection.

"Big or small problem?"

"Depends on your point of view," Paul said.

Paul had been on the ground in Turkey for four weeks. Dmitry Medkov had left four days ago, delegating daily oversight to Valentine Kuzoff, a younger lieutenant. *Bad timing to leave*, thought Paul, since the last twelve hours had thrown up the biggest challenge yet.

Paul presented known facts: Renewed fighting near Khobani the last three weeks had pushed a cluster of some two thousand refugees farther south, away from the UN's more secure supply lines and farther from the Turkish border. These mostly women and children were traveling on foot; they had converged last week in a shallow valley near Shalok and were now spread out in makeshift tents with limited access to potable water and no food. Fighting at Al Raqqa meant they could not go back there either.

The UNHCR director at the Suruç camp, a slightly framed, pretty Danish doctor, came to Valentine Kuzoff with a request: his team must expand their scope, get relief to Shalok now. It was just a two-hour drive from the border, she reasoned; trucks could deliver supplies to this group to last at least a month. A team of UNHCR aid workers had just passed north up the M4 highway yesterday morning without incident. She claimed a Turkish colonel told her most of the heavy fighting was still fifty kilometers east. The situation was fluid, but Valentine thought about it, spent an hour checking his facts, and agreed with the pretty Danish woman that this seemed a reasonable risk. He loaded up three trucks and assigned two men each. They left at noon.

Valentine's intel been right on the outboard; the three trucks reached their destination without incident. The Black Sea drivers were greeted with a mix of handshakes, appreciative smiles, and still worried stares. Dozens of Syrian women quickly organized to unload the UN medical supplies and food, while young men began to identify hidden locations in surrounding areas to bury the most scarce and valuable items.

Valentine's intel was dead wrong on the inbound return. In the next twelve hours, several hundred heavily armed Islamic State fighters lanced west to the M4. They waved black banners from atop armed trucks and shot at anything that came near their caravan. Another hundred ISIS fighters were reported about twenty kilometers south of Shalok, heading directly up.

"Can't they ride it out?" Jo asked.

"It's hard to say. I doubt it. Valentine wants to get his team back tonight. The M4 is probably open except for the last thirty kilometers."

"Not your problem, Paul. Too fucking risky."

"It is our problem, Jo. You want them to trust me or not?"

"What does Dmitry say?"

"He's not here."

She paused. *This Valentine hothead is going without or without our approval,* she thought.

"What do you need from me?" Jo said.

"Six hours of satellite coverage, starting midnight."

Jo made a series of rapid-fire calculations. Surveillance coverage on a UN relief convoy was a plausible use case with low backfire risks. Still, those Pentagon assholes would raise questions and take their pound of flesh given a short four-hour advanced notice. Eyes on Paul's crew meant they would need to divert scarce coverage from other scheduled tasks. Jo had only a limited set of tokens left to use; this was still a big ask with a lot of hair.

"Just night visuals?"

"That's right. If these six guys are beheaded, Jo, and we don't help …" Paul said.

"I get it," she replied curtly. "You do understand that if I go to bat on this, you'll need to carry the mobile Satcom link. You're the only one there who can turn on the fucking thing and use it."

"I know it," Paul said.

"Then it's your choice," she said before cutting the line.

Twenty minute later, Paul emerged outside the stone house to give Valentine the positive news.

"Coverage starts at midnight. We'll have six hours."

Valentine let out a long breath.

The rest of their plan was simple—bring enough force to engage any small ISIS group but stay nimble to maximize stealth and speed.

Paul mentally ticked off the elements of the plan as the darkness crept over the desert and Valentine went to prep the others. The men were solid. Three were trained spetsnaz; they could handle themselves if it came to a firefight. The four Kurds had been in this civil war now nearly four years; they were seasoned. The vehicles were not ideal but workable. A Turkish officer at the camp hastily accepted $25,000 for a one-time use of an American-made Humvee. MSA's six-by-six off-road truck was Russian made and heavy but still drove fast enough through desert terrain. A smaller armor-plated light vehicle would have to do the trick bringing up the rear. Moving at a fast clip, the convoy could make the trip in less than six hours, Paul concluded.

The last hour was the hardest to wait. Finally, Valentine Kuzoff took the Humvee driver's seat next to Paul. He gave a nervous smile as he revved the engine. Four Kurds followed behind in the off-road, and Valentine's two Odessa volunteers drove in the armored light utility bringing up the rear.

Paul flipped on the Satcom link. The live infrared satellite images centered on the convey and displayed the surrounding area. Up there in space, SpySat 6 tracked it all and sent those images back down to Paul's handheld device.

Nothing to be worried about tonight, Paul told himself. *This is going to work.* Then he set his watch.

22

EIGHT HUNDRED and fifty miles above the earth's surface, SpySat 6 turned its advanced optical eye on a small patch of brown earth in southern Turkey. The satellite's powerful infrared sensors locked onto the movement of three vehicles heading south, and images streamed down to the Pentagon's satellite war room, Jo's office in Lower Manhattan, and Paul's handheld Satcom.

12:05 a.m. The vehicles leave a low-rise compound just outside the sprawling Suruç refugee camp. The convoy follows a small road along a sloping ridge to an unmanned border checkpoint. The three vehicles head down another road that converges with the paved M4 road leading into northern Syria. Headlights turn off once they cross the border and pick up speed.

12:27 a.m. Valentine sets the pace in the lead Humvee at an even 120 kph. The convoy hums along through the dark night, lit only by a quarter moon and sporadic flashes of mortar fire in the direction of Al Raqqa. SpySat 6 sends down images of an empty road to Paul's handheld Satcom device.

1:05 a.m. "Are we still clear?" Valentine asks.

"Yes," Paul replies, eyes glued on the green screen propped up on the dashboard. Valentine takes a swig of water from a metal canteen and keeps his eyes on the dark road ahead.

1:25 a.m. SpySat 6's infrared sensors show a cluster of two dozen vehicles dispersed around an intersection farther south on the M4. The gathering covers a perimeter of few kilometers, too big and messy to punch through. Paul directs Valentine to steer right to go off the paved road. The convoy drives clear by a wide five kilometers. The vehicles kick up dirt and sand as they cross the desert's flat expanse in the darkness.

2:00 a.m. The convoy encounters another dirt road not on the maps; they head south faster along firmer ground.

3:10 a.m. The convoy pulls up without incident a few hundred meters away from Shalok, where the UN relief trucks are parked and the six stranded Odessa men wait. Faces light up when they recognize a smiling Valentine exit the Humvee.

"*My pribyli*, we've arrived," he shouts over to them. The six men scramble inside the six-by-six off-road truck. They take seats next to the Kurds, a sense of relief passing among them.

3:20 a.m. The convoy returns along the same route, north now for ten kilometers. Paul tells Valentine to turn left to avoid what SpySat 6 sees as additional car movement fanning out on a night patrol. The convoy turns left, travels up a smaller road, the M12, northwest along the contours of a low ridge. The men pass in between dry barley fields, now sallow and bare.

Valentine leads the way another fifty kilometers at a fast 100 kph clip. The wide horizon cuts the night sky and desert in two. A few jokes are told in the back of the middle truck. Nerves are calming.

Infrared shows Paul a clear road ahead.

Paul notices the morning star, Venus, hovering above the horizon.

4:00 a.m. The convoy slows down as the road narrows up a series of sloping hills. Valentine puts the Humvee in low gear to climb up the slope.

4:17 a.m. A slight curve in the road leads around a large rock formation jutting up from the sand. Valentine takes the Humvee slightly left to navigate the road.

4:18 a.m. The six-by-six utility pivots right along the road just behind. Its front wheel clicks down on the Russian-made PFM-7 landmine pin buried in the dirt. The explosion cracks the night sky, blowing off the truck's front wheel and sending it careening into a shallow ditch. Valentine skids the Humvee to a halt. The light utility also circles round behind the truck.

"Motherfuckers," Jo Richards shouts to herself as she watches the silent infrared images alone on the twenty-seventh floor of the World Financial Center.

4:20 a.m. Rapid machine-gun fire cuts the dry desert night air just as the men start scrambling out of the disabled truck. Two of the Kurds drop immediately. The other men scramble for cover and return fire in the darkness with their PKMs.

"There, on the ridge," Paul says, pointing to the machine gun tripod a hundred meters away. A bullet strikes an Odessa man in the lower back, entering his spleen. A fourth man goes down, hit through the upper back, into the heart.

Valentine grips the wheel, swerves the Humvee, heads over the small boulders, straight for the flashing machine gun muzzle. A black-clad fighter rises from his knees to fire a rocket from a shoulder launcher. The RPG-7 missile zooms by, too high, and skids elsewhere in a dust cloud.

The Humvee lurches forward, straight at them. Gunfire bounces off the Humvee's armored plates. The two black-clad fighters separate. Valentine runs the first one down, crushing his body beneath the Humvee's wide front wheel.

Paul unloads a semiautomatic pistol from the passenger window to drop the other man as he scrambles up a hill.

4:40 a.m. The light utility truck sweeps the perimeter. Four men from the disabled truck jump into the back of the Humvee.

"*My ikh ne brosim!* We're not leaving them," Valentine shouts angrily at his men. Two bodies are put in the back of the light utility, two in the Humvee. The vehicles speed north again.

6:04 a.m. SpySat 6 clicks off its infrared eye and pivots to its other preprogrammed tasks.

6:32 a.m. The Humvee and the light utility cross the Turkish border. Dawn breaks.

7:40 a.m. The Kurds lift the four bodies from the back of the Humvee and utility car. Two Suruç camp volunteers place the four corpses in a makeshift morgue, next to a dozen other white shrouds. The other dead men were brought in yesterday, killed in an unrelated skirmish outside Khobani two nights ago.

The four new dead men today are identified by their dog tags. Turkish nationals: Jalal Kazan, Hamdi Aziz. Two others are Ukrainian: Roman Naratov, Oleg Sidorov. The volunteer enters their names on a paper list with a ballpoint pen.

Paul waited another day to decompress before he called Jo. She picked up the line after half a dozen rings.

"Do you have any injuries from the firefight?" she asked calmly. Paul was surprised by the even, emotionless tenor of her voice.

"I'm fine."

"SpySat 6 recorded most of the action. I've handled all the usual questions on my side, Paul," she said.

"I should have taken a different road."

"Landmines are little bitches. You were lucky. The ambush wasn't set up well at night. Those assholes were spread thin, and you surprised them too."

"We went to get six and lost four." "I know it," Jo said.

"Should have taken another road," Paul repeated. "Fluid situation. Never should have gone."

"I could have taken us west, waited longer near the river until it was lighter."

Jo let the silence linger.

"You're too valuable to me, Paul. No more of this cowboy bullshit. I need you for Yuri. Time to come home."

Then Jo hung up.

Paul knew Jo was right; he had been lucky. If Valentine had swerved right, not left, up that slope, then the Humvee wheel would have been hit first; *I would be dead, and the rest gunned down.*

Later at night, Paul walked along the north perimeter of the refugee camp. More people were still pouring in each day from all the towns and small villages throughout northern Syria. The Turks prevented them from entering farther into the country's interior. *What is the endgame without a military resolution anywhere in sight? What are these tens of thousands of displaced people supposed to do in the future?*

As dusk settled, the expansive blood-red sky presented itself to him. The sky enveloped the flat horizon in a fiery hue. The scene he saw now out here alone was wordless, unframed, ever shifting, and beyond human care.

23

"I'M IMPRESSED with the progress," Emil Marek said, turning his head now to Jo Richards.

Paul stood in the small corner office of the UN Headquarters building, looking down on the traffic jam that clogged the FDR highway along the East River. He had been back just less than a month. His wool business suit still felt too tight around the shoulders.

"You have done this in record time. Smart investments, good execution," Emil continued. "You're making a difference here. High mortality rates in the past month are beginning to fall, especially among children. The worst ailments from poor sanitation like cholera are down too."

"It's been hard work," Paul said soberly.

"I have no doubt," Emil replied.

Paul showed Emil more details on the success of the MSA distribution program. The Russians were thus far playing along by allowing UN aid to cross through approved checkpoints into Syria, Jordan, and Turkey. Russian inspectors at the Odessa logistic hub were also hands off for now.

"What else can the UN do, Emil?" Jo asked. "What is Moscow's position?"

"They're reluctantly playing ball. The Europeans need to stop the influx of migrants. The Russians are waiting for the next US election," Emil said. "I'll consider this a tactical pause."

When they left Emil's office, Jo touched Paul's arm.

"Tactical pause my ass," Jo said in the elevator. "How are you doing?"

"Other than sleeping only four hours a night, perfectly fine."

"You're strong, Paul. Let it go and stay focused. We have more to do here," Jo said. "Have you reevaluated workplace security downtown?"

"Yes. Since I returned, I've been working at the Zephyr Gallery. The contractors are almost done," Paul said.

Last month, Eastern Finance had sent in a specialized security team to install new security cameras, more robust cybersecurity, and a secure room within the building's interior. Rooms were reenforced with additional concrete, and the contractors installed a new safe.

"Compartmentalize as much as possible," Jo said.

"The Chelsea gallery is becoming Fort Knox," Paul said.

"And how is Katya?"

"Helping. Rutherford continues to acquire paintings for his private collection. He's funding all these investments."

"Good," Jo said. "I want to showcase real options with a new administration. Rutherford's money can help. He is a rich son of a bitch."

The US mission security guard waved them both through the main entrance, and they took the stairs to the second floor. Jo took precautions by separately exiting the UN building via the US mission. She never liked cameras, and these New York buildings were always chock-full of them.

Jo swiped her access card on an unmarked door. The windowless room offered a small desk and what looked like a specialized refrigerator against the wall. Jo opened the cold storage freezer door and took out a metal box marked with an orange biohazard label. Cold air wafted from the box as she unsealed the lid and pulled out a small glass vial.

"This little item is about a billion dollars of US government–sponsored R&D," Jo said.

"Which means?"

"Advanced work on nanoparticles. An antidote to sarin gas. You don't need to wait for exposure to nerve agent attacks to then administer a difficult cure. This antidote acts as a shield. If the antidote is consumed, sarin will not attach to the body's enzymes. Effectively, it gives our Kurd friends a way to fight back. It can save thousands of lives, assuming it works."

"Why wouldn't it?"

"We've tested it on small sample populations but never live with larger numbers. If we could get this to the field, even in small numbers, we could test its efficacy. So far, all we've managed to do in response to Assad is a few token NATO air strikes. The White House spews words to not 'cross a line in the sand.' Assad crosses that line every day now, and we do nothing. It's a joke."[53]

Jo put the vial back into the metal box and placed it back in freezer.

"How can I help?" Paul asked.

"Help me keep going," Jo said. "We need to just keep going."

"I will try."

---

53   US President Obama issued his "red line" warning regarding Syria on August 20, 2012. Exactly one year later, a major chemical weapons attack occurred in Ghouta, a suburb of Damascus, killing approximately 1,400 people.

After Paul left, Jo exited the US mission through the opposite side along the East River. She lingered there a while near the water and reflected on her chess board positions.

No, she realized, this wasn't chess anymore; this was a goddam multilayered chemical experiment! Threading together Yuri Volkov's business, George Rutherford's money, and the UN's humanitarian goals was an approach worthy of old-school intelligence ops, the kind of scheme Bill Donovan[54] would have concocted in his day. If this chemical compound held in solid form, she could do so much more. She might quietly slip more advanced conventional weapons to the field and set up a lasting intelligence presence with the Kurds.

Approval to deploy an untested nanoparticle antidote would require oversight, and Jo loathed larger task forces, but there was hope there too. The operation was scaling. True, it was only a matter of time before Jo would need to bring in others, but she had momentum now. The Seventh Floor was going to green light more of this if she could just get the skeleton in place.

Josephine Richards breathed in the air deeply. Twenty-nine years of blood, sweat, and tears to reach this point in her career, to have this kind of a chance to tip the scales. This wasn't a career; this was a cause, almost a crusade now. She had made countless sacrifices, given up any chance to have a real family of her own, and now took no real pleasures outside the promise of her work. And work was never ending.

Her genius-driven chemistry experiment was going to succeed.

Now she steeled herself for the next combustible event.

---

54   William J. "Wild Bill" Donovan (1883-1959) is regarded as the founding father of the CIA and a pioneer of modern special operations.

CLASH

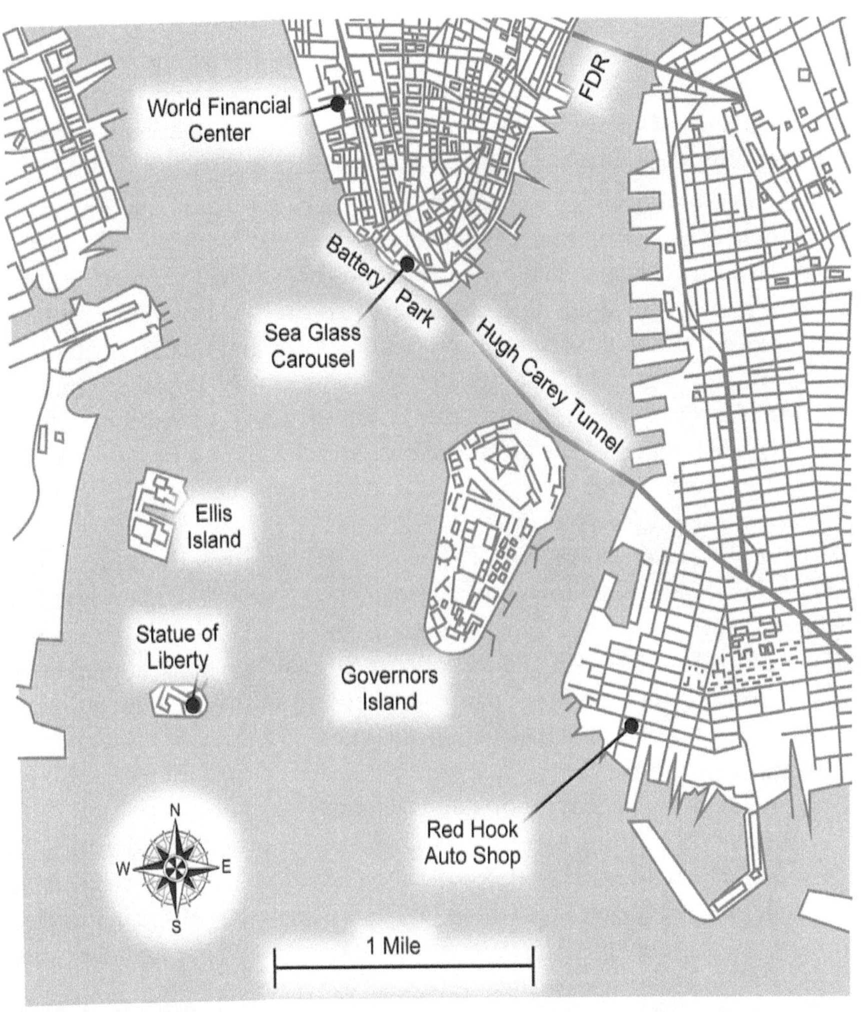

World Financial Center
Battery Park
Sea Glass Carousel
FDR
Hugh Carey Tunnel
Ellis Island
Statue of Liberty
Governors Island
Red Hook Auto Shop
N
W
E
S
1 Mile

24

JO CROSSED Chambers Street at a fast pace south down Broadway. She had been up since four, taking formal teleconference calls from a secure office the Agency maintained on the twenty-seventh floor of the World Financial Center. She paused her activities only to watch a notably chromatic sunrise while she finished a morning cigarette.

August had been a busy month. Working now from the downtown office meant higher pressure, but Jo welcomed the challenge. She was in the flow again on a live intelligence program that she had sourced, and the momentum was building. The memo she had drafted last week had been well received, although she purposely kept many operational details hidden in the version circulated. The director was now considering the option to provide her more dedicated resources in the form of a special task force and a sizable budget. If she produced more results, the traffic lights should stay green. Even these guys in their Langley seats didn't really want to know how the sausage was made.

She glanced up at Freedom Tower, now looming over the other nearby smaller buildings along downtown's morning skyline. This tallest building in North America was a shining emblem of the world's renewal. Below this glass and steel tower stood a more sober memorial: two black granite holes in the ground, thousands of names etched around the perimeter. New Yorkers spent a decade constructing this park and the vast underground memorial beneath her feet. That cavernous space below kept the rubble of 9/11 preserved as a memory of that fateful day.[55]

What a tiny group of fanatics could do if properly motivated, Jo marveled. The world had changed because the success of that clever little low-tech plot organized by a rabble of Arabs. They started small, huddled in back rooms, quietly taking their training courses. Those assholes were armed only with knives, but their plot was ingenious.

A chain of events flowed from the day those two towers crashed down. First came the country's shock and anger, and then the politicians harnessed public outrage to marshal the military. The leadership looked to

---

55   The National September 11 Memorial & Museum also occupies the most sensitive portion of the site, built primarily around and beneath the preserved footprints of the original Twin Towers.

topple regimes, take revenge against old enemies, show strength. Desert Storm, they coined the main Iraqi invasion. Now the aftermath still lingered in unanticipated ways, in the continued destabilization of governments and the rise of yet another pack of desperate people seeking an Islamic caliphate in some useless swath of infertile desert.

Jo had a ground game now. Her Black Sea network could distribute money, equipment, weapons, and, perhaps sometime soon, an antidote to nerve toxins. Best of all, this operation happened right under Putin's nose and didn't involve other regional partners. No need for erstwhile friends, the Jordanians, Lebanese, or even the Israelis. If the Syrian rebels and the Kurds in Turkey could hold their ground, then a whole generation of fighters might tip the balance, eventually topple Assad, and reconfigure the region's power dynamic. The US could recoup at least something from $2 trillion burned, five thousand American service causalities, millions of civilian deaths, and now ten million displaced.

And to think a little rabble of fanatics armed only with knives when they boarded those planes had set it all in motion fifteen years ago.

———————— ✳ ————————

Jo liked the twenty-minute walk in the morning to Battery Park.[56] She needed the exercise and the fresh salt air that blew over the little strip of green left at the tip of this manically crowded island. It was one of her few routines now within walking distance of the new office that allowed her to break up the day, clear her head, and press on with more work.

She saw Paul Drake from a distance, waiting for her at the arranged spot near the SeaGlass carousel. Paul kept his head down, face hidden by a pair of oversized sunglasses and hair covered with a biker's skull cap. He blended in now as one of the city's many document messengers or just a casual urban cyclist. Jo thought, *yes, he was a brilliant find! A hard worker, clever, useful, and a real producer. What he did in Syria was stupid, but at least he had courage.* Paul's relationship with Yuri had opened a whole new avenue of opportunity this past year. Jo could never really tell which one of her assets might deliver results. This business had too much variability. Success at this level required a rare combination of certain personality traits and lucky circumstance. But she had spun the wheel on this Paul Drake. He had taken the plunge, adapted, produced, and—most importantly—had not been killed yet. The payoff now could be substantial.

---

56 After the British took control in 1664, they installed the artillery batteries that gave the park area its name.

"How are you?" Jo asked when she approached Paul.

"Not bad today," Paul said.

"Coffee?" Jo asked Paul.

She had already had a strong cup at the office to feed her daily addiction, but that was wearing off now. She needed more.

"No thank you," Paul said.

"You sure?" Jo said. "The truck down here serves the good stuff."

"Thank you, I'm good," Paul said.

Jo walked alone over to the Coffee Kart mobile truck parked next to the pedestrian foot path. This truck had the good espresso drinks, not the cheap crap. She had found the best option through trial and error. Here it was of all places, outdoors in Battery Park.

"Long doppio, no sugar. And a water, please," she ordered.

The man in the food truck took the order, made the drink, then handed over the coffee and the bottled water through the truck's small window. He was a different face today, wearing sunglasses and a blue baseball cap with an American flag.

Jo went back to Paul, gave a quick final scan around the park, and sat next to him on the bench.

"Well? Give me a status update. What should I know for this week?" Jo said.

"It's going well. We're still ahead of schedule on what we've promised. Twenty-eight air shipments a week, plus marine container shipments for other bulk items off-loaded in Iskenderun and trucked onward."

"And the secure sites?" Jo said.

"Two are set up now. They've found four more that we can start to build out," Paul said.

"Any problems with the new equipment from Tel Aviv?"

"No, not really," Paul said. "All that made it through inspections and transit. We've been careful."

"Good, because there was another offensive near Aleppo with heavy civilian casualties. It's created more attention," Jo said. "It's important we move faster before we hit high gear with the election and everyone starts thinking about the downside." Jo took another sip of bitter coffee. Now she noticed an odd burning sensation on her lips. A tingling sensation coursed down her throat.

"Just a moment," Jo said. She coughed a few times to clear her throat. A nuisance to disrupt the flow of her thinking. She tried to cough out the thick Italian coffee grinds causing this tickle.

"As I was saying, the recent bombing near Aleppo has given me more authority to …" Jo said, and she coughed again. But now there was a burning in her chest, choking off her words. A pain leapt in her throat as if she were inhaling smoke and flames. The strange burning began to extend down to her waist and thighs. Her hands cramped.

"What is it?" Paul asked.

Jo's hands dropped the Styrofoam coffee cup. Coffee splashed sloppily on the ground. Pain now wracked her body.

"Coffee," she whispered weakly as her throat seized up.

She heard Paul's voice as if from a distant cave. Her mind raced.

Cyanide? Faster impact than a low-dose nerve agent.

Excruciating pain gripped her. Jo couldn't breathe. It was all swirling around her now. She was drowning without air. *Need to vomit before the poison shuts down organs. Need to vomit so the body can adjust,* she commanded to herself.

Need to vomit—now.

Jo's body reacted violently. She knew it was happening, but any calm response now eluded her. The poison was in her blood, quickly wreaking havoc. She felt her heart now breathing very fast, thumping hard as it pumped, and then her whole chest was bursting, and she felt dizzy and started to foam at the lips. As the deadly substance coursed through her bloodstream, her organs seized and her cells rebelled. In less than two minutes of a complete cellular rebellion against the foreign substance, Jo blacked out.

———— ✳ ————

Paul held Jo in his arms while her body convulsed, and her eyes rolled like loose marbles jangling on her face. A teenage kid in the black hoodie stopped nearby.

"Hey, man, what's wrong with her?" the kid asked.

"Get help. Call an ambulance," Paul shouted. He held Jo in his arms as she clutched at her chest and wheezed for air.

The kid in the hoody pulled out his mobile phone and dialed 911. Other people walking through the park either veered away or toward the unfolding scene. Now a woman in a white business suit stared at Jo and Paul.

"Oh, God, is she breathing? What's wrong with her?" the woman asked. Chaos mounted as others nearby came over. Paul felt the convergence of attention. He saw two NYC police offices jogging over from near the entrance of the East Coast Memorial nearby.

Paul released Jo from his arms and left the bench before the two police officers approached. He avoided eye contact with the female police officer who took Jo's limp body and hid his face from others in the crowd. The police officer put her fingers down Jo's throat to feel for why she was choking. She laid Jo's body flat on the grass and ripped open her collared shirt.

Paul needed to disappear, avoid a record, more questions, names. Paul grabbed the arm of the kid in the black hoodie.

"Tell them to pump her stomach, get the poison out," Paul ordered.

"Yeah, OK," the kid said blankly.

Then Paul walked at a quick pace toward the Coffee Kart food truck where Jo had bought the coffee. Paul pulled the handle and opened the side door. The seller was already gone; easy to disappear into a crowd at the South Ferry Station nearby. When Paul crossed Broadway, he saw an ambulance weave through traffic, lights blazing. Paul kept walking, crossed Bowling Green Park, and melted into the flow of people coming up from the Wall Street subway and flowing on to the narrow streets. Downtown's dense universe enveloped him. Now it seemed that people cluttered everywhere on the streets. They jumped off buses, darted in and out of buildings, loitered, talked, hailed cabs. There was now a whole locus swarm of people.

Paul followed a crowd of tourists behind their guide into Trinity Church.[57] Paul peeled away from the group and took a seat in a wooden pew near the last row. He put his head down as if deep in prayer. Instead, Paul kept his eyes closed to regain his composure. He kept his head down and thought hard about what to do next.

---

57   Established in 1697, Trinity Church's current Neo-Gothic structure, completed in 1846, was once the tallest building in the US and is famous for its graveyard, holding figures like Alexander Hamilton. During the 2001 World Trade Center collapse it miraculously suffered no structural damage.

25

PAUL DRAKE dropped his skull cap and sunglasses in a garbage bin as he left Trinity Church on Broadway and headed past city hall for Chinatown. There, he quickly bought new pants and a black T-shirt from a small pop-up store. He went to a dirty alley behind a garbage dumpster to change into the new clothes. Paul dialed Katya's mobile number. Was she safe?

If Perses could get to Jo like this in broad daylight …

Katya's mobile rang. No answer. Sent to voice mail.

He continued walking, shell-shocked. They had found Jo's routines, looked for weak links, very slight openings, repeated patterns.

Was I seen? Would I be blamed? And if Jo dies, what next?

Twenty minutes later, Paul called Katya again. Still no answer and no call back. To Katya, it was just an average day, oblivious to what had just happened.

A text message blinked on his mobile from Katya's number:

`Can't speak. Wait to come to the gallery. Be there @ 3:00 p.m.`

Why wait? Katya often texted him short answers, careful with mobile phones. She probably had her mundane reasons.

Now Paul walked to Chelsea as he had done so many times before. The cool morning had given way to a beautiful, early-summer day. Odd, Paul thought, how nature didn't correspond to the vicissitudes of his mental state. The day simply rolled on, ignorant of each person's trials and tribulations, the mire of any single consciousness. The taxis passed along Broadway, dropping off college students and picking up tourists. The people walking around him now didn't have any clue. To them, it was just a gorgeously lovely summer day.

Paul perched himself on a flight of brownstone stairs with clear line of sight across Twenty-Sixth Street to the Zephyr Gallery's main entrance. He waited there the final hour, watching. Satisfied there was no surveillance, Paul went down the narrow alleyway to the gallery's side entrance. He punched the six-digit security code, then entered via the back door.

Paul made his way through the inventory room, past rows of paintings arranged neatly in organized stacks. Paul punched another code to gain access to the interior office, another layer of security recently set up to protect his workspace. Paul could reach out to Dmitry once he made it to an encrypted phone, and then they would figure out what to do next. Thank God Dmitry was back in New York.

Paul saw Chloe Moreau through the open doorway that led to his new office. She sat at his office table, watching him on the security monitors as he approached.

"Where is Katya?" Paul asked when he entered the room.

Chloe didn't reply. Rather, she scrutinized him oddly. Chloe was always peering at him, demanding answers with those large, dark eyes outlined by heavy black mascara. She had no place here in his office, and he had no time now for her strange behaviors.

"What is this?" Paul asked.

Chloe lifted her hand from beneath the table. She held what looked like a 9mm Beretta pistol, muzzle pointing at him.

"Walk forward and keep your arms to your side," Chloe said.

"Is this a joke?" Paul said.

"No joke, Paul. Walk slowly forward. Keep your arms down and hands where I can see. Do it now."

A rush of blood now surged into his head. Paul stepped forward.

Chloe stood up from the table and circled him at a distance, still pointing the gun. With her left hand, she shut the office door behind him.

"There, Paul. We finally have our time alone."

Katya's eyes blinked open. Her head ached from the chloroform the two men had shoved over her face. Now, her body felt oddly frozen as she sat upright in a cold metal chair. Katya tried to move, but her arms and legs were strapped down, immobilized by a series of leather straps binding her tightly to the seat and chair arms.

What had just happened? Chloe called her into the gallery's storeroom to ask her to sign a simple inventory release for the two men wrapping up a painting for shipment to California. Katya signed the document and handed back the clipboard to the mover. Then the other man slipped behind her and shoved a rag over her face.

Unconsciousness.

Now this new reality. Splitting headache. Dry mouth.

She scanned this new place: old, empty garage space with a high ceiling, a dirty cement floor, and exposed metal roofing. The garage smelled vaguely like gasoline and spilled engine oil. The blackened windows along one wall blocked out the external light with double doors on the far wall closed and discarded cardboard boxes piled up in the corner.

A video camera on a tripod stared straight at her. The tiny red light below the lens shone bright. The camera was recording. Next to this, a foot-high black rectangular speaker stood alone atop a simple folding table. She also saw a small machine on the floor that looked like a portable electric generator. A jumble of red and white wires led away from the machine, across the floor, then finally toward her.

The wires ended in copper pads that were attached with duct tape in four places to her wrists and ankles. Katya tried to wiggle and squirm. It was impossible to move without tipping the chair over. Meaning came together: she was wired to the portable electric generator. The video camera was ready to capture the show.

Katya wasn't clear how much time had passed before the double doors opened briefly, letting in a slice of outside sunlight, then closing again. A man came into the room dressed in blue jeans, a black shirt under a combat vest, and a wool ski mask pulled over his face. He touched what seemed like an earpiece and microphone on his right ear.

"Who are you?" Katya asked.

The masked man ignored her question and mumbled some words into the headset, then sat down on a chair behind the table. A crackling series of noises came from the black rectangular speaker.

"Can you hear me?" asked a voice emanating from the black rectangular speaker. The voice tone was distorted, concealing natural speech with low metallic syllables.

"I hear you," Katya replied. She had no other choice now except to engage.

"Good, good. I apologize for this very sudden circumstance of our meeting," the distorted voice said. "I have poor manners. This is not how I intended."

She looked down the barrel of the video camera, meeting the unknown watcher's eyes with a defiant stare back.

"You have many questions, I know this. It is painful to suffer betrayal," the voice continued. "To lose trust, to know deceit. This drains the heart."

"What do you want?" Katya hissed.

"The question is not what I want. This is not right. My question is what are you willing to give?"

"I don't have anything to give," Katya spat.

"You wanted to give much before. You were eager to tell so many stories."

"I don't know what you are talking about," Katya said.

"You know. Your father knew," the voice said.

More dead silence.

The masked man came closer to Katya with a plastic bucket. He splashed water on her face and over her body. Then he returned to the table. He sat down and began to slowly turn up the power dial of the portable generator. Katya heard a slight whirring noise, then a low humming of the generator steadied as the voltage increased. The copper pads attached to Katya's four limbs grew warm and began to pulse. Katya's discomfort grew more acute as an uncomfortable vibration coursed throughout her body. The water facilitated the electric current that now passed through her.

The man turned the dial up another notch. The heat on her skin gave way to waves of pain. Her muscles convulsed as the electricity ran up from her hands and feet into her chest and torso, up her spine and into the base of her skull. Now her heart raced as if she were sprinting up the side of a steep mountain, running at a full sprint.

The masked operator turned the dial back off. The electric pain stopped, but Katya's heart continued to beat wildly, as if it was about to burst open and explode. Katya's mouth bled, as she had bit her tongue during the convulsions and gnashed her teeth.

"Painful. I know," the speaker said. "I learned this process from the Iraqi secret police and then also from the Jordanians. It seems that certain pleasures are shared amongst different tribes."

"Who are you?" Katya asked, now in Russian.

"A new path," the speaker said, answering her back in distorted, slow Russian.

"What do you want from me?" Katya said, wondering what story she could weave so the voice would continue talking and the man would take his hand away from the generator's power dial. If she kept the voice talking, maybe she could stall, hear some useful details. The voice had switched to Russian. That was a start.

"I recognize you, Katerina," the voice continued in Russian. "My people have watched you for a long time. I have studied you, waited for you so much longer than you could ever understand. I respected your father. I did. He was a good man, a true believer. And now you will help me again."

"What do you want from me?" Katya said.

"Are you afraid of death?"

She paused, not knowing how to game the answer.

"Are you afraid of death?" the same question came in that low mechanical tone.

"Yes," she said.

"Ah, of course you are. I see this. You fear because you have not made death your friend. You must make death your friend and your companion. Once you know death close like this, and you have traveled together and whispered all your secrets, then you will lose your fear."

Silence lingered before the voice started again in Russian. "When I was a boy, I read stories. Each night, a different adventure told by a beautiful woman, just like you. The king of Persia delayed this woman's execution each dawn to listen to her stories. He had killed so many other brides. For a thousand and one nights, each night, she gave her king a new reality. So many different realities, night after night ..." The voice trailed off, then suddenly demanded, "Tell me a new story, my sweet Scheherazade."

"You're insane," Katya whispered.

Katya evened her breathing for the next minute of silence before the masked man again slowly turned up the generator's power dial.

This voice from the speaker didn't want any information from her, she realized. He was toying with her in front of the camera the way a curious child toys with a tiny insect by slowly ripping off its legs, antennae, and wings.

Katya felt the hot buzz from the copper pads again, and then the waves of electricity sent painful spasms throughout her body. She clenched her teeth and began to scream. Finally, her eyes rolled back, and she lost consciousness.

———— ✳ ————

"I know you, Paul," Chloe said. "I knew you would come back here first, worried about your ice princess."

"Why do this?" Paul asked as Chloe pointed the pistol at him.

"Doesn't matter now," Chloe said coldly.

"How much did Perses promise to pay you?" Paul asked.

Paul saw a flicker of surprise in her eyes at the mention of this name.

"More than enough," Chloe said.

"Do you even know who you are dealing with?" Paul asked.

"I have an idea," she said.

"No, you don't. Whatever he pays, you will not be alive to spend it," Paul said.

"Your talk has no meaning," Chloe said. Paul could hear now in Chloe's voice a slight nervous ring. It was one thing to agree to a plan in the abstract and quite another to hold a weapon in one's hand and go through with it.

"Click on the happy face link," Chloe ordered.

Paul clicked through to the encrypted URL link. A grainy, black-and-white video emerged with no sound on his monitor. Katya appeared strapped to a chair with the wires attaching her to a machine nearby. He watched Katya. She began to squirm uncomfortably and then finally writhe in pain as electricity convulsed through her body. The soundless video clip lasted only thirty seconds.

"How to make this stop?" Paul asked.

"First, use your passcodes to transfer funds internally. I will tell you the number for the linked account," Chloe said.

"An account you control?"

"That's right. Money first. Then I want everything you have on your Black Sea plans in Turkey. Names, shipping schedules, inventories, your safehouses."

"How can I possibly get all that?"

"I know you can, Paul. I'm not blind with what you have here. No more pretending. You have remote access. Pull it all," Chloe said.

"It will take time," Paul said. "There are multiple security features," Paul said.

"Katya doesn't have time."

"And if I do this?"

"You stay, and I leave. Payments clear, I release Katya."

"So easy?"

"You can make this easy, Paul. Don't you want to make this easy for all of us? What do you even care about these Russians? They only share with you a few crumbs from their dirty plate."

As Paul typed in his passwords and began navigating the files, a stream of parallel thoughts raced through his mind. What was the logical outcome if he simply complied? Chloe had triangulated on Paul's access codes, understood the new security system, somehow gained access to a linked authorized account. He wasn't dead yet because she needed *his* passcodes and *his* active knowledge of the business database. But after he transferred money and pulled data, there was only one logical outcome. All other options seemed absurd.

"Hurry up," Chloe said as she watched him pause his typing.

"There is a secondary password. Hold on," Paul said.

His fingers typed while his mind whirred. Alternatives? A gun pointed at his head—bad odds. But Chloe still needed to pull the trigger. He was not some anonymous faraway target. She would need to do it up close. Odds were poor but better than waiting for logical outcomes to run their course. No better alternative.

Paul continued typing while he scanned for any useful object nearby. He spotted his open laptop on the desk. He could use the free chair too if he could get to it. He needed Dimitry's theater again, this time just a quick, vigorous scene to divert the audience's attention.

"What's wrong?" Chloe asked.

"The security code is sent to another device."

"Why?"

"Just how it works."

Paul picked up the laptop, opened the screen to himself, and rose from his chair.

"Here, take a look. I sent it here," Paul said, quickly improvising. "*Salaud.* Sit the fuck down," Chloe said. Paul moved one more step forward. He just needed to minimize distance and squeeze around the desk.

"Let me show you," Paul said calmly as he kept moving. One more step.

"I said sit the fuck down, or I will shoot you," Chloe hissed, backing up a pace.

"You don't understand. Look at this," Paul said, flipping the laptop's screen around to draw her eyes.

He threw the open laptop at her and ducked down toward the free chair.

She dodged the toss, squeezed the trigger, and shot twice too high. Two bullets ricocheted, shattering plaster. Paul grabbed the chair and hurled it at her hard. The chair knocked her arms as he rushed forward.

Now Paul gripped Chloe's right wrist and smashed her arm against a metal file cabinet. The gun clanked on the floor. Paul kicked it a few feet away. Chloe twisted her body away from him. He moved between her and the gun.

Chloe pulled a small knife concealed in the wide buckle of her leather belt.

"*Putain de merde,*" she hissed.

Paul rushed at her again, trading a knife slice to his right forearm for a clean, fast punch he made into her solar plexus. He didn't even feel the cut. She buckled over, and he wrestled her down to the floor. Paul trapped her wrist and peeled the knife out of her clenched hand. With his body pressed on top of her torso, Paul pinned down each arm under his knees. Paul squeezed her thin throat with his two free hands.

Squeeze. Two hands tight on Chloe's thin neck. He was smothering her now, choking out the life from her little body. She was a traitor and a liar. She deserved to die.

Paul pushed his thumbs into her larynx to close off her windpipe.

Squeeze tight and hold while she squirms just like Jo squirmed.

Now the veins in Chloe's forehead bulged. Her face began to turn purple.

Warm blood from the knife slice on his forearm dripped down on her, smearing bright red on her white face and throat.

One ...
Two ... Three ...
Four ... no air.
Enough.

Paul released his grip and lifted his knees off her arms. Chloe heaved in a deep breath, her mouth wide open, coughing and gasping.

Paul picked up the gun from the floor while she struggled to pull air into her lungs. He pulled a rag from his desk and tied a knot around his bleeding gash.

Chloe now lay on the floor in the corner of the office, panting for life, smeared in his fresh blood. He stood over her with the berretta in his good left hand.

"How much time do we have?" Dmitry asked over the phone. "I don't know," Paul said. "The plan was for twelve hours to allow bank transfers to clear."

"What else does the woman say?"

"She doesn't know where they took her but says one of Viktor's old team is involved—Mikhail," Paul said.

"We may be lucky then," Dmitry said. "I watch my men. If he is careless, he can be tracked."

Dmitry sorted his memory quickly to recover Mikhail's face from the catalogue of observations he had made at Viktor's Pominki those many months ago. Mikhail was a young, new hire to finance, still green. Probably not stupid enough to carry his own phone on a heist job. What about the expensive new smart watches HR slyly distributed last year? Those young idiots loved those gadgets. If Mikhail was careless, he might have overlooked this. Smart watches seemed innocuous. A clever little precaution might pay off big now if he could catch the signal.

"It's only been a few hours. They can't be far away," Paul said. "Somewhere easy to drive, less residential."

Dmitry furiously punched in the relevant zip code range on the computer's surveillance dashboard. He scanned the employee tracking map. Locations varied—office towers, hotel rooms, bars. Dmitry inputted Mikhail's seven-digit code into the next field. Mikhail's watch GPS signal flashed from a nearby industrial park. Dmitry homed in on the location: a block near the Gowanus Canal at the Brooklyn docks. Open parking lots. Warehouses. Dmitry cross-referenced to businesses nearest the signal. Red Hook Auto Shop. Listed as closed for two years. That had to be it.

"I see him," Dmitry said. "Brooklyn docks."

"How long before you can get there?" Paul asked.

"One hour," Dmitry said.

"You need to be quick."

"Keep them talking. I will gather my team," Dmitry shot back, annoyed, then hung up. Paul put down the phone and turned back to Chloe.

"Will he call you here?"

"Someone will soon."

"If he does, you stay calm. All in plain English with no panic button words. Understand?"

She nodded.

———————— ✳ ————————

Anton gripped the black sedan's wheel as it sped 70 mph down the FDR. He weaved between the lanes and avoided honking the horn. Any traffic violation now would kill their rescue plan in the cradle.

Dmitry, sitting in the back, breathed a sigh of relief when he saw that the Battery Park tunnel traffic into Brooklyn flowed normally. Yevgeny, his best local man for this type of operation, sat next to him. The young man was now checking the weapons he had quickly gathered: three handguns with silencers, an iron crosshair scope attached to one of the guns, and two M61 hand grenades.

No time to get more than what was in place for a break-the-glass emergency like this. This should be enough, Dmitry hoped. The quality of these two men mattered more. Both had military training. He recruited

Yevgeny straight out of Ukrainian protective services, and Anton, Viktor's former driver, cut his teeth in Afghanistan.

After the sedan emerged from Brooklyn tunnel, Anton exited to Columbia Street. He slowed down the last few blocks as they crossed the grid of smaller streets near the waterfront. "Pull over here," Dmitry told Anton in Russian. It was too great a risk to conduct a drive-by assessment. Instead, Anton stopped the sedan in a parking space several blocks away. The three men exited on foot, each concealing a weapon either inside a folded bag or stuffed inside a jacket. The broad daylight would help determine their approach, but it also exposed them. At least they had better visibility on them to assess posted security around the target building.

Dmitry crossed to the corner of a nearby brick warehouse. He slowly peeked his head around slightly to gain a view. From one hundred yards, he saw two men outside an old repair shop garage with the broken sign—Red Hook Auto Shop. The guards stood attentively with a full view of the only approach across the empty parking lot. They had a defensible position, but also the area's isolation would be an advantage. No street camera, no observation points from surrounding buildings. Dmitry could contain the scene but only if they moved quickly.

"Look there," Yevgeny said, and pointed to a third spotter in a black SUV parked at the corner of the road about thirty yards away. The driver's shape was obscured behind the car's tinted windows. Someone would need to take out this spotter too.

"We can do it, but a difficult approach across the parking lot," Anton assessed in Russian.

"I will target the two standing guards. A good shot from behind that parked car in front," Yevgeny said, holding the magnum handgun with the targeting scope attached.

"Good. Let me first go forward to close the distance," Dmitry said. "Anton—you take the spotter. Get close. Blow the car if you can't shoot through glass."

Anton nodded. Dmitry looked at each of his men. Whatever training and skills he thought they possessed would now be tested. His life was in their hands.

"Are you ready, *tovarich*?" Dmitry asked Yevgeny. The younger man nodded, knowing that Dmitry was about to take on the highest risk of them all.

The three men waited another minute to scan for lingering foot and vehicle traffic. They saw none.

"Let's go," Dmitry said. Yevgeny moved forward to a better position behind a parked car. He crouched behind the rear of the car and then began a countdown with hand signals. His fingers closed successively:

Three ... Two ... One ...

Dmitry started briskly walking across the street to the empty parking lot, his gun hidden in his coat. He closed the distance. At fifty yards, the two guards both saw him approach. They reached inside their jackets. Dmitry saw a puff of smoke on one man's chest. But the man, a Kevlar protective vest beneath his jacket, merely staggered back without falling.

Dmitry dashed ahead, arm raised toward the guards. He fired off rounds as quickly as his finger could squeeze.

Pop-pop-pop-wiz-pop-wiz.

One man's head jerked back, and he crumpled like a puppet whose strings were suddenly cut.

Pop-wiz-pop.

Return shots from a semiautomatic handgun.

Pop-pop-pop.

Dmitry ran to the side of the auto shop, out of the remaining guard's line of sight. Yevgeny took more shots from his position and moved closer to take attention off Dmitry. He would keep the remaining guard pinned down until Anton flanked, assuming Anton also took care of the spotter.

Dmitry had only precious minutes to move inside, clear out more resistance, and get her out. Dmitry cracked one of the blackened windows with the back of his elbow. He looked inside. Now he could see Katya there on the concrete floor with just another man, probably Mikhail, hovering over her in combat gear and mask.

———— ✴ ————

Inside the warehouse, Katya heard the crack of gunfire and muffled shouts. The masked man spoke something into his headset and listened for more instructions. He took out a pistol tucked in the small of his back beneath his shirt and gripped it nervously.

The man quickly switched on the generator again and then turned up the dial. The power would kick in soon.

Katya mustered her last strength to tilt her chair over. She hit the ground, then twisted over to her knees while still strapped to the chair. The electricity throbbed throughout her body as small gyrating pulses convulsed her muscles. Katya pushed with her feet, then shuffled away on her knees. The slack in the red and white wires tightened. With one final motion, she pushed away with her feet. The wires ripped off from the copper pads, breaking the circuit.

The bottom row of the blackened garage windows shattered. Glass fragments sprayed like confetti.

The masked man was now frantically looking for an escape. He ducked behind a steel beam to take cover from anyone coming through the door. Then Katya saw him stagger. He fell backward, clutching now at his throat to stop blood pouring out. He fell to his knees, gurgling.

Katya watched a little bald man climb through the broken window, walk up to the masked man, and shoot twice in quick succession into his face. He fell forward from his knees, lifeless. Dmitry moved swiftly over to her. He uncut Katya from the chair's leather straps with a sharp knife and then, with a swift and determined motion, lifted her limp arms to drape her body over his back. Katya tried unsuccessfully to stand. She could not feel her legs.

Dmitry whistled from the inside.

"*Pustoy*. Empty!" Yevgeny shouted from the parking lot. Dmitry emerged from the garage with Katya slung over his back. Yevgeny came closer to help, and they paused a moment near the parked car. They both scanned the open area for more threats.

The afternoon was now very quiet. Two bodies gathered pools of blood in the parking lot. A block away, Dmitry saw a UPS truck head down the street. But the van passed without stopping as the driver focused on his routine deliveries. He didn't notice the SUV's broken window glass or the spotter who now slumped lifeless on the front seat of the parked SUV. *Easy mark. They should have used bulletproof glass*, Dmitry thought. Another small operational planning mistake that made an enormous difference.

Then Anton brought the sedan to them in the parking lot. Dmitry put Katya in the back seat and squeezed himself in next to her. Now her head rested on his lap.

"*Te*. You," she said to him.

"Me, yes," Dmitry said. "Be still now."

Anton drove the sedan out of the parking lot, back on the road, then through a series of alleys between the industrial warehouses. Anton very calmly turned on the left-hand turn signal to gently merge the vehicle into the traffic while the three passengers sat frozen inside the car. They all stayed silent and still as the road traffic flowed normally around them in the other lanes. The sedan merged onto Highway 276, gained speed, and then headed south. The car reentered city traffic without detection.

They had caused not even a slight ripple to disturb the mundane world of routine work and common journeys.

Now Dmitry told Anton to take the highway to a private house twenty minutes east.

Dmitry released a very long sigh. No fatalities among his team, a clean extraction. Time began to decompress. They had succeeded.

He felt a tremendous pain now in his lower back, and his hand was bleeding from the cut glass he had pushed away to get into the warehouse.

Getting too old for this, the bald man knew.

"She's safe," Paul said as he put down the phone.

Chloe huddled now on the floor in the corner of the small office, holding her dislocated right arm, mascara smeared across her cheek, and a deep welt under left eye where Paul's elbow had hit hard. Paul's blood was smeared on her neck and chest.

"Are they coming here?" Chloe asked.

"Not yet," Paul said.

"When?"

"When I tell them to," Paul said. "You do understand what these Russians will do with you, don't you? Once they come, it's out of my control," Paul said.

Chloe averted her eyes and grimaced.

"That's right," Paul said. "It will be pain like you have never known. Worse than what you just did to Katya."

"I did what I was told, when I was told," Chloe said.

"If you don't cooperate with me in the next ten minutes, I will give you to them. They will find out everything. You will bleed, and you will suffer. It will be slow, no video camera, no mercy."

"You can't do that, Paul" she whimpered.

"If I contact the FBI, at least you have a chance." A glimmer of hope touched her eyes.

"Yes, Paul. You should do that."

"I will if you help me now."

"Ask," Chloe said.

"Who is Perses?"

"I don't know. I never met him. The others were a Frenchman, another Lebanese woman, a few others. We used only first names."

"When and where did you start?"

"A man came to me, two years ago when I was in trouble in my life. He took me from a bad place, a drug rehab center—you understand, offered me a way out, a new life. Gave me money, a new apartment, new clothes. Even set up an art course and English lessons."

"You knew why?"

"Not at first but later. He arranged it all—name, birthday, passport. Better for me. Move to New York, become a new person. It was just a business for all of them. Just a job. Lena paid me cash, and she taught me to watch men, steal keys, put devices on phones. She always paid when I did it. After Katya hired me, they told me to wait and watch her. There was nothing to becoming Katya's friend. Nothing to it one bit."

"Your real name then?"

"Simone," she admitted.

Paul continued his interrogation. Simone confessed more—how she was kept ignorant and simply went along with whatever she was ordered. Her handlers had been smart, Paul thought. However, he also discounted most of her confession as spin. She must still be playing a role, improvising like he would himself, lying to cover up the depth of her real tradecraft. There was the 9mm berretta, the hidden knife, the patience and skill of her long infiltration, and coordinated timing on Katya's kidnapping. Her story didn't fully add up.

Simone stared at him with her big brown eyes. She could see that Paul was drifting into a decision, doubting her.

"That's all I know," she said.

"You are a smart snake," Paul said. "You need to give me more, something I can use. Describe the Frenchman you say came to you first."

"Good-looking, brown hair."

Paul searched and found Rene's five-year-old image on his phone, the same image they had given to Nazir. He showed it now to Simone.

"Yes, Andre."

"Where is he?"

"You know that is impossible," she said.

"But you were also lovers, no? You must have been lovers, Simone. This is about more than money for you, isn't it? This is also about the thrill. Isn't that what you are really about?"

Her face went blank.

"This is your last chance. *Tell me something useful!*" Paul barked loudly. Paul's arm still dripped blood, and he stared at her now with wild animal eyes.

"Andre once took me to an apartment in Paris. It was his mistake. He used that place for other business, I'm sure of it."

"And you memorized the address, of course. Just in case."

"Sixty Rue du Cygne. Top floor," Chloe said shakily.

"There, there, Simone, you do have some bargaining chips left. What else?"

"Nothing more. I don't know Perses."

"The Russians will find out more."

"Kill me now. Just do it," she whispered.

Paul raised the gun toward her slumped, bruised body. It would be simple, and she deserved it. But Paul's gnawing voice returned. It was the same voice that stopped him from choking her. It was the same voice that made him different from others. There were lines he would not cross.

"You can't help more if you are dead," Paul said, and lowered the gun. He switched the weapon to his bloody left hand and started dialing from the office phone with his right.

He put the phone on speaker.

"Please, Paul, don't call them. I told you everything. I am begging you."

Buzz …

Buzz …

Buzz …

"Please, Paul, you can't do this," Simone sobbed.

Buzz …

Buzz …

"Please, don't."

Buzz …

Finally, a voice answered gruffly.

"Yes?"

"I have someone I need to bring in," Paul announced.

"Who is that?" FBI Agent Woods asked.

A SHADOW

Rutherford
Ranch
Route 62
Joshua Tree
National Park
Route 10
Coachella
Valley
Preserve
Palm Springs
International
Airport
Los
Angeles
111B
Jefferson
Foundation
and
Private
Gallery
Foothills of
Mt. San Jocinto
Downtown
Palm
Springs
Palm Springs
Art Gallery
N. Palm Canyon Drive
Palm
Springs
N
W
E
S
50 Miles

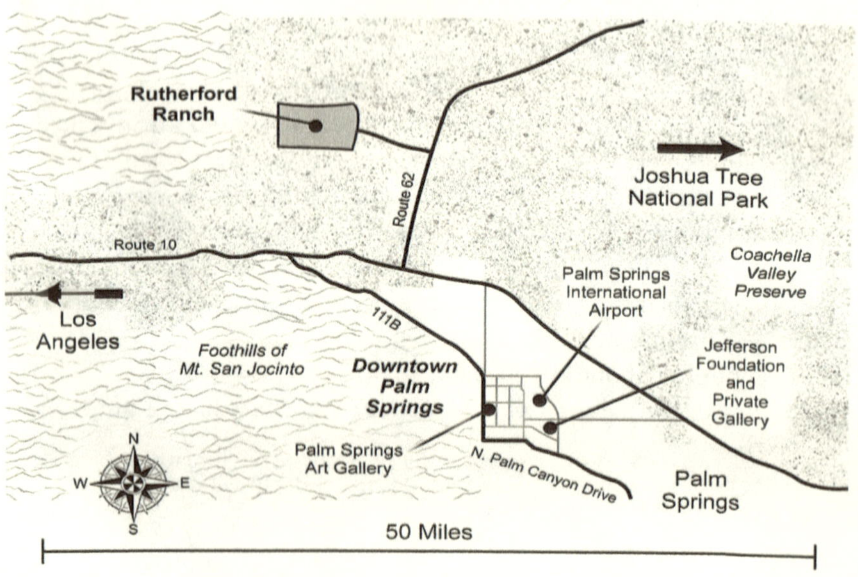

26

Y URI VOLKOV sat across from Dmitry and Paul on the twenty-second executive floor of the Peninsula Hotel in Midtown Manhattan. Yuri faced the large window looking down on Fifty-Third Street. He had slipped into New York last week. The burly immigration officer asked no questions thanks to his second Maltese passport under a different Christian name of Gregor. So far, Yuri's double life was working. No one really cared enough to check much further on Gregor's different birthdate tied to an orthodox calendar. Gregor's fictitious retirement was lived out of a two-bed flat in the Maltese capital town of Valletta. That was all the world needed to know.

Still, you could never tell with the Americans, their algorithms, new technologies, and watchlists. Coming to the US was always a risk, especially now. Yuri had thus far only left his room for lunch at Petrossian, a necessary trip to visit his most trusted American lawyer on Thirty-Fourth Street, and daily breakfasts with Katya each morning. No reason to hazard any other superfluous activities. Who knew what other hornets were stirred up during these very messy times. Best to tread lightly.

"There is one man I know of who might be this Perses," Yuri said carefully.

Paul leaned forward and quieted other distractions in his head. Dmitry also paused as he sipped the tea, anticipating that perhaps they were about to enter a place in Yuri's mind that even he had not yet glimpsed.

"Tamar Zoidze was a key Red Army man when the USSR broke apart," Yuri slowly began. "I knew him in my youth. He was one of those old guard Soviets who controlled most of the state contracts in the old system and then in the new. If you needed to build anything productive in Georgia or Turkmenistan in those days, then you needed Tamar. And Tamar had a hand in what I knew was a covert weapons program. They created an extensive stockpile."

"He is Perses?" Paul asked eagerly.

"No," Yuri continued evenly. "Tamar died of pancreatic cancer ten years ago. But Tamar had a son. Bogan was extremely ambitious, very smart. He knew how to recruit other skilled people. He took a university degree in London and spoke English well. Sergei and I met him once in

Tbilisi twenty years ago. Bogan was a very civilized, young man then. He was enthusiastic, eager. I thought that someday he might come work for me. This is before he changed."

Yuri reached over and carefully poured more tea from the porcelain pot in the three cups. Yuri took a sip from his cup, leaned back in the chair, and looked off into a corner of the Peninsula's executive floor as he pulled out distant memories from the vast reservoir of his mind.

"I was told that Tamar assigned Bogan to a special forces brigade during the second Chechen War.[58] The war there became very ugly after separatists videotaped the execution of Russian soldiers. There was a bus bombing in Georgia that infuriated Tamar and others. Political murders were common. I heard that Bogan's brigade was targeted. He retaliated with gas and other even more brutal measures. Over time, his team became known as a squad of killers—brutal raids, rapes, other atrocities. This changed him."

"The Russian government allowed this?" Paul asked.

"There wasn't much of a country then. No control."

"Why didn't we suspect Bogan before?" Dmitry asked. Yuri sighed.

"I was told by a reliable source in Moscow that Bogan was killed eight years ago. Now I know this was a careful lie that they spoon fed to me. And if Bogan is still alive, then someone at the Kremlin also must still support him and his network. Bogan has … what is the right word … evolved. They need this Perses to maintain this network, this veil of denial. Perses helps them achieve political goals in these proxy wars. He is the shadow of an unfinished humanity."

"Now what?" Paul prodded. "How do we dismantle them?"

"What about your Josephine? Have we lost her?" Dmitry asked.

"She's alive but still not responsive," Paul said. "The hospital pumped her stomach. But the cyanide sodium she drank induced seizures. Jo's brain didn't receive enough oxygen for several minutes. The doctors induced a coma. A ventilator keeps her breathing. The odds are long that she will regain consciousness anytime soon. They will move her to Walter Reed[59] in Maryland soon."

"And the traitor from the gallery?"

"The temporary solution is a detention center abroad. I suspect Poland. It's not clear if these black sites are entirely legal, but the FBI gave

---

58   The Second Chechen War (1999–2009) was a decade-long conflict between the Russian Federation and Chechen separatists that resulted in the reintegration of Chechnya into Russia.
59   Walter Reed National Military Medical Center is the world's largest multi-service military medical facility. Located in Bethesda, Maryland.

her status as a foreign combatant. Under the Patriot Act, they can hold her as long as they want."

Yuri frowned.

"We should have kept her with us," Yuri said. "Now we will never find out what else she didn't tell you. The Americans will just let her rot there, or trade her away for something useless."

"She gave me an address of a Paris flat. We can start there," Paul replied.

"Who else knows about our UN work?" Dmitry asked.

"I don't know. Jo kept a tight ship on her end. But there must be others," Paul said. "They have been funding work to create a nanoparticle antidote for certain nerve agents, including sarin. They have had success purifying a protein from bacteria that can degrade nerve agents into nontoxic chemicals."

"Will it work?" Dmitry asked.

"It can. The nanoparticle antidote stops the immune system from seeing nerve agents as hostile invaders. We were planning to start deploying doses to Kurdish fighters. There are cold storage facilitates in Odessa with more ready to be deployed."

"Then we can't stop just because of this setback. We need to continue to provide the relief and support we've agreed to do," Yuri said. "What about this strange billionaire? What is his true motive?"

"I don't know yet," Paul said.

"Why does this rich fool care about Muslim refugees in Syria?" Yuri asked.

"Syria. Iraq. Afghanistan. Vietnam. Timbuktu. The names don't matter. George Rutherford wants the world to embrace the light of American wisdom. I will find out more when I see him if you agree with my plan. George has offered to give Katya a place to recuperate at his ranch in Palm Springs."

"You think relying on an eccentric is wise?" Yuri asked.

"It's not safe to stay here," Paul said. "Rutherford has a hundred-acre ranch in a secluded area with private security and a wide perimeter. We can disappear there, get out of this viper's nest. Katya needs rest and a change. Then we can find out more about what this man knows and how he might help. We need allies. I will protect her."

"What do you think, Dmitry?" Yuri asked.

The bald man took off his silver-rimmed glasses and wiped them with the white linen napkin while searching for his answer. "I agree with Paul. There is too much danger here. We don't know enough about Perses. And we should try to get closer to this Rutherford man on his offer to help. He has been very generous with his money, and he is the best one to help us with the Americans."

"We are settled then," Yuri said conclusively to Paul. "You leave for this ranch outside Palm Springs as soon as Katya is healthy enough. Now, if you will forgive me, Paul, I must speak now with Dmitry in Russian on other matters."

"Of course," Paul said, then rose from his chair as the two old friends lowered their voices and began to speak together. Paul could not know if they were speaking about other matters or continuing with the same subjects, just without him.

Paul went to the window and looked down at the busy Midtown streets below. Fifth Avenue was crowded with cars and taxis flowing through the dense metropolis. On the sidewalk, people hurriedly walked to and from their intended destinations, each person focused on their own affair. It was a busy world of activity and distraction, oblivious to the conversation he had just now. What did any of this matter to those thousands of people below walking on the street?

All those people knew nothing of these brooding enemies and their schemes. Those strangers below didn't experience the simmering hatred Paul now felt inside like a cancer festering in his organs. And they didn't know anything about how this festering cancer, this shadow of an unfinished humanity, might metastasize and grow, until the cancer cells killed some of them too.

Paul looked at his bandaged arm. The cut was deep and still hurt, but Simone had missed major tendons. That night in Syria also flashed through his mind—another narrow escape. Blind Luck.

If Perses's network had figured out Jo's routines, how safe was he now? Perhaps it was time to think about the worst case, to make sure his family knew some fragment of the truth. If Paul was also caught in a snare, gone in an instant, there would be no time left to explain to Max, no time to let his brother know the truth of why he had made his choices. They would just read about him in the papers, or maybe not even that.

Paul owed them both at least a few words. They should know some sliver of the truth, in case he wasn't so lucky again.

27

KATYA HAD been staring at the hospital's blank white wall for more a half hour when she heard a faint knock on the door. She knew it was early evening only because the outside light from the small window had begun to soften and turn amber.

"Come in," she said.

Her eyes followed Paul as he slowly entered carrying a dozen white lilies bundled in a paper funnel.

"Very pretty," Katya said in acknowledgment.

Paul came close to kiss Katya first on the forehead; then when she pulled him closer, on the lips. He removed the old, slightly wilted roses that Yuri had bought last week and placed the fresh flowers in the frosted glass vase near her bedside. He nudged a metal chair closer to her bed and took her hand.

"You look better today," he said.

"I feel much better," Katya replied. "I can finally feel my fingertips again."

"That's progress. And your appetite?"

"A little better," she said.

"Good. It will take time."

"How's your arm?"

"No more tennis for a bit," he said.

She took a sip of water, shifted her hips, and leaned on her side. The burns on her arms and lower legs were less painful now. But she felt weak still and hated the confinement of the hospital bed. Now it was as if the years of recovery had all reversed, and she had been thrown back into the same broken world that held her before for all those long months of slow, difficult healing.

"Did Yuri agree?" Katya asked.

"He did. Are you ready for what is next?" Paul asked. "A different climate will help. Different routines."

"Yes," Katya said.

Ironic, she thought, *that Zephyr needs to close now for a few months even as it has become more successful than ever imagined.* The gallery was no longer reliant on new buyers, but still they came. The auction houses had taken notice of the volumes she was moving. Her living artists were getting paid and sending new art. What was not known to the wider industry was that George Rutherford's foundation drove this success. His support drove up the prices on oils, watercolors, and lithographs. She couldn't procure enough pictures now to meet the demand.

"I brought you some magazines and a book," Paul said. He put recent copies of *Juxtapoz*, *ArtForum*, and *Vogue* on the nightstand next to her pillow.

"You are sweet," she said.

Paul stayed with her in the room for the rest of the evening. They watched a comedy on the small television to pass the time. Katya barely watched the flickering screen. Katya wanted to tell Paul more, describe how sorry she was that it had all crashed downward so quickly. The earth had simply opened beneath them, swallowing them both into alternative plans. If she went deeper into this netherworld with Paul now, they might never reemerge, never be able to live the way she wanted to in the beginning before all this spiraled out of control and she thought it possible just to live the life she wanted. *Conserve energy, always conserve.*

Katya turned off the television after the nurse announced the end of visiting hours.

"I didn't want to bring you into this," Katya said to Paul as he gathered his coat to leave.

"You didn't do that," he replied.

"I did. I led you into this mess. It's not your cross to carry."

"I chose myself at every step. Freedom is what we do with what is done to us. Remember?"

"And you are free, Paul?"

"Maybe a little bit more than before, because of you."

"Then what do you choose next?"

"We need to destroy them. We must try, or this will never end."

After Paul left, the night nurse came in with her pain medicine. Katya swallowed two pills of oxycodone. She waited another ten minutes before turning off the lights with the remote control.

The room's darkness failed to bring peace. In the silence, she heard the echoes of that metallic voice, distorted and low: *Scheherazade. Tell me a story.* What did Perses really want from her? What did any of them really want?

In her mind, she replayed the last moments in the Brooklyn garage when the pain was at its worst. She felt herself lying on the floor again, her body on fire and her heart racing faster than she could control. She saw Dmitry stand over her tormentor's body and shoot him point-blank. The whole moment had an acrid smell of gasoline mixed with burning flesh. She had once again been on the edge of death's cliff, enough to see the void.

Cursed. No question. No way to undo all that blood. So much of her life had been built on lies and violence. It was time to embrace this uncomfortable truth, hold the pain close and feel its meaning. Paul was probably next. It was only luck really that he was still alive. Now she was dragging him further into this cycle of violence. No peace, only war.

No more hiding. No more waiting. No more weakness. If she didn't fight now, she would never escape. Perses would find her again, eventually. He had already waited years. If she did nothing, the world would crush her and her loved ones as it did those millions of others today and for those throughout history who simply ended up on the wrong side of a terrible event.

But how to fight against a shadow? With any war, it would be harder and longer than anyone planned. There might never be an end. The costs would be high.

It was simple. There was no other viable choice. She herself must do everything now to track, hunt down, and kill Perses.

28

THE GULFSTREAM jet took off from Westchester County shortly after five o'clock in the evening. In addition to the pilot and copilot, the plane carried only two passengers for the five-hour trip scheduled for arrival in Palm Springs by early evening. Katya looked out of the oval window, peering down on a blanket of shifting clouds. Paul sat next to her with his hands folded over his chest, his eyes shut, earphones for the television plugged in.

Katya peered out the window. The narrow-bodied Gulfstream was someplace over the massive American middle, those flyover states with thousands of acres of arable land and miles of rolling hills only sparsely dotted with farms and small towns. Near the front of the plane, the in-flight television screen played images picked up by satellite. The channel was set on the BBC News of the World. Even in the air, you could always stay plugged in.

"And now we turn to a special report on the crisis in Syria," the BBC newscaster announced. Paul heard this introduction through his earphones and opened his eyes. The BBC camera shots panned over the refugee camps while the field reporter continued her voiceover:

"Syrian refugees have also fled to Europe, with many crossing the Mediterranean Sea to reach the European Union. The refugees first reach islands in Greece by boat, then travel north to countries such as Germany, Switzerland, and Sweden.

"The exodus has been unrelenting. Syria's prewar population of twenty-two million people has been reduced to less than fifteen million today. As fighting continues across the country, an increasing number of health facilities have been heavily damaged or destroyed by attacks, leaving thousands without access to urgent and essential health care services."

Then the news cut to US domestic politics: "In other news, the US presidential election is entering its next phase as campaigns focus on upcoming national conventions ..."

Paul pressed the volume button down. He had seen and heard enough about the upcoming election. The leading Republican candidate, the outspoken hotel tycoon, stoked fear and hatred. Those tactics were working.

Perhaps we are in decline and just don't know it. What did Tolstoy write? One can never truly see history in its full complexity while living through it. *Too many variables*, Paul thought. If Napoleon had not had a cold at the Battle of Borodino, Europe would have taken a much different path. If Adolf Hitler had been admitted to a Vienna art school, the world might have avoided the catastrophe. If one attentive security guard had spotted the men boarding those planes in Boston on September 11, 2001, the Two Towers might still stand. And if that plot had failed, then no Iraq War, no call up of army reservists, no destruction thereafter. If Valentine had swerved right, not left, on that dirt road in Syria …

History was not a grand march toward progress led by the rational policy decisions. Instead, it was conflicts built up through millions of causes crackling through time, always unknown. History was a deaf man, answering questions no one had asked. If a man like Bogan Zoidze was left to tip the scales, even ever so slightly, what evil might emerge?

"We will gain a few hours of daylight traveling west," Katya said.

Paul turned his attention back to the sky's mutating colors outside the plane's oval window. The yellow sun hovered delicately above this sea of orange cloud. High above the rotating planet, the blood-orange light pervaded the earth's fragile atmosphere. The slight curve of the planet's horizon cut across the wide expanse, while the clouds rolled over in billowing layers beneath dark, empty space. Nature's pattern was random, silent, always shifting into new gaseous forms.

"A few more hours of added time to this day when we fly against the dusk," Paul added.

"As in the painting," Katya noted.

"Yes. Just like that painting."

"George told me he planned to install that canvas in a place of honor."

"We shall be reunited with it then," Paul said.

The painting. He had wandered to Chelsea on that first frosty winter day, then into the Zephyr Gallery as a random deviation. So much of great consequence in his life had flowed out of that single chance encounter. Everything had changed. Paul no longer had his meaningless charcoal-gray existence. He no longer belonged to a smudged-out, ordinary universe where all his actions had no consequence, purpose, or direction. Now he was authentically engaged. Now there was purpose.

Perhaps also he was one step closer to the human mystery sitting next to him and many others out there in those broken lands, struggling against each day's coming darkness, fighting for life.

"I wish I could capture this moment when the sun passes just below the horizon," Paul murmured. Katya turned to him, smiled, and pressed her delicate, thin hand into his. Their fingers interwove.

"Yes, isn't it beautiful! All this galactic dust struggling to gain form again.

Katya stared back at him with her mutating blue-green eyes. He saw a kind of stoic defiance in her pale, battered face. It was still a beautiful face, but the soul behind her eyes had hardened further against pain and loss. The universe had tried to kill the anomaly of Katerina Sergeevna Volkova twice now, only failing by a very tiny margin on each occasion. How many other unique lives in faraway cities and vast deserts out there faced the same dangers, the same long odds?

Others had not been so lucky: Sergei, Elena, Arlen, Viktor, Jo, his four men in Syria. Then there were the countless strangers, the mere statistics one only read about. Those people out there were a multitude, each a human soul as real as himself. Paul's actions perhaps tipped the scales just slightly in favor of life. Events of great consequence could be tipped by the flutter of a mere butterfly's wings, and sometimes just by the slight differences put in motion by a single person's free will.

He felt Katya's warm lips against his and touched her soft hair with his hand. They said nothing further as the lavender clouds melted into saffron.

———— ✳ ————

The morning Amtrak train from Philadelphia arrived on time at Penn Station. Throughout the whole two-hour train ride, a queasy kind of simmering anger had slowly built up inside Max Drake as he mulled over the cause for today's trip into Manhattan. His older brother, Paul, was entirely to blame.

It had been at least a year with no contact at all, except for a very short email Paul sent more than a year ago, explaining how he would be staying a few weeks in California. Then nothing. Never any replies or outreach. Paul missed Thanksgiving, Christmas, his own birthday, and even the fifth anniversary of their father's death. The building manager at Paul's former Twenty-Ninth Street apartment explained that Paul left no forwarding address. At the bank, they didn't have any clue what he might be doing for work now. They had all assumed he departed to pursue a more lucrative venture. Whatever that new life was, he was staying off the grid.

Now into these unanswered questions, a Manhattan law firm had sent this cryptic letter, delivered last week. Max had almost thrown the white envelope away among a pile of other junk mail solicitations. He called the law firm, and here he was, proceeding exactly as the lawyer instructed.

Max Drake stayed entirely underground on his way from Penn Station to Fulton Street subway station downtown. He followed the flow of morning office workers up the dirty subway stairs, then to the Chase Bank building at Maiden Lane and Pearl. A stooped, silver-haired bank officer eventually took him below to the vault. After another set of procedures and more signatures, this man directed Max to a private alcove where safety deposit box No. 4756 waited, unopened.

Max turned the tiny key and lifted the lid to reveal the box's contents. He read this letter first, tilting his head slightly so that his functioning right eye could better discern Paul's somewhat erratic handwriting. Max's left eye was glass, the original one having been crushed by a small stone a decade ago outside Fallujah.

"Don't believe the lies," Paul's strange note warned. *Shared enemy? Saving millions of people? What the hell is he talking about?*

Then there were the fifty bundles of $10,000 all neatly arranged in stacks, the small hard drive, and the single photo. Max put the photo six inches from his right eye to peer at the woman's face in detail.

Of course, there must be a woman like this one involved!

Max Drake lingered a long time in this tiny alcove, rereading Paul's letter several times without satisfaction. Finally, he bundled the contents from the box into a small duffel bag, relocked it, and left the tiny alcove.

Max headed out on the street again—now teaming with people in the early afternoon. All these human beings were darting in different directions, each one focused on a singular goal. The city was a huge, chaotic swarm of different motivations, desires, and possibilities. They were all preoccupied and distracted by countless small tasks and efforts that made up a typical day.

Someplace out there, he hoped, Paul was still alive.

Volume 2

BENEATH THE PURPLE DAWN

Life is more than crossing a field.

—*Russian Proverb*

GROUNDWORK

1 miles
Taksim
Golden
Horn
Galata
Tower
Bosphorus
Galata
Bridge
Suleymaniye
Mosque
Topkapi
Palace
Grand
Bazaar
Hagia
Sophia
Divan Yolu
Blue
Mosque
Kumkapi
ISTANBUL

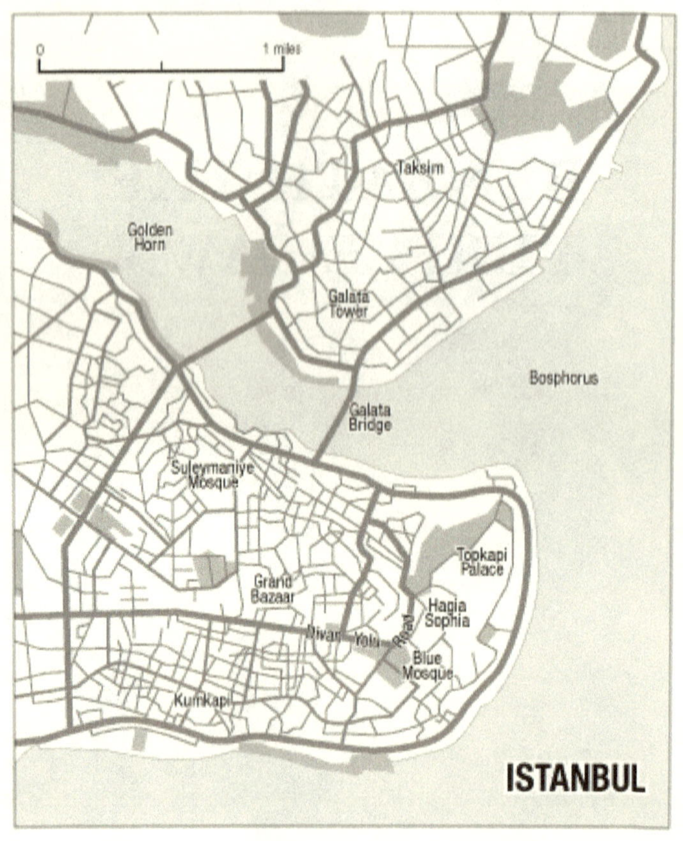

1

Istanbul, Turkey
8:35 p.m. July 5, 2018.

DMITRY IVANOVITCH Medkov took his time crossing the stop-and-go traffic along Divan Yolu Street. Dmitry disliked Istanbul, especially in the summer when the heat channeled the old city's dry dust down to the base of his throat. To make matters worse, his body hurt immensely due to an inflamed nerve in his lower back. The pain flowed from his spine out to the fingertips of both hands.

Just over the rooftops and surrounding trees, Hagia Sophia's bulky silhouette lurked. Dmitry vaguely knew of that massive old relic, once the largest church in Christendom, dedicated to the Holy Wisdom, the Logos. Hagia became the Grand Mosque when the Eastern Roman Empire's Constantinople fell to the Ottomans more than five hundred years ago.[60] Tonight, it presided like a squat sentinel observing mankind's long journey, dark against new Istanbul's fourteen-million-person sprawl and shining high towers of glass and steel. Dmitry was out of his comfort zone in this ancient, unfamiliar place. He was merely a passing ghost.

The old Russian found his way to the entrance of Tarihi, a garden restaurant tucked away a few meters off the main road. Dmitry gave his first name to the Turkish man in front, then lifted his arms for the guard to discretely pass a security wand over his body and lightly pat him down.

Colonel Hasad Atakan watched Dmitry at the door from a small table nestled beneath a leafy fig tree. The Turkish military man wore a loose tan suit, a blue silk shirt, and shiny Italian leather shoes. Atakan touched a small glass of raki mixed with water to his gray lips before lighting his next cigarette. He agreed to meet with this Russian based on a reliable recommendation from his trusted man at the Ministry of the Interior. Dmitry Medkov, he was told, worked for the United Nations High Commissioner for Refugees' main logistics firm in the region, Marine Shipping Agency, or MSA. Dmitry was MSA's key man, responsible for

---

60   Constantinople's fall in 1453 followed a 53-day siege by the Ottoman Empire's Sultan Mehmed II. It marked the definitive end of the Byzantine Empire and, by extension, the final collapse of the Roman Empire, which had lasted for nearly 1,500 years.

sending medicine and food to hundreds of thousands of Syrian refugees swelling Turkey's border camps. With so much UN donor money sloshing around, there must be some way a hard-working, senior military man might extract value, Atakan expected. These globalized Russians nowadays were always pragmatic when it came to such affairs. The ex-Soviets were ironically more capitalistic than the capitalists themselves. Such is how the world revolves, Atakan knew, one century to the next. Political ideologies came in and out of fashion while deeper hatreds kept their grip. Old wars rotted for decades, if not centuries. New wars sprang afresh. The American invasion of and withdrawal from Iraq further stoked many primitive evils. More bloodshed was sure to come from some other tremor in this unstable world.

The Turkish security guard guided Dmitry through the maze of other diners to the colonel's secluded table in the back. The two men shook hands before Dmitry sat down, lifted off his black fedora, and rubbed his bald head.

"Hot tonight," Dmitry said.

"July is uncomfortable," Atakan replied. When the waiter returned, the colonel ordered testi kebab—lamb mixed with vegetables, potatoes, and garlic. After a few more pleasantries and small talk, Atakan moved on to business. He spoke stoically of his military efforts on Turkey's southern border—more than ten thousand troops were deployed over two hundred kilometers of rough terrain to deal with the fluid situation involving the Islamic State. Nearly a hundred brave Turkish soldiers had died in the last year in skirmishes with those black-flagged fanatics. Because the UN and NATO were but sad anachronisms, Turkey took the brunt of the turmoil to protect its sovereignty. The Syrian government, a puppet regime led by Russia's strongman Bashar Al-Assad, was also no friend and couldn't be trusted.

"We'd like to extend our relief shipments to smaller camps further east. Is that possible?" Dmitry asked.

"Every new foreigner adds a burden," Atakan explained without emotion. "Your UN teams and doctors keep them in tents, but you cannot control them. Many bring radical ideas. They don't speak Turkish and shouldn't stay."

"The Syrians can work if allowed. They are just looking to escape violence, live without fear. That is only human," Dmitry suggested.

"We have enough uneducated labor here already," Atakan replied, crushing his cigarette in the ashtray. "Best these Arabic speakers go west to Europe. Germans are willing to take many. The Americans can take them in Idaho and Nebraska. Kurds should also surrender their arms and stop their attacks against us."

Colonel Atakan diverted the conversation away from the humanitarian crisis to a diatribe on the illegitimacy of Kurdish ethnic rights. After ten minutes, he paused long enough for a waiter to fill their two shot glasses with a second bottle of raki. The anise-flavored raki went cloudy as the waiter added water.

"We need local military help to stop black marketeers, especially for the medicine," Dmitry coaxed. "Our kits are trading at outrageous prices. Supplies are not reaching the real victims."

"With medicine, we can perhaps find a way to help," Atakan said, sensing an opportunity also to work both sides of what he guessed was a lucrative supply chain. At the end of the meal, Atakan believed he had negotiated well, signaled correctly, and accurately assessed the situation. "Let me look into your issues and think more on these matters," he said.

"Of course. Let's meet again. Perhaps next week," Dmitry said. He reached into his jacket, then slid an envelope across the table. Atakan glanced inside at the bundles of cash, neatly wrapped, crisp, colorful, straight from the bank.

Dmitry put on his fedora, made a slight bow, and left the table.

The colonel finished the last two cigarettes from his Murad pack while he waited for his driver Abdul to bring up the car. A good start, Atakan thought. When Abdul drove up to the curb, the colonel slipped into the backseat of the bulletproof C-Class Mercedes.

"Take me back," Atakan said gruffly in Turkish.

"Yes, bayim," Abdul replied softly.

The colonel leaned back against the rear seat's beige leather. He closed his eyes and allowed his mind to drift. A little more cash would help. So much to do these days, many mouths to feed. All his so-called superiors were biting at his heels to solve impossible political problems. Now those civilian fools in Ankara were talking about deescalating the operations against the Kurds, even though these traitors were the greatest threat to the nation's integrity. Those dirty Kurds used the regional chaos as an excuse to advance their own separatist agenda and tear Anatolia apart. Only firm tactics produced results. The Kurds would long remember death by gas; such weapons terrified them—chlorine, blister agents, mustard gas, VX, sarin. Those separatists only understood strength, brutality, and decisive action. His tactics were working along the southern border. Violent incidents against the Turkish army dropped by half in the last three months. Brutal conditions called for brutal countermeasures.

The driver Abdul brought the Mercedes down a smaller street, then turned the corner to the darkened parking lot of a closed auto repair shop. Abdul shifted the car's gear box into park.

"What is it?" Atakan asked.

"Just some air, bayim," Abdul said as he lowered the backseat window with a push of his left index finger.

Atakan refocused his attention on the moment; he turned his face towards the open window. The colonel glimpsed a slender masked figure striding quickly from the shadow of two parked cars. A primitive instinct stirred deep in Atakan's brain as if he recognized danger now leaping out of the jungle's underbrush. Yet the raki dulled his mind. Only a few seconds ticked by before the muzzle of a handgun silencer confronted his slouching eyes.

Pfif. Pfif.

Two bullets pierced Atakan's skull, one into his cheek, the other square into his forehead.

In one fluid motion, the shooter then leaned inside the open window, pointed at the driver's head, and squeezed the trigger twice more.

Pfif. Pfif.

The first bullet passed through driver's neck and lodged in the interior door. The next one hit just below his ear, passed out of the opposite cheek, ricocheted off the bulletproof windshield, and lodged in the leather front seat.

Moving quickly, the masked figure opened the driver's door, pushed Abdul's body down below the passenger seat, and slid inside. The shooter wiped the driver's blood and bits of brain from the interior of the windshield with a towel that had been wrapped around his waist. The car's engine softly purred while he cleaned the mess.

The new driver took off his ski mask, adjusted the seat back slightly for his longer legs, then rolled the Mercedes back out to the crowded main thoroughfare. He drove calmly, first to the Galata Bridge north over the Golden Horn that separated Europe from Asia, then east along Bagdat Street, away from Istanbul's densely packed residential areas. The new driver navigated the twisting roads. He cut the headlights as he drew closer to an empty lot near an abandoned tobacco-processing plant along the waterfront.

Dmitry emerged from a nearby car when he saw Valentine Kuzoff pull the Mercedes into the empty lot.

"Any problems?" Dmitry asked his Ukrainian man in Russian.

"All without incident," Valentine replied, knowing that Dmitry had kept the colonel talking while he set last-minute logistics. Flashing some money always helped distract these greedy military men. Valentine took two thick manila envelopes—one from the inside of Atakan's cheap tan suit jacket and the other from the glove compartment where Abdul had shoved it earlier in the evening.

Yevgeny Volesky threw down his cigarette before he went to help Valentine wrap the two bodies in plastic. The colonel's disappearance might be attributed to any number of causes—best to leave all this ambiguous. It was easy to place two shrouded bodies in a vat of quick-dry cement, remove the car's license plate, and burn it with petrol. These basic steps were good enough for a noisy, inefficient place like Istanbul. Off-stage disappearances were most effective when left unexplained.

Dmitry leaned over Atakan's body; he took the dead man's mobile phone, house keys, and wallet from his jacket pockets. The colonel was well known for his violent tactics against the Kurds along Turkey's long southern border with Syria, moving from one small town to the next, dropping barrel bombs full of petrol, and killing women and children indiscriminately with that most deadly of gases, sarin. Dmitry's Kurdish contacts also fingered his driver Abdul as a loyal soldier and an indifferent killer, not to mention betraying his boss for just a hundred thousand euro. They both very much deserved their violent ends.

Atakan's liquidation also served a more strategic purpose. In the future, Perses would need to deal with a different weapons buyer for his Iskenderun shipments. Change was good. Change consumed the enemy's resources. Change cost money and forced other errors. Every disruption to established transaction routines and network contacts might lure Perses out of the shadows, force him to commit an ill-advised mistake, expose a weakness.

Valentine and Yevgeny finished loading the two bodies into another van. The game continued with one less chess piece on the enemy's board. It was a dirty business, but Dmitry believed in his just cause and thus necessary methods. It was naive to expect otherwise. Everything tonight went exactly as planned. Tomorrow, he would make his way back east to the border area near Suruç. He had left Paul Drake in charge of the rest of his Odessa team for more than a week. Paul was coming along, helping with many needs at the sprawling camp. This time, Dmitry didn't need to worry about any new dangers involving Katerina Volkova. This time, Yuri's niece was safe from all these sordid wartime realities; she was hidden fourteen thousand kilometers away in the Southern California desert. Perses would not be able to drag her back into this mess as he had done before.

Now Dmitry hoped, the enemy would make his next mistake.

2

FORESTED, ROLLING mountains cut a rough outline against the coal-gray overcast sky as the Toyota Land Cruiser drove up the narrow, fenced-in, dirt entry road. The car came up past the compound's main secluded gate, then slowly rolled to a stop in front of a grove of tall blue-green juniper trees.

Two bearded men exited the car, stretched their legs, then lifted a third man out of the cargo space in the back. The guards placed their captive on his feet, legs trembling slightly, his arms cuffed behind his back and mouth gagged with a strip of black cloth. The taller man nudged the prisoner slowly up an inclined stone path to the old, two-story, wood farmhouse nestled in a tangled forest and overlooking a small mountain lake.

Bogan Zoidze, sitting at his worktable beneath a tall pine tree, watched his two Georgian men approach. He closed his book—the third volume of One Thousand and One Arabian Nights.[61] He also put down his ceramic teacup and paused a moment to consider his new arrival.

"Any injury?" Bogan asked the taller guard, Artem, in Russian.

"A few head scratches," Artem replied.

"Give him water," Bogan said.

Artem took the cloth gag off Arsalan Karay's blood-stained mouth, then pressed a bottle of cold water to the tall, muscular Kurd's chapped lips. Arsalan drank greedily before he spat out the congealed blood caked in his mouth. The Kurd's eyes flamed defiance. He held himself tall now, a fighter to the last, just as described in the latest Turkish intelligence file sent over from Ankara.

"Let him wash first, then bring him to the workshop," Bogan ordered.

Artem nodded and guided his prisoner further along a dirt road to the north side of the forested compound.

Bogan went back to his afternoon reading and his strong, bitter black tea. He was pleased that the Kurd leader had been captured but also slightly disappointed it had been so easy with such a legendary fighter. The Turkish

---

61   An expansive compendium of folk tales unified by the frame story of Scheherazade, who staves off her execution by telling the King an endless series of unfinished stories. Compiled primarily during the Islamic Golden Age.

Bayraktar drone took out Arsalan's entourage at night, even before they understood the danger hovering above them in the clear night sky. One of the Kurds was dumb enough to carry his mobile phone; that oversight was enough to give away their position. The Kurds made their next error by fleeing directly into a secondary ambush. Russian mercenaries from the Wagner Group[62] drained the remaining rebel fighters of their ammunition, leaving Arsalan no other choice but to surrender or face certain death there in the hills.

The Russian mercenaries stripped them down first, then corralled the four remaining men into a small opening in the forest. A biometric test confirmed Arsalan's identity. A few minutes later, the spetsnaz leader calmly shot the three other frightened prisoners in quick succession, each cleanly with a bullet to the back of the head. No need for unnecessary and potentially irksome witnesses, whatever anyone might say about the Geneva Convention. The mercenaries stripped the bodies of watches, jewelry, petty cash. Two plainclothes Russians then trucked Arsalan north two hundred kilometers through eastern Turkey—hooded, gagged, and handcuffed in the back of a Mercedes G-Class SUV. Artem met the Wagner men at the Turkish Georgian border, paid them two bars of gold of one kilo each, and loaded Arsalan in the Toyota's back for the last hundred kilometers over rough terrain into the hills of southern Georgia. It was an easy pick-up job once they were over the border.

On the first day at the compound, Bogan's men allowed the prisoner to wash, eat, and sleep on a small cot inside a cell in the basement of the workshop. The Turkish translator—a slight, unhealthy man with wire-rimmed glasses—asked a series of routine questions: "Where did you acquire the radar systems? Who supplied the anti-nerve agent pills? Where are the other safehouses?"

As expected, Arsalan offered vague responses, asserting ignorance. The translator didn't push more aggressively. Before he left, he gave the Kurd a pack of cigarettes—and a warning.

"The man you met this morning is the one called Perses," the translator said. "You have heard of this name?"

Arsalan nodded. He had heard of Perses from some of the Syrian fighters; however, he also assumed that this person was a myth, a demon

---

62   The Wagner Group (officially PMC Wagner) is a Russian state-funded private military company (PMC) that acts as a proxy force for the Russian government.
After a failed mutiny in August 2023, the Kremlin dismantled Wagner's autonomy. Its fighters were forced to sign contracts with the Russian military or disband. Operations are now overseen by Russian military intelligence (GRU).

invented to create fear and anxiety. Perses' terrorizing exploits seemed exaggerated, mere stories meant to scare the weak minded.

"Good," the translator said. "Be honest with him tomorrow. This will help you."

"There is nothing to say," Arsalan replied.

Arsalan finished the pack of cigarettes by midnight and managed to get a few hours of sleep on the cold cement floor. He had survived worse predicaments. He was strong, unbreakable, fearless.

Early morning of the second day, just after a breakfast of black bread and coffee, Bogan arrived at the workshop to start his process. He likened his method to a kind of medieval inquisition that always yielded an inevitable confession. Artem had already brought in Arsalan from his holding cell and prepared him for the day's process. The Kurd was standing, immobilized in iron chains against a vertical wood plank, both hands elevated above his head, and a nylon rope tourniquet tied tightly on both upper arms.

The Turkish translator repeated the key questions from a prepared list. Again, the resilient Kurd obfuscated and demurred. Unsatisfied after some ten minutes of this exchange, Bogan rose from his chair. He removed a sharp surgeon's scalpel from a toolbox. He brandished the knife in front of his captive; the clean metal blade glinted beneath the glaring overhead fluorescent lights. Arsalan's face remained impassive.

Bogan started with the fingers of Arsalan's left hand, smallest to largest. He sliced the little finger first, just below the knuckle, and placed it afterwards in a small silver bowl.

After this cut yielded the expected results—screams, shaking, wide-eyed pain—Bogan paused for the translator to repeat the questions. The translator calmly read again from his same list: "Where did you acquire the radar systems? Who supplied the anti-nerve agent pills? Where are the other safehouses?"

Bogan didn't rush his process. He allowed Arsalan time to gain his breath and composure, consider his dilemma, and adjust to the excruciating pain. Answers were cross-checked and assessed for plausibility, accuracy, and completeness. Only after a reasonable interval did Bogan continue— the ring finger was next, and a different line of questions.

The tourniquet on the upper arm prevented excessive blood loss. A shot of adrenaline kept the victim awake going into the afternoon. More questions. Better answers. Each hand, five fingers paced apart. The middle finger was next, and then the index finger.

Arsalan begged for death after Bogan took his right-hand thumb. Almost every man finally, truly broke at the thumb. A dexterous thumb gave humankind its ability to first craft tools, Bogan thought as he calmly placed this detached digit next to the others now piled in the small silver bowl. *The thumb is used to hold a brush, a pen, a sword. Now I take this thumb, and devolve this living being backward into a different creature, a lesser animal. Curious to see how far pain pushes any living being into new realms.*

When Bogan moved to the right hand, the beady-eyed Turkish translator didn't probe further for new information. There were no more questions. Arsalan only moaned now and garbled his speech. Bogan, nevertheless, continued with the little finger, then the ring finger. When he cut the middle finger of the right hand, Arsalan's forearm went slack. The stump below the knuckle barely bled.

Bogan checked for a pulse and felt none.

"Clean the blood and make sure your notes are accurate," Bogan said to the translator after he wiped down his scalpel with a towel.

Bogan carried the eight dismembered fingers in a silver bowl over to the dark storage room at the back of the workshop. He unlocked a metal cabinet with a small key, then removed a large glass jar filled with amber-colored formaldehyde. He unsealed the jar and dumped the eight fingers into the liquid. The glass jug contained almost a hundred dismembered fingers gathered in fits and starts over more than two decades—Chechnya, Syria, Russia, Iran. Fingers clustered in the jar like matchsticks—slender, fat, young, old, some still with wedding rings. All races and religions were equally reduced now to these little dismembered digits. *A curious novelty, all these lives. There is a certain terrible beauty in my work. A terrible beauty.*

In the evening, Bogan took his meal on the veranda. It was slightly cold, but otherwise a pleasant night in the mountains just north of the Armenian border. He preferred nights out here in the open mountains, far from the stench and chaos of crowded cities. Here in the mountains, the sky opened. The wide, cold, meaningless darkness stretched out above this unimportant little planet, outward into infinite space. Here, Bogan could truly think, truly plan without the interference of lesser men.

Tonight for dinner, Bogan's cook served him chicken in tomato sauce with chickpeas and okra. Afterwards, he smoked a bowl of aromatic tobacco from his dead father's old Meerschaum pipe for an hour while listening to world news on satellite radio.

More black tea helped Bogan work past midnight in his private study on the farmhouse's second floor. There was always more work to do, more requests to fulfill, more money to collect. The "Perses" persona he had invented for this past decade had steadily developed in stature and power, one victim at a time. Now Kiril in Moscow was again starting to push the boundaries for new, more ambitious political purposes. The Russians wanted their old empire back, no matter what the cost in blood and treasure. Lately, Putin's cronies were all willing to pay much more to entice skeptical partners. The most aggressive of them, Kiril, was looking for help with the Libyans. Once Bogan finished with the Kurdish problem, he could turn to this next opportunity and a host of other more lucrative ventures. The machine must move forward, always.

Bogan finished typing on his laptop.

He looked down at his own left hand, only four fingers. A long time ago now—maybe twenty years—a low-level Iranian security man had taken a scalpel to his little finger. It was only one finger then, taken mostly out of spite rather than to gain anything of real use. That mongrel scum met his end a few years later and in much greater pain than he had inflicted.

Violence begat violence, an eye for an eye, a cycle without end.

Bogan opened the page to the English book on his nightstand. He kept all his London books here in his bedroom at this cool mountain farmhouse. Turning to a marked page, he read a favorite passage from The Theory of Moral Sentiments, first published 1759, on the issue of human fingers:

> If he was to lose his little finger tomorrow, he would not sleep tonight; but, provided he never saw them, he will snore with the most profound security over the ruin of a hundred million of his brethren, and the destruction of that immense multitude seems plainly an object less interesting to him, than this paltry misfortune of his own. To prevent, therefore, this paltry misfortune to himself, would a man of humanity be willing to sacrifice the lives of a hundred million of his brethren, provided he had never seen them? Human nature startles with horror at the thought, and the world, in its greatest depravity and corruption, never produced such a villain as could be capable of entertaining it.[63]

---

63   Smith's passage explores the "arithmetic of compassion"—the phenomenon where we feel more intensely for our own minor troubles than for the catastrophic suffering of millions of strangers. Often cited as a foundational concept in both modern moral philosophy and behavioral economics.

Bogan took a shot of pomace brandy after he put down Adam Smith's book. He took off his clothes and laid down naked on the bed. It had been a very productive and satisfying day. He had by now removed so many fingers.

More to do tomorrow.

3

PALE MOONLIGHT touched upon the undulating surface of the upper Tigris River as Paul Drake wiped the sweat from the back of his neck. It was just before midnight on a breezeless, humid night. A nearly full moon hovered high in the sky and cast its dominant light in a vast field of scattered, pin-prick stars. The bright orb hovered, uncaring, distant, remote. Men had traveled to that lunar rock once, Paul briefly thought. That scientific triumph—humanity's impressive feat to launch astronauts to the moon—didn't matter down here at the river tonight, fifty years later. Tonight, the moon only hovered, an uncaring celestial rock, far above the incremental steps of something so very short as human history.

Almost done, Paul thought, as he loaded the last of the heavy, wooden crates onto the deck of the small ferry boat. His other men were nearby, just outside the old grain warehouse a few dozen meters up from the riverbank. His men were nearly done loading the rest of the cargo onto the two trucks they had driven here in the afternoon. The team had been working now for almost six hours, resting only for short water breaks.

The grain warehouse—a drab unattractive brick and stucco building on the Syrian side of the Tigris River—was ten kilometers south of the small Turkish town of Cirze. For the past year, this shabby, undistinguished warehouse served as a key logistics depot for UNHRC's relief shipments of medicine, food, and other essentials. Dmitry Medkov's Odessa team made regular visits to secure and resupply this furthermost node in their transportation network. The place was ideally situated near the river and just a short drive from the two-lane paved highway that ran south to the small town of Al-Maabadah. It was also, critically, close to the Iraq border where their Kurdish allies could move more freely without worrying about Turkish or Syrian government troops. The nearest Syrian government checkpoint was some forty kilometers north, and it was only a thinly manned outpost.

Paul's small team drove here from the Suruç camp in the east soon after Dmitry gave the order. Paul had gathered his crew quickly—two Kurds, a Turkish driver, and two older, highly capable men from Odessa. Was Arsalan Karay killed or captured? It was hard to know, but the signs they picked up in the last few days were not favorable. The MiG-29 missile dropped two days ago on a small village mosque just along the Armenian border was probably not a mere coincidence. Kurdish fighters stored small arms beneath that little mountain mosque. The basement contained specialized freezers for storing high-value, anti-nerve-toxin pills. Now all those military resources were buried under smashed stone and rubble. Only a handful of people in addition to Arsalan had known of the weapons stored there.

Paul knew this river grain warehouse from his first visit some six months ago. Beneath the basement, a false wooden plank and an iron door led into a labyrinth of tunnels and alcoves stuffed with Javelin anti-tank missiles, Kalashnikov rifles, C4 explosives, mortars, Roland mobile surface-to-air missiles, and at least thirty thousand rounds of small arms ammunition. His team's priority objective tonight was to move these various weapons to alternate sites before they might be compromised. On the second level below the main floor, the Kurds had placed their most important new defense. The eleven advanced anti-drone radar systems were by far the most critical items. Paul's former handler in the US intelligence services, Jo Richards, obtained these systems last year. She had procured the systems directly from the Israelis. Dmitry's MSA crew had smuggled them all into Syria via convoluted channels along with the UNHCR's medicine and food. Now, the Kurdish resistance fighters were tactically deploying them in more remote areas as a critical defense against increasingly sophisticated aerial drone attacks from the Turks. In just the last few weeks, the radars had already thwarted several. Eleven more radars could make a difference. Paul only cared about these radar systems. Only these advanced systems were truly irreplaceable.

He loaded the radars separately on the river ferry, not the trucks. The ferry captain finished tying down the crates on his deck. Paul untied the rope to the dock and gave the captain a hand signal to push off from the shore. The old man throttled the old diesel engine. The boat began to slowly float away from the riverbank, its motor purring softly. Boat traffic along this part of the Tigris was typically scant this late at night. It would be easy to quietly take these items ten kilometers upriver to a truck on the Turkish side and then back to a secure site inside the Suruç camp. The rest of his men planned to drive the other weapons south to several different alternative sites.

The ferry captain offered him a cigarette.

"No, thank you," Paul said, also waving his hand to refuse. It was only a short trip.

Paul first saw a fast-moving light emerge on the western horizon. The small red beacon grew brighter in the sky. It came low and fast, joined by an ominous rumble, deep and steady. The sound increased, until it grew into a thunderous clap as the fighter jet streaked overhead. Paul saw the plane's sharp nose and wings as it streaked by. Mere seconds later, the warehouse exploded with a massive boom, scattering fragments of brick, stone, and cement in a thick, expanding cloud.

Dazed, Paul saw another fire trail drop from higher in the sky. The two trucks next to the grain warehouse blasted apart in a messy cloud of flame, metal, and body parts.

The ferry captain shouted something in Turkish, panic in his voice.

Paul looked up—more lights in the sky above, circling.

We're next, Paul realized. He motioned to the terrified captain to jump overboard, then dived himself into the cold, muddy river.

Paul sank. A flash of hellish orange light and a muffled boom penetrated the river's murky darkness. He kicked his legs as a swirl of confused current sent him spinning. When he surfaced for air, pieces of flaming wood were scattered on the river's surface. The ferry was on fire, its bow now just shards of splintered wood and twisted metal.

Paul plunged back underwater. He swam away from the wreckage, kicking his legs, boots still on, arms straining against the current. He swam this way for nearly an hour, away from the flames, adrenaline pumping.

Upriver, Paul waded closer to the Turkish side of the river. He found a shallow pocket of high reeds, and rested there, waist deep in the water, his boots on the river stones buried in the soft mud. The riverbank was now strangely quiet, except for the rhythmic buzzing sounds of locusts. A small fire from the first missile still smoldered in the distance down river. Otherwise, the river was dark and undisturbed. The moon still hovered, now lower in the night sky, insensible.

As dawn climbed, Paul scurried up the riverbank. He wiped the wet mud off the geolocator strapped on his wrist and used it to gain his bearings. Valentine would pick up his signal eventually, he knew. He just needed to avoid Turkish patrols for a little while longer and find his way closer to the main highway.

Paul found a dirt walking path that led away from the river into a series of cultivated land plots that spread out flat among the scattered collection of tall palm trees. A light morning mist hung over the fertile patches of millet and sorghum fields stretching to the north. It was still too early for the rising sun to burn away the morning dew. Paul passed a few isolated houses—simple concrete boxes only—scattered among the fields. In the distance, an old, solitary man led two harnessed oxen over a brown area of untilled soil. The old farmer was intensely focused on driving his two struggling animals forward, using a whip to motivate the dumb beasts held in harness. The oxen moved forward, step by step through the soft earth. The frail old man swung his thin arms, hitting the animals with the whip. They continued forward, dragging the plough into the earth, sweating under the hot sun.

A primitive, immortal scene, Paul thought. *Mesopotamia, still unchanged, after all these thousands of years.*

Paul's legs ached as he followed the dusty walking path through the fields. A piece of debris from the ferry had smashed against his waist just after he dove underwater. The bruise was turning purple; dull pain now flared up along the right side of his lower torso. Paul concentrated on his bodily pain. The ache along his waist was a better sensation than the sharper sting of remembering anything else, especially the faces of his five dead men.

4

TIMOTHY JOHN Hastings leaned up against the wooden fence and took in the open California sky with his confident, clear gray eyes. The San Jacinto mountains loomed to the south, rugged and clean, while rolling hills spread out to the east eventually blending into the Joshua Tree National Park some thirty miles away. Tim felt particularly healthy today, breathing in the unpolluted air of a wide-open desert expanse. Here before his eyes spread out the New World in all its expansive glory. This was the real America, a big, progressive place of open horizons, rugged mountains, and unsoiled new frontiers.

Tim squinted his eyes to watch a tiny figure in the distance. He saw a rider on horseback, still tiny against the vast desert horizon. The rider gripped the reins to move the powerful gray mare to a trot. The horse gained speed as it galloped across the dry plateau towards him, its hooves kicking up clumps of dry earth. As the horse approached, Tim could see the woman's honey-colored hair flowing out from beneath a black riding cap. She rode, back arched and legs pressed against the powerful animal. Now astride this stunning mare, crossing the plateau against the backdrop of California's soaring mountains and expansive sky, this woman appeared entirely otherworldly. She galloped towards him as if out of a different time and place altogether.

"Beautiful animal," Tim shouted over to her when she was near enough to hear. The rider pulled the reins, brought the thoroughbred first to a slower trot and then to the wooden fence where Tim stood.

Tim recognized Katerina Sergeevna Volkova from the photographs that Langley's head of Russian operations, Martin Hines, emailed last week. Tim had thought her appealing from those three 4 x 6-inch digitized pictures. Those square digital photos didn't do her justice.

"And you are?" she asked him, looking down from atop the panting horse.

"Tim."

"Tim," she repeated in a deep Slavic accent. "Have we met?"

"First time," he replied. "But I want us to become fast friends, Katerina. We have much to talk about."

"Is that so?"

"It is. I'm here to help," Tim offered.

"Do I need help?"

"I've been told you might," Tim continued.

"A damsel in distress?"

"Something like that."

"Well, I don't think that's right. It's you who might need to be rescued," she quipped.

Katya dismounted the horse in a graceful motion, then tethered the muscular animal to the fence outside the Rutherford main stables. A gray-haired, lanky stableman in a faded cowboy hat came over to help her remove the heavy leather riding saddle and stirrups. Then, the stableman led the great horse to the nearby white barn where Rutherford kept four other thoroughbreds that raced each fall at the Santa Anita racetrack outside Los Angeles.

Katya carefully lifted off her black cap and unwrapped her white linen riding scarf. She splashed cold water from a nearby drinking fountain on her face and neck, before turning back to Tim.

"You came for tonight's event?" Katya asked.

"I did, yes," Tim said, meeting her blue-green eyes steady with his own. His handsome face held most women's eyes a fraction longer than most. He was tall and noticeably good-looking, with a chiseled jaw, and classic masculine, movie-star features. His mature, still firm, mid-thirties face, fit the part of a bright star, Annapolis graduate, Camp Peary–trained officer.[64] Only Tim's cold eyes revealed a decade of experience covering unpleasant conflicts in countries less touched by the bounties of the Enlightenment and the rule of law.

"I hope you will not mind if our new friendship waits a little longer. I've been riding since morning. The desert is very hot. I need to clean up before the party," she said.

Without waiting for an answer, Katya turned away and walked up the dirt path leading to the ranch's main two-story building at the top of the hill.

Hastings watched her go. *My God, she really is something,* he thought.

---

64   Camp Peary is a 9,000-acre U.S. military reservation in York County near Williamsburg, Virginia, known as "The Farm," a CIA training facility.

Earlier that morning, Tim drove two hours east down the 60 and the 10 from his West Coast office in Santa Monica at the Rand Corporation.[65] He barely registered the radio news as he drove, preoccupied with the details Marty Hines had tossed his way. The Russian desk didn't have all the facts, but the brazen poisoning of a former Kabul station chief last year in New York City had left small, anxious questions, still largely unanswered. That broad-daylight incident in Battery Park was frustratingly aggressive, even for those cruel, bloodless spiders weaving their net in Moscow. Now, Jo Richards lingered in a coma at Walter Reed, kept alive with a breathing tube. She had started something interesting via a UN logistics contract in northern Syria, but Jo's cable traffic was scant and contradictory. She was one of those old-school, no-paper types who threw everything at the wall to see what stuck. Some of it did, much of it didn't.

Hines' cross-functional task force was supposed to tie up loose ends, but these were dysfunctional times. Langley's little pop-up team was too distracted by the new administration's self-created scandals and more nuclear antics thrown up by the North Koreans and Iranians. Hines' task force had been sitting on Jo's confusing, no-win Syrian project for over a year before Rutherford's overzealous Jefferson Foundation rattled some cages with a scathing analysis of Russia's growing military influence in the Black Sea. The think tank's critique focused on the expansion of Russia's Syrian naval base and catalogued Putin's long list of historical grievances. The Russians were filling the power vacuum left after the end of the US occupation of Iraq. These uncomfortable assertions on Russian plans led to phone calls and finally to a follow-up that trickled down to Tim.

George Rutherford III. This eccentric old billionaire's involvement was another twist. The old man's sycophants were always snooping around, causing more harm than good, feeding narratives to reporters, the media, and other Beltway bandits.[66] Rutherford befriended Jo Richards when she came to him years ago with her aggressive ideas. Both were maverick personality types who naively put too much faith into their own individual ability to steer events. Rutherford endorsed Jo's world vision, gave her dire warnings more credibility in DC's congressional circles, legitimized her work. Now George introduced this Volkova woman living at his ranch.

---

65   The RAND Corporation in Santa Monica, California is an American nonprofit global policy think tank that has profoundly shaped U.S. national security and military strategy since its inception in 1946.

66   The "Beltway" refers to the Capital Beltway (I-495), the highway that encircles Washington, D.C. Private defense companies are typically headquartered in the suburbs of Northern Virginia or Maryland near this road for proximity to federal agencies, such as CIA and the Pentagon.

Maybe she had useful intel, differentiated enough to matter. Or maybe it was all smoke and mirrors just like the now infamous Chris Steele's dossier that the Democrats bankrolled in 2015; that piece of work was stuffed nicely with salacious hearsay, innuendo, and bad tradecraft.[67] Separating fact from fiction was never easy. Usually once you looked hard, there wasn't much meaningful truth left to harvest.

Hastings went back to his cabin, shaved, showered, and changed into his tailored Ermenegildo Zegna tuxedo by 7 p.m. The 75th anniversary of the Jefferson Foundation was billed as a black-tie affair; Tim needed to look the part.

Cadillacs, Porsches, Jaguars, and a few Teslas filled the parking lot inside the main area of Rutherford Ranch as the evening's sunset bathed the foothills and mountains in a deep orange glow as the temperature dipped below sixty degrees Fahrenheit. Tim had been shown the 150-person guest list: several congressmen from both parties, a coterie of donors from San Francisco's Bohemian Club,[68] a smattering of prominent technology investors, and a few other private family fortune heirs who supported Rutherford's ambitious international causes over the years.

At 8:00 p.m. George Rutherford appeared punctually in a white tuxedo, his wrinkled face beaming with a broad smile, wisps of white hair neatly combed. The 79-year-old always put on a good show. The spacious main dining hall connected to six drawing rooms, all designed in a chic, modern dude-ranch aesthetic with wide open spaces and varnished, natural redwood furniture.

Examples of the Jefferson Foundation's expansive private art collection hung on most walls—some hundred and fifty oil paintings, lithographs, and drawings covering a range of styles and historic periods. Several rooms also showed off modern bronze and marble statues. A string quartet played Bach in the main hall.

Tim mingled with the guests, surfed the conversations, kept his ears open and his smile broad. Most guests gathered tonight were too smart for their own good when it came to foreign policy. They all had money, influence, and opinions. Some were zealous patriots—so-called foreign

---

67   The Steele Dossier was a collection of 17 unverified investigative memos compiled as 2016 political opposition research. While U.S. intelligence confirmed the broader premise of Russian election interference, subsequent investigations later discredited its specific, salacious claims as uncorroborated hearsay.

68   An elite, all-male private social club in San Francisco, founded in 1872. Originally started by journalists, artists, and musicians, it evolved into a prestigious network for business and political leaders. Members have included Mark Twain, Jack London, Dwight Eisenhower, Richard Nixon, and Henry Kissinger.

policy hawks without any military service themselves. Most leaned right, although it was hard to tell since the classic definitions of liberal and conservative were all mixed up these days. Few understood the complexity of carrying out anything sustainable in war-torn, struggling places. Real conditions out there in the vast, cruel world were unimaginable for most of these wealthy, privileged donors. *There are more things in heaven and earth, Horatio, than are dreamt of in your philosophy.*[69] *Or shown on either Fox News or CNN,* Tim thought.

Tim joined a conversation with an Arizona congressman still angry about the leaking of national security secrets by Julian Assange and Edward Snowden. The politician talked loudly, frustrated that the liberal media applauded them both as free speech heroes rather than traitors. Tim also spotted a few prominent American Israelis huddled by themselves in a corner. Tim put the Israelis into a special category. The Israelis understood hard realities, but you could never really tell what Tel Aviv might have up its sleeve. He didn't blame them for their survival instincts. Israel was a tiny chunk of real estate with many enemies. They had little margin of error. Even more reason why there were limits to his trust in the realm of statecraft.

Tim caught Katya in his peripheral vision as she entered later in a stylish white gown that hugged her slender torso. She moved with a kind of natural grace; her silky, golden-tinted hair now tied up in a bun to reveal a slender, alabaster neck curving into smooth shoulders. Well-defined calf muscles supported her on heels that were just high enough, but not too much so, for her lean shape. She lifted a glass of Chardonnay from a waiter's silver tray.

Tim broke free from his conversation. Katya greeted him with a faint smile when he approached.

"White suits you tonight," Tim said. "It brings out your color."

"George told me you are staying the week," Katya replied.

"Yes, if you are also fine with that."

"I am only his guest."

"Will you make time for me if I stay?" Tim asked.

"I will try."

"Thank you," Tim said.

"Is this party what you expected?" Katya asked.

---

69   This line is from Shakespeare's Hamlet, Act 1, Scene 5, spoken by Hamlet to Horatio after encountering his father's ghost. It highlights the limitations of human knowledge, logic, and science to explain all mysteries of the universe.

"I had no expectations," he replied.

"Good. Expectations lead to disappointment."

"Rutherford should be pleased," Tim said. "More money here tonight than the GDP of a small Caribbean island."

"There is money, here, yes. But perhaps a more important question," she continued, her glossy red lips curled in a slight smile. "What do you think of the art?"

"The art?"

"Yes, the paintings. All around you," she confirmed.

Tim looked around to the walls for the first time. He had been focused on Katya, the guests, his own thoughts, and everything else imaginable except for the paintings. The paintings, he assumed, were completely irrelevant. Tim rarely looked at art. Painting had no place in his life. He dealt with hard reality, not imaginary images, myths, and long-dead visions suspended inertly inside square frames.

Katya drew Tim's attention to a series of canvases on a nearby wall. The first painting was made of sweeping primary colors that coalesced into a series of different faces drawn in vigorous lines. Curious images, Tim thought. Then, Katya directed his attention to a different canvas with geometric shapes painted in shades of red against a yellow background. Finally, there was a third large painting of two blue silhouettes in front an orange sunset.

This last painting gave Tim pause. The large, 6 x 5-foot painting reached out to him, shimmering, almost alive.[70] This painting pierced something in his consciousness. He allowed his eyes to linger.

"This one works for me," Tim said.

"I thought you might like this one. Great art mixes beauty and suffering. The artist captured that. Don't you think?"

"Something mysterious in this one," Tim said, not knowing how to describe what he saw in the detailed brushstrokes, outlines, shapes. "From your New York gallery?"

"They all are," she said.

"All?"

"Yes. Everything on display tonight. George buys art as an investment, a scarce asset. He's new to collecting but has been very active with my gallery."

---

70   The painting's title is *Against the Dusk*, as introduced in the initial chaper.

"Very active," Hastings murmured. "Wouldn't have thought Rutherford the type."

"People discover art at different stages of their journey. Art is long, and life, unfortunately, much too short," Katya said. "For me, visual arts move us beyond our divisions. It is a primal form of expression before even language. Don't you think?"

"Art?" Tim said. "Hard to define. Lots of things that people call art these days make no sense to me. I'm no expert, like you. It's not my field."

The crystalline ping of a triangle chime broke the moment. A waiter wandered into each room to signal guests to take their pre-assigned seats.

Katya and Tim went separately to their places at different round tables spaced throughout the main room.

Tim sat and smiled at the others. A bespectacled Silicon Valley investor engaged him in another conversation about the rise of crypto currency as the waiters brought out the salads, salmon, and steak. Waiters carried bottles of either red or white wine to be poured into tall glasses.

George Rutherford took the podium midway through the main course, reading his speech from a yellow notepad. George spoke eloquently about his father, the Jefferson Foundation, the importance of America's commitment to free enterprise born out of the lessons of world wars and other past tyrannies. Towards the end of his speech, Rutherford's voice grew firmer as he criticized the ham-fisted US Iraq invasion fifteen years ago and today's pointless Afghan occupation that had cost thousands of American lives, hundreds of billions of dollars, and was sure to fail. George ended by calling out the Foundation's current support for the nearly six million Syrian refugees displaced by the civil war and his commitment to a "smarter," more lasting US foreign policy to counteract the growing threat of powerful autocracies.

"History's painful lessons are clear. It will only get worse if we do not act now with greater skill and foresight to confine familiar menaces to distant shores. Every citizen of the free world bears this responsibility. Each one of us must do our part," Rutherford concluded.

The audience lightly clapped at proper moments, most already familiar with Jefferson's hawkish foreign policy positions. George thanked his three sons for their enduring support and made a final tribute to his long deceased, but beloved, wife. He called out the other donors who had recently contributed to worthy causes. More applause came while waiters served cheesecake and lemon tart along with a choice of coffee or tea.

Katya glanced at Tim before a short film about the Jefferson Foundation's current activities began to play on the main presentation screen. Tim met Katya's gaze with a firm, confident face. She faintly smiled back at him from across the high ceiling room.

Tim knew that it was always wrong to be personally involved with any foreign source. They gave you this basic warning as a central rule, and it was obvious. Mostly during his career, Tim had never been remotely tempted. He had enough success with women outside of work. But this particular human being returning his stare was different. Why was she really here, a slender beauty, sitting quietly amongst these people?

Tim took a swig of scotch, rolled the liquid around in his mouth, then swallowed.

5

KATYA LEFT the party early. After dinner, she mingled only superficially with other guests, discussed a few paintings, and steered away from politics. Tim Hastings watched her leave. She didn't say goodbye.

Tim might be useful, Katya conjectured. He looked at her with those confident, analytic eyes and winning bright smile. She could not deny that he was good-looking to the point of distraction. Most importantly, Tim had direct access to America's massive intelligence and military network that might, if properly stimulated, be stirred into action. "The System" had sensed a tiny new tingle last year. The new pinprick that the Americans felt drew a few drops of blood. Now the System was reaching out, sending one of their up-and-comers to delve more deeply into the Black Sea project, and perhaps pick up where Jo Richards left off to determine if a pinprick meant any more danger.

Katya asked for Rutherford to give Tim a comfortable, two-bedroom cabin so that he could stay the week. She needed quality time with him. George agreed immediately, enjoying his final act in life as a spy master. Rutherford had grown fond of Katya's presence; he had even begun to listen to her more, at least on subjects he thought veered into her areas of special knowledge and competency. They met at least weekly, usually in his study for iced tea with lemon in the afternoons when the sun was at its hottest outside. Whatever she needed, old George was more than willing to provide. The art purchases continued at a steady pace, although not as much as when Jo Richards was involved, and the high profits were all converted to cash to be used to further support for the Kurds in Syria and Turkey under the cover of Yuri's UN humanitarian contract.

She avoided Tim the next day after the party. Sunday was her single day of rest each week when she slept in and mostly stayed in her room to read books on the veranda. Her body needed respite from her self-imposed physical routines that included weightlifting, jogging, horseback riding, and yoga. Those weekly activities had transformed her these past months. In the past, she had always been in cities, surrounded by people, the noise and chaos of the ever-present crowd. In Paris, she had focused on cerebral priorities, nights in crowded cafés amongst other chain-smoking students. In New York, there was the Zephyr Gallery and the ever-present, dense urban pressure. But out here in the wide-open California desert, Katya felt new, clean, truly alive. Rutherford's stable of thoroughbred horses connected her to the earth. She enjoyed the freedom that riding provided. The dry, warm climate strengthened her body, cleared out old toxins. California presented a vibrant, strong, healthy future, not the sick, broken past. She slept well most nights and kept the windows open to let in the clean desert air. Geckos scurried along the walls of her room. The stars glowed bright and close.

Katya sent word to Tim's cabin that he should join her for a Krav Maga[71] session starting Monday, 7:30 a.m. sharp. She wanted Tim to see how far a seasoned trainer like Eli Gold had brought her over the past nine months.

Katya was still limbering up when Tim approached the cool, shaded exercise area beneath a grove of California fan palms nestled at the ranch's far northwest corner. Tim waved, then shook hands with Eli. The still nimble, twenty-year veteran of the Israeli Defense Forces led Katya through Krav Maga's combination of fighting techniques sourced from boxing, wrestling, judo, aikido, and karate. Katya had started as a mere beginner just nine months ago but had already reached level five—a notable accomplishment.

This morning, Tim watched Katya as she trained for defense against a knife attack. Katya moved quickly, deflecting Eli's thrust—a small wooden stick in his hand to replace a knife.

Strike–parry–catch–kick.

Each motion, a different technique, a faster response.

"Remember, in combat, it is always about the high-percentage moves. Substance over style," Eli instructed, his elbows and knees covered in thick protective pads.

Katya loosened her shoulders and neck as she practiced her throws and strikes. She moved with confidence and control.

Parry–pivot–strike–kick–block.

"Again, faster. Look for exposed knees and elbows," the trainer urged.

She kicked and struck hard enough against Eli's padded leg to make him wince.

"Good. Again."

Another strike.

"Again."

---

71   Hebrew for "contact combat", Krav Maga is a practical self-defense and military fighting system originally developed for the Israel Defense Forces (IDF).

Katya continued the exercise drills, forcing her muscles to respond without conscious thought.

"What do you think?" Katya heard Tim ask Eli at the end of the hour-long session as Katya drank water and wiped off the dust from her legs.

"She's fast and controlled. A quick learner with her feet and hands," Eli said. "But my training is not just physical; the mental is just as important. Without the mind, the body is nothing. Krav Maga doesn't have elaborate choreographies or absolutes. There are no competitions or showcases for real life self-defense scenarios. I train to avoid threats, and if it is already beyond the point of no return, to use the most effective techniques to prevail under extreme stress. I want my students to use their opponent's energy as a weapon."

"That's the right approach," Tim agreed. "Need to teach what works. Reality isn't some bullshit Hollywood fantasy."

"No, it isn't," Eli said, dropping his eyes just slightly. "The movie stops when you're dead, face down on concrete. It usually ends before most people know anything began. Lethal violence is quick terror. You don't get to take any do-over camera shots."

———————— ✻ ————————

Katya kept Tim on the move for the rest of the day—running, thirty minutes of weight training, and a two-hour hike up into the dry San Jacinto foothills. Tim mostly kept up with Katya, but when she parted with him in the late afternoon, he admitted that her boot camp routine was more strenuous than expected. "I need to ease up on the cigars," Tim quipped at the end of her fast jog around the ranch's fenced perimeter.

On Tuesday evening, after a morning of riding horses together, Tim posed more probing questions. His professional intelligence inquiries came in bits and pieces as he tried to fill in perceived knowledge gaps. How much did Tim already know? She told him about her father's liberal politics in Russia, his murder in Paris, and her long recovery after that car bomb that had nearly killed her, too. She described her successful work at the Zephyr Gallery in the Chelsea district of Manhattan. She answered questions on her uncle's ongoing UN logistics contract for refugees in Turkey and northern Syria. She even suggested the name of a Georgian war criminal, Bogdan Zoidze, as the man responsible for Josephine Richard's poisoning in Battery Park. Bogdan, her uncle believed, ran a network of arms dealers who obtained nerve toxins, thermobaric bombs, cluster munitions, and other illegal weapons for Russia's more savage, erstwhile allies. Bogan took an old Soviet alias, Perses, to both mask his role and advance a certain mythology of fear.

"Some reports I've seen claim that Zoidze was killed ten years ago in Chechnya. How does your uncle's views square with that?" Tim asked.

"Simple. Your reports are wrong," Katya answered.

"Why so confident?"

"I've spoken to Bogan. I've heard his voice."

"Only a voice?"

"That's right," she replied.

"Hard to reach conclusions based just on a voice."

"Your government has resources. They must know something more about him, too."

"Some, from years back during Russia's invasion of Grozny. He was one of many who were suspected of war crimes then, but nothing more recent," Tim replied. "Banned nerve toxins like sarin and VX have been used Syria and Iraq for years now."[72]

"Is it still getting worse?"

"Probably," Tim said cautiously. "Most incidents are difficult to trace."

On Friday afternoon, Katya and Tim drove out to the desert to meet another of Rutherford's hired trainers, Kurt Collins, at the Palm Springs Shooter's Club. The stocky former US Marine had been giving weapons training to Katya every week now for nearly a year. Collins was in high demand with all sorts of Southern California locals these days. The root causes of this renewed general interest in defensive weapon training were endless: sixty-one people killed by a demented shooter in Las Vegas just last year,[73] school shootings every week, distrust of law enforcement, an uptick in armed assault in many large cities. Americans' fears diverged from Katya's obsessions. The housewives and truck drivers didn't worry about some far away, unknown overseas terrorist. Instead, they dreaded other average people in their communities. They feared the disgruntled teenager, the unemployed marketing executive, the unassuming but paranoid right-wing nutjob who could walk into a roadside gun shop and buy an AK-

---

72   International agencies confirmed that sarin was used in massive attacks in Ghouta (2013) and Khan Shaykhun (2017), resulting in over 1,400 and 80 deaths respectively. In Iraq, the 1988 Halabja massacre remains the deadliest confirmed use of a nerve agent cocktail (including sarin and VX), which killed an estimated 5,000 civilians.

73   On the night of October 1, 2017, 64-year-old Stephen Paddock opened fire from his 32nd-floor suite at the Mandalay Bay Resort and Casino into a crowd of approximately 22,000 concertgoers. The attack resulted in 60 deaths.

47 without even so much as a background check. All these types might suddenly drop a false veneer, pull out a weapon, and senselessly kill as if playing just a video game. A mental health crisis is what they called it in Newsweek. Kurt Collin's business had never been better.

Katya's training drills lasted nearly two hours—distance shooting, accuracy at closer ranges, dynamic position shooting. Kurt timed Katya's drills with a stopwatch, first with a SIG Sauer P365, a lighter, compact handgun. Katya drew and fired one round at the target, re-holstered and repeated in four seconds. From the low ready position, she double tapped a target twice with four rounds—three and a half seconds. From a two-handed square stance, she fired, changed magazines, and fired again—five seconds. Four rounds into two separate targets—four seconds. Last drill, Katya turned 180 degrees, drew her weapon as she turned, and fired at three separate targets placed five yards apart—seven seconds.

The gunshots reverberated across the open terrain.

"Good work," Kurt said as they transitioned to a semi-automatic rifle for marksmanship drills.

Katya lay prone on the ground and took her position. She steadied her hand and peered through the scope at the targets while a solitary hawk circled the sky, scanning for brush mice hidden in the tumbleweeds. The Ruger 10/22[74] shots cut the desert air as she fired off rounds at target boards from fifty and one hundred meters. Kurt inspected the results through a long-range scope; he held up his thumb to signal his approval.

The shooting lessons continued until the waning sun turned the desert a dull orange. Kurt ended with a demonstration of various dynamic gun positions, and a discussion around situational awareness at nighttime.

"Drink in town if you are not tired?" Tim asked as Katya drove them back along Route 111 towards downtown Palm Springs.

"Let's make it dinner," Katya said.

At Bar Cecil on Palm Canyon Drive, a bottle of burgundy helped open the conversation. Tim's smooth, cool demeanor made the evening seem like a genuine date. Katya smiled at Tim's jokes, acknowledged his compliments, thanked him for joining her on rugged activities throughout the week. She didn't protest when Tim ordered a second burgundy bottle. His week with her was almost up, and he hadn't even scratched the surface. He hadn't even asked her about Paul yet.

---

74   The Ruger 10/22 is a semi-automatic rimfire rifle produced by Sturm, Ruger & Co. Since its introduction in 1964, it has become one of the most successful and customizable rifle designs in history.

"You shoot well. You have the eye," Tim said.

"Just training, like any other skill."

"Rutherford has found you top experts. You pay attention. This ranch is an unorthodox boot camp but effective," Tim said.

"I'm glad you approve. Without others here with me, it is hard to compare."

"What I don't understand is… why?" Tim pressed. "Why put yourself through all these GI Jane trials? Why all this playing with knives and guns out here by yourself? You are alone here under the hot sun. Don't you want to just return to Manhattan, run your gallery, live your life?"

Katya paused, searching for the right response. A memory of the pain she had endured in the abandoned Brooklyn auto shop flashed up. She remembered the copper pads attached to her to ankles and wrists and felt the hot rush through her spine as a masked man turned the voltage up higher until her mouth foamed. She remembered Bogan's mad discussion of Scheherazade in between sessions of intense bodily pain. She couldn't share this visceral level of detail with Tim—but it was there, always, and Neuilly-sur-Seine too, where it all began. She had escaped death twice now. Her whole universe—everything experienced now as a living, breathing, thinking human—was all on borrowed time.

"You may not believe that Bogan is alive, but I know he is," Katya said.

Tim looked at her, the corners of his mouth betraying skepticism. He reached over to take her hand.

"Listen, Katya. I want to help. You have suffered. You have lost close family members. Your parents, your brother. There are no easy answers for what happened to you these last few years."

"I am only one of many."

"Yes, I know, I know. What happens in the world is appalling. In Syria, we're doing what we can to isolate Putin's puppet Assad. The Russians are experimenting in all these broken places. They are testing us with how far they can push. Putin's goal is power. He doesn't give a shit about international norms and the human cost. But we have measures in place to stop escalation."

"Do you really?" she challenged.

"Maybe not enough for armchair critics like Rutherford, but there are limits to what we can do these days. Today, times are different. The American public doesn't want us nation-building overseas. Iraq was costly. We have our own domestic problems to worry about. We've been in Afghanistan now for what, seventeen years? When we leave, I doubt anything we've done against the Taliban will stick. We've accomplished nothing there. I'm not happy Russia props up mass murders, but we can't keep spending trillions of dollars on lost causes. Those days are over. Besides, this current president wants to cooperate with Putin and other dictators, not frustrate them. Today, it isn't about promoting freedom and democracy, no matter what eccentrics like Rutherford think. Rutherford is out of touch with what the average American cares about. Rutherford doesn't understand what motivates voters today and, more importantly, what he or she is willing to sacrifice."

"You can do nothing now to prevent worse?" she asked after a pause.

"Not unless there is a major escalation, a new war."

"It will be too late then," Katya sighed.

"Doesn't matter. We can't galvanize real action against hypothetical risks. This is just how today's politics work. The days of American leadership in the world are over. We are not that same nation anymore. There has been a generational shift, long in the making. We're divided more than ever now."

"What about justice for one of your own?"

"Jo Richards? She's only one person. One person means nothing in this world. There are nearly a thousand deaths a year in the US military just from accidents, let alone combat deaths. A single, washed-out intel person buried in Langley's lower intestines isn't even a footnote. Besides, it's not clear what happened. Jo is still breathing. I've heard she might even be making some progress in her recovery."

Katya looked away from Tim.

"I understand, Tim. I truly do," she continued. "You can't help me now. Your bureaucracy has other priorities. But soon I hope you will understand better. Soon I hope I can give you a better path to help me and help your mission."

"If I can, I will. I'm here now with you, listening, aren't I?"

"You are. But I also need to make you see as I do."

Tim furrowed his brows, not fully understanding her cryptic meaning.

"I just want you to temper your expectation," he said.

"*Da.* Yes. My expectations, are as you say in English, 'tempered.'"

Katya tilted her head back to swallow the last of the gravelly burgundy in her glass.

They left the restaurant at nearly eleven. Tim drove the car back to Rutherford's ranch in the darkness.

The guard at the ranch's main gate waved them through the secure entrance. Tim parked in the lower lot near a cluster of acacia trees at the base of a small hill.

"Let me walk you to your room," he said.

Katya nodded.

They walked up from the lower lot up through a grove of olive trees that led through a small desert flower and cactus garden area behind the guest rooms in the ranch. The sky was very clear with pinpricks of bright stars. A quarter moon hovered high in the immense translucent darkness of the unblemished California night.

"Are you still in contact with Paul Drake?" Tim asked as the crickets chirped from the rose bushes nearby.

Finally. Katya had waited the entire week for Tim to ask.

"Paul has moved on," she said.

"Where is he now?" Tim pressed.

"I'm not sure."

"Back in New York?"

"Why do you care?"

"Officially, because Paul Drake is a person of interest. Unofficially, because maybe I am jealous."

"Jealous?"

"I understand that he was once with you, romantically, I mean."

"Once, yes," she said.

"What did you see in him?"

"I don't know. Integrity maybe. Doesn't matter now. I've changed."

"Change is good," Tim coaxed.

Katya paused just outside the door to her room, then turned to take in Tim's clear blue eyes. Tim took a step forward until he stood mere inches away. Katya took his hand in her own and, as if on cue, Tim leaned in to kiss her.

Katya felt his lips on hers. She let his strong hands embrace her curving shoulders and touch her breasts. His breath quickened as he moved his lips over her smooth, slender throat. Katya's skin tingled under his firm touch, and she felt a deep, animal desire. Then, just as he pressed himself harder against her, she pushed him away.

"Not like this." she said.

"Why not?" Tim asked.

"You know."

"This is real for me," Tim urged. His hands held her waist.

"Is it?"

"Yes. I've never felt this way."

"Never?"

Tim pressed forward, kissed her neck again, undeterred. Katya gripped his wrists and pulled his much stronger hands off her body. Tim tightened his back and kept the muscles of his face frozen to hide the unpleasant mix of lust and frustration. He was unfamiliar with rejection from a woman. It had never quite happened to him before.

"What's the matter?" he whispered dumbly.

She didn't reply. Instead, she put her hand on his cheek, gave him a final look, then opened the door with her key, and slipped quietly inside.

Tim rang the doorbell twice after Katya shut the door. She didn't respond. Instead, she stripped off her clothes and spent the next twenty minutes alone in a hot shower, the water cascading over her naked body.

She ran her fingers through her hair, then moved her hands down her body, until she felt again the rough scars that ran down the length of her torso. Her body scars were always there, a permanent reminder of her life's particular path since that fateful Easter morning in Neuilly-sur-Seine. The damaged skin was as much a part of her now as any other aspect of her selfhood.

Better this way, she thought. *Tim doesn't need to touch my body. His desire to possess will be more powerful than its actual fulfillment.*

Katya put her head down on the pillow, and within minutes, drifted into a deep, dreamless sleep.

Her watch alarm rang at 6:00 a.m., just as the yellow morning light softly lifted a new day.

Katya put on a robe and made herself a cup of black tea as she finished packing her two leather travel bags. She packed only her essential items, leaving many other clothes and personal items hanging in the room's spacious closet.

Katya sorted through the rest of her remaining tasks. She tied the bubble wrap around a Motorola burner phone, sealed it in a small envelope, and addressed it to Tim. She had also prepared a letter for George the week before, thanking the old man for nearly a year of support as she healed her injuries and trained her spirit and body for what lay ahead.

After a final check of the room, she locked the door behind her, then carried her luggage out to her charcoal gray Maserati.

She stopped the car at the main gate to speak with the still sleepy-eyed guard, stationed in a small, bulletproof kiosk. The guard straightened his back as she approached him.

"Good morning, Eric."

"Good morning, Ms. Volkova."

Katya handed him the two envelopes that she had prepared the previous night.

"Please leave these for Mr. Hastings and Mr. Rutherford. Make sure they both receive them," Katya said.

"Yes, of course."

"Thank you, Eric."

He nodded back at her.

Katerina Volkova went back to her car, put on Hermes sunglasses, turned on the ignition, and pulled the Maserati out onto the two-lane Route 10 heading west to Los Angeles. As the smoothly paved road opened into wide continental space, she passed a cluster of giant white windmills, their long blades silently turning in the open desert as powerful gusts channeled along the flat expanse. She thought of Paul Drake out there somewhere. She missed Paul's voice. She missed his sincerity. Where exactly he was now, she wasn't quite sure.

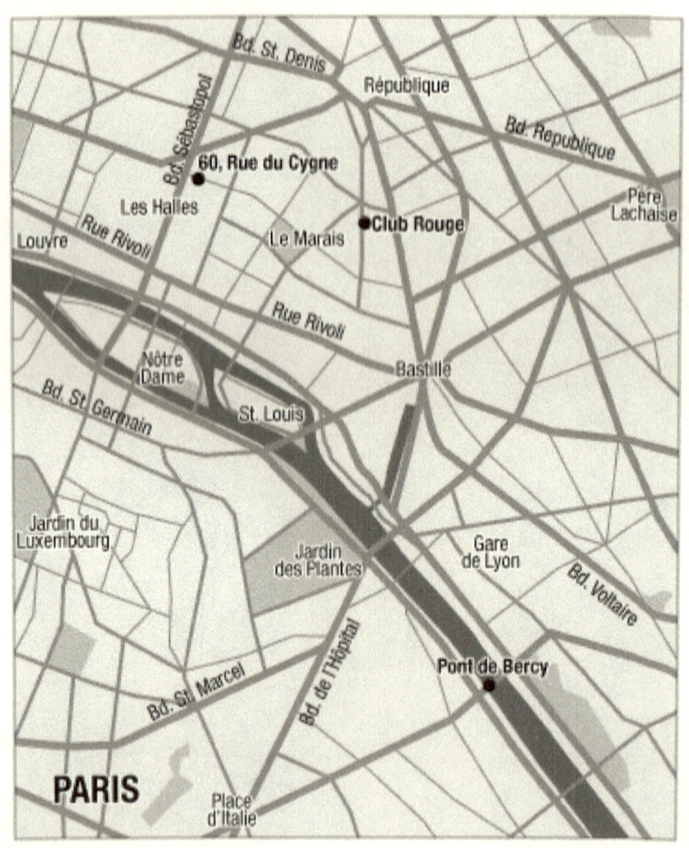

Bd. St. Denis
République
Bd. Sébastopol
Bd. Republique
60, Rue du Cygne
Les Halles
Père
Lachaise
Rue Rivoli
Club Rouge
Louvre
Le Marais
Rue Rivoli
Nôtre
Dame
Bastille
Bd. St. Germain
St. Louis
Jardin du
Luxembourg
Gare
de Lyon
Jardin
des Plantes
Bd. Voltaire
Bd. de l'Hôpital
Pont de Bercy
PARIS
Bd. St. Marcel
Place
d'Italie

6

PAUL DRAKE peered into the telescopic lens fixed on the high windows of the top floor of the Haussmann-style apartment building across the street. The low-hanging clouds glided over the picturesque, steel-gray rooftops, scattering the sunlight in an intricate display of light worthy of an impressionist's eye. Thin rectangular chimneys ending in round clay tubes jutted out of the rooftop in a somewhat haphazard sequence, and a few of the windows were left open. Seeing nothing new, Paul took his eye away from the lens and instead peered down on the street activity from the cramped, one-bedroom walk-up apartment. Central Paris' late afternoon streets bustled with businesspeople, students, and tourists. It was a pleasant, comfortable spring day.

Various tripods, sensing devices, and surveillance equipment pointed out to the top-floor apartment of 60 Rue du Cygne[75] some hundred and twenty meters away. Oleg Shevchenko was adjusting a backup telescopic recording device. The young Ukrainian needed to ensure at least one lens always stayed on target as the afternoon light shifted. On the chair in the corner, Yevgeny Volesky, another of Dmitry's acolytes, played Fortnite on an iPad to pass the time.

Paul had been in Paris for three weeks now, constantly drinking coffee and sleeping very poorly on the short, uncomfortable leather couch smashed against the wall. Paris was easier than the Syrian desert, but somehow it all felt still so uncomfortable. The waiting game was more exhausting now because of the proximity of so many oblivious people. The Parisians and the tourists went about their lives, unaware of the intrigue that played out inside this small, cramped apartment. The other human beings on the streets and in the restaurants and cafés didn't know or care about their waiting game. How could they know?

Also, there was too much at stake here for yet another disaster like that night at the river, now a distant three months ago. On many occasions, Paul still dreamt of drowning, sometimes even tasting the clammy, muddy waters in the few seconds of semiconscious disorientation before he stirred awake. Valentine still did not quite accept that it was just blind luck

---

75   Address in the Les Halles district of Paris' 1st arrondissement. Located on a narrow, pedestrian-only street dating back to the 13th century.

that had saved Paul during the missile strike while five other very capable men were incinerated inside trucks. That, to Valentine, seemed much too convenient. Valentine hated his need to explain the men's death to the families of his two Odessa men. They were blown to bits, so there were no corpses to send back for burial, and that annoyed him because it only left him with somewhat unsatisfying lies. Paul tracked down the families of the Kurds and the dead Turk driver. He wrote to them short notes in English, but that was all.

The genesis of tonight's opportunity was long in the making, starting more than a year ago. The top floor of 60 Rue du Cygne was the singular location that Paul wrung out of Simone Martin just before her arrest. The information did not come easily from this woman who had spied on Katya for nearly a year under the false identity, Chloe. Simone had insinuated herself into their lives, acting as a friend. Then, without any warning, the traitor used Katya as bait to extract money and information. She had pointed the pistol at his head in his office at the Zephyr Gallery. Lucky she didn't blow my head off in the first two seconds, Paul thought. He fought back. They struggled. She slashed him with a knife hidden in her belt; the jagged scar on his left hand was a daily reminder. It was only after Paul wrestled her to the floor and nearly choked her to death with his two hands that he was able to subdue her. It was only after he threatened to turn her over to Yuri Volkov's Russian crew instead of the Americans that she then finally offered up No. 60 as a tenuous link to her handlers. This Belle Époque Paris apartment was Simone's last bargaining chip, just enough to save her.

Nine months ago, Dmitry Medkov rented out this small room with a decent view of No. 60 across the street. Dmitry started discreetly rotating his people in to set up the surveillance system and then to monitor the cameras and other devices that kept 24/7 vigilance. Oleg Shevchenko kept the machines working as the months passed, the seasons changed, and doubts began to emerge on the quality of Simone's information and whether this entire effort here in the City of Lights was going to end up as a waste of precious time and money. Dmitry also hired lawyers to research public records on the apartment's title deeds. This secondary research led nowhere; the apartment was held in trust by an offshore company with only the name of a Swiss law firm appearing on the title.

They had lost access to Simone after her arrest, finding out later that the US District Attorney, Southern District of New York, improperly filed her extradition case. Now a pesky human rights group, Advocates for Freedom, was sniffing around the legality of holding foreign nationals without a trial. Once Simone sensed a legal escape path, she refused further cooperation. Just as Yuri Volkov predicted, the Americans tied themselves up in legal knots. Those days just after 9/11 when the spooks could grab and hold anyone were now long over. The Americans were back to their rules.

Then three weeks ago, Oleg called in a small but notable uptick in activity. Last Tuesday, a cleaning woman came to the top floor apartment. She brought new bedsheets and spent a few hours inside the room. Within 48 hours, Paul flew in from Turkey; the surveillance cameras finally struck pay dirt. At 10:15 p.m., a man walked up the five flights, slipped a key into apartment lock, and turned on the lights. In the morning, a closer camera snapped the visitor's photograph coming out to the street: Caucasian male, medium build, reddish-brown beard, sunglasses, a confident walk.

The figure captured by the camera was Andre Gauthier, alias Rene Voclain, returned at last to the City of Lights after a long hiatus. Andre had changed his appearance, but there was no doubt that this was the same man who had first approached Katya those many years ago while she was still only a student at the Sorbonne. Andre had targeted her because she was the daughter of Sergei Volkov, a liberal-minded Russian politician willing to look harder into Moscow's military programs. Andre had used his false smile and beguiling lies with Katya. He had played his part on that fateful Easter morning in Neuilly-sur-Seine. Andre was also the same man who, years later, trained Simone Martin. Now, at long last, they had him again within their sights.

"Can't we just grab him?" Paul asked, when he called Dmitry for his advice on what to do next.

"Where will that lead us?" Dmitry asked. "We take one piece from the board, and nothing changes. But you tell our enemy that we know his movements. No, Paul. Patience is what we need. If we wait and watch, we can learn more. We will learn how to perhaps checkmate their king."

"He can leave anytime," Paul said, still skeptical.

"Yes, he can," Dmitry said matter-of-factly. "But Andre is here for something."

"And if we lose him?"

"Hold steady, Paul. Use your judgement. Work with Oleg and I will send you Yevgeny soon to give you more help," Dmitry advised curtly from an unknown location, and then he hung up.

Two more weeks passed this way as Andre Gauthier settled into the Paris apartment. Paul observed at a safe distance, compiling notes on

Andre's various routines and waiting for mistakes. So far, Andre's tradecraft was superb—he never left or arrived other than by taxi and always walked the short few blocks to the busy Les Halles metro station, disappearing anonymously into the city's sprawling underground system along with all the thousands of others. Paul had tried to follow him once, but it was nearly impossible to do without being easily spotted. He had lost Andre at the first metro change. The cameras arrayed around No. 60 snapped some of Andre's movements, but without access to his mobile devices and computers, they saw only his surface veneer.

Yevgeny arrived from Odessa last week, bringing more advanced technical devices: a useful Israeli-made GPS tracking tool, a phone-tapping device to intercept wireless networks, and a new kind of surveillance intercept that used Bluetooth to mirror data on devices within ten meters. These gadgets might be helpful. Paul was working out ways to deploy all these at the next opportunity.

Still, anxiety gnawed at Paul now for days. Despite Dmitry's advice on waiting, everyone needed results and not another failure. The longer this Paris operation dragged on, the smaller seemed the chances that they would have any progress. It wasn't a question of manpower—too many of them only added risks. Andre just didn't offer up a soft underbelly. He knew his business and kept his armor tight.

This morning, Paul noted the notch up in activity. A woman came to visit Andre at 10:25 a.m. in the morning, then left after an hour. The cameras caught her details as she exited—black hair, olive skin, medium height, well-dressed in a dark blue, fashionable Versace blazer. In the afternoon, Andre drifted near the apartment window, talking actively on his mobile phone. Whatever Andre was here to do, seemed to finally to be stirring. The Frenchman went out for a smoke on the balcony later in the afternoon, dressed smartly in a blue suit as if preparing to go out. These signs convinced Paul that tonight was worth the risk to follow the target outside the usual perimeter. They needed more progress. Tonight, finally, they might be able to press an advantage.

———— ✳ ————

Andre Gauthier left 60 Rue du Cygne at 8:20 p.m. Paul waited across the street, lightly sipping a beer at a local café while Oleg stood smoking at another street corner. Yevgeny waited on a Yamaha cycle just across from Étienne Marcel metro station in case Andre slipped into a car. Yevgeny wore his motorcycle helmet, mirrored visor down.

Oleg and Paul followed behind at some twenty meters, blending into the crowded, Parisian streets. First, Andre walked toward the Centre de Pompidou—passing through the open area in front of the multi-layered, bizarrely constructed museum where teenagers skateboarded, crowds mingled, and street musicians played violins and accordions. Andre passed the Stravinsky Fountain and the Église Saint-Merry into the dense tangle of low-rise limestone buildings that blended into the Marais. They almost lost him as he merged into a thick crowd of young students and tourists milling outside a row of open-air bars and shops.

They followed as Andre walked down Rue de Quatre-Fils. Other people passed in and out of the district's many cafés. Andre took his time, as if out on a normal evening stroll, an unhurried flâneur amongst the Parisian crowd.

Andre finally came to an inconspicuous door marking the entrance to Club Rouge, a members-only club. After a brief exchange with the doorman, he disappeared within.

Paul waited a few minutes before approaching.

"*Votre card de member?*" the bulky club doorman asked.

Paul handed him a roll of crisp, purple €500 notes.

"*Merci, messieurs. s'il vous plaît entrez et amusez-vous,*" the bouncer said, opening the door.

Paul and Oleg stepped into Club Rouge's garish lobby, where chandeliers dangled from high marble ceilings and thick velvet drapes separated the rooms. The club was remodeled over the guts of a 19th century residential mansion, with many of the building's original rococo architectural features still intact. Paul followed two slender, high-heeled women into the club's spacious main room. Music blared from speakers; the smell of cigarettes mixed with perfume and sweat. Paul unobtrusively meandered to the closest bar, Oleg following. They sat on two sleekly designed, empty leather highchairs. An attractive female bartender in a skimpy, white cotton halter top and heavy dark mascara came to ask for drinks. Paul ordered two Bombay gins on ice. She poured the two drinks into two crystal tumblers without measuring out the gin, added a small stalk of rosemary in each, then placed the glasses on neat square napkins in front of them. Oleg texted the club's address to Yevgeny.

Paul scanned the club's opulent interior. The club was teeming, some patrons drinking at tables, some eating tapas-style plates, others dancing. Synthesized techno music kept the mood upbeat, chic, "a-la-mode." Young brown, black, and white women mingled with various men at small tables and in small, dimly lit alcoves. The working women were all mostly slender, girlish waifs, cool in their young bodies, distant in their eyes as part of their nightly performance art. Most men dressed well according to the moment's fashion—thin ties, tailored suits with pants short at the ankles, excessive splashes of Tom Ford and Gucci cologne. A few other younger Arab-looking men mingled in their faux luxury tracksuits, another counter-culture fashion trend that perplexed Paul. Two security guards dressed in trim black jackets watched with slightly bored expressions near the doors.

Paul spotted Andre after a few minutes sitting alone at a corner table, tucked away from the flow of the dance floor where most of the working women flowed. He was there only a few minutes more before a dark-skinned fat man with cropped black hair came over to his table and sat down. The new man wore a tight blue suit over a round, corpulent body. His pencil-thin, finely manicured black mustache seemed like a failed attempt to improve upon a dark, ugly, bloated visage. A waitress came with a bottle of champagne. Andre started a conversation.

Paul observed the two serious faces as they spoke and sipped the champagne from the orange-labeled Veuve Clicquot bottle kept cool in an ice bucket. These private clubs were good for such meetings, Paul knew. Crowded places ensured a kind of neutrality and mutual safety. Amidst this noise level and the humming activity, the men could talk business and not worry about listening devices shoved in pockets or any sudden surprises that might spring up in a less conspicuous venue. And, just as importantly, these guys just couldn't resist coming to the venues they really enjoyed. The flashy, expensive, exclusive places just appealed to their natures.

Paul slowly sipped his gin and kept his attention on Andre's table while the smoke swirled, the music throbbed, and the girls laughed. Andre pushed a small mobile phone across the table. His counterpart checked the phone's password before dropping it into the pocket of his blue suit jacket.

Oleg ordered another round of drinks when the sexy bartender came back. The young Ukrainian was doing his best to blend into the drinking action, although he seemed uncomfortable. Oleg's eyes were pink and watery from just the first gin Paul had ordered. This was Oleg's first up-close stakeout, Paul guessed. He was just the tech guy who had watched only from a distance until tonight. He wasn't one of Dmitry's older, seasoned crew more familiar with the swirl, noise, and women.

A few minutes past midnight, Andre rose, shook hands, and moved to leave by the club's back exit. The fat man with the pencil-thin mustache stayed to finish his cigarette alone at the table. A dark-skinned girl who had been lingering nearby quickly slipped into the booth next to him. The fat man poured her some champagne. He seemed lost in his thoughts and suddenly cautious.

"We need to split up here. You follow Andre," Paul said to Oleg. "Remember, keep your distance."

"Yes, Paul," Oleg replied before heading to the back exit after Andre.

Oleg gone, Paul waited at the bar until the fat man at the table finished smoking and paid the bill. Paul left first, through the lobby, just before the man appeared and waved his hand to his driver waiting next to a black Audi sedan across the street. Paul saw Yevgeny where he expected—positioned a safe distance away on his Yamaha cycle, ready to follow.

The driver opened the back door of the Audi sedan while the fat man lingered on the street. The street corner outside the club was crowded with a bevy of college-age girls, laughing and holding wine flutes. They wore high heels and slinky dresses and laughed together in a girlish, drunken fashion. The fat man watched them, amused by their antics while he smoked just one more cigarette out here in the pleasant Parisian night.

One cigarette. Time enough, Paul hoped, to close the distance to the parked Audi while the driver had his back turned. If Paul crossed the street ahead of another waiting car, then he could make contact on the sedan. It was a thirty-second window, but it might work.

Paul removed the cap of the small GPS tracking device, exposing its strong adhesive. Paul crossed the street and casually passed close to the Audi. He stuck the Israeli GPS device just inside the back wheel's arch fender, hidden above the wheel, and kept walking. The bevy of young girls crossed the street, still laughing, en route to another party elsewhere. The fat man watched them go, then tossed his last cigarette before he finally slid into the back seat of the Audi. His driver started the engine.

Paul waved off Yevgeny. No need to risk the motorcycle tail. Instead, Paul watched the car take a left on Rue de la Perle and disappear into traffic.

———————— ✳ ————————

When he left Club Rouge, Andre Gauthier purposely drifted down a smaller street as part of a security routine he used after every new meeting. These were normal transactional procedures. After eight years of working for Perses, Andre accepted that he was known to at least some intelligence services. Paris was a cesspool of many of them, especially the Arabs who now took root in the French capital like poison weeds. The likelihood of professional surveillance increased proportionally to the importance and complexity of any transaction. These Libyans were new sellers. He didn't know their level of paranoia or skill. This meant more risk.

Andre first detected his tail about five minutes after he left the club. Only a handful people were out this late in this part of the 5th arrondissement—stray lovers, solitary drunks in ragged clothes, a gaunt-looking African prostitute in an old fur coat who approached him with her *avez-vous-du-feu* routine. Andre ignored these distractions. The man behind him walked alone at a suitable distance, matched his walking pace, his head down.

Andre continued down Boulevard de l'Hôpital towards the Seine. Down by the river near the stone bridges, the quiet walking paths ran away from residential houses and cafés. These darker places would give Andre better options. The river would also hopefully ensure a whole troop of trimly dressed gendarmes didn't swoop in with sirens and police vests.

Always best to find a quiet place, Andre thought. Night helps. I need to determine if he is following me alone.

Andre carried a thin Beretta Pico[76] in a holster tightly placed in the small of his back. The gun was small enough that he didn't even notice it any longer. In tonight's case, however, the long steel blade strapped to his lower leg seemed a better alternative. If this man trailing behind him came closer, then it would be better to let it seem like a low-level street crime, a petty robbery. Police rarely looked deeply into stabbing homicides. Any poor junkie could grab a knife. Bullets made noise and left the risk of forensic identification, unwanted press, extra attention. Also, knives were simple. Up close, a blade never jammed.

Andre cupped the knife in his right hand, hidden up a jacket sleeve.

Darkness deepened as Andre turned down a flight of stairs that led to the walking path along the Seine. His follower let the distance expand a bit, but then jogged quickly down the stone stairs behind him. Now the riverbank path had only one exit two hundred meters ahead. Andre walked further along the single, narrow foot path between the high, stone breakwater wall and the dark, undulating river. When Andre saw the man approach him in the darkness under the Pont de Bercy, he pivoted, and reversed direction.

His follower paused, looked the other way to appear anonymous, but was unable to take any alternative path. Instead, the man following him just tilted his face downward and moved aside to let Andre pass.

---

76   Ultra-compact, semi-automatic handgun chambered in .380 ACP, one of the thinnest and most concealable pistols ever mass-produced.

This amateur still doesn't understand. He doesn't even realize the danger, Andre thought as he closed in.

Andre dropped the knife from his sleeve into this hand. Then, in few quick steps, he sprang upon his prey. With one thrust, Andre plunged the blade deep into the man's ribcage and then, with two more quick jabs, stuck the knife into his victim's solar plexus while his free hand covered the man's face to stifle sounds of the sudden pain.

Andre's first lethal thrust tore into his victim's lungs, the next two opened him up further. Without resistance, the man first slumped to his knees and then collapsed limply on the stone path. His legs twitched a little as the blood oozed out of the deep cuts and gathered in a black, viscous pool on the stone. Andre waited and watched as the person experienced his last moments of awareness, painfully, on the cold, dirty limestone. After a minute, the man let out a long final gasp and then stopped moving.

Andre checked his environs. The stone bridge above hid the scene in a deep shadow. The river lapped rhythmically against the stone bank, undisturbed. A small buoy chained to the side of the river, clanked lightly as it floated.

Killing fast always gave Andre a kind of guilty adrenaline rush, confirming his freedom. Everything was permitted for those strong enough to act. It felt good to be God. Limits placed on any man were false; limits were chains for lesser beings too afraid to face the truth that all of civilization was based on a false morality. The false morality of the common people didn't apply to him, acting in the shadows as he saw fit.

Andre kicked the body with his foot to turn his victim over on his back. He flicked on a cigarette lighter to better see the face: white male, clean-shaven, cropped hair, young schoolboy features. The man's open dead eyes still held a frozen surprise.

Andre searched the dead man's pockets for a wallet but found none. Law enforcement would have carried an ID, he knew. This boy carried just an unmarked key chain with a tiny steel crucifix, sixty euro, and a metro ticket. He didn't even have a phone.

Deeply unsatisfied, Andre tossed his knife in the Seine, then quick stepped to another flight of stairs that led away from the river and back into the capital city.

7

DMITRY MEDKOV made the sign of the cross over his heart as he entered the spacious nave of the L'Église Saint-Germain-des-Prés[77] in Paris' 6th arrondissement. It was mid-afternoon, just after the sun emerged from a blanket of fast-moving, white clouds. Dmitry removed his sunglasses to allow his eyes to adjust to the church's dark, ancient interior. The cooler air smelled faintly of frankincense and dry wood.

Dmitry walked down the church's nave, across the black-and-white stone tiles smoothed with age, between the restored 12th century aquamarine columns, the stained-glass windows, and the plaques marking the twelve stations of Christ's Passion. Only a few visitors at this hour of day sat quietly amongst the ancient dark mahogany pews. He spotted the back of Paul's head near the center of the church. The young American sat there alone, head lowered and eyes downcast. Dmitry hovered for almost a minute more before he sat down. Paul turned his head and looked with bloodshot eyes at the older Russian.

Dmitry Medkov had grown fond of Paul since their first meeting in Manhattan. Now after nearly three years, he could see the visible signs of stress on Paul's haggard face, with a thin beard he let grow after the French police found Oleg Shevchenko's corpse down by the river. Paul had given up much, all willingly, to join them. They put him in difficult positions—the nighttime incursion across the Syrian border, that violent day in Chelsea, the air attack on the Tigris River, and now this latest setback. Paul had spent long months in southern Turkey working with MSA's core Odessa team to distribute both aid and weapons. He spent his time with international doctors and refugees in the camps, always searching for more useful clues and ways to advance their cause. Paul was tough enough on many levels, hardened a bit above average because he had previously served in the US military. But that organized military experience was different. In the US Army, Paul was one of many in uniform. He was an officer who existed within a clear chain of command. That was a different kind of mission, supported by a vast infrastructure of professional soldiers, sanctioned by

---

77   The oldest standing church in Paris, originally founded in 558 AD as a royal abbey for the Merovingian kings. Houses the tomb of philosopher René Descartes and features vibrantly restored 19th-century frescoes by Hippolyte Flandrin.

the State. Today, in contrast, Paul lived each day mostly alone, without firm rules or established hierarchies. Dmitry knew the sense of isolation, the blurry domain of imperfect choices and unsatisfying options. This once confident, trusting young man was slowly becoming more disillusioned, jaded, detached, and angry. He was becoming, in short, more like a true Russian.

"Yevgeny said you'd be here again," Dmitry said.

"He was right. Here I am," Paul said stoically.

"It is good to stop and pause in a place like this. God's beauty is here," Dmitry said, attempting encouragement with an upbeat tone.

The silence lingered.

"There are costs to every action we take, Paul," Dmitry offered. "Oleg knew the risks when he agreed to join us. I've written to his mother in Odessa. We'll take care of his family. They will not be left behind."

"If I was smarter, then you wouldn't need to write any letter," Paul sneered back. "I could have just let Andre go and not asked Oleg to follow him. If I had just made a different choice, a better decision, the boy would still be alive."

Dmitry let out a long sigh.

"It is not your fault. Oleg was young and not well trained. He also didn't know Paris well."

"I knew all those facts, and still I made it worse. Too little, too late. Just like at the river in Syria."

"What happened at the grain warehouse wasn't your fault."

"Wasn't it? My decision to let Oleg follow Andre was my call. I told him to follow. I am the cause."

"No," Dmitry replied. "The devil usually doesn't wave a flag or come to you with a face that you can easily recognize. Mostly, he is a deceiver."

Paul turned to him, surprised.

"I didn't know you were a believer in such things," Paul said.

Dmitry tilted his head.

"Almost. I have lived, and I have seen much pain."

"Atheist then?"

"I don't know. If God does not exist, we must invent him.[78] We must believe in something absolute. Otherwise, there would be no meaning to our struggles. Our freedom would be too terrifying."

---

78 "Si Dieu n'existait pas, il faudrait l'inventer " is a line from Voltaire's 1768 poem Épître à l'Auteur du Livre des Trois Imposteurs.

"Freedom is terrifying. We are condemned to be free," Paul said.

"You know Sartre, then?" Dmitry asked, interest piqued by the reference.

"A little," Paul explained.

"Yes. Of course," Dmitry said, now leaning back. "Katerina spoke to you of these things. She reads such European books. This has always been her nature—art, history, the difficult questions. For me, I believe in free will, whether or not there is a God looking down on us. It doesn't matter to me if a higher power exists or if this is merely how men organize their hope. Those who built this church believed in a better reality. They dreamed and built this place to last a thousand years, and here we are inside the vision that they made in their own time. These builders left us something better than we had before. They created. Other men make different choices. They choose to kill and destroy. Sometimes, it is in the name of a different religion or new, invented ideology. Today, not even that is needed anymore."

"Doesn't matter how free I am if I make bad decisions," Paul said.

"Maybe," the older Russian said. "But you also succeeded. Now we have something better to go on. The Israeli GPS tracker worked. The man you saw with Andre is an important arms trader. We found him because of what you and Oleg did that night."

"How so?" Paul prodded, now leaning forward.

"His name is Nessrin Geddah. He works for a Libyan strongman, General Khalifa Haftar.[79] Haftar is a thug who leads an eastern faction against the current elected government," Dmitry explained. "After the fall of Qaddafi, Tripoli ended their chemical weapons programs in exchange for lifting oil sanctions. But Haftar did not join this treaty. Now he sits on a surplus of mustard gas, sarin, blister agents, and much more."

"And demand is strong," Paul added.

"*Da*, very strong. Haftar can use Perses' network to transport and sell his weapons," Dmitry continued. "Many buyers are back in the market— Syria, Iran, Iraq, Yemen. Putin is on the move and supports hungry client states that need his weapons. Iran just formed its Shiite Liberation Army to fight its sectarian wars. Thousands of men have become armed mercenaries and kill for money. But it will not be easy to move so many banned weapons from Libya to the Syrian theater, even with Moscow's

---

79   General Khalifa Haftar (born 1943) is the military strongman and de facto leader of eastern Libya., Haftar was a key participant in the 1969 coup that brought Muammar Qaddafi to power, then served as a top military commander until 1987, when he was captured during the war with Chad and subsequently disowned by Qaddafi.

help. You see, Paul, Oleg didn't die in vain. If we can stop Perses from brokering these weapons, then all of this will matter. Maybe we can even draw Perses out of his lair. He'll make a mistake eventually."

Paul listened more to Dmitry as the old, world-weary tactician spoke of future actions and his conjectures on the enemy's intentions. The older man's voice sounded crisp inside the church's expansive vaulted interior. As he listened, Paul's eyes also drifted up to the ancient church's latticed blue ceiling. High above his head the ceiling's perfect five-pointed stars spread out in harmonious geometric patterns against a cobalt-blue background. This restored painted ceiling was a vision of an ordered, divinely controlled universe, different than the random star patterns in the real vacuum of space.[80] Paul had always wanted to visit this oldest of Parisian churches with Katya. She would better appreciate the true artistry of the place, including the careful restoration that had been done throughout the centuries and even some more recently. Katya would probably not only know the technical details, but she could also better explain to him the meaning of an imagined moral reality conceived in the minds of anonymous medieval builders. The chance to come here with her had slipped away on their first visit. Maybe sometime in the future, it would arrive again.

"Come, let's go now," Dmitry said as he pulled Paul up by his elbow. "We have more to discuss. I need your help. We don't have time to look backwards. This war is hard. There is only the future."

"Ok," Paul said.

The two men rose from the mahogany pew. Paul followed Dmitry out through the nave, past the twelve stations of Christ's Passion, and back into the busy, distracted world of human activity along the Boulevard de Saint Germain. Dmitry hid his eyes again behind small oval sunglasses as soon as they were out on the street and back under the very strong afternoon sunlight.

---

80 The Hippolyte Flandrin designed ceiling consists of approximately 3,000 gilded five-pointed stars organized within the geometric structure of ancient ribbed vaults. A major restoration campaign started in 2013 returned the ceiling to its original brilliance.

8

MAX DRAKE left his apartment on Broad Street in Newark, New Jersey, thinking of what he was going to microwave for dinner that evening. Would it be the PF Chang's frozen Chinese sesame chicken, Stouffer's frozen lasagna, or perhaps Smithfield beef brisket, with a dash of Heinz ketchup? Should he wash down the food with a Heineken, Coors, Amstel, or a Budweiser? These critical culinary choices were the same questions Max posed to himself yesterday, and the day before that, and the day before that. Evenings blended one into the next. The world moved forward while Max remained still alone, at the dinner table, sitting in his armchair, supine on his king-sized bed, hunched in an office cubical in front of a computer screen.

Most nights Max disappeared into a 120-channel world of sports highlights, television series, movie reruns, and late-night comedy diversions. Flickering, flashing, smiling media images filled his mind day after day. It was as if all these actors populating the broadcast series were people he knew better than those in his own actual life. The scripted pantomimes were cleaner realities with a beginning, middle, and an end, completed in sixty minutes. Anytime boredom threatened, Max could switch the channel, surf the next movie, or watch another drama. Yet the screen only broadcast one way. The actors never spoke back to him through the camera lens, as he sat alone, mute. None of those performers witnessed his life, saw his memories, understood his trauma.

Max watched these screens with his one living right eye only while his inert glass eye sat dead. His left eye was a marble replica of the right—pinprick pupil, brown iris, painted white sclera. A little stone kicked up from some improvised explosive device had blasted out the original organ one afternoon ten years ago during a routine downtown Fallujah patrol. The world lost more of its depth after this event. He spent a month recovering in Germany, then was sent home, honorably discharged. There was no fanfare on his return, only a veteran's work program, and some generic support groups that didn't do him any good in terms of his readjustment. He stopped going to the support group after just a few sessions. Each month he slipped a little further away from those around him. The months turned into years. He never spoke about the war. He learned to hide his disability—a single eye was adequate for most tasks and eventually he took a job that was good enough to pay rent and distract his attention. Michter's bourbon helped with the migraines that still came at night.

During the workweek, Max took public transit each day to the title insurance firm in downtown Newark. He normally left by 7:30 a.m. to catch Bus 32. This morning, he exited his thirty-two-story apartment building about fifteen minutes early. As he walked, Max noticed a woman across the street staring at him oddly. She was dressed in a bulky denim jacket, dark sunglasses, and a blue wool cap.

His right eye passively tracked her as she crossed through the busy traffic and covered another few meters straight at him. She stepped in front of his path.

Max stopped, annoyed by some random stranger.

"Do I know you?"

"I'm Paul's friend," the woman said in a slight accent as she removed her sunglasses. Now the blood rushed up to his forehead as he recognized her blue-green eyes—the same, slightly feline, eyes from the photo that Paul had left in the Maiden Lane safe-deposit box.

"You were waiting here for me?" Max asked.

"Yes, not long," she said.

It's her, really her. In the flesh. Finally, Max thought. One question had been building up inside, swelling a little each day this past year until it was now bursting at the seams.

"Is my brother alive?" Max asked.

"Alive and well," she replied.

A spark of relief passed down his spine.

"Come. Let's take a coffee and talk more if you have a moment," she said. Max nodded.

They walked, now side by side.

The woman led him a few blocks down Broadway and then two blocks further along 12th Street. She led him to a classic 1950s diner with red vinyl booths and laminated menus. The hostess greeted them with a wide smile, then sat them in a corner booth against the window. A vintage jukebox nearby played early Frank Sinatra ballads. They ordered two coffees that were quickly brought out with tiny, pre-packaged creamers on the side.

The woman took off her blue wool hat and brushed her honey-colored hair out of her eyes. Now he saw her face more clearly—arched eyebrows, smooth complexion, delicate lips. It was a sort of neatly symmetrical face that seemed entirely otherworldly, as if drawn by the hand of a master Renaissance painter and transported here.

"You can call me Kate," she said.

"I knew you'd come eventually."

"I should have come sooner. I'm sorry."

"Fine by me. Paul has his own life. Or at least, he used to," Max said.

"Are you angry with him?"

"No. Why should I be?"

"Too much intrigue."

"He has his reasons."

"It's good that you are not angry," she said.

"I trust Paul. I always have."

Kate took a first sip of her coffee, then began to speak more about Paul. She left out specifics but indicated Max's brother was someplace on the edge of a war theater in the Middle East. Paul was trying to help. He was making a difference in other people's lives. Maybe.

The waitress came back to fill their empty mugs with a fresh refill and a smile.

"Enough about Paul. What about you? Do you still live alone?" Kate asked.

"Yes. Not one for much dating. Work keeps me busy."

"You also served in Iraq, am I right?" she asked.

"Yes. After Paul, I came in as a lowly private. Seemed like the right thing to do."

"I'm sure it was, for you."

"Paul had already finished his tours when this happened," Max said, pointing his index finger at his glass eye.

"I barely noticed. Does it bother you?"

"Not anymore. Lucky to be here."

"We both are," Kate replied, more softly now. "I understand, Max. More than you know. I too have been in dark, cold places. I don't have much of a family left myself. My father, mother, and brother are all gone now. I know what it means to have everything you really care about taken away. But in Russian, we say there is no misfortune without a blessing in it."

"That's one way to think about it."

"Has anyone come to ask about Paul?" she asked.

"An FBI man, Woods, came to see me with another man, Tom, I think. They showed up at my downtown office last month."

"Tim," she corrected. "What do you say to them?" she asked.

"Nothing. I told them Paul hadn't contacted me, and we weren't close. They left me alone after that."

"That's good," Kate said.

"What did they want?"

"Just poking around. Confused mostly."

"Do you need the money Paul left for you?" Max asked.

"Better you keep it... and the hard drive," Kate replied. "In case it gets worse for us."

"Will it get worse?"

"It might. I can't promise. Our enemy is strong. I don't know what might happen next."

Kate reached across the table and took Max's hand. He felt odd at being touched by her. He rarely had even simple contact with another person's skin.

"Is there anything else you want me to tell your brother?"

"Mom is doing well," Max said. "She's at her place in Boca Raton. She has plenty to do there, a few good friends, so she doesn't get bored. She plays a lot of Scrabble and swims every day."

"That's good. And you?"

"Tell Paul, I'm absolutely fantastic."

She held his hand tighter now.

"When this is over, Max, I promise you that everything will change," Kate said. "Whatever has been broken in the past can be fixed. We will do it together."

"If you say so," he replied, dumbly.

Kate smiled, then released his hand.

"Do you love Paul?" Max asked. He watched her eyes drift and look out the window.

"Paul must love you madly. He left it all behind just like that," Max continued, snapping his fingers. "Must be for love."

"Love is a strong word," she said.

"The right one?"

"I don't know. Perhaps I just forgot what the word means. I do know that your brother matters very much to me. Somehow, we found each other. Today, I need him more than ever."

She pulled a twenty-dollar bill from her front pants pocket and slipped it under her empty coffee cup. She rose from the table, gave Max one last look, mouthed the words "thank you," and left the diner.

Through the wide windowpane, Max watched her walk away down the street. Frank Sinatra was still singing in the background. The waitress returned to ask him if he needed anything else. That was it then. Thirty minutes for a coffee. She was gone again, back to her own mysterious universe, an unknown alien sphere.

Still, the news was good. At least, Paul was still alive.

9

A SLIM crescent moon dangled listlessly in the black night sky, high above the sprawling Turkish seaside town of Mersin.[81]

Elad Ishmail felt his mother's hand yank him forward as the other frightened, nervous people jostled and pushed near the old wooden dock. The crowd moved forward, all trying to get on the small cargo boat via a narrow set of stairs. It was nearly three in the morning; the sea air had turned cold; everyone was tired from many sleepless nights.

"*Eajal.* Hurry," his mother shouted to him angrily in Arabic. Aisha had boarded already with her two young girls, Haya and Sarah.

Elad's baseball hat had been knocked off his head by an errant elbow as they scrambled over the wobbly gang plank. Fortunately, Elad could still see the hat just beyond the railing. The sixteen-year-old boy jumped down, grabbed it from the ground with a swift sweep of his hand. Then, with his wiry, lanky arms, he climbed up again to the gang plank leading up to the ship to rejoin his mother.

Umm, as he called her, looked immensely relieved. She calmed herself by holding her hand over her beating heart.

A tall, skinny Italian herded them all en masse to the cluttered, open topside of the waiting vessel. Elad counted that there were more than three hundred of them all packed onto the deck of the small ship, huddled in family units. Men carried the luggage, and mothers kept their youngest children swaddled in blankets. The old and infirm in the shadows gripped at railings, sometimes coughed, and kept their heads bowed, fearful and uncertain.

No matter, Elad thought. *I'm strong.*

He was now the only man left in the family. His mother, aunt, and two nieces all depended on him; he needed to show them his confidence. Showing fear was the first step in a slow defeat. Besides, getting on this boat was nothing compared to what had happened to them when his father died last year. It couldn't get worse than those dark days before they

---

81   Mersin's metropolitan region of over 3.3 million people makes it one of Turkey's largest urban agglomerations, with significant population surges in recent years, partly due to more than 200,000 Syrian refugees.

crossed the border into Turkey and found their way to the UN camp at Suruç.[82] Nothing could get worse than those desperate nights of fire and violence in Aleppo.

Elad watched as the men removed the gangplank and untied the rope connecting the cargo ship to the dock. Finally, the loud motor kicked in. Slowly, the boat crawled out away into the sea's vast darkness. After a while, his adrenaline rush subsidized, and Elad watched the Mersin shore lights slowly fade in the distance. They had passed this step and were now on their way. Their luck held.

Elad felt inside the lining of his red hat. The crisp dollars were pressed there, hidden and more secure than in his pants pockets. He had earned these US dollars. The cash now needed to last.

Elad thought back to the incident that started his current journey. It began in Suruç, a month after his family arrived in the camp with nothing left of their past lives but the clothes on their backs and a single suitcase.

A security guard caught him one morning while he was leaving the camp's on-site pharmacy through a back door that he had figured out how to keep unlocked. Elad's trick to learn the door code was easy—just coat the lock with dust to record which buttons were pressed, then push patterns using these limited digits until the code worked. What Elad didn't anticipate was the surveillance camera hidden deep inside the storage room. That camera was a surprise. The security guard nabbed Elad carrying a one-pound bag of amphetamines out of the pharmacy. The drugs were worth a few hundred dollars on the black market. The guard pulled him up by his shirt, slapped him hard, and then made him wait in a hot, empty, locked room.

Elad waited until the hot afternoon before they brought him to another person, an American dressed in drab desert fatigues.

"You speak English?" the American asked.

"Yes, of course," Elad replied.

"How so?"

"School. Movies. Google," Elad said, choosing not to mention that Baba ran a computer repair store and spoke English very well.

"You know what you did was wrong," the American said. "Stealing is unfair to the others."

---

82   The Suruç Tent City Accommodation Centre was established in early 2015 to handle the massive influx of refugees—primarily Syrian Kurds—fleeing the Siege of Kobane by ISIS. At its opening, it was the largest refugee camp in Turkey, with a capacity to house roughly 35,000 people in over 7,000 tents.

Elad didn't answer. He felt no guilt. What did this arrogant American know of fairness? The Americans came and they waved their red, white, and blue flag and spoke so proudly of democracy and freedom. Then, they always left. Elad had been living with nothing for almost two years. Nothing. Many days without a single meal. No protection. No safety net. Umm and Aisha prayed nightly—Allah gave them both solace. Elad didn't feel that. In his own mind, Elad saw only a kind of slow unfolding of a process he could neither control nor influence. He had no agency himself against these external forces. They first called it "Arab Spring." But no spring came. Only the dark days, the civil war, and the bombs. Fairness? Justice? God didn't manifest his intentions. God looked elsewhere when the masked men in Aleppo broke into his father's store, lined him up against the wall, and shot him. His father died there like a dumb animal. He died there without any purpose, without any divine reprieve.

"It doesn't matter," Elad finally said, dumbly.

"You can make more money if you help us, not steal," the American offered. "I can help you if you help me. Interested?"

"How to help you?" Elad asked.

"Many ways. I need someone who can translate Arabic and help me with other jobs in the camp. You broke into the pharmacy with a clever trick. If you can use the same intelligence to help me, you'll do some good and get paid."

"US dollars?"

"Of course."

The American smiled and put out his hand. Surprised, Elad took the hand and shook it as if they were entering a business agreement.

"When to start?" Elad replied.

"We start now. I'm Paul," he said.

So began the jobs in the camp. Paul first gave him simple tasks, like helping to interview various families recently arrived from northern Syria.

The American paid cash every two weeks, small amounts but enough to buy more for Umm and Aisha. The little items made a difference—fresh oranges in the morning, wool gloves, a small gas stove for frying eggs and boiling water in the morning. On some jobs, such as laying down electric wire near the fence, Elad organized other boys in the camp. He became their de facto leader who dealt directly with Paul and then distributed payments to the others.

Camp life settled into routines. Paul organized English classes and brought in a teacher from Utah, a clean-cut Mormon in a white shirt and black pants. Paul arranged for computer classes in a stone house just outside the camp's perimeter. Elad made the most of the timed hour each day at the computer. He consumed the news in Arabic and English—articles on refugee centers springing up in Europe, opportunities to migrate. Other Syrians were getting out, finding new paths, escaping the violence. There was always a way to find a better place.

Paul brought in other donations shipped into the camp: t-shirts with funny phrases, heavy cotton socks, jeans, and sometimes decent plastic puffer coats. The coats made the most difference during the cold desert nights. One day Paul brought a whole box of red baseball hats with the angelic "A" of the Los Angeles team. The baseball hats were popular. Everyone knew Los Angeles. Land of dreams. Hollywood palm trees. Hard, tanned bodies. Money. Success.

Paul gave Elad more responsibility of over time. One morning he explained the need for his team to truck supplies into a new town that was just across the border. It was a routine task, but Paul said that it was best to have an Arabic speaker join the transport run just in case.

Elad accepted the job. The driver called himself Valentine. He was a good-looking, confident Ukrainian military man who drove fast with confidence, the radio blaring. Elad sat in the back with two of MSA's Odessa men, both of whom spoke Russian and limited English.

By late afternoon they came to small village a few kilometers just within the Syrian border. It took a few hours to unload the supplies into the basement of an unassuming residential house. Elad spoke Arabic to the villagers and gathered insights on recent activity in the area. The people in this town, mostly older residents, were grateful but also wary of strangers. They were frightened of accepting anything that might be considered foreign aid.

On the drive back, a Syrian army jeep pulled them over just a few kilometers outside the village. Valentine stopped the truck. Within minutes, another lightly armored truck pulled up, with a Syrian gunner manning a Kord heavy-caliber machine gun mounted on the back.

The two Odessa men shifted nervously, checked their rifles. Valentine calmly spoke instructions to them in Russian. His hand moved to the pistol holstered at his waist.

"I will speak with them," Elad told Valentine. Without waiting for any approval, Elad jumped out of the truck, put up his hands, and approached the Syrians. He shouted friendly words in Arabic. They allowed Elad to approach. He pointed to the UNHCR's logo painted on the truck. Elad smiled, spoke calmly, invented a story about delivering relief to many small towns. He improvised with friendly, casual gestures. Nothing to see here. Routine water, flour, and grain delivery. The Syrian driver, his face mostly hidden behind a mask, nodded, and waved them on.

Later that evening, Paul came to him.

"Valentine told me about what happened on the delivery run. That was brave diplomacy," Paul said.

"Nothing but talk," Elad said.

"You stayed calm. Told them what they needed to hear."

Elad shrugged. He was never afraid. His father had taught him they could never take your courage from you, even if you lost everything else. The only way forward was to live without fear.

"Just solved the problem," Elad said.

"Good instincts," Paul said, and handed him two twenty-dollar bills.

Paul lingered, his shoulders straight.

"Is there something else?" Elad asked.

"I need to leave soon," Paul said. "I have business elsewhere."

"Ok," Elad said. He liked Paul, but nothing was permanent. It was naive to expect anyone to stay for too long, especially an American.

"If I can find you a way to reach Europe, would you and your family want to go?" Paul asked.

"Maybe," Elad replied softly.

"I can't get you real papers. But there is a way I can get you as far as Italy. I will make sure it is safe. I will try to get you a job to start."

"Would you go if you wore my shoes?" Elad asked, hiding his excitement.

"Yes. It will be hard at first, but you'll have more opportunity there."

Umm seemed relieved when Elad told her of what the American had promised. His mother spent the next week worrying that somehow Paul might change his mind or that something else might prevent them from leaving. When the promised departure day finally came, his mother's mood brightened. In the morning, they gathered two small suitcases and quietly boarded the back of the truck. Valentine drove them about five hours along small, poorly paved roads. Paul sat in the passenger seat.

They arrived in Mersin on the southern coast of Turkey by late afternoon. The truck brought them to a parking lot on the waterfront where a group of Italian men waited. Paul spoke to the men. Afterwards, Paul brought Elad to the shaded area beneath a cluster of fig trees nearby where they could speak in private.

"I've paid these Italians to help you," Paul said. "You will get on a boat tonight with many others. Here, take this."

Elad unfolded the notes—five one-hundred-dollar bills, the gray-green image of a wise man in bifocals on each note.

"I've asked these men to find you work when you reach Italy. You will have to decide for yourself what to do after that. Understand?" Paul said.

"I understand."

"Write to me later," Paul said.

"I will."

After Paul left, Elad went back to the women, children, and elderly waiting inside the warehouse. Other families came in throughout the day. The hot warehouse smelled of sweat, dust, and clove cigarettes. The Italians slung rifles over their shoulders and kept watch as the people assembled.

Finally, night came, the air cooled, and their real new journey began. The Italians lead them out of the warehouse. Several hundred of them walked in an organized column the last hundred meters to the dock, then clambered onto this ship.

Elad felt the ocean's breeze against his face. He looked up at the stars, scattered in the open night sky. He knew the desert but had never been on the ocean until tonight. The air was salty and moist. He felt small and fragile against the universe's immeasurable expanse spreading out in all directions. Something proud and thankful swelled inside his chest. It was the promise of a better tomorrow that might soon take shape in a manner he could barely imagine.

CHOREOGRAPHY

10

"WHAT ABOUT the woman who came to Andre's apartment?" Yuri Volkov asked. "How does she fit in?"

Dmitry, Yuri, and Paul sat huddled together in discussion at a small round table at La Place Royale, a comfortable café nestled inside the Place des Vosges in Paris' 4th arrondissement. It was a lovely spring late morning, and the café buzzed with people outside enjoying the pleasant weather.

Dmitry poured the strong Mariage Frères[83] black tea from the white porcelain pot at the center of the table into three tiny cups. The tea kept them alert as they reviewed the latest surveillance efforts.

Yuri Volkov arrived late last night from London. He now sat with his hands folded across his chest. His experienced, pensive eyes stared out into the cluster of elm trees in bloom in the Place des Vosges' interior square. Dmitry kept shuffling on his chair to alleviate the pain that had again flared up from the pinched nerve in his lower back; Dmitry hadn't had the time yet for another epidural shot. Paul sat forward, two fingers at his temple as if the gesture itself might release more creative inspiration as to what they should do next.

"Her name is Isabella Portelli, maiden name Salvo, thirty-nine years old," Dmitry began. "Born in Palermo. Married ten years to Mark Portelli, a prominent businessman with joint British and Maltese citizenship. No children."

Dmitry explained further how Yevgeny followed Isabella on a shopping tour along the Rue Saint-Honoré. He slid one thousand euros into the palm of a Gucci store clerk after Isabella bought perfume and a silk scarf there. Yevgeny's bribe was enough to obtain the woman's credit card number, which then developed into a host of other details. More payments to lawyers, investigators, and security consultants outlined Isabella's known real estate ownership, offshore accounts, and business associations. She held private property in Milan, throughout southern Italy, and in Bulgaria. An investment trust listed her with sizable ownership stakes in four casinos in Belgrade, Dubrovnik, Bucharest, and Malta.

---

83   Brothers Henri and Edouard formally founded the Mariage Frères tea house in 1854. Since 1983, owned and led by Kittichat Cha Sangmanee.

"And her husband?" Yuri asked.

"Nothing criminal on record. We can assume that she holds his business interests in her name."

"Any direct links with Perses?"

"Maybe," Dmitry said.

"What is it?" Yuri prodded.

"Mark and Bogan were both students at the London School of Economics about the same time. This was a long time ago, some thirty-five years now. Neither stayed long in England. However, it's fair to assume they might have known each other as young students," Dmitry said.

"Students at the same college? That is more than coincidence," Yuri said. "I knew Bogan's father from the old Soviet days. Tamar Zoidze was a force of nature then, one of the few men in Georgia who was both a good military mind and a true patriot. Bogan was his youngest son. I met him too in Tbilisi many years ago. Bogan was a different person then. He was civilized, rational, talented, even charming. He was very smart, skilled with languages. I thought he had a very bright future."

"What happened?" Paul asked

"The Chechen War. That invasion became very savage, not just in Grozny but also in the mountain villages. Bogan volunteered to serve in an elite battalion, but it quickly fell apart for him. Each year he went deeper into this world. An official report documented he was killed about ten years ago. This was a manufactured lie. In fact, he turned into this persona, this thing called 'Perses.'"

"How could any sane person continue to help him today?" Paul asked.

"History gives the answer to your question," Yuri said. "Men always find ways to justify their sins, sometimes for pride or because of an idea, especially for profit. Bogan is no fool. He needs to hide his crimes. He needs quiet connections to the Western world. No doubt he pays his people well and punishes them if they stray. This is the same with many leaders today who show themselves as statesmen but are, in fact, mere butchers."

"What is our best theory then?" Paul prodded, turning to Dmitry.

"My information from Nessrin shows that they are arranging a sizable transaction with the Libyans," Dmitry said. "A large shipment would require maritime transport and special handling. They will not be able to use military transport, but it could be done commercially if they keep it all secret. A typical container journey from Libya's Tripoli to Batumi takes four days, first through the Bosporus Strait and then west across the Black Sea. The main challenge on this would be to avoid detection at major ports. NATO closely monitors all Russian-flagged ships in Libyan ports. A Libyan-flagged ship sent to the Black Sea would draw even more attention."

"What about using a different port outside of Libya?" Paul asked.

Yuri tilted his head and motioned for Paul to continue.

"You said Mark Portelli is Maltese. Malta is a major transshipment hub. If weapons are brought to Malta from Libya, then loaded to a Russian-flagged vessel there, then the cargo can move onward, unmolested through the Bosporus Strait and into the Black Sea. From Georgia, Perses can use land routes to Syria, Armenia, Azerbaijan, Turkey, and Iran."

"Plausible," Dmitry said. "Using a busy international container port as cover seems reasonable. But this transshipment idea is just one of many possible explanations. We don't know any more specifics."

"Which is why we need more detail," Yuri said. "We are still blind. Our talk now is only guesswork."

Yuri shifted his foot on the stone floor, then looked more closely at Paul. Yuri was somewhat surprised that Katya's young man was still sitting with them, sipping strong black tea and discussing tactics of how to foil an international weapons deal. The bond Paul had with his niece was unusually strong. Yet even though Paul was motivated, Yuri was still unsure if Paul could handle what might come next. He had invited this untested American into his world, and he was still with them now. But Yuri wondered if his so-called blank slate would prove resilient enough to handle more. Has Paul reached his limits already? The next phase will require him to make even greater sacrifices. Future choices will not be easy. Is he prepared to go even further?

Yuri lifted the porcelain tea pot. He briefly met Paul's eyes while he poured the remainder of the now lukewarm black tea into the younger man's empty porcelain cup. He watched Paul sip the tea, admitting to himself that for now none of them really had any answers.

———— ✶ ————

Katerina Volkova slept most of the way on the Swiss Air flight from Newark to Paris Charles de Gaulle. She skipped the meals, shut out the world with an eye mask, and listened to jazz piano music through her Bose noise-canceling headphones for most of the eight-hour trip.

Traffic was horrible from the airport to central Paris. It took her more than an hour just from Gare du Nord. After Katya arrived at the apartment on Rue Le Goff in the 6th arrondissement, she took a hot shower in the small bathroom and changed clothes into a more stylishly cut blue dress. Refreshed, she took her time making her way to the nearby Luxembourg Gardens. She waited for Paul now near the Medici Fountain.

The Medici Fountain was her special place here in the beating heart of old Paris. It was one of those nodes on Earth that Katya carried vividly in her mind. Her clear memories of the fountain spanned back to when she first came to France as a graduate student. She was a much different person then, still so vaguely formed, still so naive and ignorant. Now Katya was here again at the edge of the fountain's calm rectangular pool. She stood a few meters from where a large sculpture depicted Polyphemus, a giant, looming menacingly over two marble figures, the lovers Acis and Galatea. These marble figures twisted on a moss-covered dais below a rock. Such inert mythological figures, carved nearly four hundred years ago, spoke directly to her, unchanged through the long ages. In contrast, Katya's long absence from Paris following her father's death was a mere instant. Statues did not change. Only she changed. Now she was stronger in her mind and in her body from the months in Palm Springs. Physical training gave her a new kind of energy and confidence.

When Katya saw Paul walking towards her, she also felt a certain guilty joy come first into her fingertips then down her legs into her toes. Paul had grown a beard now. It made him look older, and it seemed to her as if he had lost some weight. Still, something childish in his eyes sparkled.

Paul came up to her, took her two hands, and brought his lips to hers.

"You still have the California sun on your skin," Paul said.

"You like it?"

"It's a healthy look."

They lingered at the bench next to Polyphemus.[84] The gardens were crowded this evening—families and couples enjoying the 16th century gravel paths and the comfortable shade of the tall plane trees and petunias. Katya took Paul's hand as they strolled. At first, they both spoke like excited school children of what had happened in the long months since they were last together. It was if they each were part of the same being but divided by circumstance and forced to live in separate bodies for nearly a year now. Katya told Paul about Max and his mother. Hopefully soon, she added, they might all be reunited.

---

84   Created by sculptor Auguste Ottin in 1866, the monument depicts a tragic scene from Greek mythology where the jealous Cyclops Polyphemus discovers the sea nymph Galatea in the arms of the shepherd Acis

"How did my brother look?" Paul asked.

"Fine. Maybe tired," Katya replied.

"Max needs to move on from the past," Paul mused, furrowing his brows. "It's been too long."

She didn't press for him to explain more. There was much more inside Paul she still didn't know, just as there were other people within herself that he had not yet reached. She thought momentarily of telling Paul more about her last night in Palm Springs. Nothing had happened with Tim Hastings, but she had been strangely tempted. She only resisted Tim's advances because at that moment he didn't exactly serve her higher purpose. It was better to let that incident remain unspoken for now. *Conserve energy, always conserve.*

"Anything wrong?" Paul asked.

"No, just tired from the flight," Katya replied. She focused her eyes on the marble statues placed in increments along the Luxembourg Gardens' gravel paths.

As night fell in increments of decreasing light, Paul and Katya left the garden and walked back to the Volkov's small one-bedroom walk-up apartment on Rue Le Goff. The apartment was the same as it had been on their first trip to Paris more than two years ago. Those days seemed paradoxically like yesterday and a lifetime ago. Her older brother Viktor was still alive then; she had a different life in New York. Those were good days. Back then, the gallery in Chelsea was a sanctuary, a place of beauty and freedom.

Up in the room, Paul kissed Katya's neck passionately. She removed her blue dress, and then he ran his hands over her supple breasts and across the many scars of her torso and back. She wanted time to stop while he caressed her body. Only in Paul's arms now did she feel secure. Only with Paul did she feel somehow safe and right, as it all had been when they first started dating.

After a warm bath together in the apartment's old-fashioned tub, they went back to bed without eating. They both stayed awake in the darkness and didn't speak to each other. The spring night air came in through the open window, cool and clean. Soft city street sounds murmured outside—a shout from the sidewalk, a motorcycle engine revving, a taxi horn.

Paul held Katya loosely in his arms. After he fell asleep, she listened to his breathing, this living, thinking, enigmatic other human being.

What are we together? Why him? Did she care for Paul only because he loved her and was willing to sacrifice everything for her? Would connecting with this single person, this one man, be enough? Could she ever truly trust another human being?

———— ✳ ————

When Katya opened her eyes again, a newly baked croissant and hot café allongé waited on a porcelain plate at her bedside. Fresh, new morning light through the east-facing windows cut crip rectangular light patterns on the tangled white cotton bedsheets.

Still naked, Katya leaned up straight, sipped her coffee and ate the soft, flaky croissant. No other bakeries on earth could compare with the best in Paris, she knew. Paul looked over at her and smiled. He had been reading a newspaper at the small cherrywood desk near the window. The exterior light shone on his now clean-shaven face. It was still a handsome face, she saw again.

"Coffee too strong? I asked the girl to add another espresso shot," Paul said.

"It's perfect."

"High school lessons finally paying off," Paul said, then went back to reading the International Herald Tribune, while Katya nibbled, trying to keep the croissant flakes off the bed.

She didn't want to hear anything reported in the newspaper. At this moment, this tiny one-bedroom apartment seemed like a last oasis, untouched by the vulgar, distracted world. The fury and mire of human history didn't matter at this moment. Her real, authentic self now existed only to savor the coffee and appreciate the fascinating play of sunlight through the window after a night of lovemaking with Paul. The white bedsheets felt smooth against her skin. *All that matters is that we are alive, breathing, happy together. Would I ever need more than what we have here in this little room?*

After a few minutes, Paul's serious voice broke the spell.

"Dmitry thinks we might know their next move," he said.

"Tell me, Paul." Katya rose from the bed, put on a white button-down shirt, and began to brush out the knots from her tangled, honey-colored hair. She stretched her neck and snapped her mind back to attention. They were back to planning tactics. The fantasy of an imagined escape dissipated as he summarized yesterday's conversation at Place des Vosges. She no longer thought about the play of sunlight in the room.

"Perses is looking to buy from the Libyans with Russia's help," Paul continued. "Dmitry thinks that they will ship weapons through a city called Batumi on the Black Sea. We don't know more details yet, just what he's been able to track via Nessrin Geddah."

"But you have a plan to find out more, yes?" she asked.

"Working on it."

"Working how?"

"I'm not sure," Paul admitted.

"I remember Batumi very well. A quiet, little city on the Black Sea. There is a cable car into the mountains and delicious khachapuri.[85] Have you ever eaten real Georgian food?" Katya asked.

Paul frowned.

"Why does that matter?"

"Georgian food is very spicy and never boring. There is one small place on a hilltop just near the city center that has the best khachapuri on earth. My father took me many years ago. I wonder if it is still there. I will need to google it again."

"No, no, no," Paul said. "Impossible."

"What is impossible?"

"You are not going to Georgia. Too close to Perses. His home turf."

Katya continued to brush her hair.

"All the more reason why you need my help," she said. "We don't have time to wait for the delivery of another silver plate. What's more dangerous now is if we do nothing and just let more sand slip through the hourglass. Look how long it took just to get this far, just waiting for Andre to come back to his old apartment. Still, you only see an outline from a very far distance. You know nothing yet. We must go deeper. Batumi is part of my world, Paul. They are Russian speakers there. It's only logical that I can help."

"Yuri will not agree," Paul said. "He doesn't want you more involved."

She put down her brush and turned back to stare at him directly. The feeling of security that had greeted her just after she awoke was gone, replaced by a dark, bitter mood.

"Then, why am I here?" she asked. "Should I just go back to California and hide again?"

---

85 The name combines the Georgian words khacho (cheese curd) and puri (bread). It typically consists of a leavened dough filled with various local cheeses, such as Sulguni or Imeretian cheese.

240

"No. I'm glad you came," Paul said.

Katya went over to the desk where Paul sat. She took his smoothly shaven face in her hands and kissed him. He moved his arms around her waist, his fingers lighting touching the many scars than ran jagged along her pale, naked skin.

"I wanted to see you again, too," she said. "But you both do not control my choices. I decide what I need to do."

"I know…"

"Dmitry's men must have strong contacts with shippers in Georgia. Get me close. I will do the rest," Katya said softly.

"What will you do?"

"I will do, of course, what usually works," she said, before placing another kiss on his lips.

11

T HE NEUROLOGY specialists at Walter Reed hospital in Bethesda, Maryland, had all but given up hope that Josephine Richards, Caucasian female, aged 54, might possibly regain consciousness after nearly a year in a coma. The statistical odds of a successful recovery from her type of acute brain trauma caused by cerebral hypoxia were extremely low. Most similar patients never awoke again, let alone resumed any semblance of a normal life.

Nonetheless, in the face of long odds, the lead neurologist on the case, Dr. Arthur Stein, was finally ready to admit that his original prognosis had been overly cautious. A battery of tests did indeed appear to indicate that in recent months this patient responded increasingly well to external stimulus. An attentive nurse first noticed how the patient reacted to certain louds sounds and then also to light. It was a testament to the body's natural ability to heal even after ingesting five milliliters of cyanide, Stein argued. The statistics didn't matter. Medical science could not explain all individual cases. Sometimes the human body was just strong enough to fight through even the most devastating of injuries.

When Jo finally opened her eyes, she felt as if she had been submerged for a hundred years at the bottom of a deep, primordial ocean. She didn't fully know where she was or what exactly had happened. It took her nearly a week for her lips to gain enough strength to formulate words. She started first with "water," "give," and "more rice." She saw the objects around her, but words attached to these objects only emerged again in fits and starts. Jo's fine motor skills came next. After weeks of therapy, she found a way to move her fingers again, to hold a pen, and begin to write words, even sentences.

Strangely, Jo vividly recalled parts of her life that were now long distant. It was as if the world was emerging from a confused, incomplete dream. She saw her mother's face from thirty-years ago and remembered the name of her childhood friend's brown cocker spaniel—a cute little dog with long ears and sad dark eyes. Stein explained these vivid recollections as the stimulation response of neurological clusters buried deep in her brain's tissue. Yet Jo also suffered confusing short-term memory gaps. She often forgot what she ate for breakfast. The name of the nurse who came to change her bedsheets each morning regularly slipped away.

Stein came in each week to monitor her progress and administer more tests. He adjusted her medication from week to week and increased the pace of her physical therapy.

Different nurses took Jo out to Water Reed's open garden each day, usually in the early afternoon just after lunch. Jo asked the nurses to allow her to sit without speaking in the shade of a giant willow. She breathed in the clean air and listened to the chirping robins and sparrows. Whatever happened to her memory, at least she could still smell reality now. Nature always renewed itself—the oak trees, the willows, the lavender, the sky, and the clouds. It was just as if she was a phantom, a ghost lingering among living. Only now she realized a deeper truth: the world's beauty shined whether or not the human being named Josephine Richards herself existed to subjectively experience it. The universe would continue to function perfectly well without her. The leaves would turn color each autumn, and the grass would still sprout green in spring. Nothing she did in her life changed anything about all these ongoing, continuous natural processes.

Occasionally, Jo also thought about her past before the long sleep. Before the coma, she had always been a hard worker, a true patriot, passionate about her country's purpose on the wider stage of humanity, and ready to alter the fate of others. She had devoted her entire life to serving a government that was, at least in principle, built to serve a higher good. What a shame that the world was such a messy place and that she had only imperfect tools, with an imperfect mind. Maybe she had made some positive contribution over the years. Maybe not.

The last thing Jo saw before the darkness took her was Paul Drake's face. She remembered his eyes staring at her with a kind of helpless, shocked intensity as she choked. That morning, at the tip of Manhattan, was crystal clear, etched like stone. It was as if that pain in Battery Park had just happened mere moments ago.

No, it wasn't just a moment ago. That was more than a year ago. That was a different lifetime lost in the fog of memory and still not found again.

———— ✳ ————

Valentine Kuzoff knew the Georgian port town of Batumi reasonably well. His older brother had moved there seven years ago after he married a young local woman and took up a job importing used cars from Germany. Routine business also brought Valentine at least a few times a year. The maritime business linked the major Black Sea ports together. Georgian businesses were good partners since they too were trying to emerge from the long decades of Soviet repression; most of the men he knew in Batumi also shared a distaste for Russian hegemony. The food was good, but still Valentine found Batumi to be too stuck in the past, quaintly isolated from the progress that the rest of the world had made in the last fifty years.

Founded on the site of an ancient Hellenic colony, Batumi began as a small, fortified town. In the 17th century, the Ottomans conquered and folded it into their empire only to relinquish control to Catherine the Great's expanding Russian Empire two hundred years later. Under Russian rule, Batumi thrived due to the steadily increasing Eurasian land and sea trade that accompanied the region's industrialization. In the 20th century, Stalin's Soviet Union pulled the port into its oppressive orbit for the next sixty years. The city transitioned back to the independent republic of Georgia after the Soviet collapse in 1992. Today, travelers visited Batumi by air usually with a transit via Istanbul, Tehran, or Kiev. Those who came from Georgia's less developed, mountainous interior found Batumi to be a pleasant upgrade in terms of modern conveniences, diverse restaurants, and pleasant diversions. From the city's hills, visitors gained panoramic views of the port's churches and mosques scattered along the Black's Sea's eastern shore, and nearby botanical gardens also offered visitors carefully designed hiking paths through lush foliage.

Exploring the city's best-known attractions, however, was not on Valentine's mind for his current visit. Instead, he confined himself to the bars and gambling dens along the waterfront, starting his work just after sunset. He was here only to rekindle his better business friendships. It took just a week with some generous cash payments and expensive dinners involving svelte hostesses and beluga caviar to confirm what he knew already—only a few men really controlled Batumi's lucrative commercial port contracts. The highest value contracts still went to the Medea Shipping Lines, a private company that had once been owned by several senior Soviet military men, including the influential general, now deceased, Tamar Zoidze. The man in charge of all of this today, Valentine learned, was Fyodor Abramishvili, Medea's current chairman. According to Medea's deputy director, Fyodor also appreciated life's finer luxuries and was a regular patron of the city's best casino at the Leogrand Hotel.

It was a mild Friday night, when Fyodor Abramishvili realized that he was overdue for an adventurous evening. He had just spent a miserable two weeks dealing with feckless government bureaucrats and needlessly demanding clients. To make matters worse, Fyodor's wife was needling him again to spend more time with her at their country dacha some thirty kilometers away. His wife was always nagging him about this or that responsibility. She focused her time now on their young son, already three. Her nagging about her problems and his lack of attention had become very tedious these last few years. As a result, Fyodor preferred to spend at least his Friday evenings alone, and sometimes skipped the whole weekend.

Tonight, Fyodor started with a big meal of sturgeon, caviar, herring, and black bread. He was joined by his deputy director, and they spoke mostly business over the meal. When Fyodor left the restaurant, belly full, he made his way alone to Shavsheti Street and to his favorite casino at the Leogrand. His mood brightened as soon as he stepped through the ornate entrance and saw the troop of tuxedo-clad dealers and croupiers waiting at the tables. The crowd was still light, but it would get busier, he expected, as the night progressed.

Money flowed freely at the gaming tables inside the Leogrand. The floor manager always lavished him with various perks from the moment of his arrival. He drew his chips on credit and never paid for drinks. Lean, platinum blonde waitresses served expensive scotch whiskeys and foreign vodka brands whenever asked. There was also a cigar room with all the best Cuban and Dominican brands. Romeo and Julieta No. 2 was Fyodor's preferred smoke, although he had recently begun to appreciate Fidel Castro's favorite, the Cohiba. All these bodily pleasures added to the night's raw pleasure. Some called Batumi "the Vegas of the Black Sea." That was a slight exaggeration, he conceded, but the Leogrand was good enough to deeply enjoy, all things considered.

He started with blackjack and played for an hour. His luck started to turn after a string of misfortunes suffered at the outset. Since the minimum bet at these high roller tables was five hundred dollars, mostly he played alone against the house. Occasionally, some Japanese businessman or an inveterate old Russian card player sat down. Sometimes a Chinese mainlander would join, with a steely demeanor but only a smattering of either English, Russian or Georgian. The other high rollers didn't usually last long. Besides, Fyodor didn't come to the blackjack table to socialize.

Fyodor first caught the smell of some pungent perfume as the dealer moved over a stack of chips for Fyodor's last winning blackjack hand. The young woman who sat down pushed forward a minimum bet into the betting circle with two very slender, aristocratic fingers. She received her cards, showed a four, took another hit, and then waved her hand to show a stay. The dealer busted and slid over her the winnings. The woman doubled her bet, won again, then doubled again, and lost. Fyodor won each of his bets, including the last.

"*Tibia Parteet.* Luck is with you," the woman said in Russian. Fyodor's eyes wandered to her as the dealer played out the cards. Her nipples peaked through a tight black velvet shirt. A black leather miniskirt revealed straight legs that curved up into sensual hips.

"A bit of luck, yes," Fyodor said in Russian, then sat up slightly more erect.

"Send me some luck now," she said, smiling.

"I will try," he said, watching her rummage through her Gucci purse until she found a tube of dark red lipstick and rubbed it on.

She bet again, and now Fyodor paid closer attention to how she played out her cards. He himself religiously kept to the odds and knew them precisely after many years of play. On one hand, he told her not to take another card despite her inclination to do so. His advice worked. The dealer drew a high card and busted. After this, the woman moved her chips into his betting circle to wager on his decisions in addition to her own hand. They enjoyed some success betting on his hands together. He smiled at the pleasant comments she made during the game.

"Any drinks?" a waitress asked at one of the dealer breaks.

"Vodka on ice. Russian Standard," the woman said.

"Make that two," Fyodor added, realizing that it was a very good, classic choice of drinks. An attractive woman was nothing new to the Leogrand. Many of these working beauties hovered around the card tables, whispering sweet nothings to the players to insinuate themselves for the evening. This slender pale one, however, was an exceptional find—stunning blue-green eyes, high cheek bones, delicate shoulders, and smooth white skin. Unlike the others, this one carried herself like a princess from some distant, more civilized, and romantic era. It was natural beauty too—none of those fake lips and boob jobs he so often saw wandering around most nights.

"Join me at roulette?" he asked the woman.

"Why not?"

At the spinning wheel, Fyodor finally asked the woman her name. "Natalie," she offered, from Gatchina, outside Petersburg.

Natalie gripped his arm when one of his large wagers hit red nine straight up to pay off thirty-five to one. The croupier moved over a stack of colored chips. Fyodor clanked his glass against hers in a toast. After three more Russian Standards on ice, Fyodor now felt a familiar warmth course through his arms and legs. Good vodka always eased life's uncomfortable aches. This otherworldly princess could help that, too. Natalie stood close to him, her perfume mixing with the vodka. She did not protest when he slid his hands up her dress to feel her smooth inner thigh. They switched to the baccarat table where a small crowd had gathered.

"Do you live nearby?" she asked.

"I do."

"Champagne there?" Natalie asked him.

"Of course. Dom Perignon," he replied.

"You are not tired yet?"

"Not yet. Not tonight," he replied.

"Then, let's leave before our luck changes," she whispered, her fingers on his neck, giving him a faint but scintillating massage.

Fyodor waved to floor manager to cash out his chips. After he took the cash, he felt powerful. Not only did he make money tonight, but now he could do whatever he wanted with this stunning woman. He deserved a woman like this tonight. His life was harder than anyone else assumed, and always dangerous. He deserved to reward himself with someone special, even if she cost a little extra.

Fyodor's driver took them across town and dropped them off at his luxury high-rise. The guard in the lobby immediately raised his head and came to attention when he saw the couple saunter through the door, arms entwined like newlyweds.

Fyodor kissed the Russian beauty in the elevator. Her lips were wet and sweet. She ran her delicate fingers through his smooth, straight black hair and pressed his body against her own. Aroused, he fumbled with his apartment keys before he finally opened the door.

Fyodor went to his liquor cabinet, found his best champagne bottle, twisted off the tinsel cap, and uncorked it with a pop. She stood in front of the window, waiting. Fyodor's tower room commanded a view of Batumi Bay, a shoreline dotted with minarets and onion-domed Orthodox churches. The city was dark now, except for the lattice of lights from a giant Ferris wheel that was popular with children and a few taller, more modern rectangular towers, newly built.

He poured out two flutes of champagne and handed Natalie a glass. She drank first, then she kissed him more. He drank another glass until the bottle was half empty.

"I'll be back," he said, feeling his stomach bloated after the big meal, casino drinks, and now this. He needed to prepare himself for this one, and not succumb to his own bodily frailties.

Natalie handed him his flute after he emerged from his bathroom. He finished the drink with a final gulp and then, thoroughly prepared, led her into his bedroom. She removed the rest of her black lace lingerie and slid naked next to him under the golden-colored, satin sheets.

Fyodor pressed his face into her fragrant, round breasts.

He became warm all over as Natalie pressed atop him. She was in good shape—strong arms, firm buttocks. She moved rhythmically with him; her skin pressed against his own. Her body felt soft, warm, wet. He was young again, pure, free, and strong. He noticed the jagged scars that ran down her torso, but such imperfections didn't matter now. He needed her body. He needed to possess her completely, and perhaps always assumed that something must be wrong with a divinity like this.

In the next minute, a soothing mist gently began to overtake his mind. She smiled down at him, her hands on his chest, her legs pressing against his own, entwined.

"Quiet now," she whispered.

Then, in a haze of tingling, pleasant sensations, Fyodor's world suddenly swirled in a comfortable medley of pleasure, and then went dark.

He awoke the next day with a splitting headache that spread from his temples to the base of his skull. Sunlight was pouring into the open window. He rolled over and looked to see if Natalie was there on the bed still. She wasn't. The clock on the nightstand announced it was almost 1:00 p.m.

Fyodor went to the kitchen and guzzled three glasses of water. His mouth was dry, and his throat parched. The bitch had slipped him something in his drink. He didn't precisely know what it was, but it was enough to knock him out for ten hours. He checked his personal belongings. She also emptied his wallet—ten thousand lari, more or less. She also took his gold-plated Rolex watch and some sterling cufflinks from his valet in the bathroom.

Fyodor sighed.

Russian sluts are always too good to be true.

He would have strong words with Piotr, Leogrand's owner. That bastard should have some responsibility for the quality of women he let into his place. What happened to scruples and diligence these days? Wasn't there a better way to protect the casino's most loyal patrons? Piotr should cover his losses with a new line of credit, and probably more.

Maybe the slut left an ID when she came last night, he hoped. He briefly considered the trade-offs. She had been magnificent throughout the whole evening. Even so, dreams are not reality. Her scars should have made him realize something was off. Now he was late to drive to the dacha. His wife would set in on all manner of annoying complaints. He would make sure Natalie paid a high price, if she ever dared to show her face again anywhere in his hallowed city.

12

ELAD ISMAIL began working three days after arriving in the Sicilian port town of Catania. The Syrian boy focused on making a good first impression in this new country after Paul's introduction paved the way. Just like at the camp in Turkey, Elad's critical first step was to prove himself on the job. He needed to show these hardened Italians that he could be useful, better than all the others they kept in their employment. Antonio Faraci was the first who noticed the effort and offered his support. Antonio was likeable, respected, enjoyed good connections with older powerbrokers, and spoke excellent English.

"Work hard, find your place," Antonio advised.

Elad's first job was simply to transfer crates from a small ship to several trucks and then a bonded warehouse further in Sicily's mountainous interior. The job began on Friday night and lasted through the weekend. Elad worked harder than the other local men. He also thought of a better workflow from his truck to storage, an improvement that allowed his own team of three to improve their speed by nearly a third. It was a simple packing and unpacking sequence using the equipment on hand and improvising on a technique that Valentine had showed Elad once at the camp. The foreman noticed the improvement and asked the other two older Italians how they finished a day early. They credited Elad, who had also thoughtfully bought them breakfast after the job. It was a gesture they never expected from a Syrian teenager, and they mentioned to Antonio how odd it was than an Arab kid had better manners now than an Italian.

The Italian's operation existed mostly in a gray realm outside official laws. They moved people and goods throughout many Italian ports, the Dalmatian Coast, and North Africa. Moving refugees was a new effort, driven by surging demand. Those poor souls came mostly by sea— Ghanaians, Somalians, Ethiopians, Tunisians. Each person brought a different story with the hope to create a new life, a better reality. The refugees were all fleeing some version of societal failure in their own country. Most who made it to Sicily found ways to melt into the various communities without any official help. The Sicilians accepted this approach; they had a different attitude towards authority. A work permit was like any government regulation—an unnecessary intrusion. Sicilians also knew what it meant to be outsiders in foreign lands. Many had family members who themselves had emigrated from their home country, seeking a better life.

In Elad's case, it helped also that he could easily be mistaken for an island native. He had the same dark hair and brooding features of many Sicilians. If he kept his mouth shut, mostly you couldn't tell him apart from other Italian boys. Strangers always spoke Italian to him. The words were unintelligible at first—but Elad was good with languages, and attentive. Soon, he picked up enough bits and pieces of the language to function well enough in most circumstances.

Elad found Catania to be a strange, sometimes beautiful, mostly desperate ancient city. The port town with a population of nearly six hundred thousand spread out on the slopes of Mount Etna, the volcano's rough peak always within eyesight. Etna sometimes still spewed out waves of lava and thick black plumes, as if to remind humanity of nature's power and man's ultimate frailty. Catania's baroque architecture still stood as it had for centuries, although most of the old stone masterpieces were now run-down and crumbling. The composer Bellini's stone statue in the middle of the old city was covered in grime and soot. Most downtown apartment buildings, once regal, now languished in disrepair. At nighttime, the city's denizens drank their way to pleasure. Many of Elad's fellow workers paid out their wages for love in small, cheap hotels.

Elad had no time to worry about other people's failures. He had his own problems with five mouths to feed.

Elad's rapid progress working with Antonio's people did not go unnoticed by other, younger men who thought of him as an undeserving sycophant who made them look bad. After one successful job, a lanky, disgruntled Italian man in his early twenties spat out his insults directly in the face of this arabo sporco, dirty Arab. Elad didn't wait for this insult to fester. After work, he found a place at the end of a dirty alley down by the docks. He made sure others gathered. A crowd of maybe five or six other Italians circled the two fighters. Elad was much smaller, younger, but also unafraid. The others didn't interfere after it began. Elad kept his fists tight, hitting his wiry opponent with his bare knuckles, and taking blows himself to the midsection and the stomach while the audience watched the two gladiators. Elad wrestled the other man to the ground, shoved his face into the dirty black pavement, and began to beat him senseless with his fists until Antonio's younger brother, Marco Faraci, quickly pulled him off. The Italians were surprised with how quickly Elad gained the advantage and then exploited it.

When the pain in his side didn't subside the next day, Marco took Elad to one of the better local hospitals, a private clinic just outside the city. The doctor told him that two of his ribs had been broken in the brawl. The nurse wrapped the wound properly and prescribed him opiates to last a month. The fight also started Elad's friendship with Marco. This Italian boy was also just fifteen and very eager to prove himself amongst the older men, especially Antonio who was much older at thirty, and thus more like a father figure than a brother. Marco began to spend most nights together with Elad. They enjoyed each other's company. When Marco learned of a new job, he brought in Elad. He also wanted to improve his English, so he constantly peppered his new friend with questions.

It didn't bother Elad that most of Antonio's work was illegal. Just like in Suruç, Elad needed to be fearless. So far there was nothing truly dangerous in any of the work. Antonio's men were mostly involved in petty crime, usually meant to avoid customs duties or taxes that, in their opinion, only transferred wealth to corrupt civil servants and away from real, working-class people. They smuggled in televisions, computers, mobile phones, whiskies, cigarettes, and recreational drugs. They took goods around the island, either via trucks or sometimes small boats. They ran their operation as a business, avoiding violence unless it served a purpose.

Elad's Arabic skills were useful for interacting with those who came over from North Africa or the Middle East. Sometimes Elad helped bring other Syrian families to other enclaves in different cities, such as Messina or Palermo. He helped other Syrian families settle in shelters established on the outskirts of these towns. Some of the other refugees he met had also passed through the Suruç camps in Turkey. Many others had taken different paths via Jordan or Greece.

Slowly, tentatively, Elad began to wake up in the mornings imbued with a stronger sense of certainty about the future and confidence in himself. In just six months living in this alien place, he had started a new life for himself and his family. In just a short time, he had earned enough cash to buy his own Samsung mobile phone, a decent, used, yellow Piaggio scooter, and a pair of comfortable Nike sneakers. Umm even rode his scooter to the open-air market on Sundays with the gas he could now afford. Their lives had stabilized into a difficult, but tolerable, daily struggle. Aisha began to drop hints that maybe they should consider staying longer in Italy. The Italians had a special program for new refugees to attend school with some classes in Arabic too. Aisha didn't care about the crucifix just above the school's entrance door. For now, it would be easier here. Another move to Germany or France would force them to start over yet again. She also heard from other Syrians that in those northern countries it was also hard to find decent work. Winters in those other countries were colder, too.

Elad moved the family of five into a real two-bedroom place, a tiny place on the ground floor. Umm and Aisha had their own kitchen, and the two girls their own room. The little place also had a shower and running water, and it was in an area with enough Arabic-speakers nearby for Umm to at least get by. Umm even found part-time work as a cleaning woman for a nearby apartment building.

Inch by inch, Elad was taking the lead as the man in the family. He was using all his skills and talents to transform their lives. Where it would lead to eventually, he still didn't know and didn't care.

Elad wrote Paul a brief note to his email account just after his arrival. He finally had more to share with the American, some genuinely good news. He snapped a photo of himself on his newly purchased yellow scooter, sporting a pair of aviator sunglasses.

Paul's reply from a Yahoo account came after a few days:

```
Keep up the good work.
 Watch your back.
This is just the beginning.
```

Paul finished typing a note to Elad on his small mobile phone, then looked out the window of the fifth-story room at Rue Le Goff. He watched the gray clouds gather in bilious clumps just over the Parisian rooftops. Sacré-Cœur was a distant white cupcake on Montmartre's congested top. It was just getting dark, and the City of Lights was starting to sparkle.

It's good that the Syrian boy found a way forward, Paul thought. Elad is smart. He deserved at least a chance. Progress happens in small ways. If we can't change grand designs, at least I can tilt the odds for a few.

Paul heard the shower turn off. In a few minutes, Katya emerged from the tiny bathroom, her hair still wet and a cotton robe wrapped around her lean body.

"Human again," she said.

Katya's phone rang while she was slipping into a pair of black linen trousers. She paused her efforts to answer in Russian. She laughed softly at something that was said, then placed the phone on the middle of the bed.

"Let's all speak," she said.

Dmitry's voice came over the mobile's speaker.

"Katerina, have you taken Paul to eat at A la Ville de Petrograd?"[86] Dmitry asked.

"Not yet," Katya asked. "We wait to celebrate something more."

"You must eat the herring there. The best in the world."

"We will," she said. "Do we have progress?"

Katya glanced over at Paul, listening now with a very serious expression. Two weeks had passed since she had delivered Fyodor Abramishvili's data to Dmitry's team of hackers. She had slipped Fyodor three milliliters of Rohypnol[87] into his champagne flute after he brought her back to his downtown apartment. The knock-out drug had kicked in just as his sweaty, grotesque body pressed against her skin, and his hands had touched every part of her body. She endured ten long minutes before the ugly Georgian shipping chief finally passed out. After this, four hours were enough to mirror his phone, his laptop, and his home computer to her handheld mobile device. She took his cash, Rolex, and some valuable jewelry to cover her tracks, before slipping quietly out of his building just before the dawn broke. A chartered flight took her to Istanbul, then back to Paris.

Dmitry's team used the data to gain remote access to Medea's system, to dig further into shipping plans, security assignments, recent financial transactions. It was difficult, expensive cyber work, like squeezing juice from an unripe lemon.

"The container ship is called the Archemede." Dmitry said. "On the surface, it is an average three thousand TEU feedermax with three years of service. On a deeper level, there are many military-grade changes. It has been modified with advanced lifting cranes on the main deck, a reinforced hull, bulletproof windows on the bridge, refrigeration units, and advanced internal storage chambers. The third floor is retrofitted for storing hazardous material—gas storage, sealed containers, reinforced doors. There is also a large compartment for transporting heavy vehicles, maybe armored trucks."

"Seems like the right candidate for our cargo," Paul said.

"You also might be right about Malta. The Archemede docked there six times last year. It is scheduled again next month. It makes sense to use regular routine shipping routes to hide in plain sight," Dmitry continued.

---

86   Founded in 1924 by an officer of the Imperial Guard, this historic Paris establishment serves as a cultural landmark for the Russian diaspora and specializing in authentic Slavic gastronomy.

87   A powerful benzodiazepine sedative that causes deep physical relaxation and memory loss. While used medically in some countries for severe insomnia, it is illegal in the U.S.

"We also found out that Medea has also been contracted to protect four armored vehicles to cross the Russian border at the coastal border town of Adler. Fyodor earns a nice sum to escort these armored trucks four hundred kilometers from the Russian border, then load them on to the Archemede. They are bringing over something of high value, possibly to exchange for the Libyan cargo."

"Such as?" Katya asked.

Paul leaned back as he considered how to pay the Libyans. His mind ran through the transactional options, eliminating first what probably wouldn't work: US intelligence had its fingers on commercial banks. Cash in bulk left serial numbers. Cryptocurrency payments used a distributed ledger, leaving an electronic record that was surprisingly easy to trace.

"They will pay with gold bullion," Paul offered. "Easy to store, impossible to track. Old school."

"Possibly," Dmitry said. "Russia can take gold bullion directly from the Olimpiada mine in Siberia without touching official government coffers. Separatists in Ossetia and the Donbass are paid this way. Gold is simple to process, store, and hide."

"Both superpowers are pragmatists these days," Paul said.

"Or fools," Dmitry countered. "Two years ago, the Americans paid Iran a billion dollars in cash to release a handful of hostages and make small changes to their nuclear program. The Americans have so many options and resources, but even so, they gave their money away like little bribes to small men."[88]

"If we're right about Haftar's weapons, Perses will also earn multiples on whatever it costs the Russians to invest," Paul asserted.

"What about timing?" Katya asked.

"The Archemede is scheduled to leave Batumi in four weeks, stop in Sebastopol, then sail onward to Malta."

"Four weeks? We don't have much time," Katya said. "How confident are we on this information?"

"Confident enough. My programmer still has access to Medea's systems. If plans change, and they record it, then we will know," Dmitry declared.

---

88   In January 2016, the Obama administration settled a 37-year-old legal dispute with Iran by paying $1.7 billion in cash. The payment was made in three installments of foreign currency—including euros and Swiss francs. The cash was delivered via an unmarked cargo plane on the same day that Iran released four American prisoners.

"Or Bogan has better security than we expect," Katya added. "It still seems so very thin. Not enough yet."

"The Americans could help us confirm," Paul said.

They both turned to him and paused.

"Maybe," Dmitry said. "We could bring them what we know now. They should be able to help, but I worry they may overreact. If we reach out to the Americans with this information, there is no turning back. They may not believe us. If they do, they will want to oversee any operation. Once any government becomes involved, we play a different game. We lose control."

"Could George Rutherford help outside official channels?" Paul said.

"I don't see how. Rutherford is rich, but for this we need someone who can get boots on the ground through official channels. Someone active in US intelligence service who can make things happen in Malta. Someone like your Jo," Dmitry countered.

"There is another. Tim Hastings," Katya said.

"The man from Palm Springs?" Paul asked, glancing at her. Katya had quickly mentioned Tim's name a few months back, but Paul didn't pursue more questions.

"That's right."

"You trust him?" Paul probed.

"We don't need to trust, just align. Tim has access. I'll make him listen," Katya explained.

"Good then," Dmitry said. "We reach each out to this man Tim first to see if he can help."

They spoke for another hour, putting in place the outline of plan. The debate continued, each questioning assumptions, weak logic points, and alternative explanations.

After the call, Katya switched off her phone. She slid out of the robe and into the room's small, hard bed. She heard Paul continue to work on his laptop, typing notes, and reviewing the Dmitry's latest files. Paul was always worrying about contingencies and risks. That was his nature and the result of his military and commercial training. Always second guessing himself. Always worrying about what might go wrong.

Katya put the white sheets over her naked torso. She closed her eyes, controlled her breathing, relaxed her muscles. *Conserve energy, always conserve.*

Her arms and legs felt very heavy. With her eyes closed, her mind drifted. When it was all over, then they would go A la Ville de Petrograd as Dmitry suggested. She had planned to take her father and mother there, but that had never happened. That was six years ago. She could still see her father Sergei's face, smiling, and she could hear her mother Elena's voice, too. In her memory, both were happy. She saw and heard them most clearly when she was very tired, just before sleep.

By the time Paul came over to her bed, Katya no longer stirred. He watched her chest rise and fall rhythmically. He wondered also about whether they were making the right decision to reach out to someone whom Katya had only briefly met in California. Would this Tim Hastings add more complications to an already complicated world? He would ask her more detailed questions about him in the morning, after she was fully rested.

Paul watched her for a long time this way, knowing also that he had no way to see how her memories mixed with dreams in the dark recesses of what he suspected was still a restless and troubled slumber.

Tim Hastings sat at his office desk reviewing a draft memo. It was a clean, bright day in northern Virginia. His neck hurt from sitting too long in front of the computer screen. He had not slept enough the night before thanks to a late-night fire drill involving the Saudis in Yemen again; his eyes were tired. An empty coffee mug with the faded logo of the US Naval Academy was near his keyboard. He was finished with his third round of strong Starbucks coffee, black, no sugar.

Tim's analytic output was due by the end of the week. If approved, Langley's Seventh Floor wanted to deliver his memo as part of a longer, special report requested by the Senate's Intelligence Committee. It was routine work, but not entirely simple. Tim preferred to write his own analysis rather than trust a longer memo to some junior, fresh-from-graduate-school, hack. The typical analyst always missed the pragmatic nuance and used too much academic jargon for an average reader who didn't know the international relations theory and didn't have the time to care.

Tim had turned on a light jazz station. He enjoyed jazz for these longer memos.

The bassist now was really jamming.

Congress, The White House, State Department. *What a fucking joke these days*, Tim thought. The whole vast governmental machine, broken. What the hell has happened to these humans? Feckless new appointees. Idiotic senators. Hack first-term congressmen. All these people have invented new and creative ways to hide their heads in the sand. The country has sunk to new lows.

Tim tapped his fingers on his desk as the jazz piano riff moved up an octave.

The President's snarky, novice son-in-law was the worst. Arab Israeli peace in the next eighteen months? Kim Jong Il and Putin praised as strong leaders? Absurd. No great statesmen today. Charlatans and Twitter-obsessed wackos running the show. A rogue's gallery of bald-faced, self-dealing hypocrites. This whole circus was a wet dream for autocrats. No wonder these thugs were challenging the West in so many ways, because the West itself was failing in its own disturbing way.

The piano instrumental ended in a flourish, followed by a sad, fading saxophone.

Silence. A new song, slower tempo.

Back to work.

Focus.

Come back to the title eventually with something punchier.

```
     CONTROLLED UNCLASSIFIED INFORMATION
     SPECIAL REPORT: MOSCOW'S AMBITIONS IN THE BLACK SEA AND
MIDDLE EAST
     Since the withdrawal of US ground troops from
Iraq in 2013, the Russia Federation under the explicit
direction of Vladimir Putin has strengthened its
military commitment to the Middle East and the Black
Sea region. If left unchecked, Russia is set to become a
far more dominant influence aligned with other regional
powers that have adopted adversarial positions towards
US interests and our allies. Putin has frequently
made his strategic aims clear in recent speeches and
state directives. His long-term goal is to reestablish
Russia's former sphere of influence, which the Kremlin
believes was unfairly disrupted after the collapse of
the Soviet Union in 1991. In the Middle East, Russia has
invested heavily into its naval base at Tartus, Syria.
They have also provided direct military assistance to
Iran and generous financial support for pro-Russian,
non-state actors in Georgia, Eastern Ukraine, and
Moldova. In 2014, Russia forcibly annexed Crimea, home
to a long-standing navy base at Sevastopol, and sent in
troops to support separatist movements in the Donbass
region of Eastern Ukraine. All these actions are
part of a larger strategy meant to reassert Russia's
strategic dominance as it once maintained in both the
19th century and in the Soviet era.
```

CHOREOGRAPHY

To achieve its goals, Russia has increasingly relied on military force rather than diplomacy or positive economic incentives. For example, Moscow's 2015 air campaign in support of Syria's Bashar al-Assad proved a turning point in that country's brutal civil war. Coordinated strikes successfully weakened the military resistance of pro-democracy groups, which the US failed to support following our troop withdrawal from Iraq and the rise of the Islamic State. Russia's bombing also created large-scale humanitarian challenges due to the extensive and indiscriminate nature of the strikes. Reliable intelligence sources suggest Russia's air campaign killed at least 50,000 non-combatants over a three-year period and displaced many millions more. The costs of the resultant large-scale Syrian refugee crisis have been largely borne by neighboring Turkey, Jordan, and Lebanon. An influx of refugees has also challenged European Union member states.

In contrast to Russia's strategic actions, US response has been timid and lackluster. A recent Pentagon assessment, now declassified, concluded that 2016-2018 US-led efforts to support an alliance of Kurdish and Arab militia against Islamic State militants resulted in the opposite of desired US policy goals by strengthening the Syrian government's reliance on Moscow's military. The report assessed that US strikes during this timeframe were very limited in scope and confined to strict military targets, with US forces unwilling to engage directly with the Russian mercenary groups or fighter jets.

Russia has also established much closer relations with Iran in recent years. With Russia's approval, Iran has deployed hundreds of troops to help Assad's efforts in the Syrian theater. Thousands of Shia Muslim militiamen, armed, trained, and financed by Iran, mostly from Lebanon's Hezbollah movement, now fight alongside the Syrian army and against anti-government coalition forces.

Our allies in the region remain highly concerned with this shifting balance of power in favor of Putin's strategic objectives. Saudi Arabia, a staunch Iranian rival, has also armed Syrian rebels since the start of the civil war, as did the kingdom's Gulf rival, Qatar. Our closest ally, Israel, also has increasingly expressed concerns on what it calls Iran's "military entrenchment" in both Syria and Yemen, which it views as an existential threat. Israel has also conducted air strikes with increasing frequency to thwart shipments of Iranian weapons to Hezbollah and other Shia militia. In response, some evidence suggest that

<pre>
Russia is actively helping to rebuild the chemical
weapons capabilities of its allies, including Syria,
Iran, Armenia, Yemen, and several non-state military
actors now seeking to challenge elected governments.
This alarming trend suggests....
</pre>

Ding.

A faint, but distinctive, electronic alarm interrupted Tim's typing. He paused.

Ding.

What is that?

Ding.

The source of the chime came someplace inside his desk's top drawer.

Ding.

Tim opened the drawer and pulled out a small Motorola burner phone still connected to a portable battery charger. He had forgotten the device since he shoved it in there many months ago. The tiny digital screen flashed a notice on an incoming message. He pressed a button then squinted his eyes to read the small pop-up text:

<pre>
Help me now? K.
</pre>

The incoming text also contained several encrypted files, broken into smaller sizes to be received by the phone.

Tim put the mobile phone on his desk. He turned off the jazz radio station and looked out the thin rectangular window at rows of oak and poplar trees still barely holding on to their autumn leaves.

He had blocked Katerina Volkova out of his mind for many months now. What she wanted now, he wasn't sure. He stared out at the trees and recalled their week together in the desert, her strange obsessions, their last moment, his lips pressed against her smooth neck in the darkness of that warm, dry evening.

It was wrong to be involved with any foreign target——a central rule and just plain common sense. Still, there was something deeply different about this one. Perhaps she might offer something more than useless political exercise, another memo for feckless fools and hypocrites. What had she said to him at their last dinner in Palm Springs? He couldn't recall her exact words—something about showing him a new path.

Tim turned off his computer screen and locked this station. He picked up the mobile phone and began his walk to the basement floor where the tech guys could get to work on the files. Those geeks were on the northside of the building, a bit of a hike. Still, he needed a break to clear his head from another useless memo. He resolved to grab another coffee on the way to get him through the afternoon's dying embers.

GAMES

Gozo
Gharb
Sannat
Mgarr
Comino
Cirkewwa
St. Paul's Bay
Malta
Mdina
Valletta
Mediterranean Sea
Marsaskala
Birzebugga
Malta
Freeport
MALTA

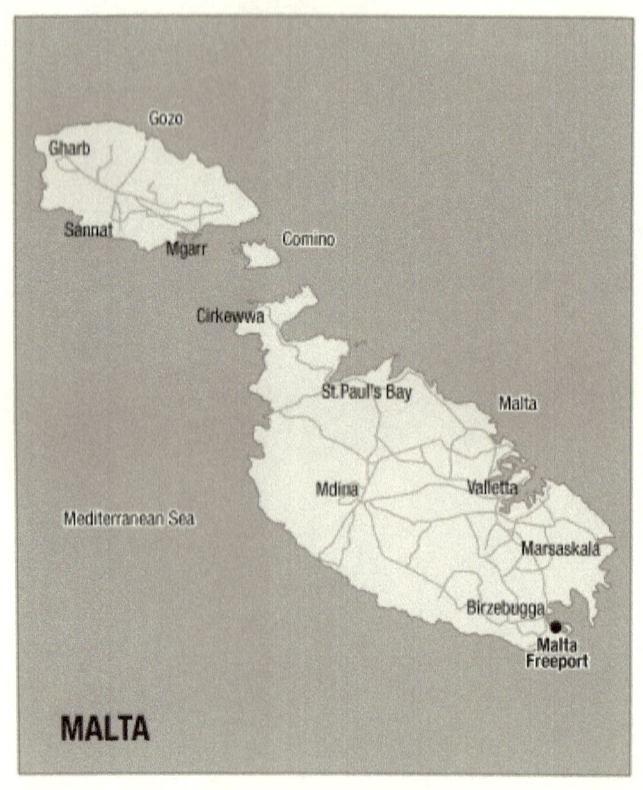

14

WHEN THE US Embassy contacted Malta's prime minister's office with a request for an urgent security meeting, Aaron Bugeja cleared his afternoon schedule. The appointment popped into his calendar as an ad-hoc coordination session with a US Sixth Fleet representative visiting from Naples.

Aaron Bugeja, a childhood friend of Prime Minister Jo Muscat,[89] was now counted among a handful of reliable men within the country's close-knit civil service. He was eighteen months into his appointment as head of Malta Security Services, the MSS, and found his current job to be more challenging than anything else in his professional career. With scant natural resources, Malta's leadership looked to follow the example of other independent island states seeking to bolster their economy within today's fast-moving, complex, and globalized world. But these were dangerous, unstable times, and Malta, as always, existed as a small island in the center of turmoil and change.

For best effect, Aaron arranged to meet at the Auberge de Castille, a formidable limestone building overlooking the Grand Harbor that dated back to the Napoleonic era. The grand building housed the prime minister's key support offices, including Aaron's small corner office.

Aaron was proud of Malta's ambitions and his island's past. He always found ways to tell the many foreigners he met how the island's 122 square miles played a pivotal role in world history. He described to visitors always how Malta served as a fortress stronghold of the Christian faith for centuries, withstanding the Ottoman's great siege in 1565 under Charles V and the Order of St. John. After Napoleon's defeat, Malta joined the British Empire to become a key shipping way station and fleet headquarters for the world's most powerful navy. When the Suez Canal opened in 1869, the island's position halfway between Gibraltar and Egypt proved a vital stop on the marine route to India. The tiny island thrived during the Victorian era when Britain's navy ruled the seas and commerce flourished among its many colonies. The Maltese were proud to be part of the British Empire at its zenith. Then came Malta's heroic defense against fascism in the 1940s,

---

89   Served as the 13th Prime Minister of Malta from March 2013 to January 2020, leading the Labour Party to significant electoral victories.

the Nazi Luftwaffe bombs, post-war decolonization, independence in 1964, and finally the country's ascension to the European Union in 2004.

Throughout these many epochs, Malta's citizens always unified and rallied against their common enemy. A unique language, and strong faith unified what in fact was a very diverse collection of people, now more than half a million. The younger generation looked ahead. In this century, Malta joined the Cayman Islands, Singapore, Bermuda, and other island states to trumpet the wisdom of Anglo-Saxon courts and the rule of law. Aaron knew this was a thin veneer though. Everyday his security team dealt with old hatreds and divisions in the form of refugees, contraband, and organized crime. In the last few years, it all seemed to be getting worse. Pressure from the other EU countries was building for Malta to clean up its act.

Two guests sat at a long table, sipping black tea, when Aaron entered the wood-lined, diplomatic room with a crystal chandelier hanging from the high ceiling. A dozen portraits of various knights of St. John hung on the room's walls, a procession of sober, long-dead faces.

The US Navy's man—Tim Hastings—shook Aaron's hand with a firm grip. He was a tall, good-looking man dressed smartly in a black suit with a thin gray tie. The woman in a stylish business suit next to him met Aaron's gaze with striking green-blue eyes.

"Allow me to introduce Katerina Volkova," Tim said. "She is affiliated with MSA, one of the shipping firms headquartered here, and a partner on our project."

Aaron tilted his head, curiosity piqued by the woman's pale, enigmatic face.

"A pleasure, Ms. Volkova," Bugeja said.

They all sat down. Aaron crossed his hands together.

"How can I help?" Aaron asked.

"As you know, the partnership between the United States and Malta is as strong as when the Maltese Knights of the Order fought alongside Washington at the battle of Chesapeake,"[90] Tim began. Tim described in a lawyerly fashion recent examples of the US-Maltese security partnership—joint maritime law enforcement training, co-sponsorship of the International Institute for Justice and the Rule of Law, financial

---

90   In 1791, 1,800 Maltese sailors and Knights of the Order served within the French Navy under Admiral de Grasse. Their combined forces defeated the British fleet, effectively blockading the Chesapeake Bay. This prevented the British from reinforcing or evacuating General Cornwallis's army, directly leading to his surrender at Yorktown and the end of the American Revolutionary War.

support for migrants. The USS Monterey had just helped the Maltese navy seize illegal oil exports out of Tripoli, an action that won Aaron plaudits as well as an annual bump to the US assistance budget.

"Yes. The United States is a very important partner. We value our longstanding relationship," Aaron said, while thinking, All standard political jargon. What else does he want to say?

Tim paused, took a sip of tea. He explained the details around the credible intelligence on a chemical weapons transshipment scheduled to pass through Malta Freeport.

"Unfortunately, these weapons are destined for the Syrian theater and possibly other conflict areas in Asia Minor and the Black Sea. We suspect Russian involvement, which, of course, Moscow's ambassador will deny," Tim explained.

"What about NATO?" Aaron prodded.

"We are not interested in triggering alliance sensitivities," Tim said.

Aaron leaned back in his chair. He wasn't entirely surprised. Most shipping companies offered up only light documentation on their containerized cargo. Other smuggling incidents involving stolen merchandise and illegal forestry products had spiked in the last few years. Aaron was already under pressure from several ministries to improve spot inspections as part of a new set of recommendations that had just been made into law. The recent murder of a prominent journalist critical of the current government also raised the stakes. Aaron needed to change the narrative away from corruption and back to Malta's historic role as an enlightened beacon of civilization in a troubled world.

"What is it, then, that you are suggesting?" Aaron prodded.

"The US Navy wants to seize the cargo and arrest those involved while these ships are here. We'll work with your courts to extradite those arrested and convicted. We will take possession of the banned material with appropriate protocols as soon as it is feasible."

"We've done similar operations before," Bugeja explained. "It's rare to have problems once ships are docked."

"Good," Tim said.

"What else?" Aaron asked, glancing now at the Russian woman.

"A high value terrorist could be involved in the related financial transaction," Tim explained. "Also, in this context, the traffic of nerve agents raises some degree of risk. We have some intelligence to indicate that the parties involved here have used extreme measures in the past."

"My team is world class," Bugeja responded. "We are well equipped to handle contingencies. Tell me more."

They spoke for another hour and agreed to meet tomorrow with a larger team to review more operational details. Aaron shook hands again at the end of the meeting. The American seemed satisfied with the offered cooperation.

Afterward, the Maltese security chief looked out the tall window, across to the Upper Barrakka Gardens, and down upon the busy Grand Harbor. On the surface, this request seemed to be reasonable. But he wondered what Tim Hastings was hiding. This was coming at him through a new channel, different from his regular interactions with the US Navy out of Naples. Also, actions involving Russia made him pause. The Russians were dirty players looking to expand their naval power. Finally, there was the woman. Why bring her into the meeting? What else aren't they telling me? He made a note to look more deeply into the commercial activities of a shipping firm called MSA.

A thousand years of such conflicts between civilizations, he lamented. It all still seemed eerily familiar. Larger powers always sought to achieve their aims—the Catholic Church, the Ottomans, the French and British, and now these so-called global superpowers jockeying for influence and arming the world with their sophisticated weapons. Once again, Malta was just a small island. This was an opportunity, and a big risk.

———————— ✳ ————————

Katya left Tim Hastings after the meeting at the Auberge de Castille. She walked through old Valletta's narrow streets towards MSA's corporate apartment at the top of Old Mint Road just a short walk away through the city's main arteries. The evening sky had just turned a deep ultramarine, and the streets were crowded with other people leaving home for work as the waning daylight shifted over the old limestone houses and the expansive sea beyond.

As Katya walked, she grew more anxious. She felt the weight of today's discussion mix with the past. She had made so many mistakes, so many errors that in hindsight seemed avoidable. First, there was that morning in Neuilly-sur-Seine; then there was her blind spot with Chloe, a woman she had so easily trusted but who was in fact working for the same men she now knew had killed her family. Perses was always one step ahead, always better informed and more creative in his approaches. Time and again, he proved his ruthlessness. She could still hear his voice from the Brooklyn garage, a kind of distorted madness taunting her. He had curiously referred to her as his Scheherazade as if it was all just a game, and she, his plaything. If she displeased him, he could behead her at any moment of his choosing.

Katya entered the low-rise building's secure, tiny lobby. She walked up the flight of stairs, then pushed open the heavy oak door to enter the small, two-bedroom apartment on the second floor. Sunlight shone in from the skylights above, giving the impression of greater space inside the otherwise cramped room. Yuri purchased the apartment as part of a deal to receive a European passport; in fact, he really hadn't used the old place; it was mothballed for most of the year except in summer when he came for a few weeks from London to attend required board meetings.

Paul waited for her at a table in the small kitchen.

"Is it on?" Paul asked.

"Tim is persuasive. And it is hard to deny the wishes of an eight-hundred-pound gorilla."

Katya recounted the long meeting. Paul listened and then pressed her on parts of the plan that he thought might go wrong. He was still uncomfortable that their plan relied primarily on local security forces, and the Americans also could not be fully trusted. Tim Hastings was not Jo. Paul knew nothing about this new man's background and his real intentions. He had never looked him in the eye.

"Let's hope we have our facts right," Katya said.

"You and I should take more precautions," Paul replied.

She looked at him somewhat puzzled.

"Such as?" she asked.

Paul rose from the kitchen table and walked over to the apartment's refrigerator. He opened the freezer door and pulled out a silver-colored pouch from inside. He unzipped the pouch and removed a small plastic container. He emptied contents of the vial out onto top the white table—a dozen, small, dull-green gel tablets.

"I brought these from Syria. Just in case," Paul explained. "With Jo, we began to distribute these capsules to the Kurdish rebels. There isn't too much organized data, but in most cases, the pills seem to work."

"Work how?"

"Protection against nerve gas. The gel contains an advanced nanoparticle defense. If you take this pill, you don't need to wait for exposure. This antidote acts as a shield so that nerve toxins cannot attach to the body's enzymes. The coating is the real innovation—that sets the timing so the drug's purified protein can be better absorbed over time. Protection can last weeks after each dose."

"You think Perses might use nerve agents here?"

"Better to be safe. He's used sarin and VX in other circumstances. Let's not take chances."

Paul picked up two gels from the table, popped them in his mouth, and swallowed.

"How safe are your little pills?" she asked.

"Not quite FDA approved," Paul said.

"So, they are entirely experimental and might not work?"

"I haven't felt any side effects. Should work on most nerve toxins," Paul said.

"Most?"

"Sarin, yes. Other gas types, probably. Nerve toxins come in many flavors—sarin, soman, VX. The pill's effectiveness will also depend on exposure levels. Let's hope none of this proves necessary."

Katya looked at him. Paul had come far with her these last two years. Her memory flashed back to when they first shared a drink and dinner on a very cold winter evening at Gramercy Tavern in Manhattan. Paul had known nothing about her then. They laughed throughout the meal and talked about singing badly at karaoke. Now here he was, plotting away in a tiny Maltese apartment, handing her experimental drugs. They were both now very, very deep inside a long and winding rabbit hole.

"Why not," she said, then took two green gels from the table and examined the tiny capsules in the palm of her hand. She clenched them between her teeth, tipped her head back, drank the water, and swallowed.

15

JO RICHARDS propped herself up on her pillow so that she could read her laptop screen better. Two weeks ago, she had agreed to be moved out of Walter Reed to a more comfortable private residence in Georgetown, a two-bedroom apartment with a decent view of the Potomac River. After an extensive series of tests and evaluations, Dr. Stein finally recommended that a routine of light work in a controlled home environment could benefit her long-term recovery.

The small Georgetown rental suited Jo for now. The bed was too soft, but comfortable enough. Taj Mahal, an Indian restaurant on Wisconsin Avenue, sent her food at least three days each week, and the pizza place nearby on M Street was decent. She could also walk down by the Georgetown canals on afternoons on those days when she had the strength, and when it wasn't too hot and humid.

Work, Jo knew, was her best curative. She focused on how to find a way back in the game. She kept a certain fantasy alive that somehow the government could overlook her medical condition, and she could reassume an active role. A sympathetic senior HR manager reinstated some of her basic office tools—a secure phone, computer access, VPN rights into a few of the classified databases. The ops guys hated residential homes, but in her case, those geeks treated her something like a hero and made an exception. Jo knew the odds. Despite her progress, and these small acts of kindness from the operations team, no one at any senior level believed that she would ever return to any viable role.

Jo didn't care what the skeptics believed. She frequently repeated the same mantra to herself each morning: the naysayers can all go fuck themselves. Nobody understood her vision. Those other so-called "intelligence officers" all walked through their duties as if living in a dream despite the obvious storm clouds that had been gathering for years. Hines' team, Jo knew, could use her insights more than they knew. Those younger guys were headstrong, arrogant, idiotic. They spent most of their time caught up in the endless stream of endlessly meaningless digital technologies while the bad guys just stayed analogue. The System still needed her, she firmly believed. There was more to intelligence work than any of those new boys really understood.

Jo's eyes first scanned the day's news. The cable traffic popped up in title format, thin rows on her laptop screen in small Courier font. Headlines appeared every few minutes as the secure news feed continuously refreshed. *Amazing how much pure bullshit our spinning world spits out each day,* she thought. NATO paralysis... another atrocity in Yemen... Russians poking our eyes again in Eastern Ukraine... the Saudi prince, that bastard, denying yet again he made the call to hack up that local journalist...

She paused on one cable, marked from the European desk. The headline piqued her interest:

```
OPERATIONAL UPDATE, DISRUPTING LIBYAN WEAPON SHIPMENTS.
```

She right clicked to open but received a blocked message.

"Assholes," she muttered to herself. Jo spent the next fifteen minutes filling out her own bio information to gain access. It took another hour before someone at Navy intelligence approved her request.

The full contents of the cable flickered on.

```
TOP SECRET/NOFORN/HUMINT
RE: OPERATIONAL UPDATE, LIBYAN WEAPONS SHIPMENTS


    A CREDIBLE FOREIGN SOURCE WITH TIES TO MOSCOW HAS
IDENTIFIED DETAILS ON A SIZABLE WEAPONS SALE INVOLVING NON-
STATE ACTORS. OUR SOURCE SUGGESTS THAT THE EASTERN LIBYAN
POLITICAL FACTION UNDER THE DIRECTION OF GENERAL HAFTAR
INTENDS TO SHIP CHEMICAL WEAPON STOCKPILES TO BUYERS IN THE
SYRIAN WAR THEATER. IDENTIFIED CARGO INCLUDES STOCKPILED
NERVE AGENTS, GAS PRECURSORS, CONTAINERIZED MUSTARD GAS,
BLISTER AGENTS, CHLORINE GAS, AND SARIN PRECURSORS.
SUSPECTED CONVENTIONAL MILITARY DEVICES INCLUDE ADVANCED
TECHNOLOGIES FOR LONG-RANGE MISSILE DELIVERY, SOPHISTICATED
ARMING DEVICES, STORAGE AND SENSING TECHNOLOGIES FOR ACTIVE
BATTLEFIELD DEPLOYMENT.
    OUR NAPLES STATION HAS ENGAGED WITH LOCAL OFFICIALS IN
MALTA TO DISRUPT HIGH-VALUE TRAFFICKING TARGET, SEIZE THE
ALLEGED ILLEGAL SHIPMENT, APPREHEND ACTIVE PARTICIPANTS, AND
DISRUPT RELATED FINANCIAL TRANSACTIONS.
    RELIABLE SOURCES ALSO CITE THE INVOLVEMENT OF KEY
GEORGIAN-BASED ARMS TRADER WITH STRONG MOSCOW TIES. RECENT
REPORTING SUGGESTS BOGAN ZOIDZE CONTINUES TO PROVIDE
SIGNIFICANT ARMS ASSISTANCE TO VARIOUS GOVERNMENTS AND THAT
A NUMBER OF NON-STATE ACTORS MAY BE DIRECTLY INVOLVED IN
THIS TRANSACTION.
```

Jo put down her laptop and looked out the small bedroom window. Her eyes saw the Potomac River, Roosevelt Island, and the traffic flowing steadily over the Key Bridge into Arlington, Virginia, while her mind churned over the report.

Fucking Russians. Thugs and bandits, all of them.

Nothing surprised her. She had warned about this nexus for the last ten years, only to be sidelined and ignored by those who didn't understand the real danger or care enough from a career perspective. Supporting Haftar's dirty rebellion was just a part of Putin's imperial ambitions to become a true alternative world power just as the Soviets had once been. Haftar was exactly the kind of compliant thug Moscow needed to fill the vacuum in North Africa, just as they were doing with good success in the Middle East. They were always looking for such leaders to emerge. A Libyan foothold would expand Russia's currently constrained naval footprint beyond the Black Sea and into the eastern Mediterranean. Even better, Libya possessed 48 billion barrels of proven oil reserves, ranked ninth in the world and the largest in Africa. Here was also another chance for Putin to enable allies in Syria and Iran with more offensive chemical and biological weapons so they too could continue to keep their grip on power. With more fear, Russia could push other loyalists forward in places like the Donbass in Eastern Ukraine or even further. It wasn't clear at what limit someone like Putin would stop. If they didn't act now, it would only get worse—just as she had so often told George Rutherford and anyone else in DC who would listen.

What piqued Jo's interest most in the cable, however, was the explicit mention of Bogan Zoidze; this was the first time she saw his name pop up in the formal cable traffic. Someone did their homework, connected the dots, and now was raising the stakes.

Jo calmed down and devised her next steps. She started with Martin Hines. At least Marty was still in his seat and hadn't quit yet for some high-paying, private-sector contracting job that paid double his current salary. Jo knew him well, having worked with Hines in Afghanistan during the early days just after the invasion when the US joint forces took out the Taliban. Hines wasn't a great thinker, but he had steadily won promotions because of his shrewd, dogged attitude. The Seventh Floor accepted Hines even while Jo floundered and squirmed for years on the fringes. Was it thanks to the old boy network? Or maybe her own inability to color fully within the lines? Still, Hines wasn't a complete moron. He could read the tea leaves. He knew the dirty tricks Russians constantly played. No doubt Hines had his fingers on this Libyan operation. If he didn't, he would know who did.

Hines didn't return Jo's call for two days. She persisted by leaving a message every six hours with his assistant. He finally called her back, just after 9:30 p.m.

"How are you, Jo?" he asked. "I've heard you've been handed a miracle. Another shot at life."

"Miracle it is, Marty. I'm indestructible. Nurses come every day to water my plants and feed me strawberry Jell-O."

"Sounds delicious. Why are you reading cable traffic and not focused on your health?"

"You know me. No rest for the wicked," Jo said.

"I know. How sad," Hines said.

"Talk to me about what the Russians are buying from Haftar," Jo persisted.

Hines let out a long breath.

"Same playbook as always," Hines said. "Putin thrives on instability."

"How can I help?"

"You can't. It's already happening. I have a top man on this project. He's building on the solid work you started."

"Which top man?" Jo asked.

"It's locked and loaded, Jo. Let it go," Hines replied coolly.

"Which top man?" Jo repeated.

"Come on, Jo. You know I can't."

"What's the confidence level?" she asked, switching tactics.

"Something useful may come in."

"Zoidze is smart. And very dangerous."

"Let's see how the intel plays out. This will happen quietly. No diplomats."

"But Yuri Volkov is involved, isn't he?" Jo asked. "Trust a Russian before our ambassador?

"That's unfair," Hines replied coolly.

"Is it?"

"Is there something about Yuri Volkov we should know that might be helpful?" Hines asked. She knew that Hines never liked how her methods stretched the boundaries. In Kabul, she acknowledged that her lone-wolf creativity and unorthodox methods had sometimes backfired. They had exchanged heated moments: Hines accusing her of leaving out critical details in her official reporting, making it nearly impossible for others higher up in the System to step in without taking on a whole gamut of new risks.

"I don't know anything about Yuri these days," Jo deflected. "He didn't send me roses while I had a breathing tube shoved down my throat."

Hines snorted.

"Thanks for the call, Jo. Get more rest. We're on the same team," Hines said, and then hung up.

Same team, my ass, Jo thought as she put down the phone. *Naval Intel doesn't know shit from shinola.*[91] *Those cowboys out in Naples have their fingers up their asses. Anything involving sailor spies usually went sideways. Boys don't know what they don't know.*

When her anger subsided, she considered the fruits of her interrogation. At least, Hines gave her something in the context of his questions. Yuri Volkov was involved. If that sly old man was in this game, then most likely her star producer, Paul Drake, was also still swimming someplace near enough to splash some waves. Paul would stay involved because of the girl from the gallery, Jo knew. Maybe he was still Hines' source for what was about to happen.

Her mind recalled Paul Drake with a strange kind of revised clarity. This time she heard his voice shouting her name while the cyanide coursed through her body and shut down her organs. It was Paul who had held her shaking body as she choked in the park. Maybe this time Paul could also help bring her truly back to life, assuming he himself had managed to stay stubbornly among the breathing.

---

91   In the US army keeping boots polished was a strict requirement, making Shinola, a popular brand of shoe polish, a staple in military barracks. The idiom relies on the fact that brown shoe polish and feces share a similar dark brown color and smeary consistency.

16

NICOLAI IVANOVIC Sokolov had been quietly living in the hilltop Vomero district of Naples, Italy, for almost ten years. His lifestyle included a bottle of smooth Chianti almost every night, fresh basil at most meals, and views of majestic Mount Vesuvius some twelve kilometers to the south.

Originally a native of St. Petersburg, Sokolov was known to his local friends simply as "Nico," a generous and friendly companion with good manners and who spoke excellent English and Italian. Ostensibly, Sokolov's work permit listed him as a managing director of PK Industrial, a commercial business specializing in retrofitting commercial ships. In fact, the Italian Russian Trade Federation, a front organization for Russia's *Federalnaya Sluzhba Bezopasnosti*,[92] the FSB, paid him a generous stipend. Sokolov built a productive track record in the last five years. He excelled at ingratiating himself with the US naval personnel at the headquarters of the US Navy's Sixth Fleet. More than ten thousand American service men from every branch of operable service called Naple's home; this base was a rich hunting ground. Sokolov's "Piazza tales," as they became known thanks to his somewhat amusing, Chekhovian writing style, had found an audience. His reporting was clear, insightful, and always right. Now his reports always went straight up to chain.

The Sixth Fleet in Naples had been a thorn in Moscow's side for seventy years—the 1958 US intervention in Lebanon, the 1973 Yom Kippur War, Serbia in 1998 were only a few of the bloodiest incidents. Most recently, US Sixth Fleet cruisers launched airstrikes on Haftar's eastern Libyan factions and some of the military men there had begun meddling in Syria to support rebels seeking to topple Assad's legitimate rule. Nicolai Sokolov kept the pulse on these dangerous imperial actions. His intelligence on the USS McFaul in 2016 and the USS Yorktown last year made a difference.

---

92   Primary internal security and counterintelligence agency of the Russian Federation, serving as the principal successor to the Soviet-era KGB. Headquartered in Moscow's Lubyanka Building, it is responsible for counterterrorism, border security, and state surveillance under the direct authority of the Russian President.

Nicolai Sokolov met Michael S. Cummings, US Navy Lieutenant First Class, four years ago at a business event organized by the Italian Maritime Association. Cummings, a native of Buffalo, New York, served as a commissioned officer, one of about three dozen such officers in Naples of similar rank. The two men drank beer first during the event's cocktail hour. Afterwards, Nico shared Cuban cigars to help keep the night moving forward.

Cummings accepted Nico's offer to the next event, followed by a few perks related to a minor retrofitting contract involving the US Navy. The first perk was a free three-night stay at a luxury villa on the Amalfi Coast, then a beachfront room on the island of Capri, a lovely place. Nico always sent over young girls for his new friend—svelte Serbians, young, pale-skinned Belarusians with gleaming eyes and perky tits. The Americans always appreciated the women; it played well to their egos and made them feel like rockstars living out a fantasy.

Mike Cummings confided more with Nico. He had stayed longer in the US Navy than he himself ever predicted—Honolulu, Yokosuka, and now Naples. But back in civilian life, Mike knew he would just be ordinary. Back in the States, he might have enough to buy a town house and a nice car, but in the navy he had rank, clout, importance. Naples was grand adventure, even if the actual job was routine and most likely he had reached the highest rank he was ever going to get in the service.

At the casino in San Giovanni Teatino,[93] Nicolai elevated his efforts after a particularly raucous evening. He argued with Mike that the world was sufficiently gray and the policy of the United States, sufficiently muddled, so that any check on America's over-the-top ambitions and out-of-control defense industry would promote world peace. Cummings should be a patriot and truly serve his own US Constitution by cooperating with other countries to ensure a natural balance of power amongst the world's most important countries. Mike listened sympathetically, albeit unconvinced. A six-figure cash payment finally tipped the scales, though. Funds were deposited into his brother-in-law's brokerage account in Florida from an unrelated bank in the Cayman Islands.

Cummings' extraction method was simple: poor physical security at the Naples' main SCIF[94] provided him a tiny window late each Thursday. Mike used these moments to photograph cables and then transmit the images to a Bluetooth device just outside the secure area. Exploiting the SCIF's simple security flaw worked like clockwork for almost two years.

---

93 Casinò Le Palme, the largest gaming house in Central Italy.
94 Sensitive Compartmented Information Facility (SCIF).

Cummings' most recent output flickered on Sokolov's laptop screen. The cable detailed a pending US operation. Sokolov didn't know exactly how his FSB colleagues might react, especially Kiril. He was merely a messenger, too far down the food chain to know the gamut of Moscow's stratagems and paranoias. The search and seizure of a Russian commercial vessel would boil some blood, another American provocation that proved how powerless Russia was to project real power outside its immediate borders. Then, there was the true wild card: Bogan Zoidze. That was a name even Sokolov had not seen for a long time in official intelligence channels. Did it matter? Some functionary three thousand kilometers away in Moscow would need to weigh in on that.

Nicolai placed the details into the context of his own reporting. Now, his Russian-language cable was almost ready. Time was the main constraint. Cummings' intel came with a week lag. It would take at least another 24 hours for Sokolov's report to land on the right desk, maybe longer since it was already Friday. Nicolai cursed Michael Cummings for his tardiness.

With trained and careful fingertips, Sokolov typed in the last fourteen-digit password to establish a secure communication with the Russian consulate in Naples. After a final check of the codes, he uploaded the report and pushed send.

17

ANDRE GAUTHIER gazed out the window. The sun raged in a dazzling display of yellow, orange, and red over the flat Mediterranean. The sky was a symphony of color, a majestic, mutating moment that played out above the world just before night fell. In the distance, he could see a sparkle of lights coming from a handful of container ships and cruise ships passing near the entrance of Malta's Grand Harbor.

Isabella Portelli poured a splash of Riesling into his wine glass. The pair had settled down now in Isabella's three-bedroom penthouse in St. Julian's just outside the island's capital of Valletta. Andre's black leather TUMI traveling bag sat in the corner.

Andre had slipped into Malta on a Turkish Air flight from Istanbul yesterday using an Algerian passport and one of his more secure aliases. He came alone as usual, a full week before the scheduled transshipment and related transaction with the Libyans. Isabella put him up in this small, one-bed hotel room. Originally, they had agreed to transact in Malta only because her husband, Mark Portelli, had convinced Andre, and then Perses, that he could offer sufficient local intelligence and security. It was easier to deal with risks in these smaller countries came the argument; Portelli had prior success moving contraband through Malta to substantiate his claims.

Now, his whole plan, meticulously arranged and negotiated with Haftar's agents, looked tenuous at best.

How did the Americans, usually so ignorant, find out about this?

Andre sipped the wine. He didn't share Kiril's bad news with Isabella because he didn't fully trust her. If it turned out she was the traitor, then Andre looked forward to dealing with her next, even if she was Mark's wife and he had bedded her the last time they were alone together in Istanbul. Andre's paranoid nature had kept him alive thus far precisely because he peeked around corners and expected to be betrayed. Was Isabella so arrogant as to think she could use her body to play him, muddle his priorities?

"There is another development," Isabella said.

"Tell me."

"Your Russian slut has come to Malta."

Andre leaned forward.

"Which one?"

"The art dealer."

"You mean Volkova?" Andre said. This incongruous little fact struck him as odd, if true. He had lost track of this woman after that botched effort in Manhattan.

"Yes, her. She's been here for ten days already."

"You are certain?"

"We pay our contact at the immigration office well. Katerina Volkova came under a Schengen visa, required for Russians," Isabella said. "Coincidence?"

"Probably not," Gauthier answered.

Andre Gauthier put down the wine glass and crossed his arms.

"Any others?"

"I only have visa data. Visas are not required for EU or US citizens," Isabella explained. "Others could have come in by ferry or on a charter flight."

"So, you don't know of any others," Andre pressed.

"No."

Andre thought back to the young face of the Russian girl as she had been in Paris. He could still picture her remarkable eyes. He was also always struck by the curious interest that Perses took in her long after they eliminated the threat of her over-zealous father. She was also Yuri Volkov's niece, and he was still a factor in this game. That old man's mere existence always bothered Andre. The Russians still made money with him, even if Yuri crossed too many boundaries to be fully trusted. It did make sense. Did they really expect a man like Yuri Volkov to never discover the truth?

"Have your man show me where she goes each night," Andre concluded.

"Yes, of course."

Andre drifted over to the window and looked down across the sea and the many ships outlined in the darkening distance as he considered what was next. Kiril was always keen to avoid entanglements involving open diplomatic issues. Perses had more than a billion and half dollars of Moscow's gold in transit for a payment to Haftar. The seller still needed to move forward since oil-rich Libya had sunk into muddled chaos ever since the Arab Spring and the NATO bombing campaign against Qaddafi. The opportunity was still intact, even with this new wrinkle.

Katerina Volkova. Unfinished business, Andre worried. *What exactly is she up to? How exactly does she fit into this mix?*

18

PAUL DRAKE waited alone for Tim Hastings at a small cedarwood table at the entrance of Alchemy, a fashionable whiskey bar squeezed between low-rise stone buildings along Straight Street. The locals still called this very long, narrow street in old Valletta "The Gut" even though the seediest aspects of this former navy nightlife center had more recently given way to posh wine clubs and trendy craft beer haunts. The British sailors were long gone. Tonight, the young crowds came from many countries, and they made the street an easy place to blend in.

Paul sipped Hendrick's gin, then crunched an ice cube in his teeth. He found Valletta to be a strange, ancient place. Everywhere he looked, he saw the lost epochs layered in the gray-yellow limestone buildings, the ornate churches, and the ramparts of the massive harbor forts strategically positioned around the Grand Harbor. It was as if this rock between Europe and North Africa bottled up many past worlds. What Malta lacked in size, it made up for along the dimension of time—a long sequence of human activity stretching back millenniums to the Romans, Normans, Ottomans, and the British. Tonight, this history seemed curled up like a spring, waiting for what would happen next, waiting for the still unwritten future.

An Italian couple at a nearby table laughed together. *I would not have predicted sitting here,* he thought. *But here I am all the same.* Only three days remained before the expected arrival of the Archemede. Then, at least, they might have results.

Paul waved his hand in a slight signal when he saw the tall, straight-shouldered American arrive. Tim met Paul's eyes with steady, penetrating blue eyes as he sat down.

"Scotch on the rocks, splash of soda," Tim ordered from the tattooed waitress when she came over to their table.

"I've been looking forward to our drink," Tim began.

"Have you?"

"Very much. I feel like I know you already," Tim persisted.

"I doubt that," Paul said.

"Oh, you're a favorite of the FBI field office in New York. It seems they still haven't quite squared away that business with Arlen Cross."

"What about him?"

"Nothing…nothing," Tim deflected. "I'm surprised, really. I didn't expect you still to be here, mixed up with all of this. But I was wrong. Here you are, deep inside a rabbit hole."

"I'm a persistent digger," Paul said.

Tim continued with small talk, pausing when the waitress arrived with his drink. He took a long swig, then put down the tumbler, and leaned forward. He stared at Paul with a kind of icy, authoritative confidence.

"Katya asked me to see you. What is it that you want?" Tim asked.

"One of my sources has come here to Malta," Paul explained. "We should watch him closely. I want to be looped in."

Tim squinted and straightened his back to show his displeasure. He didn't like being thrown new facts this late in any game.

"Which source?"

"A key one, attached to the seller."

"But you're not going to share more unless you're involved," Tim said.

"I've seen the source up close. I can help," Paul said.

"Your facts are right?"

"They are," Paul said, knowing that Dmitry's cyber team had tracked Nessrin Geddah for the last three months. A routine response to a dummy SMS first compromised the Libyan's Vodafone mobile network many months ago. After this, cell towers in each new country pinged Geddah's unique cell ID, showing him first in Tunis, then Benghazi for another week. A few days ago, the fat Libyan checked into an apartment building in St. Julian's across the harbor from old Valletta. These were all established facts that Dmitry had shared with Paul while they drank black tea together in their hotel room down by the harbor. Now, Paul was following Dmitry's advice, dangling just enough for Tim to stay involved.

"Why should I trust you?" Tim asked. "Especially after Jo Richards."

"We want the same outcome. Motives don't matter, only results," Paul said. "If I'm right, then we might also have a play on Bogan himself. We succeed, you take the credit. Think about how much someone with his access will unlock for you. It's always good to refresh the GITMO[95] lineup, no?"

"Assuming he's even involved, and we can catch him alive," Tim said.

95　Informal nickname for the US Naval Station Guantanamo Bay in Cuba, particularly referring to the military detention camp established there in 2002.

"He'll come for this. This is big enough."

Tim leaned back. He kept his eyes locked in on Paul, expression still cruel.

"Tell me, Paul. What do you want, really?"

"To help."

"Help? Help what?"

"Help stop more killing."

"All by yourself?"

"No. With you and government of the United States."

"Very noble. Thank you for your service," Tim said. "What else has Yuri Volkov promised you?"

"Nothing."

"You doing this for her then? She has convinced you that Zoidze is responsible for her parents' murder, and now here you are, serving her needs? Is that it?"

"This is much bigger than what has happened to Katya," Paul demurred. "Maybe something I do now will make a difference in a way you and I can't know today."

"It's not your fight. Our world is very old. One person can't change the course of history. Not really. Best we can do is keep the craziest bad guys within their cages, and even that is not easy."

"That's not good enough," Paul said. "If we don't do more now, we'll pay later. Many more will suffer."

"So you say," Tim said. "The only problem is that no one cares at this particular moment."

"Katya told me that you care," Paul said.

"Yeah, but this is my job. I'm paid to protect our vital national interests. I'm paid with taxpayer dollars to worry about the future. You are not."

Tim took a final swig of his scotch and soda, threw down a wad of euro bills before he slowly rose to leave the table.

"Persistence, Paul. That's what Katya must like in you," Tim added. "I'll do what I can, but you are playing with fire. This isn't a moment for unauthorized cowboy bullshit like you had before with Jo. Whatever you think you can do to help on this operation probably isn't going to. You should also think hard about what's best for Katya."

"I'll keep it in mind," Paul replied.

"You should," Tim said with a shrug.

Paul watched him walk away down the narrow street, then turn the corner without looking back.

The tattooed server came over to the table. Paul ordered another drink, bourbon this time. A guitar version of an old Beatles song, "Hey Jude," played from someplace inside the bar. A young couple laughed nearby, slightly tipsy. The night on narrow Straight Street was still beginning; more young people were just starting to fill out the bars.

Maybe Tim is right. What could any one person do that the System itself had missed? He thought of Yuri Volkov. That grizzled old Russian never trusted any bureaucracy, whatever flag was flown. The System was resourced, Yuri always said, but it was also a soulless, imperfect construct. The System could never find someone like Bogan Zoidze, buried deep in the shadows of war, lurking there. This was exactly why the Russians were working with him, always playing out a chess game at a different level, without the rules.

19

MALTA FREEPORT, a state-of-the-art container terminal on the island's eastern shore, was one of the busiest transshipment ports along the increasingly congested Mediterranean shipping routes. The port offered container storage, ground and reefer slots for a wide array of commercial ships transporting goods throughout Europe, North Africa, and the Middle East. Water depths of almost twenty meters allowed the port to accommodate any size vessel afloat today. The mainline berths could serve the latest class of 24,000 TEU vessels, up to thirty ships at any one time. Malta Freeport handled a record three and a half million containers last year as it consolidated its position as a leading global transshipment hub. Strategic routes to India and Brazil promised to add growth in the next few years. Integrated facilities for refueling, cargo storage, and crew accommodation at affordable daily rates enticed the largest shipping lines.

Malta Freeport's operations focused on efficiency. The key for any modern transshipment hub was to remain cost competitive within the global supply chain. With only a small team, the port's advanced cranes and ancillary yard equipment could unload two containers every fifty minutes from a standard feedermax ship. Today, containerized cargo was sorted according to increasingly sophisticated algorithms to maximize productivity and drive down logistics costs. Products always remained in their containers, resulting in reduced labor costs, damage, and theft. Because there were no custom duties, Malta's cargo inspections were rare, and that, unfortunately in the perspective of those involved in enforcing sanctions and regulatory regimes, enticed bad actors.

Like a tiger springing up from the underbrush, Aaron Bugeja went through the final details of his planned search-and-seizure operation. He fully intended this to be a stellar example of a joint US-Maltese operation done right. The goal was to move quickly and act decisively; legitimate shipping firms should not be spooked by tonight's intervention or perceive that these sorts of actions by local authorities were going to be threats to their own businesses.

Three days ago, the Russian commercial cargo ship Archemede docked at Berth 35 loaded with 79 twenty-foot containers stacked securely on its decks. Required documents seemed entirely routine: port of origin listed as Sevastopol, Crimea, under the auspices of the Medea Shipping line's regular monthly route. The manifest listed cargo as low-value scrap metal and various miscellaneous commercial items—hardwood timber, modular furniture, and bulk dry goods. Seventy of the twenty-foot containers were designated for transshipment onto container ships heading onward to Spain, Portugal, and Brazil. For its outbound journey, the Archemede was then scheduled to receive ten containers from a Portuguese vessel mixed with forty containers from the Libyan vessel Alethea. The Libyan containers were listed to include electrical machinery, frozen bluefin tuna and assorted canned seafood. Once loaded and refueled, the Archemede would leave no later than midnight on November 28.

Yesterday, the Libyan vessel Alethea arrived from Benghazi and docked at Berth 36. The vessel's registration indicated it carried a crew of twenty. After arrival, eleven crew members disembarked. The remaining nine, including the twenty-year-veteran captain, remained onboard. Three of the crew members belonged to the ship's security team, licensed to carry firearms. A crew carrying weapons was not unusual given the piracy threats still plaguing many commercial routes along the North African coast. The Somalis were the worst offenders; they picked out ships for any number of reasons and had recently moved beyond their typical comfort zones in the Red Sea.

The Alethea's departing eleven crew members passed a light check-in when they left Freeport's inner perimeter. Bugeja's men closely checked each of the crew's passports—nothing unusual. Libyan containers were scheduled to be lifted onto the Russian ship starting at 6:30 a.m. tomorrow. His security team was now assembling on the perimeter of the port to ensure they would never make it there.

———————— ✷ ————————

Paul Drake checked his watch—already 2:00 p.m. His stomach grumbled and he felt frustrated.

So far, the effort to monitor Nessrin Geddah these past two days had yielded no results. They had watched Nessrin's apartment building in the St. Julian's without success. Once again, Paul felt a creeping, cold sense of doubt.

Two plainclothes officers—Bella Grech and Joseph Vella—of the Malta Security Service waited with Paul Drake a few blocks away from the lobby of the high-rise apartment building. Physically, the two Maltese narcotics officers shared little in common: Grech was a dark, petite woman with long black hair, while Joe Vella was a bald, burly officer who stood a muscular six foot. Joe had broad shoulders and powerful, tattooed forearms. While Grech was friendly, Joe Vella was more guarded and kept to himself. Joe didn't hide his displeasure for being taken away from his other priorities for an assignment that essentially involved sitting for long hours in a hot car.

Vella sat alone in a dusty green Peugeot outside the apartment building, while Paul and Grech kept closer to the apartment lobby in a white Honda. Grech occasionally walked the perimeter to check the street activity.

Since his arrival, the fat Libyan left his apartment only to buy cigarettes and wine at a nearby convenience store. Last night, Geddah took a walk to a local casino. Grech followed him inside, hovered near the gaming table, and bet sporadically to blend into the casino's activity. Geddah played baccarat on the main floor for two hours. He drank three whiskey and cokes, lost a thousand euro, then returned to his apartment by midnight.

"He was unlucky," Grech told Paul when she returned.

"Any contact with other players?"

"Nothing I saw."

Paul trusted Bella Grech's instincts. In the last two days during the long, tedious afternoons, she told Paul something of her career. Bella's father was a strict police sergeant, trained in the old British system. She always respected his lifestyle and purpose. The Maltese police force was one of the oldest in Europe—tightly organized and still proud of its strong heritage. Grech and Vella had worked together now for almost four years. The two officers were young but seasoned, having spent their days stalking the darker crevices of Malta's densely crowded urban sprawl. Grech worked mostly narcotics-related organized crime as part of a special operations unit, focused on disrupting the operations of North African drug gangs. Now the gangs had stepped into lucrative human-smuggling schemes involving refugees from Somalia, Ethiopia, and Syria. Malta was again a crossroads for brazen efforts to transport people fleeing their war-torn, dysfunctional homelands. It seemed to be getting worse these recent years. The police, she admitted, could stop some crimes, but trafficking networks that extended far beyond the island's purview were notoriously difficult to shut down.

Paul's eyes were drifting when a black SUV drove up to the apartment building's lobby. A woman—black hair, slim figure, and a business suit—exited the SUV and entered the lobby.

"Hold on," Paul said, recognizing Isabella Portelli's slender form.

"You know her?"

"Yes."

"Are you sure?" Grech prodded.

"I think so."

In a few minutes, the corpulent Nessrin Geddah emerged from his apartment building behind Isabella. She went back to the driver's seat while Nessrin sat next to her in front. Paul squinted hard. Behind the tinted windows, he discerned the broad outline of a third figure in the car. He saw a bearded man sitting upright in the backseat. Isabella pulled her car out into the busy traffic of George Borg Olivier Street before he could get a better look.

Grech alerted Vella. His green Peugeot pulled out into the narrow road behind the SUV. Grech and Paul followed in the Honda. The SUV drove north through a series of twisting roads that snaked through a maze of densely packed, gray-yellow, angular stone houses. The car pulled up to a three-story square limestone house set back from the road and behind another barrier. The front gate opened; the SUV rolled inside the house's first-floor garage. The gate closed.

Vella rolled the Peugeot further up the street and stopped at a place where he could see incoming traffic. Grech positioned the Honda further back, next to several other parked cars.

The unattractive square house crouched on a treeless lot at the top of a small hill at the end of an old residential street. The house was in disrepair—an older, dilapidated, pre-war dwelling with rusted gates, broken molding, and cracks in the outer walls. Paul saw some movement inside, but the interior drapes covered the rectangular windows, limiting the view inside.

"What now?" Paul asked.

"We check the license plate and house registration. Then, wait for orders," Grech replied.

"That's it?"

"We shouldn't move too soon. Besides, they haven't done anything. Did you recognize the third man in the back?"

"Hard to see through the tinted windows," Paul said.

Bella Grech sighed.

"Doesn't matter. They aren't going anywhere. This street dead ends. We're at the only exit here. You can get some rest in the back if you like."

Bella reclined her seat and rolled down the window a few inches to let in more air. She was settling in for a longer wait throughout the humid night.

Paul folded his arms and positioned himself more comfortably in the passenger seat.

Paul looked up at the dark windows of the building at the top of the slope. The sun began to turn the sky a deep, chaotic orange. Just over the rooftops, the expansive sea spread out into the empty distance beyond.

20

A NDRE GAUTHIER lit a cigarette and inhaled a long, satisfying nicotine injection into his nervous system. For the past three nights, Isabella Portelli's local man watched Katerina Volkova from a safe distance. The man reported what he saw: she left Old Mint Street each evening, usually just after sunset when the working crowds began to fill Valletta's many restaurants, pubs, and street cafés. On Tuesday, Katya sat alone at the Queen Victoria Pub, drank a glass of wine, then walked back the same route to her apartment. On Wednesday, she sat alone at an outdoor table in Republic Square for an hour. On Thursday, she ate a meal again by herself at a café on Merchant Street.

"Did she ever meet anyone?" Andre had asked.

"Not that I saw," the local man conveyed.

Unsatisfied, Andre considered the information. It was odd for Katerina Volkova to fall into this unremarkable evening pattern. Why? He didn't have a precise answer, but likewise, didn't mull over the problem too deeply. The plan was already in motion. Other elements were now in process of being nudged and adjusted. Kiril had been clear with his warning: The Maltese would act, most likely while the ships were docked. They had already seen a certain number of security men discreetly gather at the perimeter of the port. Both ships were scheduled to leave tomorrow. Tonight, therefore, was probably the last chance that he would have to tie up loose ends.

At 6:40 p.m., Andre received a text from the lookout watching Katya's apartment. On St. Lucia's Street, he recognized her from a distance. She was dressed in a leather coat, a dark gray wool cap, and a simple, tight-fitting black outfit beneath.

Andre walked four short blocks towards the still crowded Republic Square, its perimeter surrounded by dozens of café tables and chairs. Chalk signs announced daily specials—fresh oysters, rabbit stew, grilled squid in garlic. A violinist played classical music next to a clump of short olive trees and the small crowd that had gathered to listen. Parents disciplined unruly children as they swarmed an ice cream truck situated in front of an old, neoclassical government building. Restaurant hosts smiled to passing tourists to entice them to enter inside.

A waiter sat Katya at a café table on the edge of the crowd. Andre positioned himself at Kingsway Bar nearby, about twenty meters away from her, separated by diners enjoying mulled hot wine and tea on this chilly evening. Gas-flame heaters were strategically placed amongst the tables to add more comfort; their flames flickered orange inside metal cages.

Andre ordered a gin, Bombay, mixed with tonic. The waiter returned in a few minutes with his drink. He swallowed the drink in a few gulps, squeezed the quarter lime in his teeth to suck out the juice, and settled in. The next twenty-four hours would be decisive, he knew. Perses was one move ahead. Always. Soon, they all would be running around, like headless chickens. He would be able to do as he pleased while the others were distracted.

The waiter came again. Andre ordered another drink—whiskey, neat, no ice.

He lit a cigarette, inhaled, and watched Katerina Volkova there, sitting alone. He saw that she was older now, slightly thinner. Yet, she still possessed a kind of pale, fragile beauty that made her always seem somehow removed from this universe of established laws and immutable realities. It was a shame, really, what this business required, Andre thought. She was a rare flower, completely unique. She would struggle no doubt, drawing attention with screams if he couldn't do it quickly enough. A knife would be best—faster than strangling her and more satisfying with that first, penetrating thrust. Ahhhhh. She had blossomed into such a problem. The laws of nature demanded an end to this aberration. She should have died six years ago in Neuilly-sur-Seine, then again, at that Brooklyn auto shop. Andre was just the universe's gardening tool.

He flicked his cigarette butt on the floor, then crushed it with his heel.

The restaurant diners around Republic Square's perimeter thinned out after another hour. There were only a few people left at the outdoor café tables—old Maltese men with sad eyes, a few polite German tourists, a troupe of off-beat youths dressed in faux leather jackets, and tall biker boots. The waiters wiped down the tables and stacked chairs to end another typical evening. Pairs of female Japanese tourists in their prim, clean travel outfits finished snapping selfies. The English travelers began to drift back to their hotel rooms and cruise ship cabins.

Finally, Katerina Volkova rose from her table.

She started to walk away from the square, this time east, toward the tip of the peninsula where Valletta's old forts stood solidly against the sea, away from her apartment.

At this late hour, the lower end of Valletta near Fort St. Elmo stood largely dark. Few people lived now in the crumbling apartments and massive government buildings perched at the end of these streets. This part of the ancient city stayed very quiet at night. Andre followed her at a safe distance of about thirty meters, weaving behind the many parked cars along the narrow streets.

———— ✹ ————

Katya pretended to pick at her food while she sat at the small round table in the crowded middle of Republic Square. When the handsome, young Bulgarian waiter asked her if anything was wrong with the food she had ordered, she politely asked him just to take the plate away.

"Are you sure you don't want to order a different dish?" the waiter asked.

"No, I'm fine. Thank you."

"Where are you visiting from?" he asked, lingering there, trying to engage her in small talk.

"Different places. Thank you," she said with a smile, but clearly rebuffing his attempts.

"A glass of wine?" he asked, persisting.

"No. Not tonight."

The soft murmur of human activity buzzed around her. None of these people here tonight remotely understood what played out now in her head. She repeated the mantra that she had used to calm herself, to control her feelings, and to prepare her body. When the waiter left her alone again, Katya glanced at the marble statue of a middle-aged Queen Victoria sitting proud there in the middle of the square. Grand old Queen Victoria sat on her throne, dressed in flowing robes with a scepter in one hand and a small imperial crown on her head.[96] Katya reflected on Victoria's dour marble face. *How much the world has changed since your time, Queen. How much it hasn't changed at all.*

Katya kept her solitary evening walks a secret from Tim, Dmitry, and Paul. As much as they wanted to protect her, those men were focused elsewhere, planning their actions, following their targets. Tonight, as with the other nights, Katya had sensed the surveillance of her movements

---

96   Sculpted by Sicilian Giuseppe Valenti, the statue was erected in 1891 to commemorate Victoria's Golden Jubilee. The Queen is depicted wearing a shawl of Maltese lace draped over her shoulders, a tribute to her patronage of the local industry.

on the periphery. She knew other eyes watched. One of Bujega's men perhaps? If the eyes were friendly, tonight would pass uneventfully. If Dmitry's intelligence proved right, then the port operation would disrupt the enemy, and the chess move would advance the game. Her instincts told her otherwise. If she was right, then perhaps the night would unfold in a different manner. Someone would come. Someone would seek her out, stay close to her. It was cool tonight. She dressed for the evening. Her leather coat's thick outer layer would also offer some bodily protection if it came to that.

Katya only knew with certainty after she sat at the café table in Republic Square. Her heart raced faster when she realized it was him. There he was, on the edge of tonight's crowd, smoking a cigarette alone at a small table, watching her from a distance. He simmered, a kind of cancer brooding. Other people could not perceive this evil. He was just another anonymous human to them. The rest of the crowd went about their typical evening—talking, laughing, drinking, dreaming. Humanity seemed so distracted. Each person was imprisoned in a small subjective bubble, unaware of what Katya knew, and the sharp pain she felt.

Andre Gauthier—the same confident deceiver who came to her six years ago on the steps of a Sorbonne classroom. He used the name Rene then. How naive she was at the beginning with him. All his talk about changing the world had been mere deception to gain her trust. His smile and slick words lured her further. Eventually, without too much effort, she let slip away enough information to destroy her own family, and many other lives.

At last!

Katya rose from the table and began to walk.

She walked down Republic Street away from the lingering people at cafés and bars and the brighter lights. She passed a group of loud British men and their girlfriends exiting from another bar. They stumbled drunkenly, onward to some other late-night drinking hole in the opposite direction on lower Straight Street.

Katya turned down Archbishop Street, a narrow stone path between the tall buildings that lined this densely packed part of the old city. The balcony windows that jutted slightly out of the limestone buildings in the style of old Valletta were dark tonight. The massive wood gates of Valletta's many churches were all also shut, locked tight for the evening, divinely sealed.

Katya walked toward the harbor, downward along a set of well-worn stone stairs carved into the sloping, narrow street. She smelled the fresh salt air, heard her own footsteps. She passed a statue of St. George hewn into the corner of a building on the corner of Archbishop and St. Ursula streets. George pressed his foot on the devil's neck and wielded a long sword. The devil's face—contorted pain and confusion. The hero's face—calm and certain. Artwork left here by the anonymous past to guide me tonight, she briefly thought. *Give me strength, St. George.*

The narrow street opened to the Grand Harbor at the tip of the peninsula. Scattered lights from the harbor's opposite shore below cast a dull blue haze along the ocean's surface. Old Valletta returned to its ancient medieval self. At night, the timeworn city became colder, harder—a dark place that merely tolerated the living of today's world to scurry about during the daylight hours. The night, however, returned the stones, churches, and statues back to the dead. Fort St. Elmo, empty now, guarded Malta's deepwater harbor, while a half-moon hovered above, joined by stars in the translucent sky.

Katya walked alone further along the harbor's promenade. She paused between a row of empty buildings and a wide stone wall along the edge of the harbor-side promenade.

Stay calm, conserve energy, let him come.

She stood just outside the locked iron gate that led to the Lower Barrakka Gardens. Inside the park, a Romanesque monument to a long-dead British admiral stood dark beneath a cluster of palm trees.[97] Below the wall, a sheer limestone cliff dropped down some hundred meters to the waterfront below. The second of the harbor's great forts, St. Angelo, stood in the distance on the other harbor's other side, its angular mass lit up by pinprick lights set upon its corners. A few lights shone atop smaller boats moored along the water's opposite side; a massive, eight-story cruise ship sparkled further away, nestled in the watery fingers of the harbor's inner marina.

Katya turned her head just slightly to the right as a male figure trailing her grew closer. Finally, they were alone together in a dark corner, at the edge of the Grand Harbor, the night's vast emptiness and the open sea beyond.

Andre crossed the street, no longer hiding his approach. For an instant, Andre paused, doubting himself, unclear if she recognized him. His cunning, animal eyes scanned the moment, looking for shadows, traps, other protectors. He saw none. He took two steps closer. An object dropped into his right hand from inside his sleeve.

---

97   Vice Admiral Sir Alexander John Ball, a prominent British naval officer and the first Civil Commissioner of Malta.

A knife as expected. Just like in Paris. Good.

Andre took three more steps forward. Katya backed away from the park's fence to a space behind a small wooden kiosk. In Krav Maga, aggression and overconfidence were always vulnerabilities. Eli Gold's voice spoke to her again as he had once before in the shade of tall California palms: Focus on the high-percentage moves. Use the aggressor's energy. Katya felt inside the lining of her jacket. She touched the ivory handle of the small switchblade knife and brought it out in her right hand. She pressed the switchblade's release button. The three-inch, double-edged blade locked in place.

Andre tightened his shoulders, now sealed in his decision. He lunged at her first with a stabbing motion, the tip of his blade pointed at her torso. Katya turned, grasped his forearm, and struck hard with a short, violent burst. Her explosive move isolated his elbow, rattling his nervous system.

Andre recoiled and stepped back, startled by her quick response. The blow against his elbow hurt, and nearly caused him to drop his weapon. Her leather coat was zipped up now, sleeves protecting her torso and arms. She was ready. This wouldn't be so easy as he predicted.

He came after her again, this time slashing with powerful arcs at her head. His arms cut wide slices in the air. She tactically retreated, moved her switchblade from her right to left hand, and created distance. Andre moved closer, extended his leg, waiting for her to thrust her little weapon at him. Instead, Katya slid forward in a graceful motion, and went for his right knee with a fast, sharp kick of her hard boot heel. He leaned away in pain. She quickly kicked again at the same leg to press her advantage, hitting his shin.

Andre came forward again.

She crouched forward, spun, then with a fast jab, lunged forward far enough to plunge her switchblade just below the collarbone, pricking him, although he blocked the full force of her swing with his free arm. She missed his jugular but punctured an inch below his neck. Again, she moved back to create distance.

He kept moving forward, step by step, frustrated, while she moved back, catlike.

Andre's face wrinkled in anger. Blood stains now soaked his white shirt, growing larger.

Andre thrust at her one more time, but this time without his initial strength. Her leather coat flank blocked his knife. She kicked hard at his right shin. Now, he slowed.

He lunged again and again; she jabbed twice more, quickly into his right torso and just below the armpit. Two more shallow wounds.

He grunted and stepped back awkwardly.

Reeling, Katya moved inside, trapped his arm, and with a wide arch, swung her three-inch steel blade hard at the back of his neck. The blade pierced deep, just above the trapezoid muscles and directly into his spine. She released her grip, the switchblade's ivory handle sticking out like a tiny flag. Done. Andre's knife clanked upon the stone floor. His limbs stiffened. He contorted into a violent expression of agony against the stone railing. Then in a kind of awkward, uncontrolled movement, his legs went limp, and he collapsed onto the hard granite pavement.

A black, viscous pool of blood gathered beneath his body and spread out on the ground. She watched Andre struggle, his mouth now filling up with blood and bile.

Katya walked closer, took her knife out from the back of his neck, retracted the blade, and put it back into the inner lining of her jacket.

She leaned closer, inches away from Andre's ear. The blood was oozing from the deep death wound she had driven hard into his spine.

"*Te vaya piasinca spheta.* Your song is over," she whispered.

Andre didn't answer. His eyes drifted downward. The handsome, confident face that had haunted her for years, slowly grew pale, and finally lay inert, eyes open, lips twisted.

Katya rose, stepped back. She controlled her breathing, at each breath calming down her mind and body.

One.

Two.

Three.

Four.

Conserve energy.

She looked around at the night's emptiness. No witnesses. The fight didn't take long. The quiet, external world seemed the same as it had been just five minutes ago. The harbor lights shone. The domes of medieval churches peeked over the rooftops. The half-moon hovered midway in the sky, its light reflecting on the smooth, black water. The ancient forts stood mute. All the same.

Katya breathed in the salty humid night. She shoved her bloody hands tight in her pockets, then stepped quickly over the street stones back into the darkness of old Valletta.

21

TIM HASTINGS looked at his watch. 2:13 a.m. Almost time.

Malta Freeport was quiet in the cool early morning. A bevy of tall cranes surrounded the vessels at various berths along the quay. Stacks of steel containers stored in modular fashion cluttered the holding area. Crews at the north end of the port continued their unloading routines on an around-the-clock schedule, although the early morning shift was still a small fraction of what was moved during the day. The berths were at ninety-percent capacity with ships flagged under twenty different countries.

It was fifteen minutes before the tightly bound, well-planned, operation was scheduled to begin. Success, Tim knew, would combine swift action with a sufficient show of force to intimidate any unknown elements on either of the two targeted ships.

Tim felt confident. The team of twenty was now in place, a dozen officers to board the ships and the rest ready to cordon off this section of the port. Bugeja had put together an experienced team, well versed in search-and-seizure protocols. Last year, most of this same team had conducted a half dozen similar exercises to ferret out illegal narcotics and oil exports. All these earlier efforts went smoothly without shots fired. Bugeja organized his hazmat team just outside the seizure zone with orders to intervene if the boarding team discovered any issues. The only potential downside tonight was possible exposure to nerve toxins if any of these idiots decided to play dirty. Like the others, Tim wore the heavy Kevlar vest and goggles, a gas mask strapped at his waist, just in case. He also recognized the risk if the alleged chemical weapons were not properly handled after the men seized the containers. They should have plenty of time to carefully examine the contents after securing the ships.

Tim's operational involvement meant that the Maltese could claim this as a joint security operation. Hastings had also introduced more safeguards. He asked for the US Coast Guard's cutter, the Hamilton, to patrol international waters south of Malta. The Hamilton was now close enough to react to any unexpected naval activities if tonight's actions caused any saber-rattling from the Russians or Libyans. Tim didn't expect problems, but these navies were always flexing their muscles now, looking for small excuses to create uncomfortable incidents. It was a good deterrent, a show of strength that the US Navy meant business when it came to enforcing bans against the transport and storage of chemical weapons.

2:30 a.m.

"Let's go," the Maltese team leader said to him.

Two squads of six each moved quietly to the ship's respective gangplanks. The men quietly ascended the gangplanks, moving up to the main first decks of both ships berthed next to one another. Two men each in front carried bulletproof shields.

Tim quickly crossed the gangplank onto the deck of the Archemede. He moved just behind the shields put up by the two MSS leads.

So far, so good. No topside resistance.

Two officers moved up a ladder to the ship's bridge. Tim moved down the stairs to the ship's first level, leading two of the team members with him. They moved methodically below deck, calling out warnings from compartment to compartment and steadily working from the ship's bow back to its stern. Tim held his automatic weapon ready, although pointed down to avoid unnecessary provocation with any of the remaining crew members they expected to meet beneath deck.

Three Russian crew members emerged from their sleeping quarters, hands in the air. The men were in T-shirts, jeans, and boxer shorts, apparently surprised to be confronted now by a security team in full tactical gear this early in the morning. One of the Maltese soldiers barked out instructions in English, ordering them up topside to the ship's main deck.

Tim led the way down the steep metal stairs to the second level. The door to the main interior hull was unlocked. The vehicle holding room was there. Inside the holding area, he saw four armored cars lined up in a single column. The cars were parked facing a lift area with an elaborate pulley system through the currently closed ceiling door. These were the vehicles driven from the Russian border under armed escort; these would hold their prize.

"Open these," Tim ordered.

The Maltese explosives expert quickly placed a wad of gray C4[98] on the rear door of the rear-most armored car. The man pushed the detonation rod into the C4 putty until it stuck out like a cocktail straw. The four of them sheltered behind a row of heavy metal canisters. The officer yelled a final warning then flipped the detonation switch.

---

98   A highly stable, clay-like plastic explosive developed in the late 1950s; composed mainly of specialized plasticizers that allow it to be molded by hand into any shape.

Clouds of white smoke cleared. The clean blast took off the latch and handle.

Tim tipped open the door and looked inside the back of the rear-most armored car.

He held his thumb down for the other team members to see.

Empty.

The Maltese explosives expert used the same process for the C4 explosives on the back of the next armored car—stick, shelter, detonate.

The rear padlock on the second armored car blew off, scattering bits of steel.

Again, Tim looked inside the car.

Thumbs down once more.

Tim removed his goggles and wiped off his forehead. It was smoldering hot this far beneath deck.

"We go down one more level," he told them.

Tim led the two other officers to descend a narrow ladder to the lower deck.

Tim moved down a long narrow corridor just ahead of the two Maltese security officers. He held his 9 mm Beretta handgun tightly in two hands as he entered a small, interior locker room. He saw a Russian flag hanging on the far wall—red, white, blue stripes. Some Cyrillic words were scrawled across the flag's white stripe in dark red ink. The words were illuminated by a spotlight attached to the ceiling, drawing his eyes.

Intrigued by the flag, Tim walked forward into the empty room.

Tim felt the slight pressure on his lower leg. Looking down, he saw the thin wire about six inches above the floor. Trip wire, he realized just as a high-pitched whirring sound broke the silence.

Click.

The rush of heat and an infernal cloud blasted out of a metal box rigged just inside the room. The blast tore into Tim's face, enveloping him in flames and hurtling him back some ten meters.

Tim's vision went black. Then after the powerful concussion, he regained some awareness, at first disoriented and confused. He was on the ground. He couldn't feel his body below the waist. Bits of hot metal had torn into his legs, paralyzing him. Now he was lying against a metal steel floor. A hot fire blazed in the room. The other two men were both down, inert in front of a row of plastic jugs.

He watched the flames, unable to move.

Not like this, not like this, Tim repeated to himself.

There was no pain now, only a sinking feeling, a kind of bitter regret, not to die an old man in some distant future, but rather at this instant, now. He was going to just burn here. There would never be any more new experiences, joys, thoughts, sensations. A bitter, confused swirl of regret surged just a few seconds more before the row of gasoline jugs exploded with violent finality. Then, the flames engulfed Tim Hastings' brain and body, consuming his vital essence and personality, ending all his possibilities in a violent flash.

The explosion on the third floor of the Archemede's forward deck rocked the ship. Smoke and noxious flames ran down the maze of interior hallways and reinforced steel rooms. The inferno spread, as if by careful design, up through the third floor's pipelines, to other strategically placed incendiary devices that triggered more, even larger, secondary explosions into the mainline diesel valve connected to two fuel storage tanks.

A massive, booming sound accompanied the fiery orange cloud that spewed up thirty meters from the main front deck. The stern of the Archemede shuddered.

Five hundred meters away, from a nearby hill across the bay at Marsaxlokk, Dmitry Medkov pressed the binoculars against his forehead. He watched the billowing explosion rock the Archemede's deck. Tall flames licked up against the dark, early morning sky.

It was nearly twenty minutes before fire trucks swarmed onto the dock, spraying water from powerful hoses while other men gathered around the burning ship and looked on helplessly.

Dmitry put down his binoculars and bowed his head. His lower back flared with incredible pain, and his hands tingled with a certain dejected recognition of his mistake.

22

PAUL WOKE to Bella Grech's voice speaking fast, Arabic-sounding Maltese into her mobile phone. He had nodded off sometime late last night in the Honda's back seat. The yellow morning sun was already peaking above the angular rooftops. A few residents lower down on the street were opening their windows to greet another typical, breezy seaside morning.

Paul checked his watch—7:15 a.m., two hours of sleep, enough for now.

"Trouble last night at the Port," Grech said after she put down her phone. "Time to move."

"Any actions at the house?"

"Doesn't matter. Orders to go in now," Grech said.

Paul trailed Grech by a few meters after she exited the Honda and moved closer to the limestone house. Joe Vella waited for them at a side entrance. The two Maltese officers now dangled their silver badges outside their shirts.

Grech and Vella spoke gruffly to each other in Maltese. The big officer took bolt cutters to the chains that locked the outer gate. Then, they moved on quickly to a side door that led into the house. Vella kicked open the rusted doorknob with his boot heel. Grech slipped in first, sidearm drawn in two hands.

The house smelled of mildew and dust, as if the place had not been lived in for some time. The two officers moved quietly, Grech making hand signals back to her partner to check the rooms. Paul, without a weapon, continued slowly behind them as they moved in sequence throughout the first-floor rooms. The house was sparsely furnished—old television, some chairs in the main sitting area, concrete floors with bits of debris in the corners. The bathroom was molded over as if unused for quite some time.

Grech made her way up a flight of narrow stairs to the second floor, stepping carefully, cat-like, upon old wooden floorboards. Hearing nothing, Paul followed her up the stairs to the four empty bedrooms. The beds were springboards only, no pillows or mattresses.

"Down here," Vella called to Grech from the first floor. They went down. Joe stood in front of an open cedarwood door at the back of the house. He pointed out the limestone steps that led down to a dark underground passage carved out of the stone.

"It's a tunnel. From the war. Common in old houses like this. They must have left this way last night," Grech said.

Vella took out a small flashlight from his utility kit and descended into the opening. He bowed his head to fit down the passage of unevenly carved stairs. They descended cautiously. The basement tunnel was cut out of soft limestone bedrock beneath the residential houses. After about twenty meters, the first tunnel opened to a bigger underground space with exposed pipes running parallel with the tunnel. They passed a series of alcoves that long ago were cut by hand.

"These are from the war,"[99] Grech whispered.

A sequence of rusted doors at the top of stairs, now locked with large padlocks, led up to the basements of other houses. Another twenty meters through a declining tunnel brought them to a flight of metal stairs and an exit door.

They emerged through this door into an arched chamber that appeared to be a converted wine cellar. Paul saw some two dozen wood barrels stacked one atop the other. A thin sliver of light from outside shone down into the cellar through two small windows near the ceiling. A wood door, now sealed shut, led to the outside.

Paul smelled a faint odor of organic decay just before he spotted Nessrin's body splayed out in the corner. The fat Libyan was lying face down in a pool of his own blood, his black hair tangled around a small bullet hole in the back of his skull. The exit wound had ripped open his left check.

A video camera stood on a tripod just behind Nessrin's corpse. A tiny red light below the lens glowed bright. The camera was on, recording them.

Grech went closer to the tripod. She looked deep into the lens. In response, the camera lens refracted slightly; the lens autofocused on her face, like an animal squinting down its prey.

"Knock it down," Paul shouted over. "He's watching us."

---

99   The Maltese carved a vast network of tunnels during World War II primarily to survive the relentless aerial bombing by Axis powers, as Malta was one of the most heavily bombed places on Earth. Between 1940 and 1943, over 17,000 tons of bombs were dropped on the island.

Grech obeyed, pushing over the tripod. The camera crashed on the hard stone floor.

Paul heard a faint click, followed by a steady, malignant hiss.

The sound came from someplace behind them, near a row of wine barrels at the far corner of the room. Paul looked closer—a small chrome canister in the corner spewed out a light mist from a tiny metal muzzle. The malicious, snake-like hiss continued.

Paul held his panic in check as the gas canister filled the sealed room with acrid fumes. He knew the science: sarin targeted neuromuscular junctions, blocking enzymes that relaxed muscles. Twitching quickly became paralysis; most victims suffocated.

Not good. We don't have time, a minute at most, Paul realized.

The gas hit Vella first. The big man coughed in small gasps and then more loudly. He dropped to his knees as the nerve agent went to work on his neuromuscular system. He shuddered there, confused, frightened, unable to breath.

Bella Grech smashed the two small windows at the far corner with the butt of her revolver. She also coughed, seeking fresh air, grasping at the collar of her shirt.

Stay calm. Think. You are still breathing. The antidote in your bloodstream is working. You are protected. Help them.

Paul pulled again at the main door that led to the outside. Locked, it didn't budge. The windows were very small, not enough. The only viable exit was back into the tunnel.

Vella—too big to carry. Grech—maybe.

Paul moved quickly, picking up Grech from where she crouched near him, struggling for air. He grabbed her arms and slung her body over his back.

Paul's throat and nose stung as he carried her back into the limestone tunnel. The antidote kept his muscles from seizing, but still he felt disoriented as the nerve agent attacked his cells. Paul struggled, not sure if the defense in his bloodstream would be enough. Limbs weak, eyes burning, he moved as if floating underwater without full bodily control.

He forced his legs to keep moving, staggering back into the tunnel's confined darkness. Each step burned. His fingers dug into Grech's thin arms to keep her on his back as he marched forward.

Midway back to the limestone house, Grech's body slid off. She slid off his back on to the tunnel's dusty, gray surface.

"Almost there," Paul said.

"It burns," Grech whispered, struggling to breathe.

Paul rested for a few seconds before he again picked her up, careful not to knock her head against the hard stone walls as he traversed the final section of the cramped tunnel.

Up the stairs, back into the house. Just a few more meters. A few more steps.

One.

Two.

Three.

Four.

Five.

Finally, Paul slammed the basement tunnel door shut and dropped Bella down in the corner. She slumped there on the concrete floor, her limbs slack.

"Take deep breaths," Paul told her, he himself lightheaded and disoriented.

Bella Grech didn't answer. Her tangled black hair hid her face.

"Come on, breathe deeply," Paul said again.

Again, no answer.

"Hey."

Paul touched her cheek and tilted her face upward.

Dead eyes stared back, frozen. Bella's mouth was hideously twisted as if attempting to form one last rebellion before her suffocation. Her lips were curled in agony, unable to form a final protest against a bitter, sudden, and senseless end.

23

AARON BUGEJA didn't think the situation could get any worse. Six of his security team members were already dead, killed in a series of explosions that began someplace deep inside the Archemede's hull and spread quickly to the deck and the ship's two main fuel tanks. His murdered men were seasoned officers, personally selected. Each was a colleague, a fellow Maltese compatriot. They trusted him with their lives, but still he was stupid enough to let them all foolishly walk into this disaster. The pain from the mistake had already started in the form of an intense migraine. It would likely hurt a lifetime, he suspected.

As the morning unfolded, the Maltese security crew opened containers on the Libyan ship. Some containers held low-value products; most of them were entirely empty.

Nothing. Not a goddam thing. All for nothing.

Maltese operational command phoned in more bad news at noon—two plainclothes officers asphyxiated in a botched raid in Sliema with the possible use of a high potency nerve agent in a densely packed residential area.

Aaron mentally circled through his options before he called his childhood friend, Jo Muscat, the prime minister. He dispatched a hazmat team currently active at the port to this new location, then escalated the threat alert to pull in C Company, another branch of the Maltese military. Absolutely, under all circumstances, the prime minister stressed, Aaron needed to keep details very quiet. A public panic would do no one any good, and such a scandal might have a lasting impact on the island's carefully managed reputation for safety and security.

By 2:30 p.m., Malta's anti-terrorism forces sealed off the neighborhood area, surrounding the limestone house with a flotilla of unmarked white vans. The hazmat team, fortunately, quickly concluded that the nerve agent gas had been contained underground. Although deadly when it was first released, sarin's toxicity deteriorated fast after being released into the air. The unsuspecting Sliema residents were told that the crews were meant to fix an underground gas valve that had damaged electrical wires and was emitting noxious fumes. Bugeja's security office reinforced this cover story when a new reporter picked up the story on the local evening news. The story passed by with only a minor notice, drawing even less attention than the more notable separate industrial accident involving a container ship at the Freeport docks.

"Son of a bitch," Martin Hines whispered to himself as he scanned the line item on his secure terminal screen, timestamped 8:19 a.m. EST. Hines had just finished a morning double-shot latte when he absorbed the update. Once again, his planned daily schedule was shot to hell. Dinner with his wife was out, although this loss wasn't a bad blow considering she was such an unreliable cook. At least he could pick up sushi later tonight in Arlington and flirt again with the pretty Japanese waitress there.

Hines called over to the Pentagon's image center. A second lieutenant supplied him details of the available satellite coverage that he had put in place these last few days to support Tim Hastings' operation. The most recent images from one hour ago showed black plumes of smokes still rising from the smoldering fires on the Archemede's deck.

Hines shifted his attention to managing the expected diplomatic blowback issues. This snafu probably wasn't big enough to hit the major press outlets. The damage was manageable: one agency casualty, eight dead Maltese, an angry US ambassador, and a flummoxed prime minister of a very small, unimportant EU country asking for answers. Not too bad, all things considered, he concluded.

Still, Hines mused, this was more than just bad intel. The operation had been blocked by design, a purposeful feint. They didn't seize any of Haftar's alleged weapons; and the Russians had clearly, unambiguously set them up. Hines was frustrated, yes, but these sorts of low-level operational failures offered teachable moments.

Hines picked up the phone. Jo Richards answered after two rings.

"What went wrong?" Jo asked, needing no context.

"I'm looking at nine casualties, including one of ours."

"The cargo?"

"Nothing."

"Told you he was the wrong guy for this, Marty."

"Save the postmortem, Jo. Can you help?"

"I don't know. Is there satellite coverage?"

"Some from the Pentagon."

"I'll start there. Tell them I'm coming."

"Don't make it worse," Hines said.

Three hours after the call, Jo Richards found her way to the European situation room buried deep inside the six million square feet of the world's largest office building.

Lieutenant Commander James Bedford was the senior-most officer on duty in the Pentagon's satellite surveillance center. Hines had called Bedford an hour before, alerting him to expect a female intelligence officer, and asked him as a professional courtesy to give her what she needed with respect to last night's coverage of the Mediterranean theater. Interest piqued, Bedford acknowledged the call, cleared some mundane reporting tasks, and waited for his visitor. Sometimes Langley's younger intelligence analysts were quite alluring, albeit usually in a nerdy, intellectual manner. Bedford was, therefore, surprised and very disappointed by the appearance of a ghoulish human being who slipped quietly into the main operations center at about 9:00 p.m. He wasn't quite sure of this creature's gender as it shuffled in with its cane.

Josephine Richards was dressed in a loose-fitting, tan outfit that looked like a medical gown. She leaned heavily on her cane to prop up her body above two spider-thin appendages that appeared to be shaped like human legs. Large, inflamed eyes animated the creature's gaunt face. A cluster of throbbing knotted blue veins ran across its bald head and down its forehead. Translucent skin, like rice paper, revealed the workings of nerves and sinews on two gnarled hands. The creature came at Bedford like a living zombie with one foot out of a grave and ready perhaps to jump back in. Bedford blinked twice when the creature spoke in a normal, professional voice rather than some guttural sound of a rotting dead soul. He greeted the strange ghoul, then brought it to a private workstation at one of the side rooms next to the main operations room. The ghoul put its walking cane down, sat, and fumbled to put on a set of reading glasses while other Defense Department intelligence staff sat at their workstations, managing routines matters.

"How can we help?" Bedford asked.

"I need eyes on Malta," Jo said.

"Looking for what?"

"Nothing obvious. Maybe a truck or a small plane. Most likely, a commercial marine vessel. Fishing trawler, maybe."

"We don't track commercial fishing trawlers. There are hundreds in that part of the Mediterranean, every night." Bedford explained.

"Give me a decent image analyst. It will be easier," Jo said.

"I'll check," Bedford replied to the creature, then left the alcove in search of a solution. Twenty minutes later, Caroline Pham, the Department of Defense's south European satellite image analyst joined Jo in the small room. Pham sat in front of a large image screen. The 24-year-old analyst had just arrived at her duty station an hour previously. She expected a normal shift involving a quiet review of established target sites and perhaps some slack time to talk to one of the better-looking technicians who seemed to be working up his courage to ask her out on a first date. Instead, Pham faced this creature.

"Nice to meet you," the ghoul said.

"Yes, ma'am," Pham replied. "I understand you might need some help?"

"I do. Be patient. We might be here awhile," Jo said.

"Sure. It's my job. Coffee before we start?" Pham asked.

Coffee, no. I've had enough coffee for a lifetime, Jo thought. She looked at Pham, realizing that the smooth-faced analyst knew nothing about how a tainted Turkish coffee nearly killed her. *What do any of them here know about me?* Pham was just a fresh young face, an eager cog in the government's machine, doing her little job.

"No thanks. Caffeine gives me the jitters. But you go ahead," Jo said.

"Yes, ma'am. Bottled water perhaps?"

"Water would be nice."

"Yes, ma'am. I'll get us some."

After she came with the drinks, Caroline booted up her imaging system. She felt the zombie creature's bulbous inflamed eyes study her as she typed out the system's coded commands. They went through the satellite photos, sitting close together. Pham flicked through the images—adjusting the resolution to bring out different details from the visual data gathered by the four military satellites that had arrayed their sensors on this part of the Earth. They scanned through hundreds of images for more than three hours before Pham brought one photo to Jo's attention. Spysat 9 captured the view of a boat anchored near Malta's shore, about half a mile from the Sliema location where the Maltese security team reported the sarin incident.

"Medium-sized fishing boat, most likely a deep-sea tuna long-liner," Pham suggested. "Common for Malta, Sicily, and Sardinia. If you look closely at this one, though, it has modern engines and a new radar system. Also, most tuna long-liners don't anchor this close to shore."

Caroline adjusted the resolution further down to less than five meters. Spysat 9 didn't take the best high-resolution photos, she explained, but good enough. She flicked her fingers over the keyboard and zoomed in to the highest resolution available. The overhead image was grainy; Pham focused her trained eyes on the various shadows. A man stood on the trawler's deck holding what appeared to be a semi-automatic weapon. Another figure positioned at the stern also carried what looked like a rifle.

"See them?"

"I do," Jo confirmed.

"Could be other smugglers," Pham said.

"Just for tuna?"

"Could be. Illegal fishing is big business," Pham offered.

"When was this photo taken?" Jo asked.

"Yesterday, 9:13 a.m. local time."

"And now?"

Pham flicked her fingers to check more recent photos of the same area.

"No ship," Pham said. "We can rotate for another visual, but not for another two hours. There is also cloud cover now. Hard to get more detail."

"It's enough. Nice job," the creature said. The ghoul rose from her seat and stretched her arms, before she took her cane again and shuffled out of the small room.

The Pentagon's communication center put Jo Richards through first to the US Embassy, and then via a mobile link to the operational team in Malta, specifically the man in charge, Aaron Bugeja. Jo quickly introduced herself before she launched into her assessment.

"We still may have a play," Jo asserted. "We've spotted a ship just north of the Grand Harbor."

"Your intel was wrong before. What makes you think you have it right on this?" Bugeja challenged.

"This is solid."

"Nothing I've heard since the beginning has been solid," Aaron said, unable to hide his frustration.

"I hear you. Shall we argue about it, or get these assholes?" Jo replied in an icy but calm tone.

Aaron paused.

"What else?" he asked.

"The boat has moved in the last twelve hours. We lost a live visual."

"If you are right, they won't stay here in Maltese waters," he replied.

"How much sea can you cover?" Jo prodded.

"Nothing. I can't scramble Maltese patrol ships outside territorial waters." Aaron explained.

"Can't or won't?"

"Not for this," Aaron said. Jo could hear he was already in shut-down mode.

"What do you suggest, then?" she asked.

"Italy would be easiest. Also, potentially Tunis to the west. Have you contacted your other man here?" Aaron asked.

"Not yet. How is he?" Jo said, curious, but feigning her ignorance of whom exactly Bugeja was talking about.

"He's asked to be released from our hospital. Incredible to be alive, given his nerve gas exposure."

"One lucky son of a bitch," Jo continued.

Bugeja paused for a moment to retrieve the telephone number for the Mater Dei hospital. "Call this number," he said. "Tell them you want to speak with the American. My team will put you through to Paul Drake."

PURSUIT

Isole
Eolie
Mediterranean Sea
Calabria
Palermo
Messina
Cefalù
Marsala
Etna
Catania
Agrigento
Villa
Fontesa
Siracusa
Pozzallo
Malta
SICILY

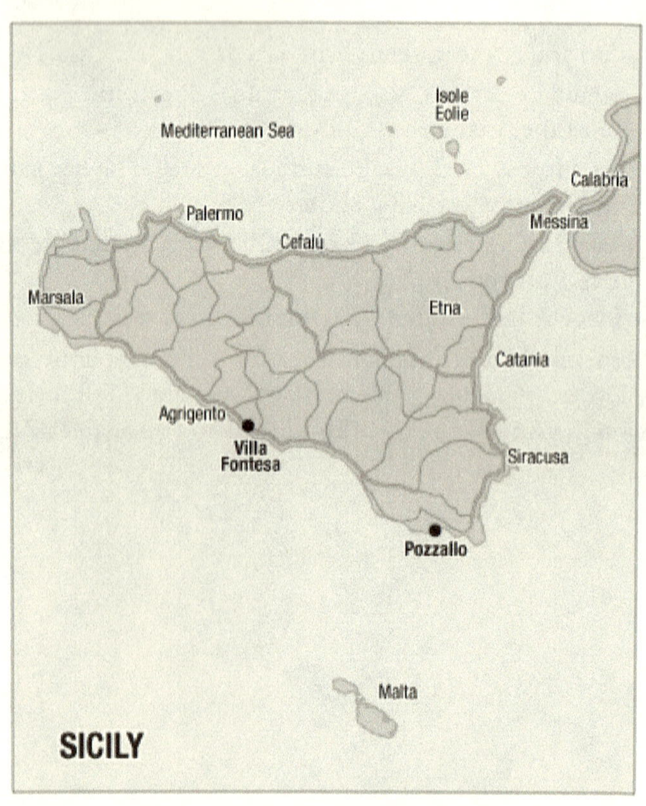

24

"INTERNATIONAL CALL for you," the female police officer said to Paul as she entered his corner hospital room at Mater Dei. The officer handed over her small Android phone, then stood back at a distance near the door, watching him with suspicious eyes. Paul assumed that she had been told about what happened in the tunnel; now they all treated him with suspicion, switching to Maltese instead of English to talk about him in his presence and watching him closely. Bella Grech was a well-liked officer and always careful.

Paul's body ached. He coughed first, not sure if he could speak. The doctors had pumped him with saline fluids for the past six hours. His throat was inflamed, his bones felt brittle, and his lower spine hurt as if it had been compressed under a heavy, hot iron. The vomiting started last night, persisting for hours, a side effect of the nanoparticle drug's defense. He loosened his neck before he put the small mobile phone to his ear.

"How are you, cowboy?" a woman said.

Paul paused, mentally adjusting to the voice.

"Jo?"

"Been a moment," she said.

"It has. I didn't think I'd hear your voice again."

"Such little faith," Jo said.

"Nothing to do with faith, just science. Doctors didn't give much hope."

"What do doctors know? You should be dead too, I'm told."

"Not yet, thanks to your green pills."

"Ah, yes. Now, that is real science put to good use."

Jo spoke quickly about what she knew: Tim Hastings killed, angry Maltese politicians, a promising clue taken from Spysat 9. Always charging ahead, even from the grave, Paul thought.

"He was here, Jo. I saw him." Paul said.

"Zoidze?" Jo asked.

"He was at the house. He killed the Libyan, and watched us die through a camera."

"We still have time. If you are strong enough, change clothes, get yourself to our embassy. I'll let our station there know you are coming."

"I'll do that," he said.

"And Paul…" Jo continued. "… good to hear your voice. Keep moving, cowboy. This isn't over," she said, then hung up.

Paul handed the Android phone back to the Maltese officer. He splashed cold water on his face, combed his hair, and put his clothes back on. Mean stares from the police officers milling around in the hospital followed him as he left. Outside the hospital's entrance, he took the lead taxi waiting in the passenger line. The ride to the US embassy took twenty minutes along the main highway inside Malta's arid interior. A constellation of different Maltese flags—a white cross against a red background, a red cross against white—waved atop tall flagpoles above the densely clustered houses along the main road.

A muscular US Marine security officer greeted Paul when he first entered the embassy's main gate. The big, young Marine with a sharp crewcut made small talk as he led Paul through a series of secure doors to a small waiting room on the ground floor. A coffee table in the center of the room had copies of National Geographic and a glossy book on the Battle of the Chesapeake, when Maltese sailors helped Washington defeat the British. Paul sat alone for ten minutes before a young female officer in a slightly oversized black blazer and loose, beige suit pants entered. She smiled widely as she introduced herself as Susan Collins, the embassy's senior consular officer. Paul rose and shook her hand. The American flag pin on the lapel of her blazer was slightly twisted.

"Sorry, I'm a mess today. I've been on calls all morning," Susan said.

"The right calls?"

"For you, yes. Feels good to break a half dozen protocols before noon. Shall we?" Susan said. She swiped an access card to open a secure door, then gestured for Paul to follow her down a flight of stairs.

Susan unlocked access to another door at the base of the stairs. They took another long tunnel to a cool, dry room with a metal cage inside that held the embassy's arsenal.

"Since the Benghazi attack on Ambassador Stevens,[100] even our smaller regional embassies have been relatively well stocked," Susan mentioned as she entered another code to unlock the cage.

---

100   On September 11, 2012, U.S. Ambassador J. Christopher Stevens and three other Americans were killed during a coordinated attack by Islamic militants on the U.S. Consulate and a nearby CIA Annex in Benghazi, Libya.

"Whatever you have will need to be good enough. I can't carry much," Paul replied. He walked into the cage and methodically looked over the weapons and tactical paraphernalia arrayed on the arsenal's steel shelves—Glock 17 pistols, grenades, semi-automatic rifles, ammunition clips. He showed Susan each tagged item for her inventory checklist before placing each inside the various pockets of a military-grade tarpaulin rucksack.

They headed back up the stairs. The gear was heavy, nearly a hundred pounds, and his legs and arms still felt weak. Susan only smiled, avoiding small talk she knew was off limits anyways. An older, heavy-set woman waited for them on the ground floor. She approached Susan for a brief conversation in whispers. Susan took an unmarked manila envelope from the woman and handed it over to Paul.

"Last item on my list. Some cash," Susan said.

"I appreciate it," Paul said stoically as he took the envelope.

"I'm just a local pharmacist filling a prescription," Susan said. "Let's get you out through the back. No cameras."

Susan led him through the embassy hallways, the rucksack slung on his back. He left through a secure back gate that led out to a small parking lot. Once he was alone, he opened the envelope: five $10,000 bundles of crisp, newly minted hundred-dollar bills. Should be enough for now.

Another taxi took him back to Valletta, again past the many red and white Maltese flags fluttering proudly above the confused maze of dull, flat limestone houses. The driver careened quickly through the narrow streets that ran along the waterfront and led finally back to the Volkov's corporate apartment on Old Mint Road.

Katya held him tightly before she let him through the door. He put down the rucksack, embracing her with two arms, his face against her slender neck. She smelled clean, freshly showered.

"How do you feel?" Katya whispered in his ear.

"Never better." Paul said.

"Are you sure? They told us nothing."

"The pills worked. Some aftereffects, but nothing to worry you," Paul demurred.

"What about the Maltese?"

"There were two with me. I couldn't help them."

"I'm sorry, Paul."

Dmitry sat at the kitchen table; he had been eating toast with butter and jam. He peered up at Paul when he entered, his eyes hard.

"Go ahead and eat something," Dmitry said. He began to cut a wedge of cheese with a small knife.

Paul sat at the table. He was feeling less queasy now and took a bite of the dry toast and then some of the hard cheese. He chewed without tasting any of the food.

"Katerina should also tell you about her night," Dmitry said.

"What about it?" Paul asked.

"Come sit down, Katerina," Dmitry insisted. "Tell Paul about your eventful evening."

Katya sat, sipped the black tea that Dmitry poured for her, and described her actions near the Lower Barrakka Gardens the night before. She spoke calmly, in a clinical manner, as if her lethal confrontation with Andre involved another person altogether and she was merely reporting it as a curious set of detached facts as one might report the results of a science experiment.

"Why?" Paul asked angrily after she finished. "Why would you be so unprofessional to confront him alone?"

"I wasn't sure it was Andre until I saw him up close. You would have stopped me, and I was always in control," she said.

"If he was better armed?" Paul said.

"He wasn't," she replied.

"*Ochen Glupy*. Very foolish," Dmitry muttered.

"It's done. You should both thank me," she said coldly. "What's next?"

Paul showed them the satellite image Jo had sent to his phone. Dmitry squinted at the small screen. Another heated conversation ensued on the reliability of this next lead. Katya and Dmitry switched back and forth from Russian to English as they debated.

"It's not much, but we must follow while we still have time."

"Follow where?" Paul pressed.

"If I were Bogan, the logical choice would be to get off this island to the nearest next country," Dmitry said. "I wouldn't risk running into the US Navy in open waters. Therefore, I would go someplace close—Sicily or Tunisia. It's a coin toss between the two. I have a few contacts in Tunisia. I will fly there tomorrow and see if they can help. You both go to Sicily."

———— ✱ ————

The following morning, Dmitry left early while it was still dark, informing Paul that Valentine planned to meet him at the airport in Tunis.

They would be in Tunis by early afternoon and would send any new relevant information. Since Nessrin Geddah had recently spent several days at a small marina just outside the airport, Dmitry suspected that this location was worth pursuing first.

Paul and Katya ate breakfast together in the apartment after the old Russian left.

Aaron Bugeja arranged for a four-man crew to take them onward by hydrofoil to Sicily as they requested. Bugeja also made it clear that this was the last official help they could expect to receive. The prime minister's private meeting with the US ambassador the night before had not gone well. Both men lacked essential details about what had happened with what, in retrospect, was dubbed a highly unorthodox operation. Muscat made Malta's position clear—no more bilateral security actions without further consultation with other cabinet members. The only tangible progress was that both men agreed to form a committee to investigate details around the Archemede debacle; the US ambassador pledged to consider further financial assistance depending on the committee's review and formal conclusions of a classified investigation.

At noon, Paul and Katya bordered the Maltese navy hydrofoil at a dock near Fort Manoel. The ocean always made Paul feel slightly uneasy; he lacked the sea legs to feel comfortable on any boat, and the strange, lingering aftereffects of the gas exposure made it worse. As he stood on the hydrofoil's deck, he felt slightly disassociated from his own body. He looked down at his own hands tightly gripping the metal railing. Was this his own body? His consciousness still perceived external reality—the sea, the railing, the motor—but his physical self didn't seem to belong to him anymore. He turned his head to watch Katya huddled in the back of the boat, her chestnut hair kept tightly bound beneath a wool sea cap. She also seemed very remote, as if appearing in a dream, very far from his own awareness locked someplace deeper inside his struggling body.

The hydrofoil chopped through the ocean, its motor humming.

Soon Paul saw the southern coast of Sicily gain form. The shore appeared as a thin, ragged line of rocks sloping up into a series of rolling hills. A long line of heavy clouds hung over the island, stymying any hope of more satellite coverage. They were chasing a shadow now with no more help from the sky.

The Maltese navy captain brought the hydrofoil to a wooden dock on the north end of the small town of Pozzallo. They jumped off, Paul carrying the heavy rucksack slung on his back. The captain exchanged a few words with an Italian officer who sauntered up to the end of the dock to meet them. The Italian gave them a quick nod and waved them onward without questions or asking for their passports.

Katya and Paul made their way to a parking lot near the main port. There, a Range Rover waited, per Aaron Bugeja's final assistance. Paul threw his rucksack into the back. Katya grabbed the keys and slipped into the driver's seat.

"It will be dark soon. I'll find us a hotel in Siracusa tonight, then we start tomorrow," she said.

"Good."

Paul unfolded a map of Sicily as Katya drove out onto a two-lane road heading north. The map showed the island's nine-hundred-mile circumference. Paul's stomach sank as he studied the island map. Sicily, the largest island in the Mediterranean, was a much greater challenge than tiny Malta. Small marinas, little coastal towns, and private villas dotted the rocky coast.

"What are you thinking?" Katya asked.

"We're not going to find anything unless we get creative."

"Creative how?"

"We need local help. It's the only way to find a needle in a haystack."

"Italian police can't help."

"That's not what I'm thinking."

"What then?"

"It's a long shot," Paul mused. The remote possibility had stirred in his brain when they were first approaching the island.

Paul typed out the text message on his phone, then pushed send.

This is Paul. I am in Sicily. Are you still here?

Within ten minutes, his phone dinged a response.

Elad: Yes.

Paul: Can you speak?

Elad: Yes.

Paul called. After several rings, Elad answered, with background street noises. The boy offered a friendly greeting: "What are you doing here? Business or pleasure?" Paul quickly got to the point.

"I'll explain more. I need your help with Antonio."

"What help?" Elad asked.

"Tell him I will pay cash to anyone who can help us find a fishing ship. Some money up-front and forty thousand dollars if we find it," Paul said. He mentally discounted twenty percent from the cash he carried—

just in case Antonio wanted to negotiate as he had done with Elad's original trip from Mersin.

"Forty thousand dollars to find a ship?" Elad repeated.

"Yes, but only if we move quickly. I need as many eyes as you can find. The ship will be hidden."

"This money is real?"

"You know I'm good for it. Trust me," Paul said. "Meet us at the main cathedral in Siracusa tomorrow at 9 a.m. Bring anyone you think can help. I'll send you a satellite picture of the boat now."

"Yes, Paul. Send me your photo. I will tell Antonio," Elad responded, his tone now businesslike and serious.

"Who was that?" Katya asked after Paul hung up. Her eyes focused on the twisting two-lane road while Paul fumbled with his phone to send the photo.

"A friend from the camps in Turkey. He lives here now," Paul. "Let's see. He's a smart kid. He knows locals who might be able help."

"A refugee kid? Will he even show up?" she asked.

"Probably. If not..."

———— ✳ ————

Paul turned over from his stomach and opened his eyes.

A new day shone brightly through the hotel's small window. Paul had fallen asleep as soon as he had undressed and put his head down on the bed's pillow. His body craved more rest, even as he knew that six hours of sleep would need to be enough for now. Katya had driven them last night to a small hotel specifically on the tiny peninsula of Ortygia, the oldest part of the Siracusa that was densely packed with hotels, churches, restaurants, museums, and shops.

Katya was standing, already fully dressed, near the window.

Paul kept the water cold as he showered, then hurried with a change of clothes after he toweled off his body. Katya led the way from the hotel. The air was crisp; the streets were just beginning to fill with early morning activity—motorcycles, busses, pedestrians on their way to work, students headed to school. Paul and Katya navigated the maze of streets until they emerged into the main city square, an open area where waiters arranged outdoor café chairs, and a cluster of Asian tourists studied their guidebooks. The façade of Siracusa's main cathedral faced down on them from the east side of the square.

Paul glanced at his watch—already 9:05 a.m.

"Will your boy come?" Katya said.

"He will."

"Did he text you?"

"Not yet."

"Expecting too much from a boy is not wise," she said.

"Let's give him a little longer. It's a few hours' drive from Catania."

Paul paced the main square. He let his eyes drift to the nearby cathedral's impressive marble front; it was graced by eighteen tall columns on the first level and twelve columns on the second.[101] Just above the cathedral's ornate entrance stood a baroque statue of a woman in flowing robes with two hands folded over her chest. A bronze halo of iron stars hovered over her head. Paul focused on the woman's calm expression looking down. She was a saint of some sort; he didn't know exactly. The statue was finely crafted; she seemed to peer directly at him as if from some remote and irretrievable past. An anonymous artisan long ago had carved that angelic figure. The cathedral builders had lifted her up to this place of prominence, and she stood like this for centuries, bearing an expression of hope.

Katya saw him looking at the statue and came closer.

"Who is she?" Paul asked her.

"Mary, I believe. It doesn't matter."

Paul closed his eyes. He didn't pray because he had never prayed to anyone for anything in his life, even at moments when despair raised its ugly head to stare at him. Instead, he calmed his mind and thought only of how strange it was just to be alive. Those long-dead builders—other human beings—were reaching across the centuries, communicating some message from a very long time ago. They were strong and they were telling him something important. What had Dmitry said? If God does not exist, we must invent him.

He felt Katya take his hand.

"We should go soon," she said.

"Give him a few more minutes."

Voices in the square murmured. Glasses clanked. A tour guide was talking to her group in Japanese, waving a yellow flag so they could see her. He could feel his limbs again. Ortygia was the heart of ancient Sicily, continuously inhabited for more than two thousand years since the ancient

---

101   The Syracuse Cathedral originated as a Greek Temple of Athena in the 5th century BC and was transformed into a Christian church in the 7th century AD. Its current Baroque appearance dates to a major reconstruction between 1725 and 1753 following a 1693 earthquake.

Greeks, long before the Christians. All those dead souls were now urging him forward, channeling some kind of energy back into his body and heart.

"Paul!" a voice shouted over the rough buzz of a scooter engine. Paul turned and saw Elad drive into the square on a yellow Piaggio. On the back of the bike, dangled another teenage boy dressed in a white T-shirt, jeans, and sandals. Both boys wore similar oversized aviator sunglasses.

Elad brought the Piaggio to a stop in front of them. The two boys hopped off the bike. Elad took off his sunglasses, and clasped Paul's hand in a firm shake.

"Just in time," Paul said.

"I'm sorry. My bike is too small for highways," Elad said.

"Glad you came."

"This is Marco, Antonio's brother," Elad said. Paul stretched out his hand. Marco was tall and thin, with gangly arms, closely cropped black hair, and very dark eyes.

"You pay forty thousand dollars?" the Italian boy asked.

"I will if you can help," Paul replied.

"Are you sure?" Marco pressed.

"Here," Paul said. He reached into his pocket and tossed over a wad of hundred-dollar bills rolled up tightly in a rubber band. "A thousand now just for driving here."

Marco took the roll and fingered the dollars. He kept his face tight to hide his surprise. Marco hadn't believed either his Syrian friend or his older brother Antonio about this American, this magical "Paul," until he touched the roll of cash. A pale woman dressed in black also stood nearby. Marco's eyes lingered on her striking features. Elad hadn't mentioned there would be a woman like this—slender, beautiful, intensely focused. She also added to the intrigue.

"I keep this for now," Marco replied, shoving the money in his front pocket. "What else about this boat you know?"

"We think a Sicilian family named Salvo is involved," Paul offered.

"Salvo? There are many Salvos in Sicily," Marco cautioned.

"But you know them? Isabella Salvo."

"I know some of this family from Palermo," Macro said.

"Good, start with that."

"Only that?"

"Start there."

Marco, motivated by the idea, took off his aviator sunglasses and reached into his back pocket for his mobile phone. He drifted away from Paul and the others to make his calls. Paul watched him as he spoke in rapid Italian on his mobile, first perhaps with his brother Antonio and then others. Marco nodded his head and waved his free hand while he walked in circles in the square. Excited moments of fast Italian punctuated otherwise long waits as new conversations began.

"Shall we take breakfast while he makes his calls?" Katya asked.

"Why not? We should eat something," Paul said.

Elad guided his yellow Piaggio over to a collection of other motorcycles parked next to an outdoor café. Paul, Katya, and Elad sat at a table beneath a wide umbrella. A tall waiter came over to them. Paul ordered three espressos and a collection of local pastries. The order came out quickly. The sugar and caffeine brought his mind further into focus.

Elad sat next to Katya. He did his best not to stare too much at her as she sipped her espresso from a tiny cup. Her blue-green eyes, Elad thought, were luminous and striking. Those gemlike eyes elevated her already attractive features to a level of loveliness that seemed to belong to a world beyond. He had never seen anyone quite like her, at least someone like this outside the pages of a magazine or on a television program.

"I'm glad you came," Katya said, turning to the Syrian teenager when it was clear he was staring.

"You are Russian?" Elad asked tentatively.

"I was born in Russia, but I left there many years ago," she answered.

"How do you know Paul?"

"Call it fate. We met in New York."

"Many years ago?"

"A lifetime ago," she replied.

Elad was struggling to ask a more interesting question when Marco returned.

"Well?" Paul asked.

"The Salvo family owns hotels in Palermo. I asked about boats and docks. There is a place in the north, a marina they use for their business," Marco said, struggling with some words. "There is also one more place in the south. I think your boat is in the south."

"Why south?" Paul probed. Marco asked Elad to translate his answer.

"He says that the south is quiet, away from people," Elad continued. "He worked there once a few years ago. He brought liquor to an old villa next to the ocean. A better place for… I don't know the English… contrabbandare."

"Show me where it is," Paul said, spreading out the map of Sicily on the café table. Marco studied the map details, pointing to both the north and south potential locations. The property along the northern coast was less than a kilometer from a main four-lane highway that led to Palermo. The coastal property in the south, however, stood more isolated along a smaller local road. Paul traced his finger along the map to the nearest town of Licata, some twenty kilometers away. It was a small town. The map only showed a handful of churches and small hotels.

"You see. South better," Marco offered.

"It seems so."

"We go look. I know a way inside."

"How?"

"I show, you pay cash?" Marco insisted.

"Yes, if the boat is there. How long of a drive?" Paul asked.

"Maybe two hours by car."

Paul looked at Katya and asked for her opinion with his eyes. She took a last quick sip of espresso and rose from her seat at the café.

"I don't have a better idea," Katya said. "Let's go."

25

THE TWO teenage boys sat in the back of the Range Rover while Katya drove along the two-lane strada provinciale SS194 through Sicily's volcanic interior. In the passenger seat, Paul inhaled the ancient, untamed island landscape. Like Malta, Sicily showed history's long imprint. They passed many smaller towns—Noto, Ragusa, Vittoria. These baroque towns now seemed left behind, remote relics of Sicily's past glory. The cement and stucco houses along the road were cracked with age, while massive ornate cathedrals soared mightily over the crumbling residential areas.

"Why must you find this boat?" Elad asked as they drove.

Paul explained Bogan Zoidze's past. Elad and Marco listened intently as Paul described Bogan's network. He told them What happened to Oleg in Paris, to Tim Hastings on the ship, and to Joe Vella and Bella Grech underground in the wine cellar.

"She died while you carried her?"

"That's right," Paul affirmed.

"If we find this man, what will you do?" Elad asked.

"Not sure," Paul said.

"Will you call police?"

"We don't need police," Katya interjected, her deep Slavic accent bringing out a certain declarative force. "When we find Bogan, Paul and I are going to kill him."

Elad glanced at Marco, who also seemed surprised by Katya's vehemency and certainty.

"How?" Elad asked.

"We're going to shoot him down with the guns we have in the back of this car. Isn't that right, Paul?"

"Maybe," Paul said.

"What if he has many guards?" Elad asked.

"We have many guns. I will kill them too."

The road curved around a series of small hills. Marco instructed Katya to take a left off the two-lane paved road at a small, unmarked intersection. She drove another few miles more slowly along a curving stretch of olive groves and oak trees. There were only a few houses dotted here and there along the road.

"There it is," Marco said, pointing out a private entrance marked by a faded bronze sign set in a low stone wall—Villa Fontesa. Katya spotted the video cameras outside the entrance; she continued driving. After few hundred meters, she slowed the car and turned into the parking lot of a small, abandoned gas station now overgrown with weeds. She brought the Range Rover to a parking place just behind the empty station's two-story stucco building. The gas station looked like it hadn't been functional for at least a decade.

"This is close enough. We can go back the rest of the way on foot," Katya said.

Paul took the pair of M22 field binoculars from the side pocket of the rucksack and tucked one of the handguns beneath his belt, under his shirt.

"Marco, you show us the way," Paul said.

"I'll carry water," Elad offered.

Marco took the lead. The four of them left the parking lot and walked along a small dirt path that led down a slope, away from the road. They followed Marco's lanky form through a grove of eucalyptus trees near the rocky coast, then down a steep descent to another narrow dirt path below the high sea cliff and along the beach. The high cliffs above dropped straight down to the isolated stretch of the island's rocky southern coast.

They walked the shore path, passing an old, abandoned shed, and a cluster of dead cypress trees. Just after a group of rocks, they climbed back up a steep hill. Slowly, cautiously, they each scrambled across the path's remaining fifty meters.

"Here it is," Marco said, pointing to the six-meter-high cement wall that loomed beyond the rocks. Barbed wire and a lattice of spikes topped a concrete barrier that surrounded the villa's private compound.

"How do we get inside the wall?" Paul asked.

"*Sì. Sì.* I find it," Marco said.

Marco trekked first another dozen meters along the high compound wall. He stopped at an uneven section where the high concrete wall curved over some larger volcanic rocks. He explored the base of a round black stone and spoke with Elad in a low voice. The two teenagers positioned themselves. Grunting with effort, they rolled the stone to the right until it revealed a dark hole at the base of the cement wall. The hole was dug out of the hard, dry earth; it was big enough to crawl through.

"Here we are. My entrance for you," Marco said, visibly relieved to find this old breach.

"You dug this to steal from them?"

"Only a few bottles they didn't count right," Marco replied smiling.

Marco crawled into the dark hole. Once descended, he pushed against another stone covering the other side and cleared away some dry underbrush. They all could see light on the other side.

"Stay here," Paul told Katya and Elad before he followed Marco into the hole.

On the other side of the wall, Paul cautiously moved behind the boy. Marco found a shaded area near a cluster of cypress trees with a vantage point that included views of the ocean, an expansive garden area, and the villa. Paul slid next to one of the cypress trees and peered through the field binoculars while Marco crouched next to him.

"Is that your fishing boat down there?" Marco asked, pointing to the boat moored at a small dock.

Paul adjusted the binocular's focus until a magnified image of the tuna long-liner snapped clear. It was the same shape and make of equipment from the overhead photo, now covered beneath an awning of sheet metal and a tan, tarpaulin cloth.

"Could be," Paul said.

Paul continued scanning. A crisscross of paths led up into a collection of old buildings on a hill crest. A stone two-story villa commanded a view above a shallow area of thick gardens. Further up the slope, Paul saw two men sitting in a shaded area next to a large garage. One guard slung a Kalashnikov over his shoulder, and the other held a semi-automatic in two hands. Both wore loose-fitting gray fatigues. Another man walked between sculpted paths of cactus trees and short European fan palms with their spiky trunks. Paul motioned for Elad to stay close to the ground since in broad daylight the guards could see them from a distance.

"We can't get closer now. I've seen enough. We go back now," Paul said.

Paul and Marco retreated from their vantage point. They crawled back through the breach beneath the concrete perimeter wall. Paul dusted off the dirt and straightened himself up after he emerged back on the other side.

"Well?" Katya asked.

"It seems we owe our friends forty thousand dollars," Paul confirmed.

"Are you sure?" Katya pressed.

"The ship is there. I saw three guards. There is a large truck and trailer at the top of the hill. It looks like they are getting ready to move again," Paul explained.

"Ha! You see! Easy work for forty thousand," Marco exclaimed. He could not contain his broad grin.

———— ✳ ————

They retraced their way back through the grove of eucalyptus trees. It was almost dark by the time they returned to the Range Rover.

"What next?" Elad asked after they all took swigs of water.

"We wait and watch," Paul said.

Katya looked at him with a stultified expression.

"Wait? For what?" she asked.

"We can tail the truck when it leaves."

"Follow them?" Katya scoffed. "Bogan's men would spot us in five minutes. No, Paul. I have seen enough. We end this tonight, while we still have the advantage of surprise. We finally have some luck. This is our only chance."

"We don't know how many there are."

"Bogan will have only a few men with him."

"How do you know that?" Paul countered.

"Because I know how he thinks," she shot back.

"And what if he isn't there at all?"

"You know he is."

"I don't," Paul replied sharply.

Paul felt Elad and Marco staring while Katya's face had hardened. He felt her eyes cut into him with a kind of intense anger. This was also a rare moment that Paul noticed Katya's semblance to her brother Viktor. There was a certain type of cruelty in Katya's eyes now, just like Viktor used to have when he was alive and determined. Her look now held the cruelty of someone in pain.

"Need to think," Paul said, backing down. He went to the Range Rover, lifted the rucksack from the trunk, and began to unzip the contents. On the ground, he methodically laid out the weapons taken from the US Embassy's arsenal in Malta: five grenades, three Glock 17 handguns, a long-range tactical rifle with an infrared laser, night goggles, a standard US Marine-issued M27 automatic rifle, and an array of additional ammunition clips for the various weapons.

Katya came to inspect the weapons. She picked up the night vision goggles and examined the tactical rifle with the infrared laser attached just below its muzzle.

"You see, Paul. Nothing to worry about. This will be enough," she said.

Paul walked away, this time without responding. He felt her eyes follow him. He picked up a long, straight branch lying in the underbrush and began to trace circles in the dirt.

Two tours in Iraq made Paul hyper-aware of multiple risks with any armed operation, however well planned. This wasn't a tennis match during which you gave your opponent one more shot after the first serve hit into the net. In combat, anything could happen with complete, utter finality. There were no second shots. Anyone could get tripped up, fragged, split open. Inches made the difference between a bullet passing right by you and one shredding your kidney. Didn't matter how much you imagined in your head how it should play out. Plans and visualization never matched what happened under live conditions. Also, tonight's whole setup didn't make for good betting odds. Perses' guards were trained killers. Katya was entirely untested. Marco and Elad were just kids who had merely stumbled into this situation earlier today.

Elad drifted over.

"You don't agree with her?" Elad said.

"Not sure."

"You think he is in this villa?"

"Probably, yes."

"Ok. I will help, like in Syria."

"You are not afraid, even after what I told you?" Paul asked.

"If what you said is true, then we must try," Elad offered.

"Even if it risks your life?"

"We have weapons. You were a soldier once. We can surprise them," Elad said.

This boy is ready to fight, Paul thought. Why? What does he believe that I don't?

"What about your family? What will they do if something happens to you?" Paul probed.

Elad didn't answer immediately.

"If I am hurt, you could do something for them?"

"Yes, I could do that," Paul replied.

"Are you sure?"

"I can call tonight."

"Then, we try. I trust you," Elad said.

Paul and Elad went back to Katya and Marco.

"Did you learn how to use an infrared targeting laser in California?" Paul asked Katya.

"Of course."

"And this type of rifle?"

"A close cousin, yes."

"But not this one. This one is different, it's a newer model issued to the military alone. You need to sync up the targeting field."

Katya stared at Paul.

"Enough debate, Paul. I can handle this weapon. You need to decide," she said, again with a deep Slavic accent that had resurfaced with her anger.

Choice. Always choice. Each choice led to unknown consequences. So many of his choices had cost other people their lives—Oleg, Tim, Vella, Grech. Was tonight worth the risk? Could they win? Was there any other way? The rock formations and thick garden inside would help. The rifle's infrared laser might give Katya a crucial advantage at night. They had surprise on their side. He just needed enough time to get close enough to Zoidze.

Elad and Katya stared at him now.

"Well?" Elad asked.

"Ok, we go tonight," Paul said. "Elad will start with a diversion near the sea cliff. Katya will keep them pinned down with the rifle. I will get to the main villa."

"What about me?" Marco asked.

"What about you? You brought us here," Paul said, reaching inside the rucksack that held the manila envelope with the cash.

"I come inside. I know the place," Marco said.

"Are you sure?"

"Why not? She fights. Elad goes. I'm not afraid," Marco said.

"Ok, then. We go together. All of us."

Paul looked at each face, and each nodded. They spoke more about the planned tactics, with Marco showing them what he remembered about the compound, although his work there was nearly two years ago and he had never been inside any of the buildings or the garage. After nearly an hour, Paul walked away from the others at the Range Rover. He dialed Jo's number on the Satcom line. Jo answered after two rings.

"Any luck?" she asked him.

Paul described the situation—the boat, villa, guards, truck, and security. Jo listened. She wanted to see Paul's face again. It was always best to read someone's face along with listening to their words. Words only delivered half the meaning, especially for critical decisions such as this. But Paul was a disembodied voice calling her from six thousand miles away. Instead of studying his expression while next to him in the field, now she merely looked out her tiny window down at the Potomac River and felt ill-informed and helpless.

"Keep your distance," Jo said. "I'll play the terrorist card with the Italians to get you help."

"You know that's not going to happen fast enough," Paul said.

"Don't even think about engaging, Paul," Jo said, her voice now firmer, like a schoolteacher. "Zoidze is a killer. He's survived more than you and I can ever know. You don't have the tools to win."

"I disagree."

"It doesn't matter if your little art-house girlfriend took some shooting classes," Jo said sternly. "Yeah, I know all about her so-called training in California. None of that matters now. Remember what happened when you followed Valentine on his little joyride to get his men in Syria? You do something stupid again like that, and you are going to get everybody killed."

"Why are we arguing?" Paul asked. "Be honest, Jo. You need me to do this. Why else send me to the embassy?"

Jo Richards took a deep breath. She turned her eyes away from the window. Susan Collins had sent her the list of weapons Paul had taken out of the Malta embassy arsenal; he had pulled a decent grab bag, she admitted to herself. She walked over to a long mirror that hung in front of her bedroom door. If she couldn't study Paul's face, at least she could observe her own. Was Paul right? The creature staring back at her looked barely human, a spiderly thing on two thin legs. The creature's eyes were inflamed, its mouth strangely twisted. The ghoul in the mirror needed closure, revenge, finality. This was their unique moment, long in the making. They were so close. Her star producer was finally ready. He was closer to the enemy than they had ever hoped possible. Now they had the upper hand.

"Listen, Paul," Jo said carefully. "You're making a mistake, but if you are going to do this, move fast and capitalize on surprise. Don't give that son of a bitch time to roll out of bed."

"This will work, Jo. I promise." Paul asserted. "I just need two favors if it doesn't," Paul continued.

"I'm listening."

"Promise me you'll help the Syrian boy's family. His mother is in Catania, last name Ishmail. Valentine can help find them. Do something for them."

"I will. And the second?"

"Tell my brother this was my decision and my decision alone. Tell him I had my reasons, and they were the right ones."

"Roger that, Paul. You have my word."

26

BOGAN ZOIDZE took a small plastic bottle from his inside vest, shook out three blue 200 milligram tablets of Captagon, and swallowed. Within minutes, the 56-year-old Georgian felt the powerful amphetamine course through his body. A rush of new, artificial energy filled his awareness. Cocaine was a better high, but Captagon kept him wired and alert for much longer. He preferred this kind of background buzz for longer days. Captagon helped his chest pains, too.

Zoidze walked from the dark main dining room to the elevated veranda at the back of the main two-story Sicilian villa. He sat down across from this old friend, Mark Portelli, on a large rattan chair. The light was waning now, the sun obscured behind a wide expanse of low-hanging, gloomy clouds. On the table, Mark had set out a plate of bread and hard cheese, a bottle of water, a bottle of vodka, and a bucket of ice. Neither man was hungry. The veranda commanded views of the villa's garden, three other cement and sandstone buildings, and the sea some hundred and fifty meters to the south. Bogan's most loyal guard, Artem, leaned against a nearby stone wall, his hands in his pockets, his ugly face vacant as usual.

Bogan's thoughts cleared as the Captagon kicked in. He returned now to the shifting problem of his current logistics.

Two nights in Sicily was too long. Italy was always the weakest link in the latest round of contingency planning. Bogan only agreed to this detour in haste and only after receiving Kiril's firm warning that the Americans had somehow unearthed enough operational details to disrupt his plans with Haftar. It was far too risky to complete the deal. The Americans had deployed their ships to patrol international waters, so it was unwise to use the tuna liner further, especially with the danger of satellite surveillance. Rather, he needed to adjust, move his chess pieces out of danger with the help of Mark Portelli's local connections. His key man, Andre Gauthier, was also missing for the past three days. No matter. Operational protocol kept information compartmentalized. Only Isabella and Mark knew about this place. Bogan could find out later what happened to Andre and if he was their betrayer. If it wasn't Andre, then someone in his own circle had made a careless mistake—or worse.

Bogan also didn't like this old coastal villa. The main building's eighteenth-century interior was too drafty, with too many marble statues, dark paintings of Christ, and rustic antique furniture. The rest of the Villa Fontesa—its walls, large garage, docking house, and storage areas—were all added later, in the early 1990s, after the Salvo family bought the property. For the past two decades, this compound had quietly served as a transit point for marine contraband entering the EU. The Salvo family trafficked mostly to and from Tunisia, Morocco, Algeria, and Libya. They made small percentages on their commercial goods. Security was adequate for such low-level activities but not ideal for the value of what his men were about to move onto the truck.

"How long to Comiso Airport?" Bogan asked.

"Three-hour drive if we stay off the main roads," Mark said.

"Security there?"

"Normally, very light. The airport is small, mostly for charter planes."

Airports risked bottlenecks, Bogan feared. The airport would be one of the first places the Americans would put on alert. Because Italy was part of NATO, it was feasible they could take direct action. A local ferry to another, more distant, airport might also lead to potential complications. Trucking the cargo further north would drag out risks; they would need to cross the Strait of Messina, and that would be tricky.

"What if we submerged your boxes underwater?" Mark asked.

"Just throw them in the sea?"

"Yes, and then you can retrieve them later."

Bogan shrugged. He hadn't clearly told Mark what exactly was in the secure boxes, only that it needed to be protected.

"Interesting. But no," the Georgian replied.

What Bogan needed, he was loathe to admit, was mighty Russia's help. He needed Moscow to step in, to assist him to adapt to new conditions and move to a better position. It was, after all, their gold. Twenty-five tons of pure bullion should be enough incentive for those bastards to help him now. Russia was a massive kleptocracy. Money kept the whole machine humming, despite whatever the Kremlin's propaganda fed the population in terms of reviving their empire and improving their lives.

Then, like manna from heaven, the phone in Bogan's shirt pocket began to vibrate. He read the income text—a short message from Kiril.

Good news. The text detailed next steps: An IL-76 commercial cargo plane would leave Belgrade tomorrow morning and reach Comiso Airport by early afternoon. The flight path was cleared. They would have ninety minutes to load the cargo on the plane, using an area at the airport that was cordoned off from other commercial areas. Then, instead of flying to Rome as declared in the official schedule, the plane would divert midair to Russian's Khmeimim Air Base in Syria, a three-hour flight time. The plane would glide right under the nose of NATO's Sigonella Naval Air Station just fifty miles away. Quick and easy. Short of a major diplomatic pushback, there was nothing to stop them. His men could push through any ragtag resistance on the ground here.

Mark Portelli saw the change in Bogan's eyes when the Georgian looked up.

"Any news?" Mark asked.

"Tomorrow morning, we drive the truck to Comiso Airport," the Georgian declared. "Make sure there are no surprises. Whatever it takes."

"You have a plane?"

"Yes."

Mark Portelli nodded, the tension in his eyes relaxing just a bit. Mark put ice cubes into two glasses, mixed water with some vodka, and handed Bogan a glass.

The two old friends clanked glasses. Bogan finished the vodka in one long gulp. It was still possible to win this game or, at least, play out the next few moves to a draw, he thought. He had some victories. The death traps successfully sprang. Neither the Libyan weapons nor his precious cargo had yet been compromised. No missiles rained down from the sky in Sicily as they might in another Arab country. In twenty-four hours, he'd be able to step away from this chess game and reset the board.

———— ✷ ————

The night cooled along Sicily's rocky southern coast as Marco led Paul, Katya, and Elad back through the eucalyptus grove and then again to a rocky footpath near the ocean. In the darkness, they furtively retraced their steps along the coast.

Katya followed behind Paul, last in line. She listened to the serene sound of the waves lapping against the rocks as she carefully treaded along the rocky path. The ocean's continuous, gentle sound seemed incongruous with the uncertainty and stress that grew more palpable in her body with each new step.

Paul put down the rucksack when they again reached the breach beneath the perimeter wall. Elad passed around a water bottle. Katya took a deep swig. She looked at the faces of the two boys, huddled in the darkness. Elad took deep breaths and rubbed his neck. Despite his earlier bravado, she could see that Marco had become nervous. He no longer smiled and touched the small silver cross that dangled around his neck.

Paul unbuckled the rucksack and handed out the rifle, handguns, and grenades as agreed to in the plan: Elad took one grenade, a Glock 17, and several ammunition clips. Marco took the second handgun. Katya grasped the infrared rifle and slid the third pistol snugly in the small of her back. Paul engaged the ammunition clip into the M27 and put four grenades in a small backpack strapped tightly on his back.

"Remember, you have only six second after you pull the pin," Paul said to Elad.

"I know. You told me this already," the Syrian boy responded.

Paul scowled. "Six seconds. Don't forget."

"I won't."

Katya observed Paul as she made his final operational check. *A shame that I pulled you down into this dark reality, she thought. You willingly followed me, but I never stopped you. Now, you are here. No time left to appreciate any of our best moments when we loved each other. If I don't survive tonight, at least we had something that mattered. It will be hard for you, Paul, but I know you can live without me. It doesn't matter if I don't live more because at least I know that...*

"Are you ready?" Paul called over to Katya in a low voice.

She nodded and pulled herself back into the moment with a long, slow inhale.

"Good. Stay focused."

"Yes, Paul. You are right," she replied, staring back at him.

"Ok. Give me fifteen minutes before you start."

"I will," Katya confirmed.

"Ok. Let's go," Paul said.

Marco crawled first through the small opening beneath the cement wall. Elad, Katya, and Paul followed. The two boys moved first toward the cluster of rocks and pine trees near the sea cliff. Paul moved in the opposite direction, along a row of low hedges that ran parallel to the perimeter wall toward the main villa. After a few seconds, Katya lost sight of Paul as he melted into a dark thicket of palm fronds and cacti. A deep, sick feeling of dread crept up into her stomach. She probably would never see him again and her own time on Earth was about to end, just like it had for all the others in her life. Stay calm. Focus. Conserve energy.

Katya moved forward. She found the place that Marco had told her about—an elevated niche between cypress and palm trees. The spot afforded a decent, partial view of the many paths through the garden and several of the buildings adjacent to the main villa. Good enough. She lay down on her stomach. Carefully, she propped the semi-automatic rifle on a flat rock, positioning her body as she had once done long ago while training with Kurt Collins in the Southern California desert. She slowed her breathing, just as she trained to do during those long hot months of careful practice. She pulled the night vision visor over her eyes and adjusted the straps and the focus settings. The space ahead appeared in glowing, greenish patterns as the thermal sensors lit up warmer shapes. She switched on the target laser. A tiny green dot, invisible to the naked eye, marked the gun's precise aim.

Katya waited, finger on the trigger, eyes adjusting to the strange greenish movements as seen through the night vision goggles. She focused on two moving green shapes—they were guards about fifty meters away. They talked in muffled low voices. The taller Georgian guard struggled to light a cigarette. He cupped his hands to protect the lighter's flame against a soft wind. Finally successful, the man took a long inhale before offering his companion his cigarette to help ignite a second.

A few more minutes. *Stay focused. The world will change after tonight, or it will end. Doesn't matter. Here I am. No turning back. At least Andre is dead, and I go on my own terms.*

Katya scanned the walkways and focused her senses.

Elad should have already started. What's the problem?

Another minute passed.

The visor felt tight around her eyes, throbbing now. She focused on the two men smoking—shifting green outlines. Still fifty meters away in her line of fire.

She heard a loud boom crack open the night. A few seconds later, Elad's pistol gunshots rang out in an erratic sequence.

Katya squinted and tightened her knuckles. The targeting laser's green dot touched the torso of the taller Georgian. She squeezed twice, dropping him as he moved towards the noise. The other guard, still thinking the threat came from elsewhere, dodged for cover behind a stone wall. His back remained exposed to Katya's view. She moved the green dot to between his upper shoulders, then squeezed the trigger three times. The man shuddered, then dropped sidewise. He lay there, suddenly motionless in an awkward, contorted heap.

Katya turned her focus to the more distant row of two-story buildings, scanning for others. The diversion was working. She tracked movement in the bushes in the direction of the villa, then heard a shout in Georgian from one of the nearby buildings. A spotlight flared from a second story window. Other electric lights switched on, lighting up the perimeter wall.

The spotlight's bright circle of white light roved down to the area where Elad had thrown the grenade and then down to the garden. The spotlight circle moved to a patch of tangled trees, paused, then moved again, searching. The bright circle of light roved up and down. Two men were dead on the path, bodies twisted. The light touched near them, then crawled up the rocks beneath her, veered at first right, and then finally, closer, up the slope, until it suddenly surrounded her.

Chort vasmi. Goddamn it!

Katya rolled to the left.

Pop. Pop. Pop. Pish. Pish. Pop. Ping. Pop. Pop. Pop.

Rock fragments and dust splattered around her. She scrambled behind the thick palm tree trunk to her right. She ripped off the throbbing visor. She had lost a grip on her rifle. It slid down the rock, a few meters away.

Pop. Pop. Wizz. Wizz.

More precisely aimed shots from somewhere near the villa pinned her down behind a squat palm tree. More shouts came from there. Her heart pounded in her throat. She felt a sharp pain in her thigh. She looked down—warm, glistening blood oozed out of the ripped, raw flesh of her right thigh.

Calm down. Think. Forget the rifle. It's gone. Keep moving. The bullet missed the bone.

Katya choked down the pain and pulled the Glock 17 from the small of her back. She crawled away, low to the ground, then slid down a rough slope into a thicket of lemon trees, and then through a densely packed grove of tangled branches. Her right leg burned. Light and shadow mixed in a confused, shifting kaleidoscope. A stone path led deeper into the garden's darkness. She spotted a stone fountain in the basin of the garden, near a high stone wall. The statue of a long-haired goddess holding a vase stood in the center of a semi-circular pool, and around the pool there were dark places to hide. She slid into a corner, crouched on her left leg, and waited.

A Georgian fighter approached from the villa, eyes alert, a semi-automatic rifle held high on his right shoulder. The man's bulky shadow cautiously approached the fountain. Katya controlled her breathing and tightened her grip on her handgun. Her right thigh burned with pain.

The man walked closer. The electric lights along the interior of the perimeter fence cast long shadows. He was moving closer in a slow, stealthy fashion in between the short garden shrubs and trees until he was no more than ten meters away. She could see the glint of a gold chain around his neck. His eyes carefully scanned the darkness, step by step.

Katya shifted her weight off from her burning leg. The man stopped motionless to listen. She held steady, completely still.

"Hey," Elad suddenly shouted from somewhere closer to the sea cliff. The Georgian turned, just long enough.

Katya raised her arms, shot twice, hitting him on the side of his Kevlar vest. He staggered back. She fired again, higher now, arms steady with a more precise aim just above that glinting gold chain on his neck. His head snapped back, his body seized, contorted. Then, like a puppet with its strings suddenly cut, he fell limp and collapsed backward into the dirt.

Paul gripped the cold metal of the M27 with both hands as he moved ahead alone in the darkness. He held the weapon's stock in the ready position, eyes focused on the shifting light along a gravel path that ran along the outer perimeter wall.

Paul found a corner position with a view of the truck inside the garage. Near the truck he observed a large man in gray fatigues, rifle propped up against a workbench. Paul paused, waiting for Elad's first distraction to begin.

The first grenade exploded with a loud crack, followed by diversionary shots near the ocean. The bulky Georgian stood up. He instinctually grabbed his weapon and put his hand to his left ear as if to listen to an earpiece. He spoke back and quickly checked his rifle and his gear.

Paul tracked his motion as he came out from inside the garage.

Almost there. Just a little closer.

Paul squeezed the M27 trigger in rapid succession.

The big Georgian twisted mid-step and sprawled forward.

Paul rose from his position, then moved towards the main villa that held the high ground over the garden and the other buildings. He jogged in a low crouch, first to a secondary point of cover, then to a short flight of stone stairs leading up to the villa's backdoor. Bursts of automatic gunfire were closer now, aimed elsewhere. There was a full firefight in the garden. He needed to move quickly now.

Paul ascended the stairs, reached the door, opened it, and slipped inside to a dark and empty room cluttered with boxes on one side near the wall. He made his way to the next room—a large table in the center, bulky furniture, some lights switched on. Across the room, he saw a row of windows that opened to the veranda, and through the windows, the movement of one… maybe two… three men.

Almost there. Stay low.

The tallest man near the veranda was facing in his direction, waiting. He spotted Paul approach, quickly knelt, and aimed. Bullets ricocheted. A stone lion statue next to Paul splintered into pieces. Paul dived down to the floor, then lay flat. The men fanned out to different defensive positions, close now, but also positioned in corners without great mobility.

Paul put his M27 down on the floor. He swung the pouch off his back and reached inside for the grenades. Five-meter kill radius. Just like tossing a baseball. Paul squatted, pulled the M67 pin, then tossed the first ball with a wide swing to the area where he saw the first shooter take cover.

The explosion scattered metal fragments and blasted out a nearby cabinet and a row of windows. It was a direct hit, confirmed by a long moan of pain.

Paul stepped closer, repeated the process: squat—pull—throw. This time at the second man. The metal ball rolled at the man's feet, and for an instant he looked down at it, not sure what he should do.

Boooooooommmmm.

Third toss. Paul launched another ball further onto the veranda with a strong shoulder action.

Booooooooooomm.

Bits and pieces of metal scattered.

Paul lifted his head over the stone half-wall to assess the damage— two down, the last one sheltering behind a stone column to the right. One more toss. Paul crouched low, pulled the pin hard. Bullets cracked plaster behind his head, forcing him back to the floor again. He flicked the last grenade with a sideways motion till it slid along the floor, a few meters away, then he scrambled fast behind an overturned cedarwood table.

Boommmarrrggggkkkkkkkkkkkkk.

Ears ringing. Searing pain—neck and back splattered with bits of metal. White smoke billowing in the room. Chaos and confusion. Paul lay among the pieces of broken and overturned furniture.

27

M ARCO SPOTTED the danger first, just as Elad had shouted down to the garden to distract the man approaching Katya. The chaos of the shooting seemed to be coming from all directions for the past ten minutes. The fear was gripping him up at the base of his throat. This fear now was the strongest emotion Marco had ever known before, although it also gave him strength as he scrambled from rock to rock, trying to see how many there were, and follow the plan to divert their attention away from Katya. He watched the spotlight as it roved. Shouts came from different directions. It was hard to understand what to do next.

Marco saw the big man in a Kevlar vest emerged from below the tuna long-liner's deck at the small dock down near the ocean. The man leaped off the boat and made his way fast up the small dirt path, his semi-automatic rifle raised in trained preparation. Marco pulled at Elad's shoulder, drawing his attention.

"Can't stay here. Separate," Elad told him in a low voice, nodding towards a cluster of pine trees. The man coming up the path could plainly see them in the transparent darkness. They needed to scramble to find better cover.

Marco dashed toward the pine trees, gripping his handgun more tightly.

The man came running fast, up from the dock; he disappeared behind a small building.

Marco reached the trees and hid behind the thickest pine tree trunk. The shooter behind the building was near enough. There was nowhere left to run. Marco tried to calm his body, hold his arms steady. He put his face out just slightly to look back at the building. Tree bark splintered a few feet only above his head. The shooter aimed too high. He wasn't behind the building now, but closer still, a bulky shadow near the rocks where the boys first hid. The man called out to others in a different language. Marco crouched down. He stuck his arm out and fired the handgun three times in the direction of the man. He couldn't see if the shots came close. Hard to think now. Wasted shots. The gun recoil was stronger than he expected.

The shooter retreated. Gun shots like firecrackers erupted from elsewhere. Marco saw a quick glimpse of Elad. He was firing down from a different angle, pinning down the Georgian.

Marco squeezed his eyes shut. Two options flashed in his mind—the first, stay hidden; the second, charge forward while the Georgian was focused on Elad. The man was firing at his friend, emptying bullets at another target. Macro opened his eyes, sucked in a deep breath of air, and decided. He spun away from his hiding place and ran straight at the man, pointing his arm ahead and squeezing the Glock's trigger repeatedly. *Pop. Pop. Pop. Pop.* Closer still. *Pop. Pop. Pop. Pop.* He dove against a stone wall. Heart thumping wildly, pulsing in his ears, Marco paused there, unsure. No more shots. The sound of the ocean filled the night again.

Elad called him over to a dark grove of trees.

"He's down," Elad said.

Marco looked; the man was splayed out on the dirt.

Elad jogged closer to Marco now.

"That was stupid," Elad said in Italian.

"Why not?" Marco replied.

"Stay low."

They waited together there, crouching against a stone wall.

———— ✳ ————

At the villa, Bogan Zoidze came forward through the smoke, testing the distance, his footsteps crushing bits and pieces of broken porcelain and plaster. He saw his attacker struggling after the explosion, defenseless now that his weapon was too far away to pick up. Did the attacker still have any more bombs? Bogan shot a few more rounds, splintering the stone wall just a few feet above where his target had just now slithered away like an animal. Artem was down already, blood pouring out of a head wound, still twitching. Mark was worse—killed instantly from a second lucky throw. Grenade fragments ripped open his torso; he was laying there, face down, blood seeping out.

Bogan kicked away a broken chair and waited for the bastard to put his head up just enough to take it off. The target had crawled further away, now out of his line of fire. But that fool had made a mistake, trapping himself in a corner. There was nowhere else to retreat to now, and Bogan had at least twenty rounds left in the current clip. That would be enough to end this one here.

Bogan moved forward to press his advantage. He took a quick step left until he saw the man's left shoulder and torso. Good enough. Bogan straightened his weapon and took aim. Suddenly, a searing pain ripped into his lower back, his arms seized, and he felt himself buckle at the knees.

Bogan was now twisted on the floor. He realized he had just been hit by something. Another shooter? He had fallen forward and lost his grip on his semi-automatic. His eyes panned right to see a figure moving closer through the smoke. A woman emerged at the top of the stairs, dragging her leg, two hands clutching a gun. Her eyes first scanned the room for threats, then focused back on him.

Bogan crawled on his elbows over the smashed wood and broken porcelain toward his semi-automatic. He wanted to crawl faster, but the pain in his back made his legs feel like jelly. No matter how he willed his legs to move, they didn't. He needed to regain his weapon. It was there, so close on the floor, less than a meter away. He still had strength in his arms even if his legs couldn't move now.

Standing in front of him, the woman used her free hand to push the rifle further away from his grasp.

Bogan saw this and stopped. He perched on his elbow, turned over to look at her, and squinted his dark eyes. She let him catch his breath.

"*Te menya ouznal?* Do you know me?" she asked.

He looked harder now.

She loomed over him, two hands on the gun that pointed at his face. His expression changed as he registered her identity. His mind raced through a flashing succession of images. Her? Sergei Volkov's daughter? He did know her.

The shadow of a slight smile crossed over his face. She saw this and smiled back.

"You do know me," she declared in Russian.

"Scheherazade," he gurgled.

"*Eta konets.* It's over," she said in Russian.

Bogan lifted himself higher on his elbows.

She didn't wait longer for Bogan to speak again. Instead, she squeezed off two more rounds at point-blank range. He felt two sharp thumps against his chest, followed by a strange loss of feeling, now throughout his entire body. After a shudder, he slumped flat. He gurgled, lips quivering, but the words in his head didn't form sounds, only the barest imprint of meaning. Now he knew he was experiencing what all the others had known before their end—a thrilling, painful, fleeting, supernatural moment. As the dark blood oozed from the two black holes near his heart, his eyes continued to follow Katya. Then, her face dissolved into something otherworldly, and the room grew very vague and dim. Oddly, he saw a path between the tall juniper pine trees he had once walked through as a boy on his way to his father's farmhouse. The trees loomed large, swirled, then melted down beneath a massive, open, starry sky.

Then, nothing.

———— ✳ ————

Elad checked his weapon — he was on his last clip, with only five bullets left. The gunfire, the explosions, and shouting had all stopped for at least ten minutes, perhaps longer. The two boys waited and listened. The last gunfire had come from the direction of the villa. He could hear the ocean's steady rhythm while he crouched in the darkness behind a cluster of volcanic rocks next to Marco.

Another ten minutes passed. Elad felt his heartbeat begin to slow. The pace of his mind's thinking decelerated. He didn't observe any movement from down in the garden, nor from any of the other buildings. The sea's consistent lapping returned the universe to its normal order after the firefight's pandemonium.

"*Andiamo*. Let's go," Elad said to Marco. Elad found the path meandering up to the main villa. They walked slowly, both boys nervously clutching weapons. Marco first saw one dead man near a stone fountain in the garden—his left eye had been shot out, leaving a grotesque black hole. Then, near the grove of olive trees and short palms, they spotted two more corpses face down, their blood-soaked bodies crumpled in awkward positions where they fell.

The two boys continued upward towards the light and movement at the main villa. Elad saw a silhouette pacing back and forth on veranda. The man held his semi-automatic rifle in a ready position, his eyes still scanning for threats. It was Paul.

"Don't shoot, it's us!" Elad shouted.

Paul squinted, then lowered the weapon.

The boys walked up the steps to the veranda. Katya slouched on a chair there. She watched Elad approach, her head tilted slightly to the side. There was a ripped cloth tied tightly around her thigh. Her face was drained of color. Her clothes were speckled with blood.

"Are you hurt?" Paul asked to Elad when he came near.

"No," Elad said. He continued past Paul into the villa's main room where small fires still smoldered; three bodies were scattered in different places among the debris.

"Which one is him?" Elad asked.

Paul nodded toward the bearded man nearest the far wall.

"Are you sure?"

"Yeah, it was him," Paul said. "Did you see anyone else alive?" Paul asked.

"I don't think so. One came up from the boat. Marco killed him." Elad said.

Paul looked over at Marco and nodded.

"Now what?" Marco asked.

"We check the compound again," Paul said. He picked up a semi-automatic from where it lay next to one of the dead men on the ground and handed it to Marco.

"Take this. It has a full clip," Paul said.

Marco and Elad walked a wide path around the main villa while Paul checked the villa's second floor, his M27 rifle ready. Elad followed Paul as he cautiously approached the two-story brick building on the north side of the garden. Paul proceeded cautiously through the front door into an empty first floor. He went up the stairs to the second floor, also empty. Paul pulled out the cord from the spotlight still shining there. It went dark.

"Let's go to the garage," Paul told the boys when he came back down the stairs.

Paul led the two boys up the small path to the open garage on the east side of the compound. When he reached the garage, he flicked on the lights. A pool of blood was now collected around the dead guard sprawled out flat just outside the garage's threshold where Paul had shot him. Inside the garage, a long, three-axel, heavy-duty trailer was hitched behind a six-wheel Mercedes Actros truck. They went to the back on the truck trailer and looked inside. Steel boxes were stacked in modular fashion. Two steel boxes remained on the garage floor atop some wooden pallets behind the trailer.

Marco went to one of the boxes. He pushed at the box without moving.

"*Pesante*. Heavy," Marco said. "What is inside?"

"Get tools. Let's find out," Paul said.

Marco looked around the garage. He brought over a crowbar and shoved the sharp edge into the side of the steel box. The Italian boy pulled as hard as he could, his face grunting with effort. Unsuccessful, Marco went back, found a large connection bolt with a sharp end. Marco used a mallet to smash the sharper end at the steel box's hinges. He pounded the bolt at the box, at first calmly and then hard, cursing in Italian, until the hammering tore at the hinge, and the pin inside loosened. Elad came over to help, switching to a crowbar to pry open the top. The veins of Elad's neck bulged as he strained his muscles. Finally, the box creaked open.

Even in the darkness, the three of them saw the metal's sparking hue. Elad pulled out one of the bricks. Stunned, the Syrian boy held the heavy twenty-seven-pound gold bar in two hands.

"How many?" Marco asked, excited.

"Six each row, six rows. I count thirty-six in each box," Elad said.

Marco pulled out two more gold bricks. He began to laugh at first in disbelief, and then in a manner that turned almost giddy.

"Is it real?"

"It is," Paul said. He went to the back door of the trailer and counted what seemed to be another fifty-eight boxes inside, stacked in four rows.

Paul searched around the garage and found a nylon sack of tools. He emptied the tools onto the cement floor. "Fill this with as many bars as you can carry," Paul said.

Marco found another sizable carrying bag further back in the garage. He dumped out the wrenches and hammers and replaced them with gold bricks from the open box.

Elad lifted his sack of seven bricks, nearly two hundred pounds. Marco stuffed eight more in his sack.

"We can take more," Marco said, his arms straining.

"It's enough. Don't be greedy," Paul said. Fifteen bricks, something like eleven million dollars, Paul quickly summed up.

Following Paul, the two boys carried the loot back toward the villa's veranda. Katya was still there as she had been before, slouched in a big rattan armchair near the edge of the terrace. She turned her eyes to the three of them when they approached.

"You found it in the truck?" she asked.

"Yes. There is much more. Many boxes, but too heavy to carry," Elad said, putting down his bag.

"Come here," Katya said, motioning him over with her hand. Elad walked over.

When he was close enough, she grabbed Elad's arm to draw him down. Surprised, he leaned closer. She pressed her lips against his cheek.

"Take the Range Rover," Katya said. "I left the keys behind the back of the left wheel."

"What about you?" Elad asked.

"Paul will help me. I'll be fine. Go," Katya repeated.

Marco glanced over at Paul, waiting for his confirmation.

"Take what you can carry now. I'll find you later," Paul said.

Marco pulled at his friend's arm, urging him to leave. They both began to walk back to the garden and the direction of the gap under the perimeter wall. Each boy struggled to carry the heavy sack slung over his back. Paul watched them merge into the darkness. Outcomes turn on the slightest of fortunes—chance encounters, tiny margins of error, he thought. A friendship, a connection, a fraction of a second. All these tenuous connections were just enough to tilt the odds.

Paul turned his attention back to Katya reclining on the chair.

"You've lost a lot of blood. I need to get you help," he said.

"Come sit first," Katya said.

"It's still not safe."

"Come sit," she repeated.

Paul acquiesced and sat next to her on the second empty rattan chair.

"The sea looks lovely from here," Katya said weakly.

"It does," Paul answered. His eyes turned to the ocean that peaked above the tangled garden and the rocks. It was still dark, but light enough now for him to see the separation of water from sky along the gentle arc of the earth's long horizon. The clouds had cleared away earlier in the night. Now a cluster of stars dotted the sky. The stars suddenly seemed very bright and near. Paul's body felt weightless again, a mere vessel that carried his awareness.

"All this," Katya continued. "Still goes on with or without us."

"Now it goes on without Bogan," Paul replied.

"Yes. That is good."

Paul emptied his mind further. He sensed the night like a newborn perceiving a borderless panorama for the first time, as if he had just emerged again outside the womb.

"It's almost morning," Paul said.

Katya didn't answer. He saw her just staring out at the ocean as a kernel of sunlight began to form more brightly in the east. The night mutated slowly from a deep, translucent black to a richer purple as a new day began to lift, minute by minute. They watched this transformation.

The dawn's soft purple slowly smeared away the remaining stars until only a few of the brightest pinpricks remained.

It was good to see another morning, Paul thought. Sunrise. Metamorphosis. Resurrection. Hope.

Good just to be alive.

Good to be with her.

28

PAUL AND Katya sat quietly as the rising daylight revealed a graveyard of men scattered throughout the smoldering compound. Paul listened to the chirping of a host of sparrows clustered in a nearby cedar tree. A pungent smell of cordite hovered heavy in the early morning air.

Paul straightened himself up and looked over to the rattan chair where Katya sat. Her eyes were now closed. In the new day's dull yellow light, he saw her gently fading there, vendetta completed, breathing very slow.

He rose from his chair and shook her shoulder. She creaked open her eyes.

"Stay with me," Paul said.

"It looks worse than it feels," Katya said, moving her hand over the makeshift bandage wrapped around her thigh.

"It will start to hurt more soon. You've lost a lot of blood. We need to keep moving. Up you go," Paul said.

She crunched her face in pain as he leaned over and lifted her body. She wrapped her arms around his neck and pulled herself onto his back. Paul's legs burned as he carried her down the stone steps to the path that led to the garage. He marched with determination, Katya lithe body draped over his back, just like with Bella Grech a few days before in that cramped, limestone tunnel. This time, he wouldn't fail. He shouldn't have wasted so much time with the boxes and the boys. This time, she'll live.

Paul made it to the truck cab inside the garage. He opened the truck's passenger seat and strained his arms and shoulders again to lift Katya inside. Then, he went to the body of the Georgian guard lying face down in a pool of dark blood at the garage entrance. Paul searched first the dead man's left pocket. In the man's right pocket, he felt a ring of metal keys.

Paul went to the back of the trailer. He pulled the trailer's heavy rear door down, sealing it, and locked the latch tightly. Then Paul went back to truck cab and slid himself into the driver's seat.

"You know how to drive this monster?" Katya asked weakly. Blood seeped onto the front seat where she sat. Was the wound more threatening that he first thought? *Why did I stupidly let her just sit there for so long?*

Paul examined the cab's unfamiliar dashboard and gear boxes. He fumbled with the keys, then finally found the truck's ignition. The big truck's engine hummed on. Paul shifted gears, and the truck lurched forward. He pressed the gas pedal with his boot, the engine kicked in, and the massive machine rolled forward.

Paul drove along the black asphalt, across the compound's front entrance to the villa's locked front gate. The truck picked up speed and rammed through the front gate, its heavy wheels easily crushing the wooden barrier.

Paul turned left on the two-lane road and drove slowly to the first intersection. He carefully steered the Mercedes truck and trailer onto the busier local road. As he drove, Paul veered near the road's gravel shoulder to let other faster cars, like darting sparrows, pass him. It was another half hour until a small road sign indicated a turnoff to the nearest town of Licata. The sign showed painted icons that indicted fuel, lodging, a church, and a hospital. Paul took the exit, then navigated through a series of small traffic circles, carefully rotating the long forty-foot trailer around the curves, nervously looking in the mirrors. On one stretch of road, a small black-and-white police car approached in the opposite direction but passed them without any incident. Katya was limp in the passenger seat, eyes closed again, still fading.

"Hey. Don't sleep," Paul warned.

"No, I won't," she replied.

"Keep your eyes open," he said again, this time more sternly.

She opened them again.

Near the town center, Paul spotted the hospital's red cross icon atop a gray two-story building next to a small church: Pronto soccorso. Emergency room. Paul eased the big truck over to the road's dirt shoulder.

"I can't fit this thing into the parking lot," Paul said.

"Doesn't matter. Close enough," Katya said.

She fell into his arms after he opened the passenger door to lift her out. She clutched his neck the last difficult thirty meters to the emergency room's front entrance. The emergency room's frosted glass doors automatically slid open. A few people lingered on plastic seats inside the local hospital's small waiting room. A young nurse came out from behind a reception desk after she saw them stagger in. An older male nurse quickly pushed forward a wheelchair. He looked at them with anxious, probing eyes.

Katya let go of Paul's neck, and he gently placed her on the wheelchair's seat.

"You know what to tell them?" Paul asked.

"That's easy," Katya replied. "I don't speak Italian. Leave me here."

"Are you sure?"

"Yes. Keep going. Nothing you can do for me here."

"I should stay."

"No, Paul. Focus," she admonished.

"I won't be long," Paul replied.

The male nurse spoke to Paul in rapid Italian. He averted his eyes and instead walked away back out through the front entrance. No one followed him out the door. Paul crossed the parking lot, walked along the road, slipped back to truck, and started the engine again.

Trancelike, Paul continued driving alone, head forward, hands tight on the wheel. He stayed away from the larger highways, passing instead along the smaller, two-lane roads. Paul didn't care exactly where he went, only that he needed to drive away from more populated cities. He had only looked at the maps of Sicily a few hours, and that now seemed a lifetime ago. Still, it seemed to make the most sense to go further into the Sicilian interior, away from the major towns and the coast. Each mile created more distance from Villa Fontesa. Each mile created more space away from last night's carnage.

After an hour, Paul followed signs to a town called Enna near the island's center. Rolling green vineyards spread out at the base of this small village, and old farmhouses were scattered haphazardly in the rolling fields. This looked to him like the ancient, untouched area of wild Sicily, higher in elevation, and very far from more trafficked areas. It was perhaps the same landscape that the Normans saw nine hundred years ago after they first arrived on their longships.

Paul spotted an old, boarded-up, concrete warehouse on the side of the road. A parking area behind the building was hidden under the shade of a grove of tall oaks. Not perfect, but remote enough, he concluded. He slowed the truck, then quietly rolled it to a dark, unobtrusive flat space that afforded a range of pervasive shadows that was also mostly hidden from the road by the abandoned, crumbling old warehouse in front. Any passing car would need to look hard to see the truck parked behind this old brick building.

Paul shut off the Mercedes' noisy diesel engine. He breathed deeply before exiting the cab to get a firmer bearing on what exactly to do now with the long trailer. He unhooked the lever beneath the trailer to lower the front landing gear. He turned the trailer's iron shaft until the two heavy landing columns braced against the dry ground, then repeated the process at the other end for the heavy trailer's rear landing gear. Finally, Paul unlatched the cables attached to the cab and eased the trailer off the steel connection hitch that linked it to the cab. It seemed like the right thing to do. He nudged the Mercedes cab forward a few feet until it separated from the heavy trailer.

It was dark by the time Paul was able to fully unhitch the trailer. Over the course of the last several hours, only a few cars passed and no one on foot. In the truck cab, Paul put his head down on the wheel and let himself drift into unconsciousness for a solid ninety minutes. He had neither slept nor eaten since the morning breakfast in Siracusa. His upper body was flaked with tiny metal fragments—he began to feel these tiny welts burn after not even noticing the pain from the last grenade that had detonated so dangerously close. A quick recharge would need to carry him for another half day at least and maybe longer.

Quarter tank of gas still left. *Hopefully enough. Keep going. Get back to her. A leg wound like what she has shouldn't be fatal. The bullet passed cleanly through, missed the bone. Even an average doctor could stitch her up, no problem. Matching blood type? They would figure it out.*

Paul drove the six-wheel Mercedes cab south, this time on the larger roads. It was easier to drive back without the long, heavy trailer swinging behind. Three hours later, he was back in Licata again just as the next morning's light also arrived. Paul followed the direction back to the town's center, specifically to the gray two-story hospital where he had dropped off Katya. He parked the truck cab next to an old stone church.

A different, older female nurse greeted him this time in the hospital's reception area. Paul was bleary-eyed from stress and lack of sleep. The older nurse spoke only halting English, but enough to answer his questions. She revealed that a surgeon had stabilized the foreign woman's leg injury last night.

"Take me to her," Paul said.

The nurse frowned and instead shoved a patient intake form into Paul's hands, insisting in her broken English that it was time for paperwork.

"Take this," Paul said, handing her one of the ten-thousand-dollar bundles from the embassy envelope. The old nurse frowned at first, but then she counted the bills and shoved all of it in the top drawer of a reception desk. Muttering some complaints, she led Paul back to a room at the end of a short hallway.

Paul pushed open the door. Katya lay there, eyes closed, a blood transfusion bag hanging from a tall metal rod next to her bed. He went inside and closed the door. Her pale face was turned away, unconscious. Her body was naked beneath the white hospital gown; a clean white bandage was wrapped around her thigh, professionally done in neat concentric rings.

Paul brought in a wheelchair from the hallway. Katya stirred slightly as he lifted her from the bed and placed her in the chair. As he removed the intravenous needle from her right forearm, she opened her eyes to look up at him with a vague expression.

"Back already?" Katya said.

"I'm very quick."

"Did you hide it?"

"For now, yes," Paul said. "Let's get you out of this gown and into some new clothes."

"They gave me drugs for the pain."

"Yes, I know," Paul said.

"I feel much better."

"That's good. Very good."

Paul quietly wheeled her out into the parking lot through a side entrance. The old nurse's eyes followed them out. However, she didn't move from her chair or protest them leaving.

Outside, a ray of sunlight found its way through the morning clouds. The fresh, natural light outlined Katya's ashen-white face. She took a breath of the open air and her lips curled into a relieved smile under the sun. It looked to Paul as if she was briefly illuminated by some divine and distant savior.

29

MAX DRAKE looked out at the busy Paris streets with his single, living, right eye. He had never really spent much time thinking about what it would feel like to walk Paris' broad boulevards, next to the orderly rows of cream-colored limestone apartment buildings. Max had visited Europe's grandest of capital cities a decade ago for a few days during a summer after high school and before his first military tour. He nebulously recalled the most superficial of details—the Louvre's massive hallways, the tiny, disappointing Mona Lisa imprisoned behind thick, bulletproof glass, hard loaves of bread, and dark, overly ornate gothic churches along the Seine. Europe's greatest city was intriguing, he admitted, but somehow left no lasting impression on his immature twenty-year-old self.

Now, ten years later, Max experienced a different city. On this cool, early spring afternoon, the streets teemed with a vibrant, unscripted reality. Every part of his body tingled. It was a magical sensation just to be in this city. Something new was about to change the direction of life. Something new was about to release him from the gray purgatory where he had been stuck alone for so many years. Something new was about to restore the full scope of his vision, even if one of his physical eyes was forever lost.

It was Paul who called him over to Paris. Again. It was always Paul, a decade after Iraq, and almost two years since his older brother had suddenly disappeared from his banking work, his apartment, his myriad routine life obligations. For many months after the woman came to see him and bought him coffee that morning at the Newark diner, he had heard nothing. Then, finally, a call. Just like that.

Paul's outreach was cryptic: find your passport, pack your bags, and come. He hinted at developments but omitted more detail. Typical Paul.

A late-night flight delivered Max first to Charles de Gaulle Airport. A taxi ride took him to a small five-story hotel in the city's center next to the Palais Royal. Max showered, changed clothes, took an espresso with an extra sugar cube at a nice, shaded café just across the street from the hotel, and began to walk to the appointed meeting place.

Rue de Saint Honoré teamed with people, most of them well dressed in spring fashion. Strangers talked amongst themselves in different languages, drifted in and out of fashionable boutiques, walked small poodles with clean, fluffy hair. They met friends, worked at jobs, talked on mobile phones, and otherwise continued with their eminently peaceful, civilized lives.

Max came to L'église de la Madeleine that loomed above the busy streets like a Roman temple with rows of commanding columns supporting its triangular portico. Paul waited inside the exterior gate, near the steps, just as promised. He was clean shaven, hair closely cropped, hands shoved inside an oversized black peacoat. Max wasn't sure exactly what emotions welled up inside him as he hugged his brother. At his core, Max felt a certain ineffable union with this other human being. They didn't look much alike except for the dark hair and a similar body type, but they shared an origin. It was Paul who convinced Max to enlist in the service after high school—it was something that their dad would have supported if he had lived longer. Now here Paul was again. For many years now, he had lost his best friend. That absence hurt.

"Come on, let's walk a bit," Paul said.

They walked at a leisurely pace away from the river. As they strolled, Max listened to his brother's story, focused on his words. Paul described his search for answers, an operation gone wrong on Malta, an underground trap, and a final, violent night on the southern coast of Sicily.

Max listened, trying to project himself into his brother's experiences. He had never been to any of the islands Paul described. He didn't know if the images conjured up by his brother's story had any connection with what Paul had gone through. Max asked clarifying questions to better understand. What to make of this fantastic, slightly unreal, cascading sequence of events? What degree of control did Paul really have over any of it?

"You took these risks?" Max asked.

"I had to. There wasn't any other way."

They passed through a small garden park, then another few blocks along a narrower, tree-lined street.

"Here we are," Paul said. Max looked across the street at a church constructed out of gray stone and graced by three triangular spires. A golden onion dome topped each of the spires, glinting now in the afternoon light. A Christ mosaic outlined in gold rested above the main entrance. Max read a wooden sign near the front of the church: Cathedrale Orthodoxe Russe St. Alexandre Nevsky.[102]

"What is this place?" Max asked.

"Katya's father was meant to take her here six years ago. He never did. Let's wait here. The service is almost over. She is inside."

"You mean Kate?"

"Kate if you like," Paul said.

The brothers waited for the congregation to drift out of the early afternoon Sunday service. Max didn't recognize Katya at first. She wore a stylish fur coat, her honey-colored hair covered in a white headscarf in a similar fashion as the other Russian women emerging from the church's interior. She walked with a cane; her left arm looped inside the arm of a white-haired old man in a tailored gray suit.

Katya smiled when she saw Paul and Max at the bottom of the stone stairs. She went first to Max and gave him two kisses on each cheek.

"I am so happy you came," she said.

"It was easy," Max said, dumbly.

The old man also reached out his hand and introduced himself as Yuri.

"We're late for our reservation. Let's go before we lose our table," the old man said.

They crossed the street toward a crowded restaurant on the corner of Rue Daru. A tall, red-haired waiter spoke to Yuri in Russian as they entered inside. The waiter led them to a round table just behind the restaurant's large front window. A La Ville de Petrograd was crowded, mostly with other Russian families from the afternoon Sunday service at Alexandre Nevsky. The restaurant showed off various Russian motifs with folk-story paintings on the brightly colored walls. Elaborate chandeliers hung from a bright blue ceiling. Busy waiters carried porcelain plates to and from the kitchen, weaving between tables spread out on the restaurant's black-and-white checkered floor.

"Have you eaten Russian food before?" Katya asked Max.

"Never," Max said.

"Try the salad olivier and the shuba," she said.

---

102   Built between 1859 and 1861 with the personal financial support of Tsar Alexander II to serve as the first permanent Russian Orthodox church in France. It is famous for its distinctive Byzantine-Muscovite architecture featuring five gilded onion domes and for hosting the 1918 wedding of Pablo Picasso to the Russian dancer Olga Khokhlova.

They ordered; the wine came first. Max sipped the glass and exchanged pleasantries as the food came out on large white plates. He took cheese and herring first.

"When I come to a place like this, and I see these people, it gives me hope," Yuri said, after he passed Max a plate of what looked like sour cream and dumplings.

"How so?" asked Max.

"Maybe someday my country will be free again. Perhaps there will be change."

"That would be good," Max replied, not knowing much about Russian politics, only that he couldn't remember any time in history when the country didn't seem to have immense problems or a brutal dictator in power.

The old man spoke a little more about political issues, but then changed the subject. He asked Max questions about his childhood with Paul. Max demurred at first, but as they spoke more, he found himself talking more freely about his family summers in Maine. Those summers were now more than twenty years ago. Their father was still alive then. He had been an avid fisherman; they all enjoyed the long days on his small fishing boat. They often brought back lobsters in nets, then boiled them at night in bitter lemon sauce and plenty of olive oil. Max's memories remained sharp and pure—he could still see his father's smile. Those were good, uncluttered days, before anything in his own life had really taken shape and before the pain of other days, misfortune, loss, failures.

Yuri Volkov smiled as he listened to Max describe his family memories. Then the older man spoke slowly, in careful English, about his own youth, even longer in the past. Yuri shared a story about ice fishing with his own younger brother when Katya was still a small child. Yuri and Sergei cooked trout over hot coals at the family's country dacha just south of St. Petersburg.

"It sounds like Maine, only in winter and much colder."

"Yes. Different, but also the same. These are the true experiences we both remember best."

"It is what is true," Max said.

Yuri took his wine glass and raised it high.

"Here is to those we have lost," Yuri said in a solemn voice, "To my brother Sergei, his beautiful wife Elena, and their eldest son, Viktor. They are still with us today if we remember."

Max, Paul, and Katya all raised their glasses.

"To fallen heroes," Paul added.

"To family and the future," Katya said.

"To family and the future," Max repeated, locking eyes first with Paul, then with her, and finally, Yuri. The old man had strange, deep eyes, he now noticed.

The meal continued another hour, then finally ended over strong black espresso coffee. Most of the other afternoon diners who had come in after the church service had already left by the time Yuri paid the check. A few new patrons drifted in for the start of the dinner menu.

Paul helped Katya to her feet; she used the cane to stay off her right leg. Paul walked her slowly to Yuri's waiting car just outside the restaurant's entrance.

"I will see you both tomorrow?" Katya asked.

"Yes, of course," Max said.

"Splendid. We'll make a day of it," she replied, smiling.

Just before Katya slipped into the backseat, Paul pulled her closer.

"All good?" Paul asked in a low voice so his brother could not hear.

"Of course, *Da*. It's been a lovely day. Spend more time with Max. He needs you," she said. Then she lightly kissed Paul on the cheek, and he shut the door.

———— ✳ ————

After the late lunch, Paul and Max drifted off by themselves back into the shifting activity of downtown Paris. They walked along Boulevard Haussmann toward the still busy traffic circle around the Arc de Triomphe. Max saw the tiny heads of people on top of the Arc, looking down from the height of the monument's terrace. The air turned chilly as night slowly descended. Paul led the way to a small stylish bar that was beginning to get crowded with young patrons despite the Sunday evening time. In the back of the bar, tucked in a private corner, the two brothers continued their long overdue reunion. Paul ordered two bourbons on the rocks from an auburn-haired young waitress with bright red lipstick and a tight-fitting black cotton halter-top.

"Jet-lagged?" Paul asked.

"Not at all."

"Enjoy the food at lunch?"

"Different," Max said.

"You seemed to connect with Yuri."

"He seems decent."

"He is," Paul said, then explained a little more about Yuri's origin.

The pretty auburn-haired waitress came back with their drinks. She smiled as she handed them the two tumblers, then moved on to the next table.

"What's next, Paul? Do you plan to come back home?" Max asked.

"I don't know. Things have changed."

"What else haven't you told me? What else happened? There is something more."

Paul looked away.

"I'm listening," Max prodded again.

"In Sicily, some of our decisions worked out well. More luck than I deserve," Paul continued.

Max sat transfixed as Paul explained his drive into the island's mountainous interior after the firefight on the coast. Max's one living eye studied Paul's face as his brother described his drive through the twisted Italian backroads after he left Katya alone at the small local hospital in Licata.

"You left an entire trailer of Russian gold in some random place in the middle of Sicily?" Max asked.

"I did. Twenty-four metric tons of it. A billion and a half dollars at today's prices."

"Where is the gold now?"

"Safe."

"Do others know?" Max asked.

"The right people do, yes. Others, no."

"What will you do with it?" Max asked.

"I'm not sure. It's not something we planned to have. Hopefully, it will be enough to help," Paul said.

"More than enough," Max said.

"Maybe," Paul replied.

Maybe? What was brother thinking? $1.5 billion?

Max finished the bourbon in one long gulp. Paul's entire narrative still sounded too fantastic, like pure fiction. How could Paul's long series of decisions and indecisions, trials and errors, have led to this strange outcome? His brother descended deep into a dark rabbit hole and emerged here, back in Paris, years later, transformed. Paul had just revealed that he possessed more wealth than he could possibly use in a lifetime. If all that had really happened, then why did his brother still seemed deeply vexed?

"What's wrong? What's bothering you?" Max asked.

"This war is not over," Paul cautioned.

"Why not? Haven't you done enough already?"

"We've just stopped a few bad guys. There are many others responsible for blood."

"Don't press your luck," Max asserted. "A few seconds difference on that ferry boat in Syria, or underground in Malta, and you wouldn't be here sipping bourbon with me."

"You are right. I was incredibly lucky. Many times. Nothing is fated."

"Stop now. You are free to do almost anything," Max pressed.

"Free. Yes, we are all free. Every day we are free, from dawn to dusk. We always have choice, no matter what the circumstances, however bad or good it all seems. We become important only because of our decisions," Paul said.

Max considered his brother's curious phrase: Important only because of our decisions. *What does he mean by that?*

"Katya has changed you," Max said. "She's made you quite the philosopher."

"Maybe she has."

Despite the late hour, neither of them felt tired. Max peered more deeply into Paul's eyes. He realized that they had only scratched the surface regarding what exactly had happened and why. There was so much more that Paul needed to explain about Katya, the old man Yuri, someone else named Dmitry, and many others. There was a whole complicated narrative inside his brother that needed unpacking. There was much, much more to carefully listen to and perhaps in his own way, finally understand. He suspected also that some plan was already slowly brewing in Paul's head.

Max caught the eye of the auburn-haired waitress as she passed. She paused and came closer to their table.

"*Avez vous besoin d'autre chose?*" she asked.

Daring to use his poor French, Max asked her to bring two more bourbons on ice.

"*Tout de suite, monsieur,*" the young woman replied, acknowledging Max's linguistic effort with a slight smile. Her gaze seemed to linger on Max's face as if trying to determine why his right eye stared at her so intensely, but his left eye rested unmoving. She offered a lingering moment that seemed to return some level of interest.

"Do you think she is pretty?" Max asked his brother after the woman disappeared back into the crowd.

"Definitely. Good bones, nice smile," Paul responded. "Ask for her number. What do you have to lose?"

"I'm not like you," Max said.

"No. You are yourself."

"Not tonight," Max said.

"Tomorrow then."

"I'll think about it."

"I'm sure she speaks English."

"Yes, with her current boyfriend," Max retorted.

"Ha! Maybe not. You can't know if you don't ask."

Paul put his hand on his brother's shoulder.

"If there is life, there is hope," Paul said. "I can't tell you what's next, but nothing is fated. The future is unwritten. What I do know now is that I sure could use your help. It's up to you to decide."

Volume 3

EASTERN LIGHT

Between stimulus and response, there is a space. In that space, is our power to choose our response.

—Viktor Frankl (b.1905, d.1997), Austrian psychiatrist, Shoah survivor (1942–1945)

WAR BEGINS

Stepana Bandery Avenue
North Bridge
Perova Boulevard
Bratyslavska Street
Zoo Kiev
Peremohy Avenue
Dnieper River
Brovarsky Avenue
Hydropark
Paul Drake Apartament
Eternal Glory Park
Antonovycha Street
Darnytske Road
Valeriia Lobanovskoho Ave
Kyiv Intern. Airport
Dnieper River
0   2,36 miles
DOWNTOWN KYIV

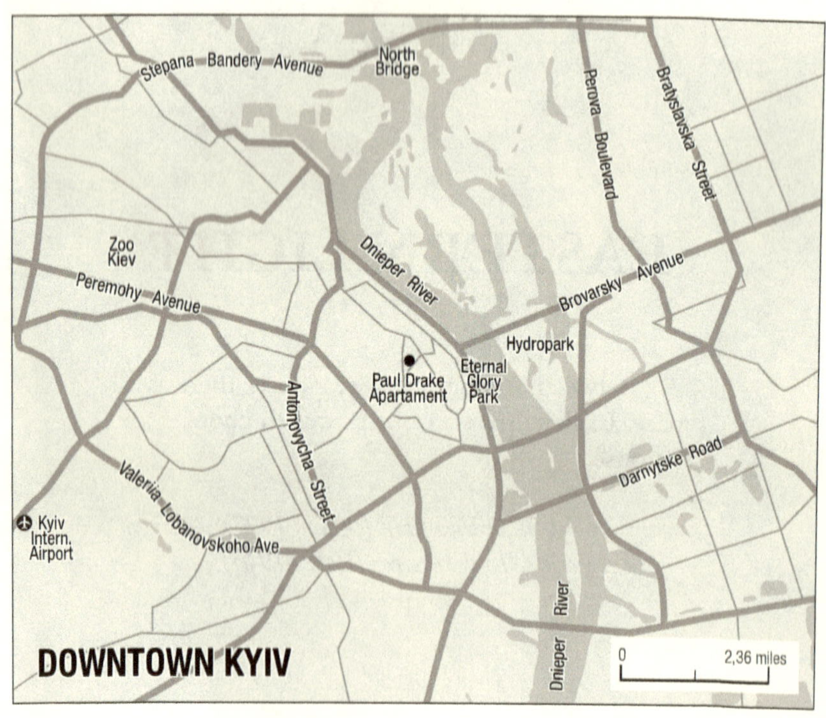

1

Kyiv, Ukraine.
March 2, 2022. 6:15 a.m.

P AUL DRAKE'S digital wristwatch alarm pulsed in sharp, staccato increments before he finally silenced it. He reemerged in the gray light, looking up at the jagged water-induced plaster cracks fanned out along the apartment's low ceiling.

Deep breaths. Exhale.

Here I am, alive… mostly, Paul thought. *Reality, again, hard in the bones. Cogito ergo sum.*[103]

Paul rolled off the hard mattress, then snatched his dangling overcoat from the back of a cracked faux leather chair. He slipped on the coat before opening the heavy fifteenth-floor balcony door. Paul's warm breath clouded into vapor. He still felt slightly unreal inside his aching body, a ghostly spirit hovering inside a jumble of automatically pulsing veins and a beating heart. Fingers touched the balcony's icy, rusty steel railing. Electrical signals shot from eye to brain until his consciousness finally registered the alien dawn's slow mutation.

Pale amber morning light danced across the patches of ice and snow along Kyiv's haphazard, jagged rooftops. Wisps of steam rose from the exhaust ducts of the larger cement and limestone apartment buildings. St. Sophia Cathedral's white bell tower and onion-domed gold crown peaked above this low, confused medley joined also by the nearby ethereal spires of St. Michael's restored monastery[104] and the ornate, turquoise-painted eighteenth-century St. Andrew's Church.[105] Groves of oak, linden, and poplar trees on Volodymyr Hill spread down to the crowded lower Podil district and the wide Dnieper River.

---

103   The Latin phrase "I think, therefore I am" is René Descartes' fundamental philosophical principle that the very act of doubting one's own existence proves that a conscious entity (the thinker) must exist.

104   Originally built in the 12th century, the monastery was demolished by Soviet authorities in the 1930s. Its reconstruction in 1999 became a national symbol of Ukraine's freedom.

105   Commissioned by Empress Elizabeth Petrovna in 1744, who laid the first three foundation stones. Completed in 1767 by the Italian architect Bartolomeo Rastrelli.

The Dnieper had served as Kyiv's civilizing artery for more than a thousand years, a commercial lifeline running down to the Black Sea that once linked a small Rus outpost to Constantinople's mighty Eastern Roman Empire, thriving still after Rome itself had long surrendered its power and succumbed to centuries of feudal darkness. This morning, more than a millennium later, the river again had become a critical defense as new barricades had sprung up on the Patona and Northern Bridges. Ukrainian army specialists hastily loaded powerful explosives along both bridges' welded iron pylons, ready to be blown if the ground invasion from the north made it this far.

Paul shuffled back inside. Only thirty minutes to meet Valentine. The shower's chilly water hit his face like an insult. A frenetic continuum of recent memories from the last few weeks replayed as Paul ran his soapy fingers through his cropped black hair. Mass panic, fear, and anger had all swirled together in those scariest first days when Kyiv had emptied like a drained bathtub. Thousands of frightened, confused, scared people clogged roads and train stations in mass shock.

Last night at dusk, Paul had first heard the whirling engines, then watched a flotilla of KA-52 Russian attack helicopters streak low and fast northward, their noses tipped slightly downward. Those four bulky machines seemed like clumsy, dangerous locusts, an advance sign of a coming mechanized plague. The KA-52s chopped their path above the urban sprawl undeterred, too fast, and too high.

That night, Paul had eaten hard cheese and black bread alone in his room. He streamed into his mobile phone a recorded emergency session of the United Nation's General Assembly. The American envoy angrily condemned Russia's violation of the UN Charter's Article 2. Other Western democracies—Poland, the Czech Republic, France, and the United Kingdom—also fumed. The world's two most populous countries, India and China, took a more cautious stance, choosing abstention rather than a principled vote. The so-called Global South had their own interests, doubts, and confusions. Paul had closed the video app after twenty minutes. Sadly, far-away diplomatic voices and high-minded institutions were irrelevant now. What had Mao said? Power comes from the barrel of a gun. True indeed, he acknowledged, before closing his eyes just after midnight.

Now Paul locked the room's door, then took the small elevator down to the building's lobby. Kyiv's early morning streets were mostly empty at this early hour, except for a few other solitary walkers, their heads hidden under hats and bodies stuffed in long coats. He walked quickly. Steel hedgehog barriers were installed at intersections, along with antitank barricades at strategic locations. At Mykhailivska Square,[106] sandbags covered a marble statue of tenth-century Princess Olga up to her long, slender neck.

At Khureschatyk Road, one of Kyiv's widest thoroughfares, Valentine Kuzoff waited at their appointed location, near a small sidewalk coffee kiosk.

"*Dobre utra*. Good morning, Paul," the handsome clean-shaven Ukrainian said with his usual wry smile.

"*Dobre*," Paul replied.

Valentine ordered two black coffees and handed the stooped old woman in the kiosk 150 hryvnia. He passed one of the Styrofoam cups to Paul.

"*Spasibo*. Thank you," Paul replied.

Paul and Valentine had grown closer these past three years. Valentine's basic English was not a barrier. Trust sprang forth from necessity. They worked well together, bonding via shared extreme moments. A few years ago in Northern Syria, there was a daring six-hour desert ride to rescue their men. Then there was the day Valentine had searched for Paul after an air attack in Turkey, eventually finding his friend dazed and alone, wandering the Euphrates Valley sorghum fields at dusk. By comparison to those prior incidents, graceful Kyiv this morning seemed manageable, even majestic in her ancient, stoic coldness. This chilly morning, the spiritual city, an ageless mother, seemed to pause her noble dance, if only for an hour. Even the bad street coffee tasted decent, bitter on Paul's tongue but warm down his throat.

A man walked closer to the coffee kiosk when he heard the two friends conversing in English on the otherwise empty street. He had a weathered dark face, a manicured black beard, and patchy white hair.

"Is the comedian gone yet?" the stranger asked in an accent Paul guessed as Turkish.

"Who? Zelensky?" Paul asked, turning to him.

"Yes. That guy," the stranger said in a derisive tone.

"He's still here," Paul replied. "He posted another video outside Gorodetsky House last night."

"The Russians want his head," the stranger continued. "I'm sure he'll get out soon, save his skin like the others."

"Maybe not," Paul replied.

---

106   One of Kyiv's oldest squares with a history spanning approximately 900 years.

"The little Jew will need more than his funny dances and jokes now,"[107] the bearded man scoffed as he lit a cigarette and took in a big nicotine-laced draw.

"What about you? Why are you still here?" Paul asked.

"Me? I own a trading business in the south. Best to wait until all this is over in a few weeks. Then we get back to normal with a better government."

"Only a few weeks?" Paul asked.

"Give or take," the stranger opined.

"Why do you think that?"

"Ha. You do not know?" he said. "These farmers will scatter like little monkeys once Russian troops arrive. This place is not a real country, you understand?"

Valentine crushed his empty coffee cup and threw it into the trash before he projected an icy stare.

"I don't think so," Valentine growled.

Paul put his hand on his friend's shoulder, knowing it was best to cut this conversation short.

"Come. We don't have time," Paul said. "Good luck to you, friend. Be safe."

The bearded stranger made a forced, uncomfortable smile. "*Dolboyob*,"[108] Valentine muttered, adding more curse words as he and Paul walked away from the main street up a sloping cobblestone road that meandered between the rows of ugly Soviet-era apartment blocks.

A few more people now appeared on the streets, each with tight, fast gaits and somber expressions. Although a few cars began to appear on the main roads, they were relatively sparse compared to the usual heavily congested traffic during a typical morning in Kyiv. And there were no children to be seen.

"How is your mother? Convinced her to leave yet?" Paul asked as they walked.

"*Nyet.* She is old. Bad knees."

"You should get her to Lviv. Safer there," Paul suggested.

"Mama never listens," Valentine said. "She hates sitting on trains. She is very, how do you, say … *upriyami*."

---

107   Prior to his 2019 election, Vladimir Zelensky was a popular television personality who played in the satirical TV series "Servant of the People" (2015–2019) about an ordinary Ukrainian who becomes its president.

108   Russian insult meaning idiotic or stupid.

"Stubborn," Paul translated.

"*Da*. Mama is stubborn," Valentine murmured.

Valentine Romanovich Kuzoff's thoughts drifted to his sixty-two-year-old mother as he led Paul along the cobblestone street and up a small hill. Mama had already survived so much turmoil and change—the fall of Soviet Communism in 1991, Ukraine's birth a year later, the so-called Orange Revolution in 2004, the Maidan Square uprising in 2016, and now this. Olga Kuzanova would rather die here on an old, cold bed instead of fleeing Kyiv and thus abandoning hope after all those prior tribulations. All alone in that crappy one-bedroom apartment, Valentine thought, and still she was not afraid. She believed she was protected by the archangel Michael, a group of long-dead saints, and what she considered to be divine justice, if an omnipresent but unknowable God exercised universal power in this way.

Olga was like most others. No fear. Only anger and puzzlement. She expected the Russians to play hardball, but this fratricidal blitzkrieg was an absurd overreach, a madman's fantasy. Putin would be locked up in an asylum if he were not sitting on his imperial throne. Lock him up, she prayed, so the rest of humanity could go on working jobs, eating borsch, watching football matches, and making healthy little fat babies. One evil lunatic should never decide the fates of millions the way Stalin and Hitler had for the long-suffering generation before.

"It's up ahead here," Valentine said to Paul, pointing to two armed men guarding the entrance to the courtyard wedged be-tween two solid five-story dark granite buildings. The taller guard recognized Valentine and motioned him in.

Inside the walled courtyard, dozens of men and women milled about, most of them dressed in khaki-colored fatigues with blue sashes on their upper arms or wrapped around their steel-gray helmets. The people came here to gather small arms—Kalashnikovs, old rifles, grenades, and Molotov cocktails. Several uniformed soldiers bearing the Ukrainian Territorial Militia insignia slowly rummaged through various wooden crates, pulling out weapons, inspecting them, and periodically handing out the small arms to new recruits.

"Well?" Valentine asked Paul.

"More than I expected, but they will be completely outgunned by professional troops," Paul said. "I hope it does not come to street battles. What is the latest update from Dmitry?"

"First truck before lunch," Valentine said, knowing that his boss, the ever-resourceful Dmitry Medkov, had quietly lifted two dozen precious Javelins from their clandestine stash on the Syrian Turkish border in just the last week.

For now, a few portable surface-to-air missiles must suffice. Paul's US Army experience would help him teach the basics to the locals. Better than nothing. If the Ukrainians could just contest the skies a while longer, then NATO or the US might step in with a no-fly zone to deny Russia air superiority, or there might even be a better response from other allies soon. Dmitry had also promised two hundred Starlink communication boxes next week, and Kyiv's basic infrastructure was still largely intact—water, electricity, tele-com towers, even heating in most buildings. But that might not last much longer after Russian generals realized their initial mistakes and changed tactics.

"I'm going inside," Paul said.

Valentine nodded and wandered over to a small group of new recruits milling about. A teenage boy and two fresh-faced girls were holding heavy older rifles as if touching them for the first time.

"You know how to use these toys?" Valentine asked one of the girls in Ukrainian.

She had rosy, smooth cheeks and tightly braided light brown hair. The girl's face was plain, he thought, except she had exception-ally beautiful large hazel eyes. A few months ago, she was probably serving out crème puff pastries as a part-time job, just a little ordinary life like any other teenager in Europe or the States. Now she caressed a clunky Soviet-made rifle with her small, much-too-soft hands.

"I know enough," the girl replied softly.

"Not afraid?" Valentine asked.

"What for?"

"How old are you, little sister?" Valentine pressed.

She squinted with hard eyes. "Why do you care?" she asked. Her two fresh-faced friends in blue jeans and faded denim jackets also scowled.

"I do not care, little sister. Just want to avoid wasting good blood on you," he replied before drifting away.

The BBC had shown satellite photos of a forty-mile-long column of tanks and trucks that had crossed over the Belorussian border. Russia's invading army, their so-called "special military operation," was now oddly stuck on a two-lane road. Rumors floated about widespread mechanical problems, fuel shortages, and basic command and control breakdowns. Were the rumors true, or were these 50,000 soldiers just waiting for their Imperial stormtrooper signal? Valentine had already experienced Russia's handiwork in Syria. Just as the Germans experimented in Spain in the 1930s, so too today's killers honed their terror tactics, hiring Wagner mercenaries, pulling in Chechen murderers to rape and slaughter. Putin invented another evil logo—the nationalistic, menacing Z—to spread their fear. The orcs painted their brutal new Z on tanks and trucks, the same as a hundred years ago when a failed Austrian watercolorist dreamed up the inverted swastika to organize followers behind his insane and violent acts.[109]

Past domestic political divisions were irrelevant now. Young and old, men and women, were all signing up, picking up weapons, ready to fight. Valentine hoped Ukraine's defense brigades could block Russian paratroopers at Hostomel airport, preventing them from establishing an air bridge to control the city. Kyiv's heavily built suburbs like Irpin and Buncha favored the defenders by a wide margin. Once the invaders became ensnarled in Kyiv's maze, a bloodbath worse than 1941 was inevitable.

"Hey there. Can you help with this one?" a lanky man said to Valentine, pointing to a heavy crate on the flatbed of a truck.

Valentine nodded and went to help.

---

109   Hitler noted in Mein Kampf that the Nazi party symbol needed to be as "highly effective as a poster" to represent his myth of racial superiority and compete with the Communist Party's hammer and sickle.

2

Palm Springs, California.
March 23, 2022. 4 p.m.

A LIGHT breeze, hot and arid, whispered over the jagged peaks of the San Jacinto Mountains, carrying with it the scent of sunbaked rock and dry brush. The sky above was a vast, cloudless azure expanse that seemed to press down on the dry mountains with its flat, inescapable, and indifferent immensity.

At the end of an unobtrusive cul-de-sac, a twelve-meter-high entrance gate lined with prickly cacti and tangled agave plants sheltered the entrance to Rutherford Ranch, fifteen miles north of downtown Palm Springs. A private security guard registered each guest's vehicle, taking down the license plate number of every Tesla, Lexus, Jaguar, and Porsche that passed through the gate. Along a stone path that led up the hill to the main building, a trail of breezy white canopies was set up in intervals to block the hot sun as guests strolled the hundred meters to the ranch's west building. The west building was the newest addition to the ranch's main three-acre property, designed with mid-century aesthetics, lofty ceilings, and large interiors ideal for social gatherings.

Inside the west building's air-conditioned interior, a low murmur of voices stirred. The room's high ceilings and varnished cedarwood floors caught conversations and sporadic bouts of laughter from the hour-old party that was now in full swing.

Chatter receded when a tuxedo-clad musician seated at a polished black Steinway grand began to play a melody, his long-trained hands dancing effortlessly across the piano's cleanly polished wood keys.

Heads turned as a tall, slightly stooped George Rutherford III appeared, celebrity-like, via the room's side doorway. From the ad-joining kitchen, several waiters wheeled out an impressive four-layer cream-colored cake to the center of the room while George shook hands and smiled broadly. The cake's top layer, iced with elaborate lavender floral swirls, held eight tall wax candles for each decade and a final one for the billionaire's eighty-first year.

Standing in the corner, Katerina Sergeevna Volkova joined in singing a resounding happy birthday chorus. Some fifty friends and family clapped as Rutherford leaned closer to the massive cake, puckered his lips, and blew. Two of the nine candles still flamed after the attempt. The tall billionaire made an enthusiastic second puff to finish them. Another round of clapping.

A blond woman in an elegant white silk dress and distinctive, red-soled Christian Louboutin high heels, who Katya recognized as the wife of a first-term Nevada congressman, shouted, "Bravo, George. Bravo!"

"Another year above ground," Rutherford replied.

"With age, wisdom," someone shouted.

"Twenty more," another voice chimed in.

George smiled at his audience, though Katya noted his small gray eyes still seemed cold and permanently aloof.

Waiters cut the massive cake as the tuxedoed piano player started a different song and voices scattered into different conversations.

A waiter handed Katya a small piece of cake. She took it and delicately ate the cream-filled slice with a slender sliver art-deco fork. The moist interior tasted sweet on her tongue, although not as good as the pastries she had picked up last week from Maison d'Isabelle, her favorite corner bakery on Rue de Saint Germain back in Paris. American cakes, she thought, always taste just a little too processed and a little too artificial. Never quite as good as the French make their own.

As Katya scanned the party for familiar faces, a remorseful memory stung. What was different this afternoon from the last time she was in this room? Who was not among the smiles?

No face here today was as appealing as that of Tim Hasting. She had first met his handsome, quick eyes here more than two years ago after, with such a rush of naïve enthusiasm, he had parachuted in to help. She now felt his absence. Tim lingered ghost-like only in her own mind, a blank void forgotten by everyone except her. *Poor Tim. You had such distinctive bright eyes. You did not deserve a life cut short because of me. The world is a lesser place without you. Now I must deal with the living without your help.*

Katya noticed George's oldest son, Skip, eyeing her from across the room. She turned to give him her necessary attention after he finally broke away to approach her.

"Thanks for coming," Skip began, his two small beady eyes encircled by gold-rimmed Prada glasses that seemed too large for his unattractive thin face. A double Windsor–knotted tie was tight around his neck, and beads of sweat dripped from his left ear.

Ever since George had invited Katya to join the Jefferson Foundation's board, this obnoxious, pot-bellied, rich brat had been poking sticks with personal questions and unpleasant, curt business emails to prove his authority. Skip could not hide his annoyance at how his father treated her, an outsider and a woman, as a peer.

"Of course. Eighty-one years is a victory," Katya replied. "Amazing your father is still so healthy."

"Blame the dry climate and the golf," Skip offered.

"In Russian, we say George is an old goat with strong horns," Katya said.

"Strong horns, yes," Skip replied wryly. "He is healthier today than when he was in his fifties. Probably owes his energy to certain younger people he keeps nearby. Especially you."

"I'm flattered," she said, her voice measured.

"You should be. Dad speaks about you often," Skip continued. "I laugh when I hear how he describes you. He sounds obsessed. Worse than my teenage son swooning about his prom date."

"Obsession is a strong word."

"Is it? Obsession is how it seems," Skip pressed.

"George and I enjoy each other's company," she countered. "Friendly conversations, I know. He tells me. You have influenced Dad's interests more than I thought possible at his age. He was never such an art connoisseur before. This place used to have empty walls. Now look at how much stuff he has bought from you. Tens of millions of dollars spent on all these paintings and sculptures in just a few years. And this is just a fraction on display. Crates of the pretty stuff you sold to him are still in storage."

"It's a good collection," Katya replied.

"Is it? I am not an expert. Art was never a thing for Dad or any of us. It was never important until he met you. He claims the value will appreciate thanks to your expert selection. Maybe that is right, or maybe it isn't."

"George's interest in collecting isn't about my tastes," Katya replied. "Art is essential. Without it, could we endure all the rest? What would be the point? One stimulation after the next. Pain. Joy. Pain again. No deeper meaning."

"I find my meaning by living well in the real world," Skip replied.

"Or perhaps what you consider the real world is all mere shadows on a cave wall?"

"Ha ha, there you go," he scoffed, lips curled in a wry smile. "That's exactly the kind of voodoo mumbo jumbo that Dad can't get out of his head!"

"It is not voodoo. It is Greek, from Plato's allegory of cave. Book seven of The Republic,"[110] Katya replied softly, putting down her empty plate. She chose not to elaborate further while Skip's adversarial puzzlement lingered. There was no point to explain to him her Sorbonne master's dissertation on how ancient Greek metaphysics influenced the development of Western art.

"Staying the night?" Skip asked.

"Sadly, no. I drive back to Los Angeles later this evening."

"Long drive at night."

"Just two hours with no traffic. I drive fast," she said.

"Moved there?"

"Visiting," Katya replied.

"Let's meet if you are free next week," Skip said. "We can have lunch at our law firm's office in Pacific Palisades. I respect Dad's foundation. He is passionate about so many critical issues. We all want him to be successful. But you should also understand that some of us in the family, well, we believe there is room for more transparency. Transparency helps everyone think long-term and stay within the parameters of ..."

Katya nodded politely while Skip driveled on about his fears of a diminished inheritance. *Now I will waste time next week stuck in an overweight lawyer's office eating roast beef sandwiches and listening to your pathetic grousing,* she thought. George never respected his four children. The old man really hated their spouses, especially Skip's third wife, Amanda, a thirty-year-old Barbie doll with oversized silicon breasts and Botox lips. The twelve grandkids, mostly in their twenties, were even worse dullards. Too much money and no purpose. No one within the family understood what George III, the patriarch, truly supported or why. The spoiled brats were all just quietly, patiently, eagerly waiting for the old man to gracefully pass on so they could live fat and self-medicated inside multimillion-dollar walled gardens.

Katya imagined the fears that rattled through Skip's mind: Who was the Russian slut really? Why had Dad fallen for the tired bromide of a young temptress during his twilight years? Was there any other explanation for why he was now squandering the family treasure on her stupid art?

---

110   This allegory depicts prisoners chained in a cave who mistake shadows on a wall—cast by puppets before a fire—for reality. One prisoner's forced ascent into the sunlight represents the painful transition from sensory ignorance to intellectual apprehension.

Was there even more recklessness to come, especially if they discovered the witch was involved with more destructive hanky-panky beneath this so-called harmless friendship? "Fancy seeing you here," a husky voice suddenly broke in during a lull in Skip's monologue. Katya turned and saw a dark, stout, slightly balding man. The man approached her for a light embrace. She grabbed the opportunity to step away from Skip with a false smile and a reluctant promise to continue next week.

Eli Gold's tan sports jacket fit tightly around his muscular shoulders, and his neck seemed too thick for his white collared shirt. He grasped Katya by the elbow with one of his large hands and pulled her over to an empty area just behind the Steinway piano.

"Nice surprise you came," Katya said.

"Too long," the Israeli trainer said.

"Much."

Katya was glad to see Eli. Now here is a man who lives in his body, she thought.

"You've been well?" he asked.

"Healthy enough," Katya replied. "Leg injury a while back, mostly healed now."

"Did not even notice. You look fit," Eli said.

"Not like before."

She owed her life to Eli's nine months of grueling physical and mental preparation out here in the open California desert. His no-nonsense Krav Maga fighting techniques had saved her life that fateful midnight overlooking Malta's Grand Harbour when she finally met Andre Gauthier, a.k.a. Rene Voclan, alone.

"Still training?" Eli asked.

"A little. I miss our outdoor sessions," Katya said.

"As do I," Eli replied. "You left without us even taking a drink."

"I know. Something came up."

"Did you resolve it?"

"*Da.* Yes. I did," she said. Gold's question prompted her to recall momentarily how she had left Andre lying in a pool of his own blood from her knife jabbed into his neck, mission accomplished, his song ended. Then she tracked down Bogan Zoidze a few days later, completing her revenge for the two murders he committed six years ago on Easter Sunday in Neilly-sur-Seine. She could still feel those moments with vivid precision.

"Shall we make up for our missed drink now?" Eli offered. A waiter delivered two new champagne flutes as he passed. They clanked the slender flutes together.

"Tell me more about all the exciting things you have been up to," Eli continued.

"My life is boring again these days, very regular," she demurred.

"I'm sure."

Katya guessed by his eyes that Eli did not expect her to explain too many deeply private details. During their numerous shared hours, the Israeli had observed the scars on Katya's torso. He knew her basic origin and saw how she moved, trained, and fought with a special kind of controlled wrath. Now he was just making polite conversation to save her from Skip. He was probably surprised to see her at Rutherford's birthday party, still breathing. Further de-tails were unnecessary.

Katya placed her half-empty champagne flute on a table. "Come, let's look at some new pictures," she said. "The big colorful one over there is by Raoul Dufy.[111] It is one of his late masterpieces in oil."

"What subject does he paint?" Eli asked.

"Little moments of true happiness," Katya said.

"Now I am intrigued," Gold replied.

"A brush in the right hands works magic. In Russian we say it is always better to see once than hear a hundred times. Let's look closer at what Dufy has done with color, over there."

———— ✸ ————

Josephine Richards sat on a green wooden bench amid the rows of acacia trees lining the path that led down to the Rutherford Ranch's main parking lot, under the shade of today's temporary tents. The hot, dry air had now cooled as the orange sun continued its daily descent behind the jagged San Juanito Mountains.

Jo had arrived in Palm Springs earlier that morning on a chartered flight from DC's Reagan National, transit via Dallas Fort Worth International. George Rutherford's smartly dressed chief of staff picked her up at the airport and drove her the short thirty minutes to the ranch in a 7 Series

---

111   A versatile French painter and designer (1877-1953) primarily associated with Fauvism; celebrated for his "stenographic" style, characterized by rapid, calligraphic brushstrokes superimposed over thin washes of vibrant, often uncontained color.

BMW sedan. She was not looking forward to the same trip in reverse on a red-eye flight tomorrow.

Jo watched various couples come and go from inside Rutherford's large ranch house. She did not recognize most of his well-heeled birthday guests. None of the others stopped by to chat. Why should any of these people voluntarily talk to someone who looked as horrid as she did now? Any normal human saw only a slightly grotesque, odd creature in baggy pants and ugly shoes. She had lost nearly all her hair since her long coma in Walter Reed National Military Medical Center. She had tried better wigs, but they all looked fake and made her seem even more unattractive.

Ah well, at least I am still alive and kicking. I still have my mind. That is what really matters. There are more important problems to worry about than my goddam bald head, she thought.

Jo raised her cane to grab Katerina Volkova's attention when she saw her appear from the west building.

Jo watched the slender Russian girl approach—flowing chestnut-hair, a luminous complexion, and a simple, sleek cream-colored satin dress that fell perfectly from her shoulders to just above her shapely calves and elegant ankles.

Katya sat next to her on the bench and reached to take Jo's hand. An odd tingle flowed up Jo's arm from the simple pressure on her delicate palm. Jo rarely touched anyone these days.

"Paul said you would be here. George has already cut the cake.

Why not come inside?" Katya asked.

"Later. Too many old farts and blowhards in one place makes me nervous. I will find George tonight after the party when I have more space," Jo replied.

"How are you?" Katya asked.

"Splendid. Give Afghanistan back to the Taliban after twenty years, now straight into another proxy war with Russia. Never a dull moment."

"*C'est plus la change, le même chose,*" Katya replied. "You have warned about Putin for a long time. This cannot be a surprise."

"Surprise? No," Jo said. "But other mindsets were, well, not so well prepared. Most did not believe a permanent UN security council member would go all in like this. Invade the whole country like Hitler did to Poland in '39? It seemed like a B-movie plot. But here we are. Truth is stranger than fiction. Fortunately, Putin's thugs are not a modern military. They do not have a viable plan. If Kyiv holds out in the next few months, there will be plenty of congressional support to send more weapons. NATO will help. Even our Germans friends might come along. Russia cannot win, not with guns, terror, or absurd propaganda. Their war machine will fail, and we are going to help make it so."

"I hope you are right. The greater the state, the more wrong and cruel its patriotism," Katya said.

Jo watched Katya's glassy eyes mutate between blue and green as the early evening light shifted. Here she was casually quoting Tolstoy as if he were a frequent dinner guest. Jo's opinion of this unusual Russian woman since those early days with her wayward brother, Viktor, had evolved considerably. Thankfully, Viktor was gone, but this strange preternatural being, Katerina Sergeevna Volkova, had also emerged stronger. Pretty face, yes, but a survivor and a killer too, Jo realized. Took guts and devious planning to sneak into that villa in Sicily and put a bullet point-blank into Bogan Zoidze's chest. She definitely proved herself with that blood act.

"How's your Uncle Yuri?" Jo asked.

"I saw him last month in London. He walks at least three kilometers every day. We played tennis in the morning."

"Did you win?"

"Barely," Katya said. "I exploited his weak backhand. He is not good on clay courts."

Jo leaned forward and balanced her cane just beneath her chin. "What's Yuri's wise opinion of this war?"

"Pointless madness," Katya replied.

"Madness is the problem," Jo said. "Back in the old days, the Politburo took care of their own. The Soviets were cruel, but they took cues from a predictable playbook, respected rules, policed themselves. Today is worse. This one untouchable bastard sits at a long table, looks across at starry-eyed Emmanuel Macron like he is a child, and then saber rattles with his arsenal of nukes. The pandemic fueled Putin's paranoia and gave him too much time to lose touch with reality. Now we face a situation that will grind tens of thousands into dust for years. None of this is good for business. Not for us, Ukraine, Russia, Europe, or anyone else."

"What would you do?" Katya asked, brushing back a strand of hair from her eyes and leaning closer as if waiting for a circus magician's big reveal.

"A different kind of change," Jo continued. "Obviously, we must send in more weapons. That is beyond debate, and long overdue. At the same time, I want to look for more subtle hands. Hands that can reach inside a very closed world. A gentle touch at first. When the time is right, a firmer grip."

"Regime change?"

"A better outcome."

"Quite fanciful," Katya countered.

"It doesn't have to be," Jo continued. "It starts with men like your uncle."

"Yuri has been in London for more than twenty years," Katya said. "He has not been to Moscow in at least five, and he is not close enough to this czar for that."

"True. Yuri acting completely alone would be nothing. There is also the problem of your father's political past. And you. But Yuri was once an influential insider. He has friends, and he has made serious money for many of them. Others will listen to Yuri, help us bridge trust among those with a broader vision who might help bring change. The willing few now. More later," Jo suggested.

"That is an overly optimistic interpretation. Russia does not work like that. Even the rich men know their own places in the scheme," Katya replied. "Look at what happened to Navalny.[112] Others cower in fear or simply bow to a reality that they cannot change. Humans do what they must to survive."

"Not all are afraid as you say," Jo said. "You've met Mikhail Petrov?"

She observed Katya's eyelids slightly flicker. "Da. I know Misha," Katya said.

"Know him very well?"

"He is a client, not a close friend. Mostly bought from our Paris gallery, sometimes from New York."

"Good aesthetic taste?"

"Everyone has their own preferences. He prefers German abstract painters, the big names—Gerard Richter, Anslem Kiefer.[113] Misha always paid top dollar. Never bargained on price."

"Petrov can afford to splurge," Jo said. "Yuri's investment bank was his lead book runner when his potash mining company listed in London.

---

112   Alexei Navalny, a prominent Russian opposition leader and anti-corruption activist, died on February 16, 2024, at age 47 while imprisoned in an Arctic penal colony. A later investigation concluded he was poisoned with a Novichok nerve agent.

113   Anselm Kiefer (b. 1945) and Gerhard Richter (b. 1932) are dominant figures in post-war German art, both centrally preoccupied with navigating the legacy of WWII, the Holocaust, and German identity.

Petrov is smarter than most. Not an ideologue or sycophant. My sources tell me that he also has some valuable connections directly with the Wagner Group's leadership, hothead lunatics like Prigozhin, running around Syria and Africa with their little commercial armies. If enough influential pragmatists like Petrov can begin to emerge, then better alternatives will evolve. Even a little pressure here and there might save us all blood and treasure. Put the world back into shape. Help bury the rotting corpse Russia has become."

"Very dangerous," Katya remarked. "My parents were murdered for much less than what you're suggesting."

"I know it," Jo said, allowing a sympathetic tone to slip into her voice. "But we have ways to help. Petrov has already reached out via a quiet channel. We believe he has an agenda and is looking for some better ways to communicate. Your uncle is my best possibility to find out what is real, what we might be able to begin together now given all the facts. We should at least explore it. Don't you think?"

"Where is Misha now?" Katya asked. "Moscow?"

"No. He is at his summer property in the South of France, an old villa just outside of Grasse, an hour from Nice. I understand it is a beautiful place, very secure, quiet, nestled up there in those rolling hills with big ocean views and stone lions guarding the gate. Have you been?"

"No, but I recall that I have sent some paintings to that property. I expect that it is a lovely place," Katya said.

Jo smiled. She watched the California desert evening light dance along the long, flowing, glimmering strands of Katya's chestnut hair. The dying light gave the young woman's unblemished skin and delicate features a glowing, radiant warm hue, sharply contrasted by the icy blue green of her unsettling, impenetrable eyes.

"Yuri can tell us where Petrov has hung your depressing German masterpieces," Jo continued. "Maybe he has found a good spot. Not a long trip from London to visit an old friend. Not long at all if you can convince him to go."

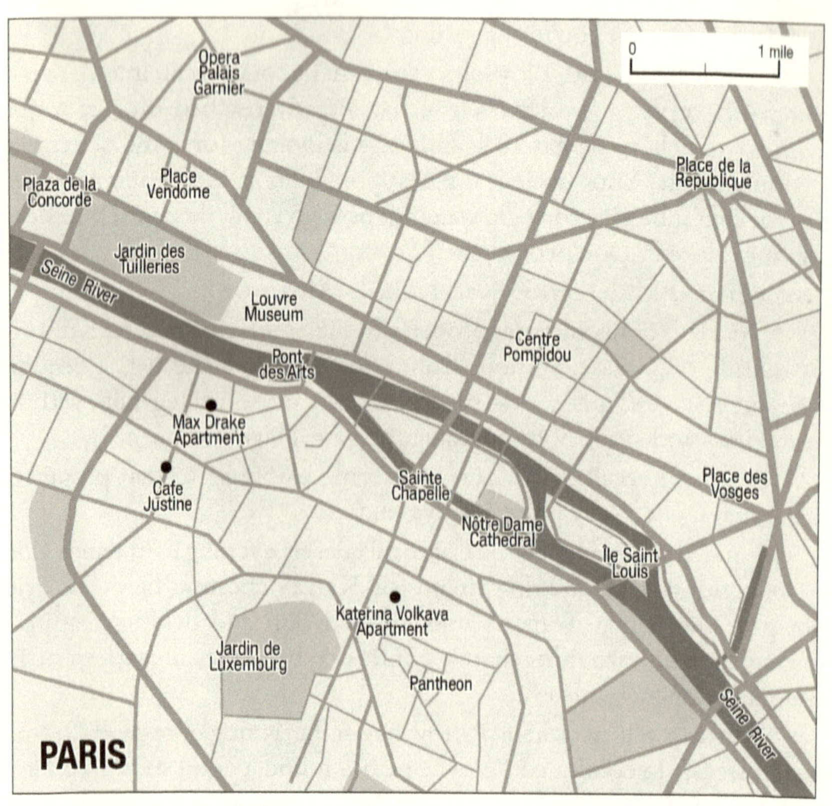
0
1 mile
Opera
Palais
Garnier
Place
Vendome
Place de la
Republique
Plaza de la
Concorde
Jardin des
Tuilleries
Seine River
Louvre
Museum
Centre
Pompidou
Pont
des Arts
Max Drake
Apartment
Place des
Vosges
Cafe
Justine
Sainte
Chapelle
Nôtre Dame
Cathedral
Île Saint
Louis
Katerina Volkava
Apartment
Jardin de
Luxemburg
Pantheon
Seine River
PARIS

3

Paris, France.
April 1, 2022. 3 p.m

MAX DRAKE reclined alone at a small round table on the terrace of Café Justine in the 6th arrondissement, just off the Boulevard Saint Germain. Paris's spring air felt clean and fresh in his lungs and cool on his skin. A row of tall London plane trees lined the wide boulevard. The trees' waxy olive-green leaves glistened, still wet, as a few pedestrians flowed back onto the sidewalk, umbrellas in hand or stowed away in posh Chanel or Louis Vuitton leather bags. The boulevard's slate-gray sidewalk stones still held small puddles, left over from the day's early afternoon rain, in various old cracks and depressions.

Max sipped a slightly sweet café allongé from a white porcelain cup while his right eye, the only functioning one, scrolled the text on his mobile phone.

```
    Do You Have Military Training? Enlist in the
Volunteer Legion Now!
    Join the International Legion of Defense of Ukraine—
Today!
    If Your Citizenship Is Other than Ukrainian but You
Are Standing With Ukraine Against the Russian Invasion
    If You Want Actively Participate in Fighting for
European Freedom and Democracy
    If You Have Combat Experience
    Now It Is Time to Act!
    Join the International Legion of Defense!
    From 1st Mar Till the End of Martial Law, Presidential
Decree No. 82/2022
    Freedom Is a Choice Join the Brave!
    Fight for Ukraine!
```

Max put down his mobile phone. Focusing too much with his one good eye always caused a headache; he had been web surfing for an hour. Instead, he gazed around at the café's typical late afternoon clientele: two skinny students in black turtlenecks, a woman resting with her designer bags after a shopping spree, an immaculately dressed middle-aged man reading Le Monde, and two silver-haired ladies talking closely together, with a tiny white poodle sitting quietly beneath the table at their feet.

Max had become a Café Justine regular this past year. The tall, bald waiter always led him to the same round corner table and the same comfortable varnished wicker chair. Sometimes he came here with his current girlfriend, Christina, for late night drinks, but often he sat alone to read and think, like Hemingway a century ago except without that dead writer's skills to capture his own life in words. Whenever Max himself tried to write anything, it just seemed silly, useless. Hard to even visualize how different this place was com-pared to his life back in Jersey, let alone write it down with the right words that would truly capture it. *I am not smart enough to express how so much has changed and why. Besides, no one cares, so I would just be writing alone for no purpose and to no end, like a precious little teenage girl. Words are not for me,* Max admitted to himself.

Justine's café terrace was one of the many small pleasures Max discovered during his almost two years in Paris. There were also the twelve-foot-high windows of his three-bedroom top-floor 61 Rue du Bac apartment with a stunning sunset view over the gray Haussmann rooftops from his west-facing balcony. Every Parisian night he rested his head on a goose down pillow and slept on silk sheets. A housekeeper cleaned the apartment three times a week, always changing the bouquets into fresh arrangements of dry lavender stalks, lilacs, and sometimes tulips. He had a private French language tutor on weekdays, a professional gym instructor, trips to Majorca, weekend jaunts to Monaco, and much more. He saw Paul often enough, at least before this latest war, sometimes also with Katya.

Yes, life was good here in the 7th arrondissement. A few gold kilos always helped ease life's little pains. Paul had grabbed a truckload of the precious metal in Sicily, more than enough to last a few lifetimes if they just quietly used it up, brick by heavy brick.

But it was not so simple, even with a few kilos shaved off from that precious metal hoard every year.

A glimmer of blue sky appeared behind the fast-moving, heavy clouds, and now the street's shallow puddles glimmered with sunlight patches.

Max put ten euros beneath the ashtray of the café's small round table. He zipped up his leather jacket and headed down Rue du Bac toward the Seine. Walking in Paris was always the best way to clear his head and think. He relied on Paris's gray limestone buildings and subdued, unified aesthetic to gain a much better perspective about a certain future that he imagined might be possible. This imagined new path suddenly loomed ahead as a vague, more pro-found new destiny.

Neither Paul nor Max had grown up rich. They came from an average American working-class family, a typical existence. His regular life back in the States had been easy and normal. Until it was not. Their dad died in 2000 from pancreatic cancer, and then, less than a year later—Max remembered it so vividly still—the Twin Towers had smashed down in a swirl of noxious fumes and debris. The world changed forever that day. Max's own singular, unimportant life changed forever too.

The Twin Towers fell at the start of Max's high school sophomore year. Paul, already in Columbia College's ROTC officer program,[114] was called up to active duty. After high school, Max enlisted to follow Paul and was sent straight to the dusty, brutal shithole of post invasion Baghdad. Max's first tour started in June 2006, year three of the occupation with 160,000 coalition troops left to clean up a broken-down, murderous mess. He forgot what they were trying to carry out that night in Fallujah— August 24, 2009—when the so-called improvised explosive device blew, killing Ron Harper, his squad captain, and sending little iron nails flying into his face. They airlifted Max to the Frankfurt army hospital to remove the metal shards from his neck, forehead, and mutilated left eye. Sixteen weeks later, he was back home, honorably discharged, injured but alive. Thank you for your service.

Then the next phase began, the hard part without any heroic, glorious, mom-and-apple-pie homecoming. Instead, he faced a de-cade of meaningless nothing, a pervasive, all-powerful loneliness. High school friends were all remote, unrecognizable. They worked jobs, dated women, watched weekend football, quoted TV sitcom characters like they were real bosom friends and not just a bunch of overpaid Hollywood actors. Former friends did not care about Iraq or him or the limits of American foreign policy. Most of them saw Iraq as a misaligned adventure, a moment when USA just needed revenge against an elusive enemy. Afterward, no one thought top-pling Saddam Hussein was a just war. The world was not saved. Max tried to rebound just like Paul had done with what seemed effortless ease. But Max could not feel it. Not really. He just was not resilient like his older brother. Instead, he settled into a routine job in Newark, New Jersey, selling whole life insurance policies for a massive soulless corporation and collecting a meager monthly veteran stipend to help cover bills. The less he thought about Iraq or the army, the better. He drifted, month after month,

---

114   ROTC stands for Reserve Officers' Training Corps, a college-based program that trains students to become commissioned officers in the U.S. military while earning a degree

year after year, movie release after movie release, pill after pill. Alone. There was certainly no alluring Christina back in New Jersey. Not even close. As Max crossed the slender Pont des Arts bridge, he glimpsed the Eiffel Tower, tall above the rooftops and against the roving clouds. In the first few weeks after the Russian invasion, Eiffel's great nineteenth-century iron tower had been lit up brightly with the defiant blue and yellow of Ukraine's national colors. New York, London, Tokyo, and Sydney had also joined with their own displays of support on iconic buildings. The special lights were beautiful, the political speeches noble. Even the British Embassy in Paris flew the blue-and-yellow Ukrainian flag next to the Union Jack as a sign of global unity.

He passed the Louvre's sprawling northern buildings, then walked through the Jardin Nelson Mandela behind the old Paris Stock Exchange. In a fenced-in park, he saw many small children clamoring on slides, gripping monkey bars, and balancing on thin wooden beams. Children's voices chirped. Mothers and fathers watched, some talking together with Starbucks cups in hand. This little urban playground was a world apart—a safe, normal, mod-ern haven where different nationalities, ages, and social classes all moved on with their daily lives, finally normalized after a much-too-long global pandemic. But just as the masks were coming off, the world slammed into its next crisis.

There was trouble back home in the States too. January 6 rioters brought the confederate flag inside the US Capitol. Despots like Putin watched the domestic chaos with glee. Dictators sensed opportunity, smelled weakness in these so-called affluent countries with their decadent habits and minuscule attention spans. Max did not have answers. He just felt in his bones that these were not normal times. Not one bit.

He turned back toward the river, toward the wider Pont Neuf bridge that crossed over the Ile de la Cité, Paris's ancient heart. Near the Henri IV statue, Max looked down at the river's undulating dark green water. He took a deep breath before calling Paul, who picked up after four rings.

"Hey," Max said. "Can you speak?"

"Some."

"Still in Kyiv?"

"Maybe," Paul replied.

"Everything all right?"

"Fine," Max said. "But we need to talk."

The conversation took place as expected. Paul gave him all the sensible answers. If Max wanted to help, there was plenty to do for the hundreds of thousands of Ukrainian refugees crossing the border, or even still in Paris, where he could remotely support MSA's important and complicated coordination. Max pressed on, focusing on how his military training could save lives now. He needed to be on the front line, to use his skills with the real fighters, not safely stowed away in rear support.

"I've read that twenty thousand foreigners have already signed up for this new international legion," Max said.

"Those are exaggerated numbers to keep up morale," Paul countered. "Most cowboys will not last a month on the battlefield. Besides, what about your eye?"

"They'll make an exception," Max replied.

"Possibly," Paul said softly.

"If you don't think I can help, then why did you want me to come to Paris?" Max finally blurted out, frustrated by his brother's frosty reception. "You are always talking about freedom, decisions, existential bullshit. I know what I am doing. Don't you trust me?"

"I do trust you," Paul said calmly. "You are thirty-five years old. You can make your own decisions."

"Then listen to what I'm saying," Max continued. "Let me do something … meaningful."

"You believe joining this new brigade in a foreign country is meaningful?"

"I do," Max said firmly.

A long silence followed. Max waited for his brother's response while an open deck cruise ship crowded with tourists passed under the ancient bridge. A few children on top of the deck waved at him, but he did not wave back.

"Listen. Things are fluid now," Paul finally said. "I plan to be in Lviv in a few weeks. We can talk in person and meet with Dmitry. See for yourself what this all is, how the wind is blowing. Then make your decision. Good enough?"

"Good enough," Max replied.

After he hung up, Max began to walk back to his apartment. He already felt a certain energy and hope kindling inside as he imagined a new destiny. Christina texted him, asking if he could make a 9 p.m. dinner date with her usual friends. He would meet her tonight and tell her about his decision tomorrow morning after he had slept on it. Christina was young. She would understand. Maybe she would wait for him until this madness stopped.

And if she does not wait for me? I do not really care, Max thought.

A woman as beautiful as Christina was just eye candy from the very beginning anyway. *Who have I been kidding? She is out of my league. She is just part of this fake Parisian fantasy that I did not earn and I do not deserve.*

Max packed light, his gear stuffed into a single tarpaulin duffel bag. The flight from Paris's Charles de Gaulle to Warsaw's Chopin Airport was a smooth two hours. A six-hour train ride then took him to the town of Peremyshl, on the Polish-Ukrainian border. The Ukrainian border guards asked him a few routine questions, flipped through his American passport, and then let him pass without any real inspection.

A crowded, hot bus then brought him the two hours to Lviv, Ukraine's sixth largest city, normally with a population of some 700,000 residents, now swelled to two million.

Max checked into a single room at an old eighteenth-century stone building later that night. After a cold shower, he fell at once to sleep on a hard bed. He kept the room's small window open to let in the evening breeze.

In the morning, he woke, ate a sausage-filled pierogi, and began to wander the town. Lviv was an old community. part of Poland for hundreds of years and then the Austro-Hungarian Empire, with architecture blending Central European styles with that of Italy and Germany. Max walked to High Castle Park, the mountaintop ruins of a fourteenth-century castle that offered panoramic views of the city's green-domed churches and tiled rooftops, all nestled neatly against the surrounding hills. Lviv belonged in a postcard, he thought, except for the tents set up in various public parks and around municipal buildings, and shrill air raid sirens that broke the nighttime quiet.

Just a few weeks after President Zelensky announced the new Ukrainian International Legion, men from dozens of different countries responded, many coming with deep prior military experience, veterans of US, Canadian, British, Polish, and even South Korean armed services. The soldiers came with much-needed tactical expertise. These trained volunteers also gave an aura of global legitimacy to Ukraine's struggle, even if their total numbers were small.

Ukraine held the world's attention, at least for now. Hundreds of journalists from all the major news networks—CNN, BBC, Reuters, Agence France Presse—had also descended in just the last few weeks. Max caught a glimpse of silver-haired Anderson Cooper, a recognizable television face, as the CNN anchor toured Lviv's historic center one early evening with an entourage of camera operators and security guards. Cooper looked paler and more fragile in person than he did all prettied up with makeup on a television screen.

Max met the first recruiting officer on his second day. The local recruiter handed him a shortlist of others who had already agreed to join: Finbar Cafferkey, an Irish political activist and veteran of the Kurdish People's Defense; Juris Jurašs, a Latvian politician; Rhee Ken, a South Korean naval officer; Conor R. Kennedy, the grandson of former United States Attorney General Robert Kennedy and great-nephew of President John Kennedy; Mamuka Mamulashvili, a commander of the Georgian Legion; and Malcolm Nance, a retired US Navy serviceman.

"You see. Heroes from all over the world coming to fight," the short-haired recruiting officer explained.

"Sounds good," Max replied, although he really did not know any of those volunteers, not even Conor, the Kennedy kid.

"You know this symbol?" the officer asked, pointing to a wall poster showing what looked like a trident with two loops on each side.

"I don't," Max replied.

"It's the *tryzub*,"[115] the recruitment officer said in broken English. "Our freedom symbol. Very old. This is what we fight for. Freedom. The future. Peace."

"I've seen it before but never knew what it was."

"Now you do," the recruiter replied. "Take this." He handed over a Zippo lighter with a small gold imprint of the tryzub. "You can help. I see this on your face. You have fought before. Now fight again. Here. With us."

"I don't smoke," Max replied.

"Take it anyway," he said.

After the meeting, Max gazed at the symbol on the Zippo more closely before he shoved it in his pocket.

Strange little complicated symbol, he thought.

---

115   "Three teeth" or trident is Ukraine's official coat of arms. The symbol first gained prominence as the ancestral sign of the Rurik dynasty, the rulers of Kyivan Rus. In the 10th century, Grand Prince Volodymyr the Great (who converted the region to Christianity) minted the trident on gold and silver coins as a mark of his authority.

4

Lviv, Ukraine.
April 15, 2022. 12 p.m.

THE BROTHERS met at noon at a well-known local place called the Italian Courtyard, behind the soot-covered sixteenth-century Dormition church. Max embraced his brother with a firm hug. But Paul's smile faded quickly, and his body language seemed restrained.

"We'll discuss your life plans at dinner with Dmitry tonight," Paul said.

"You understand why I needed to come, don't you?" Max asked.

"I understand why you think you need to be here. That does not make it smart," Paul replied.

"You are here. Is that smart?" Max said.

"That's a different situation," Paul replied.

"How?"

"It just is. I am not on the front lines taking bullets."

Later that evening, Paul led him to a restaurant with tables that spread out into the outdoor courtyard. Under the fragrant leaves of tall chestnut trees, surrounding conversations buzzed in a mix of Ukrainian, Polish, Russian, and English.

Dmitry Medkov was already sitting at the table, his black fedora tilted loosely on his bald head. Small round eyeglasses gave Yuri Volkov's key man the appearance of an eccentric professor rather than a dangerous head of security. Max knew him as Paul's mentor and friend. Dmitry was one of the very few to whom his brother turned to for honest advice, despite vast differences in age and origin. Dmitry had been borne in the Soviet Union, fought in Afghanistan, and was one of those lingering veterans now whom the Ukrainians accepted as an ally against today's regime. He had already proven himself an effective operator against Russian mercenaries in Syria.

"Let us talk while we eat. I have already ordered," Dmitry said. The food came—shuba, which was herring fish in layers of mayonnaise; a fresh loaf of black bread; and perogies, or dumplings. The dishes tasted good enough, but the bottled Polish beer had been stored in the sun for too long. Paul ate silently, his gaze drifting elsewhere. Finally, Dmitry cleared his plate and turned his attention to Max.

"So why do you want to do something as dumb as join this new international legion?" Dmitry asked.

"I'm trained. Three years of live combat experience. I can help," Max said.

"This is not your country. Not your fight."

"This is everyone's fight."

"Is it really? Where is everyone then? I don't see them here," Dmitry pressed.

"We can't let this happen," Max said. "This political bullshit about joining NATO does not help now. We need to fight the cancer before it spreads. Take a stand."

"Who is we?"' Dmitry pressed.

"Everyone. Country does not matter," Max said. He stumbled for better, more articulate arguments, regretting always that he could not speak like Paul, especially now with this old balding man peering at him through little round eyeglasses.

"Do you have any connection to the war except for Paul?"

"Do I need one?"

"You realize that Russian cruise missiles just destroyed a training center here?" Dmitry continued. "They dropped a dozen bombs exactly on that target because some recruit idiot called Mama from his mobile. They pulled at least forty bodies out of that wreckage. All burnt up while asleep, like chickens on a stick."

"I know the risks. This is not my first rodeo."

"Your combat experience was more than a decade ago and within a big US military machine. This is not the same. Zelensky's new legion is an experiment. You would be fighting alongside soldiers with many different skill levels, different countries. If captured, Russia will imprison you as an illegal foreign combatant. No diplomatic protections, no promises."

"I don't plan to be captured."

"You might be," Dmitry said.

"Never."

"War crimes are happening every day, like in Buncha. Husbands murdered, wives and daughters raped, and then all buried in pits like animals. It is a dirty way to die," Dmitry continued.

"Exactly so. I am here to stop it."

"The Ukrainian military is outnumbered, probably three to one," Dmitry stressed.

"Doesn't matter to me," Max replied.

"Do you speak Russian or Ukrainian?"

"I'll pick up what I need."

Dmitry leaned back and rubbed his thick neck.

"Only good versus evil matters to you then?" the older Russian finally asked.

"Exactly. That is the best way to think about it. Good versus evil. Sane versus insane. Simple."

"You've operated drones before?"

"Extensively in Iraq," Max replied.

"Much as changed," Dmitry countered.

"Has it?"

Dmitry turned to Paul and spoke to him as if Max were not present. "I must assume he has the basic combat skills. His English will help us in the field. Ukrainians have spirit, but they need more skilled veterans, especially when more sophisticated weapons flow into combat zones."

"What about his dead eye?" Paul asked.

"He is looking at me now. He is functional. He can be used," Dmitry said. "If we pair him up with Valentine's squad, he'll have better odds, and I know that you trust Valentine."

Paul met Max's gaze with a hard stare.

"You see what is on offer. You know the risks. Still want to do this?" Paul asked.

"Christ. Haven't you been listening? Damn right I do," Max replied loudly. A foursome of older men eating at a nearby table all raised their heads to look over.

Max felt his upper back muscles tighten. He was perplexed that his own brother still could not understand him, still could not actually hear the meaning of what he was saying. *Why don't any of them understand the words coming out of my mouth? Do I have to shout the same goddam point ten times?*

Paul's face remained calm, eyes steady, lips tight. He swallowed the last of the warm Polish beer and leaned back in his wooden chair.

"Fine," Paul replied in a low, cool voice. "Your life. You can make your own choice."

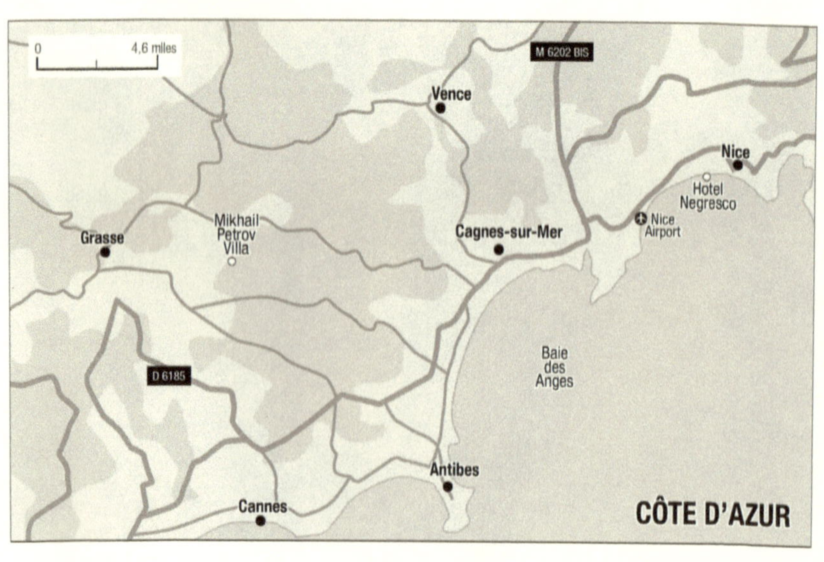

0   4,6 miles
M 6202 BIS
Vence
Nice
Hotel
Negresco
Mikhail
Petrov
Villa
Grasse
Cagnes-sur-Mer
Nice
Airport
D 6185
Baie
des
Anges
Antibes
Cannes
CÔTE D'AZUR

5

Nice, France.
June 16, 2022. 5:30 p.m.

AN UNIFORMED bellhop took Yuri Volkov's single suitcase after he arrived at the Hotel Negresco, just off the Promenade des Anglais in old Nice.

Yuri had started early at his five-bedroom house near Russell Square in the heart of London's Bloomsbury district. He had left his house quietly just before dawn, then took a taxi to the nearby St. Pancras train station, where he boarded a business class train car that carried him and a thousand other passengers via the engineering marvel known as the Chunnel on the two-hour trip to Paris's Gare du Nord. Another taxi took taken him to the busy Gare de Lyon, and from there he went south via an SNVC high-speed train, passing first through Marseilles.

Once the SNVC train left Paris's cluttered metro area, the five-hour trip was smooth and pleasant. Yuri caught up on world news on his iPad, wrote notes in his small journal, and otherwise simply blended into the crowd, indistinguishable from any typical retiree on his way to the balmy French Riviera for a brighter sun and better food. Yuri's room at the stately Hotel Negresco[116] was neatly appointed, with tall windows that offered expansive views of the slender palm trees planted in rows along the rocky beach, and the sparkling waters of the Baie des Anges beyond. He showered, changed clothes, and went downstairs to the hotel's busy restaurant. For dinner he ate a plate of *confit de canard* with thick slices of fresh country bread and a glass of red burgundy.

After dinner, Yuri strolled the palm-lined promenade, heading toward the Place Masséna, just a few blocks from his hotel. The evening temperature dipped, but it was still comfortable. Côte d'Azur's breezy summers had long attracted foreigners from colder climates—Russians, Brits, Nordics, Germans, and Americans. This year's high season had belched up droves

---

116   5-star Belle Époque hotel often described as a "museum-hotel," it is renowned for its iconic pink dome and an extensive private art collection spanning five centuries of French history.

of eager travelers after two high seasons lost to pandemic lockdowns. Nice's international airport was already back to pre-COVID traffic levels, with jets descending from around the world like clockwork. Hotels were all open for business, owners eager to recoup years of business losses. The restaurants lining the street buzzed with diners, and the ice cream kiosks busily served flavored *boules de glace* to the harried parents of impatient children.

At Place Masséna, he listened to a trio of impromptu street musicians in shorts and T-shirts harmonizing with violin, drums, and a base cello. They belted out familiar showtunes for the shifting public audience and collected tips in small wicker basket.

As the sun slowly set over the crowded open public square, colored lights illuminated the seven statues of kneeling men atop thirty-foot iron polls. The colorful statues represented peace among the world's seven continents, according to the plaque on the ground that explained the outdoor artwork.[117]

Peace among nations, Yuri thought. *A noble aspiration.*

He pulled out his phone to check his messages. An SMS in Russian came through:

```
    My driver will come tomorrow @ 9 a.m. Rue de
Rivoli & Prom des Anglais
    Looking forward
    Misha
```

Before heading back to his room, Yuri stopped on another street corner to listen to an outdoor pianist. This time the musician was a young man probably no more than twenty years old. He played a vigorous song on an old upright keyboard with tiny wheels on the base. As Yuri listened, his thoughts turned to tomorrow and to his friend Michael Petrov. He had first met the younger Russian businessman a decade ago during better times, when Russia was on a path of progress and integration, not war and isolation. Now Misha was in his late fifties. According to Jo Richards, he wanted to help. If Petrov did have a real plan, and they worked together, and the Americans quietly funneled them resources, then it might be worth the risk. Maybe, just maybe, his brother Sergei's progressive vision for Russia might eventually become a reality. Sergei's death did not need to be in vain if they could all push for change or at least stop the killing and the blood.

---

117   *Conversation à Nice* was created by the Spanish artist Jaume Plensa and installed in 2007.

Yuri dropped a twenty euro note into the musician's upturned straw hat after the kid finished a lively, impressive rendition of Beethoven's "Ode to Joy." This warm night was soft and peaceful enough to at least give way to the faint promise of hope. He was willing to trust Katya's judgment just a little now. If his only niece vouched for Jo Richards, that was at least good enough to reach out to an old friend and explore the art of the possible to end senseless bloodshed.

Yuri swallowed two strong black coffees after he showered and dressed.

At 9 a.m., a Mercedes C class sedan rolled up to the front of the hotel's main entrance. A large man with a dark beard and eyes hidden behind reflective sunglasses appeared from the shiny black car. The bulky driver motioned Yuri closer.

"I'm here to take you," he said quietly in crisp Russian.

"Good," Yuri said as the big man opened the back door for him to slip into the cold interior.

The car's pristine tan leather seats smelled new.

"There is bottled water next to the seat," the driver said.

"*Da. Spasibo,*" Yuri replied softly. "How long of a drive?"

"One hour."

Despite prior invitations, this was the first time Yuri would be visiting Petrov's vacation home in the foothills outside Grasse. Katya described it as an old late-nineteenth-century villa set in a large plot of land and isolated from more densely populated streets. A perfect hideaway for long conversations.

The Mercedes veered right onto the wide promenade, then headed out toward Nice's international airport along a busy route that included public buses, trucks, cars, and loud motorbikes.

After about twenty minutes, the driver turned off the crowded main highway. They followed the contours of the rolling hills, snaking their way around bends and gradually gaining altitude as they ascended. As they climbed farther into the hills, densely clustered apartment blocks and pastel-colored riviera-style houses slowly gave way to less tightly situated estates, most with private gardens surrounded by high stucco walls.

Yuri took in the Mediterranean to the right, a lovely smooth sea with different sized yachts drifting languorously off the rugged coast.

The Mercedes rolled down a small two-lane road and then turned down another dirt path for about two hundred meters. The car stopped in the middle of a grassy clearing nestled among a grove of tall pine trees and leafy oaks. Rather than a villa gate as expected, Yuri noticed only an old white van parked nearby.

"Why are we stopping here?" Yuri asked the driver.

"A moment," the driver replied in a crisp tone. The big man opened his front seat door, slid out, and walked behind the Mercedes.

Yuri turned his head to watch the driver through the car's tinted rear window.

Something is wrong.

A new figure—blond hair, square chin, plaid shirt, and jeans—appeared from the parked van at the edge of the grove. The new man nodded to the driver and then walked decisively to the car's rear door. The blond jerked the door open and pointed a small square pistol at Yuri's chest.

Yuri braced himself while the man loomed there, gun steady, eyes glassy and cold lips curled. They confronted each other, each awkwardly frozen for what seemed like far longer than a handful of furtive seconds.

"What is this?" Yuri finally said, dumbly.

"Easy, grandpa," the blond finally said in accented Russian. "Get out. Slowly. Show me your hands."

Yuri complied. After he got out of the car, the big driver pressed him against the trunk, frisked him for weapons, and took his mobile phone from his inside jacket pocket. At first, Yuri hoped this was part of Petrov's security routine, albeit overzealous. Then the driver pinned his arms against his back until a searing pain passed up his neck.

"He is old. Don't hit him," the blond man cautioned the muscular driver in Russian. "Just hold him down tighter."

"I am holding. Grandpa is strong. Stop playing and stick him!" the driver urged.

Yuri saw that the blond man now held a medical syringe. He jabbed the long needle into Yuri's right thigh. The two men held him while the drug coursed through his body. Yuri strained against these four hands, knowing that his effort was useless. Only a few more seconds until the injection took effect. Drugs not meant to kill, Yuri hoped, as his hands and arms began to numb.

"Take his legs," the blond man said.

They shoved him back onto the rear seat of the Mercedes. Yuri could not feel his feet as they grabbed his ankles to take off his shoes.

"Watch his head," the blond man cautioned.

Yuri strove to move but could not control his body anymore. He was just looking up at the car's interior top, arms limp and hands numb as his beating heart pushed the drug through his bloodstream. He felt himself slipping out.

Then the dark.

Mikael Andreivich Petrov gradually regained consciousness. An intense pain flared up from his right temple. He tried to ignore it and instead focus all his remaining energy to better understand his current, profoundly serious, predicament.

Petrov felt that his two hands were bound together tightly be-hind his back with a nylon rope. They had put him on a plastic lawn chair just at the back of his villa near his own sunken swimming pool. He pulled at the nylon rope to loosen it but without success.

Petrov tried again. Still tight. Not good.

Three men milled about poolside. He was not exactly sure how these thugs had entered his compound in the early morning just before dawn or how they had disabled his security alarms before barging into his upstairs bedroom while he was drifting off to sleep. His head had very quickly received the butt of a semiautomatic rifle, then lights out. Fortunately, his wife and daughter were back in Petersburg this weekend. His longtime driver and bodyguard, Ivan, was nowhere to be seen. Ivan was meant to bring Yuri Volkov from his Nice hotel later this morning. He vaguely wondered if somehow these thugs were connected to that visit. The three of them continued talking among themselves even as they saw he was awake. Two men spoke a mix of Russian and what he recognized as Serbian. The shorter man replied to them only in Russian.

Petrov watched one Serb answer his phone.

"It's done. They have him," the Serb confirmed after the call.

"OK, good," the short man replied.

Mikael quickly rolled through various survival scenarios. The three thugs were all maskless and speaking freely—not good. He needed to get creative fast. If he could find out who they were and why they came, perhaps there was a chance.

"Hey, you," Petrov called over to the short man. The man slowly sauntered over.

"What do you want?" Petrov asked. No reply.

"There is a safe in my closet. I can help you open it," Petrov said softly.

"I found it. We will take it," the short man said.

"I have so much more. Let me call my bank. I can do a wire. Easy. So easy," Petrov continued.

The short man pulled out a pack of cigarettes from his vest pocket, lit one with a Zippo, and began to puff. He pulled the smoke into his lungs and then, with a long exhale, puffed the smoke upward into the cloudless sky.

"Sorry," the short man said casually in Russian as if refusing him entrance to an opera event because the doors had already shut and the music had started.

"Give me a chance, brother," Petrov replied, trying still. "Let me pay. I will pay. Don't you know me?"

"I do know you," the short man replied.

"The security alarm. Police will be here soon," Petrov said, quickly trying a different tact.

"No. They won't," the short man countered.

"Let me pay. I have money," Petrov pressed again, still racing through his mind for a better hook, some kind of lure to change this criminal's mind.

The short man motioned for the two Serbs to come closer. "Pick him up. Let's keep moving," he said.

One of the Serbs came closer, tore the gold necklace from around Mikael's neck, and shoved it into his pocket. Then the two Serbs lifted Petrov's chair and moved him to the swimming pool's edge.

"Don't do it," Petrov begged again. "I have more. I can give you more. So much more. Just put me down. Please."

The man mumbled in unintelligible Serbian. They then tilted the lawn chair forward for him to slide off.

When he hit the water, Mikael kicked his legs in a desperate effort to keep his head above the surface. He struggled, pulling against the nylon rope, straining both shoulders. He gulped the air and wildly kicked his legs.

Petrov called out to the three men poolside who were just standing there, watching him flail. He gurgled out to them for help, but they did nothing. Each time he was able to put his head above water, it was for a shorter amount of time, a few seconds less after every herculean effort. Petrov's pain intensified in his neck and arms as he strained against the nylon rope.

Then it did not matter how hard he kicked his legs.

After a final futile effort to keep his head above the pool's surface, he finally sank. His feet touched the tiled floor, but he lacked the strength to push off from the bottom.

As oxygen left his brain, Petrov saw his wife's face. She was pouring him fresh scented black tea as always, smiling with her great big brown eyes. Then he saw his son, a tiny baby still, even though his son was already a grown young man in college. He held his baby son in his arms, such a lovely, beautiful, tiny, precious thing. His wife was saying something to him from the surface, far above the water shimmering up there. What was she saying? Her voice was sweet, melodic. She was calling out to tell him something especially important. He could not quite understand her angelic message, muffled now, high above the water's unreachable glimmering surface.

Mikhail Petrov had always loved his wife. Only she really understood him. What final secret did her shimmering form above want to tell him now?

6

Langley, Virginia.
June 20, 2022. 9:05 p.m.

DUSK'S TREMULOUS orange light gently lingered outside the double-layered soundproof windows of the George Bush Center for Intelligence.[118] The secure seven-story building and surrounding 258-acre campus stood secluded just a short twenty-minute drive from Washington, DC, off Northern Virginia's tree-lined and busy Route 123 in Fairfax County. The seven floors of double-plate glass windows were now partial mirrors for the thousands of people still working inside, reflecting different faces—calm, agitated, engrossed—at computer monitors or locked in conversation in their office cubicles or sparsely furnished conference rooms.

Martin Hines eyed Jo Richards as she threaded her way through a collection of desks outside his unremarkable corner office on the fifth floor. Hines had been in meetings for eight hours straight. His head throbbed from too much caffeine, his neck hurt from sitting hunched against his desk, and his stomach growled from the acidic bad espresso he had picked up at the first-floor cafeteria. Hines tracked Jo's motions as she entered his unlocked office door and dropped herself down on the beige couch across from his desk.

Hines locked his screen before facing this familiar monster. His long-standing colleague had never been good-looking, but now she was dreadful, more like a living zombie than a normal human being. Her bulbous eyes were enflamed. A network of blue veins fanned out along her hideously white forehead. Her lips were an odd, decaying shade of purple. She held her cane with knotted, skeletal hands attached to thin, boney arms.

"Any more details?" the zombie asked.

"Nope," Hines said.

"Your team's security advice was shit, Marty. No idea about Petrov?"

---

118   The complex was officially renamed on April 26, 1999, to honor George H.W. Bush, a former CIA Director. The headquarters campus comprises two primary structures—the Original Headquarters Building and the New Headquarters Building—which together total approximately 2.5 million square feet.

Hines cocked his head sideways.

"How could this happen?" she insisted.

"Bad guys do bad things," he replied. "I am not in charge of watching every single one of your oligarchs. Anything helpful from the locals?"

"Grasse police are investigating it as a home invasion and robbery, not political," Jo summarized. "Petrov's driver is also missing. Probably buried in a hole, legs plastered in cement."

"Yuri?" he asked.

"Nothing. Police found the GPS tracker in his shoe a mile from the villa in a little wooded clearing where they took him. Smoothly orchestrated and good attention to detail, I must admit."

"Murdering their own oligarchs is just one data point," Hines offered, switching to a more sympathetic tone. "The Russian regular army just burned up two hundred prisoners of war from the Azovstal complex after they surrendered Mariupol and were in their custody.[119] Other Russian units are raping villagers and sending stolen fur coats back to girlfriends via regular mail. This bloodletting is only beginning."

"Yuri isn't dead," Jo pushed back. "Killing Petrov was too neat, too skilled. Someone with training already surveilled Petrov for a long time and lured Yuri there, exactly on cue. This was a long play operation. We walked right into it."

"No, you walked right into it," Hines said. "Exact motives are irrelevant. Old grudge maybe. They will extract whatever information they can and use your man as an example to scare others. Yuri might get a show trial, same as Navalny, to parade the costs of disloyalty. I will ask Tom at State to put him on our priority watchlist for when he might pop up again," he continued, thinking the matter closed so he could move on to other more significant needfuls. There were certainly more important problems now rather than the fate of one of Jo's ambiguously aligned, unproven assets.

Instead, the monster glared at him with her bulbous eyes. "Put Yuri Volkov on a list? Are you kidding?" she growled. "This is on me."

"It happens, Jo. Not your fault. Not your problem. Move on," Hines said.

Jo let the silence linger while she looked out the window at the dying evening light over the tall Virginia oak and maple trees surrounding the

---

119   The incident on July 29, 2022, known as the Olenivka prison massacre, was a mass killing of Ukrainian prisoners of war held in Russian-occupied Donetsk Oblast.

main building. The window partly reflected her own hideous face, hovering there like a ghost transposed onto the darkening natural world outside.

Hines paused to fold his hands behind his head. He stretched back to ease the throbbing pain that had now moved from his neck down to his upper back and shoulders. Hines had made countless unsavory choices over the course of his extensive career. Leaving Afghanistan was a fiasco just six months ago—a string of avoidable errors and dozens of wasted US and Afghani lives during those last few frantically destructive days. Before that, there was the abandonment of the Syrian Kurds, another distasteful mess that the feckless politicians had left him to deal with and he needed to obey. And before that there was the five-year debacle of Baghdad's occupation. All these prior situations were political cul-de-sacs with no upside. These losing poker hands also reaffirmed a certain unalienable truth: allies and assets were all expendable. They were all playing cards, chess pieces, tools in a toolbox, or whatever other dehumanizing metaphor fit the moment.

"What more do you expect us to do? We make deals for American citizens, not Russians," Hines finally offered.

"I know your constraints," Jo said.

"Do you?" he challenged. "I am up to my neck handholding nitwit politicos and our so-called allies. Germans do not want to send Ukrainians their precious Leopard tanks, even with hundreds of them sitting unused, waiting for World War III."[120] Although Hines did not say it, he also knew his own personal career plans were now put on hold. Prior to the invasion, he had been a tantalizing six months from leaving Langley for a far more lucrative contracting job at Palantir, finally cashing in after twenty-five years of civil service capped at $215,000 a year. Instead, here he was, doing his patriotic best once again to muddle through another slow-moving train wreck without end.

The zombie leaned forward, close enough that Hines could see the veins in her temple pulse.

"What about stirring up Naples?" the zombie said.

"Naples?"

"Yes. Our boy Nikolai Sokolov," Jo said.

"I know the target. What about him?"

"We have had two years of constant surveillance with nothing to show. We should rattle some cages. Put the scheming little asshole into play."

---

120   Germany's Bundeswehr operates 321 active Leopard 2 main battle tanks. 18 were sent to Ukraine in the war's first year, or about 6%.

"Roll up Sokolov?" Hines asked, processing the monster's slightly more creative suggestion.

"Why not? Moscow has not recalled him yet. I own the counter intel ops. Easy to control. Nico deserves it," Jo added.

"It's an idea," Hines admitted. He had already faced internal pressure to pick up Sokolov after ample evidence implicated him in Tim Hastings's death two years ago. Sokolov had compromised the US's Seventh Fleet for years without penalty. The Maltese government was also looking for more closure on the local security officers killed at their port during that botched operation.

"Grabbing Sokolov sends a message—tit for tat," Jo continued. "Best of all, he is undeclared. Moscow will not publicly acknowledge when he just goes away."

"Who in Naples would do it?"

"Let's leave sailors out of this," Jo said. "I have better options. Other motivated players."

Hines squinted. Nothing was ever simple with Jo. Of course, she had her usual risky off-Broadway production already concocted. She had thought this all through before plopping down on his couch to make her pitch.

"You mean Volkov's niece? The curator?"

"You are paying attention, Marty," the monster replied. "Better this way. Keep it contained within interested parties. Plausible deniability. Less blowback risk."

"And less control," Hines countered. "I've already seen how this goes sideways."

"Katerina had nothing to do with the debacle in Malta. Hastings decided himself to lead a team onto that ship, and it was just bad luck how he fell into that trap."

"Maybe," Hines said. "But I spoke at Hastings's funeral, and you did not. Volkov's niece was part of that fiasco. Ditto the other asset you authorized access to the embassy arsenal. What was his name?"

"Drake. And Malta was a success, not a fiasco."

"That is what you think? Your little sideshows are unclean and uncontrolled." Hines sneered, always assuming that unvetted assets posed risks. Bad tradecraft usually led to bad outcomes.

"Come on, Marty. Paranoia is not helpful," Jo countered, leaning on her cane. "We do not have time to just play all of this out at a normal walking pace. A professional team killed Petrov, then took Yuri for a specific reason. In a proxy war, we need to use our proxies. Let me play the board. A black knight for a white bishop. We will also throw the Maltese a bone on their inquiry. This will help down the road, especially with shipping problems brewing in the Red Sea thanks to the Houthis.[121] The Maltese are a good little ally to keep happy."

"What happens after you grab Sokolov?" he pressed.

"Not sure. Step-by-step. We improve our position. Find out more."

"Not much progress if you just trade two Russians back and forth."

"I don't make simple chess moves," Jo replied.

"No. You do not. That is what worries me. Stakes are much higher now that we have a hot war on our hands."

"Are they? We always live in an imperfect world," the monster remarked.

Buzz.

Hines's desk phone distracted his attention just as he was pondering the viability of how future prisoner swaps might play into at least some progress that could be recognized by the people who mattered. He glanced at the number calling him while his mind filled back up with the dozen or so higher priority items he needed to complete before midnight. Then he needed to get up tomorrow at 6 a.m. to do it all again, and again. More headaches, more problems, and all fueled by sour, bad coffee.

Buzz.

Buzz.

"I have to take this," Hines said.

"Are you with me?" Jo said as she gripped her cane and rose from the beige couch.

"I'll sleep on it. Shut the door when you leave."

---

121   Iranian-backed militant group that controls northwestern Yemen and key stretches of the Red Sea coastline. They can disrupt shipping lanes because they occupy territory adjacent to the Bab el-Mandeb Strait, a narrow chokepoint.

7

Transcarpathia, Ukraine.
August 1, 2022. 7:30 a.m.

A SOFT, hesitant yellow dawn pushed against the light gray, cloudy summer sky. Max Drake's boots were caked in mud from the sloppy ground, which was still damp from last night's short rainstorm. A light mist hugged the tangled long grass that spread out along the foothills of the sheltered valley. Throughout the enclosed area, small clusters of armed men dressed in full khaki camouflage milled about. Some were silent and solo; others talked in small groups. All were gathering military gear and equipment for the day to come.

Max was excited, nervous, and still hungry after quickly scarfing down two slices of stale bread and a sixteen-ounce Red Bull for breakfast.

Finally! After four long weeks, we are moving on, Max thought. *About time!*

Max did not know exactly where they had been training, someplace in Ukraine's southwest, the Transcarpathia, maybe a few dozen kilometers from the Hungarian border. It was harder to know exact locations since his unit only used secure comms; precise locations were all hush-hush now.

The legion's makeshift bootcamp training this past month had been physically demanding—drills, weights, and formation jogs every day starting in the early morning and not over until the early evening at the soonest. Max had thought himself in decent physical shape before another fifteen pounds easily came off in the first two weeks and his feet blistered. By week three, they handed him a CZ 82 pistol from the Czech Republic, a Fort 222 Israeli-made semiautomatic assault rifle, a six-inch fixed blade camping knife, a helmet, a Kevlar vest, and military boots. Nothing was standard issue, but it was still decent military gear given the circumstances. Some guys snagged RPG-75s—portable, disposable, single-shot antitank weapons that had proved particularly effective in the first six months of the invasion.

Max approached Valentine as he was talking to a handful of Ukrainian medics recently pulled in to support the battalion. The tall Ukrainian broke away from that conversation and turned to Max.

"Starlink[122] loaded?" Valentine asked in his heavily accented English.

"Yes, in the first truck," Max replied, referring to the thirty communication units they had been tasked with distributing across one hundred kilometers of the southern front line.

Dmitry had made good on his promise to deliver more of these machines—a critical advantage. They expected more sophisticated stuff soon, with Max on point to keep the drones linked up to Starlink's low-altitude satellites. It should all be fine as long as Elon Musk does not reconsider and turn off the whole network because he is pissed off at some passing fart. Not the best idea to leave the fate of nations to a billionaire's whims, Max had worried when he took the order.

"Good. Ten minutes, then we go," Valentine said.

The First Battalion's 220 men divided into six squads of thirty-six men each. The battalion was mostly foreign soldiers, all with military or combat medical experience, and the rest was filled out with more experienced Ukrainians with above average English. Per Dmitry's informal recommendation, Valentine commanded Max's squad four. All six squads rolled up to the battalion commander, Vasili Rogoff. For Rogoff, this conflict was a continuation of fighting that began in 2014 when Russia took Crimea and the Donbas. Rogoff's battalion was meant to be the tip of the spear, a rapid-deployment unit with best-in-class, real-time satellite intel to disrupt and dislodge Russian defensive positions. Creative tactics were having success. Rogoff promised to do more.

Max made his way to the back of the first truck as squad four gathered into three idling six-wheeled trucks. The three foreigners he knew best were already sitting in the back: Bill Stryker, ex-UK Special Forces, age thirty-two; Colin Deacon, a former UK Marine, age thirty-four; and "Big Jacques" La Grande, Canadian Army, sniper trained, early forties. Bill and Colin had seen live combat outside Kabul and were already living in Ukraine with local girlfriends before the war. Behind them in the other two trucks were ten Poles with combat experience from UN peacekeeping missions in West Africa and a half dozen younger Romanian soldiers. The Romanians were not combat veterans, but they listened intently, spoke decent English, and seemed eager. The rest of First Battalion was pulled from southern units of the Ukrainian territorial defense force.

Max settled in as the three trucks pulled out. They drove all day, taking smaller dirt roads, rolling more cautiously across flat, expansive farmland,

---

122 Satellite internet constellation operated by SpaceX, providing high-speed, low-latency connectivity through a network of thousands of small satellites in low Earth orbit. SpaceX is owned by Elon Musk, one of the world's wealthiest tycoons.

and passing through drab, unremarkable villages. Sometimes the trucks paused for more detailed direction from the scouts ahead, then lurched onward down mostly muddy unpaved roads.

No one spoke during the drive. Max just stared out the back, watching dirt spin off the rear wheels, catching glimpses of abandoned gas stations, crappy roadside houses, and a rare beat-up local Honda or Ford truck. He now wore a black patch over his left glass eye—no need to disguise his injury as he had in the civilized world. At dusk, the honey-colored wheat fields looked very peaceful and idyllic. He envisioned that this vast landscape could just as easily have been observed during a road trip through Illinois, Kansas, or Iowa. For a precious hour, the deep brilliance of dusk infused Mykolaiv Oblast with a certain kind of lovely universal, ageless calm. Max allowed himself to simply appreciate the land's timelessness, almost—but not quite—forgetting that he was in the back of a mud-caked military truck with a motley group of armed foreigners who had never gone into combat together before.

Valentine ordered them to stop for the night an hour after dark. They decamped near a two-story abandoned farmhouse at the end of a long dirt road. The farmhouse was dark inside, with locked doors and broken windows on the ground floor. They smashed down the front door, then settled into the main room for the rest of the night.

Max joined the others for bread, sardines, processed ham from a can, and cold tea. Afterward, he found a dry, clean spot in the corner and slept six hours in a polyester bag.

The next day on the road was similar, except in the afternoon they paused near a small creek. He followed Bill and Big Jacques as they dispersed along the muddy bank as a precaution. Big Jacques annoyingly chewed tobacco and spat every few minutes. Some of the Romanians popped little blue amphetamine pills when they drank from their canteens.

Waiting there, Max heard distant artillery fire. The barrage went off in set, structured intervals, lasting about thirty minutes.

"Twenty clicks at most," Bill said. "We are getting close. Should be able to flank a few dumbass stragglers to pop our cherry."

"When?" Max asked.

"A couple of days. Maybe sooner. You hot for it?"

"Burning," Max replied dumbly and regretted it.

They drove down a small muddy road for another few hours in the evening in the direction of the artillery sounds. Word spread that two Russian brigades were jammed up moving south. Enemy units, perhaps a few hundred men, could not cross the river with heavy equipment and tanks, so they were abandoning their gear in a disordered retreat. The drones saw them heading to a different bridge about thirty kilometers south.

At midnight, Valentine ordered the trucks to stop and take cover within a thick grove of oak and popular trees. He put two five-man Javelin teams at positions farther in the woods and dispersed the rest in various covered positions for the night, a standard deployment.

Max set up his drone equipment behind the trucks, working with the options he had. These drone models were not armed like larger units, but at least they could be used to call in precise artillery targeting when needed. It was a similar reconnaissance playbook to what he had done before in northern Iraq a decade ago. Since then, drone technology had made huge strides. Now these little aerial killing machines were much more intelligent, faster, and cheaper.

After testing his basic setup, Max put himself against a fallen oak tree trunk close behind the last truck and closed his eyes. Tomorrow morning, if they decided to stay put here, he would put up two or three drones to scan along the road, a coverage area of two dozen kilometers. Better work as advertised, he vaguely worried before finally drifting off.

A sharp kick to the ribs jolted Max awake. Bill Stryker's animated face loomed over him.

"Get up," Bill barked sharply, betraying excitement. "Contact about ten minutes ago. Need to move."

Max pulled himself up to his feet, still in his boots, all laced up. "What about the drones?"

"Leave'em."

"Sure?"

"Roger that. No need," Bill replied, his face lit up by the morning's fragile dull light.

Max checked his gear, picked up his semiautomatic, fished out a spare ammunition clip from the bottom of his rucksack, and strapped on his helmet.

I feel like shit, Max thought. *Doesn't matter. I caught at least four solid hours of sleep. Today is as good a day as any.*

Max picked up the pace, jogging behind Bill deeper into the oak grove. He spotted Valentine and two others geared up behind a cluster of the tallest trees. Valentine waved them closer.

"Two tanks, twenty men." Valentine noted.

"How far?" Stryker asked.

"Two hundred meters. Ten minutes."

"Roger that."

"Check comms. Cover up over there. Wait," Valentine said in his staccato English, pointing to a place up the slope that provided better camouflage and a different angle on the road. They checked their helmet earpieces and heard Valentine's voice clearly, though not entirely intelligibly as he mixed up languages.

Max scrambled behind Stryker through the underbrush, up the slope, and to a position with a decent line of sight on the road. Max lay flat and scanned the terrain, his good eye pressed against the rifle's scope to see through the trees. Adrenaline kicked in as he licked his dry lips, the squad arrayed in various nooks along the road now, paused, hidden, listening.

Five minutes crept by.

Then he spotted movement. Two Russian T-72[123] tanks rolled slowly toward them, white Z's painted on their drab gray side armor just above the muddy caterpillar treads. There were eight men on foot—two on each of the tank's two flanks and four farther behind. A second tank brought up the rear with another four soldiers marching behind it.

The tanks lumbered forward, both tops open, the surrounding men pacing along. Max froze as they passed just thirty meters away.

Come on, guys. Take the shot.

Twenty meters.

One soldier walking alongside the first tank reached inside his vest for a pack of cigarettes and began fumbling with a lighter.

Do it.

White light flared from a stand of trees, then a fast brilliant streak rammed the first tank's turret with a *wooosh, boooom.* Another streak lit up five seconds later from a different direction in the trees. *Wooosh, boooom* into the second tank's right side. Two direct armor-piercing hits scattered metal bits.

Gunfire exploded in sporadic bursts.

Pop. pop. pop. pop. pop. pop. pop. pop. pop. pop.

Two enemy soldiers jerked, then fell back. Others scrambled.

Pop. pop. pop. Pop. pop. pop.

---

123   The most widely used main battle tank in the world. It has been manufactured in six countries, is in service with the armies of 35 nations and has fought in most major wars of the last 20 years.

One more dropped while fleeing to a ditch along the road. Silence, then another barrage. *Pop. pop. pop. pop.* Pause. *Pop.*

Pop. pop. pop from another position, like firecrackers going off at a parade.

A soldier covering near the tank ran to the ditch. Max squeezed his semiautomatic's trigger. The target snapped back, then crumbled face forward.

For a few long minutes, the T-72s crackled and burned, immobile, while three survivors in the ditch stayed down.

A Ukrainian soldier ran up to the first tank, climbed up from the back, and tossed a hand grenade into the open turret top. A muffled explosion and smoke followed. A second squad member did the same to the rear tank.

"*Se Davaisa,*" a Ukrainian lieutenant shouted at the three Russians still alive in the ditch. A boot-camp word: surrender.

The lieutenant waited, then shouted the same command twice more: "*Se Davaisa. Se Davaisa.*"

Finally, a voice shouted back.

"Move up," Valentine ordered over the comm headset. Ambush teams emerged from covered positions, guns raised at their shoulders.

The three Russians appeared slowly from the ditch, their hands high, faces distorted by terror. The Ukrainians yelled directions to them as they walked slowly forward. Then five or six from the squad sprang forward, grabbed the three Russians, and shoved each down hard. They quickly bound their hands behind their backs with thick rope, then pulled them off the dirt road and into the tangled forest.

Max followed Bill closer to the first damaged, burning Russian tank. He climbed up and checked inside the T-72. The two mangled corpses inside smelled putridly of petrol and charred flesh. There was not much else inside, so they hopped back down and checked the perimeter.

Fifteen minutes passed this way as they roamed among the dead and pulled off weapons, ammo clips, and other tactical gear. Another KIA was face down in the dirt, body twisted, uniform shredded from multiple hits. The soldier's leg still twitched despite the bits of his skull splayed out on the grass. *Brains look like raw hamburger meat,* Max thought.

Bill leaned over and yanked off the dead man's dog tags with what seemed like an angry motion.

"Stupid formation. Bad way to move," Bill remarked. "Yeah. Not smart," Max replied. "Lost little sheep."

Valentine sent six men farther up the road to see if the ambush had trigged any other enemy units nearby. The scouts reported back that the road was all clear, at least for now.

Slowly, Max's adrenalin subsided; he reverted to his normal self, drained. The squad left the tanks smoking on the road and the dead where they fell, stripped of whatever useful items they carried—ammo clips, pistols, and several cleverly stashed mobile phones with maybe useful intel instead of just porn photos and family pictures from home.

Colin started the first two-hour watch shift over the three prisoners later that night after they set up camp and a defensive perimeter. Max took his turn at about midnight. When he took his guard position, the Russian captives were all still awake, eyes staring blankly ahead.

Max was surprised how young the kids were, no more than twenty but with hollowed-out eyes and gaunt features. These raw recruits had landed in a war they did not understand, did not care about, and were not trained to fight in.

Bored, Max handed the scrawny redhead his water canteen. The exhausted prisoner took a swig and avoided eye contact when he handed the canteen back. His face was empty. Was the ambush just a nightmare he was having while lying on a warm bed in his parent's crappy Russian apartment block? Soon he would wake up. None of this would be real. Mama would be waiting in the kitchen with hot black tea and a little toasted bread with apricot jam to start the day. If only that were true.

"Any good intel?" Max asked the next morning when he saw Valentine writing in a logbook under the shade of a wide, leafy chestnut tree.

"Captain fried up in the first tank," Valentine replied in his heavy accent. "Kids say they took the road south with no orders until tanks quit. Captain found gas from diesel Toyota trucks parked at a farm. No good maps."

"Meat for the grinder," Max remarked.

"Da. They go to the *Miasorubka*. Die for nothing," Valentine replied. "We swap these three for our men. Now they are like gold." Valentine gave orders to a Ukrainian private to drive the three prisoners to a gathering point about thirty kilometers north. He ordered Max to ride in the back, transfer the prisoners to another territorial defense unit, get gas, pick up more meal packs—with ham if possible—and more .40 caliber ammo. Then circle back tomorrow morning, rendezvous point to be determined. "Got it?"

"Sir," Max confirmed, saluting.

"How was Israeli gun?" Valentine asked.

"Worked fine. No jamming."

"Hit one?"

"Maybe. Probably."

Max returned to the three waiting prisoners, who stood blindfolded with their heads down and hands tied behind their backs. He took the first redheaded, pimply faced kid by the arm, and he and the other two were pulled along to back of the first truck.

"Bad luck, brother," Max said.

The kid, no English, only slumped.

The truck engine started.

Combat was one of those experiences Max could never come close to describing. Words could never capture the mix of dread, fear, and sick thrill that swirled together during the fastest, most lethal moments. Time moved strangely then, with seconds lasting what seemed like minutes or longer. An insane possession took hold of him while the bullets whizzed by, knowing always that if just one lead projectile found its mark, death might slap down instantaneously—game over, no redo's. Oblivion stayed close during those moments as men morphed into animals, red in tooth and claw, kill or be killed.

Afterward, Max always felt the distance. Once it was over and his body functioned normally again, the external world quietly and slowly drifted away until all of it just seemed remote, like a movie playing with the sound turned extremely low. Other people he spoke to or who heard him speak in the aftermath were all oddly disconnected, their faces and expressions more like pasteboard masks than organic features of animated, sentient beings. They became like sleepwalkers. He, too, was a sleepwalker, not a creature with agency or freedom or any kind of real substance beyond a collection of organs and nerves and a basic, primitive will to live.

Max and his three prisoners bounced in the back of the military truck. He was tired now, and his hands felt heavy. Mostly though, he felt as he did before, the same as in Iraq more than a decade ago, with a familiar numbness throughout his whole body.

He felt nothing. None of it mattered.

Himself and all the others were but the quintessence of dust.[124]

---

124   Slogan used by EOD (Explosive Ordnance Disposal) teams during Iraq war. The original usage of "quintessence of dust," was spoken by Hamlet in Act 2, Scene 2 at the end of his "What a piece of work is a man" monologue, where Hamlet contrasts the theoretical beauty and nobility of humans with physical decay.

FIELDWORK

8

Yalta, Crimea, Ukraine.
August 21, 2022. 2:45 p.m.

KIRIL PETROVITCH Alekseyev crushed his latest cigarette into a porcelain ashtray cluttered with dirty butts and ash. Then he sipped the bitter black tea from his cup and chewed on the tiny leaves before swallowing.

Kiril had arrived late last night on a regularly scheduled military air transport plane from Sochi. By noon he had already finished off half a pack of Belomorkanal cigarettes.[125] He was not sure if he had brought another pack and dreaded the stale cigarettes from the noncommissioned navy guys. Now his forehead felt tense and knotted since he had not slept well all week.

Kiril kept the windows open to let the breeze refresh the dusty old two-story farmhouse. Circulating air also helped disperse er-rant houseflies. This secluded compound twenty kilometers from Yalta's town center was set on a wide elevated plateau with decent southern views of the Black Sea. A senior navy captain had cleared out the first-floor study. Outside the tall window, the sea was a grim steel blue sheet beneath heavy clouds.

A knock interrupted his thoughts. A tall wide-shouldered Russian naval officer at the interior door met his gaze.

"Sir, should I bring him up now?" the officer asked in his dull southern accent.

"Go ahead," Kiril replied in crisp, commanding Russian.

The second guard trailing behind Yuri Volkov put his hand on the old man's shoulder to help him ascend the basement stairs. The guard brought Yuri closer, locked the prisoner's ankle chain tight in a loop to a heavy metal chair, and followed the first tall officer out of the room.

Kiril reviewed the old man's state: Volkov looked frail after just four

---

125   Filter-less cigarettes with a hollow cardboard mouthpiece introduced in 1932 to commemorate the White Sea-Baltic Canal. Noted for their extreme strength, industrial-grade tobacco, and iconic map-print packaging.

weeks of captivity in the farmhouse's dank hundred-square-foot basement detention cell. He was sick the first week from the Wagner team's GHB shot. In Belgrade, they had switched him to another security units custody. The military transport plane went first to Sebastopol, then to Yalta via helicopter. *Serbian amateurs nearly killed him with an overdose,* Kiril lamented. *The old man might be strong, but he is not superhuman. Still… what to expect for the paltry sum of just $250,000. At least they delivered my package alive, barely.*

The second week, Kiril had asked his local subordinate to leave a copy of the *International Herald* and he himself had discreetly circled an article on an investigation into the death of Russian oligarch Mikael Petrov outside Grasse, France. The journalist had noted this latest death as part of a wider pattern: Sergey Protosenya, age fifty-five, was also found hanged in his spacious villa in Lloret de Mar in Spain the previous month. Protosenya "committed suicide" after allegedly murdering his wife and son in a fit of unanticipated and unexplainable madness. In St. Petersburg, two other wealthy local businessmen had plunged to untimely deaths from otherwise safe, unremarkable condominiums.

Yuri sipped icy water and ate his black bread slowly. Kiril had spent this morning refreshing himself on the old man's two-decade-old case file: longstanding interwoven concerning contacts included a younger brother, Sergei Volkov, assassinated March 27, 2016, in a Neuilly-sur-Seine car bomb, and Sergei's daughter, who survived the blast, then moved to the New York a year later along with her brother, to work at one of Yuri's private business, an art dealership.

"You've had enough to read?" Kiril began. "We have only a small collection of books here. Some plays—The Cherry Orchard, Uncle Vanya, The Seagull. Personally, I never liked Chekov. Too many unhappy bureaucrats and uninteresting women. I find these stories boring and overrated, but your preferences might differ."

Yuri gave a shallow exhale without answering.

"I did have some luck when I found *Hard to Be a God*[126] last night, a little paperback hidden up in the attic," Kiril replied. "The Strugatsky brothers are much more interesting writers than Chekov. I will send it down to you tomorrow."

"Am I here to read?" Yuri finally replied.

---

126   1964 science fiction masterpiece that explores the ethical agony of a futuristic Earth observer forbidden from using his superior power to save a medieval alien society from its own brutality.

"Of course not," Kiril said, offering his prisoner one of his few remaining Belomorkanal. Yuri refused with a terse hand wave. Instead, Kiril placed the cigarette between his own lips, lit it, and sucked in the nicotine while the pale blue smoke drifted upward.

"Why am I here?" the prisoner finally asked.

"You've been arrested to stand trial on bribery and corruption," Kiril said.

"That's your official charge?"

"Moscow lawyers will decide the exact charges once the documents are prepared. Corruption will be the easiest to prove. Your Belarus telecom venture is the softest target. I have already directed a team to seize related assets and freeze that company's bank accounts, although you made that difficult. We will have a court process, but as the sun shines, a proper and respectable judge will find you guilty. You will receive the maximum sentence but not death. In the end, you will rot for the rest of your natural life in a little room like the one you have now."

"I am already sixty-two," Yuri said with a shrug.

"Still a shame. Golden years wasted while you still can play tennis. A disappointment for the next twenty years after what you have built. What should we call it? *Sudba dlodeyka.* A turn of fate."

"Will your political masters last this long?" Yuri asked. "First, they fascinate the fools and then they muzzle the intelligent.[127] This cannot last forever."

Kiril smiled, lips surrounded by his black-haired goatee.

"Yuri Ivanovich," Kiril said. "You are right to be frustrated by today's unfortunate realities. I despise today's cronies just like you. They are all bloated, disgusting politicians. Especially Lavrov, our esteemed foreign minister. How that man remains in power, I do not know. Of course, we all know that our government's lies are pure nonsense and that we live in particularly absurd times. I personally do not assert any kind of value system. I assume my duties only as they are presented. I navigate whatever course has been set before me. A few hundred years of evidence suggests the wisdom of my approach."

"You are a very noble servant of the State," Yuri hissed back

"You and I are different? In this world, we each act according to our own interests. You have yours. I have mine. Heroes and villains are for children's stories and the brainwashed naive. What we think a better world should be does not change what the world is today."

---

127   Yuri is paraphrasing a quote attributed to the British philosopher Bertrand Russell (1872–1970) on a two-step process used by authoritarian leaders to consolidate power.

414

"Get on with it. What do you want?" Yuri said.

"Why did you plan to visit Mikael Petrov?" Kiril asked.

"He was a friend. He invited me."

"Your friend was committing treason. For a very long time."

"If true, he had his reasons," Yuri replied.

"Maybe he did," Kiril admitted. "You know, we were acquaintances from years ago. Not a close friendship, but I knew Misha at university, a class above. Two years ago, I even stayed a night at his villa. It was late summer when the hibiscus plants in his garden were all in bloom. Lovely place. A shame, all of it," Kiril said before another cigarette drag. He sat back down behind the large antique desk.

"I have a better idea than unproductive arguing," Kiril continued. "Let us use our two creative minds to solve my immediate problem. We can pretend for a moment that there is a path for us to reverse time, a way for you to simply go back to your comfortable London house and your expensive Italian dinners. We can imagine how your little basement cell goes away in a puff of smoke. Snap, you are back reclining in a nice leather chair, sipping tea with just a little bit of honey, reviewing investments and their dividend yields."

Yuri sat impassive.

"Tamar Zoidze's eldest son from Tbilisi," Kiril continued. "Bogan Zoidze. You know the name?"

Kiril took note of Yuri's very slight nod.

"Of course, you know the name very well. You held Bogan responsible for your brother's death," Kiril said. "I understand your suspicions. Bogan was a queer boy. Extremely smart but also very queer, even before the first Chechen war taught him how to truly hate. Hate made him useful with a whole new life, a new persona he created. Extreme violence against the few to bring security for the many is a particularly rare, but useful service. Now my useful little monster Perses is gone, rest in peace."

"He will not," Yuri hissed.

"I suppose not. If there is hell, Bogan belongs there. Unfortunately, hell is a myth, and Bogan also left me with practical problems in my world," Kiril continued. "I assigned him a task to transport government assets. I do not hold all the facts, but I do know that his problems began in Malta, where you own a profitable shipping business. Your niece received a Maltese visa the week Bogdan was killed."

"My niece is a company director of our Maltese shipping firm. We hold board meetings in Valetta on a routine basis," Yuri said.

"With Dmitry Medkov?"

"Possibly."

"A mere coincidence, yes," Kiril said and then continued after draining the last tea from his cup. "Unfortunately, Medkov is another traitor with tiny little thorns. He also has a long file, back to paper records from Afghanistan forty years ago, with plenty more during his twenty years with you, including your expensive little sham contract in Syria with the UNHCR. Our sources report that Medkov spends most time in Odessa now, plotting with our enemies."

"If you have your files, what do you want from me?"

"Only practical solutions."

"You want my help with your stupid war?"

"Of course not," Kiril replied. "You can offer nothing on this. Our special military operation is bigger than the man you think you are. The war is one more distraction, maybe an opportunity. Background noise, mostly, for what I have been asked to keep in line."

Kiril rose from behind the desk. He walked over, put his face a foot from Yuri's, and peered into the old man's sunken eyes. His prisoner smelled of sweat mixed with dust and mold.

"What I want is simple, old man. You will help find and return the valuable State property that Bogan lost," Kiril said in a very even, unemotional voice. "The Russian government is missing twenty-four metric tons of gold. One and a half billion dollars' worth at today's prices and going higher. If you want to avoid rotting away for the rest of your life, you are going to help me get me my precious metal back. No matter how long it takes."

9

Naples, Italy.
August 11, 2022. 7:15 p.m.

BLOOD-ORANGE SUNLIGHT scattered through a shifting bevy of fast-moving, billowing clouds above the ancient Italian city's three million inhabitants. In the distance, twenty-five kilometers south of the city's center, Mount Vesuvius's triangular shadow loomed over the city's rolling hills with the same fearful, latent volcanic power that destroyed Pompeii in a single day almost two thousand years ago.

Paul Drake wiped the sweat from the back of his neck while he reviewed surveillance footage playing back on a fifteen-inch monitor. A thin wire linked the monitor to a high-powered telescopic lens discreetly peeking out of a small disguised window. The wide-aperture, military-grade telescope picked up relevant details of a building's façade nearly two hundred meters away: two front windows with partial interior views, a tall nineteenth-century entrance door, and below this, a two-car garage door. The telescope re-corded the garage door opening and shutting each day for different vehicles, and the camera auto snapped photos of everyone leaving a car or arriving via the front entrance. Palantir's state-of-the-art Meta Four algo tracing platform did the rest, gathering up data-points, matching visual cues, correlating inputs within a vast dynamic digital network. They now had more than two years of data input into that vast treasure trove.

After Malta, the 24-7 data bots traced the leak to a node cluster within Naples's navy intelligence and the ISP of one bad apple among the Sixth Fleet's seven thousand US service members: forty-seven-year-old Michael Cummings. The bots quickly connected Cummings to a Russian national, Nicolai Sokolov, a local contractor with sporadic, low-margin work involving retrofitting navy ships retired from service. In hindsight, Sokolov was an obvious FSB agent, although it was a testament to his skill and the US Navy's ineptitude that he was not flagged sooner.

Jo had left Cummings in place. For the next year, she had fed him a smattering of relevant intelligence—half-truths mixed with disinformation to stir confusion and trace the impacts up the chain just in case there were any more higher priority vulnerabilities to suss out. Sadly, according to Jo, she had little to show for all the attention, money, and compute power churning away, unless Meta Four was using Sokolov's data in orthogonal views not clear to her small human brain.

Until now.

Paul quietly opened the tall mahogany bedroom door to check on Katya. She was awake now, sitting up in bed, wearing a white cotton tank top. Her neck glistened with sweat, and her hair was dyed jet-black. This new hairstyle was not a flippant fashion choice. Some Langley GS-11 analyst[128] had mined a pattern suggesting Sokolov preferred brunettes.

"I'll crack the window more," Paul said as he entered the tiny bedroom. The single window faced the opposite direction from their target. These past few days it had been sweltering, almost 95 degrees Fahrenheit during most of the day and still uncomfortable at night. Naples's older buildings, while stately and ornate, used ceiling fans instead of modern air-conditioning.

"A little only, please. Too many mosquitos," Katya replied.

Paul battled the old window frame until it moved. Six stories below, the old city's narrow streets churned with life. Paul smelled garlic, charred pizza bread, and oregano wafting from the crowded restaurants below.

"Anything new?" Katya asked.

"Not much," Paul replied. "Nico has not traveled much lately. He has been very careful since the war began. Hunkering down."

"Good. That means they need him here."

"I hope you are right," Paul said. "Caffé Gambrinus[129] looks like our best option. It is a big café in a crowded area. He went there, alone, three times last month, twice on Friday. Maybe he will go there tomorrow, assuming no rain."

"Tomorrow then," Katya offered.

"If he doesn't bite?" Paul continued.

"He will," Katya said confidently.

"If you spook him, no second chance."

"I will not, as you say, 'spook' him," she said. "I know his type very well."

---

128   A mid-level professional grade in the US civil service pay scale, commonly requiring a Ph.D. or 3 years of progressively higher-level graduate education.

129   An iconic coffee house serving as a cultural "drawing room" for the city since its founding in 1860. Famous patrons included Oscar Wilde, Ernest Hemingway, Jean-Paul Sartre, and various Italian Presidents.

Why are you always so sure? Paul thought without pressing her further. Katya had somehow managed to succeed before, but he disapproved of the risk-taking creature she had evolved into ever since Malta and Sicily. She had already been uncommonly lucky there. But luck could easily change. *One bad roll of snake eyes and then it simply ends, usually when least expected.*

"He'll know clumsy approaches," Paul continued.

"I'll be as natural as sunlight," Katya replied.

"You better be."

"Stop worrying," Katya said softly. "At least Yuri is alive. We have a path."

"Yes, but we can't wait too long," Paul said, referring to last week's email that Katya had received with a short cryptic message and an image of Yuri holding a recent newspaper with its date prominently shown. An untraceable ISP bounced around cyber-space, offering up a dial back but nothing more.

"I'll respond when we're done here," she said.

"Could take weeks," Paul replied.

"No, Paul. Tomorrow."

Katya lifted the bedcovers, came over to him, put her slender hands on his moist neck, and pressed her lips against his. Her glistening skin beneath the cotton underwear felt warm against his body. When she pulled back, his eyes met her two deep blue-green oval reservoirs. They were the same two gems from their first meeting in the Chelsea gallery a lifetime ago, still in constant mutation, and still inscrutable.

"Always worrying, my dearest Paul. Let go."

She kissed him again, harder. He felt her smooth, warm chest against his own.

"Trying," Paul whispered as she pulled gently away.

"Try harder. I'm taking a cold shower now."

"I smell that bad?" Paul asked.

"Only a little. I will forgive you if you join me."

"Twist my arm," he said.

Katya led Paul by the fingertips to the apartment's small bathroom. She turned on the water in the small alcove behind a tiny glass door.

Paul watched her undress. Katya lifted off her tank top, revealing the deep scars running down the length of her slender, seductive torso. The scar lines were now integral body features, including the more recent mark from two years ago where a .40 caliber bullet passed through her upper right thigh. Scars now completed her essence. He could not imagine her otherwise smooth alabaster skin without them.

Paul undressed and joined her in the shower alcove. As the cool water cascaded over their entwined bodies, he passionately kissed her neck and supple breasts. Her hands guided his fingers to her waist, then to her bare buttocks. Their lips pressed together, and his heart pumped harder.

The streams of cold water washed away the stifling heat and most, but not all, of Paul's lingering fears.

10

Naples, Italy.
August 12, 2022. 4:15 p.m.

NICOLAI SOKOLOV dabbed a clean white handkerchief to his forehead before sipping the rest of his slightly sweet chianti.

He sat under the shaded awning on the terrace of the Gran Caffè Gambrinus, just off the busy Piazza del Plebiscito. Gambrinus had proven the best place to feel the sea breeze in the afternoon while the rest of Naples sweltered. Today it had already reached 32 degrees Celsius since late morning.

The older waiters knew him as a regular. Nico usually ordered an espresso with a pistachio-flavored cannoli and a small glass of ice water. He left them generous tips to leave him alone for as long as he wanted to read the newspapers or write notes in his small black notebook.

Nico folded open *Il Mattino's* world events page.

```
IAEA    Chief   Calls   for   Maximum   Restraint   at
Zaporizhzhia Nuclear Powerplant


   Rafael Mariano Grossi, the director general of the
International Atomic Energy Agency (IAEA), called for
maximum restraint following recent reports indicating
an alarming situation at Europe's largest nuclear plant
in Zaporizhzhia, Ukraine. The plant is in the Russian
occupied part of southern Ukraine. The IAEA said it
has not been able to visit the facility since before
the conflict began. "These reports are very disturbing
and further underline the importance of the IAEA going
to the Zaporizhzhia plant. We are determined to lead a
safety mission to the site as soon as possible," Grossi
said in a statement, adding that there is a need to
"avoid any accident that could threaten public health."
On Monday, Dmytro Orlov, mayor of the Russian-occupied
city of Enerhodar, adjacent to the plant, said that an
unexplained incident at the plant left several Russian
soldiers injured. Grossi stressed that the UN nuclear
watchdog must send a mission to conduct essential safety
activities at the facility.
```

Shelling a nuclear power plant indiscriminately and hoping for the best? What a goddam mess they have made of this, Nico thought. *Incompetent hucksters running our ground combat units. Circus clowns.*

Nico understood all too well how Putin's big strategic gamble, his so-called "special military operation," was not going as planned. After the sinking of the Russian Navy's most advanced warship, the *Moskva*, in April, Nico had tasked Mike Cummings to dig up more details on how the US Navy was feeding targeting intel to Ukrainian special ops on Russia's Black Sea fleet. So far, no good answers. Cummings had not sent anything of value for months now, only useless low-level tidbits, nothing actionable or relevant to the ongoing threats. *The well is running dry. Maybe it was best to move to Sicily and restart other contacts there? A change of scenery would refresh the well and might produce more immediately useful facts, he pondered. If not Sicily, then either Istanbul or Budapest might be a better hunting ground, and it would be reasonable to ask for—*

"No, that is not going to work," a female voice said forcefully in Russian.

Nico's ears perked up. He rarely heard his native language spoken in Caffé Gambrinus.

The woman at a nearby table spoke fluent Russian into her phone. Intrigued enough, he lifted his eyes from his newspaper to slyly look her way: slender neck, round Hermes sunglasses, black hair covered under a fashionable white straw cloche with a silk purple ribbon. She was not speaking to any companion but rather to an empty chair. Small white earbuds were stuck in both ears, and her mobile phone rested on the table next to a flute of golden prosecco. "Well, if you can't make it now, there is nothing I can do," the woman continued in Russian. "Why didn't you tell me before? You are wasting my time just because you cannot decide."

Petersburg accent?

"You're not listening to what I'm saying," the woman continued. Then, in her anger, her elbow knocked the delicate prosecco flute off the café's small round table. Shards scattered, a large one near Nico's leather shoes. A few curious heads on the café terrace turned after the crash.

"Oh, God. I am so sorry," the woman said to him, switching to English and abruptly ending her phone call. She looked to the floor to assess the extent of the accident. "I'm so clumsy."

"*Nichigo Strashnago.* Never mind," Nico replied in Russian.

"Oh, you speak Russian. So embarrassing," the woman replied. Nico smiled as he bent to pick up the larger shards near his feet. "Here, let me help. Be careful. Glass is sharp," he added, still in Russian.

The head waiter saw the accident from behind the bar. He came over with a brush to sweep up the broken glass, assuring them both not to worry.

"I'm so clumsy," the woman said again in her crisp, clear Petersburg accent.

"It's nothing," Nico replied. "Here, let me buy you another."

"Certainly not," she said.

"Nonsense," Nico insisted, switching effortlessly to Italian to tell the waiter: "We will take two more, please, here at my table. Will you?"

The woman put her phone back into her small Chanel purse, removed her white earbuds and Hermes sunglasses, and moved over to the empty wicker chair at Nico's table.

Now sitting closer, Nico discerned this interesting female's face more clearly—smooth skin, classically high cheekbones, gemlike blue-green eyes. Pleasant surprise. He considered himself an expert connoisseur of Slavic females, having recruited so many of them over his very long career. This woman could hold her own against any of those professionals, and without fake Botox lips or silicon tits, he instantly assessed.

"You seemed upset on the phone," Nico offered.

"It is nothing. Just my silly sister," the woman replied. "She blames sanctions for not joining me this summer like she promised. She claims she could not get a visa, but that is nonsense. It was easy for me to get a visa myself. They talk of sanctions, but I see Russians on travel everywhere in Europe. Nobody really cares if they are willing to spend money. No, it is all about her idiotic boyfriend. He cannot leave Russia, so she wants to just spend time with him, not me. Ruined all our plans."

"On your summer holiday?" Nico asked.

"*Da. Slava Bogu.* Thank God. Finally."

"Staying long?"

"Only a week in Naples, then off to Rome."

"You've seen Pompeii?"

"Not yet. I booked a tour on Sunday, though. I have read so much about it."

"Pompeii is fascinating. Very well-preserved," Nico offered. "What else are you looking to do? What do you like?"

"I love classic art," the woman replied, brushing back a strand of her long black hair and answering softly as if admitting a bad habit or a personality flaw. Nico had expected her to say she wanted to go shopping and visit restaurants, so he paused a bit to think of a more appropriate, more cultured response.

"If you prefer sculpture, there is the Farnese Hercules[130] at the Archeological Museum," he finally offered.

"I have seen pictures of that collection. I must go there too. A few days are not enough time to truly enjoy it all."

"I know. Napoli is a special place that takes time to understand," Nico said, realizing that he also did genuinely enjoy his own ten-year residence. He had grown fond of Naples's stately, dilapidated mansions and the timeless views of Vesuvius rising against a long horizon. He also thought the Archeological Museum offered a particularly impressive collection from both the Greek and Roman eras. He had not been there in years himself.

The waiter finally came back with two prosecco glasses. Nico thanked him with another friendly flourish of his fluent Italian.

"You live here?" she asked.

"I do. I run a shipping business," Nico said.

He lifted his glass while he gazed into the young woman's eyes.

"Well then. Let us drink to your adventure, even without your selfish sister," he said.

They clanked glasses and each took a long sip.

"You are called?" he asked.

"Anya…" she said.

"Pleasure, Anya. I am Nicolai, but please call me Nico."

He furtively glimpsed at both her left and right hands. Anya wore a small, elegant gold Rolex watch on her right wrist but no rings on any of her slender, aristocratic fingers.

———— ✳ ————

Nico glanced at his Philipp Patek wristwatch while Anya exchanged pleasantries with the talkative waiter. He was surprised it was approaching eleven o'clock. They were the last couple dining among the cluster of tables, and the kitchen had already closed.

He had been with Anya already for seven hours—three hours on the terrace of Caffè Gambrinus and then another four at this magnificent dinner. When she had agreed to dine with him, he had resolved to take her to his favorite restaurant, Michelasso, which was only a short walk to the lively Via Santa Brigida area. He had watched her carefully on the stroll

---

130   Marble colossus that is a Roman copy from the early 3rd century AD, signed by the sculptor Glykon of Athens, based on a lost 4th-century BC bronze.

over to the restaurant. He liked how her hips swayed with each confident, athletic step and how she kept her back straight, poised like a trained ballet dancer and not some confused little strumpet traveling alone on holiday.

Dinner at Michelasso was superb, a perfectly orchestrated culinary experience. They had started with a plate of burrata cheese and sliced tomatoes drizzled with balsamic infusion. Then came *parmigiana di melanzane* and ricotta cheese and a very respectable bottle of Sicilian red. Roasted lamb with potatoes and swordfish came as the main course, followed by the chef's version of *tiramisu*, a moist vanilla cake dipped in coffee, and dusted with cocoa powder. While a vague professional sense of caution had always dominated Nico's life, tonight he almost regretted not living the much simpler, albeit false, narrative he provided to Anya. His invented life was just the veneer of his more sordid reality. However, he had conditioned himself to habitually deceive others so that a web of lies so often repeated also rang true even to himself. This was always the best way to play the game so that the fabric of lies was tightly woven. Tonight, his lies seemed particularly right.

Two grappa glasses came as final digestive. He felt light and satisfied. Nico had not intended to veer into politics but was intrigued by what a smart, independent woman like Anya might tell him about the popular mood back home.

"What do others back in Piter think about what's happening?" he asked.

"Depends on whom you ask. You know how most are. Stay quiet, move on with life, survive with whatever dignity they permit. Do not create an excuse for them to hurt you. The bars and nightclubs are crowded again. Everyone is just getting along with it all," Anya said.

"What do you really think?" Nico pressed.

"Me? I do not know. I have no strong opinion. There is nothing I personally can do. I would not want a brother or son to die for something as pointless as this."

"Too bad we were forced into it. No choice."

"Do you think it is going well?" Anya asked.

"Not yet, thanks to bad apples in our military. But eventually we will have victory. We just need time for the West to lose interest instead of butting their noses into our affairs. It is time for us to push back. If we don't defense ourselves now, there will be nothing left in the future."

"Let us not talk about it. It just spoils the evening. I hate politics," Anya said. "Nothing you or I can do to change it."

"I suppose not," Nico said. "We can only live, and you came to Italy to enjoy yourself."

"I did. You are helping," she said.

"Am I?"

"You are," she replied, a suggestive smile crossing her lips.

Anya excused herself to go the restroom. After she left, Nico motioned to the waiter to pay the check. When she returned, he observed how Anya had put on brighter red lipstick and rearranged her dark hair. Once again, he took in her startling movie-star good looks, especially those hypnotic, glowing blue-green eyes—timeless Russian beauty in the most classical and purest sense.

"Shall we walk a bit?" he said, holding out his hand. She took it. *Good signal.*

"Where to next?" Anya asked.

"This way, toward the water."

When they started walking, Anya's arm locked in his. He smelled more perfume on her neck, a musky, slightly sweet fragrance that mixed with the humid air.

"Thank you so much for a lovely dinner. I was so angry earlier today, maybe because of this heat. Now you have made everything better. You are an amazing listener. But you know that already, I am sure," she said as they headed along the busy streets.

"The pleasure is mine. All mine," Nico replied.

Nico could not keep his gaze from moving down along the curves of Anya's slender body. He desperately wanted to remove that cream-colored silk blouse and run his hands over her firm buttocks. He needed to feel her pale naked body next to him, innocent and pure.

Nico's mind whirred through assorted options as they walked hand in hand along the waterfront with Mount Vesuvius out there in the night's distance, stolidly imposing. *She is here for another week. Do I have time? Why not? What is the downside? She lives in St. Petersburg,. Just one night. No need to decide now, especially if she ends up being too much trouble. Slightly complicated, but I deserve it, and she will be worth it.*

"Where are you staying?" he asked.

"Two blocks this way," Anya said softly.

"Which hotel?" he asked.

"I have rented a flat. I bought some lovely amaro yesterday. We can try it together. I will mix it with some club soda for a nice nightcap."

"*Atlitchna.* Super," he said.

Anya led him down a narrow alley, away from the busier street. For a moment, Nico hesitated. But he had drunk a bottle of wine and then grappa, and Anya's musky perfume mixed with the salty ocean breeze. He checked his watch—fifteen minutes to midnight. *Early enough. I am not an old man, weak in the knees, scared of my own shadow. Besides, I need to stay healthy and keep the blood flowing strong. Use it or lose it.*

She kissed him outside the door as she fumbled with the keys. Nico held her waist tightly and moved his mouth over her slender neck, giving her light kisses on her baby-soft ivory skin. He desperately needed her now.

"Stop it," Anya said playfully but did not fully push him away.

"Why?" he asked.

"I can't open the door." She giggled.

"I am sorry. I cannot wait," he whispered back, inhaling her musky perfume.

"You need to. Please," she said before finally putting the key into the lock.

They slipped inside. Anya shut the door behind her. Inside, she kicked off her high heels.

"Give me a second," she said. "And take off your shoes."

Nico watched Anya move inside the dark room. He bent down and started to undo his shoelaces just a little so he could kick off the uncomfortable leather shoes and relax more.

"Where's the light switch?" he asked, thinking now how much he was about to enjoy this long night.

She did not answer.

Nico fumbled to find the light switch near the entrance and flicked it on.

Anya stood there stone-faced, unsmiling, with lips pursed and a little pistol dangling loosely in her hand. Nico's dream abruptly clicked off. He sensed another in the room, hovering in the corner by the window. Another man glared at him, gripping some kind of object with a square nozzle.

"Easy. Keep your hands down," Anya ordered from across the room while also raising her little pistol.

Nico stepped one foot back.

The figure in the corner strode forward with a straight outstretched arm. Three metal projectiles latched onto Nico's right pectoral muscle, delivering the Taser's searing, crackly 30,000-volt shock. Excruciating pain rampaged through Nico's upper body, ribcage, and neck.

Nico lost his balance, toppled over, and crashed into an end table. He writhed on the floor while waves of intense pain flowed from his fingertips and toes up through his spine and neck. The Taser's electric pulses paused for a moment while all those little latches still gripped onto his chest. Nico pulled against the wires weakly, without success.

The volts began anew, now with a more intense, burning pain. Unbearably so. It seared throughout his nervous system.

Warm yellowish urine from a belly full of wine flowed down Nico's white linen Armani pants as he gurgled incoherently for the agony to stop.

11

Fedorivka, Ukraine.
September 3, 2022. 1 p.m.

AFTER A short, cautious advance across a series of small dirt roads, First Battalion's squad four rolled their three armored trucks into the insignificant village of Fedorivka by early afternoon. Max's stomach growled. He had not eaten a decent meal for days, just protein bars, bread, peanut butter, and stale beef jerky. His body had continued to plod along in a mechanized fashion these last weeks, while his mind strove to shut out all the drifting, monotonous hours. *Another drab little nowhere village shithole,* Max thought just after his truck stopped. *It is depressing how poor this rural province is, and now it is much worse.*

Fedorivka offered a two-lane paved central road, a few municipal buildings, a row of unattractive cement houses, a rundown elementary school, and a damaged onion-domed church. Power lines drooped like severed tendons above the roadside shops, recently ransacked, with shattered display cases and scattered debris. Every other house's roof was smashed, and most of the windows were covered by corrugated metal sheets or wood planks. The younger villagers were long gone. Now this place was home only to the infirm, the elderly, and a smattering of caregivers unwilling to abandon the most vulnerable.

Valentine ordered two trucks to an empty lot in front of Fedorivka's main church. After a quick perimeter walk to verify no hostile threats, the Romanians started unloading the crates.

An old woman, head covered in a gray wool shawl, emerged from one of the houses and approached Valentine. Her face held two weary bloodshot eyes, cracked lips, and an enflamed nose set on a knot of heavy wrinkles. She spoke quickly to Valentine, who stood there nodding while she jabbered on.

A gaunt old man also came over and stood next to the old woman, joining the conversation. The old man repeated incomprehensible words over and over like a mantra, waving his hands, gesticulating, while Valentine nodded. Big tears rolled down the woman's cracked cheeks.

Eventually, one of the other Ukrainians came over and calmed both the villagers down.

"What are they saying?" Max asked when Valentine freed himself from the conversation.

"Nothing much. Just thanking us for coming," Valentine replied. "Happy we brought food. Russians looted every house and left them nothing. He also warned about the booby traps. You go now and check the church first. Take the metal detector."

"Will do," Max replied and went back to the truck to fish out the detector gear from the supply box.

Max strapped the bomb detector harness over his shoulder and walked over to the village church's front entrance. The northern wall was partially caved in from what looked like a small missile strike, and the exterior was riddled with bullet holes, flaking concrete, and loose bricks. Only the church's golden onion dome with its central orthodox crucifix remained undamaged, glistening there in the sun with a strange, defiant resistance.

Max swept the long stick and along the floors methodically, starting around the dusty debris-strewn perimeter. Small puddles of water gathered in a few exposed areas from the previous night of sporadic rainfall. Several beams of sunlight shone brightly through a large opening in the damaged terracotta roof. It seemed to him as if some supernatural power had bathed the damaged church interior with a quiet, otherworldly lucidity.

Max swept the detector back and forth. Two small cats, one black and one white, milled around the wooden pews, curious about the detector stick and why this new intruder was now disturbing their daily hunt for mice and rats. Max proceeded cautiously, looking for that one cleverly placed booby trap under the floor tiles, beneath one of the broken benches, inside the piano, or maybe in another unobtrusive, furtive corner.

A group of wood panels rested on the floor against the far wall. Max passed the detector over the delicately painted icons. The golden-hued icon backgrounds depicted scenes from the Passion of Christ or images of venerated saints. The images were in a flat orthodox style with pigments of ocher, sienna, and umber, all mixed with egg yolk and water. One of the large, very stylized paintings portrayed Saint Michael with a long sword in hand, his face calm as he pressed his armored foot against the dragon's sinuous body.

Max paused, suddenly curious that these anonymous painters had taken such great care delineating the stylized images. Most likely, these lacquered wood icons had been here in this small village church for at least a century, better hidden during the long decades of Soviet suppression. *Here is faith still,* Max realized. *Damaged under rubble, yes, but still here. Good versus evil, imagined by long-dead believers. These are the symbolic pictures of their hopes, dreams, and suffering.*

Max was sweeping the rest of the interior space when another soldier he vaguely recognized came through the church's entrance. "Any bombs?" he asked in a thick Romanian accent. The soldier was clean-shaven with short reddish-blond hair, and he wore an open-collared shirt too big for his skinny, boyish frame.

"Not yet," Max said.

"Valentine wants me to help."

"Help, but let me sweep first, and you follow slowly."

He nodded and then, after Max finished, cleared the rubble in front one of the larger icons depicting Christ on the cross.

"What is your name, soldier?" Max asked.

"Stefan," he said and then added, "They don't even care about churches."

"Nope, not a priority."

"Because they don't believe," Stefan said.

"Hard to say," Max replied.

"Are you a Christian?" Stefan asked.

"Sort of."

"Baptized?"

"I was told so, yes, just not that I remember."

"Almighty Christ our Lord is with us, I know it," Stefan said.

"Better that he chooses us than the orcs," Max said.

"What about the piano? Did you check it already?" Stefan asked.

"All clean," Max replied.

Stefan approached the piano and dusted the debris off the damaged bench. He leaned his rifle against the wall, sat, and removed some stones from the keys before testing a few notes for tone.

The tall, gawky Romanian started hesitantly at first with a few slow, careful movements. Then he closed his eyes and allowed his long fingers to dance over the keys. A song emerged, melodic in patterns.

Max stood still, listening. *Not perfect because of some missing piano keys but damn good still. How does this kid do it all from memory?* he thought after Stefan finished a slightly elegiac sonata.

"What did you play?"

"Chopin.[131] You know him?"

"No. Sounded nice, though. You have talent," Max remarked.

---

131   Born in Poland (1810-1849), he was recognized as a "second Mozart" by age seven.

"Hands remember. Not head," Stefan replied. He displayed his very long, slender fingers for emphasis.

"You learned as a kid?"

"Yes. Maybe you like this too?" Stefan continued, starting up again with a flourish of another song, this time a jazzier, more contemporary tune. Max snapped his fingers to the beat.

"You really are good."

"Two years at the National School in Bucharest, then a café too. My city was boring, so I play music," Stefan replied, smiling.

"Very cool," Max said.

"It was 'cool,'" he said while his hands danced.

After the jazz song, Max recognized a popular Broadway showtune, although he could not place the catchy beat, and for a moment it felt as if the church's bombed-out, decimated interior became a music hall, resonating with life.

A sharp whistle brought the music to a hard stop. Valentine glared at them from the doorway.

"Enough piano bullshit," Valentine shouted. "Done here?"

"Done. All clean," Paul replied, face suddenly flushed. Stefan dropped his smile, quickly picked up his weapon from against the wall, and slung it back over his shoulder.

"Stop fucking around. No more music class. Go clean more buildings," Valentine ordered sharply and then continued to deride Stefan in Russian.

When they passed back to the area where the others were unloading crates, at least two dozen villagers had gathered around, having slowly appeared from nearby houses and shelters. They were all animated now, eager for the fresh water, food, medicine that the squad was now unloading from the back of the trucks and handing out.

"Check over there next," Valentine said coldly, pointing at the police station, a drab two-story building with broken windows and a smashed front door, loose at the hinges.

Max entered the empty station first, leading with sweeps of the metal detector. Stefan followed. The first-floor interior was a mess—broken desks, overturned chairs, and ransacked metal cabinets with paper files scattered on the dirty cement floor. Different Cyrillic words were spray-painted in red on the walls, along with many Z letters repeated in patterns.

"You can read what they wrote?" Max asked Stefan.

"This one says: 'Property of your Russian liberators.'"

"Very poetic," Max said.

"This other one says: 'Fuck the fascist Jew Zelensky,'" the Romanian added.

"Even better. Winning hearts and minds."

"I will go check upstairs?" Stefan asked.

"Easy, Beethoven. Not too fast," Max replied. "Let me go first."

12

Budapest, Hungary.
October 3, 2022. 6 p.m.

A LANGUID late-autumn evening glow gently folded across Budapest's tangled streets as a medley of young professionals, clerks, and shop workers made their way home from a typical workday. Katya Volkova mingled among the crowd, walking along the tree-lined Andrássy út, the old city's main boulevard, toward the wide Danube River.

She had started her day late, taking a coffee alone at the ornately decorated Muvesc Café. As planned, Paul had quietly arrived the previous night by local train from Vienna. It was best to fan out, assume surveillance, and avoid stupid errors in a new, unsafe city. Operational protocol demanded separation from Paul until later.

Katya already knew Budapest's tangled street geography with a reasonable degree of precision. The capital's regal, dilapidated charm was mostly unchanged since her last visit a decade ago. Old Pest was still a quirky maze of ornate neoclassical buildings with muscular caryatids sheltering stately entrances. Across the river, Buda had been glorious once under the Hapsburgs, before two lost global wars and decades of Soviet repression. Now again the city was still lovely, but it was also under the grip of another strongman, Viktor Orban,[132] who—like Turkey's Erdogan—played upon people's fears rather than their dreams. Unlike the Poles, Orban was not keen on supporting Ukraine's cause within the NATO alliance. He was interested in his own agenda and was overly cautious with the Russians.

As she passed the grand nineteenth-century limestone Hungarian National Opera building,[133] statues of Puccini, Mozart, Litz, and Verdi peered back from its high portico. Recollections of a past life reemerged. Her parents had taken her to Budapest when she was a student. Elena, her mother, had arranged it all during Budapest's busy fall music season. Even

---

132   First elected in 1998 for four years, he was elected again in 2010 and has served as Prime Minister since.

133   When Emperor Franz Joseph I funded the project in the 1870s, he stipulated that it could not be larger than the Vienna State Opera. While architect Miklós Ybl technically obeyed, the Budapest house is widely considered more opulent.

her older brother, Viktor, had come on that trip. They had all watched Tchaikovsky's Eugene Onegin and Bizet's Carmen. The men wore crisply pressed tuxedoes, her mother wore a violet Dior dress, and she herself went in long custom-made white linen dress that hung low on her shoulders. *Golden, happy memories.*

Then Katya caught herself before memory's romance gained too much momentum.

Now each of you are mere dust specks. Gone forever. The person I was then gone too.

At the end of Andrássy út, Katya crossed an intersection into the busy Elizabeth Park near a large Ferris wheel and the ornate Danubius Fountain with bubbling, cool water splashing out of the puckered mouths of sculpted marble fish. The old well-manicured park teemed with young and old people relaxing after the long day, sitting on green benches in pairs or clustered in small groups with blankets spread out on the short, manicured grass.

Thus far, she had not spotted any visible street surveillance. Paul was out there somewhere, she knew, tracking her purposefully, meandering without too close of a presence.

After the park, she passed through the crowded Vorosmarty Square, then down another busy narrow street lined with ornate chocolate shops and busy small beer bars.

Katya approached the river. The sharp spires of the Matthias church peaked atop Buda Castle Hill on the opposite riverbank. Long ships carrying tourists motored up and down the wide river, weaving among the slower cargo barges.

Katya homed in on the arranged spot—a bronze statue of a girl called Little Princess.[134] The statue was that of a winsome girl with a pointed hat, lost in the world of her childish imagination.

A man stood near the Little Princess statue, leaning his right elbow against a footpath railing. His appearance matched her expectations: badly cut tan wool suit, slightly overweight, a small goatee at the end of a square chin, a hand nurturing a cigarette.

He flicked the cigarette to the ground when he saw her approach. "There you are. I am glad you came. Safe travels?" he started in Russian, holding out his right hand. She clasped it for a moment, playing along with his more friendly style while he sized her up.

"Of course," she answered.

---

134   A 1972 bronze statue by László Marton that depicts his young daughter playing in a bathrobe and a newspaper crown, symbolizing childhood innocence.

"Would you like one?" he continued, reaching into his jacket pocket to pull out two fresh cigarettes from a pack. She took one, and he leaned closer to give her a light. She inhaled, tilted her head back, and blew the smoke into the warm evening air through pursed lips.

"Sunset here is very nice," Katya remarked.

"Budapest is my favorite European city. Very good spas. Let us walk along the river so we can enjoy the evening with the others," he offered.

"As you like," Katya said.

They walked south along the Danube's riverside path in the direction of Gellert Hill while the sky mutated first from yellow to orange and then into a new palette of bright rose and purple. A local electric tram passed noisily just below them near the pedestrian walkway, which was crowded with locals heading home or others slowly taking café seats for dinner. She watched other faces pass. None of them paused or showed the slightest interest in why she was walking idly on this promenade with this slightly overweight, unattractive man. Whatever these two people were talking about had no bearing on their lives. Such pure anonymity was both liberating and safe. Any special interest from others was a red flag.

Never can tell with these schemers and their sham friendliness. A crowded public area is not a guarantee.

"How's my uncle?" Katya queried.

"He has books, decent food, a clean shower. He has been exercising outside every day. Just like a charming hotel," he said.

"I'm sure," she said.

They came to a walkway intersection and then turned the corner toward a group of bustling restaurants and away from the river. "Sit here for a drink?" he asked, pointing to an empty table in what seemed like a comfortable area in front of Café Mozart. Katya scanned the back of the crowded restaurant.

"Do not worry," he said, seeing her hesitation. "We will sit outside at this table near the street. Everyone can see us. If you do not like this café, we can find another."

"Here is fine," she agreed.

Katya pulled out the nearest wicker chair beside the table and sat down.

A tall smiling waiter in a white apron brought two large paper menus. Kiril ordered a Grolsch beer pint. Katya took a vodka tonic on ice.

They sat quietly until the drinks came, then each sipped the cold drinks before speaking.

Sitting this close to her, Kiril carefully examined how she tilted her head and held her shoulders back in that aristocratic, elegant manner. The photos he had studied of her had not captured her subtle grace, the glint of those bright, unsettling eyes, nor the curve of that slender neck. *Now I sympathize,* he thought regarding Bogdan Zoidze's long obsession with this particular female. As he looked at her, he was more accepting of the possibility for why others fell prey to professional lapses. Nicolai Sokolov, a highly trained and effective officer, spent ten years without incident in Naples. Yet Katerina Volkova had sprinkled fairy dust and grabbed him quietly like a baby.

"I am glad we are finally talking. It is brave of you to accept my invitation and come here for a conversation," he said.

"*Da.* We have our drinks now. Let us talk," she replied. "You start."

"I know you have questions. I expect you are angry too," he began.

"Anger is irrelevant. You have held Yuri for three months now. That is much too long for such games, Kiril Petrovitch," she replied. He creased his forehead and hid his surprise how she casually used his given name. He had been careful never to directly reveal this. Yet she already knew. *Does not matter. Easier to accelerate.*

"Tell me about what you've done in Naples," Kiril continued.

"Nico's circumstances are not as good as your hotel accommodations, but he is unharmed," Katya said.

"You are mistaken. This citizen, Sokolov, is not one of our men."

"Please, spare me," Katya replied.

"I deal with the facts," Kiril insisted.

"Is this how we want to waste time? If Nico is unimportant, then I give him to the Americans?"

"Aren't they already involved?" Kiril prodded.

"Not yet," she said. "This depends on our conversation tonight. We can spin our wheels on trivial denials, or we speak directly on how to resolve our problems."

Smart and controlled approach, Kiril admitted. *She is playing each card one at a time, but not too quickly.*

"Fine then," Kiril said. "Your uncle's case is complicated. He has been charged with many crimes. His case file is thick with hundreds of pages. So much bureaucracy is now involved, I am afraid, and our bureaucracy is very slow and complicated."

"What do you want to resolve it?" she asked.

"My own focus is not on your uncle. I am charged with more important national priorities. A valuable state asset was previously sent to a Libyan partner. If we are speaking plainly, then you know that our shipment was a payment of gold bullion. I need this found, secured, and returned, and for this I can make additional efforts for Yuri."

"Your Libyan buyers didn't take your gold?"

"You know they do not have it," Kiril replied coolly. "Your uncle has already shared that you can help. There is no other reason for us to be sitting here now if I believed otherwise."

"You only want a ransom for Yuri then?" Katya asked, using the term *vykup*.

"I would not call it this way. This word is too medieval," Kiril replied. "We are settling accounts. Resolving the most critical priority. Are you able to help?"

"Possibly," Katya continued. "But not in full."

"Whatever shortfall, I am confident Yuri has other means of compensation. Helping in this way is the key."

"How much?" she pressed.

"I am a reasonable man who, unlike many of my colleagues, believes in the wisdom of compromise," Kiril said. He took a small square wax-coated cotton napkin from the center of the round table. He took a pen from his inside jacket pocket, wrote down $600,000,000 on napkin, and slid it over. Her eyes flickered as she read it.

"We can't do that much," she said calmly, crumbling the napkin and tossing it on the floor. She finished the vodka tonic with a quick gulp.

"You understand this is life and death?" Kiril coaxed. "This is less than half of what was lost."

"I do understand. But you have misunderstood what I have in my power," Katya said, straightening her back slightly, preparing to stand.

"Have I?"

"Gravely misunderstood," she said in a low, steady, calm voice.

"Sit, sit," Kiril said. "We are talking. No harm to talk more. We will take another drink."

Kiril motioned to the waiter with his hands for two more drinks while she paused and instead leaned back in the chair. He let a few moments pass while they both listened to the violin music wafting over from another restaurant nearby. The violinist played, head crooked against his instrument, while the other diners were laughing and smiling. *Is it a*

Tchaikovsky concerto? If so, this Hungarian fool is butchering a magnificent song with such an off-key, flat rendition, he thought.

The waiter brought the two fresh drinks while the bad Tchaikovsky droned on.

"The matter is not my willingness but my ability," Katya continued after the waiter left them. "I cannot within your time limit. You have your constraints. I have mine."

"What then is possible?" Kiril coaxed.

"I can do half your amount and give you back Sokolov. Do not pretend he is irrelevant, especially if we hand him over to the Americans. Take the money, your man, and give me back my uncle. We both live another day."

"It pains me to haggle like shopkeepers," Kiril replied. "You'll transact in gold?"

She nodded.

"Then we will split the baby. Let us agree on four hundred and fifty."

She let the silence linger.

"As long as Yuri's case is expunged and he is returned unharmed. I want guarantees of no further retribution against my family or those we employ."

"What guarantees can I offer?"

"I don't know. Propose them," she countered.

"My gold will be delivered with Sokolov at a location I choose?"

"Within reason. A neutral place outside Russia," she replied.

"Of course. We will agree on a safe place," he offered. "With absolutely no government or military involvement of any sort."

"Agreed. Quiet, very safe," she confirmed.

Kiril took out another cigarette from his pack and offered it to Katya. She waved it off. He had been prepared to go as low as $250 million for the ransom, so he registered an inward pleasure that she had not low-balled him on her proposed settlement.

"I have one final condition," she continued.

Kiril squinted while he inhaled the new cigarette. "I need to see Yuri first. In person."

"Impossible. I will arrange a video so you can speak with him for as long as you like," he countered.

"Is that a joke?"

"You will see that your uncle is healthy and well-treated."

"Not through a screen while you watch and record. I want to be with him for one hour, alone and free of you."

Kiril stroked his black goatee with his left hand. She peered at him squarely with her unsettling, confident eyes while he digested the offer and considered practical details.

Why this request? Nothing much she can do if she comes to meet the old man, Kiril analyzed. *I will be able to watch her closely, crack open a few more tidbits, close the vice if she does not play ball. Four hundred and fifty million dollars for one hour of alone time works out to … a healthy $7.5 million per minute.*

"If you see him, then we have an understanding?" Kiril asked.

"If Yuri is physically unharmed, yes."

"Of course he is unharmed. I told you that he is in official custody, and we respect our laws and prioritize the health of those in our custody, whatever their crimes. When do you want to do this?" Kiril asked.

"The sooner the better," Katya replied.

"Leave with me tomorrow? There is a commercial flight to Crimea through Istanbul in the afternoon," he added.

"Up to you."

The dinner crowds had thinned out when Katya finally left Kiril sitting alone at Café Mozart. She took a different route back, zigzagging slowly and watchfully through Pest's old, narrow streets. Eventually, she headed farther away from the river to a cluster of so-called "ruin bars"[135] nestled in the old Jewish ghetto quarter, still lively with young locals at this later hour.

At midnight, Katya found Paul waiting for her as promised, alone in the back of a discreetly hidden bar. She described her conversation with Kiril while Paul listened, forehead creased, and eyes concerned.

"You didn't tell me you planned to see Yuri. That is unnecessary and reckless," Paul said. Then he chided her for another five minutes about the dangers of going off script and promising more than what they had agreed to previously during planning sessions.

"No use complaining now. I took the opportunity as it came. I will go to Crimea tomorrow," she replied tersely. "How are your efforts going? Don't you have more to do yourself here?"

"Don't change the subject," he shot back.

---

135   Makeshift bars established in the early 2000s within neglected buildings and derelict courtyards. Known for their eclectic furniture, bohemian decor, and low prices, these establishments emerged as a unique, often grungy, cultural staple.

"I am not. Surely you will make your own time in Budapest useful, as I have done tonight," she countered.

Paul let out a long breath as if to diffuse the tension of her challenge. She was glad her rebuke had the desired effect.

"Ammo is crossing the border," Paul said. "We will be in a better position soon to deliver sophisticated toys."

"With or without the Hungarian government?" Katya pressed.

"Without."

"Seems risky to act outside NATO policy."

"Calculated risks," Paul replied. "There are other sympathetic channels."

"I understand now. Your risks are calculated, but mine are reckless."

"That's not what I meant," he said, his lips pressed together.

"Good," she said. She preferred not to push back, but occasionally it was necessary to stop Paul's annoying and immature worries. She also knew that Paul hated when she implied he was not tough enough to be decisive on life and death matters. *I am unfair, but when it comes to inner strength and a next level down of cunning, I will trust myself.*

They spoke quickly after this. Paul agreed to leave the dark bar first. She lingered inside alone for another safe twenty minutes, clearing her thoughts with a glass of cold water while '80s tracks of New Order and Depeche Mode blared and the other tattooed and goth-dressed patrons nursed their last beers and cocktails.

Katya's thoughts drifted back to the early days in Manhattan when she was running the Zephyr Gallery. She had planned a completely different path for her future then. Paul had entered her gallery at a moment when she was willing to experiment with a new direction to fill a void. For those first ephemeral months in New York City, they lived anonymously in the massive city in what felt like a normal life together—fulfilling work, pleasant dinners, distracting Broadway plays, and restful weekends. Paul smiled more then. It had all changed after her older brother, Viktor, sucked Paul into her own family's problems. Then, also, her false-friend Chloe revealed herself. Chloe's betrayal nearly killed her had it not been for the quick actions of Dmitry, Yevgeny, and Anton at the Red Hook warehouse. Now here she was still with Paul, years later, staggering exits from a tiny ruin bar tucked away in the narrow streets of old Pest. Paul criticized her for taking too many risks, but she could never really remember a time without risk, except in the very beginning.

Can we ever go back? Back to those first few months and our forgetful bubble? Does any of that original romance remain now that all this has happened? When can life normalize?

She did not have even a tentative answer. It all felt too strange, too unreal.

For now, she needed to keep her mind clear for whatever new surprise tomorrow's trip to Crimea might bring.

13

Simferopol Airport, Crimea, Ukraine.
September 6, 2023. 9:30 p.m.

SIMFEROPOL WAS surprisingly busy, crowded with poorly dressed Russian tourists in track suits and blue jeans trying their utmost to ignore the war. The airport's arrival area outside smelled of sweat, garbage, and exhaust fumes.

"Hungry?" Kiril asked Katya after they left the airport's shoddy arrival area and stood waiting outside the exit doors.

"No. I ate on the plane," Katya replied.

"Terrible food, I know. Cold pasta," he replied.

"It was good enough."

Katya felt tired. Commercial flights avoided complications but were still tedious and unpleasant. She traveled clean: passport, visa card, ten thousand euros dangling in a pouch around her neck, toiletry bag, and compact carry-on bag with spare clothes. No phone, no gadgets. A black Series 3 BMW with diplomatic plates had picked her up for the drive to Franz Liszt airport. Then she had joined Kiril in first class on the Turkish Airlines flight to Istanbul. They spent an hour in transit there before they both boarded a smaller plane on a direct daily flight to Crimea. She had dozed off only a little during the last flight.

A shiny gray Toyota Lexus sedan pulled up to the curb.

"We'll take my car from here," Kiril said with a smile revealing yellow nicotine-stained teeth. He opened the back seat door for her, then went to sit in the front seat next to the skinny, bald driver.

The Lexus sedan veered through traffic and onto a larger road for about twenty minutes. They turned at a guarded gate and passed through a drab area of low-rise warehouses and rows of parked military trucks.

The driver pulled up to a high fence at the end of the road. A tall, uniformed soldier appeared from inside the gate's checkpoint booth. "It is now that I beg your forgiveness for our standard procedure," Kiril said.

The tall guard opened the sedan door, motioned for her to step out, and then placed a black cotton scarf around her eyes. Then he led her by the elbow into the back of another vehicle that smelled vaguely of motor oil and sweat.

"I will come for you tomorrow," Kiril said. "These men will help you tonight. I wish you a pleasant rest."

Katya sat silently alone in darkness for another hour's drive. The car veered and turned and eventually stopped. She heard the door crack open and felt gloved hands reach around her neck to loosen the blindfold knot and then remove it.

"You will stay here tonight," the tall guard said, pointing over to a single-story row of barracks-style rooms. He carried her small duffle bag slung over his shoulder to one of the padlocked doors, which he opened with a heavy iron latch key, and led her inside.

"Water in the refrigerator. I will be back tomorrow at 9 a.m. Be dressed then," he said.

"I will," she replied automatically.

Katya heard the click as he bolt locked the door from the outside. Rusted iron bars secured the room's two windows. Two cameras peered down from opposite corners of the low ceiling.

Katya undressed in the small bathroom. She showered with a bar of coarse soap, brushed her teeth, turned off the lights, and finally put her head down on the hard pillow to power down her restless mind.

Yuri Ivanovich Volkov waited on an uncomfortable metal bench, hands in his pockets. The late morning air felt cool and moist on his skin. High concrete walls surrounded the compound, just enough to block any view of the nearby Black Sea, although he faintly heard waves and smelled the brine. This morning, he had kept his eyes skyward for the past half hour to watch the roving clouds, silent in a constant, purposeless dance above.

Yuri had felt better this last month. His captors fed him three square meals each day and mostly left him alone in the cramped confines of a hundred-square-foot basement cell. Weeks had turned into months while the nights grew cooler. Several of Kiril's books helped pass the time. He had finished a second turn of the Strugatsky bothers' *Hard to be a God* last night to ease the boredom. He was about to take a stab at one of Tolstoy's lesser-known novels, *Resurrection*.[136]

---

136   Tolstoy's last major novel from 1899; a grim exploration of moral redemption centered on a nobleman's attempt to save a woman he once wronged.

Two familiar guards marched up the dirt path. He blinked once, then twice when he recognized the slender figure between them.

Why?

Yuri rose to his feet as the two navy guards brought Katya closer.

"You have one hour," the taller guard declared before retracing his steps back to the nearby post.

"Hello, Dada," Katya said simply and kept her distance while Yuri stood erect and gathered his attention before offering her a polite kiss on both cheeks.

"Come. We take this little path here for exercise," Yuri said. "Don't be angry," she said after more than ten paces of walking

together in silence away from the guards.

"Coming here is idiotic and dangerous. You give them exactly what they want," Yuri scolded, pressing his hand tightly around her arm.

"Of course, I do," she said. "We do not have much time. How are they treating you? Drugs? Injections? Pills?" Katya asked, ignoring his rebuke.

"Nothing that I know," Yuri replied. "Good," she said. "You must stay healthy."

"Why are you here, Katerina?" Yuri pressed again.

"I am here to see that you are healthy. And I want to tell you how sorry I am that we cannot move more quickly. Please understand. What we need to do takes more time."

"What are you scheming?" Yuri asked.

"Your freedom. The less you know, the better. Nothing foolish, nothing desperate. A fair trade. It will happen soon, I know it. Until then, you must refuse any medicine or pills that do not seem right. Most important, you cannot lose hope."

Yuri peered at her oval face, which was calm but animated with a quiet, intense passion. He had always felt like he could communicate with Katya on a deeper level, beyond words. She looked so much like Elena around the lips and he saw his brother Sergei's green-blue eyes looking back at him now. *Only you, our last survivor, will carry whatever fragile and ambiguous legacy we all might leave behind. There are no others. And here you are, pleading with this old man not to lose hope.*

"If I tell you to stop?" he queried.

"No use arguing," Katya replied. "This time will be different, I promise."

They reached the end of the dirt path and veered back while the two guards observed them from a distance with disinterested eyes.

"What else useful can you tell us about Kiril?" she prodded. "Hard to say. I have only seen him a few times. He strikes me as arrogant, but he is also a survivor and a pragmatist. Money is the most rationale choice today."

"Rational is good. Greed too."

"Do not underestimate him. Kiril has made it this far, whatever his motives. He leverages his position with the Wagner people while others scramble to recover from their mistakes," Yuri cautioned. "Whatever your plan, anticipate alternatives. Look further than what he shows you."

"Our eyes are keen," Katya offered. "I'm not alone."

"Dmitry knows how to deal with these men. He can help."

"And others will too."

Yuri frowned.

"Trusting overeager American bureaucrats is why I'm here."

"Jo made a mistake. But she has not forgotten you. She still has powerful resources that we can use," Katya suggested.

"Resources yes, but that is not the problem with Americans. Most of them today are very childish and erratic," he replied. "It is not the same country as it was years before. They are weaker today than ever before."

"Maybe that is true, but I trust Paul. He can still help us use them. We can still win," she offered.

"Win? You think this is a game?"

"What else?"

Yuri breathed out, then finally broke into a smile.

"You are making all this up as you go along. Aren't you?" he said.

"Of course," Katya replied. "Nothing wrong with creativity."

"Unless creativity kills you."

"All these men are not so smart as you think they are. They are blind to themselves, slaves to their own desires," she insisted in a resolute voice, as she squeezed his hand.

"As we all are," Yuri warned.

They walked another slow circle around the enclosed compound while continuing to talk. She asked more about his daily routines and urged him to continue to exercise and keep his mind busy. Eventually the two guards grew closer, within earshot.

"Your time is up. Back this way," the taller guard announced. "Until a better day," Yuri offered.

"It will come soon, Dada," she replied, then gave Yuri a final concentrated look, as if trying to project her own strength and confidence into his weakened resolve. Then each guard silently led them away in opposite directions.

Afterward, the taller guard walked Yuri back to the farmhouse's cold basement cell.

Yuri ate a dinner of water, mashed potatoes, and a gray hunk of something that must have been either ham or chicken or maybe just a grizzled industrialized combination of both meats.

He did not want to read tonight. Instead, Yuri took off his sandals and lay down on the thin mattress. He controlled his breathing as he gazed up at the cracked ceiling and allowed himself to drift back into the variegated past. A lifetime of disparate and vivid images flickered through his mind—places, people, past moments, all now set in the past like stone statues beyond the possibility of change. While lying on his back, he roved across multiple decades, through all his mistakes, triumphs, machinations, trivialities, and turning points. Ghostly faces whispered advice. Sometimes he listened to those other voices and many times not. There were numerous happy moments but also sharp, violent disappointments and regrets. The whole swirl of struggles, freedoms, loves, and attachments now felt far away, immaterial in the cold dampness of this tiny basement cell.

The brain is such a tiny globe of neurons and yet so vast. All this will be lost soon, wiped clean from this world with nothing remaining. My singular life is only a swirled confusion of fading, fluctuating dreams, signifying nothing. Such is the human condition.

After a few hours, Yuri turned on his side and adjusted the pillow. Whatever Katya was planning, he also knew deep down in the marrow of his old bones that Kiril Petrovitch Alekseyev was not going to let him escape this vice. Whatever small hope that Katya's reckless appearance had brought him, he knew he was already a dead man, no matter what she planned.

Occupied by Russian military
0   200 miles
Kyiv
Lviv
UKRAINE
Dnipro
Zaporizhzhia
Donetsk
MOLDOVA
Mariupol
Odessa
Rostov
RUSSIA
ROMANIA
Krasnodar
Bucharest
Sevastopol
Yalta
Constanta
Sochi
BULGARIA
Black Sea
Burgas
THE UKRAINIAN FRONT
TURKEY
as of 2023
Thessaloniki
Istanbul

14

Mykolaiv Oblast, Ukraine.
December 1, 2022. 11 a.m.

MAX FELT the frigid air whip against his cheek while the truck lurched forward. The sky's flat expanse carried off for miles as the barren winter fields met a tangle in low foothills in the distance. The mornings now were still dark, and his ankles always ached no matter how he adjusted the laces of his boots.

The first truck slowed down as they came up on roadside wreckage. Here was all that remained of a forward-deployed mechanized Ukrainian regiment. The unit had been hit by enemy artillery fire just last week, with casualty levels rumored to be above thirty per cent in just a single day. The bodies had been removed, but the hundred meter bend in the two-lane country road was still a charred graveyard of twisted metal cars, shattered tanks, and smoldering truck skeletons.

"What division?" Max asked Bill, half shouting over the truck's loud engine. Bill was now leaning out the truck's back, holding himself by one hand on the back railing to get a better view while they slowly curved around deep craters that had spit open the old asphalt road.

"Looks like the 106," Bill noted. "They moved too close. Hit with mostly 240-millimeter mortars."

"What's their range?" Max asked.

"Twenty clicks or so. The Russians are learning. They moved their big guns up from Crimea to cover new defensive lines with more Iranian drones to target us," Bill said.

"That one over there looks like an M2 Bradley,"[137] Max reported, pointing to a wreck that appeared to be one of the advanced US armored vehicles meant to tilt the war effort in Ukraine's favor.

"Definitely," Bill confirmed. "Lasted maybe a few months." "Can we still punch through this year?"

---

137   American infantry fighting vehicle developed in the 1980s to transport troops while providing heavy suppressive fire and anti-tank capabilities. It features a lethal 25mm chain gun, missile launchers, and advanced thermal optics.

"Nah, are you kidding? That window shut," Bill said. "Not until spring at the soonest. Look at this mess here. These guys took it on the chin because they moved in a large formation within range. We cannot lose numbers like this while Russia is able to still recruit so many more men."

The trucks picked up speed again as they exited the twisted metal graveyard. Bill sat back down, then tucked his chin deeper into his collar and tilted his helmet over his eyes.

Max pulled his wool hat tightly around his ears as he watched the land pass by from the back of the truck. The cold had made the last few weeks particularly grinding and unpleasant. It was hard to believe that six months had already passed in the field with most days slipping by in just a dirty haze. Squad four took only one formal break when Valentine had managed to secure them four days of rest and recuperation two weeks ago. Unfortunately, they had powered down in another unpronounceable little shithole village rather than a real city with decent food like Kyiv or Odessa. The break was good enough, though. On the last night, Max, Bill, Stefan, and Lucas had finished off three bottles of Nemiroff vodka along with Georgian-style roast chicken, beets, and too much pickled herring.

Max felt how his body continued to harden week after week under these spartan conditions. He now felt his tight muscles running down his torso, connecting hips to muscular thighs, and his forearms could now squeeze into an iron grip. When he looked at himself in the mirror, he barely recognized the stranger's face with closely cropped hair, a long dark beard, and a patch over his dead left eye.

There had been so many days these last months during which he had hardly spoken more than several hundred words all day. The external world simply entered through his five senses like a pantomime of cause and effect, a daily motion beyond his control. There was only the here and now—sights, sounds, smells, aches, and pains. He never ruminated about the past anymore. The past was a dead, immaterial illusion.

We will turn the corner in the spring, Max hoped as he considered the current state of the war. Valentine was doing a good job to keep their motley squad together. So far in the first six months, only five fatalities. One of the older Poles was hit in the head by gunfire, killed instantly during a small skirmish. Another Ukrainian officer took a shot in throat while on forward patrol. He survived for about thirty minutes but eventually bled out before any medic could help. Big Jacques lost three fingers from a shrapnel bomb last month. Valentine sent Jacques back to a military hospital in Odessa and swapped in another Canadian, Eric, into his role. Everyone agreed Eric was an upgrade since he was better trained and smarter.

Squad four inched southwards during the last few weeks, their progress marked by a trail of liberated villages. They had zigzagged through enemy lines, adapting to the ever-changing battlefield conditions. But the Ukrainian officers' demeanors had shifted dramatically as the first frigid days of winter arrived. The initial euphoria of the war's early spring and summer victories had faded. Ukraine's autumn offensive faced setbacks and staggering casualties on both sides. Credible estimates suggested Russia had thus far suffered 120,000 deaths and 180,000 wounded, while Ukraine's losses were close to 70,000 dead and 120,000 wounded. These figures were mere guesses; the true toll was probably much higher. Russia sacrificed untrained conscripts by the thousands in battles like Bakhmut simply to wear down the defenders by their sheer numbers.

As the war dragged on, millions of Ukrainians and Russians had fled their respective countries to escape the devastation and the threat of conscription. Now six million Ukrainians were abroad. Any smart Russian man below the age of thirty-five did everything possible to avoid the draft—at least three million hiding in other countries.

This war was also introducing new tactics. As a drone operator, Max knew he was at the forefront of a new kind of integrated warfare. The drones were a force multiplier. With each mission, he grew more adept to identify enemy positions and potential weaknesses. Drones, once mere surveillance tools, had evolved into deadly weapons capable of scouting out enemy positions to quickly strike or convey coordinates for pinpoint-accurate artillery fire. So far, Ukraine's drone edge was crucial to counter Russia's superior numbers and take out their leadership one by one. By neutralizing key targets and disrupting supply lines, Ukraine could level the playing field even as the enemy's regular army adapted and strengthened their defensive positions.

The trucks stopped after another half hour drive. Max watched the flashes of light just above the rolling hills in the east for a few minutes. It was from an exchange of heavy artillery fire that he guessed was at least thirty kilometers away, and there were only flashes of light and no sound.

He nudged Stefan awake with an elbow poke to his ribs. The tall Romanian opened his eyes again and stretched out his long arms.

"Time to switch. You slept three hours," Max said, marveling at how his friend could drift into a deep slumber while sitting upright in the track's back while it bounced and rumbled over the uneven roads.

"Did I miss anything?" Stefan asked.

"Nope," Max said. "Same old, same old."

CHESS MOVES

Max Drake

15

Langley, Virginia.
January 7, 2023. 5:15 p.m.

JO RICHARDS sipped a bitter double espresso, no sugar, from an eight-ounce plastic cup. She was already twelve hours into her workday and expected another six before she might check off all her tasks. Her small windowless cube was inconveniently located a long walk from the main north entrance. Still, despite her sub-optimal office placement, Jo was grateful to keep her own private cube inside headquarters' secure intestines. At least within these fortress bowels she avoided distraction and was inside the clandestine firewalls. They gave her the clean little desk out of pity and a sense of loyalty; it was still much better than stewing alone at her Georgetown apartment, passed over for dead.

Jo pressed the volume key to better hear Paul Drake's question more clearly via the video feed.

"That is the plan. What do you think?" he asked. They had been talking for more than an hour via the encrypted line; she was mostly pleased by what he had just outlined.

"It's possible that it works, but there are still issues," Jo hedged.

"Are we headed in the right direction?" Paul prodded.

"We can work with it."

"We need to," he replied. "This is their second offer. We should move faster."

"Easy, cowboy. Yuri is not going anywhere, and we have more time. Let them sweat it out."

"What about the location?"

"Chakli Island is a better choice for the exchange," Jo suggested. "That place is very remote. Map shows a small helipad and airstrip at the southern end. The closest international airport is Diagoras on the big island of Rhodes, about fifty kilometers away. The whole of Chakli is just eleven square miles. It is empty in winter except for one tiny village on the east side with a local population, three thousand, tops. You will both feel safe. You can scope out the terrain if you go there early."

"Helicopters or planes?"

"They will use choppers, definitely," Jo summarized. "Not the smaller KA-52s deployed out of Crimea. Kiril will need the medium-sized ones with better airspeed and more load capacity."

Jo pivoted her gaze to her second monitor, where she had loaded up more specific operational analytics from a database. Her eyes scanned the details:

```
Mi-17 Russian transport helicopter

1.  Medium twin-turbine transport helicopter, max speed
    450 mph. In production in Kazan and Ulan-Ude.
2.  Armed gunship versions equipped with advanced D57
    jamming tech and combat level 3 surface-to-air de-
    fenses.
3.  Twin-engine, twin-blade. Turboshaft engines for
    reliable performance. Copilot operations.
4.  Cargo compartment: Carries up to 11,000 lbs. or up
    to twenty-four passengers. External sling to lift
    and transport external loads.
5.  Russian Federation Inventory as of January 2, 2023:
    151 total in service.
6.  Relevant in-scope geography: Six in Sebastopol,
    Crimea. Eight in Tartus, Syria. Five in Tiraspol,
    Moldova.
```

"Best guess is that he will use the Mi-17, deployed now in Syria, Crimea, and Moldova," she summarized.

"Is that a problem?"

"Not a problem. A consideration. Mi-17s are respectable beasts with advanced jamming tech," Jo conveyed. "We cannot go with secondhand grade B tech. We will need something better, less bulky but still powerful enough from our recent inventory."

"Stingers?"

"Nope, not even the larger ones. Range not far enough," she replied. "Any solution must cover at least twenty-five kilometers. Smart tracking technology has advanced, but there is still a tradeoff of weight and distance. Even billion-dollar toys have payload limits. Our weapon will need a chassis. I need more time. Ask for another week."

"The more we wait, the less—" Paul pressed.

"I get it. Ask for a minimum five more days," Jo replied tersely. "Quit bitching and just leave the weapon details to me. I will get you a harpoon with enough range to skewer your whale. The rest is up to you on position and timing."

"Understood," Paul replied.

"Do you also understand that if their flight path goes north to Crimea or Moldova, then your plan will not work, no matter what I deliver?"

"Kiril won't risk transiting through Turkish airspace," Paul countered. "That would be too complicated. He will want the most direct route. Simple and fast in and out of Syria over wide-open international waters. He has every reason to stay as quiet on this as we do."

"Probabilities seems right," Jo admitted. "Best we can do. I can get six hours of satellite cover. Weather conditions are fine this time of year."

"Roger that," Paul confirmed.

"And you must scuttle my harpoon afterward. Clear on that?"
"Crystal," Paul replied.

"Make sure of it."

"Already at the bottom of the ocean," Paul confirmed.

"In all scenarios you lose your cargo. Expensive loss," Jo said.

"Depends on your perspective," Paul said.

"Doesn't seem like a trivial consideration," Jo pressed, wondering now why Paul was so nonchalant about tossing $450 million of untraceable gold bars into the Aegean Sea simply to secure Yuri Volkov.

"Cost of doing business," Paul replied coolly.

Is it? What are you hiding from me? Jo wondered but did not press. Instead of asking him more about this, Jo simply reaffirmed their next scheduled update in twenty-four hours. She had other tasks to prioritize ahead of whatever Paul Drake might be holding up his sleeve for later in the chess game. They were still a long way off from these first moves having just a reasonable chance of success. No need to obsess about many steps ahead when there was still so much that could go wrong now.

After hanging up with Paul, Jo poured herself another coffee and swallowed two aspirins to fight off the headache that had been building up since the morning.

Jo recalled the cranky voice of her first mentor, Sam Coats, a Princeton PhD and well-known military history scholar, now long dead from throat cancer after his thirty years of chain smoking. She could almost see the lanky, pale bureau chief sitting in his cluttered, book-lined office now, dressed in a trademark rust-colored cashmere sweater, a cigarette smoldering on his white porcelain ash tray. Sam had been an old-school, dyed in the wool, bad-ass operational genius.

Sam had always used the example of a village in Brittany to drive home his point on historical uncertainty and the role of luck. If it had been clear skies on the morning of June 18, 1815, outside Waterloo, then Europe and the world more generally might have traveled down a vastly different path for the last two hundred years.

But the weather on that fateful day happened to bring storm clouds in from the coast. Heavy rain threw off Bonaparte's timing by only a few hours. This critical adjustment was just long enough for the fresh Prussian troops to join up with Wellington's exhausted army. Together, the allies proved just strong enough as a single combined force to eke out a final victory.

The rest is what we all call history.

I love your historical lessons, Sam. But muskets and cannons are worlds apart from today's technology, Jo mused. *We don't pass messages by horseback anymore, either.*

That does not matter. My basic point is still valid, Sam's ghost replied. *Anything can go wrong, anytime. The fog of war moves and shifts by the hour. You cannot stop it. You will never have perfect knowledge, or all real time facts. Prepare for the worst. Your enemy is flying in with its best war machines; Russians might blast your entire crew in the first fifteen minutes, like the op you ran in Herat back in 2004. Remember that disaster?*

I do remember, and I agree there is risk, Sam, she thought. *But I was just along for the ride on that dumb Afghan fiasco. I always cut my losses when I must. Paul knows the deal. I will do what I can for him if this goes bad, though, because I owe him.*

Will you really? The ghost accused.

I will try.

Yeah, sure, try, but not too much. You serve the State, not your own morality, Sam's ghost continued. *Always best to compartmentalize. Marty's nose will stay in joint if you tag the ops with vague codes and keep it all top secret, no foreign. He only needs to approve your gameday six-hour satellite time slot, plus help batting down bureaucratic flames if it turns ugly.*

Done, she answered.

What are you calling this one? Pequod, Jo replied to the ghost.

Ah, nice literary touch. Captain Ahab's doomed whaling ship hunting the elusive white whale, Sam complimented.

I thought you would like it.

I always liked Herman Melville. Strange guy, but a great writer. Remember the book you gave me? Jo offered.

Of course—a nice little copy of Benito Cereno.[138] *Brilliant little maritime yarn on how the eyes deceive. Plenty of extra reading time available in all those isolated shitholes you served in,* Sam replied. She watched the ghost laugh before it took a long drag of his phantom cigarette.

You always had good taste, she told him.

Jo finally managed to smile before she opened her eyes and the overhead fluorescent light wiped away her long-dead mentor's lingering persona. Time was too tight to indulge conversing overlong with spirits. It was time to get back to business.

Mohammed Al Maktoum picked up her call after three rings, early morning Eastern time and late Dubai time (GMT+4). Mohammed's prepared voice was crisp and alert. After ten minutes of necessary platitudes, Jo wove in her specific but critical ask.

Jo's best option for quick procurement was the six advanced SAM[139] models still wrapped tight in the bonded warehouse about five miles outside of Dubai. She herself had arranged the clandestine sale last year as part of a much larger package the Agency approved for the "good" Sunni Arabs. The purpose of these weapons was so that the Saudis, Qatari, and UAE could defend themselves against the "bad" Shite Arabs—the Yemenis Houthis and the Iranians.[140] The six Dubai SAM launchers were big enough, originally designed for the back of a military truck with a payload of a dozen Stryker rockets, range thirty kilometers. Moving just one outside a formal consignment would be barely noticed.

"You need only one? This is nothing. Very simple," Mohammed responded.

"I appreciate the support," she replied. "Time is of the essence." "It will be all done no later than tomorrow by noon Eastern, I assure you," he replied. "You have a schedule. For me, a small favor."

"Appreciate you stepping in."

"As you would again for me," he replied.

A man like Mohammed Al Maktoum needed no further explanations; neither did Jo offer any. Their important symbiotic relationship remained in place. She needed Mohammed's support for other distasteful geopolitical matters, especially as the whole Israel-Hamas-Hezbollah-Iran disaster evolved further in the coming years. Mohammed was already in her debt.

---

138   1855 novella that follows an American sea captain's encounter with a distressed Spanish vessel, only to slowly realize a violent slave revolt has taken place on board.

139   A SAM (Surface-to-Air Missile) is a guided weapon launched from a ground-based or naval platform designed to intercept and destroy aerial targets.

140   The Sunni-Shia rift is a 1,400-year-old division that began over who should lead the Muslim community after the Prophet Muhammad's death in 632 CE.

He especially owed her for the favor four years ago concerning Arlen Cross, Mohammed's close friend from his days at a US college. Arlen's murder was the chief reason she had first contacted Paul Drake, and Jo had quietly helped Mohammed finally settle scores with the perpetrator, Viktor Volkov, a year later. A little quiet tip-off on Viktor's ill-advised stroll through Central Park had bought her years of goodwill. Now was a decent time to collect a reasonable payment of Mohammed's outstanding debt.

Ironic that this relationship has come full circle in Yuri Volkov's favor, she thought as soon as she hung up the phone.

Jo locked her computer screen, left her small office, and started down the building's main hallway connecting headquarters' north and south wings. She knew exactly where to go for the next important piece of Pequod's prep work.

As she walked, Jo kept her head down and focused on moving each foot forward, one after the next, ignoring all the other busy, distracted employees shuffling back and forth inside Langley's antiseptic interior. Those passing in the hallway in their blue and black power suits, badges dangling from necks, were the client-facing analysts who spent half their time down at State, or the White House. Most everyone else had devolved over the years into business casual, thankfully still with proper shoes.

She came to an unmarked little door next to a little brass sign, G17. Jo pressed the intercom button, then looked squarely at the small unobtrusive corner camera. She pressed the button again after an unresponsive thirty seconds.

"What is it?" the intercom voice asked.

"Need your magic touch, maestro," Jo announced.

Another long pause passed before G17's door buzzed open. She shuffled into another thin corridor that ended at yet another white unmarked secure door that now clicked open.

A rush of chilly air greeted her entrance. A long row of servers hummed in the background in front of the three workstations. Light classical music came from a little speaker on Craig Davis's exceptionally clean desk.

"You've got little Greenland in here," Jo said.

"My machines need to stay cool to be happy," Davis replied. His bald head stuck up from a bulky University of Notre Dame sweater. He stared back at her with small eyes, looking more like a bored ski lift operator at the end of a long shift than a global logistics expert.

Jo sat down on the small stool across from Davis's desk. "How's your boy finding Annapolis?" Jo started.

"He's adjusting."

"Sophomore now?"

"Senior."

"That's right," she corrected. "Losing track of time."

"Of course you are," Craig replied. "What shitshow are you roping me into now?"

"Nothing too bad. Quite simple. I need a package moved from Dubai to Greece. About a ton, sealed, wrapped. It is our stuff. I need it moved ultra dark and quiet."

"When?"

"Within three days."

"What is the order priority?"

"No billing on this, maestro."

Davis exhaled slowly while he scratched his black chin hair stubbles. "Of course there isn't," he muttered.

"That is the deal. Dark and quiet," she reiterated.

"Three days is too tight," Davis said.

"Agreed. It is not enough time. It is unfair," Jo said. "I ask only because I know your beautiful mind will color outside the lines."

"I was supposed to take Friday off."

"A day off? Didn't you already sleep in on Christmas?" she said, betraying a hint of sarcasm.

Craig Davis glared back before he moved his face closer to the largest of the six flat-screen monitors stacked in a horizontal grid. His eyes scrolled through an extensive list of digits and tracking codes across five continents.

"Where exactly is your cargo now?"

"The same UAE warehouse where we shipped six months ago."

"Good. Easier."

Jo felt the room's cold while Davis reviewed his logistic data.

"Well, maestro?" she prodded after almost ten minutes of listening to his annoying foot tapping in sync with the music.

"I might have an opening for you," Craig offered. "If I jump the queue for this, what's in it for me?"

"America's eternal gratitude," Jo replied.

"No. Really. I have a limited budget for all this customized, rinky-dink shit, Jo. Do better."

"How about season tickets for the Nationals?" Jo said. "Take your family, and I'll throw in a little American flag pin to wear on your jacket."

"I have flag pins coming out of my ass. Baseball is boring," Davis muttered.

"Hockey then?"

"Better. More action in hockey. The Capitals have a decent team this year."

"Hockey it is then," she offered. "They better be premium seats."

"A private box. Right next to the ice."

"And how complicated will this be? What is my downside?" he probed.

"The risk is on me, maestro. You just deliver and enjoy the hockey with your boy. Let me also assure you that my little jab is justified. The bad guys will not be happy. Isn't that what we are here to do? Kill bad guys?"

Craig Davis shook his head in disapproval even as his thin lips curled into a slight smile.

16

Kherson Province, Ukraine.
January 10, 2023. 7:30 a.m.

"THE FOOTPATH is easier this way," Stefan said.

"Got it," Max replied, pushing his way through a batch of scrubs and leaves covered in the melting frost. An inch of virgin snow had fallen overnight, leaving the forest ground hard and the pine needles shiny.

Max and Stefan had been tasked with a short walk through the pine grove to the nearby stream. They carried six large empty aluminum canteens to refill with the stream's icy water.

The stream ran over a clutter of small rocks, and the water was cold and clean.

Max splashed his face and neck first to push away his morning lethargy before dipping the canteens into the stream to fill them up. Max had slept decently last night, finally accustomed to sleeping outside in the standard-issue polyester bag, which kept him dry and warm, sealed tightly inside a cocoon. He had ended his shift at 11 p.m. last night, a little earlier than usual. He might be able to repeat that routine tonight if it turned out they were going to stay camped here for more than a day.

"What do you think is next" Stefan asked as they carried the heavy canisters back to the encampment. For the past few days, all the senior officers had seemed distracted, and Valentine was not his usual jovial, confident self. Something was brewing. They had parked the trucks along a ridge that ran a few hundred meters and covered them in all in drab camouflage tarpaulins. The nearby tall pines and poplar trees offered decent aerial cover.

"Not sure," Max replied. "I do not hear more than you do." "You should ask the boss," Stefan replied.

"Me? I am not Valentine's golden child. He would not tell me even if he knew."

"You told me he was good friend with your brother," Stefan said. "He is, but so what?"

In the last few weeks, First Battalion had moved step-by-step closer to the front lines. They were now about a hundred kilometers north of Kherson, the recaptured provincial capital, and less than five kilometers from very heavily entrenched Russian positions supported by seasoned and well-supplied troops based in Crimea. Max was unfamiliar with all the tactical details, but he understood, like they all did, the importance of keeping hard-fought gains. They needed to push forward as much as possible before the Russians dug further in and fortified a maze of land mines and heavy artillery. And it was still possible the enemy would launch their own counteroffensive across the river, testing the real strength of Ukrainian positions and exploiting any weaknesses they had discovered. Squad four would need to protect the army's flank before any of this happened. If necessary, they might also slice through any breach discovered and catch the enemy in a pincer movement when the time was right.

Each night for the past week, Max had sent up infrared surveillance drones, then uploaded the data and the visual feeds for the next day's analysis. Valentine feared that the Russians were moving equipment en masse because they would soon blow up the 1950s-era Soviet-made Kakhovka Dam. If they did that, vast swathes of land along the Dnieper River would be submerged and Ukraine would lose another precious power plant. Not only would that be an environmental disaster, but it would make it much harder to gain traction in a counteroffensive. The invaders did not care about the extensive human and environmental damage if a massive flood bought precious time.

All makes tactical sense, Max thought. *Sort of.*

Stefan brought his two water canisters to a circle of Romanians, then followed Max back to their own position. Since Fedorivka, Valentine had given Max more direct control over that part of the squad. Stefan and the others had been reliable backups during a short skirmish just last week. Lucas was smart, Adrian kept his cool even during the worst moments, and Roman offered solid support with his steady presence. Max was a grandpa by comparison—the Romanians were all just kids in their early twenties but not bad soldiers if they received clear instructions.

Bill was also awake when they finished the water distribution and returned to their campsite. Stefan poured the water into a portable water boiler and then into a kettle for the morning's tea. Bill had rummaged through the food containers. He grimaced when he found only cans of sardines packed in olive oil. They all began to eat after the black tea was poured.

"This tea tastes like shit," Bill said.

"Sorry we couldn't bring you a Starbucks latte," Max replied. "Latte? What about a vodka shot," Bill replied.

"Are you done with that?" Stefan asked Max.

"Take the rest," Max said, passing over an opened can of sardines that he was not eating because the little fish tasted too salty. Max preferred the usual protein bars and bread as more reliable calorie sources, and fewer gastrointestinal issues.

Stefan took the open can and used his long fingers to pick at the sardines.

"Hate those little fish," Bill said.

"Why? Can I have yours too?" Stefan said. "What do I get?"

Stefan reached into his pocket, then tossed Bill a chocolate bar. "Candy? That is all?" Bill replied. "How about more of your little

blue uppers?"

"I already gave you a fresh pack last week. You should not be using more than four a day," Stefan replied, referring to the amphetamines that most of the squad now regularly consumed.

"I'm a big boy, Beethoven. Can you get me some more of your blue pills or not?"

"Later, if you just keep it quiet," Stefan said.

"Better do that," Bill replied before passing Stefan his sardines. The bitter warm black tea coursed down Max's throat. He checked his gear and put his communication earpiece in to stay looped in with the rest of the squad. Bill talked more about what he expected Valentine to share soon on squad four's big push while Stefan listened to his musings and ate their morning fish with dirty hands.

Max glanced above the tangled pine treetops to get a better sense of the weather conditions. Was it clear enough to send up a few of the smaller drones? A slight movement above a cluster of pine trees caught his peripheral vision.

Max squinted to better see the little black dot hovering up there.

Max's good eye strained to catch the tiny detail against the bright blue sky. The drone hovered unnaturally still just above the tall treetops. The black dot silently shifted horizontally between the pines, cameras scanning.

"Get up," Max said. "Why?" Bill said.

"Get up now," Max repeated, this time sharply. He raised his Israeli semiautomatic, put the enemy's surveillance drone in the scope's crosshairs, then squeezed off a gunshot sequence that ripped open the morning silence. The drone jerked, spiraled down into the trees, and dropped into a tangle of bushes a few dozen meters away.

Bill and Stefan sprang to their feet and quickly strapped on their helmets and gear.

"Report," Valentine's voice came into Max's earpiece after just a few taut seconds.

"Drone on us. Low and close."

"Just one?"

"I think so," Max answered.

"Sure?" Valentine pressed.

"Not sure. Could have been there for a while." Valentine muttered a string of expletives.

"Round up. Back to the trucks," he finally ordered.

"Roger that," Max said.

More quick radio chatter rambled off in Ukrainian. Bill, Stefan, and the others were now combing the sky for more drones. Stefan radioed over Valentine's order to the Poles nearby. The whole squad was now alert, dozens of eyes searching the tree-tops, waiting for whatever might be next this close to what they all knew was a ring of fortified enemy positions.

Clouds shifted overhead. A cool breeze rustled through the trees. Then another sound grew louder, as if the whole forest itself inhaled one final last breath. The strange, deep inhalation rose in pitch, transformed into a sharp whistle, then crashed down in a terrific, deafening boom.

The first artillery shell hit someplace just over the crest of a nearby hill. Another shell tore through the tree line twenty meters away, mangling a thick pine truck as if it were a matchstick.

Boom. Boom.

Stefan yelled incoherently. Earth erupted. Rocks and dirt flew and wobbled as each successive explosion tore up the earth in a swirl of blue-black smoke.

Boom. Boom. Boom.

Shells rained down, heavy, incessant, deafening.

Max lifted his head and tried to steady his bearings. Stefan's eyes bulged as he looked back at Max, lips pressed together. A minute-long pause. Then another minute.

"Guns reloading. Stay down," Max thought he heard himself shout. But he did not know if he was really speaking because his jaw was clenched, his ears rang, and his body froze tight.

Stefan jumped up from his fetal position, then scrambled to a cluster of nearby trees just as the heavy shelling resumed. Mounds of dirt and stones blew out and clouded Max's eyes. Whipping rocks and earth exploded, his body quivering with each concussion. Max gnashed his teeth together, second by second, enduring the pandemonium. Pain seared along his torso and back. Cordite smoke scorched his throat and lungs, as he sprawled down flat on his stomach and covered his head.

This is it. Game over. Get ready.

Another infinitely long five minutes passed before Max decided to roll to his knees and stand up.

A horrifying silence lingered, broken by crackling fire. He was still here, eyes burning but still breathing, sensing, thinking. Max felt pain in his left torso and back where sharp, hot slices where shrapnel had ripped open his light protective gear and pierced the skin.

I feel it, yes, but doesn't seem too bad. I can move.

He saw a few stray soldiers digging out among the mottled pines and poplars, but none of the Romanians or Poles.

Bill was closest to him, lying on his side near the scattered camp equipment. Max leaned down and pushed him over onto his back to check him.

Bill Stryker's eyes were closed upon a calm, inert face. But his chest was caved in, mangled from a sizable shrapnel piece smoldering at the center of a scarlet, grizzled, catastrophic wound that had burned out his heart. Max ripped off Bill's dog tag with one quick pull. If he just went through his trained routines, there was no need to think about that smoldering hole with bright red oozing guts along a jagged rim, like a butcher's raw meat.

He shoved Bill's dog tag into his back pants pocket.

Max searched for Stefan. He strained his eye to see better around the perimeter of a smoldering crater near the tangle of pines. It was hard to get a handle on the campsite's configuration since nothing looked the same; smoke and fire confused his directional sense.

Where did Stefan run off to? He cannot have made it far.

Max started up a small hill first and began rummaging through the underbrush around the big crater's far perimeter. At first, Max thought he saw either sleeping gear or a backpack. He went closer and kicked a branch away to see the object better.

Stefan's long piano fingers spread out at the end of a detached forearm. Five meters away, Max spotted a headless torso with mangled arm stumps and twisted legs. The torso showed off ripped white bones and a headless spine wet and oozing bright red beneath the neck. He went close enough to make out the name on the torso's front jacket pocket.

Yeah. You belonged to Stefan. No fucking point getting upset about it, Max forced himself to swallow as he registered the gruesome body parts from the artillery blast. *I told you to stay down, you dumb fucking ignorant child. Now look what happened because you did not listen and you ran right to a stupid, unlucky spot.*

Max's throat continued to burn while he heard other men coughing and shouting a little up the hill, someplace beyond the haze of smoke and ash.

No use getting upset about it now. I am not going there, Max repeated to himself. *The blast took your head right off, just like that... snapped off like a twig.*

Focus. Find Valentine.

Link up. Prepare for what is next.

Max headed to where he thought Valentine had camped last night; it was farther away from the river and down the ridge. He pushed his way through a thicket of trees to another area decimated by artillery shells. He spotted movement at the rim of one of the fresh craters, still smoldering.

Squinting, Max saw a wounded soldier using his arms to crawl away from the debris, dragging limp legs behind him.

17

Kherson Province, Ukraine.
January 10, 2023. 11:05 a.m.

VALENTINE ENDURED the pain coursing throughout his entire body, especially below his midsection, where he knew he had taken the worst of the blast. The shell had struck close, just three meters away, knocking him unconscious, he was unsure how long. Pain was good. If he felt pain, that meant he was still alive and could muster up thought. If he could muster thought, he could still command and might survive.

Need to stay awake, Valentine told himself as he tried to steady his mind and focus back on what might come next. *Is this barrage step one? We are all in deep shit if enemy ground troops are close enough to move up and this was just to soften us up before a follow-up attack. What else did I also miss?*

Valentine recognized someone coming closer. He recognized Paul's brother, covered in mud and blood.

"Hang in there," Max whispered, locking gazes with him.

Max's approach forced him back into rank, and he suppressed his own pain.

"You see troops?" Valentine asked. "Nothing," Max replied.

"More drones?" "Don't think so."

"Go back to truck. Get the box. Call us in," Valentine ordered.

"Which truck?"

"Mine, under my seat," Valentine said. "Let me look at you first," Max replied.

"Fuck off. Get box. Don't waste time," Valentine repeated, this time straining and adding emphasis with a final spat of blood.

"Copy that," Max replied.

Valentine watched Max jog away through the simmering craters and splintered tree trunks.

Best-case scenario: at least two hours waiting here like sitting ducks for any medics, Valentine assessed. He knew squad four was forward deployed about fifteen kilometers from the larger mechanized Ninety-Sixth Battalion with at least four hundred men. The Ninety-Sixth would be able to support and take care of the wounded assuming they were also not hit. *Worst-case scenario: enemy ground troops swarm us, and we are all shot like dogs within a couple of hours.*

Valentine's full-on excruciating pain continued, but now it was an even, elevated level; he did not feel much beneath his waist. It was not helpful to guess whether his body had been permanently crushed. *Plenty of time to deal with all my bullshit wounds later.*

Valentine tried his best to focus. Concentrate. Let the pain wash through his body so he could adjust to the physical shock. For a few minutes it seemed like he was succeeding. The sharp pressure in his lower spine had begun to ease. He wanted to move his arms but then realized they were not moving at all. He was telling his arms to move, but his body did not obey. He was just like a punctured tire, losing air, going soft and slack.

Valentine simply sat on the ground while the pain faded and the numbness moved up from his legs to his chest, then up his neck, to his lips, nose, and eyelids. It was all going slack now, deflating. There was not even that much blood, just his bones and organs crushed on the inside.

He felt like he was lighter than air and slowly lifting off the ground as if pulled upward by invisible hands looped under his arms. He no longer sprawled on the forest floor but rather floated higher.

It was as if he could see the pine forest, marred now by smoldering craters. He looked down upon the remnants of his squad, bodies scattered in burned-out foxholes and saw Max scurrying to reach into the truck to grab the radio. Then Valentine felt himself moving up even higher until he was able to see just how small this burning patch in the woods was within the much larger forest that stretched dozens of kilometers in each direction. Rising higher still, like a weightless balloon, he saw how the forest belonged to the land and how the little stream flowed into a larger river that twisted a long way down to the sea. When he reached Earth's upper atmosphere, he marveled at how the planet smoothly curved and how it spun silently in space with such magnificent precision, a perfect little blue celestial marble. Then he moved faster away from the little blue marble like an impossible comet, flying faster than the speed of light itself. He saw the sun recede, too, until it was only a single pinprick in a vast array of millions of other tiny little pinpricks scattered randomly in a blank, empty, infinite void.

All the shit and blood and pain he had felt these last few months and years all finally faded away and dissolved.

Does not matter. Better this way. Start again with something new. No memory.

Brand new. And better.
   Again, like the stars.

———— ✳ ————

Fifteen minutes clicked off before Max finally spotted the first truck, hidden as planned under a camouflage tent and undamaged. He found the Motorola SLR5500 secure radio slid safely beneath the passenger seat just as Valentine had told him.

Max punched in the distress code. Thirty seconds passed before a remote voice answered.

"Heavy shelling. Bad hit. Many casualties," Max repeated after passing along their position's numbered coordinates, not knowing if his urgency was clear.

"Received," the voice replied.

"How long to get here?"

"Received," the voice repeated.

"How long?" Max asked again.

The radio voice switched to unintelligible Ukrainian; Max knew they would follow protocol, so further conversation was a waste of time. He slung the box's strap over his shoulder and stuffed a half dozen medical kits into his ammo bag to bring back to Valentine and others.

Max jogged past two others through the smoldering woods, shell craters, small fires, and putrid burning smells. His own back and waist still burned with pain. As he ran, his own blood also dripped down on his upper thighs. He needed to take care of his own wounds soon too.

Valentine was propped up against a tree stump in the same place he left him twenty-five minutes ago.

"Called us in. They are coming soon," Max announced.

No answer. Max moved closer. He put the Motorola radio close to Valentine, then unpacked a white gauze roll from one of the medical kits.

"Let me see your legs," Max said dumbly. As he fumbled with one of the small bottles of alcohol from the med kit to first clean off any wounds. Valentine's head remained bowed, as if he had fallen unconscious.

Max shook Valentine's shoulders, then slapped his unresponsive face.

"Come on, Boss. Wake up," Max said sternly.

Another slap, this time harder. Valentine's face still seemed to bear an expression of action, as if he would reanimate with one more slap.

Max slowed his effort after he pressed his two fingers against Valentine's right wrist for a pulse.

After he knew there was no more urgency, Max angrily tossed the med kit back to the ground. Then he sat down and paused, the queer smell of cordite and burning wood filling in his lungs.

It seemed right to wait with Valentine. *Bill, Stefan, and Valentine. Others too. No chance to fight back. If I just wait here, it will not be too long,* Max thought.

He watched blankly as two figures wandered over through the smoldering debris. They approached him directly—he recognized Roman and Lucas.

"He's gone," Max said as they moved within earshot. "You?" Lucas asked.

"Fine," Max replied.

"You have much blood on your back," Lucas said.

"Take those kits. Go help others. Bring this box to one of the sergeants. Help is coming," Max replied.

"Sir," Lucas replied and picked up the bag with the kits next to Valentine's lifeless body, while Roman obediently lifted the comm box. Then they both faded back into the tangled pine forest.

Smoke drifted, and the air brought more acrid, foul smells. *Do not care,* Max thought. *If they come, let them shoot me.*

The minutes slowed down further. Maybe an hour passed, or more. He could not follow, and he did not care anymore. *I will hear the shots, and that is that.*

Finally, Max opened his eyes again when he heard a truck roll up, and soon after, voices. The new voices wore blue sashes on their arms.

One medic, a tall, bearded man, saw him, jogged over, and spoke in Ukrainian. Then, reading Max's last name sewn into his jacket, he switched to English.

"Where does it hurt?" "Side and back."

"Let me see more," the bearded medic said. He quickly cut away Max's shirt first, then turned him over to inspect the damage. He wiped down his back and then threw powder on it. When Max lifted his arm, he felt intense pain. Bright red blood bubbled like warm wine out of a deep gash ripped into his side.

"I need to first take out the rocks and then sew you up," the medic said.

"Later," Max replied.

"Can't wait, soldier. Too much blood gone already," he replied unemotionally. "Need to do it now. This will help." He reached into his bag, pulled out a little vial, checked the needle, and then forcefully jabbed a morphine dose into Max's right upper thigh.

The drug's rush hit almost immediately, a soothing warm sensation. The acrid smell of cordite and burning trees seem less foul. The medic reached inside Max's torn flesh and removed hard fragments of stone and metal shards, then sewed up the gash in his torso as if he were sewing up a hole in a pant leg.

Another man came, tapped the medic on the helmet, and ordered him away.

"Good for now. I will come back and finish. We get you new blood quick," the medic promised. "Do not move. Keep your arms down. Breathe normally."

Max waited another twenty minutes before a different solider, a woman with a black mask covering her nose and mouth, approached him. She waved over two more men who were carrying a stretcher. They lifted him up and put him flat on his back on the stretcher.

"Why aren't you taking him?" Max asked and pointed to Valentine's lifeless body.

"Later," the masked female medic said. "You first, then we take others."

"Don't leave him."

"We do not leave. I promise, I get him next," she offered in her heavily accented English.

Max felt numb now as the warm, soothing morphine pumped throughout his body.

He did not know how long it took before the team of two carriers slid his stretcher into the back of some kind of armored vehicle. While Max lay on his uninjured side, he could see two others in the truck: One guy was cradling a mangled right hand. The other was unconscious with blood-stained bandages wrapped around his jaw and lower face.

The morphine helped Max to ease even further into what seemed like a distant remoteness, once again. None of the other wounded men or the doctors or the soldiers seemed real now. These other guys' faces were all just like pasteboard masks, fake creatures walking through a pantomime of predetermined, mechanical actions. His eyes watched it all simply transpire, but he was no longer able to really do anything about it. They were all like walking zombies without any true independent will or soul. He, too, was just a ball of quivering decaying flesh with no spirit or stable essence.

I told you to stay down, you stupid child. Why did you not listen?

Max shut his eyes when the truck engine started. It was better to feel nothing.

Morphine definitely helped.

18

Rhodes, Greece.
January 15, 2023. 2 p.m.

PAUL DRAKE kept his head down in the passenger seat while Yevgeny drove the black, manual transmission Ford Super Duty F-450 pickup. Paul's eyes focused on his phone's GPS map as they approached the secure southern gate of the Diagoras International Airport bonded warehouse facility.

A tired guard appeared from inside his post as Yevgeny pulled up. Paul handed over the pickup order, cleared a cash payment, and received a slip of paper with a printed six-digit access code. After a maze of identical-looking alleyways, the GPS brought them to warehouse 12A, a nondescript stucco building at the end of a dusty cul-de-sac.

Paul punched in the code to open 12A's large main door. A long six-wheel flatbed trailer with a massive crate covered by a white tarpaulin waited inside the cool garage. White stencils on the crate read in English and French, *Heavy load. Highly flammable. Use extreme caution when transporting*, with more Arabic translations beneath.

Yevgeny slowly backed up the Super Duty, stopped, and then after some adjustments, began to connect the powerful truck to the trailer hitch.

"Any problems?" Paul asked him after a few minutes of work. "No. Hitch fits."

"Good," Paul said. *These pesky little details matter; the unimportant stuff is usually what goes wrong*, he feared.

The package delivered two days ago all seemed in good order, just as promised, and ready for the plan's next step. Paul secured the ropes over the tarpaulin with a bit more tension, then sealed the warehouse door behind them after they drove the truck and trailer out.

Yevgeny drove cautiously with the flatbed attached, first out of the airport's bonded area then on to the island's two-lane public highway. The main road did not have much traffic so they covered the twenty-kilometer distance to the island's name-sake capital in less than an hour.

They drove first into the city of Rhodes' medieval center, an ancient place of solid stone walls and old churches built near or above a buried latticework of older Greek temples.[141]

Yevgeny parked the Ford at an open lot near Mandraki Harbor in one of the many empty parking spaces near the water.

Many marine agencies on Paul's list that they checked first at the beginning of their walk were closed for the season. The old town's harbor was not a single wharf but instead a larger area divided into commercial and private marinas. This was busiest waterfront on Rhodes, so if this did not work, Paul knew they would need to head south to try another, smaller town.

After a cluster of near-empty restaurants, Paul spotted one local rental agency with an open sign displayed prominently on its glass door, and in English.

Inside, three young men in plastic puffer coats lounged on plastic chairs, playing what looked like mobile games on their phones. After a first chat to establish Paul as a motivated international customer, one of the puffer coat trios sauntered over to the back of the agency and called out something more loudly in Greek. In a few moments, a stout, balding man wearing a blue polo shirt and a wide smile appeared through a curtain of hanging wooden beads from the agency's back office. He approached Paul, big hand outstretched, to introduce himself as the owner.

"I hear you want to rent a boat?" Stavros asked.

"Not rent. Buy," Paul explained again.

"Buy? Now?"

"Correct."

"But why not rent?"

"That's my business," Paul said. "I want to buy direct from the owner. Is that something you can help me with?"

"You pay in cash?"

"Absolutely. If you can help now, happy to pay an agency fee."

Stavros's eyes betrayed skepticism, but as Paul clarified and repeated that he was prepared to make an offer today, the Greek continued nodding and grew more animated.

"Come with me. I will help you. We do not sell here, but come, come. We take coffee and talk more at my restaurant. It is close, just a two-minute walk," he said. "I didn't catch your name, friend?"

---

141 Founded in 408 BC, the city was the site of the Colossus of Rhodes, later becoming a stronghold for the Knights of St. John (1309–1522) and the Ottomans before joining Greece in 1948.

"Mike," Paul replied.

"You come many times to Greece?"

"Passing through," Paul said.

"Better to visit us in the summer when there is swimming and many lovely ladies. In winter we have old temples to visit, though. Do you see over there? That was the temple of Aphrodite. Three thousand years old," Stavros said, pointing to the classical marble ruins while they walked a full twenty minutes to a small but well-appointed family-run restaurant along the main waterfront. The round tables outside were empty except for a thin old man sipping wine in a corner beneath the awning's shade. After they all sat, Stavros ordered three espressos quickly served in tiny white porcelain cups, each with its own small saucer.

"Are you hungry yet, friend?" Stavros asked Yevgeny as he watched the Ukrainian mix three large sugar cubes into his espresso.

"No. I just like sweet coffee," Yevgeny said in his accented English.

"Speak any Greek?" Stavros asked. Yevgeny shook his head sideways.

Stavros replied in Greek, still suspicious, even as both his guests stared blankly back. Finally satisfied, he took out a beat-up old Samsung Galaxy mobile to make his calls.

A plate of four Baklava cakes came after ten minutes, along with another round of bitter espressos with fresh pita bread and hummus.

"Please enjoy. I am working for you now. My wife's food is the best on the island," Stavros insisted while he carried on multiple telephone conversations in a staccato of fits and starts.

Yevgeny ate all the moist, honey-drenched baklava, replaced within five minutes by another full plate of the same.

"How much longer?" Paul asked after an hour had passed.

"Not long. My brother is still looking for you. He will come soon."

Another twenty minutes passed before a grizzled, balding, stocky old man in a torn gray sweater jogged over from the waterfront to their table. He handed Stavros a different Galaxy phone, smiled, and sat down.

Stavros showed several options to Paul by flipping through each boat image with quick swipes. Some images were professionally taken, but most were casual photos, hastily snapped in just the last hour.

"Go back to the previous one," Paul said when one photo of a sturdy midsized vessel caught his eye.

"This one? This one is for fishing," Stavros said.

"It looks big enough. How is the motor and range?" Paul insisted.

"Perfect! Brand new motor. She is a workhorse."

"Is it nearby?"

"Not far, just a short walk." "Shall we take a look?"

"Of course, we must," Stavros replied, rising energetically and motioning for his brother to lead the way.

Stavros's brother led them down to the docks and to another short pier crowded with different fishing vessels. Paul recognized the relevant the fishing boat at the pier's end, noting that it was in slightly worse shape than the photo showed, with slimy seaweed caked on its old, ill-kept wooden hull. They hopped on board via the stern to inspect further. Stavros showed off the motor by cycling through three different power modes. Then Paul peeked in at the two small sleeping cabins nestled beneath the boat's main enclosed cockpit.

"I told you she was an excellent boat," Stavros said with a wide smile.

"Seems like it," Paul replied. "Does this lifting crane work?"

"Are you kidding? She can lift five hundred kilos. Very good shape for you, I know it."

"Full tank?"

"I can give you more; she runs on diesel," Stavros said.

Dusk was already approaching when they returned on foot to Stavros's family restaurant, its exterior neon sign glowing brightly now in red and white above the entrance. They sat inside this time in the tackily decorated private room in the back. Stavros's wife had already laid out plates of saganaki cheese, olive-oil drenched dolmades, and lamb kebab on a large cloth-covered round table. A bottle of Roditis stood uncorked next to four wine glasses. Stavros introduced his eighteen-year-old daughter, a lanky girl with black hair, large friendly eyes, and a poor complexion. She poured wine into four glasses with a demure smile before she also sat down.

"Now we eat some before it gets cold," he insisted.

"We're already full," Paul insisted.

"Impossible."

"We can't stay long for a full dinner," Paul cautioned.

"No, not long. Food in the stomach is better business. Now we eat and we talk."

They finished the lamb and all the dolmades before Stavros proposed his price of fifty thousand euros. The relevant fine boat, in his veteran opinion, was an absolute steal, only available because the owner, his second cousin in Athens, needed cash soon to pay for a son's expensive private college. "Kids are ching-ching expensive. Always good to grab one bird now instead of looking at two far away," Stavros noted.

"For no paperwork, should we also add twenty-five percent for your transaction fee?" Paul asked.

"Mister Mike, I was about to mention this exact same amount. This is a normal charge for our island," Stavros added, trying hard to hold his smile. "We think the same. You buy in cash what you see, and we part as friends."

"Perfect," Paul said.

Paul took thick stacks of euro bills from his shoulder pack and placed them on the table. The black-haired daughter came back from the kitchen with a small black light machine, and Stavros's brother held the cash notes up to the light. The old balding brother took a bill from each stack to thoroughly inspect it, and then even repeated the process to be thorough.

More plates also emerged from the kitchen—braised lamb, rice, flatbread, and yogurt. Then it was only a matter of a handshake, broad smiles, and a final round of licorice-tasting ouzo poured into six shot glasses to celebrate a fortuitous meeting and successful deal.

"What else can I do for you, friend?" Stavros asked.

"Take-home boxes for what is left of your wife's amazing food. We will have everything still on the table. And the boat keys," Paul said.

———————— ✶ ————————

The afternoon's moment of warmth died away after sunset. The winter night air became distinctly cold as Paul powered the boat down the coast, south into the darkness. He felt alert despite the wine and the massive quantities of food working its way through his body's overloaded digestive system. Because of the cloudless night's exceptionally low light pollution, even the Milky Way's broad swath was clearly visible, a cloudy glowing smudge across the high arch of the deep black sky.

Morning light was just breaking when he met Yevgeny some thirty kilometers south down the island's east coast. Yevgeny had done his best to park the Ford Super Duty and its trailer close enough to the shore at an isolated cove.

"Good enough?" Yevgeny shouted from the truck.

"I think so," Paul shouted back.

Yevgeny slowly backed up the flatbed as close as possible to the edge of ocean's lapping waves.

The slow, demanding work with just the two of them then began in earnest. They transferred the heavy military chassis in stages, pulling apart the separate sections, then reassembling them in the boat with gloves, ropes, and levers. A sensible plan on paper, but the heavy labor stretched on for hours into the cool, quiet morning. Paul enjoyed working with his hands again, straining muscles, using pivots and ropes to swing the bulky parts onto the ship.

By noon, the SAM's bulky steel chassis was a lumpy mass beneath a dirty tarpaulin pressed on the boat's stern. They filled empty bags with rocks and sand to help stabilize the bow and brought the positioning equipment and command setup to the boat's cockpit.

For lunch they ate some more of Stavros's food from Styrofoam bins.

"How much water for our trip?" Yevgeny asked.

"Get enough for at least a week," Paul replied.

By midafternoon, Yevgeny drove the Ford for a short, final trip to buy the water, canned soup, bread, and cheese from a local market. Then he parked the truck about a kilometer from the coast and walked back to the cove. After he hopped in, Paul put the motor to work to begin a slow but steady trip farther down Rhodes's rocky, windswept, inhospitable eastern coast.

Yevgeny found a seat at the back of the cockpit and closed his eyes, exhausted from a long sleepless night. For Paul, the boat motor's steady *katuck-katuck-katuck* seemed only a frail and steady protest against the rough silence of the ancient, undulating, and unpredictable sea.

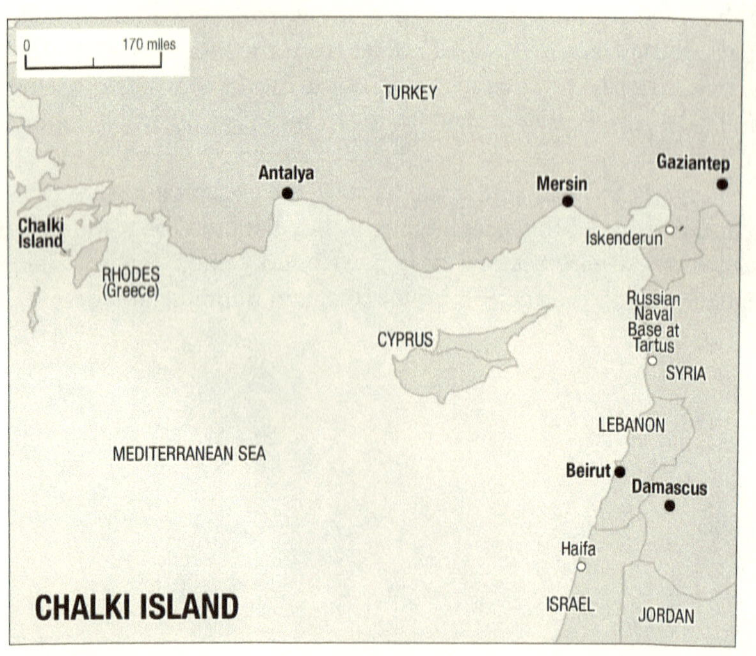

0
170 miles
TURKEY
Antalya
Gaziantep
Mersin
Chalki
Island
Iskenderun
RHODES
(Greece)
Russian
Naval
Base at
Tartus
CYPRUS
SYRIA
LEBANON
MEDITERRANEAN SEA
Beirut
Damascus
Haifa
CHALKI ISLAND
ISRAEL
JORDAN

19

Chalki Island, Northern Rhodes, Greece.
January 17, 2023. 5:15 a.m.

KATERINA VOLKOVA filled her lungs with the early morning's moist, pungent sea air while she scanned the still dark, distant horizon. It was a particularly clear sky. A three-quarter moon cast its pallid luster across the flat sea, hovering high above among the array of pinprick stars spread out across the sky's vast dark canopy. The cosmos felt close, translucent with its constellations—Orion, Cassiopeia, Andromeda, and Aquarius. She knew these old Greek names from childhood. It was a mythology that gave meaning and substance to what she also recognized was ultimately a collection of random patterns.

Katya had arrived to this tiny Greek island two days ago together with her four male companions, all handpicked to serve a specific function. The crew's boss, Dmitry, came yesterday, and now stood behind her with his quiet, steady eyes. She trusted Dmitry's judgment completely, ever since he risked his life for her in Red Hook all those years back. Dmitry's best man, Anton, waited in a truck parked two hundred meters behind the bend of the road, separated from the expected exchange point as a precaution. Dmitry had also sent his two trained sharpshooters a few hours ago to hide along the barren hillside. Dr. Hans Schmidt, Yuri's personal doctor, waited nervously near the Toyota Land Cruiser. Inside that vehicle, her captive and bargaining chip, Nicolai Sokolov, also waited locked inside, handcuffed and blindfolded.

They had all spent the last two days preparing for this dark morning. The team's first task upon arrival had been to spread out, comb the location, and confirm that there were no surprises or hidden traps waiting for them on the island. She had seen only a few local farmers, mountain goats along the trails, an abandoned sixteenth-century monastery, and a smattering of villas shuttered for the season. As expected, Chakli Island was just a forgotten, dry little place in winter, the smallest of the Dodecanese islands with its only town, Emporeio, home to less than a thousand. The hardest task had simply to be bring in their truck and cars via private ferry from the big island of Rhodes.

"Were you able to get any rest last night?" Dmitry asked as he watched her pace around the area in wide circles, sometimes squinting her eyes unsuccessfully at the nearby hill to spot the two trained marksmen.

"A few hours," she replied. Katya had slept some, but not well. How could she? Somewhere up there, unseen, in low orbit, a US military satellite was also watching. Paul had relayed Spysat's highlights ninety minutes earlier: Two Mi-17 choppers had lifted off from Tartus at 2 a.m., exited Syrian airspace by 3 a.m., and were clocking excellent time over international waters. By her own calculation, the helicopters should already be visible.

"I still can't see them," she complained to Dmitry in Russian.

"Patience. There. I see two now," Dmitry said, pointing in the distance to two small sparkles that now appeared through the morning's faint purple light.

The two lights approached in formation, low above the sea. As the choppers neared, details of the combat machines gained shape—noses tilted down, powerful rotary armed guns sticking out from just below the triangular stabilizing wings. The propeller noise reverberated over the water, steadily rising in volume until the *whomp, whomp* blared loudly as the two bulky helicopter gunships hovered above.

The two massive machines took wide circles, scanning the perimeter with bright spotlights. After two full circles, the first Mi-17 chopper descended with a booming noise and powerful wind currents scattered dust across the old, barely visible helipad. The second chopper hovered, a helmeted gunner observing, his hands on a rotary weapon that could unleash thirty .60 caliber rounds every ten seconds, should it come to that.

After a few more minutes, the second Mi-17 eventually landed on open flat ground about two hundred meters away, closer to the water.

The side door of the lead chopper slid open after the propellers slowed to a halt. Two men armed with semiautomatics, ready but pointing down, jumped onto the tarmac. Kiril Alekseyev scurried out next, wearing a Kevlar vest but no helmet and apparently unarmed.

Positive sign that he is not geared up for a firefight, Katya thought.

She felt her own pistol strapped to the small of her lower back at the ready. She visualized what she might have to do with it, just as Gold had trained her during his long sessions years before. *Any tricks—duck, roll right, take him out first.*

Kiril strode forward at an even pace, alone, his arms dangling loosely at his sides while the two others lingered near the chopper. He gave orders to his team via a small device attached to his right ear.

Katya walked forward until they stood three meters apart.

"Problems?" Kiril began in Russian.

"None at all," she replied. "We are ready."

"I want to see our cargo first," Kiril demanded.

"When you bring Yuri out," she said.

"He is in that other helicopter over there. I come unarmed. We will do this easy. Show me my cargo, as we agreed, and then Yuri will come out," Kiril insisted.

"Fine," Katya said and lifted her index finger as the signal for Dmitry to call Anton. "Your metal will be here shortly."

They stood uncomfortably in silence for what felt like an eternity while Dmitry's orders were transmitted; after ten minutes the six-wheeled truck and trailer rolled up the dirty road.

Anton came out of the truck while Dmitry opened the back of the trailer to reveal the rows of evenly stacked metal boxes.

"May I?" Kiril asked. Dmitry nodded.

Kiril lifted himself up into the back of the trailer and opened one of the unlocked metal boxes. He pulled out a heavy gold brick from the second level. With a small pocketknife, he scraped off some shavings, placed them in a small glass vial he pulled from his vest, shook the vial, and then used a small pocket light to check the liquid.

"Satisfied?" Katya asked from behind the trailer.

"Almost," Kiril said. He went farther back into the trailer, found another metal box, and pulled out several heavy bricks until he reached the bottom layer. He took out a bar from the bottom and repeated the same verification process to see if any discoloration revealed false gold. He did one more random sample on a different box at the very bottom of a corner stack.

"How many more science experiments?" Dmitry asked as the process dragged on for more than twenty minutes.

"How many tests do I need?" Kiril snapped coldly back.

"Fifty-six boxes, each with a hundred 400-ounce bars. Six and three-tenths metric tons. As agreed. We have two moving palettes there in the truck, and you can count the cargo as you load," Dmitry said.

Kiril jumped back down from the truck and straightened himself back up.

Katya kept her expression impassive. She had been right that Kiril would not have anything close to a real, thorough inspection. Nearly all the gold was real, but his spot-checks did not come close to where Dmitry had placed a single false bar—No. 1675. No. 1675 weighed the same as a gold brick and, on cursory inspection, appeared identical to a real brick. However, 1675's hollow interior held a customized low-energy responder grafted inside. Once activated, this small device would signal a precise position via a certain radio frequency—whether that would prove to be from Syrian warehouse or the bottom of the Aegean.

"You're shorter than I expected," Kiril remarked as he faced off with Dmitry.

"And you have a much older face that what I understand is your age," the older Russian replied. "Get on with it. Bring Yuri out and we will give you Nico."

"*Da, da,*" Kiril said, then spoke muffled orders into his small mic.

The armored door of the second helicopter slid open. Yuri exited in a drab gray jumpsuit. He straightened his back and kept his head high. Then, looking straight ahead, Yuri began the last final hundred meters of his long journey at a slow and steady pace.

"Can my two men start with your cargo now?" Kiril asked. Dmitry nodded, and Kiril's two men approached, semiautomatics now slung on their backs. They used rolling palettes to unload the boxes while Yuri steadily made his slow way closer.

Katya met Yuri's eyes when he finally came to her. Dr. Schmidt slid forward, took out a small penlight, and shined it into Yuri's blue eyes, inspecting his pupils.

"All fine, Uncle? Nothing strange?" Katya asked in a low voice while Schmidt also administered a thermal scan and a blood pressure test.

"Nothing I feel," Yuri replied.

"Anything else? Katya prodded.

"I don't know," Yuri replied. "Too late to care."

"The old man is healthy as an ox. Now, where is my Nico?" Kiril asked.

"This way," Katya said and brought Kiril over to Land Cruiser. She unlocked the back door, opened it, and pulled out the blindfolded Sokolov by the elbow from the back seat.

After she removed his blindfold, and then unlocked his handcuffs, Sokolov eyed her coldly. Nico had refused to speak to her since Naples; he only glared back with a simmering malice whenever she spoke to him.

Kiril took Sokolov by the elbow and spoke softly to him while the two other Russians continued to move the heavy boxes to the moving palettes. Kiril instructed Nico to make his way closer to the first helicopter.

Katya moved closer to Kiril while he stood watching his team's steady progress.

Kiril lit a cigarette as his two men worked. This time Katya refused his offer. Instead, she kept her back straight, with her line of sight always on the helmeted gunner at the deadly .60 caliber rotary machine gun.

"You trust your pilots?" Katya probed while Kiril smoked. *It is still possible once you load our gold that your trigger-happy Wagner goon will blast us,* she worried. *Keeping you close to me will help stop his itchy fingers.*

"I pay for trust. Where are your shooters? How many did you hire?" Kiril asked, peering into the dark foothills to spot any men there.

"We have enough to take your head off."

"No doubt," Kiril replied coolly. "But that would not be smart for you either. We would both end our time together in very unhappy circumstances."

"After you finish loading," Katya said. "You go last."

"Certainly. Why would I have come here to you if I wanted violence?" Kiril asked, now stepping even closer to her so that she could see his yellow teeth. "We have an agreement. Why would I risk our bright future together?"

"We have no future after tonight," she replied.

"Sure?"

She kept Kiril talking in his movie-script nonsense while Dmitry, Yuri, Anton, and Schmidt all drifted away to more remote positions. Schmidt led Yuri farther into the darkness, and Dmitry and Anton made their way in the opposite direction.

One of Kiril's men held his hand high, thumb up, while he stood next to closest Mi-17's open passenger door.

"That's it then," Kiril said. "You have your uncle back, and now your men have left us alone."

"Accounts settled?" Katya asked.

"As agreed," he replied, his lips curled into a tight smile. "Now I will walk back, and then we will find each other again under better, more civilized terms."

She wanted to say never would be soon enough, but every gesture and word needed to serve her current action, so she simply nodded as he made his way back across the landing area and pulled himself up into the first chopper.

The second helicopter's propellers spun first. It quickly gained elevation while Kiril's chopper started its noisy engine and went next vertically up into the morning sky.

Both choppers hovered for a moment there together. Then they spun around in a coordinated turn, dipped their noses downward, and propelled back east across the flat water with the noisy propellers' *whomp, whomp, whomp* gradually receding.

The two black dots eventually disappeared as the morning's new sun hovered low above the sea's rippling reflection, waves speckled with a brighter yellow morning light.

After a few minutes, Dmitry emerged from his position. "That's that," he said in Russian.

"You worried it would go sideways?" Katya asked.

"It usually does. Never know. Mercenaries also can have their own ideas."

"Kiril isn't stupid," Katya remarked. "Probably told Wagner they were picking up scrap metal."

"They all suffer from a lack of imagination. If this one was smarter, he might have lived another day," Dmitry said softly now in the early morning quiet, his voice cold against the murmur of the waves breaking against the island's rocky shore.

20

The Aegean Sea.
January 17, 2023. 7:35 a.m.

P AUL GAZED out at the dull light spreading out over the ocean's long horizon. A cluster of bilious light gray clouds lingered low in the distance, just above the Aegean's undulating waves.

Paul had vomited three times since midnight. Seasickness came as expected. The fifteen-meter tuna liner had rocked all night and smelled of gasoline and bleach. Yevgeny, up in the front, also had his challenging moments of vomiting, just not as bad as Paul.

Does not matter, Paul thought. *Game day now. We both need to power through.*

A dull tone in Paul's left earpiece broadcast the incoming transmission.

"Pequod, you there?" Jo asked.

"Go ahead Ahab," Paul replied.

"Two whales at one hundred klicks, moving east and low at two thousand feet. Pairing you now."

"Roger that," Paul said as a refreshed satellite map popped up on the small screen.

A little tracking icon moved across the map in small increments. The satellite followed the two Mi-17s in formation, moving 400 miles per hour over international waters.

"You are a lucky son of a bitch," Jo added.

"Always," Paul replied.

Paul watched the two little green icons inch their way across the black screen as they approached a targeting circle, and the distance numbers from their own location steadily clocked lower.

Thirty kilometers, then twenty, now twelve. Then ten.

Back up to twelve. Fourteen.

Fifteen.

"Pequod, confirming you have range. Harpoon away," Jo urged tersely.

"Roger that."

Paul flipped off the safety cover, pushed the button for a last red warning light, then pressed again.

A loud ignition hiss cracked, quickly became shrill, then boomed. Six missiles shot off in a quick automated sequence, twenty seconds apart.

The boat lurched, ocean water tipping into the stern, as each missile streaked out. After each launch, the missile first skimmed the ocean's surface, then, after gaining position, shot higher into an empty, open sky and out of eyesight.

"Good?" Yevgeny shouted from the boat's front after the programmed sequence ended.

Paul signaled a thumbs up. It did not matter now what was visible to them in the distance above the flat ocean. Pequod's six guided harpoons were now in search of two fast-moving proof points.

Yeah, this is it, he thought. *Decades of research, billions of US taxpayer dollars spent for world-class precision guidance systems. Better work.*

————— ✱ —————

Kiril gazed outside the thick bullet-proof oval window at the new day's sun. The morning sun rose bright above a calm Aegean Sea that spread out like a sheet of cobalt glass below.

His mission was now on its sixth hour, just an hour behind schedule. The Wagner mercenaries had performed well, followed the plan, and did as they were instructed. He was pleased that all his hires had followed procedures and kept their cool. These orcs were not paid to think, especially since he had promised their relevant bosses enough already to keep them in line. Only for a very quick moment when the two men loading the cargo realized they were moving gold bullion did Kiril think it might get ugly.

He was glad that there had not been any last-minute surprises from his counterparties. It was always hard to predict with wily opponents like Dmitry Medkov, and this was a lot of money to move.

Finally, time to relax, he thought.

Kiril pulled out a bottle of Dom Pérignon from a customized travel pouch filled with ice. He popped off the cork, let some champagne spill out, and filled two plastic flutes with the sparkling golden liquid.

Nicolai Sokolov, sitting across from him, had kept his eyes down thus far. With his head shaved, Nico looked much thinner and older than when Kiril had seen him last some five years ago in Italy. Back then, Nico was at the height of his power and widely regarded as the FSB's most effective asset in Southern Europe. Kiril offered one flute to Nico, who took it and swallowed it all in one motion.

"You don't seem as happy as you should," Kiril shouted above the propellers' constant roar.

"Just surprised," Nico shouted back, his temples still knotted and lips pursed.

"Surprised your government values you?" Kiril said.

"Do they?" Sokolov replied above the noise.

"Someone in Moscow must."

Kiril tilted the bottle again to pour another glass. Nico tipped his head back and gulped it down again.

"*Spasibo, Droog.* Thank you, friend," Sokolov said.

Kiril was not exactly sure about Nico's fate, but there was no need to raise the poor soul's anxiety level so soon after his liberation. The probable scenario would be that Nico would be interrogated for whatever intelligence value might still be extracted, especially for any new insights from his three months in captivity, wherever that had been. Something new might be marginally useful, but other than this, Sokolov's utility was certainly over. Now the system would kick in not as a matter of punishment for deficient performance but rather per a simple risk reduction calculus. A distant Siberian work camp for at least a few years would suffice while the dust settled.

I am being too generous on his odds, Kiril silently corrected himself as he knocked back his second flute of champagne. *They will surely execute Nico within a year. Oh well. I do not care. Someone else's problem.*

Kiril turned his thoughts instead to his own winning math: First, a half million paid to the authorizing Tartus Air Force captain for twenty-four-hour use of the two Mi-17 choppers. Second, $2 million for the six Wagner men. Third, another million for incidental fees. Total of $3.5 million in direct costs. Going forward, and within about a year, he planned to pay another $50 million up the chain to various FSB patrons and another $50 million directly to shell companies controlled by his key patrons and supporters within Russia's Black Sea naval command. This left him personally with $346.5 million dollars, assuming accurate spot-checks and no counterparty skimming on the gold bricks. This all was a good trade for one worthless old man already long ago marked for death. *Cash will be always king when the edifice begins to crumble,* Kiril mused, still sipping the dry Dom Pérignon. *Whatever happens next, at least now I have replenished my own war chest and spread around some targeted goodwill. A few more security steps after we land should move quickly. Then a weekend in Beirut, and I will pay a visit to—*

Suddenly, Kiril felt the chopper lurch downward. Champagne spilled out of the thin plastic flute.

As the chopper leveled out, Kiril unbuckled himself, pulled up to the cockpit door, and opened it. Both pilots tightly gripped their control sticks. A red light flashed brightly on the pilot's control dashboard.

"What is it?" Kiril fumed.

"Jamming," the pilot answered.

"Jamming what?" Kiril asked.

"Sit back," the pilot shot back angrily as his fingers danced along the control panel.

Now what? What are these two Wagner idiots up to? He wanted to scold the two pilots, until he realized that they were both fearfully engrossed in the moment.

"There," the copilot said, pointing at a tiny smoke tail low on the horizon to their right.

The pilot pushed two buttons on the dashboard. Within seconds, streams of smoke shot out from each of the chopper's sides as decoy flares.

Kiril gripped the handrail as the pilot pulled up sharply into a sudden steep ascent. A hard, hot, pounding fear leapt up inside his throat. They rolled around in the air, up first, then a sharp jerk down, another turn to the left, careening.

Through the cockpit window, Kiril saw a bright flash, followed by a deep boom. Billowing orange flames engulfed the other leading helicopter, and bits of metal scattered outward. The other chopper ahead of them in the distance whirled wildly and spiraled down.

"Get us out of—" Kiril shouted.

Boooomgaoarrggd.

The explosion hurled Kiril backward out of the cockpit, his feet in the air.

He fell back and bounced wildly against the interior walls as if inside an out-of-control carnival ride that jostled and spun him in all directions. The chopper's back tail filled with smoke. Nico screamed in pain and terror, strapped in his seat, flames now running up along his legs, burning him alive as he was strapped to the chair.

Sharp pain filled Kiril's arms and legs and neck, and he felt horrifying dread as they all twirled and bounced and screamed. Then, at the peak of unbearable pain, Kiril crossed a threshold as the chopper plummeted.

For the last moment, he saw himself float outside of his burning, broken body. Buoyant and beyond pain, time, decay, horror, and all things composed of body and flesh, his entire being was suddenly infused not with pain but a sense of wonder. He felt his consciousness expand second by second into the infinite. The bubble of his consciousness gained substance so quickly, it was as if he could feel a whole Earth within himself expand brilliantly as never before. He felt an instant of intense joy and profound understanding as the wonder and the power of his past and the future stretched his awareness to its ultimate limit.

Then Kiril Alekseyev's wonderful final infinite seconds suddenly met an end; the fragile bubble of his entire imaginary universe simply...

Popped.

Josephine Richards sat alone watching the flat screen. She had arrived this morning at 3 a.m. when it was pitch-black outside, and headquarters' main car park was mostly empty. Langley was always humming along at some foundational level, but this early Monday morning was otherwise cold and quiet.

Pequod's feed had started exactly on schedule, with an initial count of 360 minutes, moving down to zero when the coverage would end. The higher resolution live feed came with a twenty second delay, recorded from a geo-synchronized, six-hundred-mile-high orbit. Jo closed her eyes for the first two hundred minutes while the tracking sequence followed the two targets on their long flight over international waters. At minute 125, she engaged with Ahab, and then at minute 112, she noted the direct hit to the first M1-17, followed at minute 111 by another hit to the second chopper's tail. Russian decoy tech was obviously no match for our new Raytheon toys.

After this, there was not much to see. Ghost-like blossoms of fire scattered across the waves. Both choppers broke apart upon impact, little splashes on the open water. Mi-17 choppers were heavy. As expected, they sank fast. By minute 109, the video showed only a patch of oil and small floating debris on the vast ocean.

Jo switched back to Paul's channel at minute 100.

"Pequod, you stuck two whales," Jo conveyed.

"Roger that," Paul replied.

"Ready to move on?"

"In process."

"Make it quick," she urged.

"As lightning, Ahab. Out."

Jo flicked off Paul's channel. *More chatter would not help.*

The clock moved down to the final ten minutes and then hit zero and automatically turned off. A scroll of technical identifiers filled the screen. A final ringtone announced the satellite feed's end as the complex imaging system returned to its prepositioned, busy daily schedule to cover other national security priorities. The last eight hours had been coded into a level four program, full discretion, and a Pentagon service bill would be auto generated within a week for services rendered. Bespoke satellite coverage was expensive. What was she going to do about the exact amounts? Complain about an overcharge?

Jo was typing in final accounting tasks when she heard the SCIF door creak open.

The fresh-faced GS-10 analyst who had given her access to this tiny secure cubicle peered through the doorway. Mark kept his wavy hair neatly parted on the side, and he wore a dark blue wool sweater as if attending a college lecture.

"How much longer do you need the cube?" Mark asked.

"All yours. I am done," Jo replied, pulling herself up from the chair and struggling to regain her balance once she was on her feet again.

"Let me help," Mark offered as he saw Jo teeter.

"I'm good, I'm good," Jo replied. "I just sat too long for my knees. No problem," Jo replied, hiding the grimace from the pain she felt when she needed to use her aching muscles.

She kept her head down and concentrated just on walking again, one foot after the other, out of the little cube.

Jo slowly made it to the ground floor cafeteria in a slow, thoughtful twenty minutes.

The cafeteria was starting to get busy by 8:30 a.m. with breakfast. The round tables were full of young people, all those Ivy Leaguers arriving to power up the place with their Type A personalities and high-minded idealism. It was still not very easy to recruit these days, but she knew there would always be some kid out there willing to take all this shit for the noble cause. Most would not last more than a few years because the private sector defense contractors paid double, but a few might stay. Military brats and Mormons usually stayed longer than the typical Ivy Leaguer.

The cafeteria's high windows let in the early day's fresh sunlight from an enclosed inner courtyard.

She noticed the back of Marty Hines's balding head. He was at his usual spot in the cafeteria's far corner, talking intently with a younger analyst while he picked at a plate of pancakes and the analyst read out something to Marty from his iPad. No need to break up such a lovely *tête-à-tête*. She would fill Marty in later about Pequod's success once she reconciled the data and cleaned up miscellaneous security items.

She lined up with a plastic tray behind two chatty twenty-something analysts. Jo handed the cashier a twenty-dollar bill for a plate of scrambled eggs, decent rye toast with blueberry jam, and coffee. At least the subsidized food here was cheap.

For the next half hour, Jo Richards sat by herself at a small round table next to the window. She watched a murder of blackbirds in the courtyard's bare winter trees as she slowly ate her eggs.

21

Paris, France.
10th arrondissement. January 21, 2023. 11 p.m.

YURI VOLKOV now understood and accepted the inevitable—he did not have much more time.

Too bad the end will be here, like this, on a hospital bed, he silently lamented.

Yuri was still stable enough to see the external world through his burning eyes, but he had lost his ability to speak or even gesture with his hands. With compressed lungs filling with fluid, each breath wracked his chest with pain. For the past two days, different Saint-Louis Hospital[142] doctors had done their best with shots, blood transfusions, and oxygen tanks. Their efforts were obviously failing, and fast.

All to be expected. I made my peace months ago. Nothing to do now except suffer through to the end. Just a few more hours.

The blindfold from the helicopter transit ride had done the trick, he surmised. A masked soldier with blue surgical gloves had tied his wrists and wrapped the blindfold tight and firm on his face. He had detected moisture on the cloth hours before the chopper lifted off but thought it harmless.

Yuri had felt fine for the first twenty-four hours after the Chakli Island exchange. He had joined Dmitry on a chartered plane to Rome and then traveled back to Paris via the Orleans airport. That first night back in Paris, they had all felt vindicated. Katya's bold plan had worked. Hope remained after his bloodwork from the city lab came back negative on a general toxin screen. He allowed optimism to enter through a small crack. Had he just been overly cynical before?

The second night, however, hope cracked. Yuri woke from a ten-hour sleep with a high fever. Hour after hour on the third day, his fever progressed and stayed elevated at a dangerous 39 degrees Celsius. He struggled to breathe, and it was harder still to support stable awareness while the toxin ravaged through his blood, organs, and nervous system.

---

142   Founded in 1607, the hospital now employs approximately 2,500 people, including 1,000 medical staff.

Kiril's chemist had mastered a new Novichok version with a slow-release mechanism. His already weakened body was in no shape to fight.

Saint-Louis's sterile hospital room confronted him when he awoke semiconscious on the third day. Vague faces passed by at a distance. He recognized Dmitry and Katya hovering against the glaring lights. Other strangers in white medical gowns and light blue scrubs also wore sober, strained expressions.

Yuri's last coherent memory was of a cold glass of water pressed to his lips while Katya's delicate fingers wiped away his forehead sweat. He tried to muster a weak smile but was unsure if she saw his feeble attempt.

After this, Yuri sank further into a dark swirl, little by little dipping deeper into a vast dark ocean. He steadily sank into this murky inner quiet until, finally, at the bottom, he discovered a diffuse and peaceful light shimmering. He met others on the fringes of this visible sanctuary. His brother, Sergei, was there, and his wife Elena too. As they came into focus, he saw that they were much younger now, and they came to him with outstretched hands, and strange, peaceful smiles.

Where is this last place?

They were all in a weathered wood-lined dancehall. The air hung heavy with the earthy scent of pine sawdust as Yuri, Sergei, and Elena sat alone. First daylight peeked through rosy stained-glass windows, casting a soft, ethereal glow on the remnants of the previous night's raucous wedding party. Sergei, his face flushed with exhaustion and contentment, drank from a long flute, his gaze fixed on his beautiful bride. Yuri watched them both silently. He had guided his younger brother through countless challenges; he knew this morning's happiness would sustain them all for a long time. Here they all were again in a magical conversation about a future brimming with possibility. It was so very pleasing to finally speak with Sergei again and see how Elena smiles.

Then brighter rays finally streamed through the windows, bathing the empty dancehall in a very strong, brilliant light as an unreachable last dawn finally broke.

———— ✳ ————

Katya held Yuri's limp his hand as the lead doctor declared 8:52 p.m. the official time of death. The nurses detached various intubation tubes with a long-practiced, routine indifference.

Katya stayed hunched at Yuri's bedside while the others completed their tasks and drifted away. She held his limp hand, which was already turning cold.

Paul finally came back. The clock showed 11 p.m. He put his hands on her slender shoulders and forced her to rise by squeezing her with two hands.

"Come on, enough," Paul said as she released Yuri's lifeless fingers.

"I should have known," she replied.

"Not your fault," Paul replied.

"It's exactly as he warned me," she repeated.

Paul kept his hands pressed on her shoulders as they escaped the sterile room.

In the nearby empty hospital lobby, a nurse came over to ask Katya to fill out a form. The tall nurse—eyes wrinkled and hair cut short in a severe bob—began to ask them both about whether Katya wanted to authorize a final onsite autopsy.

"We need to have more documents sent over to establish Madame's legal authority as next of kin," the nurse said.

"I will arrange," Paul explained.

"M. Volkov's body must be moved to the next annex in the next hour."

"I said I will arrange it for you. You will have your paperwork tomorrow," Paul hissed back in a bitter tone.

"Of course, monsieur. As you like," the nurse responded curtly and closed her notebook with a little abrupt clap.

Outside the hospital, they both wrapped their scarfs more tightly around their necks before Paul began to search for a taxi on his phone. After midnight, the nearest driver in the 10th arrondissement was twenty minutes away.

"I want to walk back," Katya said.

"All the way to Rue du Bac? It is more than an hour."

"I need to walk, use my legs."

Katya and Paul walked back along the Canal de Saint Michel and then along Rue de Turbigo toward the river without speaking. The restaurants and cafés were all closed, with outdoor chairs stacked against walls and wrapped up in chains. Paris slept except for a few cars, taxis, and livery trucks that occasionally broke the city's cool and constant darkness.

DAYBREAK

Josephine Richards

22

Kyiv, Ukraine.
March 2, 2023. 5:30 p.m.

THE SUN'S descent cast a gold-orange glow across the wide, early spring sky. A woman, slightly hunched, dressed head to toe in black, head covered by a shawl, approached a freshly dug rectangular hole. The grave was neatly prepared at the end of a tidy row of nineteen other similar rectangles.

The woman dropped six freshly cut white tulips on the middle of the polished white oak-wood casket at the bottom of the hole.

Olga Kuzanova stared down at the coffin's shiny surface, which was engraved with an orthodox-style crucifix with two crossbars. She knew her son, Valentine, was not in the casket. For hygiene and simplicity, the army had already cremated his mortal remains two months ago. But Olga had insisted on a proper Christian burial, and the army had accommodated. Now in the day's waning light, it was easy to imagine him resting peacefully inside the casket, his earthly spirit united with an unknown infinite God.

Olga was pleased that more than five hundred people had gathered today to pay their respects to the twenty fallen heroes. But privately, she strained to hold off the simmering unanswerable questions that pulled like chains around her neck. *Why did any of this have to happen? How much longer? Wasn't it all too soon for such a handsome, smart boy to leave this world? Do the other mothers here today feel the same?*

Father Vadim's hour-long eulogy followed the orthodox tradition, full of powerful statements and deep, meaningful prayers. The yellow-and-blue flags arranged in intervals along the stone cemetery paths fluttered. None of the boys buried today would ever marry or have children. They were all gone forever.

Olga spotted Dmitry Medkov standing patiently throughout Vadim's eulogy, a black fedora tilted over his forehead. Dmitry took her by the elbow after Vadim finished, and the mourners walked back to the municipal building for another awkward, solemn hour of food and drinks. She was surprised that he came, the bald boss himself, and now held her by the elbow. Valentine had always promised that Dmitry's organization would not abandon families.

"Many people came today. I am glad for it," Dmitry said in Russian as they walked.

"The priest, Vadim, spoke well," she replied. "He told me this morning that this was his hundredth ceremony since the war began. He has blessed the souls of at least five thousand of our boys, I think."

"Too many," Dmitry replied. "And what about you? How else can I help you now? Do you have what you need?"

"The money is more than enough," she replied simply. "You are very generous. I thank you for it."

"No amount can replace your son."

"No. He was a good boy," she said.

"He was brave, and he died for justice," Dmitry replied.

"Yes. He was always a brave boy," she agreed.

As the black-clad mourners shuffled into the ugly municipal building, a baby's shrill cry cut through the heavy murmur of hundreds of slow, quiet conversations. The infant's crying continued for a full minute, despite her mother's rocking.

Dmitry brought over two short glasses of vodka from one of the tables and handed one to Olga.

"We can move you to a better apartment in Kyiv if you like," Dmitry offered.

"Thank you. My room is very comfortable, and I have quiet neighbors. My cat hates new places."

"Nothing else then?"

"You don't know?" she probed.

"Tell me," Dmitry said.

"*Pobedee.* Win," Olga said.

Now the bald man paused, and his troubled eyes peered back from behind those two small silver-rimmed oval lenses.

"*Da.* We must," he replied. "To Valentine, and to victory."

"To victory," Olga echoed, meeting Dmitry's eyes. They clanked glasses and both drained the vodka with a quick gulp.

Olga stayed only another hour before polite excuses led to Dmitry's driver driving her back to her two-bedroom apartment on Vladimirskiy Street.

Little Mishka, her old, nearly blind cat, greeted her at the threshold with soft cries. She petted him softly before opening a can of tuna to appease his hunger.

While Mishka ate, Olga boiled water and made chamomile tea from her balcony plants. After standing all day, she was relieved to remove her shoes and sit in her favorite chair.

She drank her tea slowly while staring a long time at a single framed picture on her end table. She snapped her favorite picture of Valentine on a summer trip to Yalta when he was just twenty, proudly wearing a white Ukrainian Navy uniform just after his enlistment. Her son's expression exuded confidence, as it usually did. "Oh, my little handsome boy," Olga whispered directly to the photo.

She petted little Mishka's soft fur with even strokes while she sipped her tea.

"My handsome, handsome boy," she repeated as if continuing a mantra.

Eventually, the cat retreated to another room. Then Olga closed her moist eyes and finally drifted down into sleep.

23

Lviv, Ukraine.
August 15, 2023. 2 p.m.

BILIOUS GRAY cloud cover stretched out over the long, flat horizon. Paul Drake kept two firm hands on the wheel. Two cans of Red Bull on an empty stomach kept his mind alert. The hour-long drive from the Polish border was not particularly stressful, but the 2015 Peugeot was a manual transmission, and unfamiliar roads still demanded his attention.

BBC radio news played as he drove, bringing to him the day's white noise: British royal family updates, Manchester United's latest victory, unseasonably hot temperatures in Spain and Portugal, critical reviews of a new musical opening on the West End.

Paul was nearing Lviv's old town center when he turned up the volume to listen to the radio coverage as it turned to international affairs:

> "… and now the latest international news at the top of the hour. UK and NATO officials are issuing warnings that Western military powers are running out of ammunition to give Ukraine to defend itself against Russia's full-scale invasion.
>
> Admiral Rob Bauer, NATO's most senior military official, told the Warsaw Security Forum this week that the bottom of the barrel is now visible. He said governments and defense manufacturers must be prepared to ramp up production in a much higher tempo. The admiral, who chairs NATO's Military Committee, said decades of underinvestment meant NATO countries had begun supplying Ukraine with weapons with their ammunition warehouse already half full or even emptier. 'We need large volumes. The just-in-time, just-enough economy we built together in thirty years in our liberal economies is fine for many things but not the armed forces when there is a war ongoing. We cannot stop just because our stockpiles are looking a bit thin,' Bauer said. 'We must keep Ukraine in the fight tonight and tomorrow and the day after and the day after. And if we stop, that doesn't mean Putin automatically stops.'
>
> Swedish Defense Minister Pol Jonson also warned that it was vital for Europe to improve its defense industrial base to support Ukraine for the long term. 'We're now digging

```
pretty deep now into our pockets, into our stocks,' he said.
'And in the long run, I think it's crucial that Ukrainians
also  procure  defense  material  from  Europe's  industrial
base. We learned some hard lessons about scale and volume,
especially when it comes to artillery ammunition.'

    Additionally, the UK defense ministry highlighted that
Britain  has  given  more  than  300,000  rounds  of  artillery
ammunition  and  is  committed  to  giving  'tens  of  thousands
more' by the end of the year. The US State Department says
the difficulty is that, despite attempts to ramp up production,
Ukraine is using the ammunition faster than Western powers
can  replace  it.  Analysts  say  that,  in  contrast,  Russia
appears  much  more  able  to  gear  up  its  wartime  economy  to
replenish its own stockpiles."
```

Paul switched off the station as he weaved through the tight streets of Lviv's more densely packed old center. The maze finally led to a single parking spot rented for his use. He locked the car and walked toward the city's old market square to pass a few empty hours before meeting Max.

Lviv seemed very subdued this gray afternoon, as if still half asleep. Foreign reporters did not spend as much time here now that the war had moved into its next slow, grinding phase. The world wanted a quick, uplifting narrative: struggling democracy reigns victorious over an evil invader! But this headline did not happen. Instead, the news reel just continued to roll on without any neat, heroic conclusion. Reality brought harder truths: battlefield stalemate, trench warfare, slow destruction of countless villages, and thousands killed, maimed, or displaced. Daily deaths continued far away from the cameras, faces shoved in mud, bodies mutilated. Good fathers, bad fathers, convicts, sons, brothers, all shredded up irrespective of their deeper human identities. All just fodder now. Wagner's upstart, radical leader, Prigozhin, was also dead, shot down in a plane near Moscow back in August after his very brief and ineffective mutiny.[143]

An espresso and a sugary croissant at a small café on the corner of market square helped stiffen Paul's dour mood.

At least Kiril is gone too, and the gold is back in our hands, he thought as he watched the various pedestrians go about their quiet business. *A little gold always helps.*

As planned, the hidden transponder in gold bar No. 1675 had pulsed its signal from the bottom of the Aegean. The two sunk Mi-17 choppers had fortunately settled on a sandbar less than a kilometer down.

---

143   Yevgeny Prigozhin, the leader of the Wagner mercenary group, was killed on August 23, 2023, exactly two months after his abortive mutiny against Russian military leadership.

Dmitry relied on Antonio's Sicilian team to arrange the professional dive recovery work weeks after the crashes. These were the same smugglers who had moved refugees from Syria to Europe years ago when MSA first became deeply enmeshed with the UNHCR's relief programs. Antonio's team took only seventy-two hours on location—the promise of a 15-percent success fee kept minds focused, and interests aligned.

Paul had greeted Elad Ismail as he disembarked behind the dive team's captain in Malta's Marsaxlokk harbor. Paul had demanded that Elad join Antonio's recovery effort. The young Syrian originally earned Paul's trust during their time together at the camps in Turkey, and then most definitely so during their fateful night together at Villa Fontesa in Sicily. It was only fitting he join this crew now since Elad had also risked his life to kill Bogan Zoidze and then take the Russian gold to begin with.

"Marco is getting married next month. She is from Palermo, tall and very beautiful," Elad had mentioned after the cargo was safely transferred to Dmitry's waiting team, and they were walking along the waterfront.

"Good for Marco. I wish the newlyweds the best," Paul offered then. "What about you? What is next for you?"

"If Asad falls, I'll return to Damascus," Elad said.

"To do what there?" Paul asked, surprised.

"I don't know yet, but I think I can help," Elad offered.

"Be careful what you wish for," Paul cautioned. "Asad's days are numbered. The Russians cannot afford to keep him propped up much longer. Putin does not have enough warm bodies to spare now. Russia will pull the plug if they can keep their naval bases and the Israelis agree to play ball. I give it a year at most, maybe two."

"Hope you are right," Elad replied. "Afterwards will not be easy."

"It will not be easy, but it will be better. If you have the courage to return there, I know you will find a way,"[144] Paul offered.

They had spent the rest of the evening together drinking gins at a crowded place on Straight Street in old Valetta before Paul left the next morning for Paris. Elad was thriving with his life in Sicily now. The boy had finally found security for himself and his family, all mere fantasies before. Out of all this mess, Elad had played his part. There would be more for him to do if indeed the Asad regime eventually was toppled...

"Another coffee?" the thin café waiter asked, breaking Paul's reverie.

---

144   Sill unknown at the time of this conversation, Bashar al-Assad was eventual deposed on December 8, 2024, marking the end of the Assad family's 53-year rule in Syria.

"No, thank you," Paul replied. His legs were stiff from sitting, although the hour alone had passed quickly.

The waiter counted the euros that Paul handed him as he rose and then thanked him for the tip.

Best of all, Paul concluded. *There was no need to keep Jo in the loop on all these purely private money matters. All this has nothing to do with the affairs of state. And she was grateful enough to not ask.*

The night turned colder after sunset. Paul zipped up his jacket up to the neck. He almost did not recognize his younger brother when they met at the same restaurant as the year before when Max had first arrived in Ukraine.

Max sat at a table under the expanse of a large chestnut tree with its dry leaves already turning yellow. His brother was no longer the youthful, bright-eyed thirty-five-year-old new volunteer. Max looked much thinner now, with a sharpened chin and furrowed brow like man in his fifties. The black patch worn once again over his dead eye also marked him.

They had spoken a few times over the phone after Max was admitted to the military hospital outside Kyiv. But those prior talks were insubstantial; Max was keeping more bottled up inside, as he always did.

"How many months has it been since the injury?" Paul asked.

"More than six," Max replied.

"Better to take more time. Take as long as you need," Paul said.

"Nah, I am good. I have had enough time. Felt fine since June," Max said.

"Dmitry told me that his men finally located Stefan's parents in Romania. We will do what we can for them," Paul said.

"Good. Thank you," Max acknowledged. "How were they?"

"They live in Bucharest. Stefan's father is a music teacher at a small college. His mother runs a restaurant. They had not heard from him for more than a year before the bad news."

"Sounds like Stefan. He followed his own path," Max confirmed.

"Christina came by the Rue du Bac apartment," Paul said, keeping his demeanor casual.

"Did she?"

"Yep. Just showed up after you never returned any of her calls or responded to her emails."

"What did she want?"

"Nothing. She asked me to give you this."

Paul slid over Christina's letter, still sealed, with Max's full name written with skill and care in a delicate cursive script. Max glanced at the envelope for a long moment before placing it in his jacket pocket.

"Beautifully handwritten, just like for a wedding invitation," Paul quipped.

"Thanks. I will read it later," Max said.

"Come back with me to Paris," Paul suggested. "Stay with us at the Rue du Bac apartment. See your girl again. Your stuff is still there. Stay as long as you want."

"Still not a good time," Max replied.

"When then?" Paul asked.

"Next summer if we make progress," he replied.

"Almost a year?"

"Not long," Max confirmed.

"You have a right to be discharged upon request. No one will blame you. No need to be hanging out here alone like some kind of penance."

"That's what you think?" Max asked. "There is nothing wrong with me. You are starting this again?"

"Just talking," Paul replied. "No harm in talking. I cannot roam around inside your head. You need to talk so I can understand."

"Nothing to say. You warned this was not going to be easy or quick. I have always known it," Max replied.

"That's right," Paul replied, sensing an opening. "This war will last a very long time. Not just a few more months. Years. Russia's rotten edifice still stands. Putin is firmly entrenched on his iron throne, and the world has lost interest. There is nothing really NATO, or any world leader, wants to do about it except send in just enough guns, tanks, and ammo for a stalemate. The likely scenario is also that the next US administration does nothing. Politicians clapped their hands and waved flags in the beginning, but now the world is moving on. The price of eggs is too high. There are other problems in other countries. That's just how it is."

Max gazed off in another direction before finally responding. "You still don't get it," he said finally. "I am not deaf to everything you are saying."

"You can try to apply some logic to who lives or who dies, but ultimately, it is random and it is absurd. There is no hero's culture today," Paul pressed.

"Valentine was a hero. Wasn't he your friend?" Max replied.

"He was. And you are my brother."

"Stefan was a hero, and Bill too."

"I know it hurts," Paul replied, backing off.

The waiter came over to turn on a small flame heater now that the sun was down and the air had turned colder. Paul used the pause to order another bottle of Georgian white wine, Khachapuri, and lamb kebab. He changed the dour mood after the food came, shifting tactics to reminisce more about life back home, their shared childhood memories. Maybe there was still something in Max to reconnect him back with the familiar? If Europe was not the answer, then perhaps back to the States, he gently suggested at the end of his long, discursive prodding, without any clear response.

"What about you? How's Katerina now?" Max asked after they finished their plates.

"She blames herself for what happened to Yuri. Dmitry helps on the business front, but everything has changed now that Yuri's gone."

"That's hard," Max said. "But she is not alone. She has you, right?"

"She does. I want us to normalize," Paul explained.

"What does normalize mean?" Max prodded.

"Many things. Not this. Katya wants something different."

"You mean different as in kids?" Max asked.

"Maybe. Children are not biologically possible for her, unfortunately," Paul said and then explained more details about why.

"Sorry about that," Max replied.

Paul was surprised to hear himself explain his own plans and personal struggles to Max. It felt strange to reveal his own hopes and dreams, however implausible, since he had come to Lviv to focus on his little brother's next decision, not his own.

They stayed until the waiters began collecting the chairs and folding up the tables.

"I am sorry that I need to leave tomorrow. Too much on my plate now," Paul offered as they walked back to Max's apartment.

"Great you came. That restaurant is always a good choice."

"Promise you'll let me know where they send you?"

"Sure thing."

Paul pulled his brother closer into a strong embrace. For that long moment, Max reciprocated.

"Remember what I always told you. The future is unwritten," Paul said. "You always have a choice."

"You too," Max replied.

———————— ✳ ————————

Max's temple throbbed and he felt exhausted by the time he walked up the three flights of stairs back to his one-bedroom apartment. He was glad to have finally spent more time with Paul, but likewise he still struggled to talk to his brother. Paul was always second-guessing him and judging his decisions instead of truly respecting his choices.

Max cleaned out one of the dirty shot glasses on the kitchen table. He uncorked a bottle of Nemiroff honey vodka and poured himself a shot. The vodka warmed his throat. He poured a second glass before pulling Christina's letter from his jacket pocket.

Her envelope was made of very thick, mauve-colored paper. She had signed his name in her beautiful, florid cursive script. It was a nice gesture for such a fantastic woman to handwrite a long letter and seal it all in a fancy envelope.

Christina was a very lovely woman; he had enjoyed their moments together. But that was over. Now he was just like Bogart's Rick Blaine saying 'we'll always have Paris' to Ilsa in the rain at the end of Casablanca.[145] Max had watched his favorite movie at least a dozen times. Now he was living that same script himself, but here and now, on his own terms.

Max picked up his Zippo lighter from the end table. The *trysupk* decal, the Ukrainian freedom symbol, was as clear as the day the Ukrainian recruiter had given it to him nearly two years ago.

Max went to the kitchen sink. He ignited the corner of Christina's mauve envelope with a crisp snap of the Zippo. The flame danced up the paper with surprising speed. As the paper transformed into a fragile skeleton of black ash, Max dropped the mess into the kitchen's stainless-steel basin. Chilly water carried away the final remnants. Then he slowly and thoroughly washed his hands with soap.

Tomorrow at 3 p.m. he would visit the Third Territorial Defense Battalion to learn about his next gig. So much was happening. Vasili Rogoff had recommended him to a new commanding officer. There were rumors of a planning counterattack within mighty Russia herself since the Ukrainians would soon be supplied with longer range missiles. Even the F-16s were finally getting the green light for combat. He was a sought-after commodity and eager to continue while all the so-called Great Powers

---

145   The 1942 Best Picture film is set in Vichy-controlled Morocco where expatriate Rick Blaine must choose between his love for Ilsa Lund and helping her Resistance-leader husband escape the Nazis.

pussyfooted their way back and forth, and the badly needed weapons very slowly trickled in.

Max emptied his mind while he lay there alone on the bed and eventually found a very narrow path to sleep.

24

Lviv, Ukraine.
October 30, 2023. 9 p.m.

GEORGE RUTHERFORD III's upper back ached; a knotted muscle throbbed just between his two thin shoulders. His ankles were swollen from walking in a pair of uncomfortable leather shoes. George was still jet-lagged from the time change, although he had first stayed four days at the London Mayfair before the next flight to Krakow and then across the border to Western Ukraine. He was no longer a young man, but this trip was necessary. His political loyalists needed to see for themselves what was really happening with their money.

Hell, Rutherford thought, *I am Biden's age. Old Sleepy Joe made it here back in February. I am twice the man he is.*[146]

"See you tomorrow morning at 8 a.m.?" Katya asked as she poured out the last of the red wine into George's wine glass. The waiters cleared the final porcelain dessert plate. He didn't eat much since Lviv's local food was strictly average, but it was important to share a final meal alone with Katya so that they could coordinate.

"Very good," George replied softly.

"We could meet later in the morning if you wanted," she said. "After breakfast."

"No, no. 8 a.m. is good," he replied. "Let us stay on schedule. I will make it fine."

"Thank you, George. Coming here was important. I realize your time is valuable," she offered as they walked back to his hotel. "Was the trip helpful?"

"Of course. Yes. Very much," he said.

---

146   US President Biden visited Kyiv, Ukraine, on February 20, 2023 in an unannounced visit ahead of the one-year anniversary of Russian's invasion. The derogatory nickname "Sleepy Joe" refers to a portrayal of 80-year-old Biden by his political opponents as low-energy and lacking vitality, concerns that eventually led him to withdrew from the 2024 election, albeit late in the electoral process.

Katya took his hand just before he went back into the hotel lobby. He leaned over and kissed her cheek, catching a faint perfume fragrance off her neck.

Rutherford brushed his teeth back in his room and then lay down on the hotel bed. He was exhausted, yet worries continued to disturb his restless, darting mind. Even with all his wealth, Rutherford doubted whether his efforts would have any impact on this this war, especially since all the Western democracies seemed so paralyzed with doubt and confusion. October 7 Israeli bloodshed now was added to the mix of immense and intractable problems.

Good thing Skip stayed back in California, George thought. *So much simpler without my ungrateful, sniveling progeny tailing along with unhelpful advice and self-aggrandizing agendas.*

His oldest son no longer tried to hide his frustrations, but instead did his best to obfuscate and confuse. Skip's tactics included sending a steady stream of ungrateful grandkids throughout the summer as a kind of rearguard campaign. They all feigned interest in the foundation's noble affairs and ingratiated themselves on the golf course, usually on the back nine, before launching into their demands. Their real intention, George knew, was to check what he was doing to fritter away the family's fortune while under the spell of a Russian slut with shapely calve muscles and flowing chestnut hair. Two weeks prior, back in California, George vividly recalled the tense parting with his son. It was a confrontation Skip had seemingly fueled with two tumblers of Hendrick's gin for his liquid courage.

"Why are you really doing this, Dad?" his son abruptly asked.

"Doing what?"

"Everything. This trip to Eastern Europe. The fat DC political contributions."

"If you don't see by now, then I can't help," George replied.

"It's embarrassing, Dad," Skip pleaded. "Some territorial dispute has nothing, absolutely nothing to do with us."

"Is that what Tucker Carlson told you on TV?" George had asked back.

"Come on. That is unfair. You did not really care about any of this before Katya came on the stage. First, it was her art, now you are supporting her next agenda. It is not all useless, I know, but she leads you like a puppy."

"Is that how little you really think of my agenda and our work?" George had shot back, staring his son down with hard, mean eyes.

"Isn't it obvious? Everything this vampire introduces you to has someone else taking a cut, robbing us blind."

"Vampires don't commit dollar for dollar the same amount as my foundation."

Skip returned a puzzled look. "What does that mean?"

"It means that you are talking out of your ass," George had chided. "The facts are that Katerina Volkov has made contributions alongside the Jefferson Foundation for the past year. So far, more than $50 million in cash, all earmarked for humanitarian causes. I expect we will do more together very soon in Israel."

"Paid or just pledged?"

"Paid," George confirmed. "You assumed otherwise?"

"Dirty money, no doubt," Skip had muttered. "We pay taxes, Dad," he had continued. "Foreign wars are other people's problems, not the cross to bear for this family."

"Son, if you are going to bitch and moan, then please stay home," George had retorted.

Skip had gulped the last gin and tonic before droning on with some platitudes and finally scurrying up the stairs, back to his bedroom. The whole incident had left Rutherford with a sick, bitter taste.

I was not the best father, but it is my money. I will do what I goddam please with it.

On this trip, Rutherford believed he had been wisely selective. The Jefferson Foundation sponsored two first-term Republican congressmen in swing states, a centrist Democrat senator on the important appropriations committee, and half a dozen staffers and policy wonks from inside-the-beltway think tanks. Jefferson's immediate purpose focused exclusively on humanitarian needs, including funds for five struggling government hospitals in Western Ukraine and high-impact programs administered by the Red Cross and *Médecins Sans Frontières.*

What could be controversial about such bipartisan programs? It was best to work both sides of the aisle, paying extra attention to the centrists in both parties, especially aligning against the new breed of populist Republican, the whacked-out isolationist idiots with their insane rhetoric and Putin-friendly dog whistles. The new isolationists, though, were on the rise. Older Republicans, the better ones, were now quitting politics. The younger ones were poor replacements, a reflection of America's weakness, not her strength. A new era of economic nationalism and mercantile priorities felt like it was on the verge of crashing down. Voters in Kentucky, Texas, and Michigan cared more about gas prices and the cost of eggs.

Rutherford finally turned off the lights and lay prone in darkness, still shuffling through myriad worries. He felt the stiffness of his eighty-two-year-old joints, pain in his upper back, soreness in his calves. His body presented certain natural time limits no matter how great his will or the size of his bank account. When he was gone, what would really happen to his legacy? His own family was not going to stay the course—they were no different than the rest of this Instagram-attention-deficit-disorder generation. Putin, Xi, Kim Jung Un, and the Ayatollah would all eventually win if all these ignorant numbskulls did nothing important and just let it all play out.

Who exactly is going to pick up the torch before it is too late?

———————— ✳ ————————

After breakfast and a host of handshakes, Katya changed clothes from a business suit into a more comfortable cotton shirt, long pants, and flat shoes.

She took a familiar stairwell up to the second floor of St. Paraskeva Hospital. Dr. Rodofsky's door was open, as usual, when she passed his office. He looked up from a stack of papers, offered a faint smile, and motioned for her to enter.

"Are they convinced?" Rodofsky asked in Russian.

"Always helps for donors to see their money working," she replied. "The politicians understand more now about what's really happening here."

"Good. Influential people can quickly lose interest in faraway struggles. I worry that most of them have attention spans like butterflies," Rodofsky said, and then rose from his desk.

"We will do more, I promise," Katya said.

"Walk with me now," Rodofsky said, touching her elbow to lead her back out to the tall hallway.

They chatted more about priorities as they walked. Rodofsky explained about how the hospital was short-staffed and needed to attract more skilled surgeons and trained nurses. He floated some productive ideas on how to help the current razor-thin staff do more with less, and they mulled over whether more local hospitals could partner with Polish or Hungarian faculties to help expand capacity in the most important areas.

They crossed the street to the children's annex, another old nineteenth-century limestone building, this one painted in a warm light rose color. A sleepy-eyed older guard let them pass beyond the lobby.

Dr. Rodofsky led her down a flight of stairs, explaining that the four-story annex was completely full, housing 347 orphans, ages two to fifteen. Ukrainian children with one or both parents killed were sent here under a broad government mandate. In some cases, parents made the fateful choice to voluntarily give up their children, at least for a period while one of the family's breadwinners served in uniform. In other circumstances, both parents were committed to the cause and left their offspring because they had no other options. "We must improve conditions here," Rodofsky explained. "We are already at full capacity. My new problem is that last night I was told we must take a hundred more kids. There is not enough security at other small locations. I was told they will be moved here in just four weeks."

"Why didn't you ask me to take the donors to see this?" Katya asked.

"Because I did not want our visitors to be overwhelmed by our mess. There are too many unanswerable questions for now."

A nurse came over to Rodofsky and began to discuss with him the contents of an urgent patient record; pneumonia was running through the population of children below the age of seven.

Katya drifted farther into the room.

A group of children sat quietly at a low, long wooden table while a bevy of young nurses, some no more than teenagers themselves, passed around individual milk cartons and packages of white cheese for snacks. Some few dozen children were playing, ages that seemed as young as two or three and as old as early teens. The large common room buzzed with noise like an overcrowded, understaffed daycare center bursting at the seams.

Katya watched one small girl with tawny tangled hair sitting isolated in the corner, alone. The girl hummed some kind of song and held a small stuffed white unicorn with big marble eyes.

"Hello there, kitten. What is your name?" Katya asked in Russian.

The small girl briefly looked up but continued humming. "What's your name?" Katya repeated.

Still nothing, only a continued focus on the stuffed white unicorn cradled in her small hands.

Katya went back to the entrance, where Rodofsky stood. He had been watching her with the girl out of the corner of his eye.

"Better not to speak Russian with the children here," the doctor cautioned.

"I'm sorry. I can't speak Ukrainian."

"I know you do not. Vira is from Chernihiv, near the border, so she understands Russian and a little English too. She was just ignoring you because you are a stranger. She keeps to herself, as you can see."

"What happened to her?" Katya asked.

"A missile destroyed her apartment block in the second week of the war," Rodofsky explained. "Parents, grandparents, and brother all lived on one of the top floors. The others were killed after the eight-story building came down. They were crushed instantly. Vira was tossed into the rubble. They told me it took forty hours to pull her out. Scrapes, bruises, but nothing broken, not even a finger. God's grace she survived. Nothing short of a miracle."

"How old is she?"

"Around eight, we think."

"She understands what happened?" Katya asked as they passed out of the spacious room and back into the hall.

"She doesn't say much, but she knows," Rodofsky replied. "We post all the identities of our children on a special website and in some newspapers and bulletins. Sometimes we are lucky to find a cousin or another relative. For some, eventually someone will come to take them. For Vira, though, it has been almost two years. No one has come for her yet. I do not expect that to change."

25

Lviv, Ukraine.
March 2, 2024.

A STRING of frosty winter weeks passed quickly for Katya. Dr. Rodofsky did not press her to stay longer, but after she volunteered, his broad smile made it clear he was pleased that she agreed to continue supporting the various programs already in motion. She rented a well-appointed two-bedroom apartment on Ivana Fedorova Street on a six-month lease; it was in a safe modern building only a short drive from the hospital, with good heating, tall windows, and fast broadband connections.

Most days were heads down on the hospital program's many tasks. She dove headlong into organizational needfuls, also working on the weekends. Professional calls sometimes lasted past midnight, especially when they involved ongoing fundraising efforts coinciding with one of Zelensky's frequent trips abroad. She passed New Year's Eve alone, just so she could have a moment of quiet.

Paul joined her for two weeks in late February. He was back mostly in Paris, sometimes Malta, on complicated business involving restructuring Yuri's domain. Paul carried different documents for her to review and sign as she assumed full ownership of what was mostly Yuri's profitable and stable legacy. They also carved out a few quiet nights together, and she was pleasantly surprised that Paul could still occasionally make her laugh.

"We have been productive. Anything else before I leave?" Paul asked her the morning of his scheduled departure after the coffee had been poured.

"Not at the moment," she replied.

"I am impressed with what you are doing with Rodofsky. I was skeptical you could make this work. Kids are messier than paintings. Yet here you are. You seem like a natural," he offered.

"Managing any business is similar. I try to be useful."

"You sound like Max," Paul replied.

"Each in our own way," she replied cautiously, knowing Paul still did not approve of Max's voluntary redeployment to a newly formed division on the eastern front. Max was already six months into his next role, and Paul knew only that his brother was someplace near the border of the Russian province of Kursk.

"I should be able to come back next month for at least a few days," Paul promised.

"When you come back, I want to talk more on another subject."

"About what?" Paul probed.

"Something new for us," she demurred.

"Any hints?"

"Unfair of me to say more now."

"That's how you want to leave it?" Paul protested.

"For now, yes," she replied.

"Is it about staying longer here?"

"It might be," Katya admitted before leaning closer for a final kiss.

After Paul left, Katya decided to walk to the hospital this morning instead of using her driver. It was a bright, clear spring day; Lviv's morning had begun with car honks and a busy swirl of pedestrians. *What does Paul suspect? Should I have told him more already?*

At first, Katya did not know why she went a few times every week to the children's annex. True, she wanted to see the progress. True, Rodofsky's team was putting more resources to work with remarkable success: the facility was now supported by twice as many staff, there was a new two-hundred-room dormitory, and all the children were now receiving some form of organized daily education for a four-hour minimum. True, the donors needed her, and it was her money at work.

But there was more on her mind than just these facts.

Finally, today, the warmer spring air and green buds on the old elm trees gave her a certain courage, and sense of hope.

When Katya entered the main annex room, she saw Vira in the corner. For the past few weeks, the girl had enthusiastically welcomed each of Katya's appearances. Today was no different. Vira was such a small, pale little thing, with thin legs and bruised shins but large bright brown eyes and a lovely innocent face full of enthusiasm. Vira's childish smile was always a pleasure to behold. Was it clear to them both that they shared an odd, special connection, and that this connection had pulled them so much closer over the past months?

"Good morning, my little kitten," Katya said in Russian.

"Why didn't you come yesterday?" Vira asked.

"I am sorry. I was busy with the man I brought to see you on Monday. You remember him, right?"

514

"You mean Paul?" Vira asked. Katya had taken Paul to see the progress at the children's annex and had subtly introduced him to Vira. Katya first wanted to see how well Paul and the girl naturally interacted, at least for just an hour.

"Yes, very good. What did you think of him?"

"He seemed nice," she said.

"I'm glad for it," Katya said. "Paul asked me to bring you a nice gift to say that he hopes to see you again," Katya said and pulled a piece of tinsel-wrapped chocolate candy from her small side bag.

"Can I eat it now?"

"Only a little. Save the rest for after lunch."

The young girl took the chocolate bar quickly with her tiny hand. Within seconds she had unwrapped the candy and eaten a few pieces.

"Good, no?" Katya asked. Vira nodded.

Katya had known ever since California that she might have difficulty having biological children. She had vaguely hoped motherhood might still be possible, despite the medical facts presenting very long odds. For years since her recovery, Art had become her maternal substitute. Art's abstracted creativity replaced a biological procreation. Instead of children, she focused on the manipulation of color, visions inside picture frames, imaginary dreams that others had created over centuries.

Even so, she still wondered about her family, especially now that even Yuri was gone too. *Might I someday have both?*

"I want to speak about something important," Katya began. "Will you listen carefully now?"

Vira faced her squarely in response.

"What do you think about leaving this place?" Katya asked.

"It's not good here?" Vira asked.

"It is good. But I want to take you to an even better place. You can have your own room with many new toys. The city is called Paris. You will like it. There are many nice houses, a beautiful river, many lovely chocolate stores, and nice parks where you can play outside and make so many new friends. You will go to a very good school there too."

"Everyone is going?"

"For now, it would only be you."

"Just me? Can Marina come?" Vira asked, still trying to process Katya's proposal.

"Marina's daddy will come back for her later. He will take her to her own family after he finishes with the army."

Vira lowered her eyes.

"Only I am leaving here?" Vira asked.

"Do not be afraid. You will not be lonely. You and I will live together. I will be like your new mama."

"Does it mean I can call you Mama?"

"You can if you want," Katya continued. "And you will see Paul again. Paul and I will help you speak English. You will never be bored. There is so much to do in Paris. We can even see the Olympics during the summer if we finish all the paperwork by then."

Vira puckered her lips. "What is 'Olympics?'"

"Sport games. Running, swimming, gymnastics, tennis," Katya explained. "The Olympics have all sorts of games. All the countries of the world send their best people to compete. It will be incredibly fun to watch. It only happens every four years, each time in a different city. I want to see these games in Paris with you and Paul there too."

"English hurts my head."

"You told me that you liked learning other languages. Your teacher said you are doing so great."

"Sometimes I like," Vira demurred, using English on this response to prove her point.

"If you trust me, then we will be your new family. Do you understand what I mean?"

"Do you really mean it? *Pravda.* Truth?"

"Yes. *Pravda.* If you will have me, we can be a new family, and it will be official and legal," Katya said.

Vira's eyes now welled up. She grabbed Katya's arm and pulled herself close. Her hands gripped Katya very tightly while big warm tears rolled down her tiny cheeks.

"What is wrong? Why are you crying?" Katya asked. "You don't want to come with me?"

"I do. But if I come with you, I just do not want you to die too," Vira replied.

"Do not speak such nonsense. Nobody else is going to die. Life will be very normal again. You do not know yet, but the world is so big and interesting. It will all be better when we are together. I want you to trust me to take care of you," Katya replied. "Do you understand?"

"I don't want you to die because of me," Vira insisted as the girl squeezed her body more firmly against Katya's breast.

"*Shhhh… shhhh.* It is going to be OK, little kitten," Katya said, gently patting Vira's small back. "You will be safe. No one will hurt you again. I promise. No one else is going to die."

26

Chopin Airport. Warsaw, Poland.
June 2, 2024. 4:15 p.m.

A TALL woman with heavy makeup and brown hair wrapped tightly with clips walked back along the narrow aisle. She wore a cleanly pressed dark blue uniform, and her face held a bright, constant smile, showing off her noticeably clean, straight white teeth. Vira was excited to be strapped in this big seat. She knew about airplanes, but this was her first time traveling on a real one. She sat at the very front on a big leather seat with a television screen and wide armrests. Katya was next to her, wearing a blue shirt, white pants, and slender black riding boots. Her new mommy smelled nice, like a mix of roses and lavender.

Vira's last week in Lviv had been easier than expected because Katya took her to various places in the afternoons—churches, cafés, and parks. Marina had cried when she heard Vira was leaving, but her tears faded fast. Vira had liked it when, at the end of the day, Katya took many of her best friends to eat ice cream. There were so many flavors to choose from, and her new mama was very patient while everyone looked at all the delicious choices available in the clean shop. Vira very much loved the taste of green pistachio. Sometimes she ordered two flavors and put tiny colored sprinkles on the top.

Vira held Katya's hand tightly as the plane gained speed and lifted off into the sky.

After they ascended, Vira watched the myriad clouds churn below, fluffy and white like stuffed cotton balls. The sun glinted chrome yellow in the clear azure sky stretching far away along the Earth's slightly curved horizon.

After a while, the tall uniformed woman with the bright white teeth pushed a cart through the center aisle. She served food to Vira on a tiny plastic tray. The food was delicious, especially the cheesecake and the vanilla ice cream in a small round cup. Vira ate the ice cream with a wooden spoon. It tasted sweet. The tall woman also gave her apple juice and then later handed out tiny little cookies, each wrapped in their own plastic bag.

"Can I have another cookie?" Vira asked Katya.

"You have had enough sugar. We will eat better food after the flight," Katya said.

The short flight sped by in less than three hours. The captain announced something in French and English, and then before Vira knew it, the dream above the world was over and the plane was back on the ground.

"You see," Katya said. "Easy."

Katya took her by the hand again as they left the plane and passed through a long tunnel that eventually opened into to a busy, crowded hall. This new airport was so much bigger than the one they had left from in Poland. It thronged with people, so many travelers with little roller bags or big shoulder bags, careening back and forth. Many shops were stuffed with perfumes, candies, nice clothes, watches, and other fantastic things.

Vira held Katya's hand tightly as they walked through the airport's vast halls. Sometimes they both stood on an automatic walkway, but mostly they just steadily navigated through the crowds, hands squeezed together. Katya held out their passports at the checkpoint, and then they waited for their luggage at another location. Katya pulled two suitcases from the revolving carousel before heading to the street outside.

Vira recognized Paul standing in front of a shiny black car with big wheels. Paul kissed Katya first. Then he leaned down, hugged Vira, and kissed her on the right cheek. He looked better now in a suit, with his neatly combed hair and shiny black shoes.

He handed her a white rose.

"A pretty rose for a pretty girl," Paul said as Vira took it with a smile.

While driving, Paul and Katya spoke to each other in English. Paul raised his voice to ask Vira a question, but he spoke too quickly for her to understand, so she squeezed new Mama's hand to let her know that she needed help.

"Paul asked if you are tired from the flight," Katya translated into Russian.

Vira moved her head sideways. She was not tired at all. All this—the plane, the airport, the experience of flight, the white rose—was extremely exciting, and a little overwhelming. *Or is this all a slippery trick and this man is about to trick us both, betray new Mama, and sell me into slavery? Who knows? Anything is possible,* Vira caught herself considering as the car sped up onto the highway.

The big, sprawling city looked gray and cluttered as they continued. Most buildings along the highway were ugly boxes, just like the ones back in Chernihiv. Paris's traffic was also just as bad, especially when Paul turned off the big road and navigated through busy traffic circles jammed with trucks.

Finally, Paul weaved away from other trapped cars and onto a nicer wide boulevard with fancy houses that looked better and older with big balconies and high rectangular windows all neatly ordered behind rows of very tall trees. There were so many motorcycles and bicycles darting back and forth, and many people sat outside at cafés, eating and laughing because it was still light outside, and she could feel the warm clear air through the open car window.

"That's the Eiffel Tower over there," Paul said, pointing with one hand while he drove over a stone bridge that crossed a wide river.

Through the window of the moving car, Vira saw the great tower of iron. It looked bigger and better than in the pictures she had seen in books.

"*Kak graseeva.* Pretty," Vira remarked.

They drove down a smaller street, and Paul stopped at a big iron gate. He pushed a button to open the gate like magic. Then he drove the car inside, and the gate automatically closed as he parked.

"This is your new home," Katya explained in Russian while Paul carried their luggage inside.

Vira liked the big chandelier that hung elegantly from the main room's high ceiling. A plate of strawberries on a silver tray waited at the center of a shiny table, with a bowl of cream nearby. She dipped the strawberries into the cream with her hands and ate them one by one until all six were gone. Paul handed her a white cloth to wipe her face clean.

"Don't eat too much," Katya cautioned. "Paul will take you to see your room. You can rest a little, and then we will have a real dinner later since I think you will be hungry still."

Katya's eyes seemed more greenish now, nicer in this light.

At last, Vira finally started to believe that what was happening was true. She began to believe that she had been reborn into a new life. *Maybe what new Mama promised will come true after all?*

"Do you like it?" Paul asked her after he showed her a room that had a whole row of stuffed animals and a window that looked down onto a quiet interior courtyard.

"My room?" Vira asked.

Katya kissed her on the forehead.

"It is, kitten. This is your new room," Katya said.

"All the room?"

"All of it."

"But where do you sleep?"

"Nearby. Paul and I have our own room."

Vira approached the crowded shelves. She touched the many toys with her hands to convince herself of their substantive reality. She did the same with the fluffy blankets on the bed.

Later that night, when Vira realized she was still very hungry, Katya cooked spaghetti with tomato sauce for all of them for dinner.

Afterward, she gave Vira a slice of moist, extremely sweet chocolate cake and a glass of milk served in a tall crystal glass.

Vira agreed to go to bed only when Katya insisted and after a warm bath in a beautiful large white porcelain tub with old-fashioned brass knobs. She was not tired, but after the bath it was extremely hard to keep her eyes from shutting, despite the constant excitement.

"We will have a wonderful day tomorrow. No need to do everything tonight," Katya promised.

"Good night, Vira," Paul said before he shut the door and turned off the lights.

Vira turned her body and let her head melt into a soft, silky pillow while the city's pale light cast long shadows through the tall window.

Her mind began to meander and drift through lost fragments of the old apartment where she used to live with her old mommy. That old place was not as nice as this new royal palace. Her old place was so small and old, hard to walk up all the stairs, and too hot in the summer. There was only a small, ugly bath, and the shower never had warm water most days. But she was happy there too, before the end.

New Mama said it was fine to be sad sometimes about the past. She said it was OK to cry if she wanted, anytime; whatever tears she shed just meant that Vira loved others and was loved by them too. But Vira forced herself not to cry. She wanted new Mama not to feel sad, especially when she was trying so hard with all her fancy new gifts and nice places. There was no reason to be sad, because her other mommy and daddy could both travel to any new place with her, including this big fancy room here. If she believed hard enough, Vira could feel her old family, always hovering, invisible angels protecting her. Father. Mother. Even old Grandmother too, with her old rotten teeth and crooked smile.

Vira turned over to her side. Finally, she could not resist closing her eyes. A confused medley of the day's images, deeper memories, and strange new emotions quickly carried her off to sleep.

27

Paris, France.
December 23, 2024. 4 p.m.

A WINTER sun dappled through the bare branches of the elm and chestnut trees, casting long shadows on the pavement and dirty paths. The various paths of the Tuileries Garden teemed with hundreds of pedestrians passing through after touring museums, eating at cafés, or shopping at the boutiques along Rue de Honore or Rue de Rivoli. Paris was in full holiday swing, bustling with shoppers and tourists from around the world.

It was a particularly lovely December day to be passing through the broad expanse that ran along the river, Katya noted. Although it was warm now because of the sun, Katya had wrapped a scarf around Vira's neck, and Paul kept his light leather jacket zipped up to his throat.

Two more days until Christmas and then the end of another difficult, tumultuous year.

Has it really been almost two years now since Yuri left us? We are three now, Katya thought. *Three is enough to be happy. Three is safe.* Katya considered their morning thus far. It had begun at the Center du Pompidou as an enjoyable, normal family outing during Vira's winter school break. For two hours, they wandered through an excellent collection of modern masterpieces. Katya had enjoyed sharing her enthusiasm with Paul and Vira. They had stopped at Center's rooftop café for cake and coffee just before this afternoon walk back through the Tuileries, heading eventually across the river, back to the apartment on Rue du Bac on the Left Bank.

Last night, Paul had come home with a three-meter-tall pine tree bought for a hundred euros from a vendor along the river. Tonight they planned to decorate the tall tree with ornaments and a variety of glass lights, just in time for Christmas.

"Tired yet?" Katya asked Vira in English as they crossed through the busy Les Halles market area toward the old Paris Stock Exchange.

"I'm fine, Mama," she replied, also in English.

Vira wore a wool cap with a prominent logo: Olympics 2024, Paris above five interlocking rings. Katya had bought the hat from a street vendor when they watched the thirty-third Olympic Games opening ceremony together on the banks of the Seine, gripping umbrellas in the pouring rain. For that special, albeit wet, evening, the world came together in the spirit of athletics competition. Paris hosted their athletes in grand fashion, the first time in a century. It was how the world should be—competing for medals, not murdering neighbors. Thankfully the International Olympic Committee banned Moscow's athletes, and no Russian flag flew during the games.

"Can we stop here?" Vira asked when she saw other children gathered at a large Les Halles *air d'jeux*, a renovated playground crowded with families and boisterous children scattered on the many structures.

"What do you think, Paul?" Katya asked.

"Vira deserves it after being so good all day," he replied.

"Please go ahead and take her," Katya said.

Paul pushed open the playground's metal entrance. Vira darted inside. She quickly found one of the empty slides, climbed up the stairs, and then went down. On the other more crowded structures, Vira waited patiently in line with the other children.

"Try those monkey bars," Paul suggested.

Vira saw the challenge, her face beaming. Paul helped her find her grip, and she crossed bar by bar to the other side, swinging her body to keep momentum.

Katya sat on the bench nearby, watching as Paul helped Vira more, first to try the trampoline, then to dangle from artificial climbing trees, and finally to crawl across a bridge made of nylon nets. After more than twenty minutes, as Vira scrambled herself up a colored rock wall, Paul came over and sat down next to Katya on the bench.

"I need a break," he said.

"I see that," Katya said. "It is so busy tonight. Kids are off for Christmas. Will you be able to handle all this when I go to California for a few weeks next year?"

"Of course," Paul said. "Do not worry about us."

"I can see Vira trusts you more every day," Katya said.

"She's smart," Paul noted. "Did you see how she listened so intently about all the paintings she saw today? Her English improves every day."

"Children are sponges. Change their environment, you change them," Katya offered. "She told me that she loved Chagall[147] best. His paintings really spoke to her."

"Chagall was interesting," Paul noted. "Not sure why all his figures are stretched out and floating in the sky, but nice colors. Never knew he was born in Belarus. Never really thought about what he was trying to express with all his strangeness."

"Why would you?" she asked.

Katya was about to explain more about Marc Chagall when a loud shriek erupted.

Her gaze flashed back to the playground.

In the far corner, an older, taller boy loomed over Vira, who was now pushed to the ground. Two other scrawny boys were also laughing as Vira scrambled back up to her feet. Then to Katya's horror, Vira leapt up, hands grabbing forward against the biggest boy.

"Damn it," Paul said as they both leapt up.

"Stop," Katya shouted as Vira furiously attacked the boy while they ran fast to the scene.

Vira scratched at the tall boy's face and neck, digging her nails into his skin with what seemed like a vicious animal strength. The boy instinctively hit back against the much smaller girl with his elbows. As he resisted, Vira clung to him with a savage, fearsome strength and wild eyes.

"*Lâche-moi, salope*. Get off me, bitch," the boy shouted during

their sudden, vicious combat.

Paul pulled Vira away, separating the fighters by shoving the kid back with his hand hard enough that the boy fell backward to the pavement.

"Hey. Hey. Look at me," Paul said, trying to calm Vira.

He peered steadily into her wild, distracted eyes and held her rigid body. Trapped like this in his arms, she began to growl again. Then her growl became a low, uncontrollable, painful pitch like that of a wounded coyote.

Other parents and children now circled, staring at the little drama, some looking menacingly at Paul after he pushed the boy with such force, and as the girl continue to howl so very, very strangely.

---

147   Belarusian French painter (1887–1985) and early modernist who forged a unique, poetic style blending Cubism, Fauvism, and Surrealism. Renowned for dreamlike scenes and vibrant colors.

"Please, it is OK. Everything is OK," Katya told the onlookers while Paul held Vira close to his body to calm her.

A few other mothers also stared with suspicious, judgmental eyes. Some parents talked in hushed whispers since the girl's violent outburst was not normal at all.

"Here, let me see," Katya said in French to the boy Vira had attacked. "Why did you push her?"

"She wouldn't listen," the boy replied in French.

"She didn't understand you," Katya scolded, looking around in vain for his parents.

"*Elle est retardée.* She is retarded," he added in French.

Katya quickly scrambled to pull cash from her wallet when she saw a female *gendarme* enter the playground, drawn by the commotion, the crowd's attention, and Vira's constant wail.

"Take it," Katya ordered angrily in French. "You are bigger and older. Tell this officer you are fine. It was just a mistake. Got it?" She pressed three purple five-hundred-euro notes into the boy's hand, and he squeezed them tightly in his clenched fist.

"*D'accord?* Got it?" Katya asked again.

The trimly dressed female officer approached with concerned eyes and the thumb of her right hand looped through a wide black leather belt.

Katya turned to the police officer with a fake smile, trying her best to diffuse the situation with a quick barrage of explanations and excuses while Vira thankfully finally stopped her horrible animal-like cry and instead remained limp and quiet in Paul's arms. The female *gendarme* dutifully interviewed the boy and inspected the scratches on his neck and the deep tear on his left cheek. The teenager stayed on script while Katya continued to ramble on about how her daughter had fallen and this whole incident was a misunderstanding. She should have cut the girl's sharp nails this morning. Nothing to see. Just a stupid squabble among stupid kids, Katya continued.

"Use antiseptic as soon as you can," the officer remarked to the boy.

"I will. I am fine," the boy replied and then found a slight opening in the ongoing conversation to quickly scurry away, his hand clenching Katya's cash in secret.

Paul brought Vira closer while she curled up tightly in his arms, her face catatonic.

"Is your daughter disabled?" the officer asked.

"Please," Katya began. "She will be fine. Thank you for your questions. I will take her home now. She just needs to rest."

"I understand, madame. I am a mother too," the officer said, finally switching to English. "We have services here in Paris for disabled children. I can give you some numbers."

"Yes, thank you. Extremely helpful."

"You are not French, madame?"

"No. I am Russian."

"You both live here?" the officer asked, glancing at Paul.

"We do."

"And your daughter is a Russian?"

"No. Ukrainian."

"I see, madame. But you told me just now that you are Russian, not Ukrainian."

"I was born in Russia. She is my adopted daughter."

"I see, madame."

"Is there a problem? My husband is American."

"Yes, madame. You must understand that I will take your address for now," the officer continued. "If you please, it would be best if you gave me your identification so we can contact you and make sure that your child is well and we have all your papers. I hope you understand. It is my process and the law. I must take your name and address now."

Katya reached into her pocket and brought out her French driver's license while she continued small talk about Christmas in Paris and anything else that might seem normal for two women to speak about.

Katya politely took back her license and the officer's suggested social services numbers before exchanging a final friendly and entirely false *Joyeux Noel et Bonne Année*.

"We're lucky she didn't press for more," Paul said.

"What of it? Let them," Katya said.

Vira continued to clutch Paul tightly, her face buried in his shoulder. The playground had emptied out of all the children as the early winter dusk settled, and the city was now very dark.

"It is my fault. It happened so fast," Paul said.

"My fault too. I did not watch her close enough," Katya said. "Can you carry her all the way back?"

"Of course," Paul replied. "She is still tiny enough."

Paul carried Vira cradled in his arms while she did not move and kept her eyes vaguely unfocused. They walked first across the Pont de Arts, crossing back over the wide river to the Left Bank. Then they followed Quai Voltaire along the riverbank and navigated back through a maze of smaller streets. It had turned much colder without the winter sun, and there was only intermittent auto traffic and a few occasional figures still darting around on the roads on scooters, mopeds, or bicycles.

As they walked in silence, Vira stayed oddly limp, abnormally catatonic and expressionless. It was as if no time had passed at all since the young girl was removed from the rubble of a destroyed apartment building in Cherniv. Paul carried Vira tonight the same way as it had been before, after being buried in the darkness for almost two days. She was back there again, left for dead along with all the others.

28

PAUL OPENED the rooftop door that led out to the apartment's outdoor balcony.

Katya sat alone on one of the four ornate metal outdoor chairs, her back turned to him as she peered over the gray Hausmann rooftops in the direction of the Île de la Cité just across the river to the west. Paul embraced the night's chill as he eased down into the empty chair next to her.

"You have been out here for an hour. Not cold?" he asked, noting how her warm breath steamed out in slow, even pulses. She was wrapped in a heavy fur-lined leather coat, with a white cashmere scarf wound tightly around her throat.

"I am fine. I just needed fresh air," she answered. "Is Vira still sleeping?"

"Yes. She is exhausted."

"Good."

"Sleep will help. I will call Fauchier's office tomorrow morning," Paul offered. "We can bring her to him early next year when he's back from his vacation."

"That would be helpful, Paul," Katya offered.

He noticed that her gemlike eyes betrayed a tiredness he had not seen for the last seven months, ever since Vira had arrived.

"Sitting up here reminds me of my old New York place," Katya said. "I enjoyed that room on the Upper West Side, before Viktor ruined it."

"How could I forget your old place on Ninety-Fifth Street," Paul said, thinking back to that fateful night when they had walked in on Viktor and discovered his crime. That night was still so vividly etched into his brain. What had followed since seemed both perpetually uncertain and, in hindsight, inevitable as gravity. "Your brother tossing Arlen Cross off the building's fire escape was the reason you first introduced me to Yuri and

Dmitry," Paul continued. "I can still see Arlen's face looking up at me from the alley floor."

"That was a bad night. It was from a different life," Katya said.

"Everything changes. Our view is better now," Paul offered.

"Not better. Simply different," she replied. "I always thought New York would be my home. I just wanted to run our Chelsea gallery. I did not have courage back then to even think about returning to Paris again to face them all."

"Isn't the Zephyr branch in the Marais doing well now? I thought you said the new staff were excellent and that business was finally picking up?"

"Our gallery here is fine," she said. "But it does not matter. I have other commitments. I promised Rodofsky I would be back in Lviv for at least a few weeks in the spring. Better to come back to Europe after my California trip. Besides, I am not a fan of 'Make America Great Again' rallies.[148] Too much testosterone and unthinking hate. I worry it will get much worse."

"This is why your role with Rutherford's family is even more important."

"Maybe," she offered, with a slight shrug.

A few minutes of silence passed while they both listened to the city's soft murmurs in the dark cold.

"They just finished rebuilding Notre Dame. Five years of work costing billions of dollars," Paul noted, pointing toward the lights that now embraced the massive gothic cathedral, its two tall towers just visible across the river and above the many rooftops. "I heard the bells chime a few weeks ago for the first time."

"Yes. I saw that your new president came for the opening ceremony."

"He did. And Prince William and the Pope,"[149] Paul remarked.

"Good for them. The cathedral spire fell and the whole place was nearly destroyed. All that damage because of a trivial human error," Katya reflected. "They say it was caused by a bad wire or just an errant cigarette butt. Something very stupid. Stupid and trivial, just like those asshole kids who pushed Vira down like that."

"They were just bullies," Paul replied.

---

148   So-called "MAGA" events focused on themes of national restoration and economic protectionism. Recognizable by the widespread use of red MAGA hats and merchandise; critics see them as a source of political division and xenophobia.

149   The reopening ceremony on December 7, 2024, was attended by approximately 1,500 dignitaries to mark the cathedral's restoration after a devastating 2019 fire.

"But you heard Vira scream. Too much rage and pain for such a small voice."

"She has only been with us here for seven months. Don't dwell on it," Paul said.

"Evil moves like a cloud, just slithers around the world, rolling from place to place, person to person," she continued.

"Wind clears clouds. Vira will adjust," Paul countered. "The French rebuilt Notre Dame from the ashes. Wars end. Tyrants fall."

"I wish I shared your optimism."

"We must be optimistic. We are parents now," Paul said. "Parenthood is not easy. We cannot just slip on these new roles like actors switching scripts. It is new for me too. I do not have all the answers. Optimism helps."

"Yes, Paul. You are very sincere. I believe you," she said, then reached out her slender hand to touch his cold cheek.

But even as Katya displayed tenderness, her gemlike green-blue eyes seemed to Paul still impenetrable and remote. From the very beginning, he had always known a part of her would forever remain separate. He accepted this as a foundational reality. Katya's Eastern blood was just colder than his own. She listened to his encouraging words, but he suspected that their meaning never penetrated too deeply.

"Can I really be a good mother?" Katya asked.

"You are already," Paul said sternly. "I am here with you. We are together as a family, a real family. There is only forward."

"Yes, Paul. We have only forward," she replied.

"Enough for one day. Come back inside. It is late. I'm freezing my ass off up here," Paul said.

He held her hands to lift her from the chair. After he pulled her inside, Paul shut the balcony door, locked the latch, and turned on the building's full alarm system with a memorized six-digit code, 031587—Max's birthday.

"Have you talked to your brother recently?" Katya asked as she followed him down the staircase to the apartment's main living room.

"He left a message that he might have a week's leave in the spring."

"His charming girlfriend does not call me anymore. She finally gave up," Katya said.

"Cannot blame Christina after all this time. She has better options," he said.

In the kitchen, Paul searched the pantry shelf for a bottle of Jameson's Irish Whiskey that he knew was in the back, behind the many bottles of prosecco and burgundy.

He poured the whiskey into two tumblers and mixed in ice cubes and a splash of cold soda water.

Katya sipped her glass after he handed it to her. "Not bad for American whiskey," she remarked.

"Cheap stuff still works," he said.

Paul went over to the Bose sound system and searched the device's playlist for calming music. A Yo-Yo Ma cello concerto album gently filled the late night's lengthening mood.

Paul refilled their tumblers. The bitter drink was cool on his tongue but slipped smoothly down his throat.

"Please go and check on Vira again," Katya said as she leaned her body back against the living room's plush designer couch.

"Will do," Paul replied. After the next swig, he went upstairs. He slowly cracked open the door to peek into Vira's dark room.

Her small body was hidden under the heavy quilt, inert as a stone.

When Paul came back down to the living room, Yo-Yo Ma was still playing his cello as the playlist repeated its continuous loop. Katya's glass stood empty on the end table, and her head rested against a small round pillow, her eyes closed. Disheveled chestnut-colored hair framed her pale face, timeless in its lovely beauty.

Paul went to the kitchen and poured himself the last glass of Jameson's.

His thoughts wandered while he nursed his last glass, accepting how the many conflicts and struggles would continue for years, decades, or much, much longer. Governments would keep churning out their weapons by the thousands while the satellites watched, and diplomats muddled forward. Nothing had been won, whether around the Black Sea, farther south in the Middle East, or back in the States. The last American election had also solved nothing. The country had voted to turn inward without any semblance of a coherent strategy. Putin had airlifted Assad from Damascus three weeks ago, but what came next remained uncertain. And Gaza—a catastrophe. The planet spun peacefully for some, but for millions of others it was an unresolved, venal, violent mess.

Ah, but Notre Dame de Paris has been rebuilt after her destruction, Paul assured himself. *Now I have my own family to worry about. They depend on me. Vira will be fine. Children are sponges. Sleep will rejuvenate everyone. Christmas is in two days. We will have a better day tomorrow, right as rain. After Vira opens a dozen presents, she will forget everything about those idiot playground bullies. We can afford the best professional help in the world. Everything will revert to normal. Or at least as normal as it can be for us,* he considered.

Best to connect with Dmitry soon. Look again at how I can help the cause and help my brother. So much more to do.

After another hour, Paul finally turned off the music. He found a thick cashmere blanket in the closet and draped it over Katya's resting body. When he switched off all the lights there was only darkness and faint shadows created by the pale urban light shining through the double-paned, tightly shut, twelve-foot-tall windows. Katya moved slightly when he kissed her right cheek. He was careful not to wake her as he moved the blanket higher on her bare shoulders.

They would all rise tomorrow and begin again, rejuvenated after a safe night's rest.

Cogito ergo sum.

Tomorrow brings another dawn, and new light.

REFERENCES: DRAMATIS PERSONAE

The Westerners

Paul Drake. Born 1982 in Scarsdale, New York. US Army, served in Iraq from 2004 to 2008, honorably discharged first lieutenant. Bachelor's degree from Columbia College, 2010.

Max Drake. Born 1987 in Scarsdale, New York. US Army, served in Iraq from 2007 to 2010, honorably discharged private first class. Business degree from Hunter College, 2016.

Josephine Richards. Born 1968 in Bethesda, Maryland. Bachelor's degree from University of Chicago, 1986, PhD in advanced chemistry from John Hopkins University, 1992. Career US intelligence officer.

Martin J. Hines. Born 1966 in Austin, Texas. Head of European Operations, Central Intelligence Agency. A twenty-five-year agency veteran, stationed in Afghanistan from 2014 to 2019.

George Rutherford III. Born 1941 in Los Angeles, California. Former CEO and controlling shareholder of the multibillion-dollar American Chemical Group.

Timothy John Hastings. Agency officer borne in Annapolis, Maryland. BA from Yale and Masters from the US Naval Academy.

Andrew Gauthier. Born 1975 in Marseilles, France. Key man within an illicit arms smuggling effort, including for banned chemical weapons.

The Easterners

Katerina Sergeevna Volkova (Katya). Born 1987 in St. Petersburg, Russia. Daughter of political activist, Sergei Volkov, and his wife, Irena. Master's degree in philosophy from the Sorbonne University, Paris, 2011. Lead curator of the family-owned Zephyr Gallery in Chelsea, Manhattan, since 2018.

Yuri Ivanovich Volkov. Born 1960 in Moscow, Russia, now a resident of London, England, and a Maltese citizen. Founder and owner of Eastern Finance, a global investment bank; and MSA Shipping. The elder brother of Sergei Volkov, Katya's father.

Dmitry Medkov. Born 1963 in Novosibirsk, Russia. Former spetsnaz in the Soviet Army, served in Afghanistan from 1982 to 1989. MSA's chief of security.

Viktor Volkov. Born 1982 in St. Petersburg, Russia. Katya's elder brother.

Valentine Romanovich Kuzoff. Born 1989 in Odessa, Ukraine. Previously in the Ukrainian Navy, now privately employed by MSA Shipping since 2018. Son of Olga Kuzanova.

Kiril Petrovitch Alekseyev. Born 1971 in Moscow, Russia. A division head of the state intelligence service, Federalnaya Sluzhba Bezopasnosti (FSB).

Bogan Zoidze. Born 1968 in Tbilisi, Georgia. Son of Tamar Zoidze, a leading Soviet-era general.

Nicolai Sokolov. Born 1979 in Ekaterina, Russia. An undeclared Russian intelligence officer working as the director of Ionic Shipping and Refurbishment in Naples, Italy, since 2011.

Hasad Atakan. Born 1966 in Istanbul, Turkey. Colonel in the Turkish Army.

ABOUT THE AUTHOR

Brett Andrew Strange is a Chicago native, former CIA intelligence officer, and bestselling author. He spent over a decade working overseas in regions including Southeast Asia, Europe, and the Middle East. His work often incorporates themes of intelligence tradecraft, geopolitical realities, and the personal struggles of those working in the field. A graduate of Harvard College and Georgetown University's School of Foreign Service, Strange currently resides in San Francisco with his wife and two children.

Additional resources available at
www.brettandrewstrange.com